Principal Concepts in Applied Evolutionary Computation:

Emerging Trends

Wei-Chiang Samuelson Hong
Oriental Institute of Technology, Taiwan

Information Science
REFERENCE

Managing Director:	Lindsay Johnston
Senior Editorial Director:	Heather A. Probst
Book Production Manager:	Sean Woznicki
Development Manager:	Joel Gamon
Acquisitions Editor:	Erika Gallagher
Typesetter:	Adrienne Freeland
Cover Design:	Nick Newcomer, Lisandro Gonzalez

Published in the United States of America by
Information Science Reference (an imprint of IGI Global)
701 E. Chocolate Avenue
Hershey PA 17033
Tel: 717-533-8845
Fax: 717-533-8661
E-mail: cust@igi-global.com
Web site: http://www.igi-global.com

Library of Congress Cataloging-in-Publication Data

Principal concepts in applied evolutionary computation: emerging trends / Wei-Chiang Samuelson Hong, editor.
    p. cm.
  Includes bibliographical references and index.
  Summary: "This book provides an introduction to the important interdisciplinary discipline of evolutionary computation, an artificial intelligence field that combines the principles of computational intelligence with the mechanisms of the theory of evolution"-- Provided by publisher.
  ISBN 978-1-4666-1749-0 (hardcover) -- ISBN 978-1-4666-1750-6 (ebook) -- ISBN 978-1-4666-1751-3 (print & perpetual access) 1. Evolutionary computation. I. Hong, Wei-Chiang Samuelson, 1972-
  QA76.618.P75 2012
  006.3'2--dc23
                             2012002463

British Cataloguing in Publication Data
A Cataloguing in Publication record for this book is available from the British Library.

The views expressed in this book are those of the authors, but not necessarily of the publisher.

Table of Contents

Preface xiv

Chapter 1
Ant Clustering Algorithms 1
Yu-Chiun Chiou, National Chiao Tung University, Taiwan
Shih-Ta Chou, Feng Chia University, Taiwan

Chapter 2
Three Novel Methods to Predict Traffic Time Series in Reconstructed State Spaces 16
Lawrence W. Lan, MingDao University, Taiwan
Feng-Yu Lin, Central Police University, Taiwan
April Y. Kuo, BNSF Railway, USA

Chapter 3
Self-Evolvable Protocol Design Using Genetic Algorithms... 36
Wenbing Yao, Huawei Technologies, UK
Sheng-Uei Guan, Xian Jiatong-Liverpool University, China
Zhiqiang Jiang, National University of Singapore, Singapore
Ilias Kiourktsidis, Brunel University, UK

Chapter 4
Facial Feature Tracking via Evolutionary Multiobjective Optimization 57
Eric C. Larson, Oklahoma State University, USA
Gary G. Yen, Oklahoma State University, USA

Chapter 5
Ordered Incremental Multi-Objective Problem Solving Based on Genetic Algorithms 72
Wenting Mo, IBM, China
Sheng-Uei Guan, Xian Jiaotong-Liverpool University, China
Sadasivan Puthusserypady, Technical University of Denmark, Denmark

Chapter 6
Comparative Study of Evolutionary Computing Methods for Parameter Estimation of Power Quality Signals 99
V. Ravikumar Pandi, IIT Delhi, India
B. K. Panigrahi, IIT Delhi, India

Chapter 7
A Heuristic Approach for Multi Objective Distribution Feeder Reconfiguration: Using Fuzzy Sets in Normalization of Objective Functions 130
Armin Ebrahimi Milani, Islamic Azad University, Iran
Mahmood Reza Haghifam, Tarbiat Modarres University, Iran

Chapter 8
A Scheduling Model with Multi-Objective Optimization for Computational Grids using NSGA-II 143
Zahid Raza, Jawaharlal Nehru University, India
Deo Prakash Vidyarthi, Jawaharlal Nehru University, India

Chapter 9
Extrapolated Biogeography-Based Optimization (eBBO) for Global Numerical Optimization and Microstrip Patch Antenna Design 165
M. R. Lohokare, National Institute of Technical Teachers' Training and Research, India
S.S. Pattnaik, National Institute of Technical Teachers' Training and Research, India
S. Devi, National Institute of Technical Teachers' Training and Research, India
B.K. Panigrahi, Indian Institute of Technology, India
S. Das, Kansas State University, USA
J. G. Joshi, National Institute of Technical Teachers' Training and Research, India

Chapter 10
Posterior Sampling using Particle Swarm Optimizers and Model Reduction Techniques 192
J. L. Fernández Martínez, Stanford University, University of California-Berkeley, USA & University of Oviedo, Spain
E. García Gonzalo, University of Oviedo, Spain
Z. Fernández Muñiz, University of Oviedo, Spain
G. Mariethoz, Stanford University, USA
T. Mukerji, Stanford University, USA

Chapter 11
Reserve Constrained Multi-Area Economic Dispatch Employing Evolutionary Approach 215
Manisha Sharma, M.I.T.S., India
Manjaree Pandit, M.I.T.S., India

Chapter 12
Application of Machine Learning Techniques to Predict Software Reliability 237
    Ramakanta Mohanty, Berhampur University, India
    V. Ravi, Institute for Development and Research in Banking Technology, India
    M. R. Patra, Berhampur University, India

Chapter 13
Buffer Management in Cellular IP Networks using Evolutionary Algorithms................................... 254
    Mohammad Anbar, Jawaharlal Nehru University, India
    Deo Prakash Vidyarthi, Jawaharlal Nehru University, India

Chapter 14
Using Evolution Strategies to Perform Stellar Population Synthesis for Galaxy Spectra from
SDSS 276
    Juan Carlos Gomez, KULeuven, Belgium
    Olac Fuentes, UTEP, USA

Chapter 15
A Novel Puzzle Based Compaction (PBC) Strategy for Enhancing the Utilization of Reconfigurable
Resources 287
    Ahmed I. Saleh, Mansoura University, Egypt

Chapter 16
A Comparative Study of Metaheuristic Methods for Transmission Network Expansion Planning 319
    Ashu Verma, TERI University, India
    P. R. Bijwe, IIT, India
    B. K. Panigrahi, IIT, India

Compilation of References 340

About the Contributors 367

Index 372

Detailed Table of Contents

Preface... xiv

Chapter 1

Ant Clustering Algorithms 1

    Yu-Chiun Chiou, National Chiao Tung University, Taiwan
    Shih-Ta Chou, Feng Chia University, Taiwan

This paper proposes three ant clustering algorithms (ACAs): ACA-1, ACA-2 and ACA-3. The core logic of the proposed ACAs is to modify the ant colony metaheuristic by reformulating the clustering problem into a network problem. For a clustering problem of N objects and K clusters, a fully connected network of N nodes is formed with link costs, representing the dissimilarity of any two nodes it connects. K ants are then to collect their own nodes according to the link costs and following the pheromone trail laid by previous ants. The proposed three ACAs have been validated on a small-scale problem solved by a total enumeration method. The solution effectiveness at different problem scales consistently shows that ACA-2 outperforms among these three ACAs. A further comparison of ACA-2 with other commonly used clustering methods, including agglomerative hierarchy clustering algorithm (AHCA), K-means algorithm (KMA) and genetic clustering algorithm (GCA), shows that ACA-2 significantly outperforms them in solution effectiveness for the most of cases and also performs considerably better in solution stability as the problem scales or the number of clusters gets larger.

Chapter 2

Three Novel Methods to Predict Traffic Time Series in Reconstructed State Spaces 16

    Lawrence W. Lan, MingDao University, Taiwan
    Feng-Yu Lin, Central Police University, Taiwan
    April Y. Kuo, BNSF Railway, USA

This article proposes three novel methods—temporal confined (TC), spatiotemporal confined (STC) and spatial confined (SC)—to forecast the temporal evolution of traffic parameters. The fundamental rationales are to embed one-dimensional traffic time series into reconstructed state spaces and then to perform fuzzy reasoning to infer the future changes in traffic series. The TC, STC and SC methods respectively employ different fuzzy reasoning logics to select similar historical traffic trajectories. Theil inequality coefficient and its decomposed components are used to evaluate the predicting power and source of errors. Field observed one-minute traffic counts are used to test the predicting power. The results show that overall prediction accuracies for the three methods are satisfactorily high with small systematic errors and little deviation from the observed data. It suggests that the proposed three methods can be used to capture and forecast the short-term (e.g., one-minute) temporal evolution of traffic parameters.

Chapter 3

Self-Evolvable Protocol Design Using Genetic Algorithms..36

Wenbing Yao, Huawei Technologies, UK

Sheng-Uei Guan, Xian Jiatong-Liverpool University, China

Zhiqiang Jiang, National University of Singapore, Singapore

Ilias Kiourktsidis, Brunel University, UK

Self-modifying protocols (SMP) are protocols that can be modified at run time by the computers using them. Such protocols can be modified at run time so that they can adapt to the changing communicating environment and user requirements on the fly. Evolvable protocols are SMP designed using Genetic Algorithms (GA). The purpose of this paper is to apply Genetic Algorithms (GA) to design an evolvable protocol in order to equip communication peers with more autonomy and intelligence. The next-generation Internet will benefit from the concept of evolvable protocols. In this paper, we design a Self Evolvable Transaction Protocol (SETP) with a GA executor embedded. We then use the Network Simulator (NS2) to evaluate this evolvable protocol module to demonstrate the feasibility of our new design approach.

Chapter 4

Facial Feature Tracking via Evolutionary Multiobjective Optimization 57

Eric C. Larson, Oklahoma State University, USA

Gary G. Yen, Oklahoma State University, USA

Facial feature tracking for model–based coding has evolved over the past decades. Of particular interest is its application in very low bit rate coding in which optimization is used to analyze head and shoulder sequences. We present the results of a computational experiment in which we apply a combination of non-dominated sorting genetic algorithm and a deterministic search to find optimal facial animation parameters at many bandwidths simultaneously. As objective functions are concerned, peak signal-to-noise ratio is maximized while the total number of facial animation parameters is minimized. Particularly, the algorithm is tested for efficiency and reliability. The results show that the overall methodology works effectively, but that a better error assessment function is needed for future study.

Chapter 5

Ordered Incremental Multi-Objective Problem Solving Based on Genetic Algorithms 72

Wenting Mo, IBM, China

Sheng-Uei Guan, Xian Jiaotong-Liverpool University, China

Sadasivan Puthusserypady, Technical University of Denmark, Denmark

Many Multiple Objective Genetic Algorithms (MOGAs) have been designed to solve problems with multiple conflicting objectives. Incremental approach can be used to enhance the performance of various MOGAs, which was developed to evolve each objective incrementally. For example, by applying the incremental approach to normal MOGA, the obtained Incremental Multiple Objective Genetic Algorithm (IMOGA) outperforms state-of-the-art MOGAs, including Non-dominated Sorting Genetic Algorithm-II (NSGA-II), Strength Pareto Evolutionary Algorithm (SPEA) and Pareto Archived Evolution Strategy (PAES). However, there is still an open question: how to decide the order of the objectives handled by incremental algorithms? Due to their incremental nature, it is found that the ordering of objectives would influence the performance of these algorithms. In this paper, the ordering issue is investigated based on IMOGA, resulting in a novel objective ordering approach. The experimental results on benchmark problems showed that the proposed approach can help IMOGA reach its potential best performance.

Chapter 6

Comparative Study of Evolutionary Computing Methods for Parameter Estimation of Power Quality Signals 99

V. Ravikumar Pandi, IIT Delhi, India
B. K. Panigrahi, IIT Delhi, India

Recently utilities and end users become more concerned about power quality issues because the load equipments are more sensitive to various power quality disturbances, such as harmonics and voltage fluctuation. Harmonic distortion and voltage flicker are the major causes in growing concern about electric power quality. Power quality disturbance monitoring plays an important role in the deregulated power market scenario due to competitiveness among the utilities. This paper presents an evolutionary algorithm approach based on Adaptive Particle Swarm Optimization (APSO) to determine the amplitude, phase and frequency of a power quality signal. In this APSO algorithm the time varying inertia weight is modified as rank based, and re-initialization is used to increase the diversity. In this paper, to the authors highlight the efficacy of different evolutionary optimization techniques like classical PSO, Constriction based PSO, Clonal Algorithm (CLONALOG), Adaptive Bacterial Foraging (ABF) and the proposed Adaptive Particle Swarm Optimization (APSO) to extract different parameters like amplitude, phase and frequency of harmonic distorted power quality signal and voltage flicker.

Chapter 7

A Heuristic Approach for Multi Objective Distribution Feeder Reconfiguration: Using Fuzzy Sets in Normalization of Objective Functions 130

Armin Ebrahimi Milani, Islamic Azad University, Iran
Mahmood Reza Haghifam, Tarbiat Modarres University, Iran

The reconfiguration is an operation process used for optimization with specific objectives by means of changing the status of switches in a distribution network. This paper presents an algorithm for network recon-figuration based on the heuristic rules and fuzzy multi objective approach where each objective is normalized with inspiration from fuzzy set to cause optimization more flexible and formulized as a unique multi objective function. Also, the genetic algorithm is used for solving the suggested model, in which there is no risk of non-linear objective functions and constraints. The effectiveness of the proposed method is demonstrated through several examples in this paper.

Chapter 8

A Scheduling Model with Multi-Objective Optimization for Computational Grids using NSGA-II 143

Zahid Raza, Jawaharlal Nehru University, India
Deo Prakash Vidyarthi, Jawaharlal Nehru University, India

Scheduling a job on the grid is an NP Hard problem, and hence a number of models on optimizing one or other characteristic parameters have been proposed in the literature. It is expected from a computational grid to complete the job quickly in most reliable grid environment owing to the number of participants in the grid and the scarcity of the resources available. Genetic algorithm is an effective tool in solving problems that requires sub-optimal solutions and finds uses in multi-objective optimization problems. This paper addresses a multi-objective optimization problem by introducing a scheduling model for a modular job on a computational grid with a dual objective, minimizing the turnaround time and maximizing the reliability of the job execution using NSGA – II, a GA variant. The cost of execution on a node is measured on the basis of the node characteristics, the job attributes and the network properties. Simulation study and a comparison of the results with other similar models reveal the effectiveness of the model.

Chapter 9

Extrapolated Biogeography-Based Optimization (eBBO) for Global Numerical Optimization and Microstrip Patch Antenna Design 165

M. R. Lohokare, National Institute of Technical Teachers' Training and Research, India

S.S. Pattnaik, National Institute of Technical Teachers' Training and Research, India

S. Devi, National Institute of Technical Teachers' Training and Research, India

B.K. Panigrahi, Indian Institute of Technology, India

S. Das, Kansas State University, USA

J. G. Joshi, National Institute of Technical Teachers' Training and Research, India

Biogeography-Based Optimization (BBO) uses the idea of probabilistically sharing features between solutions based on the solutions' fitness values. Therefore, its exploitation ability is good but it lacks in exploration ability. In this paper, the authors extend the original BBO and propose a hybrid version combined with ePSO (particle swarm optimization with extrapolation technique), namely eBBO, for unconstrained global numerical optimization problems in the continuous domain. eBBO combines the exploitation ability of BBO with the exploration ability of ePSO effectively, which can generate global optimum solutions. To validate the performance of eBBO, experiments have been conducted on 23 standard benchmark problems with a range of dimensions and diverse complexities and compared with original BBO and other versions of BBO in terms of the quality of the final solution and the convergence rate. Influence of population size and scalability study is also considered and results are compared with statistical paired t-test. Experimental analysis indicates that the proposed approach is effective and efficient and improves the exploration ability of BBO.

Chapter 10

Posterior Sampling using Particle Swarm Optimizers and Model Reduction Techniques 192

J. L. Fernández Martínez, Stanford University, University of California-Berkeley, USA & University of Oviedo, Spain

E. García Gonzalo, University of Oviedo, Spain

Z. Fernández Muñiz, University of Oviedo, Spain

G. Mariethoz, Stanford University, USA

T. Mukerji, Stanford University, USA

Inverse problems are ill-posed and posterior sampling is a way of providing an estimate of the uncertainty based on a finite set of the family of models that fit the observed data within the same tolerance. Monte Carlo methods are used for this purpose but are highly inefficient. Global optimization methods address the inverse problem as a sampling problem, particularly Particle Swarm, which is a very interesting algorithm that is typically used in an exploitative form. Although PSO has not been designed originally to perform importance sampling, the authors show practical applications in the domain of environmental geophysics, where it provides a proxy for the posterior distribution when it is used in its explorative form. Finally, this paper presents a hydrogeological example how to perform a similar task for inverse problems in high dimensional spaces through the combined use with model reduction techniques.

Chapter 11

Reserve Constrained Multi-Area Economic Dispatch Employing Evolutionary Approach 215

Manisha Sharma, M.I.T.S., India

Manjaree Pandit, M.I.T.S., India

The objective of Multi-area economic dispatch (MAED) is to determine the generation levels and the interchange power between areas that minimize fuel costs, while satisfying power balance and generating limit and transmission constraints. If an area with excess power is not adjacent to a power deficient area, or the tie-line between the two areas is at transmission limit, it is necessary to find an alternative path between these two areas to transmit additional power. When a MAED problem is solved with spinning reserve constraints, the problem becomes further complicated. The power allocation to each unit is done in such a manner that after supplying the total load, some specified reserve is left behind. In this paper, the authors compare classic PSO and DE strategies and their variants for reserve constrained MAED. The superior constraint handling capability of these techniques enables them to produce high quality solutions. The performance is tested on a 2-area system having 4 generating units and a 4-area, 16-unit system.

Chapter 12

Application of Machine Learning Techniques to Predict Software Reliability 237

Ramakanta Mohanty, Berhampur University, India

V. Ravi, Institute for Development and Research in Banking Technology, India

M. R. Patra, Berhampur University, India

In this paper, the authors employed machine learning techniques, specifically, Back propagation trained neural network (BPNN), Group method of data handling (GMDH), Counter propagation neural network (CPNN), Dynamic evolving neuro–fuzzy inference system (DENFIS), Genetic Programming (GP), TreeNet, statistical multiple linear regression (MLR), and multivariate adaptive regression splines (MARS), to accurately forecast software reliability. Their effectiveness is demonstrated on three datasets taken from literature, where performance is compared in terms of normalized root mean square error (NRMSE) obtained in the test set. From rigorous experiments conducted, it was observed that GP outperformed all techniques in all datasets, with GMDH coming a close second.

Chapter 13

Buffer Management in Cellular IP Networks using Evolutionary Algorithms 254

Mohammad Anbar, Jawaharlal Nehru University, India

Deo Prakash Vidyarthi, Jawaharlal Nehru University, India

Real-time traffic in Cellular IP network is considered to be important and therefore given priority over non-real-time. Buffer is an important but scarce resource and to optimize Quality of Service by managing buffers of the network is an important and complex problem. Evolutionary Algorithms are quite useful in solving such complex optimization problems, and in this regard, a two-tier model for buffer, Gateway and Base Station, management in Cellular IP network has been proposed. The first tier applies a prioritization algorithm for prioritizing real-time packets in the buffer of the gateway with a specified threshold. Packets which couldn't be served, after the threshold, is given to the nearest cells of the network to be dealt with in the second tier, while Evolutionary Algorithm (EA) based procedures are applied in order to optimally store these packets in the buffer of the base stations. Experiments have been conducted to observe the performance of the proposed models and a comparative study of the models, GA based and PSO based, has been carried out to depict the advantage and disadvantage of the proposed models.

Chapter 14

Using Evolution Strategies to Perform Stellar Population Synthesis for Galaxy Spectra from SDSS 276

Juan Carlos Gomez, KULeuven, Belgium

Olac Fuentes, UTEP, USA

In this work, the authors employ Evolution Strategies (ES) to automatically extract a set of physical parameters, corresponding to stellar population synthesis, from a sample of galaxy spectra taken from the Sloan Digital Sky Survey (SDSS). This parameter extraction is presented as an optimization problem and being solved using ES. The idea is to reconstruct each galaxy spectrum by means of a linear combination of three different theoretical models for stellar population synthesis. This combination produces a model spectrum that is compared with the original spectrum using a simple difference function. The goal is to find a model that minimizes this difference, using ES as the algorithm to explore the parameter space. This paper presents experimental results using a set of 100 spectra from SDSS Data Release 2 that show that ES are very well suited to extract stellar population parameters from galaxy spectra. Additionally, in order to better understand the performance of ES in this problem, a comparison with two well known stochastic search algorithms, Genetic Algorithms (GA) and Simulated Annealing (SA), is presented.

Chapter 15
A Novel Puzzle Based Compaction (PBC) Strategy for Enhancing the Utilization of Reconfigurable
Resources 287
Ahmed I. Saleh, Mansoura University, Egypt

Partially reconfigurable field programmable gate arrays (FPGAs) can accommodate several independent tasks simultaneously. FPGA, as all reconfigurable chips, relies on the "host-then-compact-when-needed" strategy. Accordingly, it should have the ability to both place incoming tasks at run time and compact the chip whenever needed. Compaction is a proposed solution to alleviate external fragmentations problem, trying to move running tasks closer to each other in order to free a sufficient area for new tasks. However, compaction conditions the suspension of the running tasks, which introduces a high penalty. In order to increase the chip area utilization as well as not affecting the response times of tasks, efficient compaction techniques become increasingly important. Unfortunately, traditional compaction techniques suffer from a variety of faults. This paper introduces a novel Puzzle Based Compaction (PBC) technique that is a shape aware technique, which takes the tasks shapes into consideration. In this regard, it succeeded not only to eliminate the internal fragmentations but also to minimize the external fragmentations. This paper develops a novel formula, which is the first not to estimate, but to exactly calculate the amount of external fragmentations generated by accommodating a set of tasks inside the reconfigurable chip.

Chapter 16
A Comparative Study of Metaheuristic Methods for Transmission Network Expansion Planning 319
Ashu Verma, TERI University, India
P. R. Bijwe, IIT, India
B. K. Panigrahi, IIT, India

Transmission network expansion planning is a very complex and computationally demanding problem due to the discrete nature of the optimization variables. This complexity has increased even more in a restructured deregulated environment. In this regard, there is a need for development of more rigorous optimization techniques. This paper presents a comparative analysis of three metaheuristic algorithms known as Bacteria foraging (BF), Genetic algorithm (GA), and Particle swarm optimization (PSO) for transmission network expansion planning with and without security constraints. The DC power flow based model is used for analysis and results for IEEE 24 bus system are obtained with the above three metaheuristic drawing a comparison of their performance characteristic.

Compilation of References 340

About the Contributors 367

Index 372

Preface

This book contains articles from the four issues of Volume 1 of the *International Journal of Applied Evolutionary Computation* (IJAEC). As mentioned in journal's description, this book reflects the journal's mission of publishing high-quality comprehensive interdisciplinary academic and practitioner research, and surveys that provide a reference channel for disseminating all experimental, theoretical and application emerging aspects of intelligent computation (IC) and its applications, with particular focus on breaking trends in evolutionary computation, evolutionary algorithms, evolutionary programming, fuzzy computation, neural computation, traditional probabilistic computation, and their industrial applications. Over the last years, EC in its various forms has emerged as one of the major topics in the scientific community and many EC techniques have been successfully applied to solve problems in a wide variety of fields. These articles also reflect the journal's objective of dedicating to provide a exchangeable forum academically and high quality results for innovative topics, trends and research in the field of EC, to succeed in expanding the fields and depths the most principal and critical concepts that will form the applications from EC more matured in the future.

IJAEC is intended to serve and support scientists, professionals, entrepreneurs, government employees, policy and decision makers, educators, students, and all people who are working in this scientific field or who are interested in considering and using EC techniques for their specific applications. This academic resource dedicates to provide international audiences with the highest quality research manuscripts in emphasizing computational results which have been are ideally put in the context of algorithm design; in addition, purely theoretical papers will also be encouraged. Researchers, academicians, practitioners and students will find this journal as a critical source of reference for all advanced intelligent computational applications and developments. On the other hand, along with the tremendous development in complicated public economic and business operations, EC has also been viewed as a great application and a solution to solve in a variety of business modelling. *IJAEC* is also devoted to data analysis and applications and tools used for business modelling, including all areas of pattern recognition, forecasting, classification, optimization cluster, bio-inspired systems and novel applications. A summary of the scope of IJAEC includes:

1. **Intelligent techniques:** Fuzzy computing, neural computing, and evolutionary computing; evolutionary algorithms (genetic algorithms, simulated annealing algorithms,…); evolutionary programming; probabilistic computing; immunological computing; grid computing; natural computing; expert and hybrid systems (methods); Chaos theory; and other intelligent techniques (interactive computational models);

2. **Data analysis:** Classification, regression, and optimization cluster; decision support system; statistical pattern recognition; signal or image processing;

3. **Applications and tools:** Vision or pattern recognition, time series forecasting; biomedical engineering; manufacturing systems; power and energy; data mining; data visualization; bio-inspired systems and tools and applications.

The first article in the inaugural issue of IJAEC, entitled "Ant Clustering Algorithms" by Chiou from NCTU (Taiwan) and Chou from Feng Chia University (Taiwan), of which one of the journal editors (Chiou) is a coauthor, proposes three ant clustering algorithms (ACAs) to modify the ant colony metaheuristic by reformulating the clustering problem into a network problem. The solution effectiveness at different problem scales consistently shows that ACA-2 outperforms other alternative clustering methods, including agglomerative hierarchy clustering algorithm (AHCA), K-means algorithm (KMA) and genetic clustering algorithm (GCA), in the meanwhile, ACA-2also performs considerably better in solution stability as the problem scales or the number of clusters gets larger.

The second article of this issue, entitled "Three Novel Methods to Predict Traffic Time Series in Reconstructed State Spaces" by Lan from Ta Hwa Institute of Technology (Taiwan), Lin from Central Police University (Taiwan), and Kuo from University of Maryland (USA), of which one of the journal editors (Lan) is a coauthor, deals with a more applicative topic, and embeds one-dimensional historical traffic series into appropriate multidimensional state spaces by Takens' algorithm and then to perform fuzzy reasoning to infer the future changes in traffic series based on the latest observed traffic vector. Three novel methods, called temporal confined (TC), spatiotemporal confined (STC) and spatial confined (SC) methods respectively employ different fuzzy reasoning logics to select "temporal similarity," "spatiotemporal similarity," and "spatial similarity" of historical traffic trajectories, which are confined by designated temporal, spatiotemporal, and spatial domains. The results show that the overall prediction accuracies for these three novel methods are satisfactorily high.

The third article of the issue, entitled "Self-Evolvable Protocol Design Using Genetic Algorithms" by Yao from Huawei Technologies (UK), Guan from Xian Jiatong-Liverpool University (China), Jiang from National University of Singapore (Singapore), and Kiourktsidis from Brunel (UK), of which one of the journal editors (Guan) is a coauthor, applies Genetic algorithms (GAs) to design an evolvable protocol, one of the Self-modifying protocols (SMP) designed which can be modified at run time so that they can adapt to the changing communicating environment and user requirements on the fly, in order to equip communication peers with more autonomy and intelligence. They then use the Network Simulator (NS2) to evaluate this evolvable protocol module to demonstrate the feasibility of our new design approach.

The final article of this issue, entitled "Facial Feature Tracking via Evolutionary Multiobjective Optimization" by Larson and Yen both from Oklahoma State University (USA), of which one of the journal editors (Yen) is a coauthor, describes an application of traditional patter recognition in facial feature tracking, which has received considerable attention in recent decades for its applications in video gaming, interaction, and numerous other disciplines. Of particular interest is its application in very low bit rate coding in which optimization is used to analyze head and shoulder sequences; they present a combination of non-dominated sorting genetic algorithm and a deterministic search to find optimal facial animation parameters at many bandwidths simultaneously. The results show that the overall methodology works effectively and reliably.

The first article of Volume 1, Issue 2, entitled "Ordered Incremental Multi-Objective Problem Solving Based on Genetic Algorithms" by Mo from IBM (Singapore), Guan from Xian Jiatong-Liverpool

University (China), and Puthusserypady from National University of Singapore (Singapore), of which one of the journal editors (Guan) is a coauthor, employs the incremental approach to normal multiple objective genetic algorithms (MOGA), namely IMOGA, in ordering issue investigation. Incremental approach can be used to enhance the performance of various MOGAs, which was developed to evolve each objective incrementally. Their experimental results on benchmark problems showed that the proposed approach can help IMOGA reach its potential best performance.

The second article of the issue, entitled "Comparative Study of Evolutionary Computing Methods for Parameter Estimation of Power Quality Signals" by Pandi and Panigrahi from IIT Delhi (India), of which one of the journal editors (Panigrahi) is a coauthor, presents an evolutionary algorithm approach based on adaptive particle swarm optimization (APSO) to determine the amplitude, phase and frequency of a power quality signal. Along with the sensitivity of load equipments to various power quality disturbances, power quality disturbance monitoring plays an important role in the deregulated power market scenario. They attempt to make to highlight the efficacy of different evolutionary optimization techniques like classical PSO, constriction based PSO, clonal algorithm (CLONALOG), adaptive bacterial foraging (ABF) and the proposed adaptive particle swarm optimization (APSO) to extract different parameters like amplitude, phase and frequency of harmonic distorted power quality signal and voltage flicker.

The third article, entitled "A Heuristic Approach for Multi Objective Distribution Feeder Reconfiguration: Using Fuzzy Sets in Normalization of Objective Functions" by Milani from Islamic Azad University (Iran), and Haghifam from Tarbiat Modarres University (Iran), firstly presents an algorithm for network reconfiguration based on the heuristic rules and fuzzy multi objective approach for the reconfiguration of switches in a distribution network, where each objective is normalized with inspiration from fuzzy set to cause optimization more flexible and formulized as a unique multi objective function. Secondly, genetic algorithm (GA) is used for solving the suggested model, in which there is no risk of non-linear objective functions and constraints. The effectiveness of the proposed method is demonstrated through several examples.

The final article of the second issue of 2010 is entitled "A Scheduling Model with Multi-Objective Optimization for Computational Grids using NSGA-II" and is written by Raza and Vidyarthi from Jawaharlal Nehru University (India). Their study describes an application of multi-objective optimization problem for scheduling a job on the grid. Genetic algorithm is an effective tool in solving problems that requires sub-optimal solutions and finds uses in multi-objective optimization problems. They addresses this problem by introducing a scheduling model for a modular job on a computational grid with the dual objective; minimizing the turnaround time and maximizing the reliability of the job execution using NSGA - II. Simulation study and a comparison of the results with other similar models reveal the effectiveness of the model.

The first Volume 1, Issue 3 article, "Extrapolated Biogeography-Based Optimization (eBBO) for Global Numerical Optimization and Microstrip Patch Antenna Design" by Lohokare, Pattnaik, Devi, and Joshi from National Institute of Technical Teachers' Training and Research (India), Panigrahi from Indian Institute of Technology (India), and Das from Kansas State University (USA), of which one of the journal editors (Panigrahi) is a coauthor, extend the original biogeography-based optimization (BBO) and proposes a hybrid version combined with ePSO (particle swarm optimization with extrapolation technique), namely eBBO, for unconstrained global numerical optimization problems in the continuous domain. The BBO uses the idea of probabilistically sharing features between solutions based on the solutions' fitness values. Therefore, its exploitation ability is good but it lacks in exploration ability. eBBO combines the exploitation ability of BBO with the exploration ability of ePSO effectively, which can generate global optimum solutions. The experimental analysis of eBBO, by comparing with original BBO and other versions of BBO in terms of the quality of the final solution and the convergence rate, indicates that the proposed approach is effective and efficient and improves the exploration ability of BBO.

In "Posterior Sampling Using Particle Swarm Optimizers and Model Reduction Techniques," the second article in Volume 1, Issue 3, by Martínez from Stanford University, University of California-Berkeley (USA) and University of Oviedo (Spain), Gonzalo and Muñiz from University of Oviedo (Spain), and Mariethoz and Mukerji from Stanford University (USA), presents a practical applications based on particle swarm optimizers and reduction techniques in the domain of environmental geophysics, where it provides a proxy for the posterior distribution when it is used in its explorative form to improve the drawbacks of Monte Carlo methods in solving inverse problems. The inverse problems are ill-posed and posterior sampling is a way of providing an estimate of the uncertainty based on a finite set of the family of models that fit the observed data within the same tolerance. Finally, this chapter also presents a hydrogeological example how to perform a similar task for inverse problems in high dimensional spaces through the combined use with model reduction techniques.

In the third article in Volume 1, Issue 3, "Reserve Constrained Multi-Area Economic Dispatch Employing Evolutionary Approach," by Sharma and Pandit from M.I.T.S. (India), compares classic PSO and DE strategies and their variants for reserve constrained MAED (Multi-area economic dispatch). The objective of Multi-area economic dispatch (MAED) is to determine the generation levels and the interchange power between areas that minimize fuel costs, while satisfying power balance and generating limit and transmission constraints. If an area with excess power is not adjacent to a power deficient area, or the tie-line between the two areas is at transmission limit, it is necessary to find an alternative path between these two areas to transmit additional power. When a MAED problem is solved with spinning reserve constraints, the problem becomes further complicated. The power allocation to each unit is done in such a manner that after supplying the total load, some specified reserve is left behind. The performance is tested on a 2-area system having 4 generating units and a 4-area, 16-unit system.

In "Application of Machine Learning Techniques to Predict Software Reliability," the final paper in Volume 1, No. 3, Mohanty, Patra from Berhampur University (India), and Ravi from Institute for Development and Research in Banking Technology (India) employ machine learning techniques, specifically, back propagation trained neural network (BPNN), group method of data handling (GMDH), counter propagation neural network (CPNN), dynamic evolving neuro–fuzzy inference system (DENFIS), genetic programming (GP), TreeNet, statistical multiple linear regression (MLR), and multivariate adaptive regression splines (MARS), to accurately forecast software reliability. The effectiveness of these models is demonstrated on three datasets taken from literature, where performance is compared in terms of normalized root mean square error (NRMSE) obtained in the test set. From rigorous experiments conducted, it was observed that GP outperformed all techniques in all datasets, with GMDH coming a close second.

In "Buffer Management in Cellular IP Networks Using Evolutionary Algorithms," the first paper in Volume 1, No. 4, Anbar and Vidyarthi from Jawaharlal Nehru University (India) employ evolutionary algorithms (GA and PSO) to assist to manage buffers of the cellular IP networks. Authors propose a two-tier model for buffer (gateway and base station buffer) management in cellular IP network. The first tier applies a prioritization algorithm for prioritizing real-time packets in the buffer of the gateway with a specified threshold. The packets which couldn't be served, after the threshold, is given to the nearest cells of the network to be dealt with in the second tier. Consequently, evolutionary algorithms are employed to optimally store these packets in the buffer of the base stations. Their experiments have depicted the advantage and disadvantage of the proposed models.

In the second paper in Volume 1, No. 4, "Using Evolution Strategies to Perform Stellar Population Synthesis for Galaxy Spectra from SDSS," Gomez from Katholieke Universiteit Leuven (Belgium) and Fuentes from Fuentes from University of Texas at El Paso (USA) employ evolution strategies (ES) to automatically extract a set of physical parameters from a sample of galaxy spectra taken from the Sloan Digital Sky Survey (SDSS). They pose this parameter extraction as an optimization problem and then solve it using ES. The main idea is to reconstruct each galaxy spectrum by means of a linear combination of three different theoretical models for stellar population synthesis. The goal is to find a model that minimizes this difference using ES as the algorithm to explore the parameter space. Their experimental results show that ES are very well suited to extract stellar population parameters from galaxy spectra.

The third article in Volume 1, No. 4 is "A Novel Puzzle Based Compaction (PBC) Strategy for Enhancing the Utilization of Reconfigurable Resources" by Saleh from Mansoura University (Egypt). It introduces a novel puzzle based compaction (PBC) technique to overcome the faults, such as internal and external fragmentations, from traditional compaction techniques in Field Programmable Gate Array (FPGA) fields. PBC succeeded not only to eliminate the internal fragmentations but also to minimize the external fragmentations. Moreover, the author also develops a novel formula to exactly calculate the amount of external fragmentations generated by hosting a set of tasks inside the reconfigurable chip. Experimental results have shown that PBC outperforms recent compaction techniques in which the chip utilization has reached 87%.

For transmission network expansion planning with and without security constraints, the fourth paper in Volume 1, No. 4, entitled "A Comparative Study of Metaheuristic Methods for Transmission Network Expansion Planning," by Verma from TERI University (India), Bijwe and Panigrahi from IIT (India), of which one of the journal editors (Panigrahi) is a coauthor, presents a comparative analysis of three metaheuristic algorithms, Bacteria foraging (BF), Genetic algorithm (GA) and Particle swarm optimization (PSO), for transmission network expansion planning with and without security constraints. Experimental results for IEEE 24 bus system are obtained with the above three metaheuristics and shown that BF method is a robust one and provides better results as compared to those with other two methods, in terms of least standard deviation and best convergence characteristics.

The articles in this compendium display a broad range of cutting edge topics in evolutionary algorithms, evolutionary programming, fuzzy computation, and neural computation. The preface author believes that hybrid evolutionary algorithms will play more important role in the evolutionary computation fields. These evolutionary algorithms almost have their theoretical drawbacks, such as lack of knowledge memory or storage functions, time consuming in training, and being trapped in local optimum, therefore, by hybridizing some novel search technique to adjust their internal parameters (e.g., mutation rate, crossover rate, annealing temperature, etc.) to overcome those mentioned shortcomings. Firstly, for example, in genetic algorithm (GA), new individuals are generated by the following operators, selection, crossover, and mutation. For all types of objective functions, the generation begins with a binary coding for the parameter set. Based on this special binary coding process, GA is able to solve some specified problems which are not easily to be solved by traditional algorithms. GA can empirically provide a few best fitted off-springs from the whole population, however, after some generations, due to low diversity of the population, it might lead to a premature convergence. Similarly, simulated annealing (SA) is a generic probabilistic search technique that simulates the material physical process of heating and controlled cooling. Each step of SA attempts to replace the current state by a random move. The new state may then be accepted with a probability that depends both on the difference between the corresponding function values and also on a global parameter, temperature. Thus, SA has some institution to reach more ideal solutions. However, SA costs lots of computation time in annealing process. To improve premature convergence and to receive more suitable objective function values, it is necessary to find some effective approach to overcome these drawbacks from GA and SA. Hybridization of genetic algorithm with simulated annealing (GA-SA) algorithm is an innovative trial by applying the superior capability of SA algorithm to reach more ideal solutions, and by employing the mutation process of GA to enhance searching process. GA-SA algorithm has been applied to the fields of system design (Shie & Peralta, 2005), system and network optimization (Zhao & Zeng, 2006), continuous-time production planning (Ganesh & Punniyamoorthy, 2005), and electrical power districting problem (Bergey, Ragsdale, & Hoskote, 2003). Furthermore, due to easy implementation process and special mechanism to escape from local optimum (Wang, Zheng, & Lin, 2001), chaos and chaos-based searching algorithms have received intense attentions (Liu et al., 2005; Cai et al., 2007). Applications of chaotic sequence to carefully expand variable searching space, i.e., let variable travel ergodically over the searching space, are more and more popular to be employed in evolutionary computation fields.

Secondly, several disadvantages embedded in these evolutionary algorithms are required to be improved to get more satisfied performance. For example, based on the operation procedure of SA, subtle and skillful adjustment in the annealing schedule is required, such as the size of the temperature steps during annealing. Particularly, the temperature of each state is discrete and unchangeable, which does not meet the requirement of continuous decrease in temperature in actual physical annealing processes. In addition, SA is easy to accept deteriorate solution with high temperature, and it is hard to escape from local minimum trap with low temperature (Pin, Lin, & Zhang, 2009). To overcome these drawbacks of SA, the cloud theory is considered. Cloud theory is a model of the uncertainty transformation between quantitative representation and qualitative concept using language value (Deyi, Haijin, & Xuemei, 1995). It is successfully used in intelligence control (Deyi et al., 1998; Feizhou et al., 1999), data mining (Shuliang et al., 2003), spatial analysis (Hajun & Yu, 2007), intelligent algorithm improvement (Yunfang, Chaohua, & Weirong, 2005), and so on. Based on the operation procedure of SA, subtle and skillful adjustment in the annealing schedule is required, such as the size of the temperature steps during annealing, the temperature range, the number of re-starts and re-direction of the search, the annealing process is like a fuzzy system in which the molecules move from large scale to small scale randomly as the temperature decreases. In addition, due to its Monte Carlo scheme and lacking of knowledge memory functions, time consuming is also an another boring problem. Author has tried to employ chaotic simulated annealing (CSA) algorithm, to overcome these shortcomings. In which, the transiently chaotic dynamics are temporarily generated for foraging and self-organizing, then, gradually vanished with autonomous decreasing of the temperature, and are accompanied by successive bifurcations and converged to a stable equilibrium. Therefore, CSA has significantly improved the randomization of Monte Carlo scheme, and, has controlled the convergent process by bifurcation structures instead of stochastic "thermal" fluctuations, eventually, performed efficient searching including a global optimum state. However, as mentioned that the temperature of each state is discrete and unchangeable, which does not meet the requirement of continuous decrease in temperature in actual physical annealing processes. Even some temperature annealing function is exponential in general, the temperature is gradually falling with a fixed value in every annealing step and the changing process of temperature between two neighbor steps is not continuous. This phenomenon also appears while other types of temperature update functions are implemented, such as arithmetical, geometrical or logarithmic one. In the cloud theory, by introducing the Y condition normal cloud generator to the temperature generation process, it can randomly generate a group of new values that distribute around the given value like "cloud". Let the fixed temperature point of each step become a changeable temperature zone in which the temperature of each state generation in every annealing step is chosen randomly, the course of temperature changing in the whole annealing process is nearly continuous and fits the physical annealing process better. Therefore, based on chaotic sequence and cloud theory, the CCSA is employed to replace the stochastic "thermal" fluctuations control from traditional SA, to enhance the continuously physical temperature annealing process from CSA. The cloud theory can realize the transformation between a qualitative concept in words and its numerical representation. It is able to be employed to avoid problems mentioned above.

Thirdly, the concepts of combined or hybrid models are also deserved to be considered. Please notice that the so-called hybrid model means that some process of the former model is integrated into the process of the later one, for example, hybrid A and B implies some process of A are controlled by A, some are by B. On the other hand, for the so-called combined model, it only indicated that the output of the former model is then the input of the later one, therefore, the classification results from combined models will be superior to single model. Based on this knowledge, please check clearly which types (hybrid model or combined model) your proposed model is. The combined models are employed to further capture more data pattern information from the analyzed data series. For example, inspired by the concept of recurrent neural networks (RNNs) that every unit is considered as an output of the network and the provision of adjusted information as input in a training process (Kechriotis, Zervas, & Manolakos, 1994), the recurrent learning mechanism framework is also combined into the original analyzed model. For a feed-forward neural network, links may be established within layers of a neural network. These types of networks are called recurrent neural networks. RNNs are extensively applied in time series forecasting. Jordan (Jordan, 1987) proposes a recurrent neural network model (Figure 1) for controlling robots. Elman (Elman, 1990) develops a recurrent neural network model (Figure 2) to solve linguistics problems. Williams and Zipser (Williams & Zipser, 1989) present a recurrent network model (Figure 3) to solve nonlinear adaptive filtering and pattern recognition problems. These three models mentioned all consist of multilayer perceptron (MLP) with a hidden layer. Jordan networks have a feedback loop from the output layer with past values to an additional input, namely "context layer". Then, output values from the context layer are fed back into the hidden layer. Elman networks have a feedback loop from the hidden layer to the context layer. In Williams and Zipser networks, nodes in the hidden layer are fully connected to each other. Both Jordan and Elman networks include an additional information source from the output layer or the hidden layer. Hence, these models use mainly past information to capture detailed information. Williams and Zipser networks take much more information from the hidden layer and back into themselves. Therefore, Williams and Zipser networks are sensitive when models are implemented (Tsoi & Back, 1994). For another combined model, on the other hand, some data series sometimes reveals a seasonal tendency due to cyclic economic activities or seasonal nature hour to hour, day to day, week to week, month to month, and season to season, such as hourly peak in a working day, weekly peak in a business week, and monthly peak in a demand planned year. In order to excellently deal with cyclic/seasonal trend data series, some useful trial, e.g., seasonal mechanism (Azadeh & Ghaderi, 2008; Deo & Hurvich, 2006) is also received some intentions.

Based on the discussions above, it will also become another research tendency in evolutionary computation, that is, evolutionary algorithms support systems to guide researchers how to use proper evolutionary algorithms in parameters determination for their analysis models. This is because that for any analysis models (including classification model, forecasting model, and so on), the most important problem is how to catch the data pattern, and applied the learned patterns or rules to receive satisfied performance, i.e., the key successful factor is how to suitably look for data pattern. The data pattern

Figure 1. Jordan (Jordan, 1987) networks

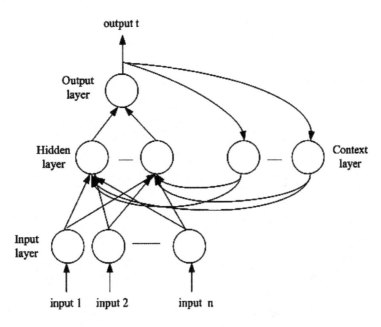

Figure 2. Elman (Elman, 1990) networks

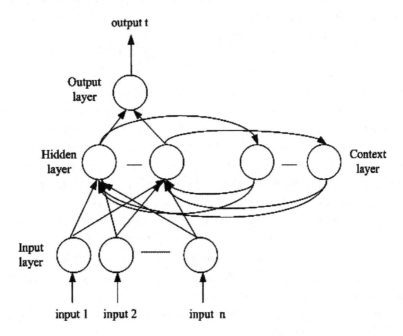

could be classified into three categories, (1) fluctuation: changing violently according to policy, or herding behaviors of investors; (2) regular pattern: annual increasing or decreasing tendency, or seasonality/cyclic; (3) noise: accidental events (e.g., 911 event, SARS event), or man-made events (e.g., product promotion event). However, each model itself has excelled ability to catch specific data pattern. For example, exponential smoothing and ARIMA models focus on strict increasing (or decreasing) time

Figure 3. Williams and Zipser (Williams & Zipser, 1989) networks

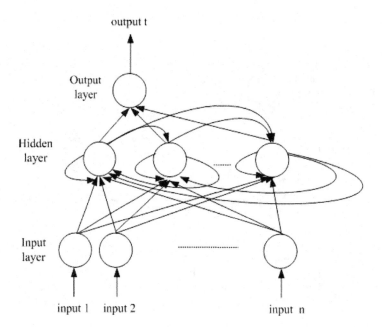

series data, i.e., linear pattern, even they have seasonal modification mechanism to analyze seasonal (cyclic) change; due to artificial learning function to adjust the suitable training rules, ANN model is excelled only if historical data pattern has been learned, it is lacks of systematic explanation how the accurate forecasting results are obtained; support vector regression (SVR) model could acquire superior performance only if proper parameters determination search algorithms. Therefore, it is essential to construct an inference system to collect the characteristic rules to determine the data pattern category. Secondly, it should assign appropriate approach to implement forecasting: for (1) ARIMA or exponential smoothing approaches, the only work is to adjust their differential or seasonal parameters; (2) ANN or SVR models, the forthcoming problem is how to determine best parameters combination (e.g., numbers of hidden layer, units of each layer, learning rate; or hyper-parameters) to acquire superior forecasting performance. Particularly, for the focus of this discussion, in order to determine the most proper parameter combination, a series of evolutionary algorithms should be employed to test which data pattern is familiar with, such as genetic algorithms (GA), simulated annealing algorithms (SA), ant colony optimization (ACO), Tabu search (TA), immune algorithm (IA), and particle swarm optimization algorithm (PSO). Based on experimental findings, those evolutionary algorithms themselves also have merits and drawbacks, for example, GA and IA could handle excellently in regular trend data pattern (real number) (Pai & Hong, 2005), SA excelled in fluctuation or noise data pattern (real number) (Pai & Hong, 2005b, 2006), TA is good in regular cyclic data pattern (real number) (Hong et al., 2006), and ACO is well done in integer number searching.

As aforementioned, it is possible to propose an intelligent support system to improve the usage efficiency of evolutionary algorithms hybridized in the analysis model, namely evolutionary algorithms support system (EASS). The main flow chart of the EASS suggested in this conclusion is given in **Figure 4**. Firstly, employ fuzzy logic to construct the inference system to pre-process the time series data, and find out or define the characteristic rules set of data pattern, such as linear, logarithmic, inverse,

Figure 4. The evolutionary algorithms support system (EASS)

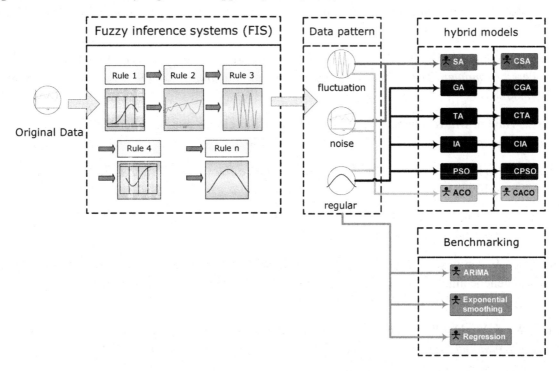

quadratic, cubic, compound, power, growth, exponential, etc. Secondly, filter the original data by those data pattern rules set, then, recognize the appropriate data pattern (fluctuation, regular, or noise). The recognition decision rules should include two principles: (1) the change rate of two continuous data; and (2) the decreasing or increasing trend of the change rate, i.e., behavior of the approached curve. Finally, decide appropriate evolutionary algorithm to be hybridized in the analysis model, in addition, to avoid trapping in local optimum, adjustment approach could be employed with associated evolutionary algorithms into these hybrid models.

This discussion of the work by the author of this preface highlights work in an emerging area of evolutionary computation that has come to the forefront over the past decade. These articles in this text span a great deal more of cutting edge areas that are truly interdisciplinary in nature.

REFERENCES

Azadeh, A., & Ghaderi, S. F. (2008). Annual electricity consumption forecasting by neural network in high energy consuming industrial sectors. *Energy Conversion and Management, 49*, 2272–2278. doi:10.1016/j.enconman.2008.01.035

Bergey, P. K., Ragsdale, C. T., & Hoskote, M. (2003). A simulated annealing genetic algorithm for the electrical power districting problem. *Annals of Operations Research, 121*, 33–55. doi:10.1023/A:1023347000978

Cai, J., Ma, X., Li, L., & Peng, H. (2007). Chaotic particle swarm optimization for economic dispatch considering the generator constraints. *Energy Conversion and Management, 48*, 645–653. doi:10.1016/j.enconman.2006.05.020

Deo, R., & Hurvich, C. (2006). Forecasting realized volatility using a long- memory stochastic volatility model: Estimation, prediction and seasonal adjustment. *Journal of Econometrics, 131*, 29–58. doi:10.1016/j.jeconom.2005.01.003

Deyi, L., Cheung, D., Shi, X. M., & Ng, V. (1998). Uncertainty reasoning based on cloud models in controllers. *Computer Science and Mathematics with Applications, 35*, 99–123. doi:10.1016/S0898-1221(97)00282-4

Deyi, L., Haijun, M., & Xuemei, S. (1995). Membership clouds and membership cloud generators. *Journal of Computer Research and Development, 32*, 15–20.

Elman, J. L. (1990). Finding structure in time. *Cognitive Science, 14*, 179–211. doi:10.1207/s15516709cog1402_1

Feizhou, Z., Yuezu, F., Chengzhi, S., & Deyi, L. (1999). Intelligent control based membership cloud generators. *Acta Aeronautica et Astronautica Sinica, 20*, 89–92.

Ganesh, K., & Punniyamoorthy, M. (2005). Optimization of continuous-time production planning using hybrid genetic algorithms-simulated annealing. *International Journal of Advanced Manufacturing Technology, 26*, 148–154. doi:10.1007/s00170-003-1976-4

Haijun, W., & Yu, D. (2007). Spatial clustering method based on cloud model. In *Proceedings of the Fourth International Conference on Fuzzy Systems and Knowledge Discovery*, 2007, (pp. 272-276).

Hong, W. C., Pai, P. F., Yang, S. L., & Theng, R. (2006). Highway traffic forecasting by support vector regression model with tabu search algorithms. In *Proceedings of the IEEE International Joint Conference on Neural Networks*, 2006, (pp. 1617-21).

Jordan, M. I. Attractor dynamics and parallelism in a connectionist sequential machine. In *Proceedings of the 8th Annual Conference of the Cognitive Science Society*, 1987, (pp. 531-546).

Kechriotis, G., Zervas, E., & Manolakos, E. S. (1994). Using recurrent neural networks for adaptive communication channel equalization. *IEEE Neural Networks, 5*, 267–278. doi:10.1109/72.279190

Liu, B., Wang, L., Jin, Y. H., Tang, F., & Huang, D. X. (2005). Improved particle swarm optimization combined with chaos. *Chaos, Solitons, and Fractals, 25*, 1261–1271. doi:10.1016/j.chaos.2004.11.095

Pai, P. F., & Hong, W. C. (2005a). Forecasting regional electric load based on recurrent support vector machines with genetic algorithms. *Electric Power Systems Research, 74*, 417–425. doi:10.1016/j.epsr.2005.01.006

Pai, P. F., & Hong, W. C. (2005b). Support vector machines with simulated annealing algorithms in electricity load forecasting. *Energy Conversion and Management, 46*, 2669–2688. doi:10.1016/j.enconman.2005.02.004

Pai, P. F., & Hong, W. C. (2006). Software reliability forecasting by support vector machines with simulated annealing algorithms. *Journal of Systems and Software, 79*, 747–755. doi:10.1016/j.jss.2005.02.025

Pin, L., Lin, Y., & Zhang, J. (2009). Cloud theory-based simulated annealing algorithm and application. *Engineering Applications of Artificial Intelligence, 22*, 742–749. doi:10.1016/j.engappai.2009.03.003

Shieh, H. J., & Peralta, R. C. (2005). Optimal in situ bioremediation design by hybrid genetic algorithm-simulated annealing. *Journal of Water Resources Planning and Management, 131,* 67–78. doi:10.1061/(ASCE)0733-9496(2005)131:1(67)

Shuliang, W., Deren, L., Wenzhong, S., Deyi, L., & Xinzhou, W. (2003). Cloud model-based spatial data mining. *Geographical Information Science, 9,* 67–78.

Tsoi, A. C., & Back, A. D. (1994). Locally recurrent globally feedforward networks: A critical review of architectures. *IEEE Transactions on Neural Networks, 5,* 229–239. doi:10.1109/72.279187

Wang, L., Zheng, D. Z., & Lin, Q. S. (2001). Survey on chaotic optimization methods. *Computing Technology and Automation, 20,* 1–5.

Williams, R., & Zipser, D. (1989). A learning algorithm for continually running fully recurrent neural networks. *Neural Computation, 1,* 270–280. doi:10.1162/neco.1989.1.2.270

Yunfang, Z., Chaohua, D., & Weirong, C. (2005). Adaptive probabilities of crossover and mutation in genetic algorithms based on cloud generators. *Journal of Computer Information Systems, 1,* 671–678.

Zhao, F., & Zeng, X. (2006). Simulated annealing—Genetic algorithm for transit network optimization. *Journal of Computing in Civil Engineering, 20,* 57–68. doi:10.1061/(ASCE)0887-3801(2006)20:1(57)

Chapter 1
Ant Clustering Algorithms

Yu-Chiun Chiou
National Chiao Tung University, Taiwan

Shih-Ta Chou
Feng Chia University, Taiwan

ABSTRACT

This paper proposes three ant clustering algorithms (ACAs): ACA-1, ACA-2 and ACA-3. The core logic of the proposed ACAs is to modify the ant colony metaheuristic by reformulating the clustering problem into a network problem. For a clustering problem of N objects and K clusters, a fully connected network of N nodes is formed with link costs, representing the dissimilarity of any two nodes it connects. K ants are then to collect their own nodes according to the link costs and following the pheromone trail laid by previous ants. The proposed three ACAs have been validated on a small-scale problem solved by a total enumeration method. The solution effectiveness at different problem scales consistently shows that ACA-2 outperforms among these three ACAs. A further comparison of ACA-2 with other commonly used clustering methods, including agglomerative hierarchy clustering algorithm (AHCA), K-means algorithm (KMA) and genetic clustering algorithm (GCA), shows that ACA-2 significantly outperforms them in solution effectiveness for the most of cases and also performs considerably better in solution stability as the problem scales or the number of clusters gets larger.

1. INTRODUCTION

Clustering, so-called set partitioning, is a basic methodology widely applied in the fields including statistics, mathematical programming (e.g., location selecting, network partitioning, routing, scheduling and assignment problems) and com- puter science (e.g., pattern recognition, learning theory, image processing and computer graph- ics). The core logic of clustering is to classify all objects into several mutually exclusive groups so as to achieve some optimal conditions. Most conventional clustering methods rapidly become computationally intractable as the problem scale

DOI: 10.4018/978-1-4666-1749-0.ch001

gets larger due to the combinatorial nature of the methods. The mathematical model of clustering for a given number (K) of clusters can be formulated as:

$$[CA] \quad Max \ F(X) \tag{1}$$

Subject to:

$$\sum_{j} x_{ij} = 1 \ \textit{for all } i \tag{2}$$

$$\sum_{j} x_{jj} = K \tag{3}$$

$$x_{ij} \le x_{jj} \ \textit{for all } i, j \tag{4}$$

$$x_{ij} = \{0,1\} \ \textit{for all } i, j \tag{5}$$

where x_{ij} denotes the relationship among objects. $x_{ij}=1$ indicates that object i is assigned to object j, (also cluster j). $x_{ij}=0$ otherwise; $i, j=\{1,2,...,N\}$, N is the number of objects, K is the number of clusters. Accordingly, $x_{jj}=1$ represents that object j is assigned to itself, indicating that cluster j has been formed. $F(X)$ is the objective function. X is the vector of x_{ij} for all i, j. Equation (2) represents that each object must be assigned to one and only one object (cluster). Equation (3) represents that a total of exactly K clusters will be formed. Equation (4) represents that the object i can only be assigned to the object which is also assigned to itself, *i.e.* the corresponding cluster has been formed.

The total number of feasible solutions of [CA] is: $|\pi_K| = (\frac{1}{K!})\sum_{j=0}^{K}(-1)^{K-j}\binom{K}{j}j^N$. That is, the solution space of [CA] is exponential to the problem size and number of clusters. For instance, there are a total of 511 feasible solutions for 10 objects ($N=10$) to be divided into 2 clusters ($K=2$). There are a total of 42,525 feasible solutions for 10 objects to be divided into 5 clusters. Brucker

(1978) and Welch (1983) proved that, for specific objective functions, clustering becomes an NP-hard problem when the number of clusters exceeds three, if one aims to find the optimal clusters. Hansen and Jaumard (1987) pointed out that even though the best algorithms developed for some specific objective functions, there would exhibit complexities of $O(N^3logN)$ or $O(N^3)$, leaving some room for further improvement.

The heuristic algorithms for clustering can generally be divided into five categories: statistics clustering, mathematical programming, network programming, neural network and metaheuristics. The algorithms for conventional statistic clustering (e.g. Ward, 1963; MacQueen, 1967) include agglomerative hierarchical clustering method, divisive hierarchical clustering method, and K-means. The algorithms for mathematical programming (e.g. Mulvey & Crowder, 1979; Trick, 1992; Moshe, *et al.*, 1996; Savelsbergh, 1997) range from dynamic programming, Lagrangian relaxation, linear relaxation, column generation and branch-and-price. The algorithms for network programming (e.g. Ali & Thiagarajan, 1989; El-Darzi & Mitra, 1995) include graph theoretic relaxations and network relaxation. The algorithms for neural networks mainly include self-organizing map (SOM) (e.g. Vesanto & Alhonierni, 2000; Wu and Chow, 2004) and adaptive resonance theory (e.g. Bartfai, 1996). The algorithms for metaheuristics have been rapidly developed recently, including genetic algorithms (e.g. Lunchian, *et al.*, 1994; Jiang, *et al.*, 1997; Lozano, *et al.*, 1998; Chiou & Lan, 2002; Garai & Chaudhuri, 2004), Tabu search (e.g. Al-Sultan, 1995; Sung & Jin, 2000), simulated annealing (e.g. Klein & Dubes, 1989; Selim & Al-Sultan, 1991), and ant colony optimization (e.g. Shelokar, *et al.*, 2004; Tsai, *et al.*, 2004; Kuo, et al., 2005; Yang & Kamel, 2006; Azzg et al., 2007).

Ant colony optimization (ACO) is a newly developed metaheuristic technique proposed by Dorigo *et al.* (1996) and Dorigo and Gambardella (1997). It is inspired by the behaviors of ant colonies in nature as they forage for food. In searching for food, ants mark the trails they used by depositing a substance called pheromone, which acts as a medium for communication information among ants. Because the pheromone will evaporate over time, the "shorter path" from nest to food will be deposited more amount of pheromone by more ants within a given period of time. Thus, the amount of pheromone will lead the following ants to find the shortest path. Compared with other conventional heuristics or metaheuristics, ACO has been proven more efficient and effective in solving such problems as traveling salesman problem (Dorigo & Gambardella, 1997), vehicle routing problem (Bella & McMullenb, 2004), quadratic assignment problem (Maniezzo & Colorni, 1999), and flowshop scheduling (Jayaraman *et al.*, 2000). Because of the excellent performance of ACO and the strategic importance of clustering, some works begin to explore the possibility in application of ACO to clustering. For optimally clustering N objects into K clusters, Shelokar, *et al.* (2004) proposed an updating procedure of a $N \times K$ pheromone matrix used to determine the clusters of each object belonging to by adopting either exploitation or exploration approaches. The performance of the algorithm was proven to be superior to those of three other clustering algorithms based on genetic algorithms, simulated annealing and Tabu search, respectively. Tsai *et al.* (2004) proposed an ACO-based clustering algorithm with different favor (ACODF) by adopting the strategies of simulated annealing to decrease the number of cities (objects) needed to be visited as number of iterations is elapsed and of tournament selection to choose a path. The algorithm has also been validated by comparing with other two hybrid methods, fast self-organizing map combining with K-means (FSOM+K-means) and genetic K-means approach (GKA). Kuo *et al.* (2005) proposed an ant K-means clustering algorithm by modifying the K-means as locating the objects in a cluster with the probability updated by the pheromone.

Yang and Kamel (2006) developed an aggregated ant clustering algorithm incorporating some parallel and independent ant colonies and a queen ant agent. The performance of the proposed algorithm has then been proven by comparing to single ant-based clustering algorithm and K-means. Azzag *et al.* (2007) proposed a hierarchical ant based clustering algorithm (AntTree) in which the ant behavior is used to build a hierarchical tree-structured partitioning of the objects. The performance of the AntTree has been proven by comparing with K-means, ANTCLASS, and agglomerative hierarchical clustering.

Although many ant-based clustering algorithms have been proposed and validated, several gaps can still be identified. Firstly, an empty cluster might be formed, once the clustering objects become more homogeneous and the number of clusters gets larger. Besides, most of abovementioned algorithms mainly utilize the pheromone to indicate the cluster which the objects should be classified to, but the similarities among objects are barely considered in the clustering process. Moreover, once an object has been clustered into a specific cluster by ACO, and then the object will never ever be re-assigned in the following clustering procedures, even the object is not belonging to the cluster which it was previously assigned to. At last, for enhancing the performance, many algorithms hybridized other algorithms, e.g. K-means, or employed complicated ant interaction structure, e.g., the aggregated ant clustering algorithm and AntTree, making the algorithm too complicated to be implemented.

To remedy these gaps, this paper proposes three ant clustering algorithms (ACAs) which are characterized with various exchanging strategies to provide a chance for the clustered objects being re-assigned. The proposed ACAs utilize several groups of K ants to collect and exchange objects according to both pheromone levels and similarities among objects. Since each ant will collect at least one object in the proposed algorithms; consequently, K clusters would be formed for sure.

The performances of the proposed three ACAs are compared with other clustering methods, including statistical clustering algorithms (agglomerative and *K*-means) and genetic clustering algorithm (GCA).

The rest of this paper is organized a follows. Section 2 presents details of the proposed algorithms. Section 3 compares the performances of three proposed ACAs. Section 4 further compares the performance of the best-performing ACA with those of statistical and genetic clustering algorithms. Finally, concluding remarks and suggestions for future research follow.

2. METHODOLOGIES

2.1. Ant Colony Optimization (ACO)

The ant colony optimization (ACO) has been proven more promising than the ant system (AS) algorithms. The algorithm of ACO is briefly narrated as follows (Dorigo & Gambardella, 1997):

- **Step 0: Initialization**: *K* ants are placed on *S* randomly chosen nodes. The initial pheromone level between any two nodes is set as a small positive constant. Set the values of all parameters including the parameter of transition rule (q_0), initial pheromone level (τ^0), pheromone decay parameter (ρ), number of ants (*K*), and maximal iteration (t_{max}).
- **Step 1: Tour construction**: In each construction step, each ant moves, based on a probabilistic decision, to a node it has not yet visited. The probability of kth ant moves from node *r* to node *s* can be computed as follows:

$$s = \arg\max_{j \in NP}\{[\tau_{uj}]^\alpha[\eta_{uj}]^\beta\} \text{' if } q \leq q_0$$

(exploitation). (6)

or visit *s* with P_{uv}^k, if $q > q_0$ (exploration)

where,

$$P_{rs}^k = \begin{cases} \dfrac{[\tau_{rs}]^\alpha[\eta_{rs}]^\beta}{\sum_{j \in J_r^k}[\tau_{rj}]^\alpha[\eta_{rj}]^\beta}, & if \ s \in J_r^k \\ 0 & , \ \text{otherwise} \end{cases}$$

(7)

where, α and β are two parameters representing the relative importance of the pheromone trail and the closeness between two nodes. τ_{rj} is the pheromone level between node *r* and node *j*. η_{rj} stands for the closeness, which is the inverse of the distance between node *r* and node *j*. J_r^k is the set of nodes that remain to be visited by the ant *k* positioned at node *r*. *q* is a random number generated from uniform distribution (0, 1). Repeat above moves until the ants have toured all nodes.

- **Step 2: Local updating**: Once an ant has completed its tour, the pheromone level on all arcs is updated by the following equation:

$$\tau_{ij} \leftarrow (1 - \rho)\tau_{ij} + \rho\tau_0$$

(8)

where, τ_0 is the initial pheromone level, which can be set as $\tau_{ij} = \tau_0 = (NL_{nn})^{-1}$, *N* is the number of arcs. L_{nn} is the total distance solved by greedy heuristic.

- **Step 3: Global updating**: After all ants have completed the tour construction, the pheromone level on the incumbent tour (T^+) is updated by the following equation:

$$\tau_{ij} \leftarrow (1 - \rho)\tau_{ij} + \Delta\tau_{ij}$$

(9)

where, $\Delta\tau_{ij} = \begin{cases} (L^+)^{-1} , & \text{if arc}(i, j) \in T^+ \\ 0 & , \ \text{otherwise} \end{cases}$

L^+ is the tour length of T^+.

- **Step 4: Incumbent tour updating**: If $\min_k\{L_k\} < L^+$, then let $L^+ = L_k$ and $T^+ = T_k$.

T_k is the tour constructed by ant k and L_k is the total length of T_k.

- **Step 5: Testing of stop condition:** If the maximal number of iterations t_{max} is reached, then terminate. T^+ is the optimal tour and L^+ is its total length. Otherwise, go to Step 1.

2.2. The Proposed Algorithms

Based on the abovementioned ACO algorithm, this paper proposes three ant-based clustering algorithms (ACAs). Our ACA algorithms will need to reformulate the clustering problem as a network problem so as to be able to draw on the strengths of the ACO algorithm. For a clustering problem of N objects and K clusters, a fully connected network of N nodes can be formed with the link cost, representing the dissimilarity of two nodes it connects. Let G(M, A) denotes the network, as depicted in Figure 1 (taking N=6 and K=2 for instance), where M is a set of nodes (objects), thus $|M| = N$. A is a set of links, $|A| = C_2^N = N(N-1)/2$. Then, K ants collect their own nodes according to the link costs and the following pheromone trail laid by the previous ants. Two of three proposed ACAs associated with different exchanging strategies are described as follows:

- **Step 0: Parameter setting:** set the values of parameters, including the number of clusters; that is, the number of ants (K), the parameters of transition rules (α, β and q_0), the pheromone decay parameter (ρ), and the number of groups of ants (H). Set the initial pheromone (τ_0) on every link equal to the inverse of the total within cluster variance ($TWCV$) of a randomly clustering result, expressed by $CP_r = \{S_r^1, S_r^2, ..., S_r^K\}$, where S_r^k is the set of objects belonging to k^{th} cluster. Subscript r indicates that the clustering result is obtained by a randomly

clustering method. $TWCV_r$ can be computed by following equation:

$$TWCV_r = \sum_{k=1}^{K} WCV_r^k \qquad (10)$$

where, $WCV_r^k = \sum_{O_i \in S_r^k} D(O_i, O_{center}^k)$. O_i represents the object i. $D(O_i, O_j)$ is the Euclidean distance function of objects i and j, defined as: $D(O_i, O_j) = [\sum_{m=1}^{M} (x_m^i - x_m^j)^2]^{\frac{1}{2}}$. x_m^i is m^{th} dimension variable of object i. M is the number of dimension variables. O_{center}^k is the center of objects belonging to S_r^k, expressed by $x_{center,m}^k = \frac{\sum_{O_i \in S_r^k} x_m^i}{|S_r^k|}$, $m=1,2,...,M$.

- **Step 1: Initialization.** Randomly distribute h^{th} group of ants (a total of K ants) to different K objects. Let $S_h^k = \{O_i\}$, $k=1,2,...,K$. O_i is object i that k^{th} ant is located. S_h^k is the set of objects collected by ant k in h^{th} group, namely the cluster k. Let P stand for the set containing all objects and CP_h be the set containing the objects been collected by ants of hth group, i.e. $CP_h = \{S_h^1, S_h^2, ..., S_h^K\}$, $NP_h = P\text{-}CP_h$.

- **Step 2: Collection.** Ants collect the objects belonging to NP_h according to the following four sub-steps:
  - **Step 2-1:** Ants collect objects in sequence, that is, $k=1, 2,..., K$.
  - **Step 2-2:** Ant k located at object u will collect the next object v according to the following equation:

$$v = \arg\max_{j \in NP} \{[\tau_{uj}]^\alpha [\eta_{uj}]^\beta\}, \text{ if } q \leq q_0$$
(exploitation). $\qquad (11)$

  or collect object v with P_{uv}^k, if $q > q_0$ and $P_{uv}^k \geq \bar{P}_u^k$ (exploration).

Figure 1. Explanatory example for re-formulating a clustering problem into a network problem (for N=7 and K=2)

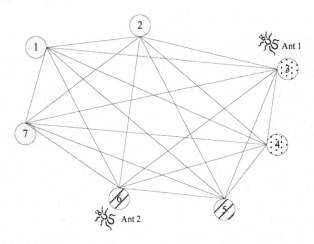

or does not collect any object, if $q > q_0$ and $P_{uv}^k < \bar{P}_u^k$.

where,

$$P_{uv}^k = \begin{cases} \dfrac{[\tau_{uv}]^\alpha [\eta_{uv}]^\beta}{\sum_{j \in NP}[\tau_{uj}]^\alpha[\eta_{uj}]^\beta}, & \forall v \in NP_h \\ 0 & , \text{ otherwise} \end{cases}$$

for $k=1,2,...,K$.

τ_{uj} represents the level of pheromone on the link between object u and j. η_{uj} represents the similarity between objects u and j, which is defined as the inverse of Euclidean distance between objects u and j. $\bar{P}_u^k$ represents the mean transition probability, defined as

$$\bar{P}_u^k = \frac{\sum_{j \in NP}P_{uj}^k}{|NP_h|}.$$ q is a random number from uniform distribution in the range between 0 and 1.

○ **Step 2-3:** If object v is collected by ant k according to Step 2-2, then let $S_h^k = S_h^k \cup \{O_v\}$.

○ **Step 2-4:** Continue Step 2-1 to Step 2-3 until $NP_h = \Phi$.

• **Step 3: Evaluation.** Compute the total within cluster variance of hth group of ants ($TWCV_h$).

• **Step 4: Exchanging.** Two strategies are proposed for ants to exchange the objects they collected, which are referred as to ACA-1 and ACA-2 hereinafter:

○ **Strategy 1:** Ant k selects a collected object w to be exchanged with the probability: $PE_w^k = \dfrac{D(O_w, O_{center}^k)}{WCV_h^k}$, $\forall O_w \in S_h^k$. That is, the farther the object to the center is, the higher probability that object would be selected. Then, the selected object w is assigned to ant l that is closest to the center, i.e. $l = \arg\min_{k=1}^{K} D(O_w, O_{center}^k)$. Let $S_h^k = S_h^k - \{O_w\}$ and $S_h^l = S_h^l \cup \{O_w\}$ for all objects selected for exchanging and all ants' collections assigned. In this paper, the ACA employing this strategy is named as ACA-1.

○ **Strategy 2:** One of the objects collected by ant k satisfying the following condition is randomly selected for exchanging:

$$D\left(O_w, O_{center}^k\right) \geq \frac{WCV_h^k}{\left|S_h^k\right|} \qquad (12)$$

Then, the selected object w is assigned to ant l that is closest to the center. The ACA using this strategy is named as ACA-2.

- **Step 5: Reevaluation.** Compute the $TWCV_h'$. If $TWCV_h' < TWCV_h$, then let $TWCV_h = TWCV_h'$; otherwise, reject the result of exchange and let $S_h^k = S_h^k \cup \{O_w\}$ and $S_h^l = S_h^l - \{O_w\}$ for all objects selected for exchange and all ants' collections assigned.
- **Step 6: Local pheromone level updating rule.** Update the pheromone level between objects by the following equation:

$$\tau_{uv} \leftarrow \left(1-\rho\right)\tau_{uv} + \rho\tau^0 \text{ for all } u,v \in A \qquad (13)$$

Let $h=h+1$. If $h \geq H$, let the optimal $TWCV$ and clustering result among groups of ants respectively be $TWCV^* = TWCV_t$ and $CP^* = CP_t$, where $t = \arg \min_{h=1}^{H}\{TWCV_h\}$, then proceed to Step 7; otherwise, go to Step 1.

- **Step 7: Global pheromone level updating rule.** Update the pheromone level between objects by following equation:

$$\tau_{uv} \leftarrow \tau_{uv} + \frac{1}{TWCV_t} \text{ for all } u,v \in S_t^k \text{ and}$$
$k=1, 2,\ldots, K \qquad (14)$

If $TWCV^* < TWCV^{**}$, then let $TWCV^{**} = TWCV^*$ and $CP^{**} = CP^*$.

- **Step 8: Testing of stop condition.** If the maximum number of iterations is reached, then terminate. The optimal clustering re-

sult is $CP^{**} = \{S^{1^{**}}, S^{2^{**}},\ldots, S^{K^{**}}\}$ and optimal $TWCV = TWCV^{**}$. Otherwise, go to Step 1.

In addition, to investigate the contributions of the exchanging strategies to the performance, the third ACA, named as ACA-3, which does not exchange any collected objects, is also developed for comparison. That is, ACA-3 is composed by abovementioned steps, except for Step 4 and Step 5.

Since every new object being collected will form a new cluster center and then affect the decisions on which object to be collected next, it may not result in an optimal clustering if only the closest object is selected. Although ACO can partly correct such a "greedy search" by further considering the pheromone. However, once an object being clustered into a cluster, the object will never ever be re-assigned to other clusters, even previous collection decision is not appropriate. Based on this, two exchanging strategies are respectively embedded into ACA-1 and ACA-2 to provide objects a chance to "escape" from the cluster they have been classified to.

Accordingly, the object to be re-assigned (exchanged) must exhibit rather different characteristics to other objects in the same cluster, that is, the object must have a longer distance to the cluster center. To identify such an object for exchanging, two exchanging strategies are designed. Strategy 1 in Step 4 is to select the object according to a probability which is proportional to its distance to cluster center. The farer the object is, the higher probability it would be chosen. Each object in the cluster has a chance to be exchanged. Therefore, it is possible to wrongly select an object for exchanging. In contrast, Strategy 2 in Step 4 is to set a threshold to first screen out the objects of which distance to the cluster center is less than average. Then randomly select an object for exchanging from the remaining objects.

3. PERFORMANCE EVALUATION AMONG THREE ACAS

To evaluate the algorithm performance for the proposed ACA-1, ACA-2 and ACA-3, a total of 30 sets of two-dimensional data at three different problem scales (containing 20, 50 and 100 objects) are examined. All objects are generated from uniform distribution within (0, 1). However, to validate the clustering solutions of the proposed three algorithms, a smaller-scale problem containing only 10 objects is used so that the global optimal solution can be easily solved by total enumeration method.

Since α, β and ρ are three essential parameters for ant colony system, this paper further examines the relative sensitivity of these parameters. Without loss of generality, we analyze the performance of ACA-2 with various values of β by fixing $\alpha=1$ and $\rho=0.5$ at different problem scales. The results are shown in Figure 2, which indicates that the proposed algorithm is insensitive to β values. In fact, only a slight variation may be found under a large-scale problem with the optimal setting

for $\beta=5$. Then, we investigate the performance of the algorithm with various values of ρ by fixing $\alpha=1$ and $\beta=5$ at different problem scales. The results are shown in Figure 3, indicating that the performance of the algorithm is slightly sensitive to ρ at problems scale of $N=20$, $N=50$, and $N=100$ with the optimal setting for $\rho=0.3$ consistently. Besides, more obvious variations can be found as the problem scale becomes larger. However, the insensitivities of these parameters to the performance might be attributed to that the data sets adopted in this paper are randomly and uniformly generated.

To validate the proposed three ACAs, a smaller-scale problem with only 10 objects forming two clusters is examined. The *TWCV* of global clustering solved by total enumeration method is 0.5660 with 6 objects in one cluster and 4 objects in another. All the proposed ACAs have achieved exactly the same result, suggesting that the three proposed ACAs can find the global optimality.

The performance of these proposed ACAs is further compared at various problem scales with 30

Figure 2. The clustering performance with different β values ($\alpha=1$, $\rho=0.5$)

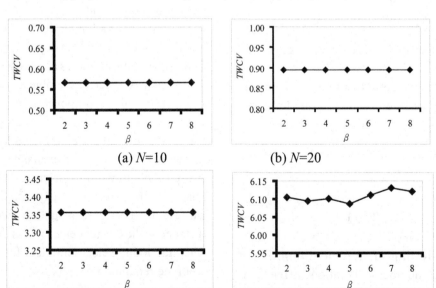

data sets. We evaluate the algorithm performance by two criteria: solution effectiveness, which is represented by the mean of *TWCV* and solution stability, which is represented by the standard deviation of *TWCV*. Since ACA-2 has the lowest means and standard deviations of *TWCV* under various problem scales, we will use ACA-2 as the base and the performance of the other two algorithms (ACA-1 and ACA-3) are tested against it whether or not a significant difference exists. The results are summarized in Table 1. It is found that, in term of solution effectiveness, ACA-2 performs better than ACA-1 with significantly lower means of *TWCV* at various problem scales and number of clusters, except for the small-scale problem (N=20) with K=3 and the medium-scale problem (N=50) with K=3 and 5. Similarly, ACA-2 also performs better than ACA-3 with significantly lower means of *TWCV* at all cases. However, in term of solution stability, ACA-2 performs significantly better than ACA-1 at the large-scale problem (N=100) with K=3 and 5 and better than ACA-3 at the medium-scale problem with K=3 and 5 and the large-scale problem with K=3, 5, 7,

and 9. Overall, it can be concluded that ACA-2 is superior to ACA-1 and ACA-3.

As shown in Table 1, both ACA-1 and ACA-2 perform better than ACA-3, explaining the importance of exchanging strategy. Without exchanging strategy, once an object has been collected by an ant (i.e. being assigned to a corresponding cluster), the object will never have a chance to leave that cluster, even the previous collection decision is inappropriate. Moreover, the exchanging strategy of ACA-2 provide a two-stage object selection process – to screen out the inappropriate objects for exchanging and then to randomly select the remaining objects for exchanging, which is better than the one-stage exchanging strategy of ACA-1.

4. COMPARISON OF ACA-2 WITH OTHER ALGORITHMS

This paper further compares ACA-2 with other three commonly used algorithms, including two statistical clustering algorithms: agglomerative

Figure 3. The clustering performance with different ρ values (α=1, β=5)

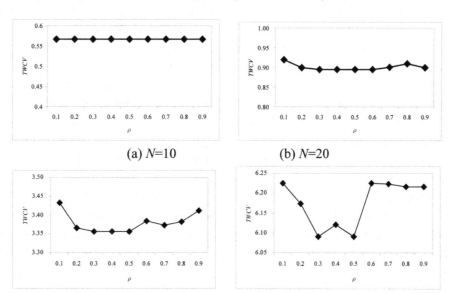

(a) N=10

(b) N=20

(c) N=50

(d) N=100

Table 1. Comparison of ACA-1, ACA-2 and ACA-3 with various numbers of clusters under different problem scales

N20	K3	ACA-2		ACA-1		ACA-3	
		Mean	Std.	Mean	Std.	Mean	Std.
		0.9016	**0.0198**	**0.9023**	**0.0199**	**0.9063***	**0.0198**
	5	0.3969	0.0047	0.4151*	0.0066	0.4249*	0.0092
	7	0.2156	0.0017	0.2386*	0.0027	0.2427*	0.0023
	9	0.1207	0.0008	0.1369*	0.0011	0.1386*	0.0011
50	3	2.7310	0.0720	2.7729	0.0820	2.8972*	0.1682*
	5	1.3749	0.0192	1.4042	0.0232	1.5227*	0.0358*
	7	0.8909	0.0116	0.9233*	0.0137	0.9554*	0.0158
	9	0.6233	0.0059	0.6478*	0.0078	0.6566*	0.0091
100	3	5.9212	0.1522	6.2558*	0.2292*	6.2459*	0.2242*
	5	3.1111	0.0324	3.2147*	0.0624*	3.2573*	0.0818*
	7	2.0710	0.0189	2.1221*	0.0207	2.1508*	0.0362*
	9	1.5160	0.0076	1.5419*	0.0101	1.5529*	0.0242*

Note: We set ACA-2 as the base and * indicates significantly greater than that of ACA-2 at $\alpha = 0.05$.

hierarchical clustering algorithm (AHCA) and K-means algorithm (KMA) and one metaheuristic clustering algorithm: genetic clustering algorithm (GCA). For the algorithmic details of agglomerative, K-means and GCA, we refer readers to the papers of Ward (1963), MacQueen (1967), and Jiang *et al.* (1997), respectively.

The comparison is made at various problem scales (N) with various numbers of clusters (K) and the results are reported in Table 2. For the small-scale problem, the solution effectiveness of ACA-2 is almost all significantly superior to that of AHCA, KMA and GCA under various numbers of clusters with an exception of GCA at K=3. In term of solution stability, however, ACA-2 performs insignificantly different from other three clustering algorithms under various numbers of clusters, except for the case of AHCA at K=5.

For the medium-scale problem, in term of solution effectiveness, ACA-2 also significantly outperforms under various numbers of clusters. The solution stability of ACA-2 is significantly

superior to AHCA only at K=3 and 5 and to KMA at K=3.

For the large-scale problem, ACA-2 still significantly outperforms in term of solution effectiveness, almost for all cases with the only exception of GCA at K=3. In term of solution stability, ACA-2 consistently performs better than AHCA under various numbers of clusters, better than KMA at K=5, and better than GCA at K=5, 7 and 9.

In sum, compared with ACHA, KMA and GCA, the proposed ACA-2 has significantly outperformed in solution effectiveness for most of the cases and is significantly better in solution stability as the problem scale or the number of clusters gets larger.

The clustering results of ACA-2 for the large-scale problem (N=100) under various numbers of clusters (K=3, 5, 7, 9) are depicted in Figure 4. It clearly shows that the objects in the same clusters are close to each other and no objects are obvi-

Table 2. Comparison of ACA-2, AHCA, KMA and GCA with various numbers of clusters under different problem scales

N	K	ACA-2		AHCA		KMA		GCA	
		Mean	Std.	Mean	Std.	Mean	Std.	Mean	Std.
20	3	0.9016	0.0198	0.9168*	0.0234	0.9359*	0.0213	0.9111	0.0218
	5	0.3969	0.0047	0.4446*	0.0110*	0.4304*	0.0113	0.4282*	0.0051
	7	0.2156	0.0017	0.2473*	0.0030	0.2439*	0.0034	0.2329*	0.0021
	9	0.1207	0.0008	0.1390*	0.0010	0.1321*	0.0009	0.1258*	0.0008
50	3	2.7310	0.0720	3.0905*	0.2283*	2.8566*	0.1591*	2.8665*	0.1102
	5	1.3749	0.0192	1.5285*	0.0413*	1.4426*	0.0221	1.5214*	0.0311
	7	0.8909	0.0116	1.0191*	0.0167	0.9436*	0.0156	0.9866*	0.0205
	9	0.6233	0.0059	0.6857*	0.0083	0.6718*	0.0100	0.6748*	0.0070
100	3	5.9212	0.1522	6.6321*	0.5983*	6.0254	0.2110	6.1253*	0.2505
	5	3.1111	0.0324	3.4196*	0.0997*	3.2281*	0.0736*	3.3866*	0.0839*
	7	2.0710	0.0189	2.2746*	0.0506*	2.1390*	0.0255	2.3188*	0.0513*
	9	1.5160	0.0076	1.6383*	0.0224*	1.5370*	0.0092	1.7461*	0.0303*

Note: We set ACA-2 as the base and * indicates the mean or standard deviation of the other algorithms significantly different (higher) at $\alpha = 0.05$.

Figure 4. The clustering results of ACA-2 for the large-scale problem (N=100)

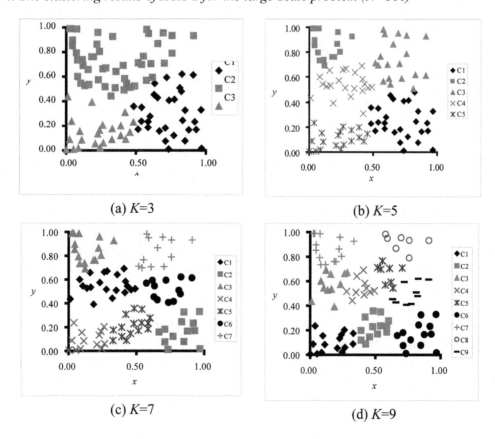

(a) *K*=3

(b) *K*=5

(c) *K*=7

(d) *K*=9

Figure 5. The improvement rates of ACA-2 over the three other clustering algorithms

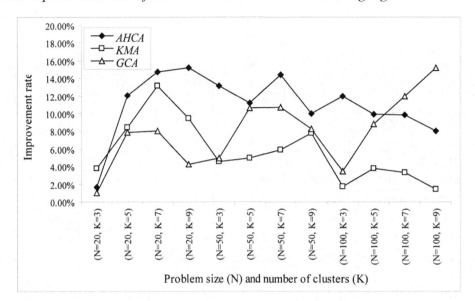

ously grouped into a wrong cluster, suggesting the satisfactory clustering results by ACA-2.

To further demonstrate how effective ACA-2 would outperform over the other three clustering algorithms, the improvement rates of ACA-2, defined as the ratio of the difference in means of *TWCV* divided by the mean of *TWCV* of ACA-2, are presented in Figure 5. It shows that, on average, ACA-2 can achieve the largest improvement over AHCA by 11.01% (from 1.69% to 15.16%), followed by 7.94% (from 1.05% to 15.18%) over GCA and then by 5.69% (from 1.39% to 5.69%) over KMA.

It is interesting to note that ACA-2 sometimes fails to significantly outperform than other clustering algorithms, including ACA-1, ACA-3, AHCA, KMA, and GCA in terms of solution effectiveness (although the mean *TWCV* of ACA-2 is still the smallest in all cases) under small number of clusters (*i.e* K=3). It may be because that in general the clustering problem with less number of clusters is much easier to be solved. The improvement room left for solving such comparatively simple problems by other clustering algorithms may be too limited for ACA-2 to achieve sig-

nificance. That explains why ACA-2 fails to significantly outperform than others algorithms.

To further compare the solution efficiency of the clustering algorithms, Table 3 provides the CPU time of ACA-2 and GCA under various scales of problems. Since AHCA and KMA are solved by statistical software, the CPU time of these two algorithms are not reported. However, according to the algorithm complexity of AHCA and KMA, their CPU time shall definitely be much less than ACA-2 and GCA. Noted from Table 3, the means and standard deviations of CPU time of ACA-2 are significantly larger than GCA, suggesting the necessity of improving the solution efficiency of the proposed algorithm. It is also worth noting that the discrepancies between ACA-2 and GCA become smaller as the clustering problem gets larger (larger *N*) and more complex (larger *K*).

5. CONCLUSION

This paper develops three ant clustering algorithms: ACA-1, ACA-2, and ACA-3. Solution effectiveness and solution stability are used as the

Table 3. Solution efficiency of ACA-2 and GCA with various numbers of clusters under different problem scales

N	K	ACA-2		GCA	
		Mean	Std.	Mean	Std.
20	3	4.3201	1.0918	1.1120*	0.3141*
	5	4.4832	1.2934	1.4282*	0.5415*
	7	4.4701	1.1071	1.2329*	0.4292*
	9	4.9111	1.5018	2.8512*	0.7221*
50	3	225.3245	24.7432	84.8665*	16.1129*
	5	238.1842	32.1122	81.5214*	14.1315*
	7	288.8210	25.6122	98.9866*	19.2710*
	9	305.2011	42.0901	108.2311*	20.1027*
100	3	923.2123	123.3235	792.1233*	81.2520*
	5	1021.0491	133.0314	834.3683*	89.1335*
	7	1123.1031	135.1904	820.2191*	73.5321*
	9	1201.1203	155.0711	860.1367*	89.3032*

Note: We set ACA-2 as the base and * indicates the mean or standard deviation of the other algorithms significantly different (higher) at $\alpha = 0.05$.

criteria for evaluating the algorithm performance. The results show that ACA-2 significantly outperforms in solution effectiveness, but insignificantly outperforms in solution stability over ACA-1 and ACA-3. A further comparison between ACA-2 and other three conventional clustering algorithms (AHCA, KMA and GCA) concludes that the proposed ACA-2 can significantly outperform in solution effectiveness almost in all cases and also performs significantly better in solution stability as the problem size or the number of clusters gets larger. In terms of improvement rates, on average, ACA-2 can lower the means of *TWCV* of AHCA, GCA and KMA by 11.01%, 7.94% and 5.69%, respectively. In other word, the clustering performance of ACA-2 has been proven.

Some future research directions can be identified. Firstly, this paper only examines the performances of proposed ant-based clustering algorithms in classifying uniformly and randomly generated data sets. The performance and the sensitivity of parameters in solving clustering problems with other specific data structures should be investigated. Secondly, the proposed algorithms can only be applied to the clustering problems with the number of clusters known or given in advance. The clustering algorithms based on ant theory that can simultaneously solve for the optimal number of clusters and optimal clustering results are worthy of exploration. Although the superiority in terms of solution effectiveness of the proposed ACA-2 has been proven, the solution stability can be further enhanced by modifying not only the exchanging strategies but also the rules to object collection and pheromone updating. Furthermore, it is worthy of comparing the performance of the proposed algorithm with other state-of-art clustering algorithms, especially ant-based clustering algorithms mentioned in Section 1. Last but not least, a hybrid method by combining the ant-based clustering algorithms with other metaheuristic algorithms is also deserved to develop. For instance, employ GAs to determine the optimal number of clusters and then use ACAs to conduct the clustering.

ACKNOWLEDGMENT

The authors are indebted to four anonymous referees who have provided very constructive comments and suggestions to improve the quality of this paper.

REFERENCES

Al-Sultan, K. S. (1995). A tabu search approach to the clustering problem. *Pattern Recognition, 28*, 1443–1451. doi:10.1016/0031-3203(95)00022-R

Ali, A. I., & Thiagarajan, H. (1989). A network relaxation based enumeration algorithm for set partitioning. *European Journal of Operational Research, 38*, 76–85. doi:10.1016/0377-2217(89)90471-2

Azzag, H., Venturini, G., Oliver, A., & Guinot, C. (2007). A hierarchical and based clustering algorithm and its use in three real-world applications. *European Journal of Operational Research, 179*, 906–922. doi:10.1016/j.ejor.2005.03.062

Bartfai, G. (1996). An ART-based modular architecture for learning hierarchical clusterings. *Neurocomputing, 13*, 31–45. doi:10.1016/0925-2312(95)00077-1

Bella, J. E., & McMullen, P. R. (2004). Ant colony optimization techniques for the vehicle routing problem. *Advanced Engineering Informatics, 18*, 41–48. doi:10.1016/j.aei.2004.07.001

Brucker, P. (1978). On the complexity of clustering problems. In M. Beckmenn, & H. P. Kunzi (Eds.), *Optimization and operations research* (LNEMS 157, pp. 45-54).

Chiou, Y. C., & Chou, S. C. (2005). *Ant-based clustering algorithms*. Paper presented at the International Conference of International Federation of Operational Research Societies, Hawaii.

Chiou, Y. C., & Lan, L. W. (2001). Genetic clustering algorithms. *European Journal of Operational Research, 135*, 413–427. doi:10.1016/S0377-2217(00)00320-9

Dorigo, M., & Gambardella, L. M. (1997). Ant colony system: A cooperative learning approach to the traveling salesman problem. *IEEE Transactions on Evolutionary Computation, 1*, 53–66. doi:10.1109/4235.585892

Dorigo, M., Maniezzo, V., & Colorni, A. (1996). Ant system: Optimization by a colony of cooperating agents. *IEEE Transactions on Systems, Man, and Cybernetics-Part B, 26*, 29–41. doi:10.1109/3477.484436

El-Darzi, E., & Mitra, G. (1995). Graph theoretic relaxations of set covering and set partitioning problems. *European Journal of Operational Research, 87*, 109–121. doi:10.1016/0377-2217(94)00115-S

Garai, G., & Chaudhuri, B. B. (2004). A novel genetic algorithm for automatic clustering. *Pattern Recognition Letters, 25*, 173–187. doi:10.1016/j.patrec.2003.09.012

Hansen, P., & Jaumard, B. (1987). Minimum sum of diameters clustering. *Journal of Classification, 4*, 215–226. doi:10.1007/BF01896987

Jayaraman, V. K., Kulkarni, B. D., Karale, S., & Shelokar, P. (2000). Ant colony framework for optimal design and scheduling of batch plants. *Computers & Chemical Engineering, 24*, 1901–1912. doi:10.1016/S0098-1354(00)00592-5

Jiang, J. H., Wang, J. H., Chu, X., & Yu, R. Q. (1997). Clustering data using a modified integer genetic algorithm (IGA). *Analytica Chimica Acta, 354*, 263–274. doi:10.1016/S0003-2670(97)00462-5

Klein, R. W., & Dubes, R. C. (1989). Experiments in projection and clustering by simulated annealing. *Pattern Recognition, 22*, 213–220. doi:10.1016/0031-3203(89)90067-8

Kuo, R. J., Wang, H. S., Hu, T. L., & Chou, S. H. (2005). Application of ant K-means on clustering analysis. *Computers and Mathematics with Application, 50*, 1709–1724. doi:10.1016/j.camwa.2005.05.009

Lunchian, S., Lunchian, H., & Petriuc, M. (1994). Evolutionary automated classification. In *Proceedings of the First IEEE Conference on Evolutionary Computation* (pp. 585-589).

MacQueen, J. (1967). Some methods for classification and analysis of multivariate observations. In *Proceedings of the Fifth Berkeley Symposium on Mathematical Statistics and Probability* (Vol. 1, pp. 281-297).

Maniezzo, V., & Colorni, A. (1999). The ant system applied to the quadratic assignment problem. *IEEE Transactions on Knowledge and Data Engineering, 11*, 769–778. doi:10.1109/69.806935

Moshe, E. C., & Tovey, C. A. (1996). Ammons J-C. Circuit partitioning via set partitioning and column generation. *Operations Research, 44*, 65–76. doi:10.1287/opre.44.1.65

Mulvey, J. M., & Crowder, H. P. (1979). Cluster analysis: An application of Lagrangian relaxation. *Management Science, 25*, 329–340. doi:10.1287/mnsc.25.4.329

Savelsbergh, M. (1997). A branch-and-price algorithm for the generalized assignment problem. *Operations Research, 45*, 831–841. doi:10.1287/opre.45.6.831

Selim, S. Z., & Al-Sultan, K. S. (1991). A simulated annealing algorithm for the clustering problem. *Pattern Recognition, 24*, 1003–1008. doi:10.1016/0031-3203(91)90097-O

Shelokar, P. S., Jayaraman, V. K., & Kullkarni, B. D. (2004). An ant colony approach for clustering. *Analytica Chimica Acta, 509*, 187–195. doi:10.1016/j.aca.2003.12.032

Sung, C. S., & Jin, H. W. (2000). A tabu-search-based heuristic for clustering. *Pattern Recognition, 33*, 849–858. doi:10.1016/S0031-3203(99)00090-4

Trick, M. A. (1992). A linear relaxation heuristic for the generalized assignment problem. *Naval Research Logistics, 39*, 137–152. doi:10.1002/1520-6750(199203)39:2<137::AID-NAV3220390202>3.0.CO;2-D

Tsai, C. F., Tsai, C. W., Wu, H. C., & Yang, T. (2004). ACODF: A novel data clustering approach for data mining in large databases. *Journal of Systems and Software, 73*, 133–145. doi:10.1016/S0164-1212(03)00216-4

Vesanto, J., & Alhonierni, E. (2000). Clustering of the self-organizing map. *IEEE Transactions on Neural Networks, 11*, 586–600. doi:10.1109/72.846731

Ward, J. H. (1963). Hierarchical grouping to optimize an objective function. *Journal of the American Statistical Association, 58*, 236–244. doi:10.2307/2282967

Welch, J. W. (1983). Algorithmic complexity: three NP-hard problems in computational statistics. *Journal of Statistical Computation and Simulation, 15*, 17–25. doi:10.1080/00949658208810560

Wu, S., & Chow, T. W. S. (2004). Clustering of the self-organizing map using a clustering validity index based on inter-cluster and intra-cluster density. *Pattern Recognition, 37*, 175–188. doi:10.1016/S0031-3203(03)00237-1

Yang, Y., & Kamel, M. S. (2006). An aggregated clustering approach using multi-ant colonies algorithms. *Pattern Recognition, 39*, 1278–1289. doi:10.1016/j.patcog.2006.02.012

This work was previously published in International Journal of Applied Evolutionary Computation, Volume 1, Issue 1, edited by Wei-Chiang Samuelson Hong, pp. 1-15, copyright 2010 by IGI Publishing (an imprint of IGI Global).

Chapter 2
Three Novel Methods to Predict Traffic Time Series in Reconstructed State Spaces

Lawrence W. Lan
MingDao University, Taiwan

Feng-Yu Lin
Central Police University, Taiwan

April Y. Kuo
BNSF Railway, USA

ABSTRACT

This article proposes three novel methods—temporal confined (TC), spatiotemporal confined (STC) and spatial confined (SC)—to forecast the temporal evolution of traffic parameters. The fundamental rationales are to embed one-dimensional traffic time series into reconstructed state spaces and then to perform fuzzy reasoning to infer the future changes in traffic series. The TC, STC and SC methods respectively employ different fuzzy reasoning logics to select similar historical traffic trajectories. Theil inequality coefficient and its decomposed components are used to evaluate the predicting power and source of errors. Field observed one-minute traffic counts are used to test the predicting power. The results show that overall prediction accuracies for the three methods are satisfactorily high with small systematic errors and little deviation from the observed data. It suggests that the proposed three methods can be used to capture and forecast the short-term (e.g., one-minute) temporal evolution of traffic parameters.

INTRODUCTION

Traffic time series is referred to as temporal evolution of traffic parameters (e.g., flow, speed, and occupancy) measured in a chronological order with identical time interval. Accurately capturing

and predicting the temporal evolution of traffic parameters is prerequisite for developing and implementing many intelligent transportation systems (Stephanedes et al., 1981; Chang & Miaou, 1999; Lam et al., 2005). A smart adaptive signal control, for instance, is oftentimes established on the basis of instantaneous or predicted short-term

DOI: 10.4018/978-1-4666-1749-0.ch002

(e.g., 5-minute) traffic data. Advanced incident detection may require even shorter-term (e.g., 1-minute) traffic data as inputs (Lan & Huang, 2006).

Techniques for predicting traffic time series can be categorized in different ways, including parametric (e.g., historical mean value algorithm, regression method, neural network algorithm, time series method, Kalman filtering, compound forecasting algorithm) versus nonparametric (e.g., nonparametric regression method, wavelet filtering method), linear (e.g., autoregressive moving average or ARMA model, autoregressive integrated moving average or ARIMA models) versus nonlinear (e.g., nonlinear ARIMA, fuzzy local reconstruction method, fuzzy neighborhood method, state-space local approximation method), among others. To save space, the present article has no intension to exhaust all the relevant works on traffic prediction. A state-of-the-art review on the traffic predicting techniques has been done by Van Arem et al. (1997) and Vlahogianni et al. (2004). However, the literature on traffic prediction is full of differing conclusions and it is never easy to make a general statement.

For example, Smith and Demetsky (1997) compared historical average, time-series, neural network, and nonparametric regression models and concluded that the nonparametric regression model significantly outperformed the other models and was also easier to implement. Durbin (2000) claimed that the state space approach has advantages over the ARMA models or ARIMA models. Smith et al. (2002) compared parametric and nonparametric models and concluded that using nonparametric regression coupled with heuristic forecast generation methods would perform better than a naïve forecasting approach, which also outperformed over a classic parametric modeling approach (e.g., seasonal ARIMA models). Taking the superior capability of neural networks to approximate a nonlinear system, however, the nonlinear ARMA (NARMA) model has been

claimed satisfactorily in nonlinear prediction (Bonnet, 1997).

A considerable number of literature adopted time series analysis for traffic prediction purposes (e.g., Head, 1995; Lee & Fambro, 1999; Lingras et al., 2000; Lam et al., 2006). Many literature showed that neural networks are one of the best alternatives for modeling and predicting traffic parameters because they can approximate almost any function, regardless of its degree of nonlinearity and without prior knowledge of its functional form (e.g., Clark, et al., 1993; Kirby et al., 1997; Ishak et al., 2003; Vlahogianni et al., 2005; Sheu et al., 2009). Other literature also elaborated the traffic predicting techniques with Kalman filtering (e.g., Okutani & Stephanedes, 1984; Sun et al., 2003; Wang & Papageorgiou, 2005), wavelet analysis (He & Ma, 2002; Li, 2002; Soltani, 2002), and multivariate state space approach (Stathopoulos and Karlaftis, 2003; Lan et al., 2007).

The aforementioned predicting techniques mainly examined the traffic series in one-dimensional state space. It has been shown that if one could scrutinize the traffic series in multidimensional state spaces, one could perhaps gain more information to better elucidate and/or to more accurately predict the real-world traffic evolutions (Lan et al., 2008a, 2008b). In view of this, the present article aims to develop three novel methods, which embed the one-dimensional traffic series into multidimensional spaces and then perform various fuzzy reasoning logics to predict the traffic evolutions.

The remaining parts are organized as follows. The use of a single time series to generate a reconstruction space to characterize the traffic evolution is described. Three novel methods adopting different fuzzy reasoning logics in temporal, spatiotemporal, and spatial confined domains, respectively, are then detailed. The criteria used for evaluating prediction performance are also explained. An empirical study is carried out, wherein one-minute traffic time series data directly extracted from freeway detectors are used to establish and validate the proposed prediction methods. The discussion of applicability of our proposed methods and concluding remarks are finally addressed.

STATE SPACE RECONSTRUCTION

Building the state space prediction models from a time series mainly involves two parts: reconstruction of the state space from data by time delay embedding and development of the methods for state-space prediction. Reconstruction of state space is to embed the one-dimensional time series into a multidimensional state space, from which one can find out more noticeable patterns for the time series evolution. Many previous works (e.g., Iokibe et al., 1995; Sakawa et al., 1998; Lan et al., 2003, 2004, 2007) have shown that state space reconstruction has the advantages for prediction. Different rationales for prediction reasoning in the reconstructed state space, however, will end up with various models which might perform diversely. Therefore, seeking for appropriate prediction reasoning logics is of critical importance. To save space, this article only highlights the very essential parts of the state space reconstruction. Readers interested in the mathematical details of mapping one-dimensional time series into appropriate multidimensional state spaces can refer to a recent work in *Transportation Research* by Lan et al. (2008b). Other books such as Abarband (1996), Kanntz and Schreiber (1997), Hiborn (2000), Sprott (2003) also provide useful guides on this subject.

Let the order of a time series be described by N state variables and represented as trajectories in the N-dimensional reconstructed state space. For a single observed variable, its trajectory can be reconstructed in an N-dimensional space by utilizing Takens' embedding theorem as follow. Let $\zeta(t)$ denote the observed time series and N and τ denote the embedding dimension and delay

time, respectively, then the vector $Z(t) = \{\zeta(t), \zeta(t-\tau), ..., \zeta(t-(N-1)\tau)\}$ represents one point of the N-dimensional reconstructed state space. Any trajectory can then be drawn in the N-dimensional space by changing t with τ fixed. When the embedding dimension N is sufficiently large, we can say that the trajectory is embedded in the reconstructed state space. Takens (1981) proved that if the observed time series is governed by some intrinsic rules, then the trajectories of the time series will follow the deterministic regularity by retaining the phase structure in the original O-dimensional state space, after the reconstructed trajectories are embedded as $N \geq 2O+1$. Thus, if the regularity can be estimated, then the data in the near future, before the deterministic causality is lost, can be predicted.

In many practices, the most important embedding parameters are the delay time and the embedding dimension. Kennel et al. (1992) proposed the method of false nearest neighbors (FNN) that guarantees an adequate embedding dimension for most purposes, stated as follows. Find the nearest neighbor $Z_l(t)$ for each point $Z_m(t)$ in a time delay τ embedding n, and calculate the distance $\|Z_m(t) - Z_l(t)\|$; iterate both points and then compute the ratio $\varepsilon_{m,l}$. If the ratio $\varepsilon_{m,l}$ exceeds a given heuristic threshold ε_{FNN}, this point $Z_m(t)$ is marked as having a false nearest neighbor. In general, the value of threshold ε_{FNN} is recommended as 10 to 15 (Abarbanel, 1996).

$$\varepsilon_{m,l} = \frac{\left| Z_m^{n+1} - Z_l^{n+1} \right|}{\left\| Z_m^n - Z_l^n \right\|}, \quad l, m = 1, 2, ..., N$$

A good estimate of the delay time τ is even more difficult to obtain. If τ is small compared with the internal time scales of the system, successive elements of the delay vectors are strongly correlated. If τ is very large, successive elements are already almost independent, and the points will fill a large cloud in the R^N, where the

Figure 1. The concept of state space reconstruction; Source: Lan et al. (2003)

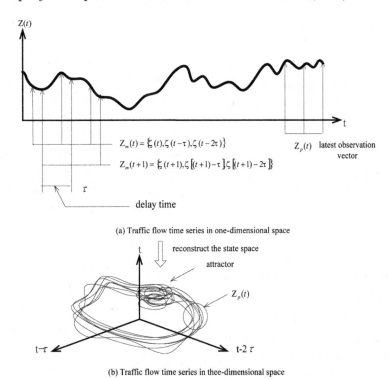

(a) Traffic flow time series in one-dimensional space

(b) Traffic flow time series in thee-dimensional space

deterministic structures are confined to the very small scales. The autocorrelation function (*ACF*) of the signal is often a good estimate for finding a compromise between these extremes.

Figure 1 illustrates the concept of state space reconstruction by embedding one-dimensional traffic flow time series into three-dimensional state spaces. After plotting the traffic time series data from the latest observations in the three-dimensional spaces, we can then investigate the historical traffic trajectories neighboring to the latest observation. If the traffic series (Figure 1(a)) is characterized with some intrinsic rules, after the state space reconstruction (Figure 1(b)), we can look for the "similar trajectories" by differencing the variables of the historical vectors, denoted as $Z_m(t)$ and the present vector, denoted as $Z_p(t)$. If the difference between $Z_p(t) - Z_p(t - v)$ and $Z_m(t) - Z_m(t - v)$ is within a threshold value, we may say that the

present vector has "similarity" to the historical ones, where v denotes the time steps before the present time t. The changes in the historical similar traffic trajectories from $Z_m(t)$ to $Z_m(t + s)$ can then be used to perform the prediction reasoning for the latest observed vector from $Z_p(t)$ to $Z_p(t + s)$, where s denotes the time steps after the present time t.

PROPOSED METHODS

The proposed three novel methods will first embed the one-dimensional historical traffic trajectories into multidimensional reconstructed state spaces and then use fuzzy reasoning to infer the future changes of the latest observed traffic vector, based on different prediction rationales for selecting the similar historical trajectories confined in the specific temporal and/or spatial domains. We use a cluster of nearby points in the state space to predict the change $\Delta\theta_{pn}(t)(i.e.\zeta_{pn}(t+s)-\zeta_{pn}(t))$ rather than just the position $\zeta_{pn}(t+s)$. Two adjustable parameters, temporal threshold value (ε_t) and spatial threshold value (ε_s), are used in this study to define the "similarity." Detailed procedures for the proposed prediction methods are described as follows.

The Temporal Confined (TC) Method

Let $\zeta_{pn}(t)$ and $\zeta_{mn}(t)$ respectively denote the present and the mth traffic trajectory in the nth dimensional state space. We refer the "temporal similarity" to a situation that the "temporal difference" between $\zeta_{pn}(t)$ and $\zeta_{mn}(t)$ is smaller than a designated temporal threshold value (ε_t). The prediction rationale for temporal confined (TC) method is to perform fuzzy reasoning for "temporal similarity." All the historical traffic trajectories are viewed as similar to the present trajectory if their temporal differences are within the domain confined by ε_t and only these trajectories are selected for fuzzy reasoning. Those trajectories with temporal differences greater than ε_t are thought as dissimilar to the present trajectory and thus will not be used for fuzzy reasoning.

To explain this concept, Figure 2 demonstrates several trajectories in which two historical vectors $Z_2(t)$ and $Z_4(t)$ are assumed dissimilar to the present vector $Z_p(t)$ such that both $\left|\zeta_{2n}(t)-\zeta_{2n}(t-v)\right|$ and $\left|\zeta_{4n}(t)-\zeta_{4n}(t-v)\right|$ are significantly larger than $\left|\zeta_{pn}(t)-\zeta_{pn}(t-v)\right|$ in the nth state space. The TC method will exclude these two vectors while conducting the prediction from $Z_p(t)$ to $Z_p(t+s)$. Theoretically, a small ε_t will encompass less historical trajectories but will enhance the degree of temporal similarity to the present trajectory. If ε_t is too small, the historical traffic data may be insufficient because too many historical observations will be ex-

cluded. If ε_t is too large, however, the prediction accuracy may be offset by including too many dissimilar trajectories for the prediction reasoning, which may lead to poor prediction. In the TC method, we assign various weights to the differencing variables of historical observations based on the degrees of similarity and then estimate the increment to infer the future change. Once the increment is estimated, the value of the present vector in the future state can be calculated. Detailed procedures for the proposed TC method are narrated as follows (Figure 2):

Step 1. Preprocess the data: Plot the one-dimensional traffic time series data $Z_p(t)$ of the latest (present) observation in the N-dimensional reconstructed state space $\left\{\zeta_{pn}[t-(n-1)\tau]\right\}$, which can be denoted as:

$$Z_p(t) = \left\{\zeta_{pn}[t-(n-1)\tau], \; n=1,2,...,N\right\}. \; (1)$$

Step 2. Extract the features: Calculate the "past" temporal differences of the latest observation $Z_p(t)$ and of the m historical observations $Z_m(t)$ between the present time t and v time steps before t by Equations (2) and (3), respectively:

$$\Delta\theta_{pn}(t) = \zeta_{pn}(t)-\zeta_{pn}(t-v), n=1,2,...,N \; (2)$$

$$\Delta\theta_{mn}(t) = \zeta_{mn}(t)-\zeta_{mn}(t-v), n=1,2,...,N; m=1,2,...,M \; (3)$$

Step 3. Define the temporal similarity and perform fuzzy reasoning: All the historical trajectories with temporal differences smaller than a temporal threshold ε_t are defined having "temporal similarity" as the present trajectory, which are expressed by Equation (4). The "fuzzy equal" reasoning to infer the

Figure 2. Temporal similarity fuzzy reasoning for TC method: a) Selection of temporal similar trajectories (Assume $M_1' = 3$; i.e., only three trajectories 1, 3, and M are selected) b) Temporal similarity membership degrees ($M_1' = 3$)

a)

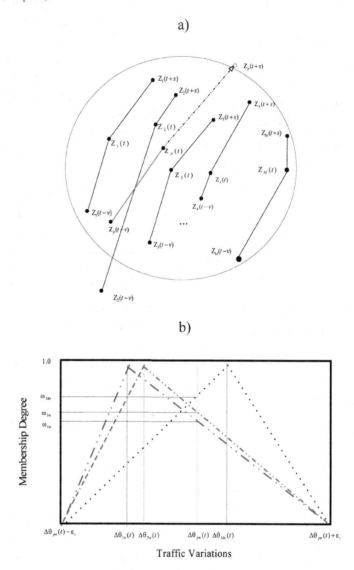

b)

future temporal difference of present vector is then preformed by Equation (5).

$$\left| \Delta\theta_{pn}(t) - \Delta\theta_{mn}(t) \right| \leq \varepsilon_t, \; m=1, 2, ..., M; \; n=1, 2, ..., N. \tag{4}$$

IF $\left| \Delta\theta_{pn}(t) - \Delta\theta_{mn}(t) \right| \leq \varepsilon_t$, THEN $\Delta\theta_{pn}(s)$ is "fuzzy equal" to $\Delta\theta_{mn}(s)$ (5)

This article uses a triangle membership function to calculate the temporal similarity membership degree for each selected historical trajectory. Each membership degree (ω_{mn}) is estimated by its membership function as follows.

$$\omega_{mn} = \frac{\varepsilon_t}{\left| \Delta\theta_{pn}(t) + \varepsilon_t - \Delta\theta_{mn}(t) \right|}. \tag{6}$$

Figure 2 demonstrates the temporal similarity fuzzy reasoning. A domain confined by a temporal threshold ε_t in Figure 2(a) shows that only three ($M_1' = 3$) trajectories $Z_1(t)$, $Z_3(t)$ and $Z_M(t)$ are used for fuzzy reasoning because their temporal differences $\Delta\theta_{pn}(t)$ and $\Delta\theta_{mn}(t)$ are smaller than ε_t; while $Z_2(t)$ and $Z_4(t)$ are not used for fuzzy reasoning as their temporal differences are larger than ε_t. Figure 2(b) further depicts the calculation (by Equation (6)) of the membership degrees for these three selected temporal differences $\Delta\theta_{1n}(t)$, $\Delta\theta_{3n}(t)$, and $\Delta\theta_{Mn}(t)$.

Step 4. Estimate the increment: Equation (7) estimates the increment $\Delta\hat{\theta}_{TCn}(s)$ for the present trajectory in the future s time steps, where

$$\Delta\theta_{mn}(s) = \zeta_{mn}(t+s) - \zeta_{mn}(t), n = 1, 2, ..., N; m = 1, 2, ..., M_1'$$

and M_1' denotes the number of historical trajectories with temporal similarity to the present trajectory.

$$\Delta\hat{\theta}_{TCn}(s) = \frac{\sum_{m=1}^{M_1'} \omega_{mn}\Delta\theta_{mn}(s)}{\sum_{m=1}^{M_1'} \omega_{mn}}, n = 1, 2, ..., N . \quad (7)$$

Step 5. Compute the predicted value: Equation (8) calculates the predicted value for the present vector in the future s time steps in the N-dimensional reconstructed state space $\hat{\zeta}_{pn}(t+s)$, from which the future state of one-dimensional traffic time series $\hat{Z}_p(t+s)$ can be obtained.

$$\hat{\zeta}_{pn}(t+s) = \zeta_{pn}(t) + \Delta\hat{\theta}_{TCn}(s) \ n=1, 2, ..., N. \quad (8)$$

The Spatiotemporal Confined (STC) Method

We refer the "spatiotemporal similarity" to a situation that not only the "temporal difference" between $\zeta_{pn}(t)$ and $\zeta_{mn}(t)$ is smaller than a des-

ignated temporal threshold value (ε_t) but its "spatial difference" is also smaller than a designated spatial threshold value (ε_s). The rationale for spatiotemporal confined (STC) method is to perform fuzzy reasoning for "spatiotemporal similarity," which satisfy the conditions of both "spatial similarity" and "temporal similarity." In other words, all the historical traffic trajectories are viewed as "spatiotemporal similarity" to the present trajectory if their "temporal differences" are within the domain confined by ε_t and their "spatial differences" are also within the domain confined by ε_s. Therefore, the STC method can be viewed as a restricted case of the TC method because we have imposed a spatial constraint to the temporal similarity trajectories. Both TC and STC methods should be theoretically identical if ε_s approaches infinity. Detailed procedures for the proposed STC method are explained as follows (Figure 3):

Step 1. Preprocess the data: Plot the one-dimensional traffic time series data $Z_p(t)$ of the latest observation in the N-dimensional reconstructed state space, as the TC method does.

Step 2. Extract the features: Calculate the "past" temporal differences of the latest observation $Z_p(t)$ and of the m historical observations $Z_m(t)$ between the present time t and v time steps before t, as the TC method does.

Step 3. Define the spatiotemporal similarity and perform fuzzy reasoning: All the historical trajectories with spatial differences smaller than a spatial threshold ε_s are defined as having "spatial similarity" to the present trajectory, which can be expressed by Equation (9):

$$\left|\zeta_{pn}[t-(n-1)\tau] - \zeta_{mn}[t-(n-1)\tau]\right| \leq \varepsilon_s,$$
$$m=1, 2, ..., M; \ n=1, 2, ..., N. \quad (9)$$

Figure 3. Spatiotemporal similarity fuzzy reasoning for STC method: a) Selection of spatiotemporal similar trajectories (Assume $M_2' = 2$; i.e., only two trajectories 1 and 3 are selected) b) Spatiotemporal similarity membership degrees ($M_2' = 2$)

a)

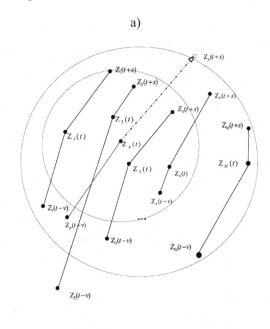

b)

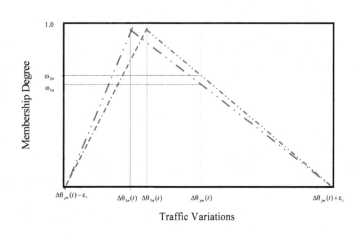

Both Equations (4) and (9) are used to define the "spatiotemporal similarity" of historical traffic trajectories. The "fuzzy equal" reasoning to infer the spatiotemporal difference of present vector is then preformed by Equation (10).

$$\text{IF} \left| \zeta_{pn}[t-(n-1)\tau] - \zeta_{mn}[t-(n-1)\tau] \right| \leq \varepsilon_s$$

$$\text{AND IF} \left| \Delta\theta_{pn}(t) - \Delta\theta_{mn}(t) \right| \leq \varepsilon_t$$

THEN

$$\Delta\theta_{pn}(s) \text{ is "fuzzy equal" to } \Delta\theta_{mn}(s). \quad (10)$$

We also use Equation (6) to calculate the spatiotemporal similarity membership degree for each selected historical trajectory. Figure 3 demonstrates the selection of spatiotemporal similar trajectories. In the spatial domain, $Z_1(t)$, $Z_2(t)$,

$Z_3(t)$ and $Z_4(t)$ are viewed as "spatial similarity" because they are within a domain confined by ε_s; but $Z_M(t)$ is not because its spatial difference $Z_p(t) - Z_M(t)$ is greater than ε_s. Moreover, in the temporal domain, as explained in the TC method, $Z_2(t)$ and $Z_4(t)$ do not have "temporal similarity" because their temporal differences between $\Delta\theta_{pn}(t)$ and $\Delta\theta_{mn}(t)$ are greater than ε_t. Consequently, only two ($M_2'=2$) historical trajectories $Z_1(t)$ and $Z_3(t)$ in Figure 3(a) are left to perform the fuzzy reasoning for prediction. Figure 3(b) further depicts the calculation of the membership degrees for these two selected spatiotemporal differences $\Delta\theta_{1n}(t)$ and $\Delta\theta_{3n}(t)$. Each membership degree (ω_{mn}) is estimated by its membership function from Equation (6).

Step 4. Estimate the increment: Equation (11) estimates the increment $\Delta\hat{\theta}_{STCn}(s)$ for the present vector in the future s time steps, where
$\Delta\theta_{mn}(s) = \zeta_{mn}(t+s) - \zeta_{mn}(t), n = 1,2,...,N; m = 1,2,...,M_2'$
and M_2' denotes the number of historical trajectories with spatiotemporal similarity to the present trajectory.

$$\Delta\hat{\theta}_{STCn}(s) = \frac{\sum\limits_{m=1}^{M_2'} \omega_{mn}\Delta\theta_{mn}(s)}{\sum\limits_{m=1}^{M_2'} \omega_{mn}}, n = 1,2,...,N .$$

(11)

Step 5. Compute the predicted value: Equation (12) calculates the predicted value for the present trajectory in the future s time steps in the N-dimensional reconstructed state space $\hat{\zeta}_{pn}(t+s)$, from which the future state of one-dimensional traffic time series $\hat{Z}_p(t+s)$ can be obtained.

$$\hat{\zeta}_{pn}(t+s) = \zeta_{pn}(t) + \Delta\hat{\theta}_{STCn}(s) \, n=1, 2,..., N.$$

(12)

The Spatial Confined (SC) Method

We refer the "spatial similarity" to a situation that the "spatial difference" between $\zeta_{pn}(t)$ and $\zeta_{mn}(t)$ is smaller than a designated spatial threshold value (ε_s). The prediction rationale for spatial confined (SC) method is to perform fuzzy reasoning for "spatial similarity." All the historical traffic trajectories are viewed as "spatial similarity" to the present trajectory if their spatial differences are within the domain confined by ε_s. Thus, the STC method can also be viewed as a restricted case of the SC method, if we have imposed a temporal confinement to screen the spatial similar trajectories. Detailed procedures for the proposed SC method are explained as follows (Figure 4):

Step 1. Preprocess the data: Plot the one-dimensional traffic time series data $Z_p(t)$ of the latest observation in the N-dimensional reconstructed state space, as the TC model does.

Step 2. Extract the features: Calculate the "past" spatial differences of the latest observation $Z_p(t)$ and of the m historical observations $Z_m(t)$ between the present time t and v time steps before t.

Step 3. Define the spatial similarity and perform fuzzy reasoning: As stated above, all the historical trajectories with spatial differences $Z_p(t) - Z_m(t)$ smaller than a spatial threshold ε_s are defined as having "spatial similarity" to the present trajectory, which can be expressed by Equation (9). The "fuzzy proportional" reasoning to infer the spatial difference of present vector is then preformed by Equation (13).

Figure 4. Spatial similarity fuzzy reasoning for SC method: a) Selection of spatial similar trajectories (Assume $M_3' = 4$; i.e., only four trajectories 1, 2, 3 and 4 are selected) b) Spatial similarity membership degrees ($M_3' = 4$)

a)

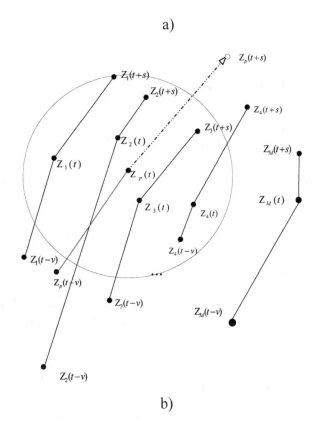

b)

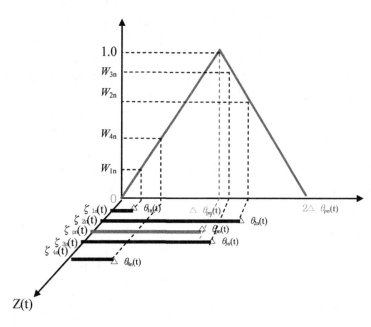

IF $\left| \zeta_{pn}[t - (n-1)\tau] - \zeta_{mn}[t - (n-1)\tau] \right| \le \varepsilon_s$

THEN $\left| \Delta\theta_{pn}(s) - \Delta\theta_{mn}(s) \right|$ is "fuzzy proportional"

to $\left| \Delta\theta_{pn}(t) - \Delta\theta_{mn}(t) \right|$. (13)

We also use a triangle membership function to calculate the spatial similarity membership degree for each selected historical trajectory. Unlike the TC and STC methods that are based on the "fuzzy equal" reasoning, however, each membership degree (ω_{mn}) of SC method is based on the "fuzzy proportional" reasoning, which can be estimated by Equation (14) as follows:

$$\omega_{mn} = \begin{cases} \dfrac{\Delta\theta_{mn}(t)}{\Delta\theta_{pn}(t)}, & if \Delta\theta_{mn}(t) < \Delta\theta_{pn}(t) \\[3mm] 2 - \dfrac{\Delta\theta_{mn}(t)}{\Delta\theta_{pn}(t)}, & if \Delta\theta_{mn}(t) > \Delta\theta_{pn}(t) \end{cases} \quad (14)$$

where $m = 1, 2, ..., M_3'$.

To explain this concept, Figure 4 demonstrates the spatial similarity fuzzy proportional reasoning. A domain confined by a spatial threshold ε_s in Figure 4(a) shows that only four ($M_3' = 4$) trajectories $Z_1(t)$, $Z_2(t)$, $Z_3(t)$ and $Z_4(t)$ are selected for fuzzy reasoning because they are within the spatial threshold ε_s; but $Z_M(t)$ is excluded because $Z_p(t) - Z_M(t)$ is larger than ε_s. Figure 4(b) further depicts the calculation of the membership degrees by Equation (14) for the four selected spatial differences $\Delta\theta_{1n}(t)$, $\Delta\theta_{2n}(t)$, $\Delta\theta_{3n}(t)$, and $\Delta\theta_{4n}(t)$.

Step 4. Estimate the increment: Equation (15) estimates the increment $\Delta\hat{\theta}_{SCn}(s)$ for the present trajectory in the future s time steps, where

$\Delta\theta_{mn}(s) = \zeta_{mn}(t+s) - \zeta_{mn}(t), n = 1, 2, ..., N; m = 1, 2, ..., M_3'$

and M_3' denotes the number of historical trajectories with spatial similarity to the present trajectory.

$$\Delta\hat{\theta}_{SCn}(s) = \frac{\sum_{m=1}^{M_3'} \omega_{mn}\Delta\theta_{mn}(s)}{\sum_{m=1}^{M_3'} \omega_{mn}}, n = 1, 2, ..., N \quad (15)$$

Step 5. Compute the predicted value: Equation (16) calculates the predicted value for the present vector in the future s time steps in the N-dimensional reconstructed state space $\hat{\zeta}_{pn}(t+s)$, from which the future state of one-dimensional traffic time series $\hat{Z}_p(t+s)$ can be obtained.

$$\hat{\zeta}_{pn}(t+s) = \zeta_{pn}(t) + \Delta\hat{\theta}_{SCn}(s), n = 1, 2, ..., N. \quad (16)$$

CRITERIA TO EVALUATE PREDICTION PERFORMANCE

In literature, measuring the prediction errors of a time series can use different criteria including mean error (*ME*), mean percent error (*MPE*), mean absolute error (*MAE*), mean absolute percent error (*MAPE*), root-mean-square error (*RMSE*), root-mean-square percent error (*RMSPE*). The problem with *ME* or *MPE* is that they may be close to 0 if large positive errors cancel out large negative errors. To overcome this problem, *MAE* or *MAPE* is often used instead. However, the value of *MAE* or *MAPE* is generally smaller than that of *RMSE* or *RMSPE* because *RMSE* or *RMSPE* penalizes heavily (with squared effect) for large individual errors. Obviously, *RMSE* or *RMSPE* is more desirable than *MAE* or *MAPE*. Unfortunately, use of the above-mentioned criteria will come across two major shortcomings. First, the value has no upper bound. Second, there is no rule-of-thumb standard to judge if the prediction errors are too large to be acceptable for prediction purposes. As such, these criteria (particularly, the *MAPE* and *RMSPE*) are primarily used for the comparison of relative prediction power between different models, say, new models with benchmark models.

To judge if a prediction model is acceptable, in econometric literature, the most useful criterion is perhaps the Theil inequality coefficient (U), which is defined as follows (Pindyck and Rubinfeld, 1998):

$$U = \sqrt{\frac{1}{T}\sum_t (\hat{x}_t - x_t)^2} \Bigg/ \left(\sqrt{\frac{1}{T}\sum_t x_t^2} + \sqrt{\frac{1}{T}\sum_t \hat{x}_t^2} \right)$$
(17)

where $\hat{x}_t$, x_t respectively represent the predicted and observed values at time t and T is the number of observations. The good feature of U is that it can take values between zero and one. The closer to zero U is, the more accurate the prediction is. If U=0, $\hat{x}_t = x_t$ for all t and it is a perfect prediction. If U=1, on the other hand, the predictive performance is as bad as it possibly could be. In practice, a value of U not greater than 0.2 will indicate the prediction model acceptable.

Note that the numerator (without the square root) of U can be further decomposed into the following three proportions: the bias (U^M), the variance (U^S), and the covariance (U^C).

$$U^M = (\bar{\hat{x}} - \bar{x})^2 \Big/ (1/T)\sum_t (\hat{x}_t - x_t)^2$$
(18)

$$U^S = (\hat{\sigma}_t - \sigma_t)^2 \Big/ (1/T)\sum_t (\hat{x}_t - x_t)^2$$
(19)

$$U^C = 2(1-\rho)\hat{\sigma}_t \sigma_t \Big/ (1/T)\sum_t (\hat{x}_t - x_t)^2$$
(20)

where $\bar{\hat{x}}$, $\bar{x}$, $\hat{\sigma}_t$, σ_t are the means and standard deviations of the series $\hat{x}_t$ and x_t, respectively, and ρ is their correlation coefficient. The bias proportion U^M is an indication of systematic error; the variance proportion U^S indicates the ability of the prediction method to replicate the degree of vari-

ability; the covariance proportion U^C measures unsystematic error. Ideally, one would hope that both U^M and U^S are close to zero and U^C close to one. For any value of $U > 0$, the ideal distribution of inequality over the three prediction error sources is $U^M = U^S = 0$ and $U^C = 1$. A large value of U^M or U^S (normally, above 0.2) would mean that a systematic bias is present or the fluctuation of actual time series data considerably differs from that of predicted data; in this case the prediction method must be abandoned even though the overall U statistic is low (less than 0.2). This rule-of-thumb standard provides useful information to judge if a prediction model is satisfactory or not, without the need to compare with any benchmark models. Namely, with the information of U and its three components, one can not only judge if the prediction model is acceptable but also know where the sources of predictive errors come from. Hence, Theil inequality coefficient is used to evaluate the prediction performance in this study.

PREDICTION RESULTS

This article carries out a field study with traffic flow data directly drawn from 16 detector stations of the United States I-35 Freeway in Minneapolis, Minnesota. Averages of the lane-specific traffic counts are accumulated over one-minute interval. At each station the one-minute-flow data for ten workdays' morning peak hours (from 6 AM to 9 AM) are extracted. The average flow rates for these 16 stations range from 16.8 to 33.8 vehicles per minute per lane, or equivalently, with average headways from 3.57 seconds (moderate flow) to 1.78 seconds (near saturated flow). The data points for the first nine days are used to establish the proposed prediction methods (i.e., recognition of similar trajectories); the data points for the last day are reserved for validating the predictive accuracy.

Three parameters of the TC method, including delay time (τ), embedding dimension (N) and temporal threshold (ε_t), need to be determined in advance. While for the STC and SC methods, additional parameter, spatial threshold (ε_s), must be determined. The delay time is determined by the autocorrelation function (*ACF*) when *ACF* reaches zero at the first time. The method of false nearest neighbors (FNN) is used to determine approximate embedding dimension, which is around five to seven. We have assigned different values, on a trial-and-error basis, to the temporal threshold (ε_t) and spatial threshold (ε_s) and found that the prediction errors converge when either one of these two threshold values exceeds six, holding the other threshold fixed. Thus, the values from four to six are used for these spatial and temporal thresholds in the sensitive analysis. A total of 27 combinations (ε_s=4, 5, 6; ε_t=4, 5, 6; N= 5, 6, 7) are attempted accordingly and the optimal combination of (ε_s, ε_t, and N) that minimizes the prediction errors is finally reported. Without loss of generality, the number of prediction step (s) is set equal to 1.

Table 1 summarizes the prediction results by the three proposed methods with the information of U as well as its components U^M, U^S, and U^C for diagnosing the sources of prediction error. Recall that the data points for nine days are used for establishing the prediction methods; while the data points for the last day are reserved for validating purposes. Figure 5 illustrates the predicted flow time series overlaying the observed ones in the last (10th) day. It provides evidence that the proposed three methods can satisfactorily predict the one-minute traffic time series. From Table 1, we note that the values of U range from 0.099 to 0.197 for TC method, from 0.089 to 0.180 for STC method, and from 0.085 to 0.171 for SC method. Even for the worst case, the value for U is less than 0.2, strongly indicating that these three methods can satisfactorily predict the drastic variations of one-minute traffic time series.

We further investigate the sources of prediction error by examining both the bias and variance proportions for U statistic, which are far less than 0.2 throughout all stations. It robustly indicates that the three novel methods have small systematic bias as well as little deviation from the observed data. From Table 1, in general, station 32 performs the worst while station 52 does the best job. STC method performs somewhat better than TC and SC when traffic volumes are light; however, SC is slightly superior to STC, which is slightly better than TC when traffic volumes get heavier. As anticipated, higher traffic volumes would generally associate with smaller U values, indicating that the proposed three methods perform better prediction in heavy flow than in moderate flow circumstances.

DISCUSSION

Accurately predicting the traffic time series, especially when measured in short time intervals, has become a prerequisite in the development of advanced traffic management and transport information systems. Prediction of shorter-term traffic dynamics (e.g., 1-minute traffic or shorter) is generally more challenging than the prediction of longer-term dynamics (e.g., 5-minute traffic or longer) because more conspicuous fluctuations can be observed in the shorter-term traffic trajectories evolution. Capturing and predicting the traffic trajectories evolution with our proposed methods is due mainly to the macroscopic traffic variations (trend) and the microscopic traffic variations (fluctuations surging along with the trend). We further discuss such underlying traffic features and some potential applications of our methods to real world traffic congestion management.

The day-to-day traffic patterns at a given roadway can be attributed to deterministic-like dynamics, which are regarded as some intrinsic rules governing the regularity. What do the real meanings or phenomena imply for such intrinsic

Table 1. Prediction performance and sources of prediction error

Station no.	Traffic volume (veh/min/lane)	Prediction method	ε_s	ε_t	Embedding dimension N	Delay time τ (minutes)	U	Sources of prediction error		
								U^M	U^S	U^C
32	16.8	TC	-	6	6	44	0.197	0.000	0.106	0.894
		STC	4	5	6		0.180	0.001	0.076	0.923
		SC	5	-	6		0.171	0.000	0.079	0.921
49	21.9	TC	-	6	7	27	0.167	0.000	0.151	0.849
		STC	4	4	7		0.129	0.002	0.021	0.977
		SC	4	-	7		0.141	0.002	0.056	0.942
45	23.7	TC	-	6	5	22	0.162	0.001	0.156	0.843
		STC	4	4	7		0.146	0.000	0.019	0.981
		SC	4	-	7		0.161	0.009	0.035	0.956
48	23.9	TC	-	6	5	25	0.170	0.000	0.153	0.847
		STC	4	4	6		0.136	0.000	0.016	0.984
		SC	4	-	5		0.143	0.000	0.092	0.908
44	24.8	TC	-	6	5	20	0.148	0.001	0.142	0.857
		STC	4	6	6		0.133	0.002	0.030	0.968
		SC	5	-	5		0.128	0.000	0.075	0.925
50	25.6	TC	-	5	5	23	0.127	0.001	0.147	0.852
		STC	4	6	7		0.119	0.001	0.045	0.954
		SC	4	-	7		0.114	0.002	0.018	0.980
39	27.8	TC	-	6	5	28	0.188	0.000	0.164	0.836
		STC	4	5	7		0.124	0.001	0.003	0.996
		SC	4	-	7		0.134	0.000	0.009	0.991
43	28.9	TC	-	6	5	29	0.182	0.002	0.167	0.831
		STC	4	4	6		0.144	0.001	0.005	0.994
		SC	4	-	7		0.163	0.005	0.050	0.945
41	29.9	TC	-	6	5	29	0.166	0.001	0.176	0.823
		STC	4	4	7		0.113	0.002	0.002	0.996
		SC	4	-	7		0.117	0.001	0.002	0.997
42	31.9	TC	-	6	6	29	0.124	0.001	0.185	0.814
		STC	4	6	7		0.106	0.006	0.006	0.988
		SC	5	-	7		0.109	0.003	0.005	0.992
52	31.9	TC	-	6	5	27	0.099	0.004	0.111	0.885
		STC	4	5	5		0.098	0.013	0.107	0.880
		SC	7	-	5		0.085	0.006	0.023	0.971
51	32.5	TC	-	6	7	24	0.125	0.001	0.174	0.825
		STC	4	5	6		0.089	0.000	0.007	0.993
		SC	4	-	6		0.096	0.002	0.024	0.974

continued on following page

Table 1. Continued

53	32.5	TC	-	6	6	27	0.112	0.002	0.127	0.871
		STC	4	6	5		0.094	0.001	0.072	0.927
		SC	5	-	5		0.092	0.001	0.056	0.943
54	32.8	TC	-	6	6	27	0.119	0.001	0.123	0.876
		STC	4	6	5		0.105	0.000	0.081	0.919
		SC	5	-	5		0.096	0.006	0.028	0.966
56	33.2	TC	-	6	5	28	0.107	0.003	0.142	0.855
		STC	4	6	5		0.105	0.008	0.134	0.858
		SC	5	-	5		0.095	0.005	0.061	0.934
55	33.8	TC	-	6	5	27	0.103	0.003	0.155	0.842
		STC	4	5	5		0.100	0.002	0.046	0.952
		SC	5	-	5		0.093	0.000	0.061	0.939

Note: The bias proportion U^M is an indication of systematic error; the variance proportion U^S indicates the ability of the method to replicate the degree of variability; the covariance proportion U^C measures unsystematic error. For a satisfactory prediction method, U value should be small (practically, no greater than 0.2). The ideal distribution for $U > 0$ is that both U^M and U^S should be close to zero (less than 0.2 is acceptable) and U^C close to one (Pindyck and Rubinfeld, 1998).

rules in our daily life? We may consider most trip makers get to work by 9 am and take off at 5 pm on workdays. They might depart from homes or work places at approximately the same times, using the same modes, and/or choosing the same routes everyday. Such macroscopic regularities perhaps cause "similar but not exactly the same" traffic patterns from day to day. Moreover, due to the constraints of travel demand, roadway capacity, speed limit, and so on, the observed traffic flows would never go beyond two extreme values: zero (free or jam) flow and maximum (capacity) flow. Thus, if we investigate the traffic time series of successive days, many recurrent curves would exhibit. The macroscopic regularities perhaps dominate the shape (trend) of such deterministic-like traffic patterns.

However, not all drivers are completely confined by such macroscopic regularities. Individual driver in any circumstance always controls his/her vehicle at a desired speed with safe spacing and clearance so as to best interact with roadway environments and neighboring vehicles. The presence of human behavior is perhaps the key factor

making the traffic dynamics more complicated than many other physical systems that do not involve human behavior. Besides, roadway traffic is composed of heterogeneous vehicles with diverse powers or maneuver capabilities. Due to the heterogeneity across drivers and vehicles, the microscopic irregularities of traffic dynamics, especially measured in short time intervals, should be considerably fluctuated surging along with the macroscopic regularities.

The major advantage of embedding one-dimensional traffic series into multidimensional state spaces is to find out more noticeable trajectories evolution—both regularities and irregularities. The proposed three novel methods have embedded the one-dimensional historical traffic trajectories into multidimensional spaces and then utilized different fuzzy reasoning logics to infer the future changes of the latest observed traffic vector, confined in some designated temporal and/or spatial domains. With this advantage, our proposed methods should be applicable practically in the recurrent and non-recurrent congestions management.

Figure 5. Predicted and observed flow time series (United States I-35 Freeway in Minneapolis, Minnesota, Station 55 as an example): a) TC Method b) STC Method c) SC Method (Solid line denotes the observed data; dot line denotes the predicted data)

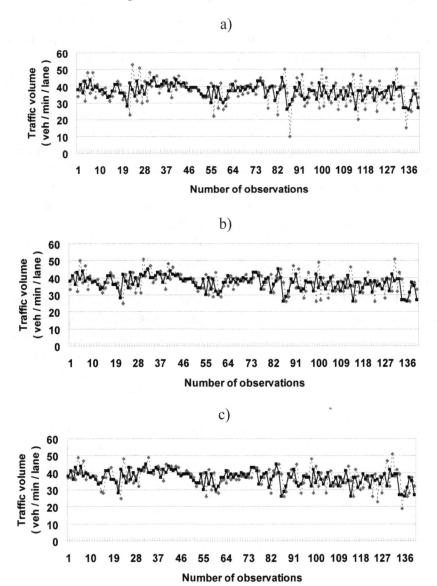

For most recurrent congestions which are due mainly to trip makers' macroscopic regularities and roadways' limited capacities, the effective means include altering the service process more closely matching the arrival patterns, making the arrival process more closely matching the service capacity, and imposing proper service disciplines to cut down the size of delays. The main challenge is to determine the proper timing to actuate the control (e.g., ramp metering) mechanism. We can apply the proposed methods to accurately predict the temporal traffic (flow, occupancy, speed) variations. Proper metering rates can then be actuated accordingly to hold back the incoming vehicles so as to smooth out the peak traffic and to reduce the congested delays altogether.

For most non-recurrent congestions which are due perhaps to unexpected incidents, the most effective means is expediting the diagnosis and removal of incidents in order to retrieve the roadway capacity. The major challenge is to diagnose the incidents as soon as possible because the overall delays can be proportional to square of the incident duration. Our proposed methods perform fuzzy reasoning by "temporal and/or spatial similarity" of historical traffic trajectories to infer the present data to the future time steps. If the short-term traffic dynamics predicted by the proposed methods have significant deviation from those detected by the roadway detectors for consecutive two or three time steps and the alarm signals are actuated accordingly, then it can advise the traffic managers to verify the likely incidents in situ (e.g., through the remote CCTV). Consequently, the congestions due to such incidents could be alleviated, or at least mitigated, immediately.

CONCLUSION

We have developed temporal confined (TC), spatiotemporal confined (STC), and spatial confined (SC) methods to predict the short-interval traffic dynamics, in terms of one-minute flow time series, in reconstructed state spaces. The TC method performs fuzzy reasoning by "temporal similarity" of historical traffic trajectories to infer the present data to the future time steps. The STC method performs fuzzy reasoning by both "spatial similarity" and "temporal similarity" of historical trajectories to make the prediction inferences. The SC method only conducts fuzzy reasoning by "spatial similarity" to make prediction inferences. Validation of the predicted data with the field one-minute flow time series data directly extracted from 16 detector stations of the United States I-35 Freeway has shown that all

of the proposed methods have yielded satisfactory prediction accuracy, according to the Theil inequality coefficient. The small bias and variance proportions of Theil inequality coefficient further indicate that the predicted results have small systematic bias and little deviation from the observed data. In conclusion, the proposed three novel methods are acceptable for traffic time series prediction purposes.

The present article only dealt with the one-minute flow time series. Future study can use the proposed novel methods to examine the same traffic data measured in different time intervals, such as five-minute or ten-minute. Of course, other traffic parameters such as speed and occupancy time series can also be examined by the proposed methods. In addition to the proposed "fuzzy equal" and "fuzzy proportional" concepts in selecting similar historical trajectories, future study may incorporate other recognition techniques (e.g., considering the turning directions of the trajectories in the reconstructed state spaces) to refine the degrees of "similarity." Sensitivity analysis can be carried out by either varying the temporal threshold or varying the spatial threshold under the best combination of other fixed parameters. More sophisticated methods to determine the embedding dimension, temporal threshold, and spatial threshold of the traffic time-series data are also challenging and deserve to explore.

ACKNOWLEDGMENT

The authors would like to thank Dr. C. J. Lan, former professor of University of Miami, for providing the field traffic time series data. This work is part of the research projects granted by the ROC National Science Council (NSC-91-2211-E-009-048 and NSC-92-2211-E-009-058).

REFERENCES

Abarbanel, H. D. I. (1996). *Analysis of observed chaotic data*. New York: Springer-Verlag.

Bonnet, D., Labouisse, V., & Grumbach, A. (1997). δ-NARMA neural networks: A new approach to signal prediction. *IEEE Transactions on Signal Processing, 45*, 2878. doi:10.1109/78.650106

Chang, J. L., & Miaou, S. P. (1999). Real-time prediction of traffic flows using dynamic generalized linear models. *Transportation Research Record, 1678*, 168–178. doi:10.3141/1678-21

Clark, S. D., Dougherty, M. S., & Kirby, H. R. (1993). *The use of neural networks and time series models for short term traffic forecasting: A comparative study*. Paper presented at Transportation Planning Method Conference, PTRC 21st Summer Annual Meeting, Manchester, UK.

Durbin, J. (2000). The Foreman lecture: The state space approach to time series analysis and its potential for official statistics. *Australian and New Zealand Journal of Statistics, 42*(1), 1–23. doi:10.1111/1467-842X.00104

He, G., & Ma, S. (2002). A study on the short-term prediction of traffic volume based on wavelet analysis. In *Proceedings of the IEEE 5th International Conference on ITS* (pp. 731-735).

Head, K. L. (1995). Event-based short-term traffic flow prediction model. *Transportation Research Record, 1510*, 45–52.

Hilborn, R. C. (2000). *Chaos and nonlinear dynamics*. New York: Oxford University Press.

Iokibe, T., Kanke, M., & Yasunari, F. (1995). Local fuzzy reconstruction model for short-term prediction on chaotic time series. *Fuzzy Set, 7*(1), 186–194.

Ishak, S., Kotha, P., & Alecsandru, C. (2003). Optimization of dynamic neural network performance for short-term traffic prediction. *Transportation Research Record, 1836*, 45–56. doi:10.3141/1836-07

Kantz, H., & Schreiber, T. (1997). *Nonlinear time series analysis*. Cambridge, UK: Cambridge University Press.

Kennel, M. B., Brown, R., & Abarbanel, H. D. I. (1992). Determining embedding dimension for phase-space reconstruction using a geometrical construction. *Physical Review, 45A*, 3403–3411.

Kirby, H., Dougherty, M., & Watson, S. (1997). Should we use neural networks or statistical models for short term motorway traffic forecasting? *International Journal of Forecasting, 13*, 43–50. doi:10.1016/S0169-2070(96)00699-1

Lam, W. H. K., Chan, K. S., Tam, M. L., & Shi, J. W. (2005). Short-term travel time forecasts for transport information system in Hong Kong. *Journal of Advanced Transportation, 39*(3), 289–306.

Lam, W. H. K., Tang, Y. F., & Tam, M. L. (2006). Comparison of two non-parametric models for daily traffic forecasting in Hong Kong. *Journal of Forecasting, 25*(3), 173–192. doi:10.1002/for.984

Lan, L. W., & Huang, Y. C. (2006). A rolling-trained fuzzy neural network approach for freeway incident detections. *Transportmetrica, 2*(1), 11–29. doi:10.1080/18128600608685653

Lan, L. W., Lin, F. Y., & Huang, Y. S. (2004). Confined space fuzzy proportion model for short-term traffic flow prediction. In *Proceedings of the 9th Conference of Hong Kong Society for Transportation Studies* (pp. 370-379).

Lan, L. W., Lin, F. Y., & Kuo, A. Y. (2003). Testing and prediction of traffic flow dynamics with chaos. *Journal of the Eastern Asia Society for Transportation Studies, 5*, 1975–1990.

Lan, L. W., Sheu, J. B., & Huang, Y. S. (2007). Prediction of short-interval traffic dynamics in multidimensional spaces. *Journal of the Eastern Asia Society for Transportation Studies, 7,* 2353–2367.

Lan, L. W., Sheu, J. B., & Huang, Y. S. (2008a). Features of traffic time-series on multidimensional spaces. *Journal of the Chinese Institute of Transportation, 20*(1), 91–118.

Lan, L. W., Sheu, J. B., & Huang, Y. S. (2008b). Investigation of temporal freeway traffic patterns in reconstructed state spaces. *Transportation Research, 16C,* 116–136.

Lee, S., & Fambro, D. B. (1999). Application of subset autoregressive integrated moving average model for short-term freeway traffic volume forecasting. *Transportation Research Record, 1678,* 179–188. doi:10.3141/1678-22

Li, S. (2002). Nonlinear combination of travel-time prediction model based on wavelet network. In *Proceedings of the IEEE 5th International Conference on ITS* (pp. 741-746).

Lingras, P., Sharma, S. C., & Osborne, P. (2000). Traffic volume time-series analysis according to the type of road use. *Computer-Aided Civil and Infrastructure Engineering, 15*(5), 365–373. doi:10.1111/0885-9507.00200

Okutani, I., & Stephanedes, Y. J. (1984). Dynamic prediction of traffic volume through Kalman filtering theory. *Transportation Research, 18B,* 1–11.

Pindyck, R. S., & Rubinfeld, D. L. (1998). *Econometric models and economic forecasts* (4th ed.). Singapore: Irwin/McGraw Hill.

Sakawa, M., Kosuke, K., & Ooura, K. (1998). A deterministic nonlinear prediction model through fuzzy reasoning using neighborhoods' difference and its application to actual time series data. *Fuzzy Set, 10*(2), 381–386.

Sheu, J. B., Lan, L. W., & Huang, Y. S. (2009). Short-term prediction of traffic dynamics with real-time recurrent learning algorithms. *Transportmetrica, 5*(1), 59–83. doi:10.1080/18128600802591681

Smith, B. L., & Demetsky, M. J. (1997). Traffic flow forecasting: Comparison of modeling approaches. *Journal of Transportation Engineering, 123*(4), 261–266. doi:10.1061/(ASCE)0733-947X(1997)123:4(261)

Smith, B. L., Williams, B. M., & Oswald, R. K. (2002). Comparison of parametric and nonparametric models for traffic flow forecasting. *Transportation Research, 10C,* 303–321.

Soltani, S. (2002). On the use of the wavelet decomposition for time series prediction. *Neurocomputing, 48,* 267–277. doi:10.1016/S0925-2312(01)00648-8

Sprott, J. C. (2003). *Chaos and time-series analysis.* New York: Oxford University Press.

Stathopoulos, A., & Karlaftis, M. G. (2003). A multivariate state space approach for urban traffic flow modeling and prediction. *Transportation Research, 11C,* 121–135.

Stephanedes, Y. J., Michalopoulos, P. G., & Plun, R. A. (1981). Improved estimation of traffic flow for real-time control. *Transportation Research Record, 795,* 28–39.

Sun, X., Munoz, L., & Horowitz, R. (2003). Highway traffic state estimation using improved mixture Kalman filters for effective ramp metering control. In *Proceedings of 42nd IEEE Conference on Decision and Control* (pp. 6333-6338).

Takens, F. (1981). Detecting strange attractors in turbulence. In *Dynamical Systems and Turbulence, Warwick 1980* (LNM 898, pp. 366-381).

Van Arem, B., Kirby, H. R., Van Der Vlist, M. J. M., & Whittaker, J. C. (1997). Recent advances in the field of short-term traffic forecasting. *International Journal of Forecasting*, *13*, 1–12. doi:10.1016/S0169-2070(96)00695-4

Vlahogianni, E. I., Golia, J. C., & Karlaftis, M. G. (2004). Short-term traffic forecasting: Overview of objective and methods. *Transport Reviews*, *24*, 533–557. doi:10.1080/0144164042000195072

Vlahogianni, E. I., Karlaftis, M. G., & Golias, J. C. (2005). Optimized and meta-optimized neural networks for short-term traffic flow prediction: A genetic approach. *Transportation Research*, *13C*, 211–234.

Wang, Y., & Papageorgiou, M. (2005). Real-time freeway traffic state estimation based on extended Kalman filter: A general approach. *Transportation Research*, *39B*, 141–167.

This work was previously published in International Journal of Applied Evolutionary Computation, Volume 1, Issue 1, edited by Wei-Chiang Samuelson Hong, pp. 16-35, copyright 2010 by IGI Publishing (an imprint of IGI Global).

Chapter 3
Self–Evolvable Protocol Design Using Genetic Algorithms

Wenbing Yao
Huawei Technologies, UK

Sheng-Uei Guan
Xian Jiatong-Liverpool University, China

Zhiqiang Jiang
National University of Singapore, Singapore

Ilias Kiourktsidis
Brunel University, UK

ABSTRACT

Self-modifying protocols (SMP) are protocols that can be modified at run time by the computers using them. Such protocols can be modified at run time so that they can adapt to the changing communicating environment and user requirements on the fly. Evolvable protocols are SMP designed using Genetic Algorithms (GA). The purpose of this paper is to apply Genetic Algorithms (GA) to design an evolvable protocol in order to equip communication peers with more autonomy and intelligence. The next-generation Internet will benefit from the concept of evolvable protocols. In this paper, we design a Self Evolvable Transaction Protocol (SETP) with a GA executor embedded. We then use the Network Simulator (NS2) to evaluate this evolvable protocol module to demonstrate the feasibility of our new design approach.

INTRODUCTION

Rooted in the autonomic computing research (Kephart & Chess, 2003), autonomic communications (AutoComm) aim to achieve the self-governance of a communication system or network with the assistance of the self-* capabilities, which include self-management, self-configuration (Milcher, 2004), self-optimisation, self-healing (Liu, Zhang, Jiang, Raymer & Strassner, 2008), self-protection and self-monitoring (Gu, Strassner, Xie, Wolf & Suda, 2008). The rapid development of this field has attracted considerable attention from academia and industry in recent years. In Europe, the European Commission (EC) funded a number of projects on AutoComm, e.g. CAS-

DOI: 10.4018/978-1-4666-1749-0.ch003

CADAS, ANA, HAGGLE under the Situated and Autonomic Communication (SAC) Initiative of the Sixth Framework Programme (FP6). Under the Seventh Framework Program (FP7) Auto-Comm research received further funding from the EC (Ref. projects EFIPSANS, SOCRATES, et al.) and has been recognized as a core feature of the future Internet. As pointed out in (Strassner, Fleck, Lewis, Parashar & Donnelly, 2008), the number of international conferences that focus on "autonomics" or "autonomically inspired" topics has increased rapidly in recent years, and the voice advocating standard organizations to make the movement towards the development of interoperability standards for autonomic systems are getting louder. It is evident that this surge of enthusiasm towards AutoComm will accelerate as more industrial companies become involved and relevant standards activities start.

The ultimate goal of autonomic communications is to "achieve the autonomy of communication networks with minimum human administration" (Gu et al., 2008), and the self-* capabilities of AutoComm systems are the key to achieving this goal. Gu, et al. identified the principal characteristics of an AutoComm system that distinguish it from conventional communication systems in (Gu et al., 2008). Dobson, et al., summarised the main challenges for AutoComm and reviewed the related work towards tackling some of the challenges in their survey paper (Dobson et al., 2006). In (Raymer, Meer & Strassner, 2008), researchers from the Architecture Expert Group of the Autonomous Communication Forum presented their design of the architecture of autonomic network system. In this architecture, based on the knowledge about the local network situation that is constantly being monitored, the Autonomic Management (AM) element produces and rectifies the network management policies according to the high level business targets, and the Autonomic Control (AC) mechanism proactively configures and adjusts the operations of the network devices according to the latest technical

policies. It is clear from many recent literature that, most of the current research on AutoComm has been focused on adding the *autonomic management* and *autonomic control* mechanisms into the existing policy based network management (PBNM) mechanism (Gu et al., 2008; Jennings et al., 2007; Raymer et al., 2008).

The principle of AC element is straightforward. It monitors the local network's situation, and feeds the observed data to the AM and PBNM elements. Taking the observed network situational data and the constraints from the PBNM as the reference target, the AC element applies the adaptive control theories to adjust the Policy Enforcement Point (e.g. a server or a router). This is illustrated in Figure 1.

The challenge is, when the AM changes its technical policies as reacting to the variation of the network environment and the PBNM accordingly translates the policies into target constraints, the AC has to find an optimal way to adjust the attainable network resources to meet the changing constraints. In Gu et al. (2008), Jennings et al. (2007), and Raymer et al. (2008), traditional control theories have been proposed as potential solutions for this problem. However, these studies assumed that the systems being controlled could be represented by linear models. In the complicated network environment, this assumption cannot always be held because network problems often involve complex nonlinear dynamics, chaotic disturbances and randomness that traditional algorithms are unable to conquer.

Genetic Algorithms (GA) (Miettinen & Neittaanmaki, 1999) has been successfully applied to complex optimization problems like adaptive control, optimal control problems, wire routing, scheduling etc. In this paper, we adopt GA as an effective tool to address the complex control problem in AutoComm systems. Rather than focusing on adjusting the configuration of network devices (Gu et al., 2008), and services such as web services (Lu, Abdelzaher, Stankovic & Son, 2001), or queue management for TCP-based streaming

Figure 1. The architecture of an autonomic communication system

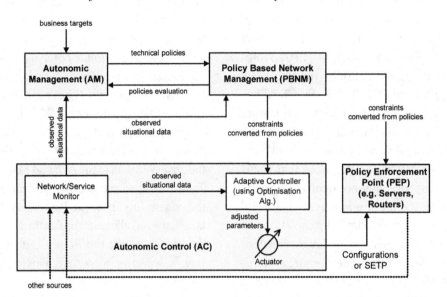

traffic (Hadjadj, Mehaoua & Skianis, 2007), we take a completely different approach in this paper. We focus on the use of GA to control and optimize the communication protocol between two network nodes under the constraints imposed by the PBNM. More specifically, we have designed an evolvable protocol which can be controlled and optimized by the AC and GA in order to equip the communication peers with better autonomy and intelligence.

Self-modifying protocols (SMP) are protocols that can be modified at run time by the computers using them. Such protocols can be modified at run time so that they can adapt to the changing communicating environment and various requirements on the fly. The concept of SMP was first proposed in (Sheng-Uei & Zhiqiang, 2000) which also provides a collection of case studies. Evolvable Protocols are the SMP designed using Genetic Algorithms (GA) or computational intelligence algorithms.

This paper is structured as follows. First we introduce the concept of self-modifying protocols and our design method using GA. Next section presents a Self Evolvable Transaction Protocol (SETP) designed with a Genetic Algorithm

executor. Then we describe the prototype and introduce our simulation model. The simulation results obtained along with their evaluation are presented in the final section before the conclusion of the paper.

SELF-MODIFYING PROTOCOLS AND OUR EVOLUTIONARY APPROACH

A self-modifying protocol is a set of rules that can be changed by the systems communicating with the help of that protocol. The idea is that network nodes of the future will use their communication protocols in much the same way as we do in ordinary meetings. For example, when two friends are conducting an informal conversion, a third person enters the scenario. The topic may be changed from one to another. The interesting point is that every person involved is able to cope with these changes right away. Each person is able to incorporate the new rules into his conversation scheme, and to proceed with the new communication protocol.

When communicating by means of self-modifying protocols, two nodes are not committed to one particular type of interaction. Instead, they are enabled to adapt the rules of interaction to the circumstances under which they communicate. With self-modifying protocols, modifications are introduced and processed on the fly, to the desired benefit of the system.

To date, there are not many protocols that allow modification by the computers that use them. Existing inter-agent languages and protocols, like KQML and COOL, do not pay much attention to the autonomous change of protocol performatives. Finin et al. claim that KQML pays attention to how agents structure conversations (Finin, McKay, Fritszson, & McEntire, 1994). It is left unspecified how to structure or re-structure a multi-agent conversation. COOL comes closer to the realization of a self-modifying protocol (Barbuceanu & Fox, 1994). The conversation rules can in theory be modified by the agents that use them.

GA has received increased interest in recent years, particularly with regard to the manner in which they may be applied for practical problem solving. The main reason for us to adopt GA as an optimization method is due to its robustness to a changing environment. Traditional methods of optimization are not robust to dynamic changes in the environment and often require a complete restart to provide a solution. In contrast, GA can be used to adapt a system to find out a solution to dynamic changes. The available population of evolved solutions provides a basis for further improvement and in most cases it is not necessary to reinitialize the population at random.

In our self-modifying protocol design, GA is applied as a vehicle for protocol auto-configuration controlled by the AC. This evolutionary process will result in an optimal modifying direction for the protocol to adapt to the changing communication environment and requirements from the PBNM.

In the following section, we use an example to demonstrate and verify this approach. We present a Self Evolvable Transport Protocol when QoS constraints and information of the real-time transport quality are taken as the input by the AC.

SELF EVOLVABLE TRANSACTION PROTOCOL

Existing Transport Protocols

The Internet protocol suite includes two transport service protocols, TCP and UDP, providing virtual circuit and datagram service, respectively (Braden, 1985). TCP can provide reliable transfer of packets. However, TCP has a high cost as a result of its circuit setup and teardown phases. UDP avoids the overhead of TCP connection setup. However, UDP has two potentially serious problems: (1) unreliable communication; and (2) the limitation of a data object size to the 548-byte maximum in a single UDP packet.

Currently, real-time services like RTP (Real-time Transport Protocol) utilize UDP-based transport protocols to deliver packets. But the application requirement may vary at different time, UDP can't meet the reliability requirement well. In addition, since no flow control mechanisms are used for UDP-based real-time services, the network itself must participate in the work of managing resources and regulating traffic in order to achieve some level of QoS support.

Although TCP can carry RTP messages as well in order to provide a good reliability guarantee, real-time applications can easily forgo the complexity of TCP because they do not normally need its services. Most audio playback algorithms, for example, can tolerate missing data better than lengthy delays. Instead of introducing delays with retransmissions, these applications prefer the transport layer to simply forget about missing data.

A number of RFCs published in the past few years provide the instruments for tuning TCP under different network situations. For example, the Explicit Congestion Notification (ECN) between two routers defined in RFC 3168 allows the routers to slow down the transmission rate of TCP packets when congestion occurs. RFC2582 specifies the NewReno modification for the TCP fast recovery algorithm in order to enhance the transmission of wireless TCP traffic. The NewReno algorithm changes the way that a sender can increase their sending rate during fast recovery when multiple segments in a window of data are lost and the sender receives a partial acknowledgement. RFC2018 and RFC2883 introduce the use of selective acknowledgement (SACK) option for acknowledging the retransmission of a particular lost segment, and dealing with the duplicated acknowledgments. RFC 3517 specifies how to recover from the loss of segment of received data when SACK is used. RFC 4138 specifies how to detect spurious retransmission timeouts with TCP and SCTP. Moreover, receivers can change the scale factor to tune the size of the TCP receive window up to 1G bytes (RFC1323). In the latest Windows products (Vista, Server 2008), Microsoft implemented this mechanism and the Compound TCP (CTCP) which allows the sender to aggressively maximize the window size based on the monitored bandwidth-delay product.

Although these patches can, to a certain extent, improve the adaptability of TCP in the local network situations, the intrinsic, rigid nature of TCP and many other transport protocols is not changed. This motivates us to design a protocol that is born with self-adaptability and self-configurability. Note that in this paper, we have no intention to design a transport protocol to replace TCP or UDP or other transport protocols. Space limit here has also determined that we cannot address all the detailed issues that have been discussed about TCP. Our main goal is to explore the feasibility of the idea of evolvable protocol through SETP. We hope that this tentative attempt may shed some light on the design of the future self-adaptive protocol.

Self-Modifying Reliability Mechanism

Many applications require that a transport protocol provide reliable transactions – error-free, in sequence, and without duplication. However, it should also be possible for the application programs to request that reliability to be relaxed for particular transactions. Our objective is to design a self-modifying protocol based on which future transport protocols can provide satisfactory solutions for applications with a flexible reliability requirement.

Retransmission

In general, a Request or Response is retransmitted periodically until acknowledged, up to some maximum number of retransmissions. SETP uses a parameter Retries that indicate the number of retransmissions before giving up.

Retransmissions are required either because of overruns or bad link quality which often happens in wireless networks. Lessons from the studies of TCP tell us that we have to deal with these two situations differently. While rate control is often used to deal with the network congestion, the reduction of packet size and increase of transmission rate are more effective when dealing with bad link quality. For this reason, selective retransmission as well as rate control and packet size adjustment is applied in SETP.

Rate Control

Rate-based flow control adjust inter-packet gaps of packets in a packet group to control the arrival rate at the receiver. A client is expected to estimate and adjust the interpacket gap time so as not to overrun a server or intermediate nodes and also not to waste available network bandwidth. The interpacket gap is expressed in 1/32 of the Maximum Transmission Unit (MTU) packet transmission time. The minimum interpacket gap is 0 and the maximum gap that can be specified in the protocol is 7 packet times[1]. The maximum gap can be changed subject to different design requirements.

Packet Size

Many hosts find it efficient to send a large amount of data as a single blast of packets rather than pacing the flow. But the maximum number of bytes per packet is determined by the network maximum packet size. In SETP, to facilitate selective retransmission and buffering, a message is divided into packet groups. Each packet group is identified by a transaction identifier. The data segment is viewed as a sequence of segment blocks allowing the portions of the segment to be specified by a 32-bit mask.

The Trade-Off among Packet Size, Retransmission and Rate Control

When interpacket gap is too small or packet size is too large, congestion is likely to happen. It will lead to the increase of data loss and delay jitter which are two important QoS parameters. The protocol may recover with a selective retransmission and suitable retry times. In other cases, the interpacket gap time is increased or packet size is decreased to avoid congestion, but the bandwidth usage will drop which leads to the extension of transmission time. When coping with the problem from bad quality links, the protocol can adjust the packet size and selectively retransmit lost packets. It is expected that SETP can achieve a tradeoff among the above protocol parameters to meet the specified requirement.

Packet Format

SETP assumes an underlying delivery service that provides end-to-end (best-effort) datagram delivery, such as provided by the IP protocol. The packet format, as shown in Figure 2, is structured as message control block (MCB) and segment data. MCB specifies the control information for communication.

Part of the SETP MCB format refers to the minimal format of Versatile Message Transaction Protocol (Cheriton, 1988).

- **Gene:** 9-bit chromosome representation specifying the protocol's different forms.
- **FUN:** Function Code: 1 bit - type of packets. If the low-order bit of the function code is 0, the packet is sent to the Server, else it is sent to the Client.
- 0 --- Request 1 --- Response
- **Send Time:** 32 bits---system time when sending this packet.
- **Client:** 32 bits--- identifier for the client entity associated with this packet.
- **Server:** 32 bits--- entity identifier for the Server associated with this transaction.
- **Transaction:** 32 bits--- identifier for this message transaction.
- **Delivery Mask:** 64 bits---identifier indicating the transmission of the ith segment with a 1 in the ith bit position. Each bit corresponds to one 512-octet data segment.

Figure 2. Packet format

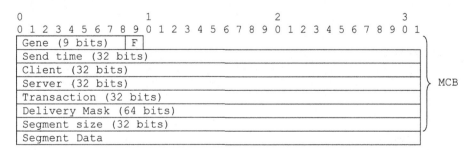

- **Segment Size:** 32 bits --- size of data segment in octets
- **Data Segment:** 0-512 octets--- the segment portion corresponding to the Delivery Mask.

The gene field of this packet format only uses nine bits for the simulation in the next section. If there are more communication mechanisms to be optimized besides packet size, retransmission, and rate control, the size of the gene field can be extended.

One General Communication System Model

In our previous self-modifying protocol research work (Sheng-Uei & Zhiqiang, 2000), we have designed one general Self-Modifying and Self-Regulating communication mechanism (Figure 3) for the implementation of self-modifying protocols. Our current work is based on this model.

When the communication process at each peer faces a problem and needs modification, it raises some event to its Daemon which is a process controlling the self-modifying process. The Daemon starts a negotiation process with its own peer

after it stops the original communication process. The communication process is required to transmit parameters related to the communication problem to the negotiation process. Then the latter process searches for the problem's solutions in the Problem-Solution Table, and derives one or more solutions. Next, some negotiation protocol is conducted between the two peers by the negotiation processes. As a result, one of the solutions is agreed by these two peers. The solutions are transmitted back to the communication process. According to these solution parameters, some modules in the old protocol are modified. At last, the Daemon sends a signal to the communication process to restart communication based on the new protocol.

Client and Server Operations of SETP

In SETP implementation, we also adopt the above self-modifying communication mechanism (Figure 3), but a more "intelligent" GA executor is used to optimize self-modification instead of the Problem-Solution Table (Figure 4).

When the user's QoS requirement or the communication environment are changed, and the current protocol can't adapt to the change, the

Figure 3. SMP communication system model

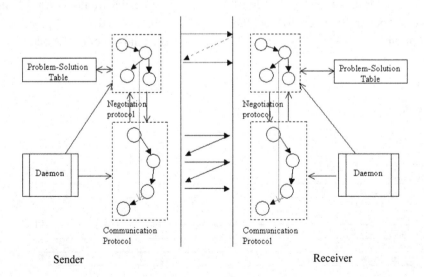

Figure 4. SETP communication system model

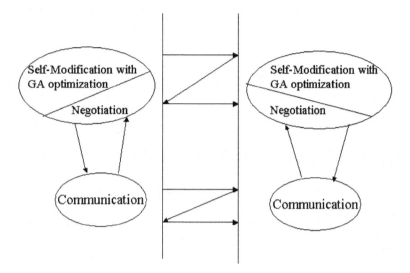

negotiation process is started. With the help of GA executor, an optimal protocol configuration is achieved after generations of negotiation by the two peers. Then the protocol is self-modified to this new configuration and starts a new communication process.

SETP itself includes the negotiation protocol in Figure 3 The client and server state transitions of negotiation are illustrated in Figure 5.

A client can be in one of the following states:

- **AwaitingResponse:** Waiting for a Response packet group to arrive with the same (Client,Transaction) identification.
- **ReceivingResponse:** Waiting for additional packets in the Response packet group it is currently receiving.
- **Processing:** During the communication process, it includes operation system states associated with initialization of packets for transmission. During the negotiation process, it includes GA computing, creating gene field, adjusting packet size, adjusting interval gap, and packet header formatting.

The client goes into the *AwaitingResponse* state after the transmission starts. Then on receipt of a packet response, it goes into the *ReceivingResponse* state. In the *ReceivingResponse* state, if it receives from the server a retransmission request with the Delivery Mask indicating lost packets, it will retransmit the lost packets to the Server. The response messages received from the Server are used to derive the QoS. If the current QoS performance can't satisfy the use's requirements, the negotiation process is started.

The GA executor used in the negotiation process will be described in the following section. The executor creates a group of chromosomes for each evolutionary generation. Each chromosome represented in the gene field in a packet needs to experience a negotiation process as shown in Figure 5. In the negotiation process, according to the corresponding bits in the gene field, packet size and interval gap can be adjusted. And the QoS derived from the response messages received from the Server will be sent to the GA executor to compute the fitness value for the next evolutionary generation. The measurement of network performance parameters will be discussed. At the end of GA optimization, an optimal candidate is selected and the negotiation process is finished.

The Server's state transition diagram includes the following states:

Figure 5. State transition diagram of SETP (communication and negotiation processes)

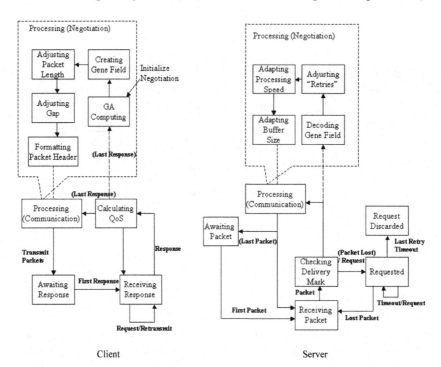

Client

Server

- **AwaitingPacket:** Waiting for a message packet group.
- **ReceivingPacket:** Waiting to receive additional packets in a packet group.
- **CheckingDeliveryMask:** Checking lost packets according to the delivery mask.
- **Requested:** Request for Retransmission has been sent and the Server is counting down toward timeout.
- **RequestDiscarded:** The Server has reached the last timeout so no further retransmission request can be sent.

Processing: During the communication process, it includes operation system states associated with processing the received packets; During the negotiation process, it includes gene decoding, adjusting retransmission retry times, adapting processing speed, and adapting buffer size.

The Server generally starts in the *Awaiting-Packet* state. On receipt of a packet, the Server

moves into the *ReceivingPacket* state. After receiving subsequent packets that constitute the message, the Server enters *CheckingDeliveryMask* state. When some packets are found lost, the Server can request the Client for retransmission, and it enters Requested state. In the Requested state, the Request will be resent on timeout until the lost packets have been received. And the maximum time requesting for retransmission is decided by the Retries parameter. On the last timeout, the Server moves into the *RequestDiscarded* state, which means it gives up retransmission.

In the *CheckingDeliveryMask* state, the Server keeps a *"current_mask"* record which keeps record of all the fragments received. When a new packet's mask (*"new_mask"*) is received, it will perform an "OR" bit-operation on the *"current_mask"* and *"new_mask"* to derive a new *"current_mask"*. We assume the packets are transmitted in order, so if the Sever finds out a packet missing according to the *"current_mask"*, it will send a retransmission request. Timeout is indispensable for repetitive retransmission. Moreover, the Server records the retransmission times it has requested for each packet. When the record is larger than the maximum retransmission retry times ("Retries"), the Server gives up retransmission.

During the negotiation process, the Server *Processing* state will implement gene decoding, adjusting *Retries* parameter according to the gene field, adapting processing speed and buffer size according to the packet size and interval gap received from the Client, which are also represented by the corresponding bits in the gene field.

In the above state transition diagram, the Client plays an active role by sending large amounts of data to the Server. Likewise, the role can be reversed: when the Client requests large amounts of data from the Server, the operations of adjusting packet size and gap will be done by the Server according to the gene field of the request packet received. In brief, it is the gene field in SETP packets that triggers the negotiation function on packet size, interval gap, and retransmission times between the Client and Server.

SIMULATION

GA Executor

In SETP, a GA executor is used to optimize self-modification.

GA Problem Formulation

To derive a suitable protocol configuration using the GA evolutionary process, the AC will derive the target QoS constraints from the PBNM. The objective function is defined as the difference between the Target QoS and the Achieved QoS which are actually delivered. In order to form a single fitness value, these objectives are combined by a linear weighted function. In another word, the aim of the genetic operation is to achieve a minimum fitness value, which means the Achieved QoS can satisfy the target QoS requirements optimally (Table 1).

Chromosome Representation

The configuration of SETP can be coded in a chromosome with a (9-bit) long binary string representing three different portions. A sequence of the gene layout in the SETP packet format is shown in Figure 6.

The interpacket gap is expressed in 1/32 of the MTU packet transmission time. In our simulation, the unit is set as 0.03s.

When self-modification is needed, it is the gene field in the packet format that synchronizes the modification process on each peer. If both sides cooperate well with the current gene format and achieve a successful communication meeting the QoS requirements, this gene format will survive with a good fitness value through GA optimization. Otherwise, the unqualified gene format will be eliminated.

Optimization Template and GA Parameters

Figure 7 is a template for the GA optimization process, performed by each communication peer.

1. **Population Size (adjustable):** A population pool size is set as 10 chromosomes.

Table 1. Problem Formulation

Given	Target QoS, a sequence of gene layout
Minimize	Difference between the Target QoS and Achieved QoS (Linear weighted function used to create a fitness value)
Variables	Protocol parameters and structure (Chromosome Coding)

Figure 6. Chromosome representation 9

Packet size	Retransmission	Rate Control

0   3   6   9

1. Packet size

Genes	Representation
000	Packet size=100 bytes
001	Packet size=200 bytes
...	...
111	Packet size=800 bytes

2. Retransmission

Genes	Representation
000	Without Retransmission
001	Selective Retransmission with Retries=1
...	...
111	Selective Retransmission with Retries=7

3. Rate Control

Genes	Representation
000	Interpacket gap=0 (No Rate Control)
001	Interpacket gap=1
...	...
111	Interpacket gap=7

Figure 7. A template for GA optimization process

```
GA executor( )
        {
                // initialize a random population of individuals
                init_population P;
                //evaluate the fitness of all individuals in the initial
                 population
                evaluate P;
                // evolution cycle
                while not terminated do
                        // select a sub-population for offspring production
                        P' = select_parents P;
                        // recombine the "genes" of selected parents
                        recombine P';
                        // perform mutation
                        mutate P';
                        // evaluate its new fitness
                        evaluate P';
                        // select the survivors from actual fitness
                        P = survive P, P';
        End
        }
```

2. **Selection:** In this simulation, the parent randomly selects 6 chromosomes for recombination.

3. **Crossover:** The essence of GA operation lies in the method of mixing the gene structure. A total of four crossover methods can be adopted in this simulation. The probability associated with the crossover operation is the crossover rate, which can be selected by the user.

    a. **Singe-point crossover:** A single crossover point with the range [1,9] can be randomly selected. An example is shown below:
        000100010 and *100100110* (crossover)
        ---- > 0001*00110*

    b. **Two-point crossover:** Two-point or Multi-point crossover is allowed. An example is shown below:
        000100010 and *100100110* (crossover)
        ---- > 000*100*010

    c. **Uniform crossover:** A uniform crossover mask is required during uniform crossover operations. Such a mask with the same length as the chromosome is randomly generated. An example with the mask "110010100" is given below:
        000100010 and *100100110* (crossover)
        ---- > 00*01*00*10*

    d. **Heuristic crossover:** In the heuristic crossover, the binary coding is converted into in an integer and then computed according to the following formula to yield an offspring:
        Offspring = parent1 * α + (1- α) * parent2, where $\alpha \in$ [0,1].
        An example is shown below:
        000100010 and 111011001 (crossover)
        ---- > 001111001
        (34) (473) 34*0.8+473*0.2=121.8 --> 121 (α=0.8)

    e. **Mutation:** Mutation is another important genetic operation. This can prevent premature convergence from occurring. Since binary coding is adopted in the simulation, only bit mutation is implemented. Here users have two options. The bit to be mutated is either from a user-specified bit location or a system-generated random location. The mutation rate can be set by the user.

4. **Evaluation:** With the Network Simulator (NS2), the protocol configured by the corresponding chromosome is simulated to acquire the Achieved QoS. Then its fitness value can be calculated by the objective function (Formula 1):

$$
\begin{aligned}
Fitness = \; & \omega_1 \times \frac{|rtt\_achieved - rtt\_planned|}{rtt\_planned} \\
& + \omega_2 \times \frac{|jitter\_achieved - jitter\_planned|}{jitter\_planned} \\
& + \omega_3 \times \frac{|throughput\_achieved - throughput\_planned|}{throughput\_planned} \\
& + \omega_4 \times \frac{|error\_achieved - error\_planned|}{error\_planned}
\end{aligned}
$$

(1)

Four quantitative critical performance criteria for networks are used to represent the QoS desired which are round trip time (transit delay), jitter (delay variation), throughput, and error/loss rate. This formula calculates the difference between the Achieved QoS and the Target QoS. ω_i represents the weight of the ith QoS parameter, which measures the importance of this parameter to the user.

5. **Survival:** Since the fitness value represents the difference between the Target QoS and Achieved QoS, the ten chromosomes with small fitness values survive from the combination of the last population and the new offspring created.

6. **Termination Criteria:** The program is terminated either when
    ◦   The maximum number of generations is reached. The user sets this figure.

- ○ The pre-defined fitness threshold is reached by all chromosomes (protocols) or one of the chromosomes in the population accounting for the choice of "average fitness" or "best fitness".
- ○ There are only several fixed chromosomes appearing repeatedly in the successive generations, which means these chromosomes have the best fitness values.

Network Performance (QoS) Measurement

For Equation 1, the four performance criteria (delay, delay variation, throughput, and loss rate) need to be measured to calculate the fitness value. In SETP, there is a timestamp field to record the sending time of a packet. So the round trip time (delay) can be measured by the difference between the local system time receiving the packet and the timestamp. It is also straightforward to measure throughput and loss rate, since every SETP packet has the fields of Segment Size and Delivery Mask. Jitter (delay variation) is not as clearly defined. Some authors understand jitter as the difference between the longest and the shortest delay in some period of time. Others define jitter as the maximum delay difference between two consecutive packets

in some period of time. We chose the definition standardized in RFC1889 (Schulzrinne, Fokus, Casner, Frederick & Jacobson, 1996).

If packets i and j are time stamped with timestamps S_i and S_j when they are sent and are received at time R_i and R_j, respectively, then $D_{ij} = (R_j - S_j) - (R_i - S_i) = (R_j - R_i) - (S_j - S_i)$ is the difference in transit time in time stamp units. In order to measure delay variation, we look at the difference in transit time between two consecutive packets, thus $j = i+1$. If packets arrive at exactly the same rate they were sent, D_{ij} is zero. For a packet that is late relative to the previous packet, D_{ij} is positive. If the next packet arrives in time, that is with average delay, D_{ij} is negative for this new pair of packets. Thus, one late packet leads to two non-zero D_{ij} values. Figure 8 shows an example of seven packets that are sent out at equal time intervals but arrive irregularly.

According to the definition in (Schulzrinne et al., 1996), jitter is a smoothed function of $|D_{i-1,i}|$:

$$J_i = J_{i-1} + (|D_{i-1,i}| - J_{i-1})/16 = 15/16 * J_{i-1} + 1/16 * |D_{i-1,i}| \qquad (2)$$

Equation 2 is a simple example of a class of estimators called "recursive prediction error" or "stochastic gradient algorithms". Here, we are not making predictions, but we aggregate the $|D_{i-1,i}|$ observations into a stable estimate of the current

Figure 8. Example of irregular arrivals and resulting delay differences

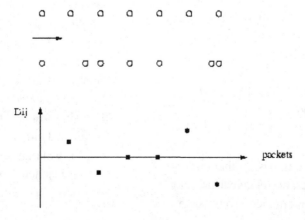

jitter. Thus, jitter is a sort of running average of all $|D_{i-1,i}|$ from the beginning of the measurement up to the current packet. Recent packets have a larger weight than older packets.

Lost packets are simply ignored in the jitter calculation. They could be understood as packets with infinite delay, but that would be impractical for the calculation. Including them in the jitter measurement has no benefits.

When protocol configuration is changed for optimization, the network performance parameters being measured will experience a short period of variation. In order to obtain a group of accurate QoS parameters, we discard transient data collected during the start of the simulation which is also called as "Warm Up Time". We measure 100 transmissions to calculate the average and accumulated QoS results in the system reaching the "steady" state.

Network Topology

In this simulation, we created a new protocol function by adding two modules into the simulator framework, SETP.cc and SETP.tcl, based on the underlying functions (e.g. IP) supported in NS2. SETP.cc defines the GA executor and the detailed protocol implementation. In SETP.tcl, the simulation network topology is defined as shown in Figure 9.

There can be two types of traffic flow transmitting through this network topology. From n0 to n2, then to n3, and transiting back to n0, this flow uses the SETP protocol we created. Another flow, from n1 to n2, then ending at n3, can be set as CBR (Constant Bit Rate) traffic or VBR (Variable Bit Rate) traffic which has an exponential distribution. The packet size of this flow is set as 50 bytes, and the interval gap or its mean value for VBR traffic is set as 5ms. Each link in the topology has a bandwidth of 0.1Mb and an average transmission delay as 10ms. From n2 to n3, an Error Model is set to simulate packet drop. The Error Model operates in the unit of *pkt*(packet),

ranvar(randomvariable) of *uniform,* and its error rate can be set from the input.

In the GA executor, the population size is set as ten chromosomes which represents ten types of protocol configurations. In NS2, we define ten groups of network topology (Figure 9) in the simulation, so that ten protocol configurations can be simulated in parallel to speed up the GA optimization.

SIMULATION RESULTS AND DISCUSSION

Evolution under Environment Change

When only one SETP flow moves in the network topology, from n0 to n3 with the packet size as 50 bytes and the interval as 5ms, this results in a bandwidth of 0.08 megabits per second for the link n2 to n3. But when another CBR flow starts its transmission from n1 to n3 with the packet size as 50 bytes and the interval gap as 5ms, there is a total bandwidth of 0.16Mb/s which exceeds the link capacity of 0.1Mb/s. So obviously overflow happens, some packets will be discarded.

In this case, the weights of all QoS parameters in Equation1 are given the same value as 1. The loss rate of the link from n2 to n3 is set as 0.01. The crossover method is the single-point crossover. The crossover rate and mutation rate are 0.8 and 0.01 respectively. The Target QoS parameters are the round trip delay of 50ms, the delay jitter of 1.0ms, the throughput of 6000bps and the error rate of 0.01. In this case of workload change, the Achieved QoS may be unable to meet the Target QoS, so that self-modification is needed. We simulate this case and measure the change of average fitness value for each generation.

In Figure 10, Y represents the average fitness value for a generation, and X represents the generation number. We can see that the average fitness value decreases with the increasing generation

Figure 9. Network topology

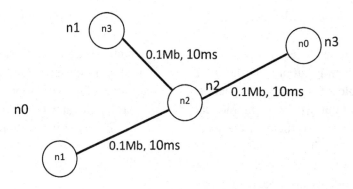

number. After ten generations, the fitness value is stable at the minimum value, which means that the difference between the Achieved QoS and the Target QoS has been minimized after ten GA generations. From the tenth generation, the chromosome "001110101" is selected, so its corresponding protocol configuration (packet size: 200 bytes, retransmission times: 6, interval gap: 0.15s) can meet the environment change. After optimization, the SETP gene field will be changed to "001110101", and both peers will implement modifications according to this new configuration.

We also perform this simulation in the case that another flow is set as VBR traffic which has an exponential distribution. The result is that the same chromosome is selected after ten generations though some different data are observed during the optimization process. This shows that our simulation can achieve similar results under the exponential traffic condition in a real network.

Evolution under User Requirement Change

Another case is due to user requirement change. SETP needs self-modification to meet a changed Target QoS requirement.

The simulation is performed with only one SETP flow. The Target QoS parameters, link loss rate, crossover method, crossover rate and mutation rate are all set the same as the previous simulation. And we set the weights of jitter and

Figure 10. Average fitness value for each generation

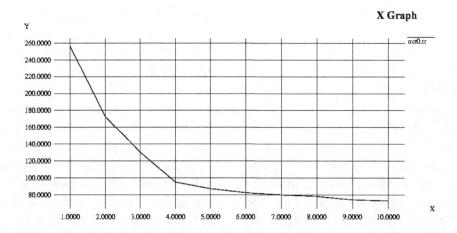

error rate as 9, much larger than the other two with weights as 1. This means the delay jitter and error rate are more important requirements for applications such as MP3 real-time playback on the Web.

The simulation results for the best chromosome of each generation are shown in Table 2. We can see that during the optimization process the Achieved QoS parameters move closer to the Target QoS, especially the delay jitter and the error rate which have the larger weights. Therefore, it is feasible for users to adapt the weight of each parameter in order to favour some desired QoS requirement.

We also perform this simulation for the applications which has a high requirement on the round trip delay and error rate, such as a real-time stock update system. In this case, we set the weights of round trip delay and error rate as 9, much larger than the other two with weights as 1.

The simulation results for the best chromosome of each generation are shown in Table 3. We can see that during the optimization process the Achieved QoS parameters move closer to the Target QoS, especially the round trip delay

and the error rate which have the larger weights. Therefore, it is feasible for users to adapt the weight of each parameter in order to favor some desired QoS requirement.

Comparison of Different Crossover Methods

Crossover has always been regarded as the primary search operator in GA. In this simulation we also compare the effects of different crossover methods.

In Figure 11, Y is the average fitness value, and X is the generation number. Four curves represent the simulation results using four types of crossover scheme. We can see that the average fitness values converge to the minimal value very quickly for the single-point and two-point crossover schemes. However, this tendency may lead to a local minimal point instead of a global optimization if the protocol has a wide choice for optimization. Compared with the heuristic crossover, the uniform crossover has a smooth and steady optimization process which tally with our expectation and the analysis result of the work in (Lin & Yao, 1997).

Table 2. QoS Results (Case 1): The best chromosome for each generation

Original QoS		67.5	13.2	4342.5	0.325
Generation	Chromosome (decimal)	RTT (ms)	Jitter (ms)	Throughput (bps)	Error Rate
1	259	90.2	0.8	8731.0	0.373
2	338	103.4	15.0	11504.3	0.314
3	71	66.1	0.3	4379.8	0.216
4	504	114.2	14.9	18765.0	0.157
5	306	95.4	1.4	12275.9	0.122
6	114	66.2	0.6	4883.0	0.118
7	83	72.1	0.7	8351.5	0.122
8	57	83.9	1.3	8139.3	0.073
9	223	69.4	1.2	5346.5	0.036
10 (Achieved QoS)	312	70.2	0.9	7054.0	0.018
Target QoS		50	1.0	6000.0	0.01

Discussion

About Network Topology

In SETP, which is a transport-level protocol, the GA executor adapts three parameters: packet size, retransmission, and rate control. This handles three key functions provided by the transport layer - breaking messages into packets, achieving reliable end-to-end communication, and performing end-to-end flow control. These functions have no direct relation with the network topology. That's why we adopt a simple network topology (Figure 9) here. For a real network, SETP may need further extensions to operate on a complicated network topology.

The protocol implementation includes both client and server operations, so that the node attached with the SETP agent in NS2 is able to function either as a client or a server for different transactions at the same time.

About the Objective Function

To achieve a suitable protocol configuration using GA, the user should specify his intended QoS as

Target QoS. However, most users have no idea about these network performance parameters. So some heuristic values can be suggested as the default QoS values for user-specified applications according to the network status. Some expert advice can be provided to guide the user to adapt the weights in the objective function in order to meet his special requirement. For example, in the simulation (Sec. 5.2), the application is an MP3 real-time playback on the web. Because the data transferred is compressed, the error rate requirement is higher than the transfer of normal sound files. And due to the real-time requirement, the delay jitter also has a strict demand. With the expert advice, large weight values are suggested for this application.

In the objective function (Equation 1), we use absolute values to calculate the difference between Achieved QoS and Target QoS. The formula proves to obtain the closest quality required by the application. On further thoughts, we found it can't obtain a reasonable result for some practical cases. For example, assume the fitness value is decided only by error rate, for two Achieved error rate, one is larger than the other, but they

Table 3. QoS Results (Case 2): The best chromosome for each generation

Original QoS		67.5	13.2	4342.5	0.325
Generation	Chromosome (decimal)	RTT (ms)	Jitter (ms)	Throughput (bps)	Error Rate
1	504	143.2	19.4	4052.9	0.345
2	9	129.2	1.9	5773.6	0.211
3	231	112.4	2.3	4837.4	0.204
4	132	101.5	3.4	5848.2	0.187
5	34	93.4	5.4	4234.7	0.132
6	59	137.6	8.4	6535.9	0.093
7	2	79.4	0.9	3090.0	0.046
8	434	126.2	7.6	12017.4	0.007
9	246	72.2	8.3	5901.1	0.001
10 (Achieved QoS)	66	113.7	19.9	9847.8	0.003
Target QoS		100	20.0	6000.0	0.002

Figure 11. Comparison of different crossover methods

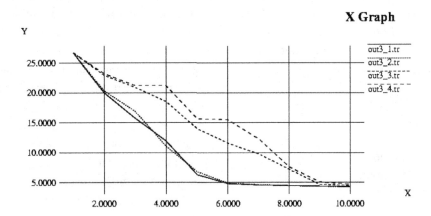

Equation 3.

$$Fitness = \omega_1 \times \frac{p_1 \left| rtt\_achieved - rtt\_planned \right|}{rtt\_planned}$$

$$+ \omega_2 \times \frac{p_2 \left| jitter\_achieved - jitter\_planned \right|}{jitter\_planned}$$

$$+ \omega_3 \times \frac{p_3 \left| throughput\_achieved - throughput\_planned \right|}{throughput\_planned}$$

$$+ \omega_4 \times \frac{p_4 \left| error\_achieved - error\_planned \right|}{error\_planned}$$

$(p_i > 1$ If Achieved QoS > Target QoS; else $p_i = 1$)

both have the same difference from the Planned error rate. According to the objective function, these two Achieved error rates will achieve the same fitness value. But, for most applications, a smaller error rate is preferred when there is a large gap between these two Achieved error rates. For other QoS parameters, the same problem exists. Therefore, some improvement is added to the objective function to handle the above case (Equation 3).

A penalty coefficient p_i guarantees that the smaller Achieved QoS will achieve a smaller fitness value in the above case. In another word, the chromosome with Achieved QoS smaller than

Target QoS has the priority to be selected compared to the chromosome with Achieved QoS larger than Target QoS. For example, in the simulation shown in Table 3, the best two chromosomes selected in the 10th generation are 66 and 246 (decimal), which are the best chromosome in the 10th and 9th generation respectively. According to the objective function in Equation1:

F(246)=9*|72.2-100|/100+|8.3-20|/20+|5901.1-6000|/6000+9*|0.001-0.002|/0.002=7.604

F(66)=9*|113.7-100|/100+|19.9-20|/20+|9847.8-6000|/6000+9*|0.003-0.002|/0.002=6.379

53

So the chromosome of 66 with a smaller fitness value is selected as the best chromosome. If the objective function in Equation3 is adopted, we get a different result: (we set the penalty coefficients of round trip time and error rate as 1.5)

$$F(246)=9*|72.2-100|/100+|8.3-20|/20+|5901.1-6000|/6000+9*|0.001-0.002|/0.002=7.604$$

$$F(66)=1.5*9*|113.7-100|/100+|19.9-20|/20+|9847.8-6000|/6000+1.5*9*|0.003-0.002|/0.002=9.246$$

We can see that the chromosome of 246 is selected as the best chromosome which is also a more reasonable solution for practical use.

About the Mutation Operation

In a previous section, we compared the optimization process with different crossover methods. As for the mutation operation, its main function is to prevent premature convergence from occurring, so that the global optimization can be guaranteed with GA. As SETP is a protocol with a simple self-modifying mechanism, we found that there is no difference between local and global optimization in our simulation. So mutation has no obvious effect on the simulation results. In our future work, a more complicated self-modifying protocol for a real network will be designed in which mutation is indispensable for global optimization.

About GA Computational Cost - Time

In the case of evolution under environment change, the time cost for each generation step is 1.9 seconds when Nam trace view is not invoked in NS2. For the case of evolution under user requirement change, the time cost for each generation is 1.1 seconds. In these simulations, a suitable chromosome can be selected after about ten generations, so the run-time overhead of SETP for optimization process is around 10-20 seconds.

The time cost in our simulation includes the NS2 network environment setup time, GA calculating time and the time to simulate packet transmission. Different simulations need different network environment setup time in NS2. For example, the difference of time cost above is just because another CBR flow is needed in the first case which leads to the additional setup time cost. The time cost for the GA executor is just calculating time which can be neglected compared with the time to simulate packet transmission.

To obtain the fitness value of each chromosome, we need to simulate the packet simulation process and measure the network performance parameter for each protocol configuration. In our simulation, the population size is set as ten chromosomes which represent ten types of protocol configurations. And we define ten groups of the same network topology in our simulation, so that ten protocol configurations can be simulated in parallel to speed up the GA optimization.

CONCLUSION

In this paper, evolvable protocols are proposed to adapt to the changing communicating environment and user requirements on the fly. We have shown that genetic algorithms can be applied to design such an autonomous and intelligent protocol. A practical self evolvable transaction protocol named SETP is designed to meet different QoS requirements dynamically. Due to the evolutionary ability provided by a GA executor, SETP has a simple packet format, adopts a straightforward client/server operation paradigm, and requires no complicated negotiation during the communication process. In our simulation we have created an SETP protocol agent in NS2, evaluated its performance, and demonstrated the feasibility of our approach.

REFERENCES

ANA. (n.d.). *Autonomic Network Architecture project*. Retrieved from http://www.ana-project.org/

Aoul, H., Mehaoua, A., & Skianis, C. (2007). A fuzzy logic-based AQM for real-time traffic over internet. *Computer Networks*, *51*, 4617–4633. doi:10.1016/j.comnet.2007.06.007

Barbuceanu, M., & Fox, M. (1994). *COOL - a language for describing coordination in multi-agent systems* (Tech. Rep.). Toronto, Ontario, Canada: Enterprise Integration Laboratory, University of Toronto.

Black, D. et al. (1998). An architecture for differentiated service. *RFC 2475*.

Braden, R. (1985). *Towards a transport service for transaction processing applications* (RFC 955). Los Angeles: UCLA OAC.

Carreras, I., Chlamtac, I., De Pellegrini, F., Kiraly, C., Miorandi, D., & Woesner, H. (2006). A biological approach to autonomic communication systems. In *Transactions on Computational Systems Biology IV* (LNCS 3939, pp. 76-82).

CASCADAS. (n.d.). *CASCADAS project*. Retrieved from http://www.cascadas-project.org/index.html

Cheriton, D. (1988). VMTP: Versatile Message Transaction Protocol. *RFC 1045*.

Diao, Y., Hellerstein, J. L., Parekh, S., Griffith, R., Kaiser, G. E., & Phung, D. (2005). A control theory foundation for self-managing computing systems. *IEEE Journal on Selected Areas in Communications*, *23*, 2213–2222. doi:10.1109/JSAC.2005.857206

Dobson, S., Denazis, S., Fernández, A., Gaïti, D., Gelenbe, E., & Massacci, F. (2006). A survey of autonomic communications. *ACM Transactions on Autonomous and Adaptive Systems*, *1*(2), 223–259. doi:10.1145/1186778.1186782

EFIPSANS. (n.d.). *EFIPSANS project*. Retrieved from http://www.efipsans.org

Elsayed, T., Hussein, M., Youssef, M., Nadeem, T., Youssef, A., & Iftode, L. (2003, December). ATP: Autnomous Transport Protocol. In *Proceedings of the 46th IEEE International Midwest Symposium on Circuits and Systems (MWSCAS'03)* (Vol. 1, pp. 436-439).

Finin, T., McKay, D., Fritszson, R., & McEntire, R. (1994). KQML: An information and knowledge exchange protocol. In T. Yokoi (Ed.), *Knowledge building and knowledge sharing*. Amsterdam, The Netherlands: IOS Press.

Gu, X., Strassner, J., Xie, J., Wolf, L. C., & Suda, T. (2008, January). Autonomic multimedia communications: Where are we now? *Proceedings of the IEEE*, *96*(1), 143–154. doi:10.1109/JPROC.2007.909880

Guan, S.-U., & Jiang, Z. (2000). *A new approach to implement self-modifying protocols*. Paper presented at the IEEE International Symposium on Intelligent Signal Processing and Communication Systems. HAGGLE. (n.d.). *HAGGLE project*. Retrieved from http://www.haggleproject.org/index.php/Main_Page

IETF. *RFC1323*. Retrieved from http://www.ietf.org/rfc/rfc1323.txt?number=1323

Jennings, B., Meer, S. V. D., Balasubramaniam, S., Botvich, D., Foghlu, M. O., & Donnelly, W. (2007). Towards autonomic management of communications networks. *IEEE Communications Magazine*, *45*(10), 112–121. doi:10.1109/MCOM.2007.4342833

Kephart, J. O., & Chess, D. M. (2003). The vision of autonomic computing. *Computer*, *36*(1), 41–50. doi:10.1109/MC.2003.1160055

Lin, C.-L., & Guan, S.-U. (1996). The design and architecture of a video library system. *IEEE Communications*, *34*(1), 86–91. doi:10.1109/35.482251

Lin, G., & Yao, X. (1997). Analysing crossover operators by search step size. In *Proceedings of the IEEE International Conference on Evolutionary Computation* (pp. 107-110).

Liu, Y., Zhang, J., Jiang, M., Raymer, D., & Strassner, J. (2008, March). A case study: A model-based approach to retrofit a network fault management system with self-healing functionality. In *Proceedings of the 15th Annual IEEE International Conference and Workshop on the Engineering of Computer Based Systems (ECBS 2008)* (pp. 9-18).

Lu, C., Abdelzaher, T. F., Stankovic, J. A., & Son, S. H. (2001 June). Feedback control approach for guaranteeing relative delays in web servers. In *Proceedings of the IEEE Real-Time Technology and Applications Symposium,* Taipei, Taiwan (pp. 51-62).

Miettinen, K., & Neittaanmaki, P. (1999). *Evolutionary algorithms in engineering and computer science*. New York: John Wiley & Sons.

Milcher, B. (2004). Towards an autonomic framework: Self-configuring network services and developing autonomic applications. *Intel Technology Journal, 8(*4). Retrieved from http://developer.intel.com/technology/itj/index.htm

Mortier, R., & Kiciman, E. (2006, September). *Autonomic network management: Some pragmatic considerations*. Paper presented at SIGCOMM'06 Workshops, Pisa, Italy.

Motlabs.com. (n.d.). *Evolution of reconfiguration management and control system architecture* (IST FP6 project, E^{2}RII, Deliverable 2.1). Retrieved from https://e2r2.motlabs.com/Deliverables/E2RII_WP2_D2.1_060807.pdf

Raymer, D., van der Meer, S., & Strassner, J. (2008 March). From autonomic computing to autonomic networking: An architectural perspective. In *Proceedings of the Fifth IEEE Workshop on Engineering of Autonomic and Autonomous Systems (EASE 2008)* (pp. 174-183).

Schulzrinne, H., Fokus, G. M. D., Casner, S., Frederick, R., & Jacobson, V. (1996). *RTP: A transport protocol for real-time applications* (RFC 1889). Palo Alto, CA: Xerox Palo Alto Research Center, Lawrence Berkeley National Laboratory.

SOCRATES. (n.d.). *SOCRATES project*. Retrieved from http://www.fp7-socrates.org

Strassner, J., Fleck, J., Lewis, D., Parashar, M., & Donnelly, W. (2008, March). The role of standardization in future autonomic communication systems. In *Proceedings of the Fifth IEEE Workshop on Engineering of Autonomic and Autonomous Systems (EASE 2008)* (pp. 65-173).

Zhang, L., Deering, S., Estrin, D., & Zappala, D. (1993). RSVP: A new resource reservation protocol. *IEEE Network Magazine*.

ENDNOTE

[1] These choices were made heuristically. They can be fine tuned according to network traffic and application scenario.

This work was previously published in International Journal of Applied Evolutionary Computation, Volume 1, Issue 1, edited by Wei-Chiang Samuelson Hong, pp. 36-56, copyright 2010 by IGI Publishing (an imprint of IGI Global).

Chapter 4
Facial Feature Tracking via Evolutionary Multiobjective Optimization

Eric C. Larson
Oklahoma State University, USA

Gary G. Yen
Oklahoma State University, USA

ABSTRACT

Facial feature tracking for model–based coding has evolved over the past decades. Of particular interest is its application in very low bit rate coding in which optimization is used to analyze head and shoulder sequences. We present the results of a computational experiment in which we apply a combination of non-dominated sorting genetic algorithm and a deterministic search to find optimal facial animation parameters at many bandwidths simultaneously. As objective functions are concerned, peak signal-to-noise ratio is maximized while the total number of facial animation parameters is minimized. Particularly, the algorithm is tested for efficiency and reliability. The results show that the overall methodology works effectively, but that a better error assessment function is needed for future study.

INTRODUCTION

Facial feature tracking has received considerable attention in recent decades for its applications in video gaming, man-machine interaction, model based coding, and numerous other disciplines. Analyzing a head and shoulders sequence remains to be one of the most needed, yet challenging problems in video processing today. Even so, years of research has reduced the problem of facial analysis to a numerical optimization in which classical search methods are often used. See Pearson (1995) for an excellent review of the evolution of model based coding and Pandizic *et al.* (2003) for the current state of the art.

DOI: 10.4018/978-1-4666-1749-0.ch004

A dominant amount of attention for facial feature tracking has been spent applying it towards model-based facial coding (MBFC). In model-based coding, the idea is to analyze an object (i.e., the face) and send high level information about the animation of the object like movement and rotation, instead of sending raw video. The decoder uses knowledge of the model and renders the appropriate animation. The face, however, is a particularly difficult object to model because it requires not only rigid body motion, but also deformations to create expression. Modern facial models can recreate a human likeness with remarkable clarity. Figure 1 shows three reconstructed facial models and the original frames.

Using a model to transmit video opens the possibility for transmission using dynamic bandwidths (i.e., sending video at different bandwidths dynamically depending on the conditions of the transmission channel). In transform based coding, dynamic bandwidth means increasing or decreasing the compression thresholds, reducing video quality when the compression is high. In MBFC, dynamic bandwidth means sending a dynamic number of parameters of the face, resulting in less movement of the model at high compression but not necessarily less quality.

This application promises to revolutionize video telephony and teleconferencing by drastically reducing the bandwidth required for transmission (Eisert, 2003). But there is no free lunch. The bandwidth reductions in MBFC must be paid for in computational analysis. Despite the advances in facial analysis, current work has been limited in several aspects. Before MBFC can be adequately implemented, the following factors need addressing:

1. **The limitations of gradient-based optimization:** This type of analysis, while showing promise for real-time implementation, inherently relies upon a gradient *approximation*. This approximation limits the problem scope to facial sequences involving movements built into the gradient approximation training (i.e., small head movements).

2. **The use of static facial parameters:** Current algorithms use a hand selected set of animation parameters on the face, or use all facial animation parameters. It is unclear if bandwidth could be further reduced using a dynamic set of animation parameters, or what the ideal set of parameters is that adequately represents all facial animation sequences.

Figure 1. Selected frames of a model-based video. Top: the original video frames. Bottom: frames synthesized from a model based coder. The frames are generated using a facial model; they are rendered sequences derived from stretching a facial "texture" over the three dimensional facial wireframe. See (Eisert, 2000).

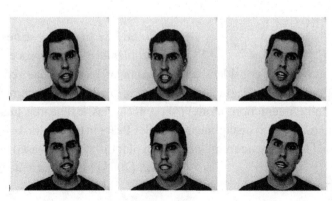

3. **The prohibitive use of computationally complex algorithms:** The use of direct methods to analyze head and shoulder sequences in real time has been completed only by reducing the number of animation parameters optimized. The resultant frames are not considered high enough quality to be realistically rendered.

In this paper, we address all of the stated concerns by formulating the analysis and synthesis into a multiobjective optimization problem (MOP). In short, we want to design a facial coder that *simultaneously* finds a high quality representation of the face while uses a minimal amount of animating parameters. Therefore, when sending a frame of a video sequence, we can choose the most accurate facial analysis based upon the available bandwidth. In this way, we want an optimization that finds the entire Pareto front in trade-off between maximizing quality and minimizing number of parameters. If we know what bandwidth we can send at, then we know how many animation parameters we can use for facial analysis. We then choose the highest quality solution with the available bandwidth from the converged Pareto front.

As an example, imagine participating in a video telephone call in your car (passenger seat, of course). Ideally, you send a high fidelity animation of your face to the other participant. But, if you enter a tunnel or are far away from a cellular tower, the available bandwidth drops off. Knowing this, your phone grabs lower bandwidth frames from the Pareto front of the analysis, avoiding dropped frames in the video. To the best of our knowledge, no one has attempted to address facial analysis in terms of this multiple objective optimization framework. This is a highly significant problem and we believe the solution will open the door for real-time, robust facial analysis, and finally bridge the gap between what model-based facial coding *promises* to do and *can* do.

The attempt to move toward a MOP and reduce complexity appears, at first glance, to be counter-

intuitive. However, the genetic algorithm has been shown to be an ideal solution for many problems having multiple objectives (Deb, 1999; Schaffer, 1985). We chose to use NSGA-II because it has been shown to be an efficient means of solving MOPs while maintaining accuracy and diversity (Deb *et al.*, 2002). Without loss of generality, other multiple objective genetic algorithms could be used as well, such as rank-density based genetic algorithm (RDGA) (Lu & Yen, 2003) or dynamic population multiobjective evolutionary algorithm (Yen & Lu, 2003).

Even with the efficiency of NSGA-II, it is loath to perform in real time. Therefore, in this experiment, we enhance the speed of convergence of the NSGA-II search by adding an additional deterministic optimization search. In addition, we investigate if careful tuning of the algorithms can reduce complexity and successfully find crucial animation parameters.

In the remainder of this paper we briefly discuss the history of facial analysis algorithms for model-based coding in Section II. After which Section III discusses the changes made to NSGA-II, combining it with the deterministic algorithm to make it more appropriate to this specific application. Section IV then presents the results of the simulations and interprets the findings. Lastly, Section V concludes and summarizes the paper.

PARAMETERIZED FACIAL ANALYSIS

In 1982, the first proper digitally parameterized face was introduced using synthesis parameters from the facial action coding system (Parke, 1982). The next year, improving upon the animation of the parameterization, a deformable wireframe of the human face was introduced, not only easing the usability of the model but also expanding the amount of faces that the model could represent (Forchheimer & Kronander, 1989).

This parameterization opened the door for MBFC and, more specifically, what came to be known as analysis-by-synthesis coders. These systems start with a "guessed" set of facial parameters, create a head and shoulders frame from the guess, and measure the difference between the synthetic frame and input video frame. If the error is large, a new guess is made. Otherwise, the guess is accepted as an accurate facial analysis. Figure 2 shows a common representation of the analysis by synthesis loop.

The means of finding new guesses, compensating motion, and finding an appropriate means of calculating error evolved over the next decades. The work was pioneered by Forchheimer and Kronander (1989), Aizawa and Harashima (Choi *et al.*, 1994; Aizawa *et al.*, 1989), Buck (1993), Diehl (1991), and Pandizic (Pandizic *et al.*, 2003). Although the problem is far from answered, this research made it well realized. Indeed, the problem of rigid body head motion is largely considered solved.

MBFC became so popular and well understood that the MPEG-4 framework was introduced with facial coding parameters similar to those in the facial action coding system (Pandizic & Forchheimer, 2002). MPEG-4 defined the model of a human face using facial definition parameters (FDPs) and animation of the face using facial animation parameters (FAPs). By mapping points upon the texture of a person's face to a wireframe definition model of the face, the system could represent the likeness of any human being. FAPs realistically represent all possible facial movements (rigid and deformable). While these FDPs and FAPs standardize parameters for MBFC, they do not provide the actual analysis and synthesis steps.

Specifically, MPEG-4 provides 66 low level FAPs to animate a face. For model-based coding, these are the parameters that need to be optimized. The FDPs are part of the model and are known beforehand at the coder and decoder. The FAPs must be found using optimization techniques, such as analysis-by-synthesis.

Recently, Eisert (2003) has shown that FAPs and shading parameters can be found using gradient based approximations and least squares estimation. In (Ahlberg & Forchheimer, 2003; Dornaika & Alberg, 2004), it was shown that real time facial analysis could be achieved using a gradient training approach and active appearance models. These results, however, were shown to be prone to inaccuracies under large head motions, and in (Dornaika & Ahlberg, 2006) it was shown

Figure 2. A typical analysis-by-synthesis coder. Animation parameters are iteratively solved for by synthesizing a facial image and measuring the error between the synthetic image and video frame. Once the animation parameters produce an adequate analysis of the image, they are transmitted across the channel or sent to a quantization stage.

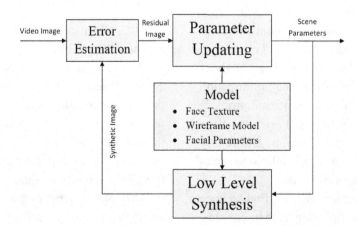

that more robust and accurate results (though with less speed) could be achieved using direct optimization techniques. Our algorithm builds upon the work done in (Dornaika & Ahlberg, 2006) by integrating the optimization techniques known as evolutionary multiobjective optimization, specifically the improved version of the non-dominated sorting genetic algorithm, NSGA-II.

AN APPLICATION SPECIFIC NSGA-II

Specifications

Many FAPs can be gleaned from surrounding FAPs. For example, it is unlikely that a person raises the inner portion of their lip without raising the outer portion. Likewise, few people can wiggle their ears. Therefore, the dimensionality of the search space was reduced from 66 to 18 sets of FAPs. This grouping is similar to what taken in (Eisert, 2003; Dornaika & Ahlberg, 2004).

The algorithm implemented is largely similar to NSGA-II. No adjustments were made to the domination and diversity sorting. The population is crossed-over and the resultant set of children and parents are combined, sorted, and eliminated according to rank and nearest neighbor distance. In an effort to speed convergence, the MOP is terminated before convergence and a directed search is performed using an individual from the Pareto front. The *Stopping Criteria* for NSGA-II is chosen as when the average *PSNR* of the population increases less than 0.5dB, signifying that the population is not approaching convergence quickly. Additional components needed to implement the NSGA-II are detailed below:

Objective Functions: First, the initial and rendered images are converted into grayscale versions using the transformation,

$$\mathbf{I} = 0.3 \times \mathbf{R} + 0.59 \times \mathbf{G} + 0.11 \times \mathbf{B}, \tag{1}$$

where **I** is the gray scale image and **R**, **G**, and **B** represent the red, green, and blue color channels, respectively. Since the aim is to reduce the error between the synthetic image and the input video frame using an FAP sequence, each FAP set must be rendered and compared to the original image. In order to assess error between the source and rendering, we chose to use peak signal-to-noise ratio (*PSNR*). *PSNR* is a widely accepted and computationally convenient form of image quality assessment. It is based upon the mean-squared error and is defined as,

$$PSNR = 10 \log_{10} \left(\frac{255^2}{D} \right) \tag{2}$$

$$D = \frac{1}{MN} \sum_{m=0}^{M-1} \sum_{n=0}^{N-1} E(m,n)^2 \tag{3}$$

where $E(m,n)$ is difference between pixels at m, n in the distorted and reference images of size $M \times N$.

Secondarily, we want to minimize the number of FAP sets used. This function is straightforward, defined as,

$$N_{FAP} = \sum_{i=1}^{18} FAP(i), \tag{4}$$

where

$$FAP(i) = \begin{cases} 0, & \text{if FAP set is not used} \\ 1, & \text{if FAP set is used} \end{cases}.$$

This objective function does not specify which FAPs are selected, only the number used. The MOP results in a Pareto front, maximizing *PSNR*, while simultaneously minimizing the number of needed FAP sets.

Initialization: Each individual in the population is a collection of FAP sets. The population for the first video frame (where no previous frame is known) is initialized using a Gaussian random number generator (Carter, 1994) with standard deviation, σ, of 30 and a mean of half-way between the bounds of each FAP. FAPs with abnormally large bounds are renormalized so that a σ of 30 is appropriately random. After the first frame, subsequent frames of the video sequence are initialized using a Gaussian random number generator with σ of 10 and mean equal to the FAP in the previous frame. This exploits knowledge that additional frames are likely to be similar to previous frame.

Crossover: Parents are selected for crossover using tournament selection. Half of the current population is chosen to produce two children each. A random crossover point is chosen, whereby each child gets a different and opposite set of genes from each parent. The dual children set is then copied and mutation is forced upon the copied offspring.

Mutation: The forced mutation occurs on every FAP in the individual using the addition of a Gaussian random number. The mean of the Gaussian is set to zero and the standard deviation changes with increasing generations. At early generations search is accelerated using a large σ, but the variance is decreased by a parameter, $\alpha < 1$, promoting a more local search. The mutated individual is defined as,

$$FAP_{new}(i) = FAP(i) + \eta(0, \alpha^{n-1} \times \sigma) \qquad (5)$$

where σ is the starting standard deviation, n is the current generation, and $\eta(\mu,\sigma_n)$ is the normal distribution with mean μ and standard deviation σ_n. The α parameter is similar to the cooling schedule parameter implemented in simulated annealing (Kirkpatrick *et al.*, 1983).

Constraint Handling

Each FAP is subject to upper and lower bounds $g_{low}(x)$ and $g_{high}(x)$. The constraints are handled according to the NSGA-II recommendations.

Individuals considered infeasible are placed in several dominated fronts, where each front is established by how much the constraints are in violation. This behavior is ensured using penalty functions that always place the *PSNR* of the infeasible individual lower than the lowest individual. Moreover, infeasible individuals are never allowed to dominate. Additionally, more sophisticated designs such as Venkatraman and Yen (2005) and Tessema and Yen (2009) can be applied with the same success.

Local Optimization

The genetic MOP is allowed to search and partially converge upon the Pareto front. At this point, the Pareto front consists of individuals using different FAPs. However, once the bandwidth requirements are established (i.e., the allowed number of FAPs), the individuals in the Pareto front must be chosen.

To choose the individual with proper bandwidth, the individual with (1) the highest *PSNR* but (2) not over the allowed number of FAPs is chosen and used as a starting point for the deterministic optimization. The deterministic search is only performed on FAPs used by the individual chosen from the Pareto front. The deterministic search is fast, especially if the number of FAP sets used by the individual is minimal. The search method chosen is similar to that used in Dornaika and Ahlberg (2006) and is based upon a cyclic optimization (Edgar *et al.*, 2001; Reklaitis *et al.*, 2006).

In cyclic optimization, each dimension of the search space is varied one by one while the objective function is improving. We used this approach with a coarse discrete step size for each dimension. Once every parameter has undergone the cyclic step estimation, the direction of steepest descent is approximated using the difference between the original FAP set and the new FAP set. A line search along the direction is then performed. This continues until the cyclic search cannot find an improving direction. Obviously, this method is *not* resilient toward deep local minima. However, it is hoped that the genetic MOP will have pushed the solution close enough to convergence that the local optimum found is also global.

Pseudo-code for the combined NSGA-II and cyclic optimization algorithm can be seen in the Appendix.

NUMERICAL RESULTS

The algorithm was simulated using a population size of 32 with a maximum number of 25 generations set for NSGA-II and a maximum number of 15 iterations set for the deterministic algorithm. Stopping criteria for NSGA-II was evaluated as when the average *PSNR* of the population increased less than 0.5dB, in order to achieve an efficient convergence. Table 1 summarizes the main results from the experiment. It shows the best *PSNR* and average *PSNR* obtained over ten runs of the algorithm. The results are divided into three bandwidths. High bandwidth individuals are considered those using 14 to 18 parameters. Medium bandwidth individuals are considered those using between 7-13 parameters. Low bandwidth individuals are considered those using 6 parameters or less.

The high bandwidth optimizations are evaluated only once because the deterministic algorithm was used exclusively. This was chosen because the Pareto optimization results were unexpected; no individuals used all the FAP sets, and therefore, the NSGA-II algorithm was irrelevant for high bandwidth transmission. Multiple trials are not necessary because the deterministic algorithm convergence is dependent completely upon the starting point.

The video sequence chosen was from ISTface (2009) and is a cartoonish representation of a human face. Although the sequence is not completely realistic, it can be considered well designed for proof of the concept of the algorithm. For a more realistic result, additional parameters for shading

are needed and better models of a human face. We acknowledge this limitation of our optimization and hope, in near future more research can lead to a suitable rendering software.

Table 1, column 1, shows *PSNR*s achieved after the deterministic optimization has taken course. At medium bandwidths, the results are as accurate as those found in (Eisert, 2000), and can be considered mostly good fits to the face. In (Eisert, 2000), the facial model used 18 animating parameters and achieved a *PSNR* of approximately 30dB, on average. In Pique and Torres (2003) the facial analyses achieved were in 29.5dB to 31.5dB range. And, in Huang and Tao (2001) the resultant facial fits ranged from 25dB to 31dB, at low bit rates.

In addition, the medium bandwidth *PSNR* results do slightly better on average than the low bandwidth results with averages of 29.43dB compared to 27.26dB. Also, at low bandwidths, the best *PSNR*s are 1-5dB lower than at medium bandwidths and the average *PSNR*s are 1-6dB lower.

Interestingly, most of the medium bandwidth results and many of the low bandwidth results outperform those of the high bandwidth. This can be attributed to the complication of the search space using the deterministic algorithm. As mentioned previously, the deterministic search has problems with multimodal surfaces. Higher dimensions inevitably create more local maxima to stifle the algorithm. As can be seen from Table 1, the deterministic search prematurely converges in a local optimum. Moreover, the optimum has a consistently lower *PSNR* and can be considered an analysis failure. This finding reinforces the need for a dynamic FAP set allocation, but in the respect that it increases efficiency and convergence rather than providing dynamic bandwidths.

Also shown in Table 1, column 3, are the selected FAP sets and the number of times each set was selected in superscript parentheses. At maximum, the set could be selected ten times, once for each run. These results provide a means for

Table 1. Fap simulation summary

Max Bandwidth (Uncompressed)	Frame No.	Selected FAP Sets[a]	Best PSNR	Mean PSNR (Over 10 runs)	Mean Function Evaluations
High	0	All, 0-17	31.20 dB	NA	512
(~7.2 Kbits/s	1	All, 0-17	26.82 dB	NA	298
At 25 fps)[b]	2	All, 0-17	28.04 dB	NA	375
	3	All, 0-17	28.35 dB	NA	417
	4	All, 0-17	27.10 dB	NA	365
	5	All, 0-17	30.34 dB	NA	386
	6	All, 0-17	30.65 dB	NA	358
	7	All, 0-17	27.33 dB	NA	389
	8	All, 0-17	26.97 dB	NA	338
	9	All, 0-17	28.59 dB	NA	436
	10	All, 0-17	31.39 dB	NA	417
Medium	0	$0^{(6)} 1^{(6)} 2^{(2)} 3^{(2)} 4^{(1)} 5^{(4)} 6^{(6)} 7^{(1)} 8^{(3)} 9^{(2)} 10^{(5)} 11^{(5)} 12^{(1)} 13^{(4)} 15^{(10)} 16^{(9)} 17^{(1)}$	30.57 dB	28.93 dB	335.40
(~4.8 Kbits/s	1	$0^{(7)} 1^{(5)} 2^{(2)} 3^{(2)} 4^{(1)} 5^{(5)} 6^{(4)} 7^{(2)} 8^{(4)} 9^{(4)} 10^{(3)} 11^{(6)} 12^{(6)} 13^{(5)} 14^{(4)} 15^{(10)} 16^{(10)} 17^{(5)}$	35.14 dB	29.46 dB	285.80
At 25 fps)[b]	2	$0^{(6)} 1^{(5)} 2^{(2)} 3^{(3)} 4^{(2)} 5^{(4)} 6^{(5)} 7^{(4)} 8^{(4)} 9^{(6)} 10^{(3)} 11^{(7)} 12^{(4)} 13^{(7)} 14^{(7)} 15^{(10)} 16^{(10)} 17^{(5)}$	32.09 dB	29.78 dB	303.20
	3	$0^{(6)} 1^{(4)} 2^{(5)} 5^{(5)} 6^{(6)} 7^{(3)} 8^{(3)} 9^{(4)} 10^{(3)} 11^{(5)} 12^{(4)} 13^{(5)} 14^{(5)} 15^{(10)} 16^{(10)} 17^{(5)}$	33.20 dB	30.07 dB	279.60
	4	$0^{(2)} 1^{(4)} 2^{(2)} 3^{(1)} 5^{(5)} 6^{(6)} 7^{(2)} 8^{(2)} 9^{(2)} 10^{(4)} 11^{(4)} 12^{(1)} 13^{(2)} 14^{(6)} 15^{(8)} 16^{(8)} 17^{(5)}$	34.29 dB	30.42 dB	285.70
	5	$0^{(3)} 1^{(6)} 2^{(4)} 3^{(1)} 4^{(1)} 5^{(2)} 6^{(5)} 7^{(2)} 8^{(5)} 9^{(3)} 10^{(7)} 11^{(3)} 12^{(7)} 13^{(3)} 14^{(5)} 15^{(10)} 16^{(7)} 17^{(3)}$	32.90 dB	30.60 dB	315.10
	6	$0^{(7)} 1^{(6)} 2^{(5)} 5^{(2)} 6^{(3)} 7^{(4)} 8^{(7)} 9^{(7)} 10^{(5)} 11^{(3)} 12^{(5)} 14^{(4)} 15^{(10)} 16^{(10)} 17^{(4)}$	32.60 dB	30.13 dB	299.30
	7	$0^{(9)} 1^{(5)} 2^{(5)} 3^{(1)} 4^{(1)} 5^{(5)} 6^{(4)} 7^{(6)} 8^{(7)} 9^{(4)} 10^{(5)} 11^{(6)} 12^{(6)} 13^{(6)} 14^{(5)} 15^{(10)} 16^{(10)} 17^{(5)}$	31.91 dB	29.22 dB	330.80
	8	$0^{(6)} 1^{(2)} 2^{(4)} 4^{(2)} 5^{(6)} 6^{(6)} 7^{(2)} 8^{(5)} 9^{(5)} 10^{(2)} 11^{(3)} 12^{(4)} 13^{(7)} 14^{(6)} 15^{(10)} 16^{(10)} 17^{(5)}$	30.97 dB	28.80 dB	290.80
	9	$0^{(4)} 1^{(5)} 2^{(3)} 3^{(1)} 4^{(1)} 5^{(6)} 6^{(5)} 7^{(4)} 8^{(5)} 9^{(4)} 10^{(4)} 11^{(3)} 12^{(5)} 13^{(3)} 14^{(5)} 15^{(10)} 16^{(10)} 17^{(4)}$	30.96 dB	28.10 dB	293.70
	10	$0^{(9)} 1^{(1)} 2^{(2)} 3^{(2)} 4^{(1)} 5^{(4)} 6^{(3)} 7^{(3)} 8^{(4)} 9^{(4)} 10^{(2)} 11^{(6)} 12^{(5)} 13^{(4)} 14^{(6)} 15^{(10)} 16^{(10)} 17^{(4)}$	30.21 dB	28.22 dB	313.30
Low	0	$0^{(5)} 1^{(2)} 2^{(1)} 3^{(1)} 5^{(1)} 6^{(2)} 7^{(2)} 8^{(3)} 9^{(3)} 10^{(3)} 11^{(2)} 12^{(1)} 13^{(3)} 14^{(5)} 15^{(5)} 16^{(5)}$	29.95 dB	25.92 dB	309.22
(~2.4 Kbits/s	1	$0^{(3)} 1^{(1)} 2^{(2)} 5^{(3)} 6^{(2)} 7^{(1)} 8^{(5)} 9^{(1)} 10^{(1)} 11^{(4)} 12^{(4)} 13^{(2)} 14^{(2)} 15^{(8)} 16^{(7)} 17^{(6)}$	33.73 dB	29.39 dB	242.11
At 25 fps)[b]	2	$1^{(2)} 2^{(1)} 5^{(2)} 6^{(1)} 7^{(1)} 8^{(3)} 9^{(3)} 10^{(2)} 11^{(4)} 12^{(3)} 13^{(3)} 14^{(5)} 15^{(9)} 16^{(7)} 17^{(5)}$	32.11 dB	27.20 dB	242.22
	3	$2^{(2)} 5^{(3)} 6^{(3)} 7^{(2)} 8^{(1)} 9^{(4)} 10^{(5)} 11^{(1)} 12^{(3)} 13^{(5)} 14^{(3)} 15^{(8)} 16^{(7)} 17^{(4)}$	32.60 dB	27.72 dB	273.00
	4	$0^{(1)} 1^{(2)} 2^{(4)} 3^{(1)} 5^{(4)} 6^{(2)} 7^{(2)} 8^{(1)} 9^{(4)} 10^{(3)} 11^{(4)} 12^{(3)} 14^{(3)} 15^{(9)} 16^{(6)} 17^{(5)}$	35.16 dB	27.97 dB	278.56

continued on following page

Table 1. Continued

Max Bandwidth (Uncompressed)	Frame No.	Selected FAP Sets[a]	Best PSNR	Mean PSNR (Over 10 runs)	Mean Function Evaluations
	5	$0^{(3)}$ $1^{(4)}$ $2^{(1)}$ $3^{(1)}$ $4^{(1)}$ $5^{(2)}$ $6^{(2)}$ $7^{(1)}$ $8^{(4)}$ $9^{(3)}$ $10^{(2)}$ $11^{(2)}$ $12^{(2)}$ $13^{(1)}$ $14^{(4)}$ $15^{(9)}$ $16^{(8)}$ $17^{(5)}$	32.60 dB	29.77 dB	282.44
	6	$1^{(3)}$ $2^{(1)}$ $3^{(1)}$ $5^{(4)}$ $6^{(2)}$ $7^{(3)}$ $8^{(2)}$ $9^{(3)}$ $10^{(3)}$ $11^{(3)}$ $12^{(3)}$ $14^{(6)}$ $15^{(8)}$ $16^{(8)}$ $17^{(2)}$	30.00 dB	27.41 dB	272.11
	7	$0^{(1)}$ $1^{(3)}$ $2^{(4)}$ $5^{(2)}$ $6^{(2)}$ $7^{(4)}$ $9^{(3)}$ $10^{(3)}$ $11^{(3)}$ $12^{(3)}$ $13^{(2)}$ $14^{(1)}$ $15^{(8)}$ $16^{(9)}$ $17^{(5)}$	29.45 dB	26.66 dB	252.33
	8	$0^{(2)}$ $1^{(2)}$ $2^{(3)}$ $4^{(2)}$ $5^{(2)}$ $6^{(1)}$ $7^{(3)}$ $8^{(2)}$ $9^{(2)}$ $10^{(1)}$ $11^{(2)}$ $12^{(1)}$ $13^{(4)}$ $14^{(1)}$ $15^{(7)}$ $16^{(9)}$ $17^{(3)}$	29.27 dB	26.95 dB	258.56
	9	$0^{(2)}$ $1^{(1)}$ $2^{(3)}$ $3^{(2)}$ $5^{(1)}$ $7^{(1)}$ $8^{(1)}$ $9^{(1)}$ $10^{(3)}$ $11^{(3)}$ $12^{(2)}$ $13^{(1)}$ $14^{(1)}$ $15^{(7)}$ $16^{(8)}$ $17^{(4)}$	28.79 dB	25.68 dB	229.00
	10	$0^{(2)}$ $1^{(1)}$ $3^{(1)}$ $5^{(3)}$ $6^{(3)}$ $8^{(1)}$ $9^{(1)}$ $10^{(3)}$ $12^{(4)}$ $14^{(1)}$ $15^{(2)}$ $16^{(7)}$	27.78 dB	25.17 dB	220.56

This table summarizes the results from all trial frames encountered. Note: high bandwidth individuals were never present in the Pareto front. Therefore, the Best PSNR resulted from analysis by the deterministic algorithm only and the mean PSNR is meaningless.

[a]The selected sets are numbered 0-17 and represent sets of animation parameters that control specific facial movements. The superscript number enclosed in parenthesis beside each set indicates the number of times that FAP set was chosen from the Pareto front. A value of 2 or 3 implies that the set is a crucial set for analyzing the face. Outliers are considered sets that were only chosen once and are not crucial to analysis.

[b]Note that these rates are raw FAP data. Bandwidth can further be reduced using transform based quantization such as the DCT. For example, in [3] an 18 dimensional FAP set was sent at 1 Kbits/s.

quantifying how well the algorithm finds crucial FAP sets for analysis of a particular frame. The medium bandwidth sets are mostly in agreement with one another; with a marginal number of outliers (i.e., FAPs selected only a few times) present in frames 0, 1, 5, and 7. The low bandwidth sets show many outliers, with marginal numbers in all frames. It is surprising that many of the outlier FAP sets control mouth movements and eye movements. These are considered important parameters for decoding a human face. In contrast, both the bandwidths show agreement in FAP sets 15, 16, and 17, which control head pitch, yaw, and roll, respectively.

It is interesting that the low bandwidth sets chosen also have some consensus for FAP sets 12 and 14. These sets control the rightmost eyebrow position and arch. We believe this result highlights a flaw in using *PSNR* that may also explain the absence of mouth and eye movement FAP sets. Deviations in the eyebrow affect the MSE (and,

subsequently, the *PSNR*) more than deviations of the mouth because the contrast between eyebrow and skin is greater than lip and skin, resulting in higher pixel differences from slight eyebrow deviations. This is not encouraging. Studies show that human perception of faces is governed strongly by the position and deformation of the mouth (Jiang *et al.*, 2002). Also of note is that FAP sets 7 and 8 are not present in the selected FAPs for low bandwidth optimizations, except as outliers. These sets control the eyelids opening and closing on the face, movements that are distracting if not present in a video sequence.

In light of this, it may be more appropriate to use a form of quality assessment that takes structure into account, such as structural similarity (Wang *et al.*, 2004), Eigen-face reconstruction (Ahlberg & Forchheimer, 2003; Dornaika & Ahlberg, 2006), or a geometric distortion metric. However, all structurally based metrics increase computation time.

Figure 3. Three different Pareto fronts from different frame optimizations are above. Specifically, frames 0 (a), 8 (b), and 10 (c) from Table 1. The blue dots represent individuals in the NSGA-II non-dominated front. Note that the algorithm is prematurely stopped so that the additional optimization can take place. The red lines indicate the improvement for two individuals chosen at low and medium bandwidths (sets of FAPs) using the cyclic optimization technique. Notice here that the MOP does well at isolating important sets of FAPs, so that the additional optimization has less dimensions to optimize on, and subsequently, finds the optimum faster and more efficiently.

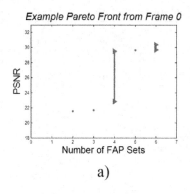
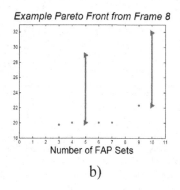
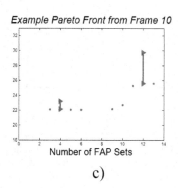

a)   b)   c)

The efficiency of the algorithms can be seen in Table 1, rightmost column. On average, the number of function evaluations is not statistically different for the sets of data. This is proven in that the error-bars from the two sets of data have large overlap, signifying that the NSGA-II function evaluations overshadow the deterministic evaluations. On average, 75.6% of the function evaluations are spent in the NSGA-II optimization and only 25.4% of the evaluations are spent in the deterministic evaluations. Once the deterministic evaluation takes over, it takes 77.44 function evaluations for the deterministic search to converge, on average.

Figure 3 shows three example premature Pareto fronts from the NSGA-II optimization. The aim is to maximize *PSNR* and minimize the number of FAP sets. Figure 3 also shows the improvement in two individuals using the deterministic optimization, one at low bandwidth and another at medium bandwidth. It can be inferred from these graphs that relative improvement is dependent upon two factors. First, improvement depends upon how close to convergence the individual is. For instance, graph (a) shows little improvement

for the medium bandwidth individual because it starts at 30dB. Secondly, and more importantly, improvement depends upon the found FAP sets. If crucial sets are not found, little improvement is possible. For instance, graph (c) shows little improvement for the low bandwidth individual at a low *PSNR*, but large improvement for the medium bandwidth individual around the same *PSNR*. Graph (b), on the other hand, shows excellent improvement for both individuals, indicating the crucial sets were found for individuals in each bandwidth.

On average, the improvement from the deterministic optimization was 2.81dB, for medium bandwidths, and 2.04dB, for low bandwidths. When the resultant *PSNR* was above 29dB (i.e., the crucial FAP sets were found), the improvement was, on average, 2.23dB and the standard deviation of the improvement was 2.54dB. The standard deviation here highlights that the deterministic algorithm can help considerably when the original convergence of the NSGA-II optimization is low. In fact, the deterministic optimization improved the *PSNR* by 4dB or greater on 27.79% of the

Figure 4. Histograms of the resultant data for low and medium bandwidth optimum individuals. Trend-lines are added for ease of analysis. The low bandwidth histogram has two marked peaks, at 23 dB and 30 dB. This dichotomy highlights that low bandwidth individuals are more susceptible to failure when crucial FAP sets are not found. This is seen somewhat also in the medium bandwidth optimums, but with markedly less convergence failures.

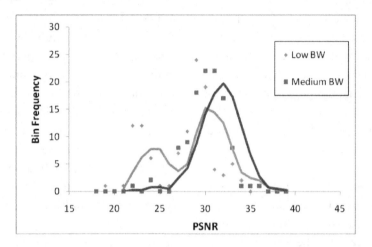

Figure 5. The ideal and resultant optimized facial expressions and head pose for medium and low bandwidth solutions. The original video sequence was chosen such that the 18 parameter sets could not completely define the head motion and deformation. Although the analysis is cartoonish more than realistic, it proves the concept of FAP evaluation using our algorithm. In a realistic scenario, the shading parameters would need to be optimized for in addition to the FAPs.

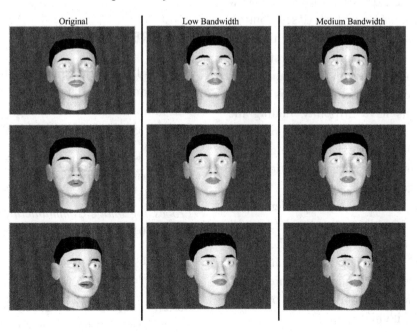

trials conducted. If we consider *PSNR*s above 29dB to be good facial analyses, then 78.1% of the medium bandwidth optimums are acceptable. In contrast, only 27.82% of the low bandwidth optimums are acceptable.

Figure 4 shows a histogram of the found *PSNR*s for medium and low bandwidth individuals, using 1dB bins. Trendlines in the data show that the medium bandwidth individuals are less susceptible to convergence failure and most results lie in the 26dB to 35dB range. Low bandwidth individuals lie mostly in the 20dB to 25dB range with a significant amount in the upper range of 29dB to 31dB.

Figure 5 shows three example facial analyses and the original images. The first and third rows can be considered adequate fits to the eye movements of the data except for the low bandwidth individual in row one. All analyses do excellent tracking of the head yaw, pitch, and roll. The mouth parameters are somewhat close, but have obvious problems. It is apparent from these examples that subtle mouth deformations completely change the expression of the face. Row two is a complete failure of the FAP sets controlling eyelid closing and opening. In fact, the eyelid movement was identified correctly only once by a medium bandwidth optimization.

The convergence of the first frame is of note. Many algorithms have difficulty finding the original facial analysis because no previous knowledge of the frames exists. This algorithm, however, with sufficient Gaussian mutation, finds the analysis quite well.

The final *PSNR*, then, is dependent upon many factors. It was shown that the deterministic algorithm does not perform well when using many FAP sets. The surface is too multimodal. It was also shown that if crucial FAPs are found, the deterministic algorithm finds an optimum efficiently, and with high quality.

CONCLUSION

The results of an application-specific NSGA-II algorithm for facial analysis were presented with the aims of reducing complexity, increasing reliability, and providing a means for allocating bandwidth dynamically. Specifically, two objectives were selected, maximizing PSNR and reducing the number of animation parameters. It was found that, for the test frames implemented, the algorithm does well at finding head pose and eyebrow movements but has difficulty with mouth and eyelid deformations. No individual was found that needed all animation parameters to be successful. Mostly, 6 to 11 animation parameter sets were needed to fully analyze a facial scene. Most problems with the algorithm were traced to the choice of quality assessment, *PSNR*. However, the algorithm performed well at finding the accentuating characteristics that PSNR provides. Currently, we are working to extend the reliability of the analysis using a different means of assessing rendering quality.

REFERENCES

Ahlberg, J., & Forchheimer, R. (2003). Face tracking for model-based coding and face animation. *International Journal of Imaging Systems and Technology*, *13*, 8–22. doi:10.1002/ima.10042

Aizawa, K., Harashima, H., & Saito, T. (1989). Model-based analysis-synthesis image coding (MBASIC) system for a person's face. *Signal Processing Image Communication*, *1*, 139–152. doi:10.1016/0923-5965(89)90006-4

Buck, M. (1993). *Model based image sequence coding*. Berlin, Germany: Kluwer.

Carter, E. F. (1994). The generation and application of random numbers. *Forth Dimensions*, *16*, 202–214.

Choi, C. S., Aizawa, K., Harashima, H., & Takebe, T. (1994). Analysis and synthesis of facial image sequences in model-based image coding. *IEEE Transactions on Circuits and Systems for Video Technology, 4*, 257–275. doi:10.1109/76.305871

Deb, K. (1999). Multi-objective genetic algorithms: problems, difficulties, and construction of test problems. *Evolutionary Computation, 7*, 205–230. doi:10.1162/evco.1999.7.3.205

Deb, K., Pratap, A., Agarwal, S., & Meyarivan, T. (2002). A fast and elitist multiobjective genetic algorithm: NSGA-II. *IEEE Transactions on Evolutionary Computation, 6*, 182–197. doi:10.1109/4235.996017

Diehl, N. (1991). Object motion estimation and segmentation on image sequences. *Signal Processing Image Communication, 3*, 23–56. doi:10.1016/0923-5965(91)90028-Z

Dornaika, F., & Ahlberg, J. (2004). Fast and reliable active appearance model search for 3D face tracking. *IEEE Transactions on Systems, Man and Cybernetics. Part B, 34*, 1838–1853.

Dornaika, F., & Ahlberg, J. (2006). Fitting 3D face models for tracking and active appearance model training. *Image and Vision Computing, 24*, 1010–1024. doi:10.1016/j.imavis.2006.02.025

Edgar, T., Himmelblau, D., & Lasdon, L. (2001). *Optimization of chemical processes*. New York: McGraw-Hill.

Eisert, P. (2000). *Very low bit rate coding*. Unpublished doctoral dissertation, Fraunhofer Institute for Telecommunications, Germany.

Eisert, P. (2003). MPEG-4 facial animation in video analysis and synthesis. *International Journal of Imaging Systems and Technology, 13*, 245–256. doi:10.1002/ima.10072

Forchheimer, R., & Kronander, T. (1989). Image coding– from waveforms to animation. *IEEE Transactions on Acoustics, Speech, and Signal Processing, 37*, 2008–2023. doi:10.1109/29.45550

Huang, T. S., & Tao, H. (2001). Visual face tracking and its application to 3D model-based video coding. In *Proceedings of Picture Coding Symposium*, Seoul, Korea (pp. 57-60).

ISTface. (2009). *wow25.fap* (Program from Instituto Superior Technico, standard FAP animation sequence).

Jiang, J., Alwan, A., Keating, P. A., & Edward, T. A. (2002). On the relationship between face movements, tongue movements, and speech acoustics. *EURASIP Journal on Applied Signal Processing, 11*, 1174–1188. doi:10.1155/S1110865702206046

Kirkpatrick, S., Gelati, C. D., & Vecchi, M. P. (1983). Optimization by simulated annealing. *Science, 220*, 671–680. doi:10.1126/science.220.4598.671

Lu, H., & Yen, G. G. (2003). Rank-density-based multiobjective genetic algorithm and benchmark test function study. *IEEE Transactions on Evolutionary Computation, 7*, 325–343. doi:10.1109/TEVC.2003.812220

Pandizic, I. S., Ahlberg, J., Wzorek, M., Rudol, P., & Mosmondor, M. (2003). Faces everywhere: Towards ubiquitous production and delivery of face animation. In *Proceedings of the 2nd International Conference on Mobile and Ubiquitous Media*, Norköping, Sweden (pp. 49-56).

Pandizic, I. S., & Forchheimer, R. (2002). *MPEG-4 facial animation: The standard, implementation, and applications*. New York: John Wiley.

Parke, F. I. (1982). Parameterized models for facial animation. *IEEE Computer Graphics and Applications*, *2*, 61–68. doi:10.1109/MCG.1982.1674492

Pearson, A. (1995). Developments in model-based image coding. *Proceedings of the IEEE*, *83*, 892–906. doi:10.1109/5.387091

Pique, R., & Torres, L. (2003). Efficient facial coding in video sequences combining adaptive principal component analysis and a hybrid codec approach. In *Proceedings of IEEE International Conference on Acoustic, Speech, and Signal Processing*, Hong Kong, China (pp. 629-632).

Reklaitis, G., Ravindran, A., & Ragsdell, K. (2006). *Engineering optimization, methods and applications* (2nd ed.). New York: John Wiley.

Schaffer, J. D. (1985). Multiple objective optimization with vector evaluated genetic algorithms. In *Proceedings of the 1st International Conference on Genetic Algorithms*, Pittsburgh, PA (pp. 93-100).

Tessema, B., & Yen, G. G. (2009). An adaptive penalty formulation for constrained evolutionary optimization. *IEEE Transactions on Systems, Man, and Cybernetics. Part A, Systems and Humans*, *39*, 565–578. doi:10.1109/TSMCA.2009.2013333

Venkatraman, S., & Yen, G. G. (2005). A generic framework for constrained optimization using genetic algorithms. *IEEE Transactions on Evolutionary Computation*, *9*, 424–435. doi:10.1109/TEVC.2005.846817

Wang, Z., Bovik, A., Sheikh, H., & Simoncelli, E. (2004). Image quality assessment: From error visibility to structural similarity. *IEEE Transactions on Image Processing*, *13*, 600–612. doi:10.1109/TIP.2003.819861

Yen, G. G., & Lu, H. (2003). Dynamic multiobjective evolutionary algorithm: Adaptive cell-based rank and density estimation. *IEEE Transactions on Evolutionary Computation*, *7*, 253–274. doi:10.1109/TEVC.2003.810068

This work was previously published in International Journal of Applied Evolutionary Computation, Volume 1, Issue 1, edited by Wei-Chiang Samuelson Hong, pp. 57-71, copyright 2010 by IGI Publishing (an imprint of IGI Global).

APPENDIX

The pseudo-code for the combined NSGA-II algorithm and cyclic optimization is included here.

```
for {each individual in the population}
    create new params from previous frame params

while {average error is not improving quickly}
    assess PSNR of population
    assess Number of FAP sets for each individual
    perform crossover of population
    combine new and old population
    perform dominance/nearest neighbor sorting
    select top individuals

Select individual in Pareto front with best PSNR and under the maximum number
of available FAP sets

while {a search direction of improvement can be found}
    for {each dimension}
            step 20 units
-if the step is favorable, another step is made
            -Else, choose next dimension

find direction of steepest descent from original point and improved point

    while {step size scaling constant < 0.0001}
take step in the steepest descent direction
-if the new point is favorable, increase step size by two,
-else, decrease step size by a factor of ten.

    Update starting individual with new individual
```

Chapter 5
Ordered Incremental Multi-Objective Problem Solving Based on Genetic Algorithms

Wenting Mo
IBM, China

Sheng-Uei Guan
Xian Jiaotong-Liverpool University, China

Sadasivan Puthusserypady
Technical University of Denmark, Denmark

ABSTRACT

Many Multiple Objective Genetic Algorithms (MOGAs) have been designed to solve problems with multiple conflicting objectives. Incremental approach can be used to enhance the performance of various MOGAs, which was developed to evolve each objective incrementally. For example, by applying the incremental approach to normal MOGA, the obtained Incremental Multiple Objective Genetic Algorithm (IMOGA) outperforms state-of-the-art MOGAs, including Non-dominated Sorting Genetic Algorithm-II (NSGA-II), Strength Pareto Evolutionary Algorithm (SPEA) and Pareto Archived Evolution Strategy (PAES). However, there is still an open question: how to decide the order of the objectives handled by incremental algorithms? Due to their incremental nature, it is found that the ordering of objectives would influence the performance of these algorithms. In this paper, the ordering issue is investigated based on IMOGA, resulting in a novel objective ordering approach. The experimental results on benchmark problems showed that the proposed approach can help IMOGA reach its potential best performance.

DOI: 10.4018/978-1-4666-1749-0.ch005

INTRODUCTION

Background

In the real world, there are many optimization problems which have more than one objective. They are called multi-objective optimization problems (MOPs). In MOPs, the presence of multiple objectives results in a set of optimal solutions (named the Pareto-optimal set), instead of one optimal solution. Without further information, one Pareto-optimal solution cannot be declared as better than another. Given the Pareto-optimal set, users can get a clear idea on how one objective will benefit from the deterioration of one or more other objectives. In that case, they could evaluate the cost and choose the Pareto-optimal solution which most satisfies their requirements. That is why MOGAs are increasingly used (Tamaki et al., 1996). MOGAs maintain a population of solutions and thus can find a number of solutions which are uniformly distributed in the Pareto-optimal set in a single run. This distinguishes it with classical methods such as weighted sum approach or ε-constraint method and goal programming (Taha, 2003), which can only find one Pareto-optimum in a single run. The aims of MOGAs are to find as many Pareto-optimal solutions as possible, and to ensure a good spread of the solutions. No prior knowledge about the objectives is assumed. In contrast, the goal programming method converts the original multiple objectives into one single goal and obtains only one compromised solution in a single run. Preemptive method (Taha, 2003) is one of the goal programming methods, which assigns different priorities to the objectives according to prior knowledge. It is different from the objective ordering discussed in this paper.

So far, a number of MOGAs (Deb et al., 2002; Fonseca & Fleming, 1993; Fonseca & Fleming, 1995; Fonseca & Fleming, 1998; Knowles & Corne, 2000; Kursawe, 1991; Laumanns et al., 1998; Schaffer, 1985; Srinivas & Deb, 1994; Zit-zler & Thiele, 1998; Zitzler & Thiele, 1999) have been suggested. However, almost all of them treat the objectives of an MOP as a whole and evolve them together. Only in VEGA (Schaffer, 1985), appropriate fractions of the next generation are selected from the whole of the old generation according to each of the objectives separately. But the objective space is still explored as a whole, as the overall fitness corresponded to a linear function of the objectives. Because of the weighted-sum fitness, VEGA can only solve the MOPs with convex Pareto fronts (Schaffer, 1985).

In order to explore the objective space in a more powerful manner, IMOGA was designed to evolve the objectives one-by-one and it benefits from inheritance. The superiority of IMOGA over other MOGAs has been shown in (Chen & Guan, 2004), where IMOGA outperformed three well known MOGAs, NSGA-II (Deb et al., 2002), SPEA (Zitzler & Thiele, 1999) and PAES (Knowles & Corne, 2000), on all the problems tested. The development of IMOGA arose from an idea that performance of a certain tool will improve as its task gets easier. It is assumed that the performance of a MOGA will improve, or at least would not degrade as the objective set gets smaller, and the Pareto-optimal points are likely to remain Pareto-optimal after objective increment. Applying this rationale, if the initial solutions from the first few objectives contain better candidates, upon subsequent objective increment, they are most likely to stay, and also improve the accuracy and quality of the solutions. Thus an incremental approach can be more efficient. This incremental approach can also be applied to the mentioned state-of-art MOGAs, NSGA-II, SPEA and PAES, resulting in INSGA-II, ISPEA and IPAES. Performance of the obtained incremental algorithms has been shown better than the original ones (Chen, 2003). In fact, the concept of incremental evolution has been also successfully applied in supervised learning, which works both in the input and output spaces (Guan & Li, 2001;

Guan & Li, 2002; Guan & Li, 2004; Guan & Liu, 2002; Guan & Liu, 2004; Guan & Zhu, 2003). However, the objective ordering problem still remains. With regard to the IMOGA, the objectives were handled according to the original order they were given. Whether this is a good choice is questionable. This issue is discussed in this paper.

Challenges and Proposed Solution

According to our subsequent study, the performance of IMOGA fluctuates a lot as the objective order changes. Generally the original objective order does not result in the best performance. This can be seen from the following example, which is a 4-objective problem solved by IMOGA.

As shown in Figure 1, the performance of IMOGA varied as the objective order changes, which is measured by the distance between the found solutions and the true Pareto front. When the objective functions of this problem were evolved in their original order, the distance was 2.065759. If the positions of the last two objective functions were exchanged, the distance was increased to 2.837251, i.e. the performance dropped by 37.35%. Whereas, if the middle two functions

were exchanged, the distance was decreased to 1.921137, i.e. the performance was improved by 7%. This finding suggests investigating the issue of objective ordering. Therefore, the aims of research are to evaluate the effect of objective ordering in incremental multi-objective problem solving, and to find out metrics for ranking the objective ordering so that the best objective order can be found.

This paper has different aims and contents from one of our earlier papers about IMOGA (Chen & Guan, 2004). That paper presented a new genetic algorithm approach for solving MOPs. It theoretically analyzed the effect of objective increment on Pareto-optimal and non-Pareto-optimal points. Based on the analysis, it presented the IMOGA procedure and a new method of diversity preservation as well as the technique of integration to enhance the quality of individuals. In that paper, the order of objectives was not taken into account. The objectives were evolved in their original order. Whereas, this paper focuses on objective ordering for incremental MOP solving. To highlight further the contribution of this work, it should be noted that the objective ordering issue is a specific issue arising from the

Figure 1. Performance fluctuation of IMOGA with objective order changing

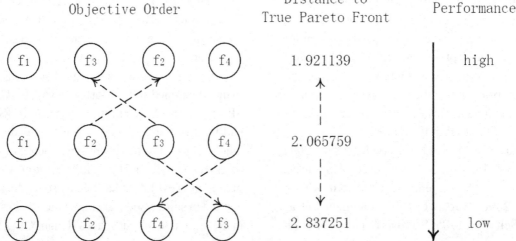

aspect of incremental MOP solving. The incremental MOP solving not only refers to the IMOGA introduced in one of our early papers. It can also be applied to other state-of-the-art MOGAs such as NSGA-II, SPEA and PAES, resulting in incremental NSGA-II (INSGA-II), ISPEA and IPAES. In (Chen, 2003), it was shown that the performance of those state-of-the-art MOGAs could be improved by employing the incremental strategy. The objective ordering is yet considered in this thesis. Therefore, the objective ordering is an open issue in the area of incremental MOP solving. IMOGA is only used as a vehicle for this study. This paper analyzes why objective ordering has influence on the performance of incremental MOP solving. Based on the analysis, two ordering approaches are designed. Experiments are then conducted to compare and verify these approaches. Lastly, we explain why the two ranking metrics are reasonable and why one of the approaches is recommended.

Due to the incremental nature and the limited resources used for the intermediate phases of IMOGA, two factors associated with objective ordering are believed to have impact on the final performance of IMOGA. One is the conflict level between adjacent objectives and the other one is the difficulty in handling individual objectives. However, these two factors are difficult to evaluate for the various forms of objective functions. Some researchers have studied the relationship among objectives within the context of evolutionary multi-objective optimization (Purshouse & Fleming, 2003; Schroder, 1998). Purshouse and Fleming (2003) categorized the relationship into conflicting, harmony and independent, and analyzed the effect of each category on evolutionary multi-objective optimization (EMO). Their analysis is consistent with the assumption made in this paper that MOPs with more conflicting objectives would be harder to solve. Schroder (1998) defined the level of conflict as a weighted-sum of the crossings between pairs of objective regions.

But this method requires additional preference information to partition each objective range into a number of regions. In this paper, comparison-based methods to rank objective pairs and individual objectives are proposed for objective ordering. The major idea is that the conflict level of each objective pair can be compared by the range of their Pareto fronts, and the difficulty in handling each individual objective can be compared by the performance of the optimization algorithm solving them. With the comparison results, the objective pairs can be ranked by their ranges (of the Pareto fronts) and the individual objectives can be ranked by their performance (of the optimization algorithm solving them). After ranking, we shall evolve as early as possible the objective pairs with smaller ranges and/or the objectives with better performance. An ordering strategy is drawn comprising both metrics. The results show that the range metric plays a major role in ordering while the objective performance metric plays a minor role. Based on this strategy, the found best objective order would be consistent with the optimal order obtained by exhaustive searching experiments.

With regard to the choice of metrics for evaluating the performance of IMOGA, hyper-volume metric developed by Zitzler and Thiele (1999) is used with minor revision, and will be elaborated further in the following sections.

The rest of the paper is organized as follows. First, the ideas and the implementation of IMOGA are elaborated, followed by the introduction of the hyper-volume metric used to evaluate IMOGA. Then, the effect and principles of objective ordering is stated: two possible approaches of ordering are described and the complete IMOGA with the objective procedure is given. The results and findings of the experiments are given, followed by some analysis on the results. The next section explains the reason why the recommended ordering approach works.

INCREMENTAL MULTI-OBJECTIVE GENETIC ALGORITHM

The objective ordering problem discussed in this paper is an issue rooted in IMOGA. In this section, we briefly recapitulate how IMOGA works and introduce the performance indicator used for evaluating IMOGA in this paper.

Procedure and Resource Limitation of IMOGA

IMOGA originated from the idea of objective increment. With regard to the objective increment and its effect, they have been analyzed in details in (Chen & Guan, 2004). To summarize, most Pareto-optimal solutions will remain Pareto-optimal after objective increment. This finding showed the continuous existence between the Pareto-optimal sets before and after objective increment, and thus implied the feasibility to solve an MOP by taking objectives into consideration incrementally. As described in (Chen & Guan, 2004), the procedure of IMOGA can be shown in Figure 2.

Remarks: What needs to be noted is that the positions of the first two functions are equipotent and exchangeable.

As shown in Figure 2, the whole evolution is divided into as many phases as the objectives number, and one more objective is considered in each phase. Each phase is composed of two stages: single-objective evolution (SOE) and multi-objective evolution (MOE). An independent population is evolved by SOE to optimize one specific objective. Next, the better-performing individuals obtained by SOE and last MOE are joined together by an operation of integration. The resulting population then becomes an initial multi-objective population, to which a multi-objective evolution based on the incremented objective set is applied. The pseudo code of IMOGA is given in Figure. 3. Please consult (Chen & Guan, 2004) for details of the implementation of IMOGA.

It may be argued that the cost of IMOGA should be much higher than normal MOGAs. In fact, except the last MOE, the resources including population size and evolution generations are limited for the other MOEs. So the total cost of

Figure 2. Procedure of IMOGA

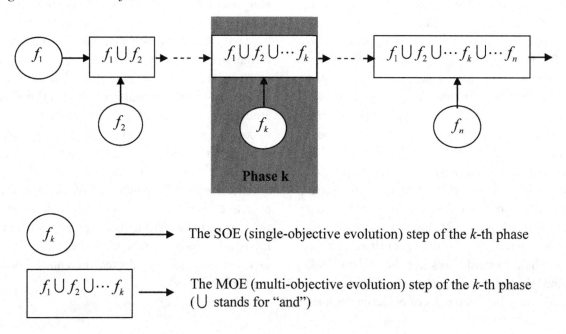

The SOE (single-objective evolution) step of the k-th phase

The MOE (multi-objective evolution) step of the k-th phase ($\bigcup$ stands for "and")

Figure 3. Pseudo code of IMOGA

Randomly initialize a population;

Perform SOE on the population with the first objective;

Select s individuals to form the first multi-objective population (MOP);

Set $k = 1$;

Until (ALL THE OBJECTIVES HAVE BEEN EVOLVED) ***Do***

{

   $k = k + 1$;

   Randomly initialize a population;

   Perform SOE on the population with the k th objective;

   Select s individuals to form the k th single objective population (SOP);

   Integrate the k th SOP with the $(k-1)$ th MOP to form a new population;

   Perform MOE based on the objective set from the first to the k th objective;

   Select the best m individuals to form the k th MOP;

}

IMOGA can be kept comparable with that of normal MOGAs. The resource limitation, such as population size and evolution time, is the major reason why objective ordering has impact on the performance of IMOGA.

Hyper-Volume Metrics

As indicated by Zitzler (1999), multi-objective optimization is quite different from single objective optimization in that there is more than one goal: 1) Convergence to the Pareto-optimal front; 2) Good (in most cases uniform) distribution of the solutions found. There has been an increasing interest in performance evaluation of multi-objective optimization and a lot of metrics have been proposed (Hansen & Jaszkiewicz, 1998; Knowles et al., 2000; Knowles & Corne, 2002; Zitzler & Thiele, 1998; Zitzler, 1999; Zitzler et al., 2000). Since we aim at comparing the

performance of IMOGA with various objective orders, we need a metric that can measure the two goals mentioned above. The hyper-volume-based scaling-independent metrics developed by Zitzler and Thiele (1998) were chosen because they can measure the convergence to the pareto-optimal front, as well as the uniform distribution of solutions.

As described in (Zitzler & Thiele, 1998), there are two volume-based metrics involved.

1. S calculates the size of dominated objective space covered by a set of Pareto-optimal solutions.
2. D calculates the difference in coverage by two sets of Pareto-optimal solutions. Let $A, B \subseteq X$ be two sets of Pareto-optimal solutions. The function D is defined by

$$D(A, B) := S(A + B) - S(B),$$

which gives the size of the objective space weakly dominated by A but not by B.

In the two-objective case, when a minimization problem is considered and the maximum values of f_1 and f_2 are equal to $f_1\_\max$ and $f_2\_\max$ respectively, the metrics mentioned above can be visualized in the Figure 4.

As shown in Figure. 4, the shaded area represents $S(A)$, the objective space covered by A, and the area filled with diagonal represents $D(A,B)$, the objective space covered by A but not covered by B. Similarly, $S(B)$ and $D(B,A)$ can also be found in Figure 4.

Assume the Pareto-optimal front obtained by IMOGA is denoted as I, while the sampled set of the true Pareto-optimal front is denoted as T. To reveal the relationship of these two sets of Pareto-optimal solutions, we should consider both $D(I,T)$ and $D(T,I)$ according to the definition of D.

Ideally, $D(I,T)$ should always be zero as all the Pareto-optimal points should be contained in the true Pareto front. However, what should be noted is that some $D(I,T)$-error may be introduced by the sampling of the true Pareto-optimal front. As shown in Figure 5, $D(I,T) > 0$ because

$P \in I$ but $P \notin T$. In this case, P is actually a point on the true Pareto-optimal front, as it cannot be dominated by any point in T. The reason why a non-ideal $D(I,T)$ happens is that an ideal true Pareto-optimal front contains all the non-dominated points in the objective space, while in practice a finite set of true Pareto-optimal points cannot completely cover the whole true Pareto-optimal front. Nevertheless, if the resolution of the sampled true Pareto-optimal front is high enough so that $|T| >> |I|$, where $|\cdot|$ represents the number of points in a set, this kind of bias would be negligible. Therefore, the size of the true Pareto front used is set much larger than the desired solution number.

With regard to the Pareto-optimal front found by a multi-objective optimization algorithm, it is required that the true Pareto-optimal front should be covered as much as possible. That means $D(T,I)$ need to be minimized. Thus, we define a hyper-volume metric η to evaluate the performance of IMOGA based on Zitzler's volume-based metrics, $\eta := \dfrac{\alpha}{V}$, where $\alpha = D(T,I)$ and $V = S(T)$. Using IMOGA with various objective ordering to solve a certain multi-objective optimization problem, the less the η, the better is the

Figure 4. 2D Visualization of hyper-volume metrics

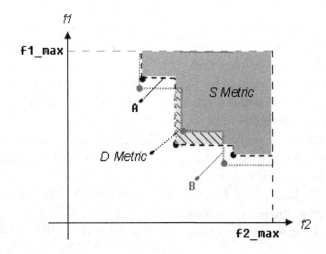

Figure 5. Hyper-volume error introduced by sampling

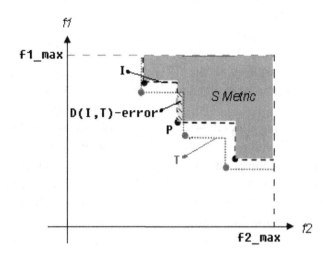

found Pareto-optimal front, thereby the better the objective order is. The values of η is used to compare the performance of IMOGA with different objective order.

OBJECTIVE ORDERING FOR IMOGA

In IMOGA, the objective functions were introduced into the incremental evolution procedure following their original order. But we found that the objective order has significant impact on the final performance of IMOGA. In this section, the effect of objective ordering is illuminated and the principles for objective ordering are concluded. Based on the discussion, two objective ordering approaches are proposed, which aim at finding the best objective order for IMOGA to achieve its best performance.

Effect and Principles of Objective Ordering

For IMOGA, the initial population after objective increment is generated by integrating the solutions obtained before objective increment and the solutions obtained by SOE on the newly

added objective. Chen and Guan have analyzed in detail the effect of objective increment on the solutions found before objective increment (Chen & Guan, 2004). It has been shown that IMOGA could benefit from the inheritance, as the solutions with good quality obtained in the earlier phases can help the search in the latter phases. On the other hand, any inaccuracy incurred in the earlier phases may mislead the evolution in the latter phases, resulting in premature or bad solution spread, and thereby offset the advantages of IMOGA. The qualities of the solutions obtained by SOE and MOE fluctuate due to the following two factors respectively:

1. **The difficulty of individual objective:** It has been proved in (Chen & Guan, 2004) that most of the Pareto-optimal solutions remain Pareto-optimal after objective increment. 'Pareto-optimal' is defined for multi-objective problems. With regard to the stage of SOE, in which only one single objective is involved, the concept of 'Pareto-optimal' is equivalent to 'global optimal'. That is to say, the optimal solution found in SOE in an earlier phase will probably remain Pareto-optimal during the following phases of IMOGA. The more accurate these solutions

are, the larger the non-Pareto-optimal space they would dominate. And they could help eliminate non-Pareto-optimal solutions in the population more effectively. Thus, the objective whose solution is closer to the optimal solution would better be evolved earlier.

2. **The level of conflict among objectives:** For MOPs, the spread of solutions results from the conflict among objectives. If there is "conflict" between two objectives, it means that any one of them cannot be improved without the deterioration of the other. Considering IMOGA, the Pareto front is expected to be constructed part-by-part as the objectives will be evolved one-by-one. This is realized by generating the initial population for a high dimensional search by copying and integrating the solutions found in the one-dimensional lower search with the solutions found by SOE on the incremented objective. According to (Chen & Guan, 2004), the Pareto-optimality of the solutions found before objective increment will remain after objective increment. So if the initial population of a certain phase is generated based on a more accurate Pareto set found in the previous phase, less search effort will be wasted on non-Pareto-optimal solutions. In other words, it would give more effective guidance on the search after objective increment and result in more accurate results which will be the base of search for the next phase. That means this positive effect will ripple from one phase to the next till the last phase. Therefore, objective pairs which are easier to get accurate results would better be evolved earlier, where high accuracy includes smaller distance to the true Pareto front, good coverage and spread of the solutions. Since IMOGA evolves the objective space dimension by dimension, it will be computationally ineffective if abundant resources, like population size and number of

generations, are wasted in the earlier phases. To make the computation time of IMOGA comparable to other MOGAs, the resources (and efforts) for evolution in the initial and intermediate phases are limited. So the objective pairs with less conflict are more likely to obtain better results. There is no conflict problem in the initial phase because only one objective is being evolved. With regard to the intermediate phases, different objective ordering will make a difference, which can be seen from the following example.

Given a 3-objective problem: $f_1 = x^2$, $f_2 = (x+1)^2$, $f_3 = (x-1)^2$, $x \in [-2,2]$, there are three phases, including the initial phase, the intermediate phase and the ending phase. To consider the conflict between the objective pair which is evolved in the intermediate phase, there are three possible objective orders: 123, 132 and 231. The objective pairs evolved in the intermediate phases are (12), (13) and (23), respectively and the corresponding Pareto-optimal solutions are $x \in [-1,0]$, $x \in [0,1]$ and $x \in [-1,1]$. If we use ten bits to encode the solutions, the number of Pareto-optimal solutions obtained in the intermediate phases should be 256, 256 and 512 respectively. Given the same amount of computation resources (including population size and computation time), an algorithm would perform better in terms of the difference between the found Pareto-optimal front and the true one, as the problem gets easier. With regard to the example above, the intermediate phases having 256 solutions is easier than the one having 512 solutions using the size of the Pareto-optimal set as the criterion for comparison. So, if solved by the same algorithm with the same resources, the solutions derived in the intermediate phases with less Pareto-optimal solutions would be closer to its true Pareto-optimal front. Thereby more useful information could be passed to the last phase to effectively guide the search.

From the analysis above, it can be inferred that if we can rank the objectives according to their difficulty or rank the objective pairs according to their conflict, we may be able to get good objective order for IMOGA. Unfortunately, the objective functions can be in various forms, continuous or discrete, differentiable or non-differentiable, convex or non-convex, neither the conflict among the objectives nor the difficulties of them could be measured directly by any deterministic approach. Nevertheless, it is believed that for a certain algorithm, given the same computation resources, the performance would get better as the task gets easier. Therefore, the difficulties of different individual objectives could be ranked according to the qualities of the corresponding solutions obtained using a specific optimization algorithm. Similarly, the conflicts in different objective sets could be ranked according to the characteristics of the corresponding Pareto-optimal solutions using a specific multi-objective optimization algorithm.

Therefore, the metrics for ranking the objectives/objective sets can be summarized as follows:

1. SOE aims at finding solutions approaching the true global optimum of the individual objective as close as possible. So the quality of solutions, namely the difficulty of the corresponding objective, can be evaluated by their distance to the true optima.

2. MOE in any intermediate phase needs to find a Pareto-optimal front with a good spread. Since the spread of Pareto-optimal front results from the conflict among the objectives, the conflict in objective sets can be estimated and compared by the number of Pareto-optimal solutions obtained by a certain multi-objective optimization algorithm with certain computation resources. This metric would be biased when the resolution of solutions for the objective functions are different, which is discussed later in Section IV.D.

Based on these two metrics, two possible objective ordering approaches can be proposed. The detailed procedure is described in the next subsection.

Objective Ordering Approaches

For ease of description, some definitions are given as follows.

1. **Relative Accuracy (RA):** For any objective in the objective set, the Euclidean distance between the solutions obtained by the associated SOE and the true optimum (obtained earlier), divided by the objective value of the true optimum, is called *relative accuracy*.

2. **Objective Pair:** A pair of any two objective functions is called an *objective pair*, which is denoted as (i, j), where $i, j = 1, 2, ..., n$, $i \neq j$ and n is the number of objective functions. So the total number of objective pairs should be $\binom{n}{2} = \dfrac{n(n-1)}{2}$.

3. **Conflict Level (CL):** For a specific problem, the *conflict level* of each objective pair is assigned according to the number of Pareto-optimal points obtained by a certain algorithm. The more the Pareto-optimal points, the higher is the conflict level: CL of the objective pair having the smallest number of Pareto-optimal points is set to 1, CL of the objective pair having the second smallest number of Pareto-optimal points is set to 2, etc. $CL_{i,j}$ represents the conflict level of objective pair (i, j) and $CL_{i,j} = CL_{j,i}$.

4. **Cumulative Conflict Level (CCL):** Given a sequence of objectives and a new objective, *cumulative conflict level* is the sum of CLs between each objective in the original sequence and the new objective.

5. **Niche:** Each location in the sequence of objectives is called a *niche*. l_i represents the i th niche, where $i = 1, 2, ..., n$.

Based on the analysis given in Section III.A, two objective ordering approaches are proposed for IMOGA. Both of them consider the two ranking metrics RA and CL, but the priorities vary.

a. Difficulty based objective ordering approach (DOOA)

As mentioned, IMOGA would prefer objectives with smaller RA being evolved earlier. DOOA is designed based on this observation.

1. Calculate the relative accuracy of each objective, RA_i, $i = 1, ..., n$.
2. Choose the objective order in ascending RA as the best order for IMOGA. If ties appear, the objective that results in the smallest CL for the later stage will be chosen.

b. Conflict level based objective ordering approach (CLOOA)

IMOGA would prefer objective pairs with smaller CL being evolved earlier. CLOOA is based on this observation.

1. Rank the objective pairs according to the number of Pareto-optimal solutions found, and assign the rank of each objective pair as its conflict level, $CL_{i,j}$.
2. Choose an objective pair with the minimal CL to fill in l_1 and l_2.
3. Set $k = 0$.
4. $k = k + 1$. Scan the remaining objective functions to calculate the CCL. And choose the objective function corresponding to the smallest CCL to fill in l_{k+2}. According to the definition of CCL, when the p th objective function is considered, $CCL_{k,p} = \sum_{u=1}^{k+1} CL_{O_u,p}$, where O_u denotes the objective function which has been assigned

to l_u. If ties appear, the objective with the smallest relative accuracy wins.

5. Repeat the procedure described in 4 until only one objective function is left and fill that objective function into l_n.

Next, the whole procedure to employ the ordering approaches to get a certain objective order for IMOGA is described in the following section.

IMOGA with Objective Ordering Procedure

To implement any of the two ordering approaches, values of both RA and CL are required. These can be computed based on the two ranking metrics before applying the complete procedure of IMOGA with objective ordering, which is shown by the flowchart in Figure 6.

The procedure of objective ordering induces some additional cost. If this cost is too high, it makes no sense to do the objective ordering. The complexity analysis is given as follows.

In the objective ordering procedure, the basic operations and their complexities in the worst case are (n is the number of objectives and m is the population size for 2-objective IMOGA):

1. Run the 2-objective IMOGA for all the objective pairs: $O\left(\frac{n(n-1)}{2} \cdot 2m^2\right) = O\left(n^2 m^2\right)$;
2. Compute the RA values for all the objectives: $O(n)$;
3. Assign the CL values for all the objective pairs: $O\left(\frac{n(n-1)}{2}\right) = O\left(n^2\right)$;
4. Order the objectives according to their RAs and CLs: $O\left(n^3\right)$;
5. Moreover, the global optimum of each single objective is required for the calculation of RA. Generally, the difficulty of solving

Figure 6. Flowchart of IMOGA with objective ordering

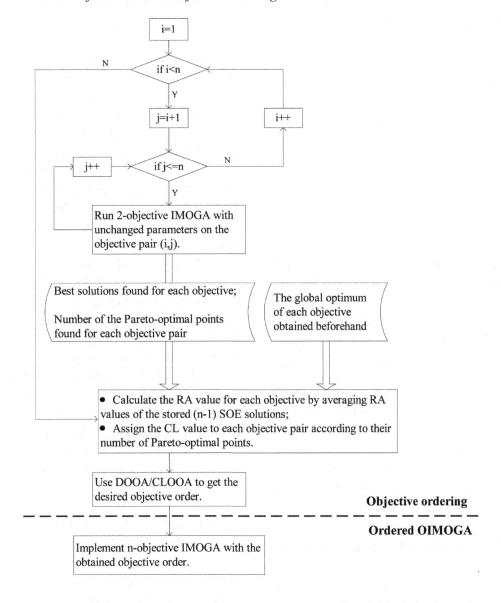

MOPs comes from the conflict among objectives, rather than the individual objectives. So mostly simple mathematical analysis can be made to get the global optima of each individual objective, which is what we have done for all the problems shown in this paper. Even if such analysis is not feasible for some objectives, their global optima could be obtained by optimization algorithms, either decisive algorithms like linear programming or heuristic algorithms like GA. In other words, the computation effort of obtaining the global optimum of each individual objective is a constant. Thus, the complexity of obtaining the global optimum of each objective is $O(n)$.

Normally, the population size used in MOGA is much larger than the objective number,

$m \gg n$. Therefore, the total complexity of the objective ordering process is $O\left(n^2 m^2\right)$.

On the other hand, the complexity of the n-objective IMOGA is $O\left(nM^2\right)$ (M is the population size for n-objective IMOGA) (Chen & Guan, 2004).

So the overall complexity of IMOGA with objective ordering is

$$
\begin{cases}
O\left(nM^2\right), & if \ \dfrac{M}{m} \geq \sqrt{n} \\
O\left(n^2 m^2\right), & otherwise
\end{cases}.
$$

Also, the population size is usually increased rapidly with the increase of objective number. For instance, in our experiments the population size used for 2-objective and 4-objective IMOGA is 100 and 1000 respectively. In other words, there is $M \gg m \gg n$. Thus, the condition $\dfrac{M}{m} \geq \sqrt{n}$ will be satisfied in most cases and the overall complexity of IMOGA with objective ordering will be $O\left(nM^2\right)$. Since the computation complexities of IMOGA and other state-of-the-art MOEAs such as NSGA-II, SPEA and PAES are all shown to be $O\left(nM^2\right)$, the computation load of objective ordering is reasonable and acceptable.

As shown in Figure 6, we have to choose either DOOA or CLOOA for ordering. Although either in DOOA or in CLOOA the two ranking metrics are considered, apparently they are emphasized respectively. So we will test DOOA and CLOOA separately to find out which metric is crucial in deciding the objective ordering in the following section.

EXPERIMENTAL RESULTS AND ANALYSIS

In this section, the ordering approaches are validated by experiments.

Experiment Scheme

Originally, IMOGA evolves an objective set in the original order. The aim of the experiments done in this paper was to test whether the performance of IMOGA could be improved further by the proposed objective ordering approaches. Thus, a series of comparison experiments were designed. Firstly, the ordering approaches were tested with a 4-objective problem in which the difficulty of each objective is the same. Secondly, a 3-objective problem was tested, which reflects the situation of multiple objectives with the same conflict level. Lastly, two problems with different difficulties and conflict levels were tested. The general steps for comparison include: 1) The best objective order was obtained by each proposed ordering approach; 2) Implementing n-objective IMOGA with each of the possible $n!$ objective orders. The performance of IMOGA with each order was evaluated by the metric η as stated in Section II.B. The objective order corresponding to the best performance was marked; 3) Comparing the best objective orders obtained in the above two steps respectively. All the test problems were minimization problems and were done on a Pentium IV 2.0GHz PC.

2-Objective IMOGA and Metrics used for Evaluation

As described in Section III, the ranking metrics RA and CL should be obtained by the 2-objective IMOGA. Given an objective pair, the 2-objective IMOGA is run 20 times with initial seeds from 1 to 20. The parameters of the 2-objective IMOGA were set as follows.

1. For each problem, the algorithm is given 0.5s to evolve in each run.
2. Each decision variable is encoded in 30 bits.

3. Crossover: one-point crossover at the input variable boundary only, with a probability of 1.

4. The mutation rate for each decision variable is $1/d$, and for each bit it is $1/l$ (d: the number of decision variables, l: the number of chromosome bits).

5. Stopping criteria for single-objective evolution: the enhancement of the fittest individual is less than 0.1% in the last ten generations or the generation number is more than 1000.

6. The initial population size for single-objective evolution is 100, and 25 best individuals are selected into the integration operation.

7. The population size for multi-objective evolution is 1000.

All the parameters above follow the settings recorded in (Chen & Guan, 2004). According to (Chen & Guan, 2004), the 2-objective IMOGA with these settings can achieve splendid performance in the sense that it can find a Pareto front very close to the true Pareto front with excellent spread and coverage. This guarantees the validity of the following evaluation metrics used for ranking:

1. N is the number of Pareto-optimal solutions obtained by the 2-IMOGA implemented on an objective pair. The larger the N, the higher conflict level will be assigned to this objective pair.

2. δ is the RA of each individual objective. The solutions obtained by the SOE steps of the 2-objective IMOGA are used to evaluate δ.

$$\delta = \frac{\sum_{j=1}^{k} |y_j - Y|}{|Y|},$$

where k is the number of solutions obtained by SOE associated with the objective, y_j is the objective value of the jth solution and Y is the true optimal value of this objective. The closer the solutions approaching the true optima, the less difficulty this objective possesses.

What should be noted is that:

1. Since the first two niches are equipotent, there is no ordering issue for 2-objective IMOGA.

2. For the fairness of comparison, the parameters of the 2-objective IMOGA should be fixed.

3. Since every possible objective pair should be evaluated, the number of SOEs associated with the same objective will be $n-1$. So, the repeated number of experiments for evaluating the difficulty of any individual objective is $20 \times (n-1)$.

4. It is assumed that the true optimum of each individual objective is known, which can be obtained either by numerical methods or well-received heuristics such as GAs and/or neural networks.

Experimental Results

With regard to the second step of the experiment scheme mentioned in Section IV.A, n-objective IMOGA will be applied to solve the test problems. The parameter setups for the n-objective IMOGA are kept unchanged from one objective ordering to another and roughly the same as the setups of the 2-objective IMOGA described in Section IV.B. The parameter setup that are different from one problem to another are listed in Table 1.

To get rid of the influence of objective difficulty on performance, we set all the objectives with the same difficulties. In this way, how the conflict level affects the objective ordering can

Table 1. Parameter setups for the n-objective IMOGAs used in each problem

Problem	# of bits for encoding	Computation time (s)	Population size of SOEs	# of solutions inherited from SOEs	# of Gen. for inter. MOEs	Desired final solution #
1	8	3	20	5	5	256
2	10	10	100	15	5	1500
3	8	10	50	15	5	400
4	5	10	50	10	5	1000

Remarks: '# of bits for encoding' is the number of bits used to encode each decision variable;
'Computation time' is the total time to which the n-objective IMOGA is limited;
'Population size of SOEs' is the number of chromosomes used in each SOE;
'# of solutions inherited from SOEs' is the number of solutions inherited from a SOE to form the initial population for the following MOE;
'# of Gen. for inter. MOEs' is the number of generations a MOE evolves its population;
'Desired final solution #' is the number of final Pareto-optimal solutions, also the population size of the last MOE.
1) Problem 1

be seen clearly. A 4-objective problem is defined as follows.

$$f_1 = (x_1+2)^2 + x_2^2$$
$$f_2 = (x_1+1)^2 + x_2^2$$
$$f_3 = (x_1-1)^2 + x_2^2$$
$$f_4 = (x_1-2)^2 + x_2^2$$

with the constraints: $-2 \leq x_1, x_2 \leq 2$

For this problem, the conflict level between any objective pair is decided only by the first variable. The projections of the objectives along the first variable can be shown in figure. 7.

From Figure 7, it can observed that the Pareto set of Problem 1 covers the whole range of x_1. For different objective pairs, the coverage of the Pareto solutions and the corresponding conflict level are listed in Table 2.

As mentioned at the beginning of this section, the two-objective IMOGA was used to rank the

Figure 7. Projection of the objective functions in problem 1

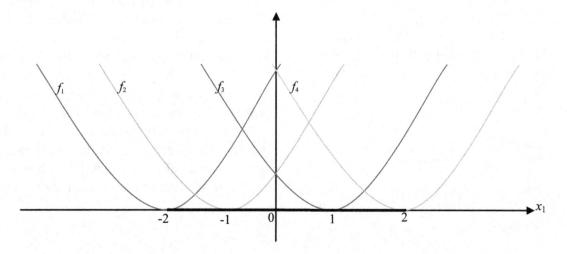

Table 2. True conflict level between objective pairs in problem 1

Objective pair	12	13	14	23	24	34
Proportional range covered by corresponding Pareto solutions	1/4	3/4	1	1/2	3/4	1/4
CL	1	4	6	3	4	1

objective pairs and assign conflict levels to them. The results are shown in Table 3.

Comparing the CL item in Table 2 and Table 3, it can be seen that the CL assignment obtained by the 2-objective IMOGA was consistent with the intuitive analysis. Since the factor of objective difficulty had been eliminated, the two ordering approaches DOOA and CLOOA would get the same result and the ordering only depends on the CL. As remarked in Figure. 2, the first two functions are equipotent and exchangeable. In this case, we only need to assign an objective pair to the first two niches without considering the order between those two objectives. Considering CLOOA, either (1, 2) or (3, 4) could be selected to fill in the first two niches l_1 and l_2, as they have the lowest CL. Say (1, 2) is selected. Thereafter we have $CCL_{3,3} = 7$ vs. $CCL_{3,4} = 10$, which means selecting objective 3 for l_3 could benefit the third phase of IMOGA. Then the remaining objective 4 will fill in l_4. So **(12)34** is one of the best objective orderings obtained by the proposed ordering approach, where the brackets stand for exchangeability. Similarly, **(34)21** could be obtained as the other candidate.

To show the validity of the proposed approaches, the 4-objective IMOGA was used to solve the problem with different objective orders. The performance of this 4-objective IMOGA was measured by the hyper-volume metric η. 256 true Pareto-optimal points were found beforehand by a brute-force method for evaluation of η. That is, each pair of two possible solutions in the feasible output space was compared to find those non-dominated solutions. Table 4 shows the average results over 20 runs with initial seeds from 1 to 20.

It should be noted that, since the first two niches are exchangeable, the slight difference of performance results due to the exchange of the first two objectives could be caused by the random initial setting. So, the performance of these two equipotent orders was averaged for comparison, denoted as $\bar{\eta}$. For the ease of comparison, the results in Table 4 were sorted in ascending order according to $\bar{\eta}$. As can be seen from Table 4, the order **(12)34** and the order **(34)21** give similar optimal performance. So both the two orders are regarded as optimal orders.

From this experiment, it can be concluded that the optimal objective orders found by the proposed ordering approaches are consistent with the optimal objective orders found by exhaustive search using 4-objective IMOGA.

Table 3. Assigned conflict level of all possible objective pairs in problem 1

Objective Pair	12	13	14	23	24	34
N	256	768	1024	512	768	256
CL	1	4	6	3	4	1

Table 4. Performance comparison of 4-objective IMOGA with different objective orders for problem 1

Order of objectives	η	$\bar{\eta}$
1234	0.076958	0.076979
2134	0.077000	
3421	0.077001	0.077074
4321	0.077147	
3214	0.119999	0.124236
2314	0.128472	
2341	0.127594	0.124355
3241	0.121115	
3124	0.226651	0.226561
1324	0.226471	
4231	0.226374	0.227425
2431	0.228476	
1423	0.382944	0.391459
4123	0.399974	
4132	0.398629	0.399942
1432	0.401254	
1243	0.572139	0.575882
2143	0.579624	
3412	0.697808	0.700969
4312	0.704129	
1342	0.860990	0.853981
3142	0.846971	
2413	0.887645	0.854828
4213	0.822011	

2. Problem 2

It is a 3-objective objective ordering problem as shown below:

$$f_1 = x_1 x_2 + x_2 x_3 + x_3 x_4$$
$$f_2 = 1 + \left(x_1 - x_2\right)^2 + \left(x_3 - x_4\right)^2$$
$$f_3 = 1 - \exp\left(\frac{x_1 + 2x_2 + 3x_3 + 4x_4}{10}\right)$$

with the constraints: $1 \leq x_1, x_2, x_3, x_4 \leq 10$

The true optimal value of each objective in Problem 2 is: $f_{1\_\min} = 3$, $f_{2\_\min} = 1$ and $f_{3_\min} = $ -22025.5, respectively.

Firstly, three 2-objective problems corresponding to the three possible objective pairs were solved by the 2-objective IMOGA. And they were ranked according to their number of Pareto-optimal solutions, resulting in the conflict levels. The results are shown in Table 5.

It can be seen from Table 5 that there are two objective pairs with the same CL. In this case, it can be seen clearly how the objective difficulty impact on the objective ordering. On the other

Table 5. Conflict level of all possible objective pairs in problem 2

Objective Pair	12	13	23
N	1	550	1
CL	1	2	1

Table 6. Relative accuracy of each SOE in problem 2

Objective associated with SOE	f_1	f_2	f_3
δ	0.021713	0.00024	0.010004

hand, the relative accuracy of each SOE, namely the difficulty of each objective, is evaluated and the results are shown in Table 6.

Secondly, we can find from Table 6 that the best objective ordering based on DOOA should be **(23)1**. The steps of CLOOA are described as follows. 1) We chose the objective pair with the smallest CL. There was a tie between (1, 2) and (2, 3). So, the objectives difficulty should be considered. 2) Since $\delta_3 < \delta_1$, (2, 3) was chosen for the first two niches. 3) The third niche was filled in with the remaining objective 1. Thus, **(23)1** is the optimal objective order.

Lastly, to show the validity of the proposed approaches, a 3-objective IMOGA was used to solve the problem with different objective orders. 9457 true Pareto-optimal points were found beforehand by a brute-force method for the evaluation of η. The results are shown in Table 7, which shows the average over 20 runs with initial seeds

from 1 to 20. As can be seen from Table 7, the optimal order is **(23)1**.

From the experiment above, it can be concluded that the optimal objective orders found by both DOOA and CLOOA were consistent with the true optimal objective order found by exhaustive searching using 3-objective IMOGA.

3. Problem 3

It is a 3-objective objective ordering problem as shown below:

$$f_1 = 2 - \exp\left(-\sum_{i=1}^{3}\left(x_i - \frac{1}{\sqrt{3}}\right)^2\right)$$

$$f_2 = 2 - \exp\left(-\sum_{i=1}^{3}\left(x_i + \frac{1}{\sqrt{3}}\right)^2\right)$$

$$f_3 = x_1 + x_2 + x_3$$

with the constraints: $-4 \leq x_1, x_2, x_3 \leq 4$

The true optimal value of each objective in Problem 3 is: $f_{1\_\min} = 1$, $f_{2\_\min} = 1$ and $f_{3\_\min} = -12$, respectively. The conflict level of each objective pair and the accuracy of each individual objective are shown in Table 8 and Table 9, respectively.

From Table 9 we can find that the best objective ordering based on DOOA should be **(23)1**. To apply CLOOA, we chose the objective pair with the smallest CL based on Table 8 to fill in the first two niches, which is (1, 2). So, the third niche is filled in with the remaining objective 3. Thus, CLOOA gave **(12)3** as the optimal objective order for handling this problem by IMOGA.

Table 7. Performance comparison of 3-objective IMOGA with different objective ordering for problem 2

Order of objectives	123	213	132	312	231	321
η	0.019299	0.019055	0.022095	0.0228232	0.017338	0.018892
$\overline{\eta}$	0.019177		0.022459		0.018115	

Table 8. Conflict level of all possible objective pairs in problem 3

Objective Pair	12	13	23
N	98	149	168
CL	1	2	3

Table 9. Relative accuracy of SOEs in problem 3

Objective associated with SOE	f_1	f_2	f_3
δ	0.001899	0.001740	0.001716

To validate the proposed approaches, a 3-objective IMOGA is used to solve the problem with different objective orders. A total of 378 true Pareto-optimal points were found beforehand by a brute-force method for evaluation of η. The results are shown in Table 10, which shows the average over 20 runs with initial seeds from 1 to 20. As can be seen from Table 10, the optimal order is **(12)3**.

Comparing the experimental results, it can be concluded that the optimal objective order found by CLOOA was consistent with the true optimal objective order found by exhaustive searching using 3-objective IMOGA, while the optimal objective order found by DOOA was not.

4. Problem 4

It is a 4-objective objective ordering problem as shown below:

$$f_1 = (x_1 - 2)^2 + 4x_2^2$$
$$f_2 = x_1^2 + (x_2 - 3) \times (x_3 - 3)$$
$$f_3 = x_1 x_2 x_3$$
$$f_4 = \frac{1}{x_2^{1.5} \times x_3^{2.5} \times x_4}$$

with the constraints: $1 \leq x_1, x_2, x_3, x_4 \leq 10$

The true optimal value of each objective in Problem 4 is: $f_{1\_min} = 4$, $f_{2\_min} = -13$, $f_{3\_min} = 1$ and $f_{4\_min} = 10^{-5}$, respectively. The conflict level of each objective pair and the accuracy of each individual objective are shown in Table 11 and Table 12, respectively.

According to the rules of DOOA, the best objective order should be **(43)21**. On the other hand, the ordering steps based on CLOOA, are shown in Figure. 8.

To validate the proposed ordering approaches, a 4-objective IMOGA was used to solve the problem with different objective orders. A total of 6224 true Pareto-optimal points were found beforehand by the brute-force method for the evaluation of η. Table 13 shows the results, which are the average over 20 runs with initial seeds from 1 to 20.

For the ease of comparison, the results in Table 13 were sorted in ascending order according to $\bar{\eta}$. It can be seen that the optimal order is **(13)24**, which has the lowest value of $\bar{\eta}$.

From the experiment above, it can be concluded that the optimal objective orders found by DOOA and CLOOA are different, and only the one obtained by CLOOA is consistent with the optimal objective order found by exhaustive searching using 4-objective IMOGA.

Table 10. Performance comparison of 3-objective IMOGA with different objective orders for problem 3

Order of objectives	123	213	132	312	231	321
η	0.009875	0.009561	0.012139	0.012067	0.012497	0.013045
$\bar{\eta}$	0.009718		0.012103		0.012771	

Table 11. Conflict level of all possible objective pairs in problem 4

Objective Pair	12	13	14	23	24	34
N	93	1	363	361	277	408
CL	2	1	5	4	3	6

Analysis of the Experimental Results

From the experimental results above, it can be observed that:

1. As shown in Figure 9, the objective ordering for IMOGA does have impact on the final performance of the IMOGA, and the variance of performance would become clearer as the number of objectives increases. So it is important to find the optimal objective order to get the best performance of IMOGA, especially when the number of objectives is large.
2. The metric CL plays a decisive role in determining the ordering for IMOGA. CLOOA can find the optimal objective order from Problem 1 to Problem 4 without exception.
3. The metric RA could be used as a secondary factor in considering the ordering for IMOGA. For the tested problems, DOOA only finds the optimal objective order for Problem 2. However, we cannot get rid of this metric, as it would help determine the ordering in the case of CL tie which can be seen in Problem 2.
4. The time required in the ordering process comprises of getting the optimum of each objective, running 2-objective IMOGAs and calculating values of the two ranking metrics. Considering GA is used to search the optimum of the single objectives in the test problems, it will not take more than 0.2s for

Figure 8. Procedure of CLOOA

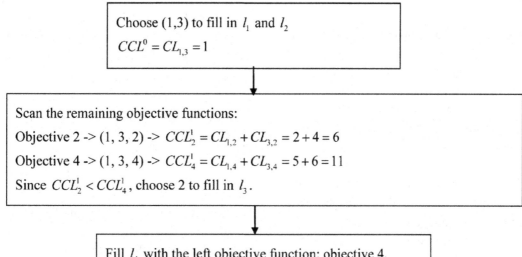

Table 12. Relative accuracy of SOEs in problem 4

Objective associated with SOE	f_1	f_2	f_3	f_4
δ	0.004209	0.002456	0.0014516	0

any one. Each 2-objective IMOGA was given 0.5s to run. The time required to evaluate the two ranking metrics was extremely short, which can be ignored. Therefore, the computation loads of objective ordering for 3-objective problem and 4-objective problem are about $0.2 \times 3 + 0.5 \times 3 = 2.1s$ and $0.2 \times 4 + 0.5 \times 6 = 3.8s$. Compared to the computation time taken for the *n*-objective IMOGA, these loads are acceptable, which is consistent with the complexity analysis presented previously.

Therefore, it can be concluded that IMOGA can achieve its potentially best performance with objective ordering at an acceptable cost. CLOOA is an approach to objective ordering that can find the optimal objective order for IMOGA.

DISCUSSION

To explain why the two ranking metrics RA and CL can be used to determine the objective order for IMOGA and why CL is more important in the objective ordering procedure, we visualize the ordering effect on a minimization problem with three conflicting objectives. As shown in Figure 10, it is assumed that:

- The three center points O_1, O_2 and O_3 are the global optima for the three objective functions respectively.
- Each circle represents a local optima circle, on which all the points have the same objective values. And the bigger the circles

the larger the objective values. (The local optima circles could be expanded to the whole feasible input space, not limited to those shown in the figures.)

- The density of the local optima circles implies the difficulty of an objective function. The distance between two center points implies the number of Pareto-optimal solutions of the two corresponding objective functions.

It can be seen from Figure 10 that the Pareto set of $f_1 \cup f_2$, $f_1 \cup f_3$, $f_2 \cup f_3$ should be O_1O_2, O_1O_3 and O_2O_3, respectively. Assume that O_1O_2, O_1O_3 and O_2O_3 have equal lengths, the numbers of Pareto-optimal solutions for the three objective pairs would be the same if the resolution is fixed. Also, it can be seen that the densities of the local optima circles surrounding O_1 and O_3 are the smallest and the biggest respectively, which means that the SOE_1 will most likely get O_1 while the SOE_3 will be most likely trapped on local optima circles.

Therefore, if f_1 and f_2 are the two objectives firstly evolved, it can be assumed that O_1 and O_2 are found by SOE_1 and SOE_2, respectively. Through integration, O_1 and O_2 can be inherited into MOE_1, which evolves $f_1 \cup f_2$ mainly by using local searching (mutation), i.e. $(x_1(t+1), x_2(t+1)) = (x_1(t) + \Delta_1, x_2(t) + \Delta_2)$. Thus, under the guidance of O_1 and O_2, the Pareto set O_1O_2 will be found most likely. In contrast, if f_1 and f_3 are the two objectives firstly evolved, as shown in Figure 10, the light green arc may be found by SOE_3, as SOE_3 will be trapped most likely. Then, under the guidance of O_1 and this arc, the light green line might be found as the Pareto set by MOE_1. Also, this biased Pareto set would make false guidance in the following MOE_2.

Similarly, the effect of the number of Pareto-optimal solutions can be illustrated by Figure. 11, in which the three objective functions have the

Table 13. Performance comparison of 4-objective IMOGA with different objective orders for problem 4

Order of objectives	η	$\bar{\eta}$
3124	0.000153	0.000171
1324	0.000189	
1234	0.000188	0.000219
2134	0.000250	
4213	0.000270	0.000266
2413	0.000263	
4123	0.000270	0.000275
1423	0.000280	
2314	0.000291	0.000291
3214	0.000291	
3412	0.000387	0.000365
4312	0.000343	
1342	0.000328	0.000374
3142	0.000420	
2143	0.000386	0.000402
1243	0.000417	
2431	0.000395	0.000407
4231	0.000419	
2341	0.000406	0.000409
3241	0.000411	
1432	0.000509	0.000453
4132	0.000398	
4321	0.000461	0.000460
3421	0.000458	

same possibility of being trapped on local optima circles, while the numbers of Pareto-optimal solutions of the objective pairs are different. The objective pair $f_1 \cup f_3$ has a larger number of Pareto-optimal solutions than the other two pairs, as $O_1O_2 = O_2O_3 < O_1O_3$.

Actually, if the resources for evolution are more than enough, different ordering would not make a big difference. However, in IMOGA the resources for intermediate phases are limited for computational efficiency. Thus, if the Pareto set is too large, e.g. $f_1 \cup f_3$ is evolved first, it is very likely that only part of it is found by MOE_1 and

passed to MOE_2. Hence, the guidance in MOE_2 from the inherited solutions would be non-uniform, as shown by the light green arrows in Figure. 11, which may result in incomplete or poorly distributed final Pareto set.

The reason why the difficulty of individual objective has less influence in objective ordering may be that the bias incurred by the error of SOEs has chances to be rectified. Even if the SOE associated with an objective of great difficulty is likely to be trapped and the obtained local optima will be inherited into the subsequent MOEs, once the global optimum of the objective is found in

Figure 9. Performance of IMOGA measured by hyper-volume metrics under different objective orders from problem 1 to problem 4

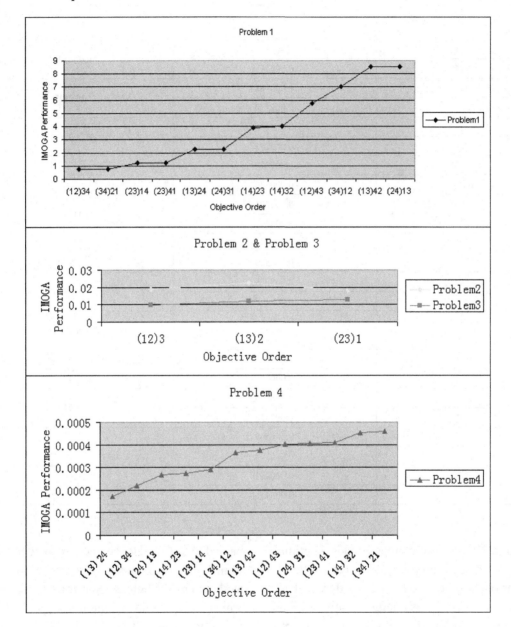

those MOEs all the biased Pareto-optimal solutions resulting from the local optima will be dominated and discarded. In contrast, the poor spread of Pareto-optimal solutions incurred by the objective set with high conflict level could not be improved because those solutions are non-dominated to each other and would not be discarded. Thus, the CL

plays a decisive role in determining the ordering for IMOGA.

Besides, there are two issues that should be noted. One is the equipotence of the first two niches. It can be seen from the procedure of IMOGA that the positions of the first two niches are equipotent and exchangeable. But why the IMOGA performance varies by exchanging the

Figure 10. Three conflicting objectives with different difficulties

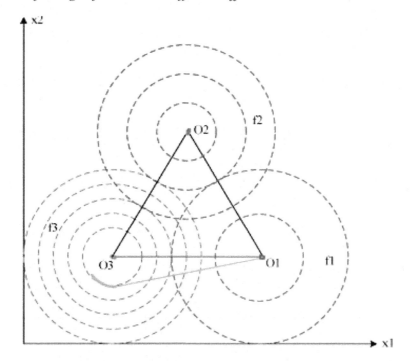

first two objectives? In fact, this is because we feed the same initial seeds into IMOGA with different objective ordering for fairness of comparison. In this case, the series of random numbers generated in each IMOGA is the same. So, exchanging the first two objectives is equivalent to exchanging the initial populations for the first two SOO, which results in slightly different final performance.

The other issue is the distribution and resolution of solutions. To use the number of solutions N as the metric for evaluating the conflict level, the solutions need to be distributed uniformly and the resolution of solutions should be kept unchanged, which means that the number of bits used to encode the chromosomes should be fixed for a problem. Otherwise, the metric N may be biased because using either a fixed resolution to sample surfaces with uneven distributions or different resolutions to sample uniformly distributed surfaces will result in different number of solutions.

CONCLUSION

This paper first summarized the IMOGA approach and stated the necessity of objective ordering for IMOGA. Since the objective functions are evolved one by one in the procedure of IMOGA, the ordering of introducing objectives should be considered. To compare the performance of IMOGA under different objective orders, we introduced the hyper-volume metric that can measure the distance between the Pareto optimal front found by IMOGA and the true one, as well as the spread of this found front.

Also, we analyzed why objective ordering has influence on the performance of IMOGA. Two factors were emphasized, one is the difficulty of individual objective function and the other is the level of conflict among objective functions. Since incremental inheritance mechanism is applied in IMOGA, the solutions found in the earlier stages should be made as accurate as possible. Thus,

Figure 11. Three conflicting objectives with the same difficulties

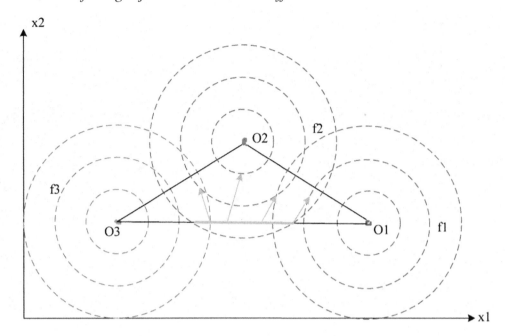

the principle of objective ordering is that the objective functions with less difficulty and the objective pairs with lower conflict levels should be handled with priority. Nevertheless, these two conditions may not be satisfied together. So we need to make one as major while the other one as minor. Based on this concept, we proposed two objective ordering approaches, DOOA and CLOOA, emphasizing the metric of difficulty and the metric of conflict level, respectively.

Experiments on four test problems were conducted and for each problem the performance of IMOGA with various objective orders was compared. The results indicate that objective ordering would affect the performance of IMOGA, and CLOOA has potential to obtain the optimal objective order for IMOGA, which is not necessarily the original order of the objective set. So with objective ordering, the performance of the original IMOGA could be improved further. Please note that IMOGA has already been shown better than three state-of-the-art MOGAs as reported in (Chen & Guan, 2004).

Subsequently, explanations on the reason why the two ranking metrics are reasonable and why CLOOA is recommended were given. Two important issues in the experiments were discussed at last, including the equipotence of the first two niches and the distribution and resolution of solutions that needs to be noticed for using the proposed objective ordering procedure.

REFERENCES

Chen, Q. (2003). *Objective Increment, Its Effect and Application in Multi-Objective Optimization Evolution*. Unpublished master's thesis, National University of Singapore, Singapore.

Chen, Q., & Guan, S. U. (2004, June). Incremental Multiple Objective Genetic Algorithms. *IEEE Transactions on System. Man and Cybernetics B, 34*(3), 1325–1334. doi:10.1109/TSMCB.2003.822958

Deb, K., Pratap, A., Agarwal, S., & Meyarivan, T. (2002, April). A fast and elitist multiobjective genetic algorithm: NSGA-II. *IEEE Transactions on Evolutionary Computation, 6*(2), 182–197. doi:10.1109/4235.996017

Farhang-Mehr, A., & Azarm, S. (2002). Diversity assessment of Pareto optimal solution sets: An entropy approach. In *Proceedings of the Congress Evolutionary Computation, 1,* 723–728.

Fonseca, C. M., & Fleming, P. J. (1993, July 17-21). Genetic algorithms for multiobjective optimization: Formulation, discussion and generalization. In *Proceedings of the Fifth International Conference on Genetic Algorithm,* San Mateo, CA (pp. 416-423).

Fonseca, C. M., & Fleming, P. J. (1995). An Overview of Evolutionary Algorithms in Multiobjective Optimization. *Evolutionary Computation, 3*(1), 1–16. doi:10.1162/evco.1995.3.1.1

Fonseca, C. M., & Fleming, P. J. (1998, January). Multiobjective optimization and multiple constraint handling with evolutionary algorithms. I. A unified formulation. *IEEE Transactions on System. Man and Cybernetics A, 28*(1), 26–37. doi:10.1109/3468.650319

Guan, S. U., & Li, P. (2002). A Hierarchical Incremental Learning Approach to Task Decomposition. *Journal of Intelligent Systems, 12*(3), 201–226.

Guan, S. U., & Li, P. (2004). Incremental Learning in Terms of Output Attributes. *Journal of Intelligent Systems, 13*(2), 95–122.

Guan, S. U., & Li, S. C. (2001, December). Incremental Learning with Respect to New Incoming Input Attributes. *Neural Processing Letters, 14*(3), 241–260. doi:10.1023/A:1012799113953

Guan, S. U., & Liu, J. (2002). Incremental Ordered Neural Network Training. *Journal of Intelligent Systems, 12*(3), 137–172.

Guan, S. U., & Liu, J. (2004). Incremental Neural Network Training with an Increasing Input Dimension. *Journal of Intelligent Systems, 13*(1), 45–70.

Guan, S. U., & Zhu, F. M. (2003, November). Incremental Learning of Collaborative Classifier Agents with New Class Acquisition – An Incremental Genetic Algorithm Approach. *International Journal of Intelligent Systems, 18*(11), 1173–1193. doi:10.1002/int.10145

Hansen, M. P., & Jaszkiewicz, A. (1998). *Evaluating the Quality of Approximations to the Nondominated* Set (Tech. Rep. No. IMM-REP-1998-7). Copenhagen, Denmark: Technical University of Denmark, Institute of Mathematical Modeling.

Knowles, J. D., & Corne, D. W. (2000). Approximating the nondominated front using the pareto archived evolution strategy. *Evolutionary Computation, 8*(2), 149–172. doi:10.1162/106365600568167

Knowles, J. D., & Corne, D. W. (2002). On metrics for comparing nondominated sets in congress on evolutionary computation. In *Proceedings of the Congress on Evolut. Comput. (CEC'02),* Piscataway, NJ (Vol. 1, pp. 711-716).

Knowles, J. D., Corne, D. W., Oates, M. J., et al. (2000). On the assessment of multiobjective approaches to the adaptive distributed database management problem. In M. Schoenauer, et al. (Eds.), Parallel Problem Solving From Nature—PPSN VI (pp. 869–878). Berlin: Springer-Verlag. doi:10.1007/3-540-45356-3_85doi:10.1007/3-540-45356-3_85

Kursawe, F. (1991). A variant of evolution strategies for vector optimization. *Parallel Problem Solving from Nature,* 193-197.

Laumanns, M., Rudolph, G., & Schwefel, H. P. (1998). A spatial predator-prey approach to multi-objective optimization. *Parallel Problem Solving from Nature, 5,* 241–249. doi:10.1007/BFb0056867

Purshouse, R. C., & Fleming, P. J. (2003, April). Conflict, Harmony, and Independence: Relationships in Evolutionary Multi-Criterion Optimization. In *Proceedings of the Evolutionary Multicriterion Optimization* (pp. 8-11).

Schaffer, J. D. (1985). Multiple Objective Optimization with Vector Evaluated Genetic Algorithms. In *Proceedings of the Genetic Algorithms and their applications: First International Conference on Gen. Algo.* (pp. 93-100). Philadelphia, PA: Lawrence Erlbaum.

Schroder, P. (1998). *Multivariable Control of active magnetic bearings*. Unpublished doctoral dissertation, University of Sheffield, Sheffield, South Yorkshire, England.

Srinivas, N., & Deb, K. (1994). Multiobjective optimization using non-dominated sorting in genetic algorithms. *Evolutionary Computation, 2*(3), 221–248. doi:10.1162/evco.1994.2.3.221

Taha, H. A. (2003). *Operations Research: An Introduction*. Singapore: Prentice-Hall.

Tamaki, H., Kita, H., & Kobayashi, S. (1996, May 20-22). Multi-objective optimization by genetic algorithms: A review. In *Proceedings of the IEEE Conference on Evolutionary Computation (ICEC'96)*, Piscataway, NJ (pp. 517-522).

Zitzler, E. (1999, December). Evolutionary Algorithms for Multiobjective Optimization. *Methods and Applications*. Zurich, Switzerland: Swiss Federal Institute of Technology (ETH).

Zitzler, E., Deb, K., & Thiele, L. (2000, April). Comparison of multiobjective evolutionary algorithms: Empirical results. *Evolutionary Computation, 8*(2), 173–195. doi:10.1162/106365600568202

Zitzler, E., & Thiele, L. (1998). An evolutionary algorithm for multi-objective optimization: the strength rateto approach. *Swiss Federal Institute of Technology, TIK- Report*, (43).

Zitzler, E., & Thiele, L. (1999, November). Multiobjective Evolutionary Algorithms: A Comparative Case Study and the Strength Pareto Approach. *IEEE Transactions on Evolutionary Computation, 3*(4), 257–271. doi:10.1109/4235.797969

This work was previously published in International Journal of Applied Evolutionary Computation, Volume 1, Issue 2, edited by Wei-Chiang Samuelson Hong, pp. 1-28, copyright 2010 by IGI Publishing (an imprint of IGI Global).

Chapter 6

Comparative Study of Evolutionary Computing Methods for Parameter Estimation of Power Quality Signals

V. Ravikumar Pandi
IIT Delhi, India

B. K. Panigrahi
IIT Delhi, India

ABSTRACT

Recently utilities and end users become more concerned about power quality issues because the load equipments are more sensitive to various power quality disturbances, such as harmonics and voltage fluctuation. Harmonic distortion and voltage flicker are the major causes in growing concern about electric power quality. Power quality disturbance monitoring plays an important role in the deregulated power market scenario due to competitiveness among the utilities. This paper presents an evolutionary algorithm approach based on Adaptive Particle Swarm Optimization (APSO) to determine the amplitude, phase and frequency of a power quality signal. In this APSO algorithm the time varying inertia weight is modified as rank based, and re-initialization is used to increase the diversity. In this paper, to the authors highlight the efficacy of different evolutionary optimization techniques like classical PSO, Constriction based PSO, Clonal Algorithm (CLONALOG), Adaptive Bacterial Foraging (ABF) and the proposed Adaptive Particle Swarm Optimization (APSO) to extract different parameters like amplitude, phase and frequency of harmonic distorted power quality signal and voltage flicker.

DOI: 10.4018/978-1-4666-1749-0.ch006

INTRODUCTION

In recent years, power quality has become a significant issue for both utilities and customers. Power quality issues (Arrillaga, Watson, & Chen, 2000; Bollen, 2000 ; Dugan, McGranaghan, & Beaty, 2000) and the resulting problems are the consequences of the increasing use of solid state switching devices, non-linear and power electronically switched loads, unbalanced power systems, lighting controls, computer and data processing equipment as well as industrial plant rectifiers and inverters. These electronic types of loads cause quasistatic harmonic dynamic voltage distortions, inrush, pulse type current phenomenon with excessive harmonics and high distortion. A power quality (PQ) problem usually involves a variation in the electric service voltage or current, such as voltage dips and fluctuations, momentary interruptions, harmonics and oscillatory transients causing failure or mal-operation of the power service equipment. In order to improve electric power quality, the sources and causes of such disturbances must be known before appropriate mitigating action can be taken. However, in order to determine the causes and sources of disturbances, one must have the ability to detect and localize these disturbances. Estimation of amplitude and phase of fundamental, as well as harmonic signals has been one of the important tasks in measurement, control, relaying protection, distribution automation, and intelligent instrumentation of power system. Accurate power fundamental frequency is a necessity to check the state of health of the power index, and a guarantee for accurate quantitative measurement of power parameters, such as voltages, currents, active power, reactive power, and energy, and so on, in multifunction power meters under steady states. It is more difficult to precisely estimate the fundamental frequency of power systems in presence of harmonics and noises than under sinusoidal condition. It is essential to seek and develop some effective algorithms for accurate estimation of the instantaneous fundamental frequency of power systems under non-sinusoidal conditions.

Several methods employing digital algorithms have been developed for the estimation of parameters like amplitude, phase and frequency of power quality signals. Algorithms based on Fast Fourier Transform (FFT) have been widely used for the purpose (Chen, 1997; IEEE Standard, 1993). The FFT method suffers from the major problem such as resolution, spectrum leakage and picket-fence effects. As the system frequency deviates from the nominal value, the leakage error becomes more (Probabilistic aspects Task Force, 1998). Some of the pit falls of DFT was suggested in (Girgis & Ham, 1980). The leakage effects of system frequency variation on the measurements of harmonic and flicker have never been accurately determined, so some serious errors might happen in the related measurements. Digital algorithms based on Least Error Square (LES) state estimation technique (Lobos, Kozina, & Koglin, 2001; Sachdev & Giray, 1985; Soliman & El-Hawary, 1999), Least Absolute Value (LAV) estimation (Soliman, Christensen, Kelly, & El-Naggar, 1992) are more common to estimate the parameters of a power quality signal. The above algorithms are not suitable for the non-stationary signals. The other digital algorithm based on Kalman Filtering is a stochastic dynamic filtering algorithm, mostly suitable for non-stationary signals. This method leads to fast and accurate estimation of power system signal amplitude and phase. This method has been applied for finding the parameters of the voltage flicker signal, harmonic signals and has been reported in (Dash, Jena, Panda, & Routray, 2000; Routray, Pradhan, & Rao, 2002). However the algorithm requires an accurate guess of system frequency. The use of Fourier Linear Combiner for harmonic estimation in distorted power signals is reported in (Dash, Swain, Liew, & Rahman, 1996; Dash, Pradhan, & Salama, 2002). Another method based on sample count and interpolation estimation technique is reported in (Aghazadeh, Lesani, Sanaye-Pasand, & Ganji,

2005) for frequency and amplitude estimation of power system signals. Besides the above digital techniques, some of the intelligent techniques like Artificial Neural Network (ANN), Expert system (ES) has been applied for amplitude, phase and frequency estimation of distorted power signals (Kandil, Sood, Khorasani, & Patel, 1992; Martins, Oliveira, & Goncalves, 2000; Mori, 1992; Osowski, 1992). Soft computing techniques like Genetic Algorithm (GA) (El-Naggar & AL-Hasawi, 2006; El-Zonkoly, 2005), Simulated Annealing (SA) (Soliman, Mantaway, & El-Hawary, 2004) have also been applied for power quality analysis. A new algorithm integrating both least square and GA has been reported in (Bettayeb & Qidwai, 2003), where the advantages of both least square and GA have been combined for harmonic estimation. Another literature (Mishra, 2005) combines least square and bacterial foraging optimization approach for harmonic estimation. However in this literature the authors have estimated the amplitude of harmonics using least square algorithm and phase of the harmonics using GA or Bacterial Foraging.

Particle Swarm Optimization (PSO) is one of the most robust evolutionary optimization technique proposed by Eberhart (Eberhart & Shi, 2001; Shi & Eberhart, 2001). A lot of new dimensions have been given to the basic PSO and have been successfully applied to many of the engineering optimization problem (Ho, Yang, Ni, & Wong, 2006; Lei, Qi, Hui, & Qidi, 2005; Li, Gao, Zhang, & Li, 2006; Senthil Arumugam, Chandramohan, & Rao, 2005). In this paper we have tried to extract the amplitude, phase and frequency of fundamental as well as that of the harmonics present in a power quality signal using a few evolutionary computing techniques. The newly proposed Adaptive Particle Swarm Optimization (APSO) is a modified version of the original PSO. The paper briefly describes the evolutionary techniques like Clonal Algorithm, Bacterial Foraging and Particle Swarm Optimization and the proposed adaptive particle swarm optimization. The formulation of the problem and the results obtained by all the above mentioned algorithms are reported in the paper in the subsequent sections. The results of the proposed APSO algorithm are compared with those of the existing methods.

AN OVERVIEW OF EVOLUTIONARY ALGORITHMS

Clonalog

The Clonal Selection Principle describes the basic features of an adaptive immune response to an antigenic stimulus. De Castro and Von Zuben (1999) presented a clonal selection algorithm, which took into account the affinity maturation of the immune response, in order to solve complex problems, like learning and multi-modal optimization. Their algorithm constitutes an implementation of the biological processes and does not account for any mathematical sophistication to enhance its performance in particular tasks.

The Clonal Selection Principle establishes that only those cells that recognize the antigen are selected for proliferation and differentiation. When a B cell receptor (antibody) recognizes an antigen with a certain affinity, it is selected to proliferate. Regarding immune cells, the proliferation is asexual: the cells divide themselves and produce exact copies (clones). They undergo a mutation process with high rates (hyper mutation) that, together with a high selection pressure, result in a B cell with antigenic receptors with higher affinity. In the end of this process the B cells with higher antigenic affinities are selected to become memory cells with long life spans. This clonal selection principle is shown in Figure 1. The Clonal Selection Algorithm (CLONALOG) (Castro & Timmis, 2002) was initially proposed to solve machine learning and pattern recognition problems. Due to its adaptive features, the algorithm was later applied to optimization problems. The block diagram representation of clonal selection algorithm is given in Figure 2.

Figure 1. Clonal selection principle

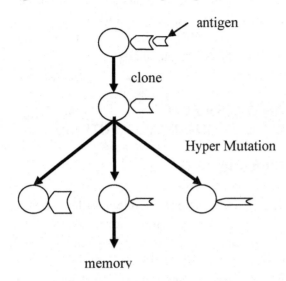

The clonal selection algorithm step-by-step procedure:

1. Generate a set (P) of candidate solutions, composed of the subset of memory cells (M) added to the remaining (Pr) population (P = Pr + M).
2. Determine (Select) the n best individuals of the population (Pn), based on an affinity measure.
3. Reproduce (Clone) these n best individuals of the population, giving rise to a temporary population of clones (C). The clone size is an increasing function of their affinity.
4. Submit the population of clones to a hyper mutation scheme, where the hyper mutation is proportional to their affinity. A matured antibody population is generated (C*).
5. Re-select the improved individuals from C* to compose the memory set M. Some members of P can be replaced by other improved members of C*.
6. Replace d antibodies by novel ones (diversity introduction). The lower affinity cells have higher probabilities of being replaced.

The main features of the clonal selection theory:

*   Generation of new random genetic changes subsequently expressed as diverse antibody patterns by a form of accelerated somatic mutation.
*   Phenotypic restriction and retention of one pattern to one differentiated cell (clone).
*   Proliferation and differentiation on contact of cells with antigens.

It could be argued that a genetic algorithm (GA) without a crossover would be a reasonable model of clonal selection. However the GA does not account for two important properties of CS algorithms: the proliferation rate of the antibody is proportional to its affinity, while the mutation is inversely proportional to it (Castro & Zuben, 2002).

Bacterial Foraging

The Bacterial Foraging algorithm was introduced by K. M. Passino for solving distributed optimization and control problems (2002). Animals search for and obtain nutrients in a way that maximizes the ratio E/T (where E is the energy obtained and T is the time spent on foraging) or maximizes the long term average rate of energy intake. Evolution optimizes the foraging strategies, since animals that have poor foraging performance do not survive. Some animals forage as individuals and others forage as groups. While to perform social foraging an animal needs communication capabilities, it can gain advantages in that it can exploit essentially the sensing capabilities of the group, the group can gang-up on large prey, individuals can obtain protection from predators while in a group, and in a certain sense the group can forage with a type of collective intelligence. This activity of foraging led the researchers to use it as an optimization process. The foraging behavior of *E. coli* (bacteria present in our intestines) can be explained by four processes namely, chemotaxis,

Figure 2. The clonal selection algorithm block diagram

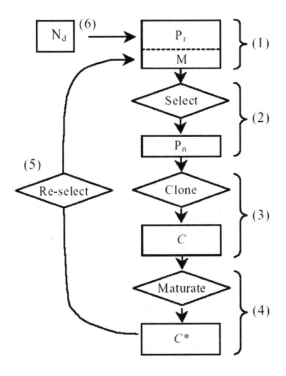

swarming, reproduction, and elimination and dispersal as presented below.

- **Chemotaxis:** The locomotion is achieved by a set of rigid flagella which enable the bacteria to swim. This left-handed helix configured flagellum either rotates counter clockwise to create the force against bacterium to push the cell or rotates in clockwise direction to pull at the cell. This mechanism of creating rotational forces to spin the flagellum in either direction is named as biological motor. An *E. coli* bacterium can move in two different ways, it can swim or it can tumble. The bacterium moves in a specified direction during swimming and during tumbling it does not have a set direction of movement and there is little displacement. Generally, the bacterium alternates between these two modes of operation in its entire lifetime. This al-

ternation between the two modes enables the bacteria to move in random directions and search for nutrients.

- **Swarming:** When any one of the bacteria reaches the better location, it should attract other bacteria so that they converge in that location. In order to meet these criteria, the E. coli cells provide an attraction signal to each other so that they swarm together. The swarming pattern seems to form based on dominance of the two stimuli (cell-to cell signaling and foraging). This can be achieved by a cost function adjustment based upon the relative distances of each bacterium from the fittest bacterium. When all the bacteria have merged into the solution point this adjustment is no more to be performed. The effect of swarming is to make the bacteria congregate into groups and move as concentric patterns with high bacterial density.

- **Reproduction:** After the end of chemotaxis event the final population of bacteria undergoes the reproduction stage, where the least healthy bacteria die and the other healthiest bacteria split into two at the same location thus ensuring that the population of the bacteria remains constant.

- **Elimination and Dispersal:** A gradual or sudden changes in the location may occur due to consumption of nutrients or some other influence. This may cause the elimination of a set of bacteria and/or disperse them to a new environment. This reduces the chances of convergence at local optima location.

The Bacterial Foraging Algorithm

Step1: Initialization

a. Number of bacteria (S).

b. Number of parameters (p) to be optimized.

c. Swimming length (Ns) is the maximum number of steps taken by each bacterium when it moves from low nutrient area to high nutrient area.

d. Nc is the number of chemotactic steps taken by each bacterium before reproduction (Nc >Ns).

e. Nre and Ned are the number of reproduction and elimination dispersal events.

f. Ped is the probability of elimination and dispersal.

g. Specifying the location of the initial position of bacteria by random numbers on [0, 1].

h. The values of $d_{attract}$, $\omega_{attract}$, $h_{repellent}$, and $\omega_{repellent}$.

i. Random swim direction vector $\Delta(i)$ and run length vector C(i) = [C(1); C(2); … C(p)],where C(1), C(2),.., C(p) are the run length vector corresponding to the each parameter respectively.

Step2: Iterative Algorithm for Optimization

This explains the main part of the algorithm, i.e., evaluation of chemotaxis, swarming, reproduction, elimination and dispersal process. It starts with the calculation of *J error* for the initial bacterial population inside the innermost chemotaxis loop. Any i^{th} bacteria at the jth chemotactic, k^{th} reproduction and l^{th} elimination stage is represented by $\theta^i(j,k,l)$ and its corresponding error value is given by *J error* (*i, j, k, l*). (Initially, *j=k=l=0*).

The algorithm works as follows.

1. Starting of the Elimination-dispersal loop (*l=l+1*)

2. Starting of the Reproduction loop (*k=k+1*)

3. Starting of the chemotaxis loop (*j=j+1*)
   a. For all *i* = 1, 2, …, S, calculate *J error* (*i, j, k, l*)
   b. *J error* (*i, j, k, l*) is saved as *J errorold* so as to compare with other *J error* values.

c. Tumble: Generate a random vector $\Delta(i) \in R^p$ with each element being a random number in the range [-1,1].

d. Move:

$$\theta^i(j+1,k,l) = \theta^i(j,k,l) + C(i)\frac{\Delta(i)}{\sqrt{\Delta(i)^T \Delta(i)}}$$

(1)

This results in a step size *C(i)* in the direction of the tumble for i^{th} bacterium.

e. Calculate *J error* (*i, j+1, k, l*)

f. Swimming loop:
   Let m = 0 (counter for swim length)
   While m < N_s
   m = m+1;
   If *J error* (*i, j+1, k, l*) < *J errorold*, then *J errorold* = *J error* (*i, j+1, k, l*) and

$$\theta^i(j+1,k,l) = \theta^i(j+1,k,l) + C(i)\frac{\Delta(i)}{\sqrt{\Delta(i)^T \Delta(i)}}$$

(2)

This $\theta^i(j+1,k,l)$ is then used to calculate new *J error* (*i, j+1, k, l*).
   Else m = N_s

g. Go to the next bacterium (*i*+1) till all the bacteria undergo chemotaxis.

4. If *j* <Nc, go to step 3 and continue chemotaxis since the life of bacteria is not over else continue.

5. Reproduction:
   a. For the given *k* and *l*, and for each *i* = 1,2,...S, let $J^i_{health} = \sum_{j=1}^{Nc+1} J_{error}(i,j,k,l)$
   be the health of *i*th bacterium. The bacteria are sorted according to ascending order of J_{health}.
   b. The bacteria with the highest J_{health} values die and those with minimum values split and the copies that are

made already, now placed at the same location as their parent.

6. If k <Nre go to step 3 to start the next generation in the chemotactic loop else go to step 7.

7. Elimination - dispersal: For i = 1, 2 ...S, a random number is generated and if it is less than or equal to Ped, then that bacterium is dispersed to a new random location else it remains at its original location.

8. If l <Ned go to step 2 else stop.

Step3: An Adaptive Strategy for Run Length Vector

The run length vector $C(i)$ plays an important role in the convergence of bacterial foraging. A small value of $C(i)$ causes slow convergence whereas a large value may fail to locate the minima by swimming through them without stopping. A careful selection of $C(i)$ has to be, therefore, done. Here an adaptive scheme to update $C(i)$ is used which ensures the convergence of bacterial foraging algorithm. Initially assuming the $C(i)$ as 0.05 and during the evaluations it will be reduced as given in following steps.

Steps of Adaptive strategy:

a. Assume $C(i)$ = 0.05.

b. Run the chemotaxis stage.

c. Now adjust the runlength $C(i)$=min{$(C(i)$ − 0.0005),0.00001}.

d. Do steps (b) and (c) until all elimination and dispersal as well as reproduction stages are completed.

Particle Swarm Optimization (PSO)

J.Kennedy and R.C.Eberhart introduce a concept for the optimization of nonlinear functions using particle swarm methodology. The performance of particle swarm optimization using an inertia weight is compared with performance using a constriction factor is also explained. Similar to other evolutionary algorithms, the Particle Swarm Optimization method conducts search using a population of particles, corresponding to individuals. Each particle in the swarm represents a candidate solution to the problem. It starts with a random initialization of a population of individuals in the search space and works on the social behavior of the particles in the swarm like bird flocking, fish schooling and the swarm theory. Therefore, it finds the global optimum by simply adjusting the trajectory of each individual towards its own best location and towards the best particle of the swarm at each generation of evolution. However, the trajectory of each individual in the search space is adjusted by dynamically altering the velocity of each particle, according to the flying experience of its own and the other particles in the search space.

Classical PSO Algorithm

The position and the velocity of the ith particle in the d-dimensional search space can be represented as Xi = $[x_{i1}, x_{i2}, ..., x_{id}]^T$ and Vi = $[v_{i1}, v_{i2}, ..., v_{id}]^T$, respectively. Each particle has its own best position (pbest) Pi(t) = $[p_{i1}(t), p_{i2}(t), ..., p_{id}(t)]^T$ corresponding to the personal best objective value obtained so far at generation 't'. The global best particle (Gbest) is denoted by Pg(t) = $[p_{g1}(t), p_{g2}(t), ..., p_{gd}(t)]^T$, which represents the best particle found so far at generation 't' in the entire swarm. The new velocity of each particle is calculated as follows:

$$v_{ij}(t+1) = \omega v_{ij}(t) + c_1 r_1 \left(p_{ij}(t) - x_{ij}(t) \right) + c_2 r_2 \left(p_{gj}(t) - x_{ij}(t) \right)$$

$$j = 1, 2, ..., d; \quad i = 1, 2, ..., n \qquad (3)$$

Where c_1 and c_2 are constants named acceleration coefficients corresponding to the cognitive and social behavior, ω is called the inertia factor, n is the population size, r_1 and r_2 are two independent random numbers uniformly distributed in the range of [0, 1]. Thus, the position of each particle at each generation is updated according to the following equation:

$$x_{ij}(t+1) = x_{ij}(t) + v_{ij}(t+1)$$
$$i = 1, 2, \ldots \ldots n \quad and \quad j = 1, 2, \ldots \ldots d \tag{4}$$

Equation (3) shows that the new velocity is updated according to its previous velocity and to the distance of its current position from both its best historical position and the global best position of the swarm. Generally, the value of each component in V_i can be clamped to the range $[V_{imin}, V_{imax}]$ to control excessive roaming of particles outside the search space $[X_{imin}, X_{imax}]$. Then the particle flies towards a new position according to eqn (4). The process is repeated until a user-defined stopping criterion is reached. During the iterative process the value of ω is reduced from ω_{max} to ω_{min}. This strategy is called as time varying inertia weight.

Constriction Based PSO Algorithm

The modification of classical PSO algorithm for dynamic adaptation of range is given by Eberhard and Shi (Eberhart & Shi, 2000). The method of incorporating the constriction factor is mentioned in eqn (5), where k is a function of c_1 and c_2 as illustrated in eqn (6).

$$v_{ij}(t+1) =$$
$$k\left(v_{ij}(t) + c_1 r_1\left(p_{ij}(t) - x_{ij}(t)\right) + c_2 r_2\left(p_{gj}(t) - x_{ij}(t)\right)\right) j \backslash$$
$$= 1, 2, \ldots, d; i = 1, 2 \ldots, n \tag{5}$$

$$k = \frac{k1}{\left|2 - \phi - \sqrt{\phi^2 - 4\phi}\right|}; k1 = 2, \phi = c_1 + c_2, \phi > 4. \tag{6}$$

Adaptive PSO Algorithm

In simple PSO method the inertia weight is made constant for all the particles in a single generation. But the most important parameter that moves the current position towards the optimum position is inertia weight (ω). In order to increase the search ability, the algorithm should be redefined in the manner that the movement of swarm should be controlled by the objective function. In our Adaptive PSO, the particle position is adjusted such that the highly fitted particle (best particle) moves slowly when compared to the low fitted particle. This can be achieved by selecting different ω values for each particle according to their rank, between ω_{min} and ω_{max} as in the following form.

$$\omega_i = \omega_{min} + \left(\omega_{max} - \omega_{min}\right) * \frac{Rank_i}{Total\ Population} \tag{7}$$

So from (7) it can be interpreted that the best particle takes the first rank and inertia weight for that particle is set to minimum value and for the lowest fitted particle it will take the maximum of inertia weight and makes that particle to move with a high velocity. The velocity of each particle is updated using (8), and if any updated velocity goes beyond v_{max}, then limit it to v_{max} using (9).

$$v_{ij}(t+1) = \omega_i v_{ij}(t) + c_1 r_1 (p_{ij}(t) - x_{ij}(t)) + c_2 r_2 (p_{gj}(t) - x_{ij}(t)) \tag{8}$$

$$v_{ij}(t+1) = sign(v_{ij}(t+1)) * \min\left(\left|v_{ij}(t+1)\right|, V_{jmax}\right)$$

$$j = 1, 2, \ldots, d; \quad i = 1, 2, \ldots, n \tag{9}$$

The new particle position is obtained by using the (10) and if any particle position goes beyond the range specified, then it is adjusted to its boundary using (11).

$$x_{ij}(t+1) = x_{ij}(t) + v_{ij}(t+1), j=1,2,\ldots,d; i=1,2,\ldots n \tag{10}$$

$$x_{ij}(t+1) = \min(x_{ij}(t+1), range_{jmax}) \; x_{ij}(t+1) = \max(x_{ij}(t+1), range_{jmin}) \tag{11}$$

The concept of re-initialization is introduced to the proposed APSO algorithm after a specific number of generations if there is no improvement in the convergence of the algorithm. The population of the proposed APSO at the end of the above mentioned specific generation is re-initialized with new randomly generated individuals. The number of this new individuals is selected from k least fit individuals of the original population, where 'k' is the percentage of total population to be changed. This effect of population re-initialization is in a sense similar to the mutation operator in GA (Koumousis & Katsaras, 2006). This effect is favorable when the algorithm prematurely converges to a local optimum and further improvement is not noticeable. This re-initialization of population is performed after checking the changes in 'Fbest' value in each and every specific number of generations.

The Procedure of Adaptive PSO

Step 1: Get the input parameters like range [min max] for each variables, c_1, c_2, samples of the signal, Iteration counter=0, V_{max}, ω_{min} and ω_{max}.

Step 2: Initialize n number of population of particles of dimension d with random positions and velocities.

Step 3: Increment Iteration counter by one.

Step 4: Evaluate the fitness function of all particles in the population, find particles best position pbest of each particle and update its objective value. Similarly find the global best position among all particles and update its objective value.

Step 5: If stopping criterion is met go to step (11). Otherwise continue.

Step 6: Evaluate the inertia factor according to (7), so that each particles movement is directly controlled by its fitness value.

Step 7: Update the velocity using (8) and correct it if $v_{new} > v_{max}$ using (9).

Step 8: Update the position of each particle according to (10) and if new position goes out of range set it to the boundary value using (11).

Step 9: The Elites are inserted in the first position of the new population in order to maintain the best particle found so far.

Step 10: For every 5 generations, this $F_{Best,new}$ value (at the end of these 5 generations) is compared with the $F_{Best,old}$ value (at the beginning of these 5 generations), if there is no noticeable change then re-initialize k % of the population. Go to step (3).

Step 11: Output the Gbest particle and its objective function value.

MATHEMATICAL FORMULATION

The aim of the present paper is to find the amplitude, phase and frequency components present in a power quality signal. As a first step to look into the problem the power quality data is prepared by either direct substitution or obtained from Matlab simulink based models or practical measured data such as available in TOPS processor (TOP). In this section the various mathematical models used for describing the voltage flicker signal, harmonic distorted signal and fault signal are explained.

Simulation of Voltage Flicker Signal (El-Naggar & AL-Hasawi, 2006)

The equation of voltage flicker signal can be represented as

$$v(t) = \left\{ A_1 + \sum_{i=1}^{m} A_{fi} \cos\left(2\pi f_{fi} t + \phi_{fi}\right) \right\} \cos\left(2\pi f_1 t + \phi_1\right) \tag{12}$$

where v(t) is the instantaneous voltage magnitude at time t, A_1, Φ_1 and f_1 are the amplitude, phase and power frequency of the fundamental component, A_{fi}, Φ_{fi} and f_{fi} are the amplitude, phase and frequency of the ith flicker component, m the number of flicker modes. Here the actual problem is to estimate the various parameters mentioned above like A_1, Φ_1, f_1, A_{fi}, Φ_{fi} and f_{fi}.

Simulation of Harmonic Voltage Signal

The harmonic voltage signal is modeled as

$$v(t) = a\,e^{-bt} + \sum_{i=1}^{m} A_i\,cos(2\pi f_i t + \phi_i) \qquad (13)$$

where i = 1 for the fundamental component and equals 2,3,..,m for harmonic components, m is the number of harmonics considered. Here also the problem is to estimate the values of different parameters present in the model i.e. a, b, A_i, Φ_i and f_i.

Simulation of Fault Signal

The fundamental model for transient system is derived as follows.

Steady state current is given by

$$i_{ss} = \frac{v}{z} \sin\left(wt + \theta - \phi\right) \qquad (14)$$

Transient current is given by

$$i_{tr} = ke^{-\frac{Rt}{L}} \qquad (15)$$

The total current now becomes

$$i = \frac{v}{z}\sin\left(wt + \theta - \phi\right) + ke^{-\frac{Rt}{L}} \qquad (16)$$

When t = 0 then current i= 0;

$$0 = \frac{v}{z}\sin\left(\theta - \phi\right) + k \qquad (17)$$

$$i = \left|\frac{v}{z}\right|\sin\left(wt + \alpha\right) + \left|\frac{v}{z}\right|\sin\left(\alpha\right)e^{-\frac{Rt}{L}} \qquad (18)$$

It can be re written as

$$i(t) = A\sin\left(wt + \alpha\right) + Be^{-\beta t} \qquad (19)$$

The above current wave can be given along with sinusoidal damped oscillation as

$$i(t) = A\sin\left(wt + \alpha\right) + Be^{-\beta t} + C\,e^{-\gamma t}\sin\left(2\pi f_{tr}t + \phi\right) \qquad (20)$$

where A, w, α, B, β, C, γ, f_{tr} and Φ are amplitude of the fundamental, frequency of the fundamental, phase of the fundamental, amplitude of the transient part, time constant of transient part, amplitude of the sinusoidal damped oscillation, time constant of damped oscillation, frequency of damped oscillation and phase of the damped oscillation respectively.

Fitness Function

Let f_s is the sampling frequency for the digital data to be collected and N is the number of data points in one cycle of the signal. The main necessity of the problem is with the available signal data we have use curve fitting concept so that the actual wave and estimated wave are exactly matching each other. The objective function for this problem can be stated as

$$Min\ J = \sqrt{\frac{\sum_{i=1}^{k}\left(s(i) - \bar{s}(i)\right)^2}{k}} \qquad (21)$$

where, k is the total number of samples (N*number of cycles considered), $s(i)$ is the actual sample value at ith time interval and $\bar{s}(i)$ is the estimated sample value calculated using any one of the above explained model.

SIMULATION RESULTS

The comparison of the results obtained from Clonalog, Bacterial Foraging and APSO for Voltage flicker signal as well as Harmonic signal is considered for this study. The algorithms for all the five methods are implemented in Matlab–7(MATLAB) programming language and the developed software program is executed on 3GHz, 512 MBRAM Pentium IV PC.

Parameter Settings for Evolutionary Algorithms

For a fair comparison of all the five methods the total number of function evaluation is made equal. All the five algorithms are terminated either when the specified number of function evaluation is exceeded or the specified tolerance limit is exceeded. The specified tolerance value for J is considered as

1e-6. The number of state variables for each case is different and is equals to the number of model parameters need to be estimated. A brief discussion regarding the selection of various variables for the evolutionary algorithms is given in Box 1.

Voltage Flicker Signal

The equation of the voltage flicker signal can be represented by

$$v(t) = A_1 \cos(2\pi f_1 t) + A_{f1} \cos(2\pi f_{f1} t) \cos(2\pi f_1 t)$$

$$(22)$$

Where, $v(t)$ is the instantaneous flicker magnitude at time 't'. A_1 is the fundamental voltage amplitude, f_1 is the fundamental power frequency, A_{f1} and f_{f1} are the amplitude and frequency of the voltage flicker. For the simulation of the voltage flicker signal the parameter values chosen are A_1=1.0, A_{f1}=0.2, f_1=50 and f_{f1}=5.

The proposed APSO algorithm was implemented for estimating the magnitude and frequency of the fundamental (A_1 and f_1), magnitude and frequency of the flicker (A_{f1} and f_{f1}) and

Box 1.

1) Classical Particle Swarm Optimization:
  Number of generations: 200
  Population size:60
  Vmax = (Max Range-Min Range)/3;
  C1=2.1; C2=2.1; ω_{min} =0.4 and ω_{max} =0.9;
  Time varying inertia weight is used here.
	2) Constriction Particle Swarm Optimization:
	  Number of generations: 200
	  Population size:60
	  Vmax = (Max Range-Min Range)/3;
	  C1=2.1; C2=2.1;

3) Adaptive Bacterial Foraging:
  Number of Bacteria S: 10 Number of chemotactic steps Nc: 5
  Swimming Length Ns: 4 Number of Reproduction steps Nre: 40
  Depth of attractant: 0.01 Width of attractant: 0.04
  Height of repellent: 0.01 Width of repellent: 10.0
  Number of Elimination and Dispersal events Ned: 6
  Probability of elimination and dispersal Ped:0.02 Run length vector initial value C(i): 0.05	

4) Clonalog:
Number of generations: 60 Number of antibodies: 40
Maximum no of clones: 10 Percentage shuffle: 0.03
Multiplication factor for reproduction: 0.1 Hyper mutation probability: 0.08
Mutation control rate: 0.8
	5) Adaptive Particle Swarm Optimization:
	Number of generations: 200
	Population size:60
	  Vmax = (Max Range – Min Range)/3;
	  C1=2.1; C2=2.1; ω_{min} =0.2 and ω_{max} =0.8;
	  Ranking based inertia weight calculation is used here.
	  Re-initialization percentage k=8%;

the result was compared with Classical PSO, Constriction PSO, CLONALOG and Adaptive Bacterial Foraging (ABF) approach. A voltage flicker signal of three cycles is simulated and all the algorithms are tested on this signal. In order to demonstrate the effectiveness of each of the evolutionary algorithm the number of samples per fundamental frequency cycle of the signal was varied. The number of samples per cycle is taken as 16, 32, 64, 128 and 256 respectively. We can obtain these samples per cycle by choosing different sampling frequency i.e. 800 Hz, 1.6 kHz, 3.2 kHz, 6.4 kHz and 12.8 kHz respectively. The estimation of parameters $A1$, A_{fl} and f_{fl} for different samples per cycle is shown in Figure 3 (a-c), and the obtained parameter values for the best case for all the five methods are compared in Table 1 for 64 sample case. The original and reconstructed waveform using APSO is shown in Figure 3(d). The convergence of performance index J for all the methods is shown in Figure 4. It is observed that APSO has a better convergence property as compared to other techniques. Table 2 and Table 3 represents the performance of all the above mentioned evolutionary techniques for estimation of amplitude and frequency of fundamental and flicker for 50 run case, where we have considered two sampling cases and it is observed that the APSO performs better than the others. As the captured power quality signals may contain noises, we have tested the proposed algorithm with flicker signal added with noise. Figure 5 shows the actual, noisy flicker signal (added with 10dB white Gaussian Noise) and estimated flicker signal using APSO. The estimated parameters of the voltage flicker signal by APSO in noisy case (with different noise levels) are reported in Table 4 for 50 different trials by means of average and standard deviations. From the results shown, it is evident that the proposed adaptive particle swarm optimization works better than other methods in all conditions.

The robustness of the proposed algorithms is evaluated by running the algorithm (to find the flicker parameters) 50 times on the same captured signal (with and without noise). Each time the estimated parameters are found out and the results of 50 runs are summarized in Table 2 – Table 4. The execution of each algorithm is stopped if the error reaches tolerance limit of 1e-6 or the algorithm is evaluated for 12000 evaluations. It is observed that the Classical PSO, Constriction PSO, Clonal algorithm and adaptive bacterial foraging are evaluated for 12000 evaluations in each case as the convergence criteria are not met, whereas the proposed APSO converges to the tolerance limit of 1e-6 within 3000 evaluations. The average error and standard deviation for these five algorithms were compared. The Adaptive Bacterial Foraging gives better results than the clonalog but APSO performs better than all other four algorithms. It is observed that APSO estimates the flicker parameters more accurately in each run.

Simulation of Harmonic Voltage Signal

The harmonic voltage signal can be modeled as

$$\nu(t) = a\, e^{-bt} + \sum_{i=1}^{m} A_i\, cos(2\pi f_i t + \phi_i) \qquad (23)$$

where i = 1 for the fundamental component and equals 2,3,..,m for harmonic components, m is the number of harmonics considered. The first part of Equation (23) represents a decaying dc component. The actual values taken for producing the test signal are as follows. a=0.2, b=0.02, A_1=1.4141, A_3=0.7071, A_5=0.3536, φ_1=60°, φ_3=30°, φ_5=25° and f_1= 50 Hz. The estimated values of different parameters of the signal (sampling frequency 3.2 kHz) for no noise case for 50 trial runs employing all the five techniques are reported in Table 5. The performance of APSO for this estimation is shown in Figure 6.

It is observed that the APSO performs better in estimating the amplitude, phase and frequency

Figure 3. Estimated value of (a) fundamental magnitude, (b) flicker magnitude, (c) flicker frequency, and (d) actual and estimated voltage flicker signal

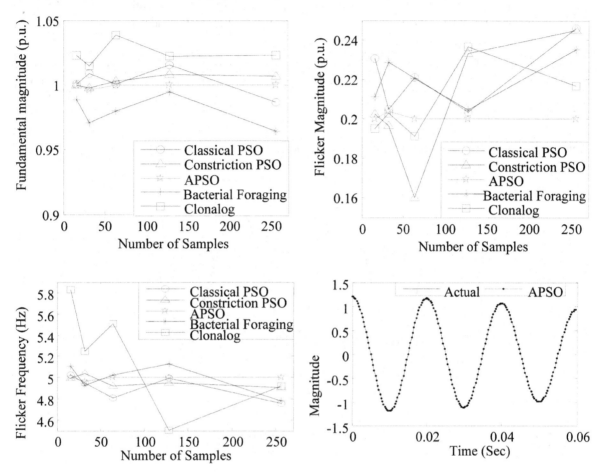

Figure 4. Comparison of error for different schemes without noise

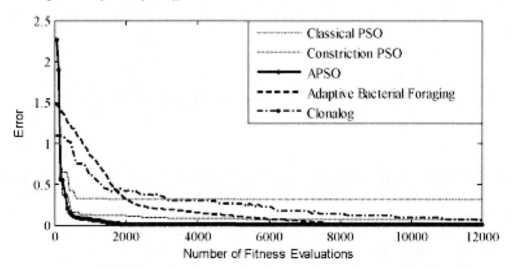

Table1. Comparison of estimated values for flicker signal [for 64 samples - best]

Parameter	Actual Value	Classical PSO		Constriction PSO		Clonalog		ABF		APSO	
		Est.	Err %	Est.	Err %	Est.	Err %	Est.	Est.	Err %	Est.
A_1	1	1.0003	0.03	0.99919	0.081	0.9812	1.88	1	0.00	1	0.00
A_{fl}	0.2	0.19772	1.14	0.20286	1.43	0.19868	0.66	0.20025	0.125	0.2	0.00
f_1	50	50.0	0.00	50.001	0.002	50.062	0.124	50	0.00	50	0.00
f_{fl}	5	5.0012	0.024	5.022	0.44	5.4066	8.132	5.0028	0.056	5	0.00

Figure 5. Estimated voltage flicker signal for 10dB noise

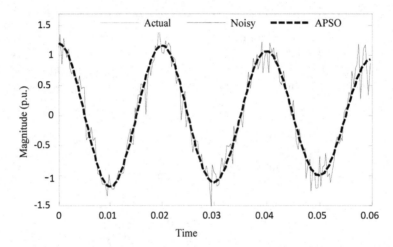

Figure 6. Error plot showing the best along with average error for 32 sample harmonic case

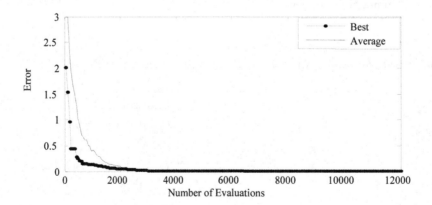

of the fundamental as well as of the harmonics more accurately than the other methods. The estimated parameters of the harmonic distorted signal in noisy case using APSO are reported in Table 6. To compare the performance of the pro-posed algorithm the test signal is mixed with different noise levels and the test signal is obtained having different SNRs. For each noisy signal having a particular value of SNR the algorithm is tested for 50 trial runs.

Table 2. Comparison of estimated values for flicker signal [for 64 samples – 50 trials]

Parameter	Actual Value	Classical PSO		Constriction PSO		Clonalog		ABF		APSO	
		Avg.	Std.	Avg.	Std.	Avg.	Std.	Avg.	Std.	Avg.	Std.
A_1	1	0.98762	0.069211	0.98197	0.073025	1.0383	0.069682	0.97992	0.079846	1	6.2084e-006
A_n	0.2	0.19594	0.087787	0.20738	0.074529	0.19136	0.061712	0.2203	0.077235	0.2	5.887e-006
f_1	50	50.001	0.0044744	50	0.0034985	50.001	0.060132	50	0.001806	50	1.4868e-006
f_n	5	5.3883	1.9836	4.9828	2.0213	5.5073	1.7426	5.0213	0.98594	5	9.8858e-005
Error	0	0.089926	0.11882	0.097265	0.10802	0.010552	0.0040875	0.0033818	0.001467	7.8828e-007	1.6391e-007

Table 3. Performance comparison of different methods for voltage flicker signal [32 sample case – 50 trials]

Parameter	Actual Value	Classical PSO		Constriction PSO		Clonalog		ABF		APSO	
		Avg.	Std.	Avg.	Std.	Avg.	Std.	Avg.	Std.	Avg.	Std.
A_1	1	0.98222	0.085965	0.9668	0.096224	1.0145	0.075902	0.97117	0.082675	0.99599	0.028322
A_n	0.2	0.20674	0.079563	0.20166	0.077961	0.20295	0.064052	0.22901	0.079764	0.20393	0.027766
f_1	50	50	0.004775	50.002	0.0084158	50.003	0.067279	50	0.0023624	50	0.00029168
f_n	5	5.1697	2.0162	4.8256	2.2467	5.2465	1.4036	4.9286	1.0476	4.9662	0.23916
Error	0	0.090461	0.11559	0.10928	0.12002	0.011949	0.0055163	0.0034637	0.0017691	9.9575e-005	0.00069836

Table 4. Comparison of actual and estimated parameters of voltage flicker signal using APSO for various white gaussian noise levels (50 run average 64 sample case)

Noise level	A_1		A_n		f_1		f_n	
Actual	1		0.2		50		5	
	Avg.	Std.	Avg.	Std.	Avg.	Std.	Avg.	Std.
No Noise	1.0	6.2084e-006	0.2	5.887e-006	50	1.4868e-006	5.0	9.8858e-005
40	1.0001	5.2584e-007	0.19993	2.4344e-007	49.999	5.8508e-007	5.0001	1.9558e-006
35	0.99952	8.5965e-008	0.20019	3.2288e-008	50	8.7847e-008	5.0137	1.5223e-007
30	1.0027	1.1486e-007	0.20347	1.1202e-007	50.004	2.743e-008	4.9678	3.6405e-007
25	0.99821	4.6364e-008	0.19602	4.8504e-008	49.995	5.0781e-008	4.9849	5.7359e-007
20	1.0024	1.0221e-005	0.21658	1.8489e-005	49.989	1.6577e-005	4.8767	0.0002167
15	1.0165	0.00036505	0.18858	0.00038712	49.991	0.00031523	5.1145	0.0032948
10	1.0166	0.0042793	0.18137	0.01099	49.999	0.0012695	5.0562	0.038491
5	1.0113	0.0014326	0.19799	0.0023567	49.963	0.00098063	4.9699	0.013871

Table 5. Estimated values of amplitude, phase and frequency of harmonicsignal [64 Samples]

Parameter	Act. Val	Classical PSO		Constriction PSO		Clonalog		ABF		APSO	
		Avg.	Std.	Avg.	Std.	Avg.	Std.	Avg.	Std.	Avg.	Std.
a	0.2	0.20577	0.022937	0.20168	0.0037666	0.20476	0.027234	0.19974	0.014839	0.2049	0.032094
b	0.02	0.027749	0.011801	0.029001	0.010295	0.019957	0.011727	0.020104	0.011717	0.023151	0.0088
A_1	1.4141	1.4162	0.0051283	1.4152	0.0023114	1.423	0.049616	1.3578	0.2801	1.4126	0.0066409
A_3	0.7071	0.60866	0.24814	0.6072	0.2475	0.69883	0.03465	0.55087	0.29556	0.70824	0.0072399
A_5	0.3536	0.21939	0.17355	0.26887	0.15264	0.33799	0.04867	0.27662	0.14868	0.35224	0.0092799
Φ_1	60	60.825	1.4978	60.697	1.585	60.554	3.1475	51.046	46.58	59.996	0.23239
Φ_3	30	31.355	66.173	15.245	71.474	29.415	9.8675	6.9282	69.631	30.032	0.66971
Φ_5	25	-12.43	105.56	24	72.202	23.346	16.888	-4.0539	67.447	25.34	3.0236
f_1	50	49.924	0.13327	49.938	0.14882	49.993	0.20717	49.967	0.14854	49.999	0.027014
Error	0	0.27424	0.32197	0.20214	0.33249	0.18054	0.085939	0.21880	0.12431	0.032556	0.11064

Table 6. Comparison of actual and estimated parameters of harmonic signal using APSO for various white gaussian noise levels [64 sample]

Parameters		Actual	No Noise	40	35	30	25	20	15	10	5
						Noise Level					
a	Avg.	0.2	0.2049	0.23073	0.24232	0.19174	0.2383	0.2521	0.23088	0.19694	0.16271
	Std.		0.032094	0.054067	0.055925	0.049982	0.052024	0.040674	0.048351	0.043327	0.049637
b	Avg.	0.02	0.023151	0.026578	0.025676	0.024282	0.025174	0.025466	0.025437	0.022418	0.022652
	Std.		0.0088	0.0078114	0.0078663	0.0087705	0.0079121	0.006941	0.0082091	0.008561	0.009133
A_1	Avg.	1.4141	1.4126	1.3824	1.3773	1.3871	1.3803	1.3733	1.374	1.3661	1.3337
	Std.		0.0066409	0.029315	0.037271	0.033675	0.030711	0.029102	0.03357	0.03097	0.027758
A_3	Avg.	0.7071	0.70824	0.68717	0.67787	0.68283	0.67279	0.67302	0.69498	0.68584	0.67995
	Std.		0.0072399	0.03929	0.045604	0.04602	0.047797	0.050919	0.037631	0.05751	0.041785
A_5	Avg.	0.3536	0.35224	0.31379	0.34081	0.31361	0.32706	0.3443	0.34353	0.33374	0.26256
	Std.		0.0092799	0.080645	0.066823	0.082746	0.063016	0.051512	0.068691	0.073996	0.10319
Φ_1	Avg.	60	59.996	60.494	60.585	60.175	59.711	60.268	59.135	61.528	58.439
	Std.		0.23239	2.0203	1.4281	1.5523	1.4174	2.1747	1.5716	1.6806	2.0672
Φ_3	Avg.	30	30.032	31.72	31.353	32.127	29.943	30.141	29.396	32.572	29.618
	Std.		0.66971	6.6395	4.872	5.2399	4.4954	6.1707	4.8063	4.7084	5.9148
Φ_5	Avg.	25	25.34	27.008	23.909	28.98	29.021	24.863	21.969	22.549	18.824
	Std.		3.0236	35.653	32.296	32.281	26.236	17.586	25.874	26.369	49.704
f_1	Avg.	50	49.999	49.985	49.988	49.988	49.999	50.001	50.014	49.972	50.008
	Std.		0.027014	0.053343	0.039734	0.040265	0.037372	0.054872	0.041369	0.039507	0.049177

Figure 7. Waveform of test signals with (a) 10dB noise, (b) 20 dB noise, (c) 30dB noise, and (d) 40 dB noise

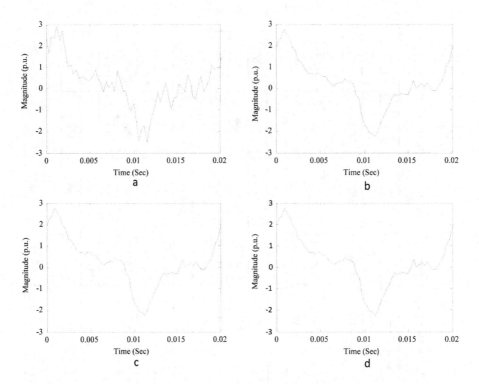

Figure 8. Waveform of actual and estimated harmonic signals with (a) 10dB noise, (b) 20 dB noise, (c) 30dB noise, and (d) 40 dB noise

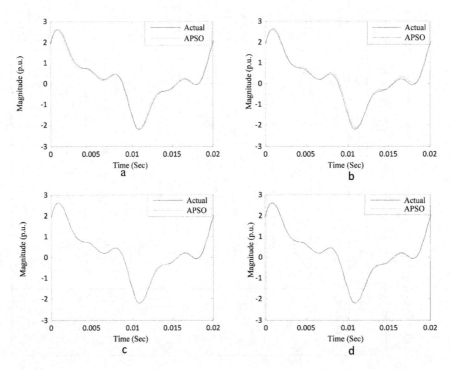

Figure 7 represents the noisy harmonic signal of one cycle fundamental frequency at different noise levels (SNR 10 dB to 40 dB) and the sampling frequency of the signal is 3.2 kHz. The proposed APSO algorithm was applied to the noisy signal and the estimated and actual signals are plotted in Figure 8 for all the 4 cases of noise. It is observed that the proposed approach is an efficient one in estimating the signal more accurately i.e., the amplitude, phase and frequency of the fundamental and harmonics are estimated more accurately. Mostly in relaying application, the power system engineers are interested in extracting the magnitude and phase of fundamental more precisely from a harmonic distorted signal and sometimes the signal containing a decaying dc component.

Figure 9 demonstrates the extraction (estimation) of the fundamental component from the harmonic distorted signal containing a decaying dc component (as described in Equation 12). It is

observed that the amplitude and phase of the fundamental are estimated almost having an accuracy of 100% up to SNR of 20 dB. But in the case of SNR 10 dB although the amplitude is extracted more accurately there is an error of phase estimation within 4%. Figure 10 demonstrates the estimation of magnitude and phase of the fundamental as well as the harmonics for a 50 run case using APSO.

For testing the proposed APSO algorithm for higher harmonics the following equation is consider for producing the data samples and the sampled datas are collected at 64 samples / cycle.

$$v(t) = 1.0 \, s \in (\omega t + 10°) + 0.1 \, s \in (3\omega t + 20°)$$
$$+0.08 \, s \in (5\omega t + 30°)$$

$$(24)$$

Figure 9. Waveform of actual and estimated harmonic signals of fundamental with (a) 10dB noise, (b) 20 dB noise, (c) 30dB noise, and (d) 40 dB noise (a) (b)

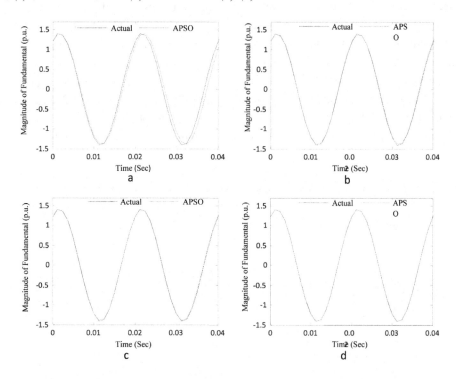

Table 7.Estimation of harmonic magnitude and phase angles

Order of Harmonic	Actual Magnitude	Estimated Magnitude	Actual phase	Estimated phase
1	1	0.9985	10	9.9547
3	0.1	.099	20	20.0012
5	0.08	0.08001	30	29.9967
9	0.08	0.079954	40	40.001
11	0.06	0.06097	50	49.9982
13	0.05	0.050019	60	60.0027
19	0.03	0.029914	70	69.99127

The actual and estimated waveforms are shown in Figure 11 and the estimated values are given in Table 7.

Simulation for Practical Fault Signal

To demonstrate the efficacy of the proposed algorithm a practical system is considered as shown in Figure 12. The system consists of two 100MVA, 230Kv voltage sources, two 5MW loads, one 10 MW loads, three pi-section model of transmission lines, one fault simulation block and one three phase measurement unit. The various types of faults are created and the data is stored. The types of faults simulated are Line-Ground fault (LG) occurs between phase *a* and ground, Line-Line fault (LL) occurs between phases *a* and *b*, Line-Line-Ground fault (LLG) occurs between phases

a, *b* and ground and three phase symmetrical fault (LLLG) occurs between all three phases and ground. The model used here is

$$i(t) = A\sin(wt + \alpha) + Be^{-\beta t} + C\,e^{-\gamma t}\sin(2\pi f_{tr} t + \phi) \quad (25)$$

where A, w, α, B, β, C, γ, f_{tr} and Φ are amplitude of the fundamental, frequency of the fundamental, phase of the fundamental, amplitude of the transient part, time constant of transient part, amplitude of the sinusoidal damped oscillation, time constant of damped oscillation, frequency of damped oscillation and phase of the damped oscillation respectively. The estimated value of each parameter is listed in Table 8. The actual and estimated waveforms are compared in Figures 13-16.

The applicability of the algorithm for practically measured data is tested with the captured signal in the laboratory. Three phase voltage signal is captured with a sampling frequency of 800 Hz (16 samples per cycle) and the signal is presented in Figure 17. The estimated values of fundamental magnitude, phase and frequency is reported in Table 9. It is observed that the maximum amplitude of all the three phase voltages is 1 and having a phase difference of 120°. The maximum amplitude, phase and frequency errors are 0.2%, 0.11% and 0.002% respectively.

A three phase fault is simulated in a power system using MATLAB SIMULINK and the noisy

Figure 10. (a)Estimated magnitudes and (b) estimated angles of 1ˢᵗ, 3ʳᵈ & 5ᵗʰ harmonic

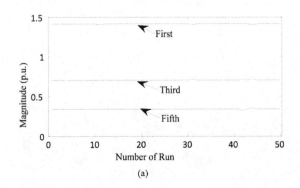

(a)

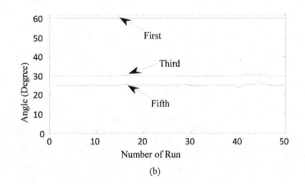

(b)

Figure 11. Estimated harmonic voltage signal

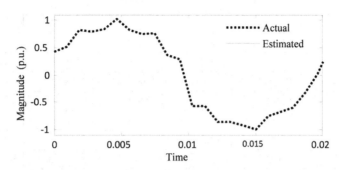

Figure 12. Simulink model for transmission line fault simulation

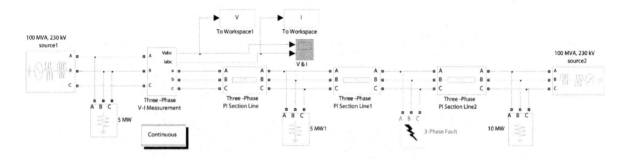

Figure 13. Waveform comparison of actual and estimated signal for LG fault

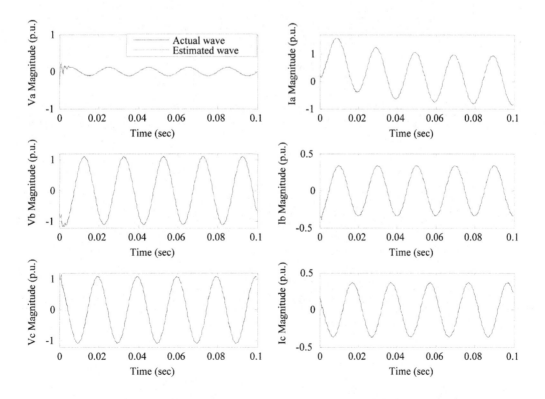

Table 8. Estimation of parameters for fault case

Type of Fault	Parameter	Va	Vb	Vc	Ia	Ib	Ic
LG	A	0.1115	1.0995	1.0802	0.8801	0.3391	0.3664
	F	50.0325	50.0022	49.9858	49.9986	49.9878	50.0091
	α	355.5940	222.1661	100.3534	286.0845	271.7956	145.3448
	B	0.0344	0.0530	0.0034	0.9580	-0.0588	-0.0735
	β	622.3423	738.1532	642.9910	35.3326	691.8682	816.0385
	C	0.3853	-0.1634	0.0840	-0.0635	0.0428	0.0693
	γ	676.5289	743.1146	233.6615	563.3953	540.0993	909.2090
	f_{tr}	513.4765	746.2867	923.1752	300.4111	547.0556	553.3881
	Φ	312.6179	132.1115	115.1813	344.4308	38.5315	132.6811
LL	A	0.5282	0.5756	1.1009	0.9925	0.0641	0.0363
	F	49.9933	50.0005	49.9995	50.0003	5.0000	5.0000
	α	285.2029	276.9820	100.8831	317.6066	13.0936	14.9683
	B	-0.0231	0.0104	0.0002	0.8727	-0.0873	-0.0000
	β	571.0527	434.1753	633.0298	30.5468	3.0517	20.6414
	C	-0.2473	0.2109	-0.0000	-0.0465	0.0057	0.0000
	γ	634.4634	447.6785	578.0172	510.7549	100.0000	100.0000
	f_{tr}	741.5216	729.2935	966.3133	728.2396	83.2336	44.8656
	Φ	79.4141	211.4628	144.7883	270.8200	18.2548	25.2804
LLG	A	0.0788	0.1110	1.0765	0.9288	0.0899	0.3418
	F	50.0577	50.0053	49.9702	49.9993	5.0003	50.0046
	α	320.9305	268.3153	102.0928	288.6774	16.2181	147.0353
	B	0.0432	0.0649	0.2905	1.0091	-0.0735	-0.0923
	β	630.7249	621.3196	999.9991	31.4223	2.9117	646.3531
	C	-0.4201	-0.7965	-0.4154	-0.1045	0.0165	-0.1324
	γ	565.2868	978.2782	820.4448	762.2282	100.0000	849.5466
	f_{tr}	501.0285	546.1347	570.1226	501.3165	54.7048	481.1212
	Φ	308.7622	51.3692	94.9587	242.2986	35.2527	142.0768
LLLG	A	0.0517	0.0525	0.0523	0.9425	0.9423	0.9426
	F	50.1850	50.1039	50.1251	50.0005	49.9995	49.9964
	α	7.8420	250.4429	129.5231	284.9090	164.9730	45.0161
	B	0.0275	0.0461	-0.0697	1.0172	-0.7284	-0.2943
	β	827.5786	795.3254	948.7028	30.5535	30.5769	32.0929
	C	0.4355	0.8181	1.2250	0.0924	0.1678	-0.2441
	γ	449.0178	440.1160	430.8368	523.0563	440.2158	417.8889
	f_{tr}	727.3680	730.4324	728.4409	727.7602	726.5338	728.2801
	Φ	237.1608	98.6396	359.5012	126.8449	0.9413	214.6550

Figure 14. Waveform comparison of actual and estimated signal for LL fault

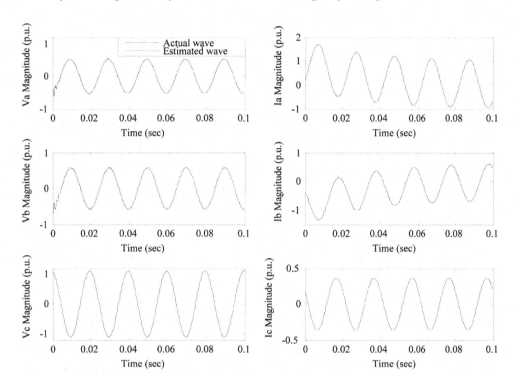

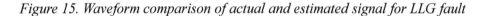

Figure 15. Waveform comparison of actual and estimated signal for LLG fault

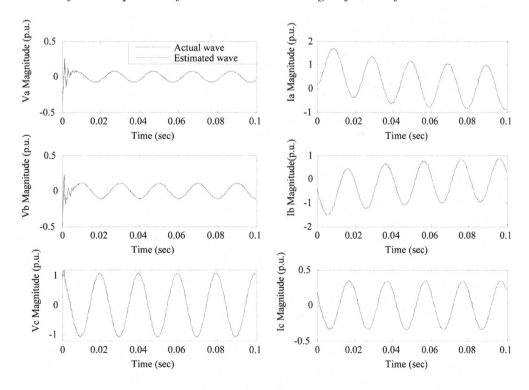

Figure 16. Waveform comparison of actual and estimated signal for LLLG fault

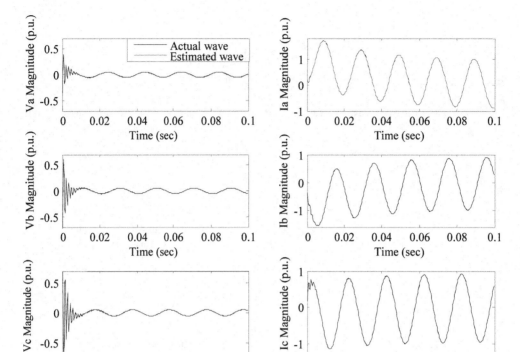

Figure 17. Practical voltage signal

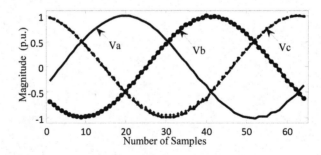

Figure 18. Actual and estimated signal for phase-A

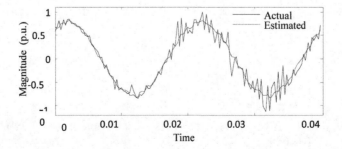

Figure 19. Actual and estimated signal for phase-B

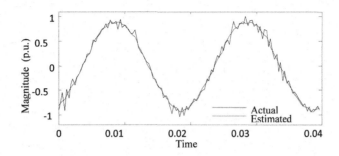

Figure 20. Actual and estimated signal for phase-C

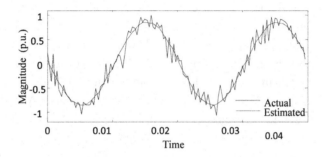

Figure 21. Actual and estimated wave comparison for real measurement

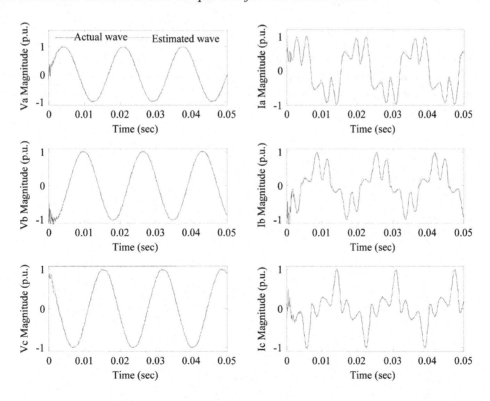

Table 9. Estimated values of amplitude, phase and frequency for practical data

Parameter	APSO		
	V_a	V_b	V_c
A_1	1.00	0.998	0.9993
Φ_1	-15.75	-135.8	104.33
f_1	49.99	49.99	50.01

Table 10. Estimated values for real noisy data

Parameter	Phase A	Phase B	Phase C
A_1	0.7816	0.9022	0.8531
f_1	50.065	50.023	49.969
Φ_1	54.814	-65.757	174.717

data of the three phase voltages are sampled at 6.4 kHz. The proposed algorithm is applied to the data of two fundamental cycles after the inception of the fault for the extraction of frequency, phase and amplitude. The results are demonstrated in Figures 18 to 20 and also reported in Table 10.

To show the performance of the algorithm for the practical measurement the real measured data given in TOPS software (TOP) is considered. The actual and estimated waveform for this case is shown in Figure 21. and the values are listed in Table 11.

Simulation for Practical Arc Furnace Signal

The estimation of parameters present in the arc signal is not so easy, since it may contain flicker and inter harmonic components along with the normal nth order harmonic components. There is no exact model representing the arc signal because of its characteristics are continuously varying with time. In this section before going to the estimation of parameters in real arc data given in TOPS software (TOP) we firstly estimated the parameters of generated data for inter harmonics obtained by direct substitution.

The model used in this case has dc decaying component a=0.2 p.u., b=0.02 p.u., fundamental harmonic component A_1= p.u., f_1= Hz and Φ_1=60°, third harmonic component A_3=0.3536 p.u., f_3=150 Hz and Φ_3=25°, and inter harmonic component A_{i1}= 0.7071p.u., f_{i1}= 75Hz and Φ_{i1}= 30°. The actual and estimated waveform for this case is shown in Figure 22 and the estimated values are listed in Table 12.

The flicker model is also included in the above for estimating the parameters present in the real arc furnace data given in TOPS software. The estimated values of various parameters are listed

Figure 22. Actual and estimated wave comparison for inter harmonic case

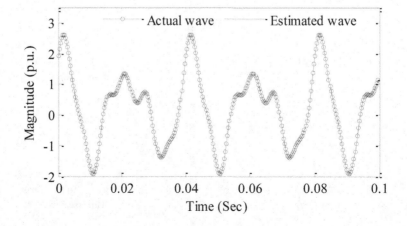

Table 11. Estimated parameter values for real data

Parameter	Va	Vb	Vc	Ia	Ib	Ic
a	0.009636	2.633e-006	2.8586e-011	0.015727	0.019098	0
b	0.0189	0.0156	5.6815e-006	0.0068783	0.018002	0.016933
A_1	0.99573	1.0139	1.0139	0.75003	0.62963	0.46265
A_3	9.4873e-010	8.2997e-014	7.1818e-005	0.20635	0	0.20292
A_5	1.5725e-009	2.596e-016	9.3996e-007	0.34452	0.30481	0.28569
A_7	0.0016255	0.0046024	0.001357	0.11987	0.083647	0.11447
A_9	0	0	4.4226e-006	5.776e-014	0	7.2489e-017
f_1	60.049	59.986	59.907	59.811	60.11	59.862
Φ_1	2.8325e-007	240.6	121.56	24.854	250.72	161.78
Φ_3	9.901	360	321.18	98.093	262.32	256.69
Φ_5	134.38	360	165.29	171.46	271.7	34.639
Φ_7	40.381	201	135.38	0	182.97	106.08
Φ_9	350.91	228.93	360	2.1917e-010	166.12	285.88
C	-0.34807	0.49938	0.5	0.36937	0.44016	-0.4761
γ	997.92	1000	993.89	1000	1000	1000
f_{tr}	1500	1500	100	626.21	914.38	380.79
Φ	3.3131	358.06	219.78	360	358.12	360

Table 12. Estimated parameter values for inter harmonic case

Parameter	a	b	A_1	f_1	Φ_1	A_3	f_3	Φ_3	A_{i1}	f_{i1}	Φ_{i1}
Value	0.1996	0.0212	1.4154	49.9981	60.0823	0.3529	149.9746	25.3526	0.7067	75.0186	29.6866

Figure 23. Actual and estimated waveform for arc signal

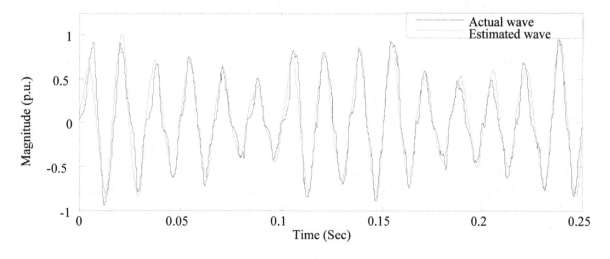

Table 13. Estimated parameter values for arc data

Parameter	a	b	A_1	A_3	f_1	f_3	Φ_1	Φ_3	A_{i1}	A_{i2}
Value	0.0352	0.0081	0.6203	0.0521	59.7581	179.274	0	113.5865	0.0419	0.0787
Parameter	A_{i3}	f_{i1}	f_{i2}	f_{i3}	Φ_{i1}	Φ_{i2}	Φ_{i3}	A_{f1}	f_{f1}	Φ_{f1}
Value	0.0362	35.4925	82.009	91.7741	195.16	192.748	122.267	0.0014	9.082	0

Table 14. Kruskal Wallis test result of APSO versus

Case	Classical PSO	Constriction PSO	Clonalog	ABF
Flicker 64 sample	4.0880e-011	1.1546e-014	3.3751e-014	1.5543e-015

in Table 13 and wave form comparison is shown in Figure 23.

STATISTICAL ANALYSIS

When conducting some experiments with several approaches, we often want to compare the performance of the methods that we used. It can be achieved by using some statistical methods that conclude that whether there is some significant difference between the methods or not. The Kruskal Wallis test is a non-parametric alternative to the one-way independent sample test ANOVA and it is an extension of Wilcoxon test. The standard command line function available in Matlab is used to perform the Kruskal Wallis test. The function takes the samples as input and returns the probability value p. The standard level of significance is 5%. If $p < 0.05$, indicating that the difference is significant. For null hypothesis, the test gives the p value as 1, since all the samples are identical. The error values obtained for the flicker signal of 64 sample case by APSO in 50 trials are compared with the result of other methods using Kruskal Wallis test and obtained p values are reported in Table 14. The values in table lead the conclusion that the proposed method is significantly different from others.

CONCLUSION

This paper presents a new approach based on an evolutionary optimization algorithm based on Adaptive Particle Swarm Optimization (APSO) to estimate the magnitude, phase and frequency of flicker and harmonic distorted power quality signal. Several experiments were performed and compared with the other evolutionary algorithms like classical PSO, constriction PSO, Clonal Algorithm and Adaptive Bacterial Foraging. It is observed that the proposed algorithm is able to extract different parameters of the power quality signal more accurately for the pure as well as noisy signals. The effect of sampling frequency and noise present in the measured signal are studied with the proposed algorithm and observed that the APSO is more robust than the other methods. Furthermore, it is observed that the algorithm is more robust in the presence of severe noise conditions and decaying DC component.

ACKNOWLEDGMENT

The authors acknowledge the financial support by the Department of Science and Technology, Government of India, for the research project SR/S3/EECE/46/2007.

REFERENCES

Aghazadeh, R., Lesani, H., Sanaye-Pasand, M., & Ganji, B. (2005). New technique for frequency and amplitude Estimation of Power Signals. *IEE Proceedings. Generation, Transmission and Distribution, 152*(3), 435–440. doi:10.1049/ip-gtd:20041255

Arrillaga, J., Watson, N. R., & Chen, S. (2000). *Power System Quality Assessment.* New York: John Wiley & Sons.

Bettayeb, M., & Qidwai, Q. (2003). A Hybrid Least Squares-GA based Algorithm for Harmonic Estimation. *IEEE Transactions on Power Delivery, 18*(2), 377–382. doi:10.1109/TPWRD.2002.807458

Bollen, M. H. (2000). *Understanding Power Quality Problems: Voltage Sags and Interruptions.* New York: IEEE Press.

Castro, L. N., & Timmis, J. (2002). *Artificial Immune System: A New Computational Intelligence Approach.* New York: Springer Verlag.

Castro, L. N., & Zuben, F. J. (2002). Learning and optimization using Clonal Selection principle. *IEEE Transactions on Evolutionary Computation, 6*(3), 239–251. doi:10.1109/TEVC.2002.1011539

Chen, M. (1997). Digital Algorithms for measurements of voltage flicker. *IEE Proceedings. Generation, Transmission and Distribution, 144*(2), 175–180. doi:10.1049/ip-gtd:19970683

Dash, P. K., Jena, R. K., Panda, G., & Routray, A. (2000). An extended complex Kalman filter for frequency measurement of distorted signals. *IEEE Transactions on Instrumentation and Measurement, 49*, 746–753. doi:10.1109/19.863918

Dash, P. K., Pradhan, A. K., & Salama, M. A. (2002). Estimation of Voltage Flicker Magnitude and Frequency Using Fourier Linear Combiners to Improve Power Quality. *Electric Power Components and Systems, 29*, 1–13.

Dash, P. K., Swain, D. P., Liew, A. C., & Rahman, S. (1996). An Adaptive Linear Combiner for On-Line Tracking of Power System Harmonics. *IEEE Transactions on Power Systems, 11*(4), 1730–1735. doi:10.1109/59.544635

De Castro, L. N., & Von Zuben, F. J. (1999). *Artificial Immune Systems: Part I – Basic Theory and Applications* (Tech. Rep. No. RTDCA 01/99).

Dugan, R. C., McGranaghan, M. F., & Beaty, H. W. (2000). *Electrical Power Systems Quality.* New York: McGraw-Hill Int.

Eberhart, R. C., & Shi, Y. (2000). Comparing inertia weights and constriction factors in particle swarm optimization. In *Proceedings of the 2000 Congress on Evolutionary Computation* (Vol. 1, pp. 84-88).

Eberhart, R. C., & Shi, Y. (2001). Particle swarm optimization: developments, applications and resources. In *Proceedings of the Congress on Evolutionary Computation* (pp. 81-86). Piscataway, Soul: IEEE.

El-Naggar, K. M., & AL-Hasawi, W. M. (2006). A Genetic based algorithm for measurement of Power System Disturbances. *Electric Power Systems Research, 76*, 808–814. doi:10.1016/j.epsr.2005.06.012

El-Zonkoly, A. (2005). Power system model validation for power quality assessment applications using genetic algorithm. *Expert Systems with Applications, 29*, 941–944. doi:10.1016/j.eswa.2005.06.013

Girgis, A. A., & Ham, E. M. (1980). A Quantitive Study of Pit Falls in the FFT. *IEEE Trans. on AES, 16*(4), 434–439.

Ho, S. L., Yang, S., Ni, G., & Wong, H. C. (2006). A Particle Swarm Optimization Method With Enhanced Global Search Ability for Design Optimizations of Electromagnetic Devices. *IEEE Transactions on Magnetics, 42*(4), 1107–1110. doi:10.1109/TMAG.2006.871426

Kandil, N., Sood, V. K., Khorasani, K., & Patel, R. V. (1992). Fault identification in an ac-dc transmission system using Neural Networks. *IEEE Transactions on Power Systems*, *7*(2), 812–819. doi:10.1109/59.141790

Koumousis, V. K., & Katsaras, C. P. (2006). A sawtooth genetic algorithm combining the effects of variable population size and reinitialization to enhance performance. *IEEE Transactions on Evolutionary Computation*, *10*(1), 19–28. doi:10.1109/TEVC.2005.860765

Lei, W., Qi, K., Hui, X., & Qidi, W. (2005). A modified adaptive particle swarm optimization algorithm. In *Proceedings of the IEEE International Conference on Industrial Technology (ICIT 2005)* (pp. 209-214).

Li, D., Gao, L., Zhang, J., & Li, Y. (2006). Power System Reactive Power Optimization Based on Adaptive Particle Swarm Optimization Algorithm. In *Proceedings of the 6th World Congress on Intelligent Control and Automation*, Dalian, China (pp. 7572-7576).

Lobos, T., Kozina, T., & Koglin, H. J. (2001). Power System Harmonics Estimation using Linear least squares method and SVD. *IEE Proceedings. Generation, Transmission and Distribution*, *148*(6), 567–572. doi:10.1049/ip-gtd:20010563

Martins, R., Oliveira, A. D., & Goncalves, W. A. (2000). Expert Systems for the Analysis of Power Quality. In *Proceedings of the IEEE International Conference on Electric Utility Deregulation and Restructuring and Power Technologies*, City University, London (pp. 90-95).

MATLAB. (n.d.). *Math Works INC* (version 7.3). Retrieved from http://www.mathworks.com

Mishra, S. (2005). A Hybrid Least Squares-Fuzzy Bacterial Foraging Strategy for Harmonic Estimation. *IEEE Transactions on Evolutionary Computation*, *9*(1), 61–73. doi:10.1109/TEVC.2004.840144

Mori, H. (1992). An Artificial Neural Network Based Method for Power System Voltage Harmonics. *IEEE Transactions on Power Delivery*, *7*(1), 402–409. doi:10.1109/61.108934

Osowski, S. (1992). Neural Network for estimation of harmonic components in a power system. *IEE Proceeding. Part C*, *139*(2), 129–135.

Passino, K. M. (2002). Biomimicry of bacterial foraging for distributed optimization and control. *IEEE Control Systems Magazine*, *22*(3), 52–67. doi:10.1109/MCS.2002.1004010

Probabilistic aspects Task Force of the Harmonics Working Group Subcommittee. (1998). Time Varying Harmonics: Part – I – Characterizing Measured Data. *IEEE Transaction on Power Delivery, 13*(3), 938-944.

Routray, A., Pradhan, A. K., & Rao, K. P. (2002). A novel Kalman filter for frequency estimation of distorted signals in power system. *IEEE Transactions on Instrumentation and Measurement*, *51*(3), 469–479. doi:10.1109/TIM.2002.1017717

Sachdev, M. S., & Giray, M. M. (1985). A Least Square Technique for Determining Power System Frequency. *IEEE Transactions on Power Apparatus and Systems*, *104*(2), 437–444. doi:10.1109/TPAS.1985.319059

Senthil Arumugam, M., Chandramohan, A., & Rao, M. V. (2005). Competitive Approaches to PSO algorithm via New Acceleration Co-efficient Variant with Mutation operators. In *Proceedings of the sixth Intern. Conf. on Computational Intelligence and Multimedia Applications* (pp. 225-230).

Shi, Y., & Eberhart, R. C. (2001). Fuzzy Adaptive Particle Swarm Optimization. In *Proceedings of the Evolutionary Computation*, *1*, 101–106.

Soliman, S. A., Christensen, G. S., Kelly, D. H., & El-Naggar, K. (1992). Least Absolute Value Based On Linear Programming Algorithm for Measurement of Power System Frequency from a Distorted Bus Voltage Signal. *Elect. Mach. and Power Systems, 20,* 549–568. doi:10.1080/07313569208909620

Soliman, S. A., & El-Hawary, M. E. (1999). Measurement of Voltage Flicker Magnitude and Frequency in a power systems for power quality analysis. *Elect. Mach. and Power Systems, 27,* 1289–1297. doi:10.1080/073135699268588

Soliman, S. A., Mantaway, A. H., & El-Hawary, M. E. (2004). Simulated Annealing Optimization Algorithm for Power System Quality Analysis. *Electric Power and Energy Systems, 26,* 31–36. doi:10.1016/S0142-0615(03)00068-1

Standard, I. E. E. E. (1993). *IEEE Recommended Practices and Requirements for Harmonic Control in Electrical Power System* (pp. 519–1992). Washington, DC: IEEE Press.

TOP. (n.d.). *TOP, The Output Processor* (version 6.2). Retrieved from http://www.pqsoft.com

This work was previously published in International Journal of Applied Evolutionary Computation, Volume 1, Issue 2, edited by Wei-Chiang Samuelson Hong, pp. 29-59, copyright 2010 by IGI Publishing (an imprint of IGI Global).

Chapter 7

A Heuristic Approach for Multi Objective Distribution Feeder Reconfiguration:
Using Fuzzy Sets in Normalization of Objective Functions

Armin Ebrahimi Milani
Islamic Azad University, Iran

Mahmood Reza Haghifam
Tarbiat Modarres University, Iran

ABSTRACT

The reconfiguration is an operation process used for optimization with specific objectives by means of changing the status of switches in a distribution network. This paper presents an algorithm for network recon-figuration based on the heuristic rules and fuzzy multi objective approach where each objective is normalized with inspiration from fuzzy set to cause optimization more flexible and formulized as a unique multi objective function. Also, the genetic algorithm is used for solving the suggested model, in which there is no risk of non-linear objective functions and constraints. The effectiveness of the proposed method is demonstrated through several examples in this paper.

1. INTRODUCTION

In the original configuration of a distribution network there are some normally open (N.O.) and some normally closed (N.C) switches. Clearly, in order to reach specific purposes, we can close some of N.O switches and open corresponding N.C ones.

The whole mentioned operation for reaching a new optimized configuration is named "Reconfiguration of distribution networks".

In general, reconfiguration methods can be divided to two groups: "General" and "Specific". In the specific methods, one initial answer is obtained and is used in a specific algorithm to reach further answers up to an improvement point considering the constraints of the problem. In general methods,

DOI: 10.4018/978-1-4666-1749-0.ch007

an algorithm is used for solving the problem and a large range of answer are obtained, among which by performing an operation the most improved answer is selected as a final one.

So far, several different techniques have been presented to resolve the network reconfiguration problem. For instance, Civanlar et al. in (Civanlar, Grainger, Yin, & Lee, 1998) described a formula to estimate the loss change resulting from the transfer of a group of loads from one feeder to another feeder. In Baran and Wu (1989) a heuristic algorithm was employed to minimize the power loss and load balancing, while Liu, Lee, and Vu (1989) developed a global optimality condition for the problem and two solution algorithms.

Shirmohammadi et al. (Shirmohammadi & Hong, 1989) described a technique for the reconfiguration of distribution networks to decrease their resistive line losses and included results pertaining to large scale system examples. In Wang, Chiang, and Darling (1996) explicit loss reduction and line flow formulas were developed to determine efficiently the switching operations.

Recently, AI-based approaches have been described to solve the problem and the results of such methods as the expert system (Liu, Lee, & Venkata, 1988), Genetic algorithm (Nara, Shiose, Kitagawa, & Ishihara, 1992), neural network (Kim, Ko, & Jung, 1993), simulated annealing (Chang & Kuo, 1994), evolutionary programming (EP) (Lin, Cheng, & Tsay, 1999), and fuzzy logic (Zhou, Shirmohammadi, & Liu, 1997; Prasad, Ranjan, Sahoo, & Chaturvedi, 2005) are all encouraging. Where their methodologies in (Zhou, Shirmohammadi, & Liu, 1997) combined the optimization techniques with heuristic rules and fuzzy logic for efficiency and robust performance and (Prasad, Ranjan, Sahoo, & Chaturvedi, 2005) presented a fuzzy mutated genetic algorithm for optimal reconfiguration of radial distribution systems. This method involves a new chromosome representation of the network and a fuzzy mutation control for an effective search of solution space.

As it is clear, in the most introduced methods a uni-objective function is considered for solving the problem and due to the importance of the power loss minimization, reconfiguration with the purpose of reduction in loss is highly signified.

In this essay four objectives, included in one multi-objective function with weight factor related to each objective are considered as following:

1. Minimization of the system's power loss;
2. Minimization of the deviation of nodes voltage;
3. Minimization of the branch current constraint violation;
4. Load balancing among various feeders.

For normalization of each function, fuzzy sets are used to make reconfiguration more flexible not only to satisfy realistic objectives and soft constraints, but also to supply rigorous mathematical and heuristic approaches within the problem-solving process.

The fuzzy set theory provides an excellent framework for integrating the mathematical and heuristic approach into a more realistic formulation of the reconfiguration, while keeping an efficient computation (Huang, 2002). Owing to the non-commensurable characteristics of the objectives, a conventional approach that optimizes a single objective function is inappropriate for this problem. The fuzzy sets is therefore adopted to simultaneously consider the multiple objectives and to obtain a fuzzy satisfaction maximizing decision.

Meanwhile, Genetic algorithm is considered to be an efficient method for solving the large-scale combinatorial optimization problem, due to its ability to search global or near global optimal solutions and its appropriateness for parallel computing in which there is no risk of non-linear objective functions and constraints.

Finally the numerical results of the proposed method used on a simple network are provided for more study.

2. PROBLEM FORMULATION

As mentioned earlier, reconfiguration of distribution feeders is done by means of changing the state of switching points for reaching specific purposes.

Continuously, each one of the objective functions is used to make a model and is normalized for forming a multi-objective function inspired by fuzzy sets.

As a result a membership function is attributed to each object, which shows its satisfaction level. It is clear that since each one of these functions obtain a quantity between unit and zero (and not only 0 and 1) in "fuzzy logic", by using this theory, above-mentioned multi-objective optimization problem becomes more flexible.

The membership function consists of a lower and upper bound value together with a strictly monotonically increasing and continuous function for different objectives which are described below.

2.1 Membership Function for Power Loss Reduction

The basic purpose for this membership function is to reduce the real power loss of the system, and can be define it as (Das, 2006):

$$p_i = \frac{Ploss(i)}{ploss0} \quad for \quad i = 1, 2, ..., N_k \quad (1)$$

Where:

N_k: total number of branches in the loop including tie-branch, when k th tie-switch is closed;

Ploss (i): total real power loss of the radial configuration of the system when i th branch in the loop is opened;

Ploss 0: total real Power loss before network reconfiguration.

Regarding the above mentioned equation if P_i is high, power loss reduction is low, and hence, a higher membership value is assigned. The

Figure 1. Membership function for power-loss reduction

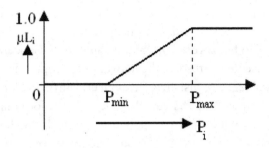

membership function for power loss reduction is given in Figure 1.

From Figure 1, function of μ_{Li} can be written as:

$$\mu_{Li} = \frac{p_i - p_{min}}{p_{max} - p_{min}}, for \ p_{min} < p_i < p_{max}$$

$$\mu_{Li} = 0 \quad for \quad P_i \leq P_{min}$$

$$\mu_{Li} = 1 \quad for \quad P_i \geq P_{max} \quad (2)$$

This means that by assuming $x_{min}=0.5$ and $x_{max}=1.0$, if the loss reduction is 50% or less, the unity membership value is assigned and if the loss reduction is 100% (or more), the zero membership value is assigned.

2.2. Membership Function for Maximum Node Voltage Deviation

The basic purpose of this membership function is to reduce the deviation of nodes voltage, and can be defined it as:

$$y_i = max \left| V_{ij} - Vs \right|$$

For, $i = 1, 2, ..., N_k, J = 1, 2, ..., N_B$ \quad (3)

Where

N_k: total number of branches in the loop including the tie-branch, when k th tie-switch is closed;

N_B: total number of nodes of the system;

V_s: voltage of the substation (in per unit);

$V_{i,j}$: voltage of node j corresponding to the opening of the i th branch in the loop (in p.u.).

If the maximum value of nodes voltage deviation is less, then a lower membership value is assigned and if deviation is more, then a higher membership value is assigned.

Considering Figure 2, which shows the membership function for maximum node voltage deviation, it can be written:

$$\mu_{Vi} = \frac{y_i - y_{\min}}{y_{\max} - y_{\min}}, for\ y_{\min} < y_i < y_{\max}$$

$$\mu_{Vi} = 0 \quad for \quad y_i \leq y_{\min}$$

$$\mu_{Vi} = 1 \quad for \quad y_i \geq y_{\max} \tag{4}$$

This means that by assuming $y_{\min}$=0.05, if the substation voltage is 1.0 p.u., then the minimum system voltage will be 0.95 p.u. and if the minimum system voltage is greater than (or equal to) 0.95 p.u.,the zero membership value is assigned, meanwhile, by assuming $y_{\max}$=1.0 the minimum system voltage will be 0.90 p.u.and if the minimum system voltage is less than (or equal to) 0.90 p.u.,the unity membership value is assigned.

2.3. Membership Function for Maximum Branch Current Loading Index

The basic purpose for this membership function is to minimize the branch current constraint violation, and can be define it as:

$$Z_i = \max \left[\frac{I(i,m)}{I_c(m)}\right]$$

For, $i = 1, 2, ..., N_k, m = 1, 2, ..., N_{B-1}$ \qquad (5)

Figure 2. Membership function for maximum node voltage deviation

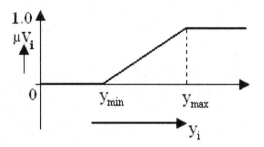

Where:

N_k: total number of branches in the loop including tie-branch, when k th tie-switch is closed;

$|I(i,m)|$: magnitude of current of branch m when the i th branch in the loop is opened;

$I_c(m)$: line capacity of branch m;

$N_{B:}$ total number of the nodes of the system.

When the maximum value of branch current loading index Exceeds unity, the maximum membership value is assigned and as long as it is less than (or equal to) unity, a lower membership value is assigned.

Considering Figure 3, which shows the membership function for maximum node branch current loading index, it can be written:

$$\mu_{Ai} = \frac{y_i - y_{\min}}{y_{\max} - y_{\min}}, for\ z_{\min} < z_i < z_{\max} \quad \mu_{Ai} = 0$$
for, $z_i \leq z_{\min}$

$$\mu_{Ai} = 1 \ for, z_i \geq z_{\max} \tag{6}$$

This means that by assuming $Z_{\min}$=1.0 until the branch currents of the system are less than or equal to their respective line capacity, unity membership value is assigned and if $Z_{\max}$=1.15, 15% overloading is allowed for each branch and if in any branch, the current is greater than (or equal to) 1.15 times the line capacity, a zero membership value is assigned.

Figure 3. Membership function for maximum branch current loading index

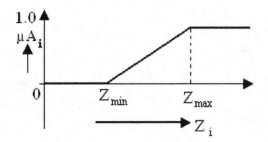

2.4. Membership Function for Feeder Load Balancing

Load balancing is one of the major objectives of feeder reconfiguration and an effective strategy to increase the loading margin of heavily loaded feeders is to transfer part of their loads to lightly loaded feeders.

For balancing the load of the feeders we can model the "Feeder Load Balancing Index" in this way:

$$FLB_{i,j} = \frac{IFF_{i\max} - IF_{i,j}}{IFF_{i\max}}$$

For, $i = 1, 2, ..., N_k, j = 1, 2, ..., N_F$ (7)

Where:

N_k: total number of branches in the loop including tie-branch, when k th tie-switch is closed;

N_F: total number of feeders;

$IF_{i,j}$: current of feeder j corresponding to the opening of the i th branch in the loop;

$IFF_{i\max}$: maximum of all the feeder currents corresponding to the opening of the i th branch in the loop.

With this definition and regarding that:

$$Ui = \max (FLB_{i,j}) \qquad (8)$$

If the value of U_i is low, a better load balancing can be achieved, hence for a low U_i a low value of membership, and for a high U_i a high value of membership is assigned.

Considering Figure 4, which shows the membership function for the load balancing index, it can be written:

$$\mu_{Bi} = \frac{u_i - u_{\min}}{u_{\max} - u_{\min}} \quad , for \quad u_{\min} < u_i < u_{\max}$$

$$\mu_{Bi} = 0 \quad for \quad u_i \leq u_{\min}$$

$$\mu_{Bi} = 1 \quad for \quad u_i \geq u_{\max}$$

$$(9)$$

If $u_{\min} = 0.1$ and $u_{\max} = 0.5$, $u_{\min}$ indicates that the maximum deviation of feeder currents will be 10% with respect to the maximum value of feeder current and if this deviation is less than (or equal to) 10%, a zero membership value is assigned and $u_{\max}$ indicates that if this deviation is greater than 50%, the unity membership value is assigned.

3. THE MODEL OF MULTI-OBJECTIVE FUNCTION

In this section the four objective functions introduced in the previous part are combined by means of weight factors, in a way that one weight factor is considered for each mentioned purpose and the four objective functions, normalized by the introduced method are modeled in the form of a single multi-objective function as follows:

$$F_{Multi} = \sum_{x=1}^{4} W_x \cdot F_x \qquad (10)$$

In this equation, if $x = 1, 2, 3$ & 4 then F_x is successively the objective function of power loss minimization, minimization of the deviation of nodes voltage, minimization of the branch current constraint violation and load balancing

Figure 4. Membership function for the load balancing index

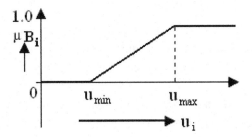

among various feeder where constants of w_1 to w_4 successively are corresponding weights for each one of these functions. Hence regarding to system conditions and considered objectives, can lead the solution of multi-objective problem toward suitable purposes by changing the value of w_1 to w_4. Meanwhile using this multi-objective function, system operational constraints- such as maintaining the structure of network in the radial form- should be considered.

4. SOLVING THE OPTIMIZATION PROBLEM USING GENETIC ALGORITHM

Genetic algorithm is one of the optimization methods based on heredity and evolution. This algorithm is one of the statistic searching methods and due to the fact that the offered model of reconfiguration of distribution systems is a non-linear problem with binary variants, it can be considered as an appropriate method for reaching an improved configuration with proposed objective functions.

In this algorithm, first the state of tie-switches are encoded by a set of binary values, then -considering the objective function- a fitness function is considered for each string of numbers, so that in the next stage the initial population will be chosen, in a way that we can use the probability of roulette for this choice.

The suggested fitness function for creating the initial population can be written as:

$$F_{\text{Fitness}} = \frac{1}{1 + \sum_{x=1}^{4}(W_x . F_x) + \sum_{y \in SC} A_i . B_i} \tag{11}$$

In which $\sum_{x=1}^{4} W_x . F_x$ is the weighed set of objective functions and demonstrates the final multi-objective function and F_{Fitness} is the fitness function. Meanwhile $\sum_{y \in SC} A_i . B_i$, is considered as a penalty factor in the fitness function for covering the constraints of the problem, in a way that A_i is the corresponding penalty factor to the i th constraint and B_i is the rate of violation from the corresponding limitation and SC is the set of constraints.

The suggested fitness function (Equation 11) is used to evaluate the fitness value of initial population, consequently the roulette is divided in according to the quantities of fitness function of each string and with each circulation, and one string for creating a new generation is selected.

The act of creating a new generation is done by the genetic operators such as cross-over and mutation. Afterward the fitness quantity for each one of the newly created strings is calculated by above-mentioned offered equation and strings with more fitness are chosen as the next generation. Absolutely the strings with high fitness values are more probable to be transferred to the next generation.

This process will be continued until the best answer in successive repetitions has no improvement and the resulted binary string shows the information of the final optimized configuration.

4.1. Chromosomes Structure

The binary decision variables denote the on/off status of switches to be determined in the reconfiguration. Where '0' denotes 'open' of the switch and '1' represents 'close'. The fitness value of each individual is evaluated by decoding the 1/0 status of switches to obtain the network configuration (Huang, 2002).

For preserving the radial property, one branch must be opened from the set of branches forming the loop. In proposed method, the chromosome consists of substrings of binary codes (that can get decimal values). Each tie line represents one substring as shown in Figure 5.

The leftmost bit of a substring is the status of the tie line (1≡Close, 0≡ Open) and it is followed by other bits representing the branch to be opened if the status bit is 1.

4.2. Fitness Scaling

Fitness scaling converts the raw fitness scores that are returned by the fitness function to values in a range that is suitable for the selection function. The selection function uses the scaled fitness values to select the parents of the next generation. The selection function assigns a higher probability of selection to individuals with higher scaled values.

The range of the scaled values affects the performance of the genetic algorithm. If the scaled values vary too widely, the individuals with the highest scaled values reproduce too rapidly, taking over the population gene pool too quickly, and preventing the genetic algorithm from searching other areas of the solution space. On the other hand, if the scaled values vary only a little, all individuals have approximately the same chance of reproduction and the search will progress very slowly.

Rank fitness scaling, scales the raw scores based on the rank of each individual instead of its score. The rank of an individual is its position in the sorted scores: the rank of the most fit individual is 1; the next most fit is 2, and so on.

The rank scaling function assigns scaled values so that;

- The scaled value of an individual with rank n is proportional to $\frac{1}{\sqrt{n}}$.
- The sum of the scaled values over the entire population equals the number of parents needed to create the next generation

Note that Rank fitness scaling removes the effect of the spread of the raw scores.

4.3. Mutation

Although, in general, the genetic mutation probability is fixed throughout the whole search process, due to the fact that in practical application of distribution feeder reconfiguration, a small fixed mutation probability can only result in a premature convergence, an adaptive mutation process is used to change the probability, i.e. (Ah King, Radha, & Rughooputh, 2003)

$$p(k+1) = \begin{cases} p(k) - p_{step} & if \quad f_{\min}(k): unchanged \\ p(k) & if \quad f_{\min}(k): decreased \\ P_{final} & if \quad p(k) - p_{step} < p_{final} \end{cases}$$

$p(0)$=1.0

p_{step}=0.001

p_{final}=0.05

where,

k:generation number
p:mutation probability.

and minimum mutation probability in this paper is given as 0.05

This is clear that the mutation scale will decrease as the process continues and as is mentioned, the above adaptive mutation not only prevents premature convergence, but also leads to a smooth convergence.

Figure 5. Introducing a typical chromosome structure

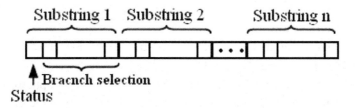

Figure 6. Flowchart of proposed method

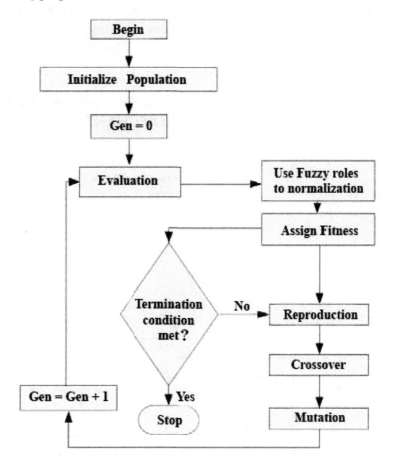

The proposed GA algorithm creates a binary vector (Mask) and changes the genes if the corresponding cell has just "1" value.

Note that the cell with "0" value will cause no change to the corresponding gen.

This Mask can be produced by following steps:

1- For i=1 to "number of genes" do:
2- Generate a random value (Rnd) between 0 & 1
3- If Rnd < P(iteration)
then Mask(i)=1
else
Mask(i)=0

4.4. Crossover

Crossover operator specifies how the genetic algorithm combines two individual, or parents, to form a crossover child for the next generation. In this paper the scattered crossover method is used which it creates a random vector and selects the genes where the vector is a 1 from the first parent, and the genes where the vector is a o from the second parent, and combines the genes to form the child. For example, if P1 and P2 are the parents

P1=[a b c d e f g h]

P2=[1 2 3 4 5 6 7 8]

And the binary vector is [1 1 0 0 1 0 0 0], the function returns the following child:

Child 1= [a b 3 4 e 6 7 8]

(This kind of crossover is accessible in MATLAB software).

4.5. Other Factors

In this paper the population size of 100 is considered. More over the crossover factor for this population size is considered as 0.7, which demonstrates an acceptable fast convergence by means of several experimental executions. This factor determines the percentage of population which will contribute to produce crossover children.

5. PROPOSED METHOD FLOWCHART

A flowchart describing the main process for proposed method is shown in Figure 6.

Table 1. Line and load data

Bus	R (pu)	X (pu)	P (MW)	Q (MVAr)	V (pu)
4-1	0.07	0.11	2.0	1.6	0.991
5-4	0.08	0.11	3.0	1.5	0.988
6-4	0.09	0.18	2.0	0.8	0.988
7-6	0.04	0.04	1.5	1.2	0.985
8-2	0.11	0.11	4.0	2.7	0.979
9-8	0.08	0.12	5.0	3.0	0.971
10-9	0.11	0.11	1.0	0.9	0.977
11-9	0.11	0.11	0.6	0.1	0.971
12-9	0.08	0.11	4.5	2.0	0.969
13-3	0.11	0.11	1.0	0.9	0.994
14-13	0.09	0.12	1.0	0.7	0.955
15-13	0.08	0.11	1.0	0.9	0.992
16-15	0.04	0.04	2.1	1.0	0.991
11-5	0.04	0.04			
14-10	0.04	0.04			
16-7	0.09	0.12			

Figure 7. Initial sample network structure

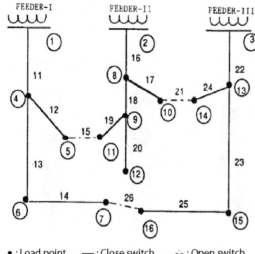

• : Load point   —— : Close switch   -‑- : Open switch

Table 2. The numerical results of experiments

Test Case	Loss(kW)	Voltage Deviation Index (VDI)
Base Network	488.46	3.54
Loss Reduction	252.53	2.63
Minimization of Loss - Considering the Voltage Deviation Index	251.33	1.53

6. NUMERICAL RESULTS

For examining the efficiency and improvement, the suggested model is developed in MATLAB, on a Pentium-4 PC (1.86GHz & 2GB RAM), and is performed on a sample three-feeder network related to reference (Civanlar, Grainger, Yin, & Lee, 1998). The convergence tolerance for the three-phase power flow execution is set at 0.001 and the most important system parameters and its structure are shown in Table 1 and Figure 7.

•: Load point
——: Close switch
-‑-: Open switch

For examining the efficiency of the suggested multi-objective function, an experiment is carried out on the mentioned sample network in two ways:

In the first way the only purpose is to minimize the power loss and in the second the two main purposes – namely minimization of loss and minimization of voltage deviation- are considered. The Table 2 designates the numerical results of these two experiments.

In order to show the improvement of the multi-objective optimization method introduced, the Figure 8 is provided, which shows the deviation of voltage of feeders both before and after the reconfiguration of experimental network. As shown in the related graph, the voltage deviation is significantly improved after reconfiguration by means of suggested method.

Also, in order to compare the results of suggested method with other references, the proposed method is applied to two other tested systems; they are called Baran (Baran & Wu, 1989), and Lopez (Lopez, Opazo, Garcia, & Poloujadoff, 2002).

Table 3 represents the power loss after reconfiguration for proposed method in comparison to some other available methods.

It was clear from these experiments that the resultant power losses were less than or equal to those found by the techniques applied in Liu, Lee, and Vu (1989), Shirmohammadi and Hong (1989), Lopez, Opazo, Garcia, and Poloujadoff (2002) and Zhu (2002) (see Table 3).

As the last study, Table 4 provides a comparison between suggested method and methods presented in Huang (2002) and Hsiao (2004). This comparison depicts better results in loss reduction and voltage deviation for proposed method while minimization of "power loss" and "voltage deviation" are considered as two main purposes of this multi-objective reconfiguration.

Figure 8. The voltage deviation of feeders, after/before reconfiguration

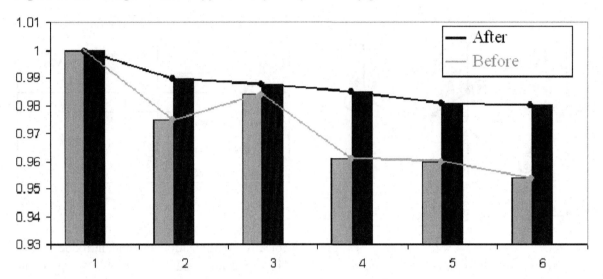

Table 3. Power loss after reconfiguration in 3 tested systems; a comparison between proposed & other methods

System	Ref.	%Loss after reconfiguration	%Loss after implementation of proposed method
I. Civanlar[1]	[3]	0.583	0.485
	[16]	0.569	
	[17]	0.569	
II. Baran[2]	[4]	1.402	1.363
	[16]	1.395	
	[17]	1.395	
III. Lopez[15]	[4]	0.0946	0.0926
	[16]	0.0926	

Table 4. Result of proposed method; comparison with 2 other methods (considering minimization of loss & voltage deviation)

Reference number	Reduction in loss (%)	Max. deviation of bus voltage (pu)	Proposed Method	
			Reduction In loss (%)	Max. deviation of bus voltage (pu)
[13]	44.6	0.0712	49.2	0.0422
[18]	49.5	0.0253	51.9	0.0218

7. CONCLUSION

In this paper a new heuristic multi-objective algorithm has been proposed to solve the network reconfiguration problem in radial distribution systems. In this modeling four objective functions are normalized according to a method based on the fuzzy sets and are placed besides each other by a suggested equation with weight factors to create a unique multi-objective function.

Regarding to the suggested method that is a non-linear model, the genetic algorithm is used to solve the optimization problem.

In order to examine the suggested method, several experiments have been done to compare the results with some other methods applied in reliable articles.

The obtained results in this essay designates its efficiency in the multi-objective reconfiguration of distribution networks, in a way that the operator by the help of this method and regarding to the conditions of the network can perform an effective multi objective reconfiguration – with minimization of power loss, minimization of the deviation of nodes voltage, minimization of the branch current constraint violation and load balancing - and create a optimal balance among these four purposes.

8. REFERENCES

Ah King, R. T. F., Radha, B., & Rughooputh, H. C. S. (2003). A real-parameter genetic algorithm for optimal network reconfiguration. *IEEE International Conference on Industrial Technology, 1*, 54-59.

Baran, M. E., & Wu, F. F. (1989, April). Network reconfiguration in distribution systems for loss reduction and load balancing. *IEEE Transactions on Power Delivery, 4*(2), 1401–1409. doi:10.1109/61.25627

Chang, H. C., & Kuo, C. C. (1994). Network reconfiguration in distribution system using simulated annealing. *Electric Power Systems Research, 29*, 227–238. doi:10.1016/0378-7796(94)90018-3

Civanlar, S., Grainger, J. J., Yin, H., & Lee, S. S. H. (1998, July). Distribution feeder reconfiguration for loss reduction. *IEEE Transactions on Power Delivery, 3*(3), 1217–1223. doi:10.1109/61.193906

Das, D. (2006). A Fuzzy Multi objective Approach for Network Reconfiguration of Distribution Systems. *IEEE Transactions on Power Delivery, 21*(1), 202–209. doi:10.1109/TPWRD.2005.852335

Hsiao, Y. T. (2004, February). Multiobjective evolution programming method for feeder reconfiguration. *IEEE Transactions on Power Systems, 19*(1), 594–599. doi:10.1109/TPWRS.2003.821430

Huang, Y. C. (2002, September). Enhanced genetic algorithm-based fuzzy multi-objective approach to distribution network reconfiguration. In *Proceedings of the IEE Gener. Transm. Distrib. Comf.* (Vol. 149, No. 5, pp. 615-620).

Kim, H., Ko, Y. K., & Jung, H. (1993, July). Artificial neural networks based feeder reconfiguration for loss reduction in distribution systems. *IEEE Transactions on Power Delivery, 8*, 1356–1366. doi:10.1109/61.252662

Lin, W. M., Cheng, F. S., & Tsay, M. T. (1999). Feeder loss reduction by switching operations with a hybrid programming technique. In *Proceedings of the IEEE Transm. Dist. Conf.* (Vol. 2, pp. 603-608).

Liu, C. C., Lee, S. J., & Venkata, S. S. (1988, May). An expert system operational aid for restoration and loss reduction of distribution system. *IEEE Transactions on Power Systems, 3*, 619–629. doi:10.1109/59.192914

Liu, C. C., Lee, S. J., & Vu, K. (1989, April). Loss minimization of distribution feeders: optimality and algorithms. *IEEE Transactions on Power Delivery*, *4*(2), 1281–1289. doi:10.1109/61.25615

Lopez, E., Opazo, H., Garcia, L., & Poloujadoff, M. (2002, July). Minimal loss reconfiguration based on dynamic programming approach: Application to real systems. *Power Compon. Syst.*, *30*(7), 693–704. doi:10.1080/15325000290085145

Nara, K., Shiose, A., Kitagawa, M., & Ishihara, T. (1992, August). Implementation of genetic algorithm for distribution systems loss minimum reconfiguration. *IEEE Transactions on Power Systems*, *7*(3), 1044–1051. doi:10.1109/59.207317

Prasad, K., Ranjan, R., Sahoo, N. C., & Chaturvedi, A. (2005, April). Optimal reconfiguration of radial distribution systems using a fuzzy mutated genetic algorithm. *IEEE Transactions on Power Delivery*, *20*(2), 1211–1213. doi:10.1109/TP-WRD.2005.844245

Shirmohammadi, D., & Hong, W. H. (1989, April). Reconfiguration of electric distribution networks for resistive line losses reduction. *IEEE Transactions on Power Delivery*, *4*(2), 1492–1498. doi:10.1109/61.25637

Wang, J. C., Chiang, H. D., & Darling, G. R. (1996, February). An efficient algorithm for real time network reconfiguration in large scale unbalanced distribution systems. *IEEE Transactions on Power Systems*, *11*, 511–517. doi:10.1109/59.486141

Zhou, Q., Shirmohammadi, D., & Liu, W. H. E. (1997, May). Distribution feeder reconfiguration for service restoration and load balancing. *IEEE Transactions on Power Systems*, *12*, 724–729. doi:10.1109/59.589664

Zhu, J. Z. (2002). Optimal reconfiguration of electrical distribution network using the refined genetic algorithm. *Electric Power Systems Research*, *62*, 37–42. doi:10.1016/S0378-7796(02)00041-X

This work was previously published in International Journal of Applied Evolutionary Computation, Volume 1, Issue 2, edited by Wei-Chiang Samuelson Hong, pp. 60-73, copyright 2010 by IGI Publishing (an imprint of IGI Global).

Chapter 8
A Scheduling Model with Multi–Objective Optimization for Computational Grids using NSGA–II

Zahid Raza
Jawaharlal Nehru University, India

Deo Prakash Vidyarthi
Jawaharlal Nehru University, India

ABSTRACT

Scheduling a job on the grid is an NP Hard problem, and hence a number of models on optimizing one or other characteristic parameters have been proposed in the literature. It is expected from a computational grid to complete the job quickly in most reliable grid environment owing to the number of participants in the grid and the scarcity of the resources available. Genetic algorithm is an effective tool in solving problems that requires sub-optimal solutions and finds uses in multi-objective optimization problems. This paper addresses a multi-objective optimization problem by introducing a scheduling model for a modular job on a computational grid with a dual objective, minimizing the turnaround time and maximizing the reliability of the job execution using NSGA – II, a GA variant. The cost of execution on a node is measured on the basis of the node characteristics, the job attributes and the network properties. Simulation study and a comparison of the results with other similar models reveal the effectiveness of the model.

INTRODUCTION

The effort to attain a cooperative, collaborative, and high performance computing environment with ubiquitous presence has led to grid formation. Aided with the enormous reach of the

World Wide Web, the grid promises to provide a future computing platform with almost every computing capability. The grid is an aggregation of heterogeneous resources spread in various administrative domains working together to solve a problem. Being a part of the grid enables the user to compute anything anywhere irrespective

DOI: 10.4018/978-1-4666-1749-0.ch008

of his own computational capabilities or presence (Prabhu, 2008; Tarricone & Esposito, 2005; Taylor & Harrison, 2009).

A grid, being composed of a number of heterogeneous participants with their own administrative domains and policies, poses a number of challenges for job execution. These challenges range from the topology of the grid affecting the job submission to discovering the suitable resources for the job and conveying the results back to the user. Since the resources constituting the grid are scarce and the access could be under some economic policy, it is always desired to get the job executed in the most reliable manner with minimum turnaround incurred for better utilization of the grid. Reliability is the ability of a system to perform and maintain its functions in routine circumstances, as well as in hostile or unexpected circumstances. As the composition of the grid is dynamic the resources are prone to failures. Thus, under the dynamic and unreliable grid conditions it becomes essential that the job execution takes place in a reliable manner. This reliable execution further adds strength to the objective in which turnaround is minimized. The catch here is that it is not always necessary that scheduling the job on the resources with the objective of turnaround minimization may result in most reliable execution of the job and vice versa. Since optimization of one objective may not result in the optimized solution for the other objective, the two possibly conflicting objectives need to be met simultaneously. The best way to attain this is to have the solutions explored and accept the ones with better results corresponding to both the objectives. Going this way, solutions are obtained which may not be optimum for any of the objectives but certainly better when seen as a trade off between the two objectives. This is the approach adopted in the multi-objective optimization problems (MOP). Finally, with the requirements in hand, the user or the system zeroes in on the best solutions as per the need and the domain knowledge.

A number of job schedulers for the grid are available in the literature with various approaches towards scheduling the jobs. Schedulers to minimize turnaround (Raza& Vidyarthi, 2008) and maximizing reliability of job execution (Raza, & Vidyarthi, 2009b) have been reported. A batch scheduling scheme to minimize makespan and flowtime using Cellular Mementic Algorithms is proposed in (Xhafa, Alba, & Dorronsoro, 2007). A high level timed Petri net to model the workflow of grid tasks is proposed in (Yaojun, Changjun, & Xuemei, 2005) whereas a Game Theoritic approach is used in (Rzadca, Tryatram, & Wierzbicki, 2007). A scheduling model considering the availability of the computational resources, communication delays and the resource reservation is reported in (Aggrawal & Aggrawal, 2006).

Genetic algorithm is an effective tool for solving an optimization problem that involves navigation through a big search space. It is based on the Darwin's theory of evolution with "survival of the fittest". GA works with exploration of various solutions simultaneously making use of the past information for the future. This, coupled with mutation, avoids the false peaks to move towards the global optima. With suitable modifications, GA finds use for multi-objective optimization problems employing specialized fitness functions along with the diversity preserving mechanisms. The set of solutions at any time in a MOP is known as Pareto-optimal solutions which are accessed from time to time. The solutions are said to be acceptable if they satisfy the given objectives without being dominated by others. The use of evolutionary algorithms like GA for MOP is much better in comparison to the classical optimization techniques which stress on the conversion of the problem to a single optimization problem by considering one Pareto-optimal solution at a time. Further, the decision on the precise use of weights itself creates a bottleneck in the performance and effectiveness for the classical methods.

The rest of the paper is organized as follows. The use of the GA in solving multi-objective optimization problems. The next section describes the model in terms of the scheduler, notation used, fitness function for turnaround time and reliability estimates and the algorithm for job scheduling using NSGA-II. The simulation study and performance comparison of the model with the simple GA and non GA based similar models is then presented.

MULTI OBJECTIVE OPTIMIZATION USING GA

There are several multi-objective optimization algorithms reported in the literature. Some of them are Vector Evaluated GA(VEGA) (Schaffer, 1985), Multi Objective GA (MOGA) (Fonseca & Fleming, 1993), Niched Pareto GA (NPGA) (Horn, Nafpliotis, & Goldberg, 1994), Pareto Envelop Based Selection Algorithm (PESA) (Corne, Knowles, & Oates, 2000), Pareto Archived Evolution Strategy (PAES) (Knowles & Corne, 1999), Non Dominated Sorting GA (NSGA) (Srinivas & Deb, 1994), NSGA-II (Deb, Agarwal, & Meyari-van, 2002; Deb, Agarwal, Pratap, & Meyarivan, 2000), Strength Pareto Evolutionary Algorithm (SPEA) (Zitzler & Thiele, 1999) and SPEA-2 (Zitzler, Laumanns, & Thiele, 2001). VEGA is the simplest implementation of the multi-objective GA scheme with only minor changes required in simple GA to convert it into a multi-objective GA with the least computational complexity. The problem with VEGA is that each solution is not tested for the remaining objectives and converges to individual best solutions only. Also, no diversity mechanism is available in VEGA. MOGA offers the advantage of easy fitness assignment and sharing with diversity preservation by niching but the convergence is too slow. NPGA offers very simple selection operator using the tournament selection but have problems related to niche size parameter and with an extra parameter for the tournament selection. The niche count is used as a tie breaker in tournament selection. NSGA

also ensures diversity by niching and offers the fitness assignment based on the non dominated sorting with fast convergence but has problems with the niche size parameter. Further VEGA, MOGA, NPGA and NSGA lack elitism. PESA, PAES, NSGA-II, SPEA and SPEA-2 on the other hand are elitist algorithms. PESA is a pure elitist algorithm with an ease of implementation but the performance depends on the prior information about the objective space. PAES on the other hand uses Pareto dominance to replace a parent if offspring dominates. The disadvantage here is that it is not a population based approach and performance depends on the cell sizes. SPEA uses ranking based on the external archive of non dominated solutions with no parameter for clustering required. But the complex clustering algorithm proves to be a problem. An evolutionary algorithm outperforming SPEA with both objective function values and faster search along with even lesser computational efforts has been proposed (Sarker, Liang, & Newton, 2001). Another approach using Differential Evolution (DE) algorithm showing promising results over SPEA has been suggested (Sarker & Abbass, 2004). SPEA-2 is an improved SPEA but has computationally expensive fitness and density calculations. NSGA-II is an elitist algorithm based on ranking the individuals using non dominated sorting. The crowding distance parameter ensures the diversity in the population resulting in least user intervention but has a problem that crowding distance works in objective space only. A model with the aim of maximizing performance and simultaneously minimizing performance variance using Radial Basis Function (RBF) network is also reported (Ray & Smith, 2006).

Deb et al. (Srinivas & Deb, 1994) proposed the NSGA as an evolutionary algorithm for multi-objective optimization problems. It was noticed that the algorithm had a computational complexity of $O(MN^3)$ for M objectives and N population size. This resulted in a computationally expensive algorithm with increase in the population size. The algorithm lacked elitism as the fruitful solutions could be lost in the process. Further, the diversity is ensured by the use of a sharing which requires the specification of the sharing parameter from the user (Deb, Agarwal, & Meyarivan, 2002; Deb, Agarwal, Pratap, & Meyarivan, 2000). These issues are addressed in the NSGA-II algorithm with the new algorithm having a computational complexity of $O(MN^2)$. The algorithm is elitist as the parents are combined with the offspring and are then sorted to result in various fronts with the individuals ranked accordingly. The new population for the next generation is then created containing the best of the previous generations decided by the front or rank of the individual. This way good solutions are not lost in the process thus exhibiting elitism. Diversity among the solutions is ensured by the use of the crowding distance operator thus eliminating any need of user specifications as is there in the sharing parameter in the NSGA. In case of a tie breaker an individual with higher crowding distance as compared to its peers with the same rank is selected. A model to distribute the solution set evenly in order to maximize the spread of solution set has been proposed to enhance the optimization ability of multi-objective evolutionary algorithms (Tan, Goh, Yang, & Lee, 2004).

GA has been used extensively for many optimization problems. Channel allocation schemes for mobile communication using GA has been reported in (Khanbary, Omer, & Vidyarthi, 2008; Zomaya & Wright, 2002). A modified GA scheme is also used for the same purpose of channel allocation (Khanbary, Omer, & Vidyarthi, 2009). Scheduling being an optimization problem has also attracted attention of the use of GA. Various approaches in scheduling in Distributed Computing Systems have been exhaustively discussed in (Vidyarthi, Sarker, Tripathi, & Yang, 2009). A GA based task scheduler is proposed in (Aggarwal, Kent, & Ngom, 2005; Jianning & Huizhong, 2005). Minimization of the turnaround for the job submitted is very much desired in the grid system

and has got attention in GA based approaches in (Raza & Vidyarthi, 2009a, 2009c). Maximization of reliability is also an equally important requirement and has been addressed in (Limaye, Leangsuksun, Yudan, Greenwood, Scott, Libby, & Chanchio, 2005; Vidyarthi, Tripathi, Sarker, & Yang, 2005; Vidyarthi & Tripathi, 2001).

The use of multi-objective evolutionary algorithms for scheduling jobs on computational grids has been proposed in (Crina, Ajith, & Bjarne, 2007). A review of the multi-objective optimization using GA is compiled in (Konak, Coit, & Alice, 2006; Amaki, Kita, & Kobayashi, 1996; Coello, 2000). Maintaining diversity in the solutions generated midway is an important task and is addressed based on minimum spanning tree in (Zheng & Miqing, 2008) Scheduling of the job for a multiprocessor system to minimize the finishing time and the waiting time using GA is proposed in (Moattar, Rahmani, & Derakhshi, 2007). Dynamic multi-objective optimization is reported in (Chun-an & Yuping, 2007) by dividing the time period into random sub periods and applying static multi-objective optimization during each sub period. A niched Pareto multi-objective optimization is discussed in (Horn, Nafpliotis, & Goldberg, 1994). Deb et al. proposed the NSGA and gained much appreciation with the improvement of NSGA in the NSGA-II being used for multi-objective optimization. NSGA-II has been used extensively in the optimization problems with some of them as reported in (Alexandre, Dias, & Vasconcelos, 2002; Lu, Sheng-Wu, Jie, & Ji-Shan, 2006; Mikkel, 2003).

Most of these models run short of the scheduling requirements over grid resources in the sense that nature of the job in terms of the resource requirements and interactive job handling has not been addressed. Even the resource attributes like effect of node speed and existing workload on the nodes does not find a mention in the allocation strategy. Further, most of the work focuses on only a few parameters in determining the fitness function thus invariably missing the real grid picture.

Majority of the models reported in the literature have handled the reliability based scheduling of the job by first scheduling the job and then estimating its reliability rather than scheduling the job based on the most reliable resources at that time. Also, not all the parameters that affect the reliability have been used for reliability estimation.

THE PROPOSED MODEL

The proposed model schedules the job on the grid satisfying the dual objective of minimizing the turnaround time and maximizing the reliability of the job execution. This dual objective optimization problem is solved using NSGA-II algorithm. The process generates the result in the form of many pareto fronts with each member corresponding to a turnaround time and reliability offered to the job. With further domain knowledge and the job requirements, the user or system can pick the solutions which satisfy the needs most.

The grid, under consideration, consists of number of clusters. The clusters are interconnected with a high speed network. The cluster may be specialized in catering to a job of a particular specialization. For example, the cluster specializing in graphic specific application may be preferred for execution of the graphic related jobs. Each cluster, in turn comprises of a number of computational resources called nodes. In this work, each node is considered to be consisting of a single processor only whereas in practice a node may contain multiple processors. The current cluster state is reflected in the Cluster Table (CT) associated with the Cluster Scheduler (CS) available at each cluster. The CT enables the model to keep track of the grid composition i.e., the number of nodes available in the cluster along with their attributes and the number of jobs pending with them. Following information is assumed to be available with each CT

1. Number of clusters in the grid
2. Specialization of the clusters
3. Number of nodes in each cluster
4. Hamming distance between various nodes in the cluster to give insight of the minimum number of links traversed for the data exchange between two participating nodes
5. Processing speed of each node in the cluster

The architecture of the scheduler is shown in Figure 1.

The job can be submitted at any of the constituent nodes from where it is dispatched to all suitable clusters matching the specialization of the job. Cost of execution for the job is then calculated at each selected cluster and is informed to the node on which the job was submitted. This cost corresponds to an allocation pattern for the modules of the job under consideration. Thus, for each solution there is an allocation pattern and an associated cost in terms of the turnaround time and the reliability offered to the job. Finally, the user/system decides in favor of the best solution(s) satisfying the requirements. Accordingly, the cluster offering that solution is selected and the job is allocated to its nodes as per the suggested allocation pattern. The modules assigned to each node are then internally scheduled according to

Figure 1. Grid scheduler

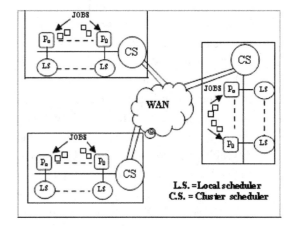

its own local scheduling policy by its Local Scheduler (LS).

The job, demanding execution, is assumed to be submitted with the following information.

1. Specialization of the job; this specifies the job requirements in terms of the resource requirements for its execution.
2. Number of modules in the job.
3. Order of execution of the modules as per its Job Precedence Graph (JPG).
4. Size of each module in terms of the number of instructions.
5. Information about the loop structure, if any, in the module.
6. The number of bytes required to be exchanged between the modules for interacting modules.

This information may be collected during the compilation (data flow analysis) and is exclusive to this model.

The data structures and parameters used in the model are as follows.

a. Cluster table (CT) for each cluster C_n indicates the status of the cluster with the following attributes

$$C_n (P_k, S_n, f_k, T_{prfk})$$

It contains information about the number of nodes P_k, the cluster specialization S_s, the clock frequency of each node f_k, and the time to finish existing modules T_{prfk} on the nodes. The CT is updated periodically to reflect the dynamic grid conditions.

b. Job type J_j representing the job specialization for various jobs. For example J_0 may stand for graphic specific job, J_1 for multimedia, J_2 for database specific job etc. The type J_p may corresponds to the job type which does not have any specialization or does not require

a specialized treatment in terms of resource requirements.

c. E_{ijkn}: Processing time of a module m_i (Size I_i) of job J_j on node P_k of cluster C_n.

$$E_{ijkn} = I_i * (1/f_k) + n * \alpha \qquad (1)$$

Where 'n' is multiplication factor to account for the loop constructs in the module and 'α' is the average time taken in the loop. E_{ijkn} reflects the computational capabilities of a node. It will be less for nodes with high clock speed and vice versa.

d. B_{ihj}: Bytes exchange between modules m_i and m_j of job J_j. This reflects the communication for the interactive modules.

e. Chromosome structure: GA requires a chromosome for the initial population. For the scheduling problem, the chromosome structure should be able to reflect the allocation of modules to the various nodes under consideration. Further, the structure should also support allocation of multiple modules on a single node. For the purpose, a chromosome of size (number of genes) equal to the number of modules of the job is generated dynamically such that each gene represents the allocation of a module to a node. Starting from the left hand side, the first gene corresponds to the node allocation for the first module, the second gene referring to the node allocation for the second module and so on till the last gene corresponding to the last module as shown in Figure 2.

For example, a typical chromosome for a job with four modules is shown in Figure 3. The allocation considers a cluster with five nodes. The chromosome structure can be interpreted as module 1 being allocated to node 3, module 2 on node 2, module 3 on node 3 and module 4 on node 1.

Figure 2. Chromosome structure

Node No. for Module1	Node No. for Module2	Node No. for Module3	Node No. for Module 4	Node No. for Module5

Figure 3. Allocation of nodes to the modules

3	2	3	1

Notation

The Notation used in the proposed model is as listed below.

- J_j: Submitted job with specialization j
- m_i: i^{th} module of the submitted job
- Ii: Number of instructions in the module mi C_n: n^{th} cluster in the grid
- Sn: Specialization of cluster Cn Pk: k^{th} node of a cluster
- f_k: Clock frequency of node P_k
- N: Number of clusters comprising the grid M: Number of modules in a job
- K: Number of nodes in the cluster
- g: Generation number for the population
- E_{ijkn}: Processing time of a module mi of job Jj on node Pk of cluster Cn.
- B_{ihj}: Communication between interactive modules m_i and m_h of job 'J$_j$' in form of number of bytes that needs to be exchanged
- D_{kln}: Hamming distance between nodes P_k and P_l of a cluster C_n. This corresponds to the number of links that connects nodes P_k to P_l.
- Xijk: Vector indicating the assignment of module mi of job Jj on node Pk. It assumes a binary value. It is 1 if the module is allocated to the node and is 0 otherwise.
- λ_{kn}: Failure rate of node P_k of cluster C_n

- μ_{ij}: Failure rate of the module m_i of job J_j
- ζ_{kln}: Failure rate of the link connecting nodes k and l of cluster C_n
- Tprfk: Time to finish the current load for a node P_k of a cluster Cn corresponding to the allocation pattern suggested by chromosome f. This represents the execution time needed for the execution of the modules already assigned to the node. The same is denoted as 'T_{prk}' for the non GA scheduling models.
- NEC_{kifn}: Turnaround time offered to module m_i of job J_j by node P_k of cluster C_n for chromosome f.
- $ChromCost_{fn}$: Turnaround time offered by chromosome f of cluster C_n. This is calculated for chromosome f as the maximum of the NEC_{kifn} over all the nodes P_k on which allocation has been made.
- $ModRel_{ik}$: Reliability of execution of module m_i on node P_k. This is the reliability with which a module can be executed on a node and is a function of the reliability of the module, reliability of the node in consideration and the reliability of the links which participates in data exchange for the interactive modules, residing on different nodes. Thus the same module may have a different reliability of execution over different nodes.
- $ChromRel_{fn}$: Reliability with which a job can be executed as per the allocation pattern

of chromosome f of cluster C_n. It is also a function as mentioned for $ModRel_{ik}$. While using GA, various chromosomes are randomly populated with each gene representing a node for execution of the corresponding module. This result in possibly different nodes assigned to various modules and in turn different reliability offered to the job by each chromosome.

- $ClusCost_{jn}$: This corresponds to the execution cost in terms of the turnaround time and the reliability offered to the job J_j offered by the first Pareto front member chromosomes of the cluster C_n.

- $ClusRel_{jn}$: Reliability of execution of a job J_j at cluster C_n.

- f_{gn}: This is the set of chromosomes which finally gets selected by the user, offering the best turnaround and reliability till that generation

- NoOfFronts: This provides the number of fronts in the current generation

- SizeOfFront(): This provides the number of front elements in each front

- $GridCost_{moj}$: This corresponds to the execution cost offered by the grid to the job submitted in terms of the turnaround time and reliability offered by the chromosomes / solution(s) finally selected by the user/ system.

- *Sendall*: Send modules of the job along with its attributes to all the clusters for cost evaluation.

- *Receiveall*: Receive '$ClusCost_{jn}$' and '$ClusRel_{jn}$' from all the selected clusters at the calling node.

Fitness Function

The model aims the dual-objective with scheduling of job to those grid resources which offers a satisfactory turnaround time to the job in addition to provide the most reliable environment for its execution. This is achieved by first finding the clusters matching the specialization of the job and then scheduling it to those nodes of the cluster which provides best tradeoff between both the objectives.

It is desired that the fitness function should reflect the contributions from various factors affecting the turnaround and the reliability offered to the job. These factors include the effect of the computing resource (nodes) involved in the execution of the job, characteristics of the job and the network links supporting the data exchange between various nodes.

The attributes of the nodes that affect the job allocation is the clock frequency of the node f_k and the time required T_{prfk} for the jobs already allocated on these nodes. Faster the nodes involved in computation, lesser will be the turnaround time offered to the job. Similarly, lesser the time required to finish the existing workload lesser will be the turnaround offered to the job. The same logic applies for estimating reliability also as a node is desired to be available till the job(s) finishes. Thus, faster the node, sooner it will finish the job and more reliable it will be. With lesser existing workload, the failure chance of the current job also reduces increasing the probability of successful execution of the job.

The application itself affects the cost of execution. If there is a job with high degree of interaction between its modules, the turnaround time will increase and the reliability decreases as it will take a longer time to finish.

The contribution of the network is viewed by the data exchange amongst the interacting job modules. This interaction is enabled by the various network links connecting the nodes executing those modules. This affects the turnaround and reliability as both of them depends on the availability of these links for interaction.

Considering all the factors mentioned above the turnaround offered by a node P_k to a module m_i of a job J_j for the allocation pattern corresponding to chromosome 'f' can be written as

$$NEC_{kifn} = E_{ijkn}.x_{ijk} + \sum_{h=1}^{i-1} w\left(B_{ihj}.D_{kl}\right)x_{ijk}.x_{hjl} + T_{prfk}$$

$$(2)$$

where

$$T_{prfk} = \sum_{\substack{forall \\ g \neq j}} \left(E_{igkn}.x_{igk} + \sum_{h=1}^{i-1} w\left(B_{ihg}.D_{kl}\right)x_{igk}.x_{hgl} \right)$$

$$(3)$$

The turnaround offered by each chromosome f can be calculated as

$$ChromCost_{fn} = \max(T_{prfk})_{for\ all\ k\ on\ which\ allocation\ has\ been\ made}$$

$$(4)$$

Similarly the reliability offered to any module m_i by any node P_k can be written as presented in Equation 5.

For any chromosome f, with all the modules allocated to a node, the reliability offered by the chromosome to the job becomes Equation 6.

Thus, each chromosome corresponds to a turnaround and reliability offered to the job as per Equation (4) and (6) which is used in NSGA-II to determine the dominance of the chromosome over other members. This information is further used to create Pareto fronts.

After convergence of the result, the set of chromosomes f_{gn}, in the first Pareto front are eventually selected for each cluster under consideration. The solutions, corresponding to this set forms the cost offered by the cluster ClusCost$_{jn}$, in terms of the turnaround time and reliability offered to the job. This set is then conveyed to the user/system for the final decision. As mentioned earlier, out of all the solutions available from various clusters, the user/system selects the best suiting the needs. This solution provides the final cluster selection and the job is allocated to the nodes as per the allocation pattern suggested by the selected chromosome. The turnaround time and reliability offered by this solution becomes the cost offered by the grid GridCost$_{moj}$ to the job.

The Algorithm

The model uses the NSGA-II algorithm to schedule the job on the grid resources with the aim of meeting the objectives of minimizing the turnaround time of the job while maximizing the reliability with which the job can be executed. Each job has its own requirements in terms of the appropriate

Equation 5.

$$\mathrm{ModRel}_{ik} = \exp\left\{ -\left[(\mu_{ij} + \lambda_{kn})\left[E_{ijkn}.x_{ijk}\right] + (\mu_{ij} + \xi_{kl})\left[\sum_{h=1}^{i-1} w(B_{ihj}.D_{kl})x_{ijk}.x_{hjl}\right] + \lambda_{kn}\left[T_{prfk}\right] \right] \right\} \quad (5)$$

Equation 6.

$$Chrom\,\mathrm{Re}\,l_{fn} = \prod_{i=1}^{K} Mod\,\mathrm{Re}\,l_{ik}$$

$$= \prod_{i=1}^{K} \exp\left\{ -\left[(\mu_{ij} + \lambda_{kn})\left[E_{ijkn}.x_{ijk}\right] + (\mu_{ij} + \xi_{kl})\left[\sum_{h=1}^{i-1} w(B_{ihj}.D_{kl})x_{ijk}.x_{hjl}\right] + \lambda_{kn}\left[T_{prfk}\right] \right] \right\} \quad (6)$$

resource needed for the execution of the job specified as its specialization. This is taken care of in the model by first searching then evaluating only those clusters which match the specialization of the job. The clusters matching the job's resource requirements are then further evaluated for the turnaround time and the reliability offered to the job using the fitness function as described in the earlier section. After meeting the convergence criterion, these clusters produce a set of chromosomes which are the non dominated solutions in the first Pareto front. These chromosomes correspond to some values of turnaround time and reliability offered to the job. All these chromosomes/ solutions are then sent to the node on which job was submitted. The system analyzes the solutions received from various selected clusters and decides on the solution(s) of the interest. Accordingly, the job is allocated to the cluster from which the selected chromosome has emerged and the cluster table (CT) can be updated according to the allocation pattern suggested by the selected chromosome.

The cost estimation for each selected cluster is estimated using NSGA-II. In this, first a population of chromosomes of size Pop Size is generated dynamically in each cluster. These chromosomes are then randomly populated. Using tournament selection operator, the chromosomes are then mated to generate an off-spring population of size equal to the original population. The parent chromosomes and the off-springs are then combined together. This produces a generation of population of size twice that of the original population. It results in preserving the best chromosomes for future use thus inducing elitism in the algorithm. Mutation is effectuated after every few generations to avoid local optima. The population is then sorted based on non dominance. The result is ranked by placing individuals in appropriate fronts with individuals in same front having same rank and the first front members being the non dominated solutions. The population is then restored back to its original value by filling the members starting from the first front. It is possible that the number of members

in the last front may exceed the number of elements remaining to restore the population back to its original size. This situation is resolved by the use of crowding distance selection operator in NSGA-II. The decision is taken in favor of the individuals having higher crowding distance as compared to its peers. This helps in preserving diversity in the solutions. The process is repeated over the generations till the result converges. The obtained first front members represents the non dominated chromosomes considered as the best and are referred as $ClusCost_{jn}$. This set of chromosomes is given back to the calling node on which the job was submitted. Finally, the solution is selected. This solution(s) now becomes the $GridCost_{moj}$. Since the cost estimation has factored major hardware and software contributions affecting scheduling, the resulting allocation pattern is a uniform one. The algorithm for the same is shown in Algorithm 1.

SIMULATION STUDY

A simulation study for the model was carried out to analyze the performance by altering various parameters. The experiments were carried out in MATLAB 7. The various simulation parameters for the grid are listed below in Table 1.

In the experiments the effect on turnaround time and reliability for the submitted job is observed over the generations for varied grid architecture. For each generation the members of the first front represent the non dominated solutions which are best in that generation. These non dominated solutions are observed over the generations. When saturation condition is met, these first front members depict various solutions in terms of the various combinations of turnaround time and reliability offered to the job. It is noticed that the result converges by 50 generations. Several experiments were conducted to analyze the performance of the proposed model. Some of these results in terms of the final first front mem-

Algorithm 1.

```
Alloc (Job)
{
Submit the job in the form of modules
// Submit the job J_j in the form of modules m_i (i = 1 to M)
```
Sendall // *Send the jobs to all the clusters for evaluation of their suitability for the job execution*
```
For all clusters C_n (n = 1 to N) do
{
```
Access the specialization S_n of the clusters with the job // *check for the suitable clusters*
```
If it matches, do
// Evaluate the turnaround time and reliability offered by these clusters
Compute E_{ijkn}
// Calculate the processing time of the nodes, for all the modules, as per eq. (i)
Generate population
// Generate 'PopSize' chromosomes with number of genes equal to the number of modules
// and randomly populate these chromosomes by allocating nodes to the genes
Calculate_Cost()
{
Perform Crossover
// Using tournament selection select mates and perform crossover
Perform Mutation
// Mutation is performed every fifth generation to avoid local optima
Combine the parent and off-spring chromosomes
// This results in a new population double the size of the original population
Perform non dominated sorting
// This results in generation of Pareto optimal fronts with ranked individuals
Restore population
// This results in generation of new population of size PopSize again
```
NewPopulation=0
```
SizeOfNewPopulation=0
```
Count=0
```
FrontCount=1

Calculate NoOfFronts
// This gives the number of fronts in the present generation
Calculate SizeOfFront()
// This gives the number of chromosomes in each front
```
do
```
{
If ((SizeofFront(FrontCount) + SizeOfNewPopulation)<=PopSize)
{
New Population=New Population U Front(FrontCount)
// Enter the front members in the new population
SizeOfNewPopulation=SizeOfNewPopulation+SizeOfFront(FrontCount)
// Update the size of the new population
FrontCount=FrontCount+1
// Move to the next front
}
} // Repeat the process for the fronts which fully become part of the new
// population
Remaining=PopSize-SizeOfNewPopulation
// Calculate the remaining entries in the new population

Calculate Crowding distance for Front(FrontCount)
// Crowding distance required to decide which individual should go to the new population
SortFront(FrontCount)
// Sort the front elements in the descending order of the crowding distance
Select
// Select only the first few chromosomes entries equal to the remaining entries in
// the new population
New Population=New Population U Front (FrontCount)
// Finish filling the selected members in the new population.
```

continued on following page

Algorithm 1. Continued

// This restores the population to PopSize again
} *Repeat the process till the result converges*

Receiveall // *Receive ClusCost$_{jm}$ from all the selected clusters*
Select cluster for the job execution // *Select the cluster as selected by the user*
Allocate the job
// Allocate the job to the selected cluster as per the allocation pattern suggested by the selected
// chromosome
Update grid
// Update the cluster table of the selected cluster to reflect the accommodation of the new job
}
}

Table 1. Grid parameters

S. No.	Parameter	Notation Used	Range
1	Number of Clusters	N	1-5
2	Number of Nodes in a Cluster	K	5-15
3	Clock Frequency of Nodes	f_k(MHz)	10-20
4	Intra Node Distance	D_{kl}	1-10
5	Time to finish Previous Workload	T_{prfk} (μS)	10-30
6	Number of Modules in a Job	M	5-15
7	Number of Instructions in a Module	I_i	500-3000
8	IMC	B_{ihj} (Bytes)	5-20
9	Population Size	PopSize	25
10	Probability of Crossover	---	100%
11	Probability of Mutation	---	20%

Figure 4. Turnaround time v/s reliability with NSGA-II based model

Figure 5. Turnaround time v/s reliability with NSGA-II based model

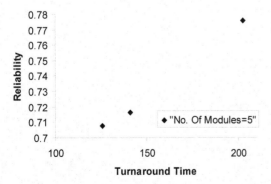

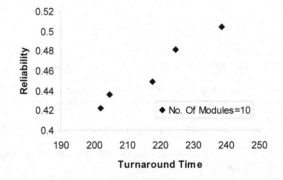

Figure 6. Turnaround time v/s reliability with NSGA-II based model

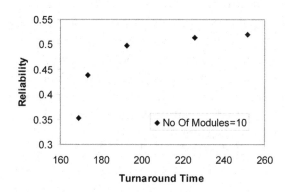

Figure 7. Turnaround time v/s reliability with NSGA-II based model

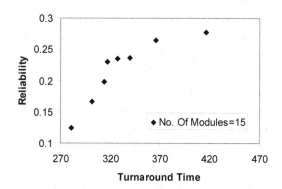

bers obtained for various grid architectures and jobs are shown in Figures 4-7. The result presented here and in the following section corresponds to the cluster which provides the best solutions out of all the clusters selected for evaluation.

It is observed that the NSGA-II algorithm helps in providing the non dominated solutions as is evident from Figures 4-7. Each point in the graph corresponds to a solution representing a chromosome in terms of turnaround time and reliability offered to the job. A study of the results reveal

that out of all the solutions the terminal points correspond to those solutions which gives a satisfactorily optimized value for one parameter but a poor solution to the other parameter. Thus the terminal points are the solutions which offer either a good turnaround poor reliability or a good reliability poor turnaround time to the job. The solutions between these extremities represent the solutions which are a tradeoff between the turnaround time and the reliability. Finally, the desired solution is selected by the user/system as per the needs.

Figure 8. Turnaround time v/s reliability with 5 modules

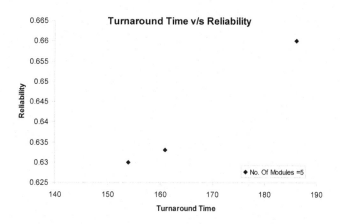

Performance Comparison with Other Similar Models

An exhaustive simulation study was conducted to study the sensitivity of the proposed model. Some more results (Figures 8-12) were obtained on the line of the results presented in Figures 4-7. These experiments also produced the results and observations similar to that of Figures 4-7. These results are compared with the results obtained using a similar model allocating jobs based on the single objective of either minimizing the turnaround time or maximizing the reliability of the job submitted as produced in (Raza & Vidyarthi, 2008). Though these models, now referred as the non GA models, optimize a single objective function only but are useful in determining the performance of the proposed model because of the basic allocation strategy being the same in both the cases. The model (Raza & Vidyarthi, 2008) optimizes the turnaround time on the basis of estimating the turnaround time of each module and allocating them sequentially while preserving the module precedence according to the JPG. The turnaround offered to each module on a node of the cluster can be calculated using Equation (2). The module is allocated to that node which offers the minimum turnaround. The new turnaround on the selected node now becomes its time to execute the previous workload T_{prk}, accounting to all the allocated modules so far on the node. This process is repeated for the remaining modules while updating their respective T_{prk}. When all the modules get allocated, the node with highest T_{prk} gives the turnaround offered to the job by that cluster. Similarly, the model maximizing the reliability of the job allocation too works on the same basis and allocates job modules to those nodes which offer them the maximum reliability. Therefore, these two models can provide us the desired benchmark for evaluating the results of the proposed model. Further, the results are compared with the simple GA based models (Raza & Vidyarthi, 2009a, 2009b) which also optimizes only one of the parameters viz. turnaround time and reliability. The GA based models use the same chromosome structure as used by the proposed NSGA-II based model. These models differ only in the selection of chromosomes for mating to reproduce the next generation. The simple GA based model considers the best chromosome in the current generation and mate it with the current population to reproduce the new generation.

The performance of the proposed model is compared with the non GA and simple GA based models on the same grid architecture. The perfor-

Figure 9. Turnaround time v/s reliability with 10 modules

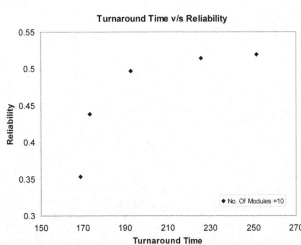

Figure 10. Turnaround time v/s reliability with 15 modules

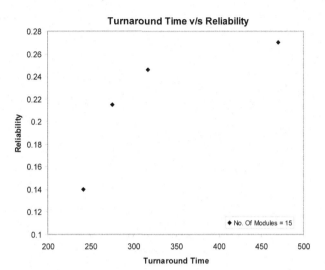

mance is evaluated in terms of the turnaround and the reliability obtained from the proposed NSGA-II based model and comparing these results with the turnaround time and reliability obtained from the non GA and simple GA based models. Further, the load balancing is observed for all the models by evaluating the allocation pattern of the job modules obtained from each model. Figures 8- 12 shows the various solutions obtained from the proposed NSGA-II based model in terms of the turnaround time and reliability offered to the job.

A comparative study of the results for the turnaround time and the reliability obtained from the above experiments for various models is presented in Table 2 in which various solutions offered by the NSGA-II based model are compared with the results obtained from the simple GA based and non GA models optimizing only one parameter. Table 3 presents the best solution offered by the NSGA-II based model for comparison with the results obtained from simple GA based and non GA models while Table 4 reflects the percentage

Figure 11. Turnaround time v/s reliability with 20 modules

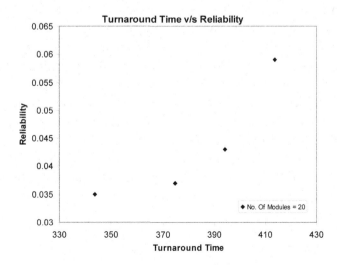

Figure 12. Turnaround time v/s reliability with 25 modules

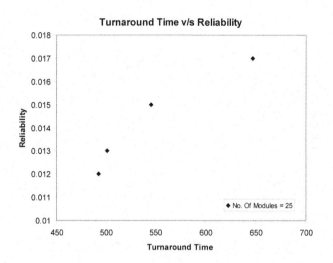

loss or gain (+/-) by the NSGA-II based model as compared to the results obtained from the simple GA based models and non GA based models.

It is observed from Table 3 and Table 4 that out of all the models considered for comparison, the simple GA based models provide the best solutions. It has already been proved by the authors in their previous work (Raza & Vidyarthi, 2009a, 2009b) that simple GA based models work better than the non GA models. Further, it has been established by the authors that if a model is scheduling the job in order to optimize only one parameter, the same allocation does not ensure the optimization of the other parameter. In particular, if the model schedules the job with the objective of maximizing the reliability of the job, the same allocation provides a poor turnaround time as compared to the turnaround time obtained by scheduling with the objective of minimizing the turnaround time. The proposed NSGA-II based scheduling model provides an allocation for the job in order to meet the dual objective of minimizing the turnaround time while simultaneously maximizing the reliability. Thus the turnaround time and reliability obtained may not be the best

as compared to the simple GA based model (with single objective) but is certainly a good solution if optimization of both the turnaround time and the reliability together are concerned. On the other hand, the simple GA based models provide good results for the optimization of only one parameter and at the same time the same allocation provides a very poor result with the other parameter. The comparison of these results with the set of solutions suggests that the NSGA-II based model provides a good compromise solution which may not be the best optimized solutions with respect to one objective but are certainly better if seen as a tradeoff between the two optimization parameters. Therefore, NSGA-II based models prove to be a better choice if optimization of more than one parameter is concerned.

It is always desired from a scheduling model that the load is distributed evenly on the nodes capable of executing the job. The allocation of modules for the results discussed above is presented in Table 5. It is observed that the allocation is uniform across the nodes of the cluster ensuring proper load balancing for the jobs submitted.

Table 2.Comparison of NSGA-II results with simple GA based and non GA based models

Experiment cor-responding to	NSGA – II Based Model		Simple GA Based Model		Non GA Model	
	Turnaround Time	Reliability	Turnaround Time	Reliability	Turnaround Time	Reliability
Figure 7	{ 154.000, 161.000, 186.142 }	{ 0.630, 0.633, 0.660 }	152.142	0.691	157.666	0.274
Figure 8	{169.142, 173.571, 192.714, 225.625, 251.571 }	{ 0.353, 0.438, 0.497, 0.514, 0.519 }	148.500	0.432	150.333	0.107
Figure 9	{ 241.800, 275.400, 316.625, 470.600 }	{ 0.140, 0.215, 0.246, 0.270 }	222.000	0.209	238.555	0.017
Figure 10	{ 343.833, 374.666, 394.000, 413.666, 604.200 }	{ 0.035, 0.037, 0.043, 0.059, 0.073 }	286.666	0.0762	357.666	0.00013
Figure 11	{ 492.800, 501.300, 545.625, 647.25 }	{ 0.012, 0.013, 0.015, 0.017 }	494.000	0.023	418.888	0.000

Table 3. Comparison of best NSGA-II results with simple GA based and non GA based models

Experiment cor-responding to	NSGA – II Based Model		Simple GA Based Model		Non GA Model	
	Best Turn-around Time	Best Reliability	Turnaround Time	Reliability	Turnaround Time	Reliability
Figure 7	154.000	0.660	152.142	0.691	157.666	0.274
Figure 8	169.142	0.519	148.500	0.432	150.333	0.107
Figure 9	241.800,	0.270	222.000	0.209	238.555	0.017
Figure 10	343.833	0.073	286.666	0.0762	357.666	0.00013
Figure 11	492.800	0.017	494.000	0.023	418.888	0.000

Table 4. Comparison of NSGA-II results with simple GA based and non GA based models for % loss and gain

Experiment corresponding to	NSGA – II Result Comparison with Simple GA Based Model		NSGA – II Result Comparison with non GA Based Model	
	% Gain/Loss in Turn-around Time	% Gain/Loss in Reliability	% Gain/Loss in Turn-around Time	% Gain/Loss in Reli-ability
Figure 7	-1.22%	-4.4%	+2.3%	+140%
Figure 8	-14%	+20%	-12.5%	+385%
Figure 9	-8.9%	+29%	-1.3%	+1488%
Figure 10	-19%	-3.9%	+3.8%	+56054%
Figure 11	-0.2%	-26%	-17%	+∞%

Table 5. Job allocation pattern for NSGA-II based, simple GA based and non GA model

Experiment corresponding to	Allocation Pattern for the Job Modules				
	NSGA – II Based Model (Best Solution)	Simple GA Based Models		Non GA Models	
	Dual Objective Optimization of Minimizing the Turnaround Time and Maximizing the Reliability	Objective of Minimizing the Turnaround Time	Objective of Maximizing the Reliability	Objective of Minimizing the Turnaround Time	Objective of Maximizing the Reliability
Figure 7	5,2,3,6,5	5,5,2,3,1	5,6,6,5,5	5,2,3,6,1	5,6,6,6,5
Figure 8	10,6,6,10,13,3,10,11,14,6	11,11,7,11,13,12,1,9,12,14	10,6,4,10,6,13,14,13,6,11	9,6,10,9,12,11,6,14,7,4	13,13,13,6,6,13,13,13,13,6
Figure 9	13,2,13,2,2,2,6,1,8,12,4,11,7,12,13	12,7,13,1,2,1,5,9,13,10,4,7, 12,14,6	13,9,8,11,2,1,8,10,6,1,12,1 ,8,12,12	12,9,6,10,11,10,4,7,6,9,1 4,13,12,11,1	12,12,12,12,12,12,12,12,12,12 ,12,12,12,12
Figure 10	8,3,13,13,12,13,10,6,11,6,2,13,6,1, 5,14,12,4,10,14	11,7,11,14,8,4,8,10,9,9,4,3,2, 1,11,12,6,10, 14	12,6,13,12,13,12,6,9,6,13,4, 3,2,6,1,12,6,10, 14	9,6,10,11,12,4,9,7,14,13, 6,11,10,1,7,2,12,8,5,3	6,6,6,6,6,6,13,6,6,13,6,6,6,6,1 3,6,6,13
Figure 11	12,7,10,12,3,10,10,11,12,9,6,12,13 ,12,11,9,8,5,2,3,6,11,10,1	1,5,8,14,3,10,14,2,9,10,8,4,5, 2,6,3,10,9,4,4,13, 8,6,11,12	12,6,10,2,12,3,13,6,10,10 ,2,6,6,6,6,13,10,14,3,11, 6,6,2,10	12,6,6,6,6,6,6,6,6,6,6 ,6,6,6,6,6,6,6,6,6,6,6	12,9,10,11,6,9,10,7,14,4,13,12 ,11,1,2,8,14,10,6,9,7,3,13,5,4

CONCLUSION

A scheduler for the grid is expected to ensure minimum turnaround time while providing the most reliable environment to the job. The requirement gains paramount importance for the computational grid in which the resources are scarce and unreliable. Scheduling the job with the objective of providing the minimum turnaround time ensures optimum use of these resources. Further, reliability infusion takes care of the fact that the jobs get completed without any failure which otherwise would result in a substantial increase in the computational cost.

GA is a popular tool to be used for optimization. NSGA-II is an elitist algorithm with computational complexity of $O(MN^2)$. The algorithm is elitist as the parents are combined with the offspring and are then sorted to result in various fronts with the individuals ranked accordingly. The model uses NSGA-II for scheduling which has been very popular for the NP Hard problems.

Since turnaround time and reliability offered to a job are a function of various hardware and software grid constituents, the fitness function for turnaround time and reliability estimates takes into account the factors like computational resource attributes, job characteristics and network contributions to reflect a true grid picture. Further, the chromosome structure used enables the model to accommodate the possibility of multiple modules allocation on a single node.

The performance of the model is studied and compared with other similar models optimizing only one parameter without using GA and using GA. It is found that the proposed NSGA-II based model ensures proper load balancing for the job allocation and provides good solutions considering the problem of dual objective optimization as a tradeoff between turnaround time and the reliability which is not the case with the simple GA based or non GA models. The proposed model is a prime candidate as the scheduler for computational grid.

ACKNOWLEDGMENT

The authors would like to thank the anonymous reviewers for their valuable comments and suggestions to improve the quality of this paper.

REFERENCES

Aggarwal, M., Kent, R. D., & Ngom, A. (2005). Genetic Algorithm Based Scheduler for Computational Grids. In *Proceedings of the Nineteenth International Symposium on High Performance Computing Systems and Applications (HPCS'05)* (pp. 209-215). Washington, DC: IEEE.

Aggrawal, M., & Aggrawal, A. (2006). A Unified Scheduling Algorithm for Grid Applications. In *Proceedings of the International Symposium on High Performance Computing in an Advanced Colloborative Environment (HPCS'06)* (pp. 1-7).

Alexandre, H. F., Dias, & Vasconcelos, J. A. (2002). Multiobjective Genetic Algorithms Applied to Solve Optimization Problems. *IEEE Transactions on Magnetics*, *38*(2), 1133–1136. doi:10.1109/20.996290

Amaki, H., Kita, H., & Kobayashi, S. (1996). Multi-Objective Optimization By Genetic Algorithms: A Review. In *Proceedings of IEEE International Conference on Evolutionary Computation* (pp. 517-522).

Carlos, A., & Coello, C. (2000). An Updated Survey of GA-Based Multiobjective Optimization Techniques. *ACM Computing Surveys*, *32*(2), 109–143. doi:10.1145/358923.358929

Corne, D. W., Knowles, J. D., & Oates, M. J. (2000). The Pareto Envelope-Based Selection Algorithm For Multiobjective Optimization. In *Proceedings of the Sixth International Conference On Parallel Problem Solving from Nature*, France. Berlin: Springer Verlag. Retrieved from http://www.lania.mx/~ccoello/EMOO/knowles00d.ps.gz, 98-105

Deb, K., Agarwal, S., & Meyarivan, T. (2002). A Fast And Elitist Multi-Objective Genetic Algorithm: NSGA-II. *IEEE Transactions on Evolutionary Computation*, 6(2), 182–197. doi:10.1109/4235.996017

Deb, K., Agarwal, S., Pratap, A., & Meyarivan, T. (2000). A Fast Elitist Non-Dominated Sorting Genetic Algorithm For Multi-Objective Optimization: NSGA-II. In *Proceedings of the Parallel Problem Solving from Nature VI Conference*, France (849-858).

Fonseca, C. M., & Fleming, P. J. (1993). Multiobjective genetic algorithms. *IEE colloquium on Genetic Algorithms for Control Systems Engineering* (Digest No. 1993/130). London, UK.

Grosan, C., Abraham, A., & Helvik, B. (2007). *Multiobjective Evolutionary Algorithms for Scheduling Jobs on Computational Grids*. Retrieved from www.softcomputing.net/ac2007_2.pdf

Horn, J., Nafpliotis, N., & Goldberg, D. E. (1994, June 27-29). A Niched Pareto Genetic Algorithm For Multiobjective Optimization. In *Proceedings of the First IEEE Conference on Evolutionary Computation, IEEE world congress on computational intelligence*, Orlando, FL, USA (pp. 82-87).

Jensen, M. T. (2003). Reducing the Run-Time Complexity of Multiobjective EAˢ: The SGA-II and Other Algorithms. *IEEE Transactions on Evolutionary Computation*, 7(5), 503–515. doi:10.1109/TEVC.2003.817234

Khanbary, L., Omer, M., & Vidyarthi, D. K. (2008). A GA-Based Effective Fault-Tolerant Model for Channel Allocation in Mobile Computing. *IEEE Transactions on Vehicular Technology*, 57(3), 1823–1833. doi:10.1109/TVT.2007.907311

Khanbary, L., Omer, M., & Vidyarthi, D. P. (2009). Channel Allocation in Cellular Network Using Modified Genetic Algorithm. *International Journal of Artificial Intelligence*, 3(A09), 126–148.

Knowles, J., & Corne, D. (1999, July 6-9). The Pareto Archived Evolution Strategy: A New Baseline Algorithm For Pareto Multiobjective Optimisation. In Proceedings Of The Congress On Evolutionary Computation (CEC99) (pp. 98–105). Washington, DC: IEEE.

Konak, A., Coit, D., & Smith, A. (2006). Multi-Objective Optimization Using Genetic Algorithms: A Tutorial. In *Reliability Engineering and System Safety* (pp. 992-1007). Atlanta, GA: Elsevier Ltd.

Limaye, K., Leangsuksun, B., Liu, Y., Greenwood, Z., Scott, S. L., Libby, R., & Chanchio, K. (2005). Reliability-Aware Resource Management For Computational Grid/Cluster Environments. In *Proceedings of the sixth IEEE/ACM International Workshop on Grid Computing* (pp. 211-218).

Lin, J., & Wu, H. (2005). *A Task Duplication Based Scheduling Algorithm on GA in Grid Computing Systems* (LNCS 3612, pp. 225-234). Berlin: Springer-Verlag.

Liu, C.-a., & Yuping, W. (2007). Dynamic Multiobjective Optimization Evolutionary Algorithm. In *Proceedings of the Third International Conference on Natural Computation* (pp. 456-459).

Moattar, E. Z., Rahmani, A. M., & Derakhshi, M. R. F. (2007). Scheduling in Multi Processor Architecture Using Genetic Algorithm. In *Proceedings of the fourth International Conference on Innovations in Information Technology* (pp. 248-251).

Prabhu, C. S. R. (2008). *Grid and Cluster Computing*. PHI Learning Private Limited.

Qin, H., Zhou, J., Li, Y., Liu, L., & Lu, Y. (2008). Enhanced Strength Pareto Differential Evolution (ESPDE): An Extension of Differential Evolution for Multi-objective Optimization. In *Proceedings of the Fourth International Conference on Natural Computation (ICNC '08)* (pp. 191-196).

Ray, T., & Smith, W. (2006). A Surrogate Assisted Parallel Multi-objective Evolutionary Algorithm for Robust Engineering Design. *Engineering Optimization, 38*(9), 997–1011. doi:10.1080/03052150600882538

Raza, Z., & Vidyarthi, D. P. (2008). A Fault Tolerant Grid Scheduling Model to Minimize Turnaround Time. In *Proceedings of the International conference on High Performance Computing, Networking and Communication Systems (HPCNCS'08)*, Orlando, Florida (pp. 167-175).

Raza, Z., & Vidyarthi, D. P. (2009a). GA Based Scheduling Model for Computational Grid to Minimize Turnaround Time. *International Journal of Grid and High Performance Computing, 1*(4), 70–90.

Raza, Z., & Vidyarthi, D. P. (2009b). Maximizing Reliability with Task Scheduling in a Computational Grid Using GA. *International Journal of Advancements in Computing Technology, 1*(2).

Raza, Z., & Vidyarthi, D. P. (2009c). A Computational Grid Scheduling Model To Minimize Turnaround Using Modified GA. *International Journal of Artificial Intelligence, 3*(A09), 86–106.

Rzadca, K., Tryatram, D., & Wierzbicki. (2007). Fair Game-Theoritic Resource Management in Dedicated Grids. In *Proceedings of the IEEE International Conference on Cluster Computing and the Grid (CCGrid'07)* (pp. 343-350).

Sarker, R., & Abbass, H. (2004). Differential Evolution for Solving Multi-Objective Optimization Problems. *Asia-Pacific Journal of Operational Research, 21*(2), 225–240. doi:10.1142/S0217595904000217

Sarker, R., Liang, K., & Newton, C. (2002). A New Evolutionary Algorithm for Multiobjective Optimization. *European Journal of Operational Research, 140*(1), 12–23. doi:10.1016/S0377-2217(01)00190-4

Schaffer, J. D. (1985). Multiple Objective Optimization With Vector Evaluated Genetic Algorithms. In *Proceedings of the International Conference on Genetic Algorithm and Their Applications* (pp. 93-100).

Srinivas, N., & Deb, K. (1994). Multi-Objective Optimization Using Non-Dominated Sorting In Genetic Algorithms. *IEEE Transactions on Evolutionary Computation, 2*(3), 221–248.

Tan, K. C., Goh, C. K., Yang, Y. J., & Lee, T. H. (2006). Evolving better population distribution and exploration in evolutionary multi-objective optimization. *European Journal of Operational Research, 171*(2), 463–495. doi:10.1016/j.ejor.2004.08.038

Tarricone, L., & Esposito, A. (2005). *Grid Computing for Electromagnetics*. Boston: Artech House Inc.

Taylor, I. J., & Harrison, A. (2009). *From P2P and Grids to Services on the Web- Evolving Distributed Communities* (2nd ed.). New York: Springer Verlag.

Vidyarthi, D. P., Sarker, B. K., Tripathi, A. K., & Yang, L. T. (2009). *Scheduling in Distributed Computing Systems*. New York: Springer Verlag.

Vidyarthi, D. P., & Tripathi, A. K. (2001). Maximizing Reliability of Distributed Computing System with Task Allocation using Simple Genetic Algorithm. *Journal of Systems Architecture, 47*(6), 549–554. doi:10.1016/S1383-7621(01)00013-3

Vidyarthi, D. P., Tripathi, A. K., Sarker, B. K., & Yang, L. T. (2005). Performance Study of Reliability Maximization and Turnaround Minimization with GA based Task Allocation in DCS. In Yang, L. T., & Guo, M. (Eds.), *PART III - Scheduling and Resource Management, High Performance Computing: Paradigm and Infrastructure* (pp. 349–360). New York: John Wiley and Sons.

Wang, L., Xiong, S.-W., Yang, J., & Fan, J.-S. (2006). An Improved Elitist Strategy Multi-Objective Evolutionary Algorithm. In *Proceedings of the Fifth International Conference on Machine Learning and Cybernetics*, Dalian, China (pp. 2315-2319).

Xhafa, F., Alba, E., & Dorronsoro, B. (2007). Efficient Batch Job Scheduling in Grids using Cellular Memetic Algorithms. In *Proceedings of the IEEE International Symposium on Parallel and Distributed Processing (IPDPS 2007)*.

Yaojun, H., Changjun, J., & Xuemei, L. (2005). Resource Scheduling Model For Grid Computing Based On Sharing Synthesis Of Petri Net. In *Proceedings of the Ninth International Conference on Computer Supported Cooperative Work in Design*.

Zheng, J., & Li, M. (2008). An Efficient Method for Maintaining Diversity in Evolutionary Multi-objective Optimization. In *Proceedings of the Fourth International Conference on Natural Computation* (pp. 617-624).

Zitzler, E., Laumanns, M., & Thiele, L. (2001). *SPEA2: Improving the Strength Pareto Evolutionary Algorithm*. Zurich, Switzerland: Swiss Federal Institute Techonology.

Zitzler, E., & Thiele, L. (1999). Multiobjective Evolutionary Algorithms: A Comparative Case Study And the Strength Pareto Approach. *IEEE Transactions on Evolutionary Computation, 3*(4), 257–271. doi:10.1109/4235.797969

Zomaya, A. Y., & Wright, M. (2002). Observation on Using Genetic Algorithms for Channel Allocation in Mobile Computing. *IEEE Transactions on Parallel and Distributed Systems, 13*(9), 948–962. doi:10.1109/TPDS.2002.1036068

This work was previously published in International Journal of Applied Evolutionary Computation, Volume 1, Issue 2, edited by Wei-Chiang Samuelson Hong, pp. 74-94, copyright 2010 by IGI Publishing (an imprint of IGI Global).

Chapter 9
Extrapolated Biogeography-Based Optimization (eBBO) for Global Numerical Optimization and Microstrip Patch Antenna Design

M. R. Lohokare
*National Institute of Technical Teachers'
Training and Research, India*

S.S. Pattnaik
*National Institute of Technical Teachers'
Training and Research, India*

S. Devi
*National Institute of Technical Teachers'
Training and Research, India*

B.K. Panigrahi
Indian Institute of Technology, India

S. Das
Kansas State University, USA

J. G. Joshi
*National Institute of Technical Teachers'
Training and Research, India*

ABSTRACT

Biogeography-Based Optimization (BBO) uses the idea of probabilistically sharing features between solutions based on the solutions' fitness values. Therefore, its exploitation ability is good but it lacks in exploration ability. In this paper, the authors extend the original BBO and propose a hybrid version combined with ePSO (particle swarm optimization with extrapolation technique), namely eBBO, for unconstrained global numerical optimization problems in the continuous domain. eBBO combines the exploitation ability of BBO with the exploration ability of ePSO effectively, which can generate global optimum solutions. To validate the performance of eBBO, experiments have been conducted on 23 standard benchmark problems with a range of dimensions and diverse complexities and compared with original BBO and other versions of BBO in terms of the quality of the final solution and the convergence rate. Influence of population size and scalability study is also considered and results are compared with statistical paired t-test. Experimental analysis indicates that the proposed approach is effective and efficient and improves the exploration ability of BBO.

DOI: 10.4018/978-1-4666-1749-0.ch009

INTRODUCTION

Scientists have been drawing inspiration from nature and natural creatures for years to solve complex search problems of real word. Global numerical optimization problems frequently arise in almost every field of engineering design and scientific applications. Many evolutionary algorithms (EAs) have been introduced to solve global numerical optimization problems in the continuous domain. Since 1960s genetic algorithm (GA) (Back, 1996; Michalewicz, 1992) based on principle of natural selection has been playing a dominant role in the optimization world. There are many different EAs for global optimization, such as particle swarm optimization (PSO) (Eberhart & Shi, 2004; Kennedy & Eberhart, 1995), differential evaluation (DE) (Kaelo & Ali, 2006; Storn & Price, 1997), evolutionary strategy (ES) (Yao & Liu, 1997), evolutionary programming (Yao, Liu, & Lin, 1999), bacterial foraging optimization algorithm (BFA) (Passino, 2002), and so on. Getting trapping in local minima of the objective function is the major challenge in global numerical optimization problems. This issue becomes more challenging when the dimension is high.

Biogeography-Based Optimization (BBO) (Simon, 2008) is biology inspired and population based optimization technique and based on mathematical models of biogeography (MacArthur & Wilson, 1967). BBO mainly uses the idea of probabilistically sharing features (Migration operator) between solutions based on the solutions' fitness values. This is similar to other EAs, such as GA and PSO. In BBO, like PSO, solutions remain continue from one generation to next, but in GA solutions "die" at the end of each generation. Reproduction strategies like GA and ES are not used in BBO. Unlike PSO solutions, solutions of GA and BBO do not have tendency to follow global best to clump together in similar groups. In BBO, migration is used to change the solutions directly, while in PSO velocity modulation is used to change the solutions. DE solutions also change directly, but it depends on differences between other DE solutions. BBO is applied to the sensor selection problem for aircraft engine health estimation and for general benchmark functions (Simon, 2008). The Markov analysis, on simple unimodal, multimodal and deceptive benchmark functions with low mutation rates proves that BBO generally outperforms both, GA with single-point crossover (GASP) and GA with global uniform recombination (GAGUR) (Simon, Ergezer, & Du, 2009). This is because a BBO individual use its own fitness before deciding how likely it is to accept features from other solutions. BBO is a new global optimization algorithm and has shown its ability to solve optimization problem.

PSO is a population-based, self-adaptive stochastic optimization algorithm molded after the simulation of the social behavior of bird's flocks (Kennedy & Eberhart, 1995). PSO is similar to other EAs in the sense that both approaches are population based and each individual has a fitness function. In PSO the interaction of the individuals are relatively similar to the arithmetic crossover operator used in EAs (Carlos, Coello, & Lechuga, 2002). However, PSO is influenced by the simulation of the social behavior rather than the survival of the fittest (Eberhart & Shi, 2001) also in PSO each individual benefits from its history whereas no such mechanism exists in EAs (Carlos, Coello, & Lechuga, 2002). The PSO method is becoming very popular due to its simplicity of implementation and ability to quickly converge to a reasonably good solution. However, it has a number of drawbacks, one of which is the presence of problem dependent parameters. It suffers from premature convergence when multimodal problems are being optimized. In PSO, loss in the diversity takes place due to the fast rate of information flow between particles, which results in creation of similar particles. This may increase the possibility of being trapped in the local minima. Several modifications of the PSO have been proposed to address these problems. Recent ePSO (Arumugam, Rao, & Tan, 2009) gives quality optimal solution with faster convergence. In ePSO, by considering the basics of the PSO algorithm, the current particle position is updated by extrapolating the global best particle position and the current particle positions in the search space.

To improve the performance of BBO many modified versions of BBO have been suggested for global numerical optimization and to solve real word problems. In oppositional BBO (Ergezer, Simon, & Du, 2009), BBO performance is accelerated by incorporation of opposition-based learning, dynamic scaling and weighted reflections. Real Coded BBO (RCBBO) (Gong, Cai, & Ling, 2009a) is the extension of BBO with integration of three different mutation operators, RCBBO-G (Gaussian mutation), RCBBO-C (Cauchy mutation), and RCBBO-L (Levy mutation). Modified BBO (MBBO) (Lohokare 2009b) is applied for standard benchmark function optimization and for calculation of resonant frequency of circular microstrip antenna. Still there are several open search questions that should be addressed for BBO so that it gives better convergence. In this paper, authors propose a hybrid version of BBO, namely eBBO. In eBBO, extrapolated mutation operator of ePSO is integrated in mutation scheme of BBO. eBBO combines the exploitation ability of BBO with the exploration ability of ePSO effectively, which can generate global optimum solution. Next, each function is experimented with directly encoded floating-point vector initialization to solve continuous global optimization problem. The proposed technique is validated on 23 standard benchmark problems and five performance criteria are applied to compare eBBO with other algorithms. Influence of population size and scalability study is carried out to show the performance of eBBO comparing with original BBO. Results of both the algorithms are also compared with statistical paired t-test.

The remainder of this paper is organized as follows. Firstly, the basic concept of BBO and PSO algorithms are briefly described. Next, the motive of hybridization and proposed hybrid version eBBO technique is presented. Thirdly, to validate the performance of eBBO experimental results comparing with BBO and with other modified versions are demonstrated. Finally, eBBO and BBO are shown as soft computing tool for calculating the design parameters of MSA such as length and width, followed by the conclusion.

BASIC CONCEPT

Biogeography-Based Optimization

Biogeography is the study of distribution of species in nature and its mathematical model can be made analogous to general problem solutions. Mathematical models of biogeography are available that describes the species migration phenomena related to their emigration rates μ and immigration rates λ from one island to another, speciation process by which new species arise and their extinction processes. Each possible solution is an island and their features that characterize habitability are called suitability index variables (SIV). The goodness of each solution is called its habitat suitability index (HIS) (Simon, 2008). In BBO each problem solution can share its features with other solutions. The probability that a given solution shares its features is proportional to its fitness, and the probability that a given solution receives features from other solution is inversely proportional to its fitness. In BBO, a habitat H is a vector of N (SIVs) integers initialized randomly. Before optimizing, each individual of population is evaluated and then follows Migration and Mutation step to reach global minima. In Migration the information is shared between habitats that depend on emigration rates μ and immigration rates λ of each solution. Each solution is modified depending on probability P_{mod} that is a user-defined parameter. Each individual has its own λ and μ and are functions of the number of species K in the habitat and is expressed by Equation (1) and (2) (Simon, 2008).

$$\lambda_k = \frac{EK}{P} \quad (1)$$

$$\mu_k = I\left(1 - \frac{K}{P}\right) \quad (2)$$

where; E= maximum λ, I= maximum μ, P = population size.

The immigration and emigration curves are straight lines for the case of $E=I$. Habitat with few species (low HIS, poor solution) has low μ and high λ, while habitat with more species (high HIS, good solution) high μ and low λ. Poor solutions accept more useful information from good solution, which improve the exploitation ability of algorithm.

Habitat modification (Migration) algorithm is described in Box 1 (Simon, 2008).

In BBO, the mutation is used to increase the diversity of the population to get the good solutions. Mutation operator modifies a habitat's SIV randomly based on mutation rate m for the case of E=I. The mutation rate m is expressed as (3) (Simon, 2008).

$$m(s) = pmutate * \left(1 - \frac{p_i}{p_{max}}\right) \quad (3)$$

where; *pmutate* is a user-defined parameter and P_{max} =argmax P_i, i = 1,...,p.

Habitat Mutation algorithm is described in Box 2(Simon, 2008).

Particle Swarm Optimization

In PSO, a swarm of individuals (called particles) fly through the search space. Each individual represents a potential solution (fitness). Particle changes their positions by velocity flying around in a multi-dimensional search space. A point in the D-dimensional space represents the position of a particle. The velocity of a particle represents the magnitude and the direction of the movement and changes according to its own flying experience and the flying experience of the best among the swarm. Firstly, each particle begins at its random position with a random velocity. In each generation, particles velocity and position is updated by following equations (4) and (5) respectively.

$$v_i(t) = w \times v_i(t-1) + c_1 \times r_1(t) \times (pbest_i - x_i(t-1)) + c_2 \times r_2(t) \times (gbest_i - x_i(t-1))$$

$$(4)$$

$$x_i(t) = x_i(t-1) + v_i(t) \quad (5)$$

where; t denotes the current iteration, *pbest* records the i-th particle's position that attains its personal best fitness value up to the present iteration, while *gbest* records the position that attains the global best fitness value among all up to the present iteration. The new velocity is related to the old velocity weighted by w, and also associated to the

Box 1.

```
Select H_i with probability α λ_i
If H_i is selected
    For j = 1 to P
        Select H_j with probability α μ_i
        If H_j is selected
        Randomly select an SIV σ from H_j
        Replace a random SIV in H_i with σ
        end if
    end for
end if
```

Box 2.

```
For j = 1 to N
    Use λ_i and μ_i to compute the probability P_i
    Select SIV H_i(j) with probability α P_i
    If H_i(j) is selected
    Replace H_i(j) with a randomly generated SIV
    end if
end for
```

position x have the particle itself and that of the personal best (*pbest*) and global best (*gbest*) by factors c_1 and c_2 respectively. c_1 and c_2 are called an acceleration co-efficient, namely cognitive and social parameter respectively. w is the inertia weight, which is employed to control the impact of the previous history of velocities on the current one. Two random functions r_1 and r_2 in the range from 0 to 1 are applied independently to vary the relative pull of the personal and global best particles. In PSO, proper control of global exploration and local exploitation is crucial to find the optimum solution efficiently. The PSO suffers from premature convergence when multimodal problems are being optimized.

A number of variations to the original PSO have been proposed to make PSO faster and reliable. Ratnaweera, Halgamuge & Watson (2004) introduced time varying acceleration coefficients c_1 (2.5 to 0.5) and c_2 (0.5 to 2.5) and inertia weight factor in PSO. Further self organizing hierarchical particle swarm optimizer concept is added to enhance global search. In gregarious particle swarm optimization algorithm (GPSO) (Pasupuleti & Bhattiti, 2006), particles are re-initialized with random velocity when stuck in local minima. The algorithm also adopts a reactive determination of step size based on the feedback from last iterations to avoid premature convergence. In GLBestPSO (PSO with global-local best parameters) (Arumugam, Rao, & Chandramohan, 2008), inertia weight (w) and acceleration co-efficient (c) are proposed in terms of global best and local best position of the particles. Wang, Cui and Zeng (2009) improved the convergence speed and the capacity of global searching of PSO by group decision making with all the individuals. Cui, Cai, Zeng and Sun (2008) incorporated fitness uniform selection strategy (FUSS) with a weak selection pressure and different forms of random walk strategies (RWS) in PSO to balance between exploration and exploitation capability. In ePSO, the position of the particles is directly updated without using velocity equation. Extrapolation

operation involves both the current particle position and the global best particle position. It also includes two extrapolation coefficients (e1 and e2) linearly decreasing with the generations from 0.999 to 0.36, which are much similar to the time varying inertia weight (TVIW). A random function is also included to incorporate the stochastic behavior into the algorithm's search to find the optimal solution. The position update operator for each particle is given by (6).

$$x_i(t) = [gbest] + [e_1 \times Rnd \times gbest] + [e_1 \times (gbest - x_i(t-1)) \times \exp(e_2 \times ((f(gbest) - f(x_i(t-1))) / f(gbest)))]$$

$$(6)$$

Where; $e_1 = e_2 = exp$ (- *current generation/ Max. no. of generation*)

Rnd is the random function, which varies between [0, 1)

gbest is the particle position where the best fitness solution is found;

x_i *(t)* is the current particle position in i^{th} generations.

f *(gbest)* is the fitness value at gbest position.

$f(x_i(t))$ is the current particle's fitness value.

The first term in the Equation (6) is the main operator for extrapolation which refines the search towards the global optimum value. The second term ensures the movement of the current particle towards the gbest position. The third term gives the step size for the movement for the updated position. The difference between *f(gbest)* and *f(xi(t))* is high at initial stage of the simulation, so the particle will move more distance towards the gbest position and in later stages the difference will be reduced since the current particle will be close to the gbest position. During the early stages of the simulation, the step size will be large and at the final stage of the simulation, the current particle's fitness will become closer to the gbest particle's fitness value and hence the step size is reduced to smaller value.

EXTRAPOLATED BBO (EBBO)

In hybrid evolutionary algorithm, the best features of different algorithms are combined to avoid individual disadvantages. Hybridization of EAs has the capability of handling several real world problems (Grosan, Abraham & Ishibuchi, 2009) and gives outstanding performance compared with the algorithm acting separately (Tseng & Liang, 2006). Researchers have tried to improve the quality of optimal solution over multimodal and high dimensional functions by fusion of BFA with PSO (Biswas, Dasgupta, Das, & Abraham, 2007) and GA (Kim, Abraham, & Cho, 2007). Tseng and Liang (2006) combined ACO, GA and local search (LS) to solve the quadratic assignment problem (QAP). Mo and Guan (2006) combined PSO and incremental evolution strategy to solve function optimization problem. Hendtlass (2001) hybridized PSO with DE to form a combined swarm differential evolution algorithm. Sun, Zhang and Tsang (2004) combined DE with Estimation of Distribution Algorithm (EDA). It uses the probability model to determine promising regions in order to focus the search process on those areas. Hong, (2009) used support vector regression (SVR) model with a hybrid evolutionary algorithm (chaotic genetic algorithm, CGA) to forecast the electric loads, CGA is applied to the parameter determine of SVR model. Hybrid versions of BBO are also proposed like intelligent BBO (IBBO) (Lohokare Summary: A concept for the optimization of nonlinear functions using particle swarm methodology is introduced. The evolution of several paradigms is outlined, and an implementation of one of the paradigms is discussed. Benchmark testing of the paradigm is des. et al., 2009a) combined with BFA, DE/BBO (Gong, Cai, & Ling, 2009b) combined with DE and BBO/ES (Du, Simon, & Ergezer, 2009) combined with ES. They are tested for global numerical optimization.

The exploitation ability of BBO is good because migration operator can efficiently share the information between solutions. However, it is slow at exploration of the solution. In BBO, if a solution is selected for mutation, then it is simply replaced by a random solution. Due to this random mutation BBO lacks in exploration ability. This procedure may result in creating too many infeasible solutions and may slow down the algorithm considerably. On the other hand, ePSO is good at exploring the search space and locating the region of global minima. EAs like GA, DE, PSO, ES and BBO are equivalent to each other under certain special conditions due to their similar features and can be expressed in terms of each other. BBO is similar to GAGUR as migration strategy in BBO is conceptually similar to a combination of two ideas from GAs: global recombination, and uniform crossover (Simon, Ergezer, & Du, 2009). PSO is equivalent to a continuous GA with intermediate fitness-based global recombination, if a particle's velocity at each generation is independent of its previous velocity, and the best position is probabilistically selected based on fitness (Simon, Ergezer, & Du, 2009). In ePSO, the position of the particles is directly updated without using velocity equation and the position of particle is extrapolated by using the global best and current particle's position and fitness values in the search space. This equivalency of EAs makes the natural feasible way of integration. Based on these considerations, in order to balance the exploration and the exploitation of BBO, in this work, authors propose a hybrid approach, called eBBO, which combines the exploitation ability of BBO with the exploration ability of ePSO effectively. In eBBO, while integrating the extrapolated ePSO operator is updated and is given by

$$H_{i(j)}(t) = [H_{gbest}] + [e_1 \times Rnd \times H_{gbest}]$$
$$+ [e_1 \times (H_{gbest} - H_{i(j)}(t-1))$$
$$\times \exp(e_2 \times ((f(H_{gbest}) \qquad (7)$$
$$- f(H_{i(j)}(t-1))) / f(H_{gbest})))]$$
$$+ [e_1 \times (H_{gbest} - H_{i(j)}(t-1))]$$

Where; H_{gbest} is the SIV where the best fitness solution is found

$H_{i(j)}(t)$ is the current SIV in i^{th} generations.
$f(H_{gbest})$ is the fitness value at gbest position.
$f(H_{i(j)}(t))$ is the current SIV fitness value.

In updated version last term related to difference between SIV with best fitness solution and the current SIV is additionally added. This term ensures the self-replication of SIV selected for mutation more towards the SIV with best fitness solution. Updated version has shown better convergence towards global minima. Hence, keeping all the above point in view, the authors proposed the extrapolated mutation algorithm in Box 3.

eBBO Algorithm

In eBBO, migration is same as basic BBO to maintain its exploitation ability. However, mutation scheme is modified by integrating extrapolated mutation operator from ePSO. In eBBO, authors have selected habitat SIVs to be mutate only for the worst half (j = N/2 to N) of the solutions (poor solutions only) based on the habitat's Mutation Rate for the case of E=I. where; E and I are maximum λ and μ. Mutation Rate is higher at worsts half of the solutions. A solution is selected for mutation that is proportional to species count probability existence which is computed from λ and μ. In eBBO and BBO, elitism is implemented by setting immigration rate λ equal to zero for the *keep*=2 best solutions, where *keep* is a user-defined parameter, to prevent the best solutions from being corrupted by immigration. In BBO, the

Box 3.

```
For j = N/2 to N
    Use λi and μi to compute the probability Pi
    Select SIV Hi(j) with probability α Pi
    If Hi(j) is selected
        Replace Hi(j) as per equation (7)
    end if
end for
```

duplicate habitats are simply replaced randomly, but in eBBO the duplicate habitats $H_{i(j)}$ is replaced with feasible solution generated by sharing the information from current best SIV solution ($H_{best(j)}$) and is expressed as (8).

$$H_{i(j)} = \left(H_{best\ (j)} + \left(H_{i(j)} - H_{best\ (j)}\right) \times rand\ ( )\right)$$
$$(8)$$

The proposed eBBO algorithm is described in Box 4.

eBBO also follows migration and mutation step to reach global minima until computational limitations are exceeded, as described in migration and mutation algorithm.

COMPARISON OF EXPERIENTIAL RESULTS OF EBBO AND BBO

To validate the performance of eBBO, experiments have been conducted on twenty three benchmark functions. These functions were divided into three categories: unimodal functions, multimodal functions with many local minima, and multimodal functions with a few local minima. The details of benchmark functions are shown in Table 1 (Cai & Wang, 2006; Yao, Liu, & Lin, 1999). Functions f_1-f_{13} are high–dimensional and scalable problems. Functions $(f_1$-$f_5)$ are unimodal. Function f6 is the step function, which has one minimum and is discontinuous (Yao, Liu, & Lin, 1999). Function f_7 is a noisy quartic function, where *random* [0, 1) is a uniformly distributed random variable in [0, 1). Functions f_8-f_{13} are multimode functions

Box 4.

Initialize Parameters:
      P= population size
      G= Maximum number of generation
      Keep =Elitism parameter
      P_{mod} =Island modification probability *Pmutate*=Mutation probability

Step1: Initialize the population P randomly.
Step2: Initialize species count probability of each Habitat
Step3: Evaluate the fitness for each individual in P.
Step4: Get H_{gbest} and $f(H_{gbest})$.
Step5: **While** The termination criteria is not met **do**
Step6: Save the best habitats in a temporary array
Step7: For each habitat, map the HSI to number of species S, λ and μ
Step8: Probabilistically choose the immigration island based on the immigration rates.
Step9: Migrate randomly selected SIVs based on the selected island in Step7.
Step10: Mutate the population probabilistically as per (7)
Step11: Evaluate the fitness for each individual in P.
Step12: Sort the population from best to worst
Step13: Replace worst with best Habitat from temporary
Step14: Check for feasibility of each individual SIV.
Step15: Check for duplication of habitat, duplicate habitat is replaced as per (8)
Step16: Update H_{gbest} and $f(H_{gbest})$.
Step17: g=g+1
Step18: **end while**

where the local minima increase exponentially with problem dimension (Yao, Liu, & Lin, 1999). Functions f_{14}-f_{23} are low dimension functions that have a few local minima.

Experimental Setup

In the original BBO algorithm, each solution (individual) is a vector of integer that limits the combination. The granularity or precision is limited. In eBBO, each individual is directly encoded by floating point to solve the continuous global optimization problem. Following parameters are set for all experiments except the cases otherwise mentioned.

- Number of Monte Carlo simulations=50 (Gong, Cai, & Ling, 2009a)
- Population size (islands) =100 (Brest, Greiner, Boskovic, Mernik, & Zumer, 2006; Gong, Cai, & Ling, 2009a; Yao, Liu, & Lin, 1999)

- Number of variables of each function (SIVs) =30 (Gong, Cai, & Ling, 2009a)
- Habitat modification probability=1 (Simon, 2008), (Gong, Cai, & Ling, 2009a)
- Mutation probability =0.005 (Gong, Cai, & Ling, 2009a)
- Value to reach: VTR (Suganthan et al., 2005) =10^{-8}, except for f07 of VTR = 10^{-2}.
- Maximum Number of Fitness Function Evaluation (max_FFEs) (Suganthan et al., 2005): for f_1, f_6, f_{10}, f_{12} and f_{13} max_FFEs=150000; for f_3-f_5, max_FFEs = 500000; for f_2 and f_{11}, max_FFEs = 200000; for f_7-f_9, max_FFEs = 300000.

Following performance criteria are selected for comparison of algorithms.

1. Error (Suganthan et al., 2005) =f(x)-f(x†), where x* = global optimum of the solution. Best minimum error is recorded when the Max_FFEs is reached in 50 runs. Mean

Table 1. Benchmark functions used for experimental performance

Function (F)	D	S	f_{min}
	30	$[-100,100]^d$	0
$f_2 = \sum_{i=1}^{d} \mid x_i \mid + \prod_{i=1}^{d} \mid x_i \mid$	30	$[-10,10]^d$	0
	30	$[-100,100]^d$	0
$f_4 = \max_i \{\mid x_i \mid, 1 \leq i \leq d\}$	30	$[-100,100]^d$	0
	30	$[-30,30]^d$	0
$f_6 = \sum_{i=1}^{d} [\mid (x_i + 0.5) \mid]^2$	30	$[-100,100]^d$	0
	30	$[-1.28,1.28]^d$	0
$f_8 = -\sum_{i=1}^{d} (x_i \sin(\sqrt{\mid x_i \mid}))$	30	$[-500,500]^d$	-12569.5
	30	$[-5.12,5.12]^d$	0
$f_{10} = -20 \exp\left(-0.2\sqrt{\frac{1}{d}\sum_{i=1}^{d} x_i^2}\right) - \exp\left(\frac{1}{d}\sum_{i=1}^{d} \cos(2\pi x_i)\right) + 20 + \exp(1)$	30	$[-32,32]^d$	0
$f_{11} = \frac{1}{4000}\sum_{i=1}^{d} x_i^2 \quad - \prod_{i=1}^{d} \cos(\frac{x_i}{\sqrt{i}}) + 1$	30	$[-600,600]^d$	0
	30	$[-50,50]^d$	0
$f_{13} = 0.1\left\{\sin^2(\pi 3 x_1) + \sum_{i=1}^{d-1}(x_i - 1)^2[1 + 10\sin^2(3\pi x_{i+1})] + (x_n - 1)^2[1 + \sin^2(2\pi x_d)]\right\}$ $+ \sum_{i=1}^{d} u(x_i, 5, 100, 4).$ where $\quad u(x_i, a, k, m) = \begin{cases} k(x_i - a)^m, & x_i \succ a \\ 0, & -a \leq x_i \leq a \\ k(-x_i - a)^m, & x_i \prec -a \end{cases}$	30	$[-50,50]^d$	0
$f_{14} = \left[\frac{1}{500} + \sum_{j=1}^{25}\frac{1}{j + \sum_{i=1}^{2}(x_j + a_{ij})^6}\right]^{-1}$	2	$[-65.536, 65.356]^d$	0.998
$f_{15} = \sum_{i=1}^{11}\left[a_i - \frac{x_1(b_i^2 + b_i x_2)}{b_i^2 + b_i x_3 + x_4}\right]^2$	4	$[-5,5]^d$	0.003075
$f_{16} = 4x_1^2 - 2.1x_1^4 + \frac{1}{3}x_1^6 + x_1 x_2 - 4x_2^2 + 4x_2^4$	2	$[-5,5]^d$	-1.0316285

Table 1. Continued

$f_{17} = \left(x_2 - \dfrac{5.1}{4\pi^2}x_1^2 + \dfrac{5}{\pi}x_1 - 6\right)^2 + 10\left(1 - \dfrac{1}{8\pi}\right)\cos x_1 + 10$	2	[-5,10]x[0,15]	0.398
$f_{18} = \left[1 + \left(x_1 + x_2 + 1\right)^2 \left(19 - 14x_1 + 3x_1^2 - 14x_2 + 6x_1 x_2 + 3x_2^2\right)\right]$ $\times \left[30 + \left(2x_1 - 3x_2\right)^2 \left(18 - 32x_1 + 12x_1^2 + 48x_2 - 36x_1 x_2 + 27x_2^2\right)\right]$	2	$[-0,1]^d$	3
$f_{19} = -\displaystyle\sum_{i=1}^{4} c_i \exp\left[-\sum_{j=1}^{n} a_{ij}\left(x_j - p_{ij}\right)^2\right]$	3	$[-0,1]^d$	-3.86
$f_{20} = -\displaystyle\sum_{i=1}^{4} c_i \exp\left[-\sum_{j=1}^{n} a_{ij}\left(x_j - p_{ij}\right)^2\right]$	6	$[-0,1]^d$	-3.32
$f_{21} = -\displaystyle\sum_{i=1}^{5}\left[\left(x - a_i\right)\left(x - a_i\right)^T + c_i\right]^{-1}$	4	$[-0,10]^d$	-10.1532
$f_{22} = -\displaystyle\sum_{i=1}^{7}\left[\left(x - a_i\right)\left(x - a_i\right)^T + c_i\right]^{-1}$	4	$[-0,10]^d$	-10.4029
$f_{23} = -\displaystyle\sum_{i=1}^{10}\left[\left(x - a_i\right)\left(x - a_i\right)^T + c_i\right]^{-1}$	4	$[-0,10]^d$	-10.5364

and slandered deviation of the error is also calculated.

2. NFFE$_S$ (Suganthan et al., 2005): The number of fitness function evaluations (NFFE$_S$) is also recorded when the VTR is reached. The average and standard deviation of the NFFE$_S$ values are calculated.

3. Number of successful runs (SR) (Suganthan et al., 2005): The number of successful runs is recorded when the VTR is reached before the max_FFEs condition terminates the trial.

4. Convergence response (Suganthan et al., 2005): Error (log) verses Number of fitness function evaluations (NFFEs).

5. Acceleration rate (AR) (Rahnamayan, Tizhoosh & Salama, 2008): This criterion is used to compare the convergence speeds between eBBO and other algorithms. AR= NFFEs$_{other}$/ NFFE$_{S\ eBBO}$, where AR>1 indicates eBBO is faster than its competitor.

eBBO and BBO results are compared with statistical paired t-test, which determines whether two paired sets differ from each other in a significant way under the assumption that the paired differences are independent and identically normally distributed (Goulden, 1956).

Overall Performance

Authors have compared the results of eBBO with BBO and Real Coded BBO (RCBBO) (Simon, Ergezer & Du). Real Coded BBOs (RCBBOs) are the extension of BBO with integration of three different neighborhood search (mutation) operators, RCBBO-G (Gaussian mutation), RCBBO-C (Cauchy mutation) and RCBBO-L (Levy mutation). The parameters used for eBBO and RCBBO are set as per the experimental setup. The parameters used for BBO are set as in (Simon, 2008) and mutation probability is set as

Table 2. Best error values on all test functions, where "Mean" indicates the mean best error values found in the last generation. "Std Dev" stands for the standard deviation. Hereafter, a result with boldface mans better value found

F	eBBO		BBO		eBBO vs BBO	RCBBO-G	RCBBO-C	RCBBO-L
	Mean (Std Dev)	SR	Mean (Std Dev)	SR	t-test	Mean (Std Dev)	Mean (Std Dev)	Mean (Std Dev)
f_1	**6.22E-27** (2.17E-26)	50	6.97E-01 (2.93E-01)	0	-16.811*	1.39E-03 (5.50E-04)	2.11E-03 (7.41E-04)	1.63E-03 (6.60E-04)
f_2	**4.46E-23** (1.28E-22)	50	2.21E-01 (4.35E-02)	0	-35.902*	7.99E-02 (1.44E-02)	9.15E-02 (1.51E-02)	8.04E-02 (1.42E-02)
f_3	**4.98E+01** (8.04E+01)	0	4.40E+02 (1.78E+02)	0	-13.217*	2.27E+01 (1.03E+01)	3.90E+01 (1.91E+01)	4.80E+01 (2.19E+01)
f_4	**7.68E-08** (1.37E-07)	22	9.74E-01 (2.03E-01)	0	-33.825*	3.09E-02 (7.27E-03)	3.02E-02 (5.29E-03)	2.68E-02 (5.09E-03)
f_5	**5.16E+01** (4.37E+01)	0	7.79E+01 (8.86E+01)	0	-3.454*	5.54E+01 (3.52E+01)	6.45E+01 (3.43E+01)	5.27E+01 (3.91E+01)
f_6	**0.00E+00** (0.00E+00)	50	7.00E-01 (8.86E-01)	38	-5.584*	0.00E+00 (0.00E+00)	0.00E+00 (0.00E+00)	0.00E+00 (0.00E+00)
f_7	**1.88E-03** (3.60E-03)	50	2.60E-03 (5.00E-03)	14	-0.774*	1.75E-026 (.43E-03)	1.95E-02 (6.96E-03)	1.87E-02 (5.11E-03)
f_8	**8.13E-09** (2.21E-14)	50	5.02E-01 (2.26E-01)	0	-15.714*	-	-	-
$f_{8\#}$	**-1.26E+04** (5.87E-12)	-	-1.26E+04 (2.08E-01)	-	-	-1.26E+04 (2.20E-05)	-1.26E+04 (2.65E-05)	-1.26E+04 (1.93E-05)
f_9	**0.00E+00** (0.00E+00)	50	7.42E-02 (2.49E-02)	0	-21.048*	2.62E-02 (9.76E-03)	3.39E-02 (1.51E-02)	2.77E-02 (1.02E-02)
f_{10}	**1.45E-14** (9.93E-15)	50	2.99E-01 (6.04E-02)	0	-35.081*	2.51E-02 (5.51E-03)	3.34E-02 (6.15E-03)	2.89E-02 (5.15E-03)
f_{11}	**6.57E-03** (9.00E-03)	27	4.15E-01 (1.23E-01)	0	-23.509*	8.49E-02 (5.44E-02)	3.57E-02 (3.78E-02)	2.99E-02 (3.20E-02)
f_{12}	**3.75E-32** (6.58E-32)	50	4.37E-03 (6.12E-03)	0	-5.050*	3.28E-05 (3.33E-05)	5.21E-05 (5.69E-03)	2.73E-05 (2.49E-05)
f_{13}	**1.08E-26** (2.76E-26)	50	3.97E-02 (1.44E-02)	0	-19.524*	3.72E-04 (4.63E-04)	6.96E-04 (1.02E-03)	5.84E-04 (8.82E-04)

* The value of t with 49 degree of freedom is significant at α = **0**.05 by two-tailed test.

\# Indicate the fitness value results of f_8 for f(x†), where x† = global optimum of the solution.

0.005 since it gives better results with mutation operator for larger population size (Simon, 2008). Table 2 shows the experimental results of mean and slandered deviation of error on each function after completion of 50 Monte Carlo simulations for unimodal and multimodal functions with many local minima. The results show that eBBO gives better performance for all the unimodal as well as multimodal benchmark functions as compared with BBO and RCBBO. eBBO can obtain the VTR over all 50 runs within the MAX_NFFE$_S$ for 9 functions However, BBO may trap into the local minima for all the functions. For unimodal functions f_3, f_4 and f_5 eBBO may get trapped in local minima still its performance is better than BBO and RCBBO. For multimodal functions (f_8-f_{13}) eBBO gives better results which are much more important as they reflects the algorithms ability to escape from getting trapped in local minima and converge to near-global optimum. Table 3 shows

Table 3. NFFES required obtaining accuracy levels less than VTR. "NA" indicates the accuracy level is not obtained after MAX_NFFE$_S$

F	eBBO			BBO			eBBO vs BBO
	Mean	Std Dev	SR	Mean	Std Dev	SR	AR
f_1	56110	3559.251	50	NA	NA	0	NA
f_2	73670	4640.076	50	NA	NA	0	NA
f_3	NA	NA	0	NA	NA	0	NA
f_4	491498	14486.144	22	NA	NA	0	NA
f_5	NA	NA	0	NA	NA	0	NA
f_6	17138	2141.132	50	119042	16882.8	38	8.69
f_7	43864	39947.48	49	205000	23896.2	14	5.23
f_8	59948	2831.762	50	NA	NA	0	NA
f_9	72220	16458.023	50	NA	NA	0	NA
f_{10}	84870	4800.818	50	NA	NA	0	NA
f_{11}	120422	71312.352	28	NA	NA	0	NA
f_{12}	45416	2520.314	50	NA	NA	0	NA
f_{13}	54302	2238.94	50	NA	NA	0	NA

Figure 1. Mean error curves of BBO and eBBO for selected functions population size=100 dimension=30 (a) f_1 (b) f_4 (c) f_6 (d) f_9 (e) f_{11} (f) f_{13}

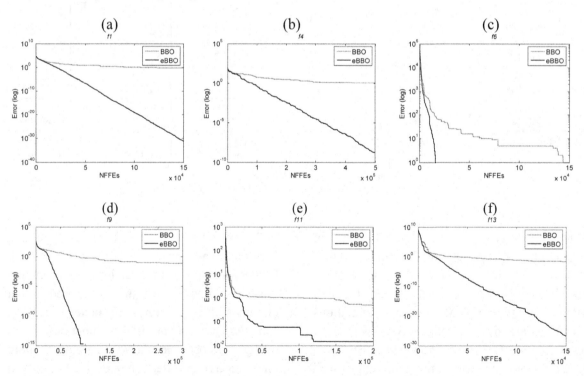

the average and standard deviation of NFFE$_S$. The results show that eBBO requires less NFFE$_S$ to reach the VTR than BBO on all functions. Figure 1 shows the selective convergence graphs of eBBO and BBO for unimodal and multimodal functions with multiple local minima. It shows that eBBO converges faster than BBO for all benchmark functions.

Functions (f_{14}-f_{23}) are low dimensional functions that have only a few local minima. They appear simpler than multimodal function with many local minima. To get the representative comparison with RCBBO for these functions the experiments are conducted for mean best fitness values and standard deviation after completion of 50 Monte Carlo simulations. The experimental results are given in Table 4. Out of ten functions eBBO gives better performance for nine functions

when compared with BBO and eight functions when compared with RCBBO. Figure 2 shows the mean best fitness curves of BBO and eBBO for selected multimodal functions with a few local minima. It shows that eBBO has the ability to get global minima.

Overall results indicate that performance of eBBO is better than RCBBO and significantly better than BBO. The results also indicate that integration of extrapolated mutation operator from ePSO balance the exploitation and exploration ability of the algorithm. It has the ability to escape from the local minima and get converge to the optimum value. Based on the t-test results, it can be seen that the integration of extrapolated mutation operator from ePSO has a big effect on the BBO. The convergence graphs of eBBO and BBO for unimodal, multimodal with many local min-

Table 4. Best fitness values on all test functions, where "Mean" indicates the mean best error values found in the last generation. "Std Dev" stands for the standard deviation.

F	eBBO Mean (Std Dev)	BBO Mean (Std Dev)	eBBO vs BBO t-test	RCBBO-G Mean (Std Dev)	RCBBO-C Mean (Std Dev)	RCBBO-L Mean (Std Dev)
f_{14}	**0.998012** **(5.53E-03)**	0.998014 (5.28E-03)	-0.062*	0.998017 (5.53E-05)	0.998086 (4.56E0-04)	0.998069 (4.46E-04)
f_{15}	0.000805 (2.05E-04)	0.000878 (2.33E-04)	-1.513*	**7.86E-04** **(1.80E-04)**	1.17E-03 (2.28E-03)	1.17E-03 (2.78E-03)
f_{16}	**-1.031314** **(4.86E-04)**	-1.031092 (6.95E-04)	-1.948*	-1.031010 (9.01E-04)	-1.031100 (7.90E-04)	-1.03112 (5.88E-04)
f_{17}	**0.3982139** **(4.56E-04)**	0.398334 (7.00E-04)	-0.169*	0.398414 (6.77E-04)	0.398470 (1.06E-03)	0.398289 (5.52E-04)
f_{18}	**3.005476** **(6.31E-03)**	3.007536 (9.55E-03)	-1.445*	3.009504 (1.12E-02)	3.008666 (1.15E-02)	3.006942 (1.02E-02)
f_{19}	-3.862644 (1.55E-04)	**-3.862668** **(1.49E-04)**	0.759	-3.862480 (3.65E-04)	-3.862540 (2.74E-04)	-3.86247 (4.67E-04)
f_{20}	-3.307568 (3.90E-02)	-3.293204 (5.14E-02)	-1.640*	**-3.316910** **(2.36E-02)**	-3.307480 (3.90E-02)	-3.31228 (3.26E-02)
f_{21}	**-7.453849** **(3.46E+00)**	-6.394933 (3.50E+00)	-1.656*	-5.513410 (3.35E+00)	-4.618730 (3.32E+00)	-561985 (3.45E+00)
f_{22}	**-8.086827** **(3.32E+00)**	-7.793875 (3.34E+00)	-0.413*	-6.800220 (3.52E+00)	-6.869030 (3.51E+00)	-7.06758 (3.48E+00)
f_{23}	**-9.094935** **(2.72E+00)**	-7.845428 (3.30E+00)	-2.036*	-7.284800 (3.38E+00)	-7.250110 (3.47E+00)	-7.46472 (3.49E+00)

* The value of t with 49 degree of freedom is significant at α = **0.**05 by two-tailed test.

Figure 2. Mean best fitness curves of BBO and eBBO for selected multimodal functions with a few local minima (a) f_{14} (b) f_{16} (c) f_{18} (d) f_{19} (e) f_{21} (f) f_{23}

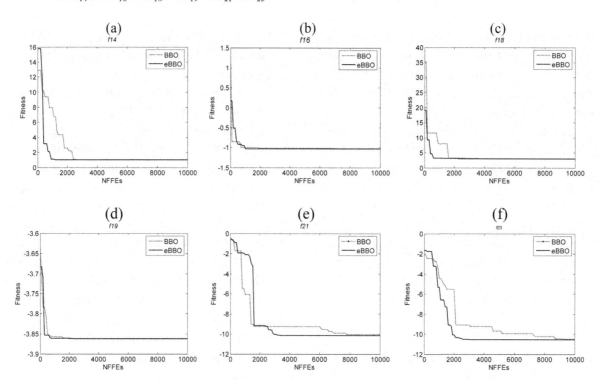

ima and low dimensional functions with few local minima shows that eBBO has better convergence rate than BBO. The majority results of eBBO, RCBBO and BBO algorithm for the low dimensional functions (f_{14}-f_{23}) have no significant difference, so these functions are not used while conducting the further experiments.

Influence of Population Size

Increasing the population size will increase the diversity of possible movements, promoting the exploration of the search space. However, the probability to find the correct search direction decreases considerably (Feoktistov & Janaqi, 2004). In this section, the influence of population size is investigated by changing the population size to 50, 100, 150 and 200, keeping the remaining parameters same. The results for different population size are shown in Table 5. The results show that

eBBO exhibits higher overall successful runs and more robustness than BBO for all the functions with different population size. Results of unimodal functions, f_1, f_2, f_4, f_6 and f_7 give better performance for all population sizes. For function f_3, accuracy decreases as population size increases. Results for multimodal functions are good for different population and reaches VTR over all 50 runs within the MAX_NFFEs except function f_{11} that gets trapped in local minima. Figures 3 through 5 gives some representative convergence graphs of eBBO and BBO with fixed dimension of 30 and changing population size. The result shows that eBBO gives higher convergence velocity than BBO.

Effect of Dimensionality

In this section, the influence of scalability (problem dimensions change) is investigated on the

Table 5. Influence on the performance with different population size for functions f01-f13 (Dimension=30)

F	Population size=50					Population size=100				
	eBBO		BBO		eBBO vs BBO	eBBO		BBO		eBBO vs BBO
	Mean (Std Dev)	SR	Mean (Std Dev)	SR	t-test	Mean (Std Dev)	SR	Mean (Std Dev)	SR	t-test
f_1	**1.75E-48 (6.31E-48)**	50	6.42E-01 (2.83E-01)	0	-16.055*	**6.22E-27 (2.17E-26)**	50	6.97E-01 (2.93E-01)	0	-16.811*
f_2	**1.08E-38 (2.46E-38)**	50	5.29E-01 (1.02E-01)	0	-36.589*	**4.46E-23 (1.28E-22)**	50	2.21E-01 (4.35E-02)	0	-35.902*
f_3	**1.70E+00 (4.33E+00)**	0	1.98E+02 (9.71E+01)	0	-14.366*	**4.98E+01 (8.04E+01)**	0	4.40E+02 (1.78E+02)	0	-13.217*
f_4	**8.25E-12 (2.25E-11)**	50	8.26E-01 (1.74E-01)	0	-33.560*	**7.68E-08 (1.37E-07)**	40	9.74E-01 (2.03E-01)	0	-33.825*
f_5	**4.76E+01 (3.67E+01)**	0	8.49E+01 (3.55E+01)	0	-4.634*	**5.16E+01 (4.37E+01)**	0	7.79E+01 (8.86E+01)	0	-3.454*
f_6	**0.00E+00 (0.00E+00)**	50	1.00E-01 (3.03E-01)	45	-2.333*	**0.00E+00 (0.00E+00)**	50	7.00E-01 (8.86E-01)	38	-5.584*
f_7	**1.30E-03 (6.40E-03)**	50	5.30E-02 (3.45E-02)	0	-10.170*	**1.88E-03 (3.60E-03)**	50	2.60E-03 (5.00E-03)	14	-0.774*
f_8	**8.13E-09 (4.04E-13)**	50	3.68E-01 (1.33E-01)	0	-19.563	**8.13E-09 (2.21E-14)**	50	5.02E-01 (2.26E-01)	0	-15.714*
f_9	**0.00E+00 (0.00E+00)**	50	7.17E-02 (2.76E-02)	0	-18.341*	**0.00E+00 (0.00E+00)**	50	7.42E-02 (2.49E-02)	0	-21.048*
f_{10}	**8.78E-15 (3.37E-15)**	50	2.71E-01 (6.27E-02)	0	-30.563*	**1.45E-14 (9.93E-15)**	50	2.99E-01 (6.04E-02)	0	-35.081*
f_{11}	**9.00E-03 (1.18E-02)**	26	4.08E-01 (8.71E-02)	0	-32.709*	**6.57E-03 (9.00E-03)**	27	4.15E-01 (1.23E-01)	0	-23.509*
f_{12}	**1.57E-32 (5.53E-48)**	50	4.00E-03 (6.30E-03)	0	-4.550*	**3.75E-32 (6.58E-32)**	50	4.37E-03 (6.12E-03)	0	-5.050*
f_{13}	**1.35E-32 (1.11E-47)**	50	3.53E-02 (1.57E-02)	0	-15.962*	**1.08E-26 (2.76E-26)**	50	3.97E-02 (1.44E-02)	0	-19.524*
F	Population size=150					Population size=200				
	eBBO		BBO		eBBO vs BBO	eBBO		BBO		eBBO vs BBO
	Mean (Std Dev)	SR	Mean(Std Dev)	SR	t-test	Mean (Std Dev)	SR	Mean (Std Dev)	SR	t-test
f_1	**2.89E-18 (6.82E-18)**	50	8.53E-01 (3.12E-01)	0	-19.308*	**9.69E-14 (1.52E-13)**	50	9.88E-01 (3.23E-01)	0	-21.598*
f_2	**1.35E-16 (2.55E-16)**	50	2.13E-01 (3.65E-02)	0	-41.407*	**3.31E-13 (5.80E-13)**	50	2.32E-01 (4.50E-02)	0	-36.399*
f_3	**1.53E+02 (1.45E+02)**	0	6.42E+02 (2.72E+02)	0	-10.966*	**2.90E+02 (1.95E+02)**	0	9.76E+02 (4.66E+02)	0	-10.078*
f_4	**2.81E-05 (1.01E-04)**	0	1.06E+00 (2.63E-01)	0	-28.654*	**3.31E-13 (5.80E-13)**	50	1.24E+00 (2.66E-01)	0	-32.868*
f_5	**5.10E+01 (3.93E+01)**	0	8.55E+01 (3.64E+01)	0	-4.441*	**5.16E+01 (4.37E+01)**	0	9.08E+01 (3.21E+01)	0	-4.338*
f_6	**0.00E+00 (0.00E+00)**	50	8.80E-01 (8.24E-01)	18	-7.550*	**0.00E+00 (0.00E+00)**	50	9.60E-01 (9.68E-01)	20	-7.012*

Table 5. Continued

f_7	**1.40E-03** **(1.90E-03)**	50	7.10E-03 (3.10E-03)	42	-11.246*	**1.20E-03** **(2.20E-03)**	50	6.60E-03 (2.80E-03)	45	-10.458*
f_8	**8.13E-09** **(4.04E-13)**	50	5.42E-01 (2.33E-01)	0	-16.466*	**8.13E-09** **(4.34E-14)**	50	5.78E-01 (2.29E-01)	0	-17.862*
f_9	**0.00E+00** **(0.00E+00)**	50	1.00E-01 (5.59E-02)	0	-12.684*	**0.00E+00** **(0.00E+00)**	50	9.47E-02 (3.18E-02)	0	-21.041*
f_{10}	**3.37E-10** **(4.91E-10)**	50	3.45E-01 (8.13E-02)	0	-29.973*	**1.79E-08** **(2.06E-08)**	50	3.53E-01 (5.96E-02)	0	-41.910*
f_{11}	**5.00E-03** **(6.80E-03)**	30	4.94E-01 (9.91E-02)	0	-34.413*	**3.27E-02** **(9.28E-02)**	35	5.09E-01 (1.27E-01)	0	-22.109*
f_{12}	**2.21E-28** **(5.35E-28)**	50	5.52E-03 (6.15E-03)	0	-6.352*	**3.41E-16** **(8.78E-16)**	50	8.10E-03 (1.42E-02)	0	-4.015*
f_{13}	**1.62E-18** **(4.45E-18)**	50	4.52E-02 (1.65E-02)	0	-19.427*	**3.54E-14** **(1.07E-13)**	50	5.30E-02 (1.86E-02)	0	-20.211*

* The value of t with 49 degree of freedom is significant at $\alpha = 0.05$ by two-tailed test.

Figure 3. Mean error curves of BBO and eBBO for selected functions population size=50 dimension=30 (a) f_3 (b) f_5 (c) f_8 (d) f_{10} (e) f_{11} (f) f_{13}

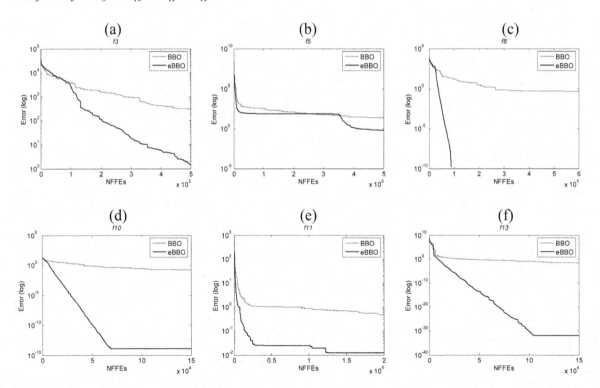

Figure 4. Mean error curves of BBO and eBBO for selected functions population size=150 dimension=30 (a) f_1 (b) f_2 (c) f_4 (d) f_7 (e) f_{10} (f) f_{12}

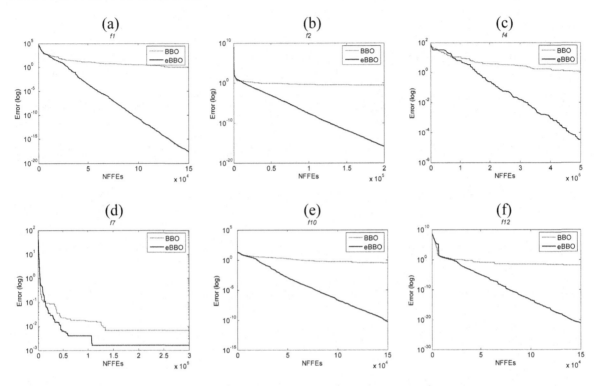

Figure 5. Mean error curves of BBO and eBBO for selected functions population size=200 dimension=30 (a) f_2 (b) f_4 (c) f_6 (d) f_7 (e) f_9 (f) f_{11}

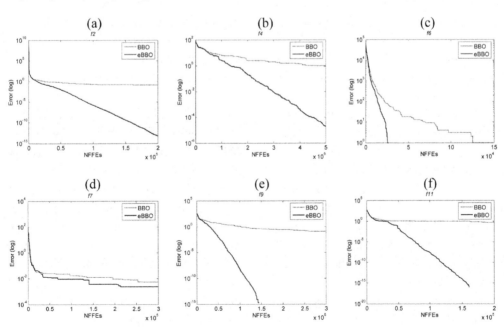

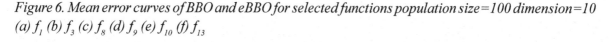

Figure 6. Mean error curves of BBO and eBBO for selected functions population size=100 dimension=10 (a) f_1 (b) f_3 (c) f_8 (d) f_9 (e) f_{10} (f) f_{13}

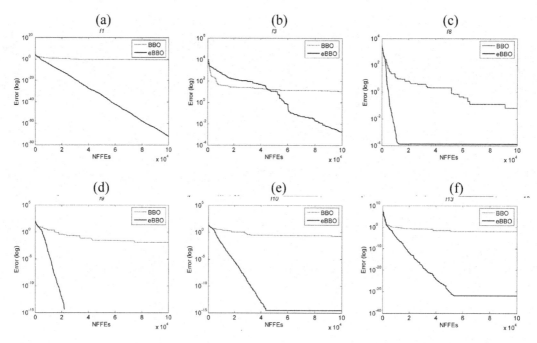

performance of eBBO and BBO for the scalable functions (*f1-f13*), dimensions= 10, 50, 100. The results are recorded in Table 6 after D x 10000 NFFE$_S$ (Ergezer, Simon & Du, 2009; Suganthan, *et al;* 2005) Increasing problem dimension, sometime algorithms fails to solve the problem before reaching the MAX_NFFE$_S$ and that results in decrease in the SR value. Figures 6 through 8 shows some representative convergence graphs for different dimensions. The results show that eBBO gives excellent performance for all functions with different dimensions as compare to BBO. eBBO gives robust performance for the functions f_1, f_2, f_6, f_7, f_9, f_{10}, f_{12} and f_{13}. For f_4 function scalability affects more, increasing the dimension decreases the accuracy as well as the SR value. Function f_8 gives the good performance for dimension 10 and 50 but for dimension 100, accuracy is decreased slight below the VTR, which makes the SR value to 0. For functions, f_3, f_4 and f_5 accuracy decreases as dimensions increases. Function f_{11} may get

trapped in local minima with different dimensions. Convergence graphs for different dimensions indicate that eBBO has faster convergence than BBO. The results indicate that diversity controlled mutation operator has the ability to accelerate BBO in general; especially the improvements are more significant at higher dimensionality.

CALCULATION OF OPTIMIZED PARAMETERS OF RECTANGULAR MICROSTRIP PATCH ANTENNA

Miniaturized Microstrip patch antenna (MSAs) are of great interest in the recent time specially in wireless communication systems and biomedical applications due to their attractive features such as ease in fabrication and integration with solid-state devices etc. (Bahl & Bhartia, 1980). In the changing scenario of wireless communication technology, demands for MSA with size reduction,

Table 6. Scalability study for functions f01-f13 at MAX_NFFE$_S$ = D x 10000

F	D=10						D=50					
	eBBO		BBO		eBBO vs BBO		eBBO		BBO		eBBO vs BBO	
	Mean (Std Dev)	SR	Mean (Std Dev)	SR	t-test		Mean (Std Dev)	SR	Mean (Std Dev)	SR	t-test	
f_1	8.00E-61 (5.63E-60)	50	6.74E-02 (4.69E-02)	0	-10.171*		3.54E-50 (1.13E-49)	50	3.05E-01 (1.18E-01)	0	-18.219*	
f_2	3.00E-28 (2.12E-27)	50	4.80E-02 (1.57E-02)	0	-21.615*		3.41E+03 (1.42E+03)	50	2.39E-01 (3.93E-02)	0	16.971*	
f_3	1.40E-03 (3.30E-03)	0	1.94E+01 (1.70E+01)	0	-8.050*		3.32E+03 (1.60E+03)	0	4.68E+03 (1.42E+03)	0	-4.366*	
f_4	8.07E-14 (4.86E-13)	50	3.76E-01 (1.77E-01)	0	-15.025*		1.01E-01 (9.48E-02)	0	3.02E+00 (5.27E-01)	0	-38.561*	
f_5	6.04E+00 (5.69E+00)	0	2.37E+01 (2.67E+01)	0	-4.507*		1.15E+02 (5.05E+01)	0	1.73E+02 (4.76E+01)	0	-5.333*	
f_6	0.00E+00 (0.00E+00)	50	0.00E+00 (0.00E+00)	50	-		0.00E+00 (0.00E+00)	50	0.00E+00 (0.00E+00)	50	-	
f_7	1.20E-03 (1.90E-03)	50	3.20E-03 (1.70E-03)	50	-6.019*		2.28E-03 (6.09E-03)	50	2.90E-02 (1.41E-02)	2	-12.030*	
f_8	9.10E-13 (0.00E+00)	50	1.44E-01 (9.92E-02)	0	-10.278*		9.72E-09 (2.40E-10)	50	8.08E-01 (2.36E-01)	0	-24.266*	
f_9	0.00E+00 (0.00E+00)	50	2.61E-02 (1.45E-02)	0	-12.743*		0.00E+00 (0.00E+00)	50	1.35E-01 (4.03E-02)	0	-23.622*	
f_{10}	2.59E-15 (5.02E-16)	50	1.34E-01 (6.59E-02)	0	-14.400*		1.45E-14 (3.32E-15)	50	1.22E-01 (2.19E-02)	0	-39.504*	
$f11$	1.63E-02 (1.60E-02)	12	1.55E-01 (4.94E-02)	0	-19.580*		5.50E-03 (7.80E-03)	28	2.74E-01 (6.63E-02)	0	-28.141*	
$f12$	1.57E-32 (5.53E-48)	50	1.50E-03 (2.60E-03)	0	-4.200*		1.57E-32 (5.53E-48)	50	1.30E-03 (1.30E-03)	0	-7.242*	
$f13$	1.35E-32 (1.11E-47)	50	7.40E-03 (5.90E-03)	0	-8.751*		1.35E-32 (1.11E-47)	50	1.38E-02 (6.30E-03)	0	-15.327*	
F	D=100											
	eBBO		BBO		eBBO vs BBO							
	Mean (Std Dev)	SR	Mean (Std Dev)	SR	t-test							
f_1	1.40E-41 (2.67E-41)	50	5.80E-01 (1.28E-01)	0	-31.948*							
f_2	3.04E-25 (4.49E-25)	50	4.96E-01 (4.42E-02)	0	-79.303*							
f_3	2.87E+04 (6.25E+03)	0	4.35E+04 (1.33E+04)	0	-8.283*							
f_4	1.76E+00 (1.38E+00)	0	5.23E+00 (5.31E-01)	0	-17.694*							
f_5	2.57E+02 (4.95E+01)	0	3.40E+02 (4.51E+01)	0	-8.495*							
f_6	0.00E+00 (0.00E+00)	50	0.00E+00 (0.00E+00)	50	-							

continued on following page

Table 6. Continued

f_7	**5.93E-03 (6.52E-03)**	**50**	4.75E-02 (1.53E-02)	0	-17.171*					
f_8	**2.70E-08 (5.75E-13)**	**50**	1.43E+00 (3.72E-01)	0	-21.891*					
f_9	**0.00E+00 (0.00E+00)**	**50**	2.55E-01 (4.75E-02)	0	-37.896*					
f_{10}	**3.57E-14 (3.94E-15)**	**50**	1.29E-01 (1.91E-02)	0	-47.775*					
f11	**1.43E-02 (1.02E-02)**	**10**	3.48E-01 (7.15E-02)	0	-32.509*					
f12	**1.57E-32 (2.89E-48)**	**50**	1.40E-03 (1.00E-03)	0	-9.960*					
f13	**1.35E-32 (2.89E-48)**	**50**	2.35E-02 (7.60E-03)	0	-21.964*					

* The value of t with 49 degree of freedom is significant at $\alpha = \mathbf{0}.05$ by two-tailed test.

Figure 7. Mean error curves of BBO and eBBO for selected functions population size=100 dimension=50 (a) f_3 (b) f_4 (c) f_6 (d) f_9 (e) f_{11} (f) f_{12}

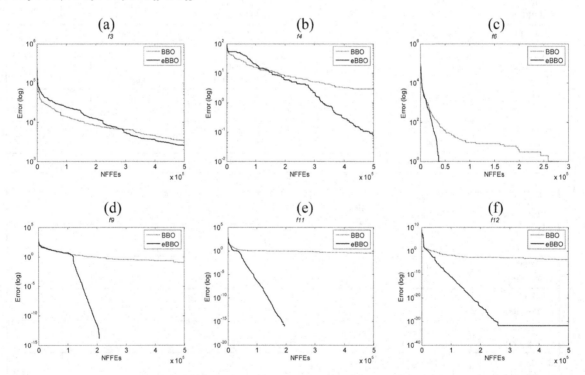

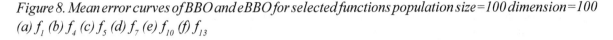

Figure 8. Mean error curves of BBO and eBBO for selected functions population size=100 dimension=100 (a) f_1 (b) f_4 (c) f_5 (d) f_7 (e) f_{10} (f) f_{13}

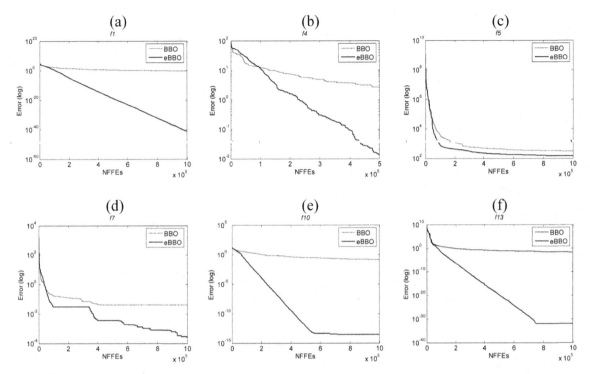

high gain, wide bandwidth, multiple functionality, and system level integration using soft computing techniques. As MSA is inhomogeneous and the radiation appears at the edges of the patch, the physical properties are difficult to determine when designing an antenna for a specified frequency and substrate material (Kara, 1997). The antenna performance characteristics depend largely on the physical dimensions of the patch, the diameter and position of the feed probe, the relative permittivity, and the thickness of the substrate. Although several formulas using different levels of approximation are available in the literature to design the physical properties of rectangular MSA elements (Bahl & Bhartia, 1980; Kara, 1997; Pozar & Schaubert, 1995), there appears to be no reliable general method that gives these properties. The designer has thus been forced to obtain the required physical properties by a trial-and-error technique. Also, due to inherent narrow bandwidth, the resonant

frequency or the dimension of the patch antenna must be predicted accurately. Nature inspired soft computing tools such as GA (Pattnaik, Khuntia, Panda, Neog, & Devi, 2003) and PSO (Yilmaz & Kuzuoglu, 2007) are also used for this problem. In this section, BBO, eBBO are applied to calculate the design parameters such as length 'L' and width 'W' of these antennas for given resonant frequency (f_r), dielectric constant (ε_r) and thickness of the substrate (h). For experimentation considered antennas are electrically thin and dimensions are taken from (Kara, 1996b). Figure 9 illustrates a typical rectangular MSA with side length, width, height and the feed point location. The parameters of BBO and eBBO are set as given previously to evaluate 10^3 NFFEs with one Monte Carlo simulation. A population member consists of a vector (SIVs) of fraction numbers, with each element in the vector representing change in length (L) and width (W) of the antenna. These are passed as search space variables in search space domain of BBO and eBBO.

The resonant frequency of rectangular MSA is determined by h, ε_r, L and W and is given as (Kara, 1996b).

$$f_r = \frac{c_0}{2(L + \Delta W)\sqrt{\varepsilon_e(W)}} \qquad (9)$$

where; c_0 is the velocity of the electromagnetic waves in free space and $\varepsilon_e(W)$ is the effective dielectric constant, which is given by (10).

$$\varepsilon_e(W) = \frac{\varepsilon_r + 1}{2} + \frac{\varepsilon_r - 1}{2\left(1 + \dfrac{10}{\mu}\right)^{0.5}} \qquad (10)$$

$\varepsilon_r(W)$ is the relative permittivity of the substrate, and $\mu = W/h$.

ΔW is the line extension and is given by

$$\Delta W = 0.412h\frac{[\varepsilon_e(W) + 0.300](\mu + 0.264)}{[\varepsilon_e(W) - 0.258](\mu + 0.813)} \qquad (11)$$

Later Kara (1996a) refined resonant frequency formula is given by (12). In this formulation,

the effective dielectric constant $\varepsilon_e(w)$ is given by (12).

$$\varepsilon_e(W) = \frac{\varepsilon_r + 1}{2} + \frac{\varepsilon_r - 1}{2\left(1 + \dfrac{10}{\mu}\right)^{cd}} \qquad (12)$$

where ;

$$c = 1 + \frac{1}{49}\ln\left[\frac{\mu^4 + \left(\dfrac{\mu}{52}\right)^2}{\mu^4 + 0.432}\right] + \frac{1}{18.7}\ln\left[1 + \left(\dfrac{\mu}{18.1}\right)^3\right]$$

$$d = 0.564\left(\frac{\varepsilon_r - 0.3}{\varepsilon_r + 0.3}\right)^{0.053}$$

and this time, the line extension ΔW is given by

$$\Delta W = 0.824h\frac{[\varepsilon_e(W) + 0.300](\mu + 0.264)}{[\varepsilon_e(W) - 0.258](\mu + 0.813)} \qquad (13)$$

The fitness or HIS of a population member is calculated by taking the difference between measured resonant frequency (f_r) and calculated resonant frequency (f_{rcal}). f_{rcal} is calculated by using the formulation given in (Kara, 1996b; Kara, 1996a) respectively, we can define two separate

Figure 9. Rectangular microstrip patch antenna

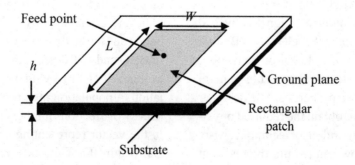

Table 7. Experimental dimensions of Rectangular Microstrip Antennas and comparison of optimization results for 'L' and 'W'

(f$_r$) GHz	Experimental values (Kara, 1996b)				GA (Pattnaik, et al; 2003)		PSO-f$_1$ (Yilmaz & Kuzuoglu, 2007)		PSO-f$_2$		BBO-f$_1$		BBO-f$_2$		eBBO-f$_1$		eBBO-f$_2$	
	(ε$_r$)	(h) mm	(L) mm	(W) mm	(L) mm	(W) mm	(L) mm	(W) mm	(L) mm	(W) mm	(L) mm	(W) mm	(L) mm	(W) mm	(L mm)	(W) mm	(L) mm	(W) mm
6.2	2.55	2.0	14.12	13.37	14.382	8.975	14.294	8.978	14.290	8.972	14.106	13.732	14.17	12.374	14.128	13.224	14.136	13.291
8.45	2.22	0.17	11.85	7.90	11.867	9.456	11.844	9.412	11.852	9.408	11.848	7.678	11.849	7.217	11.853	8.085	11.882	7.798
7.74	2.22	0.17	12.9	8.50	12.9	19.337	12.888	19.314	12.887	19.333	12.955	10.882	12.973	10.029	12.959	10.488	12.962	10.006
3.97	2.22	0.79	25	20.00	25.306	13.007	25.104	13.023	25.101	13.042	25.047	21.688	25.105	19.084	25.068	20.659	25.062	19.736
5.06	2.33	1.57	18.6	17.20	18.6	18.4	18.603	18.442	18.606	18.414	18.622	17.724	18.619	17.787	18.687	15.897	18.642	17.191
5.6	2.55	1.63	16.21	15.00	16.07	13.34	16.178	13.440	16.232	13.568	16.075	13.638	16.142	14.456	16.216	14.913	16.186	15.055
4.805	2.33	1.57	19.6	18.10	19.573	21.696	19.612	21.703	19.609	21.756	19.638	18.635	19.629	17.834	19.586	18.207	19.613	17.973

fitness functions to be minimized, as $f_1 = f_r - f_{rcal1}$ and $f_2 = f_r - f_{rcal2}$. In designing patch antenna, patch width is an important consideration as it affects the bandwidth, the efficiency, the H-plane radiation pattern, the resonant frequency and the cross polarization (Kara, 1997; Pozar & Schaubert, 1995). A small width results in a large bandwidth, and low antenna efficiency and gain. A large width, however, results in the excitation of high-order modes, which may distort the radiation pattern, decrease the bandwidth, and increase the efficiency. In proposed method, while selecting the patch width authors have applied the boundary restriction that the width must be less than $\lambda_d/2$ (Kara, 1997), where λ_d is the wavelength in the dielectric substrate and also according to Derneryd (1978) $W \approx 0.3\, \lambda_0$. The experimental results using BBO and eBBO are presented in Table 7. The results are also compared with GA and PSO. These results are in good agreement with those in the literature.

CONCLUSION

In this paper, the authors have presented an improved variant of BBO named as 'eBBO'. Extrapolated mutation operator from ePSO is used to balance the exploitation and exploration ability of the algorithm to escape from getting trapped in local minima and converge to near-global optimum. Thus improving accuracy eBBO is formulated to optimize functions of continuous variables. The experiments are conducted on both the unimodal $(f_1 - f_7)$ and multimodal $(f_8 - f_{13})$ high dimensional benchmark functions. Influence of population size and dimensionality are carried out to show the performance of eBBO comparing with original BBO. Experimental analysis shows that eBBO can solve continuous global optimization problem with better accuracy and fast convergence rate compared to BBO. According to simulation results, and with the evidence from two-tailed t-test, eBBO have performance that is statistically significantly better than the original BBO. In this work, authors only consider the unconstrained function optimization. For future work, the performance of eBBO can be tested for constrained optimization problem. eBBO and BBO are also used as soft computing tools for calculating the design parameters of rectangular MSA with thin substrates. The result shows that BBO and eBBO technique gives better performance in terms of accuracy as compared with other published results with application of boundary restriction while selecting the width of the patch. The proposed soft computing tool to calculate the design parameters of rectangular MSA may be used as an alternate CAD simulation tool where both length and width are to be adjusted simultaneously in order to achieve the required resonant frequency specially in miniaturized structure.

REFERENCES

Arumugam, M. S., Rao, M. V. C., & Chandramohan, A. (2008). A new and improved version of particle swarm optimization algorithm with global-local best parameters. *Journal of Knowledge and Information System, 16*(3), 324–350.

Arumugam, M. S., Rao, M. V. C., & Tan, A. W. C. (2009). A new novel and effective particle swarm optimization like algorithm with extrapolation technique. *International Journal of Applied Soft Computing, 9*(1), 308-320.

Back, T. (1996). *Evolutionary algorithms in theory and practice*. Oxford, UK: Oxford University Press.

Bahl, I. J., & Bhartia, P. (1980). *Microstrip Antennas*. Dedham, MA: Artech House.

Biswas, A., Dasgupta, S., Das, S., & Abraham, A. (2007). Synergy of PSO and Bacterial Foraging Optimization-A Comparative Study on Numerical Benchmarks. In Corchado, E., Corchado, J. M., & Abraham, A. (Eds.), *Innovations in Hybrid Intelligent Systems, Advances in intelligent and soft computing* (*Vol. 44*, pp. 255–263). Berlin: Springer. doi:10.1007/978-3-540-74972-1_34

Brest, J., Greiner, S., Boskovic, B., Mernik, M., & Zumer, V. (2006). Self-adapting control parameters in differential evolution: A comparative study on numerical benchmark problems. *IEEE Transactions on Evolutionary Computation, 10*(6), 646–657. doi:10.1109/TEVC.2006.872133

Cai, Z., & Wang, Y. (2006). A multiobjective optimization-based evolutionary algorithm for constrained optimization. *IEEE Transactions on Evolutionary Computation, 10*(6), 658–675. doi:10.1109/TEVC.2006.872344

Carlos, A., Coello, C., & Lechuga, M. S. (2002). MOPSO: A Proposal for Multiple Objective Particle Swarm Optimization. In *Proceedings of the Congress on Evolutionary Computation Vol.* (Vol. 2, pp. 1051-1056). doi: 10.1109/CEC.2002.1004388

Cui, Z., Cai, X., Zeng, J., & Sun, G. (2008). Particle swarm optimization with FUSS and RWS for high dimensional functions. *Applied Mathematics and Computation, 205*(1), 98–108. doi:10.1016/j.amc.2008.05.147

Derneryd, A. G. (1978). A Theoretical Investigation of the Rectangular Microstrip Patch Antenna Element. *IEEE Transactions on Antennas and Propagation, 26*(4), 532–535. doi:10.1109/TAP.1978.1141890

Du, D., Simon, D., & Ergezer, M. (2009). Biogeography-Based Optimization Combined with Evolutionary Strategy and Immigration Refusal. In *Proceedings of the IEEE Conference on Systems, Man, and Cybernetics* (pp. 997-1002). doi: 10.1109/ICSMC.2009.5346055

Eberhart, R., & Shi, Y. (2001). Particle swarm optimization: Developments, applications and resources. In *Proceedings of the IEEE congress on Evolutionary Computation* (Vol.1, pp. 81-86). doi: 10.1109/CEC.2001.934374

Eberhart, R., & Shi, Y. (2004). Special issue on particle swarm optimization. *IEEE Transactions on Evolutionary Computation, 89*(3), 201–228. doi:10.1109/TEVC.2004.830335

Ergezer, M., Simon, D., & Du, D. (2009). Oppositional Biogeography-Based Optimization. In *Proceedings of the IEEE Conference on Systems, Man, and Cybernetics* (pp. 1009–1014). doi: 10.1109/ICSMC.2009.5346043

Feoktistov, V., & Janaqi, S. (2004). Generalization of the strategies in differential evolution. In *Proceedings of the 18th International Parallel and Distributed Processing Symposium* (pp. 165-170). doi: 10.1109/IPDPS.2004.1303160

Gong, W., Cai, Z., & Ling, C. X. (2009a). *A real-coded Biogeography-Based Optimization with neighborhood search operator.* Retrieved from http://academic.csuohio.edu/simond/bbo

Gong, W., Cai, Z., & Ling, C. X. (2009b). *DE/BBO: A hybrid differential evolution with biogeography-based optimization for global numerical optimization. Manuscript submitted for publication.* Retrieved from http://academic.csuohio.edu/simond/bbo

Goulden, C. H. (1956). *Methods of Statistical Analysis.* New York: Wiley.

Grosan, C., Abraham, A., & Ishibuchi, H. (Eds.). (2007). *Hybrid Evolutionary Algorithms*. Berlin: Springer.

Hendtlass, T. (2001). A combined swarm differential evolution algorithm for optimization problems. In L. Monostori, J. Vancza, & M. Ali (Eds.), *Proceedings of the 14th International Conference on Industrial and Engineering Applications of Artificial Intelligence and Expert System, Engineering of Intelligent Systems* (pp. 11-18). Berlin: Springer.

Hong, W. C. (2009). Hybrid evolutionary algorithms in a SVR-based electric load forecasting model. *International Journal of Electrical Power & Energy Systems*, *31*(7-8), 409–417. doi:10.1016/j.ijepes.2009.03.020

Kaelo, P., & Ali, M. M. (2006). A numerical study of some modified differential evolution algorithms. *European Journal of Operational Research*, *169*(3), 1176–1184. doi:10.1016/j.ejor.2004.08.047

Kara, M. (1996a). Formulas for the Computation of the Physical Properties of Rectangular Microstrip Antenna Elements with Various Substrate Thicknesses. *Microwave and Optical Technology Letters*, *12*(4), 234–239. doi:10.1002/(SICI)1098-2760(199607)12:4<234::AID-MOP15>3.0.CO;2-A

Kara, M. (1996b). The Resonant Frequency of Rectangular Microstrip Antenna Elements with Various Substrate Thicknesses. *Microwave and Optical Technology Letters*, *11*(2), 55–59. doi:10.1002/(SICI)1098-2760(19960205)11:2<55::AID-MOP1>3.0.CO;2-N

Kara, M. (1997). Empirical Formulas for the Computation of the Physical Properties of Rectangular Microstrip Antenna Elements with Thick Substrates. *Microwave and Optical Technology Letters*, *14*(2), 115–121. doi:10.1002/(SICI)1098-2760(19970205)14:2<115::AID-MOP12>3.0.CO;2-A

Kennedy, J., & Eberhart, R. (1995). Particle swarm optimization. In *Proceedings of the IEEE International Conference on Neural Networks*, *4*, 1942–1948.

Kim, D. H., Abraham, A., & Cho, J. H. (2007). A hybrid genetic algorithm and bacterial foraging approach for global optimization. *Information Sciences*, *177*(18), 3918–3937. doi:10.1016/j.ins.2007.04.002

Lohokare, M. R., Pattnaik, S. S., Devi, S., Panigrahi, B. K., Bakwad, K. M., & Joshi, J. G. (2009b). Modified BBO and Calculation of Resonant Frequency of Circular Microstrip Antenna. In *Proceedings of the World Congress on Nature and Biologically Inspired Computing* (pp. 487-492). doi: 10.1109/NABIC.2009.5393365

Lohokare, M. R., Pattnaik, S. S., Devi, S., Panigrahi, B. K., Das, S., & Bakwad, K. M. (2009a). Intelligent Biogeography-Based Optimization for Discrete Variables. In *Proceedings of the International Symposium on Biologically Inspired Computing and Applications* (pp. 1088-1091). doi: 10.1109/NABIC.2009.5393808

MacArthur, R., & Wilson, E. (1967). *The Theory of Biogeography*. Princeton, NJ: Princeton University Press.

Michalewicz, Z. (1992). *Genetic Algorithms + Data Structures= Evolution Programs*. New York: Springer.

Mo, W., & Guan, S. U. (2006). Particle Swarm Assisted Incremental Evolution Strategy for Function Optimization. In *Proceedings of the IEEE Conference on Cybernetics and Intelligent Systems* (pp. 1-6). doi: 10.1109/ICCIS.2006.252276

Passino, K. M. (2002). Biomimicry of bacterial foraging for distributed optimization and control. *IEEE Control Systems Magazine*, *22*(3), 52–67. doi:10.1109/MCS.2002.1004010

Pasupuleti, S., & Bhattiti, R. (2006). The Gregarious Particle Swarm Optimizer (G-PSO). In *Proceedings of the 8th Annual Conference on Genetic and Evolutionary Computation* (pp. 67-74). New York: ACM.

Pattnaik, S. S., Khuntia, B., Panda, D. C., Neog, D. K., & Devi, S. (2003). Calculation of optimized parameters of rectangular microstrip patch antenna using genetic algorithm. *Microwave and Optical Technology Letters, 37*(6), 431–433. doi:10.1002/mop.10940

Pozar, D. M., & Schaubert, D. H. (Eds.). (1995). *Microwave Antennas: The Analysis and Design of Microstrip Antennas and Arrays.* New York: IEEE Press.

Rahnamayan, S., Tizhoosh, H. R., & Salama, M. M. A. (2008). Opposition-based differential evolution. *IEEE Transactions on Evolutionary Computation, 12*(1), 64–79. doi:10.1109/TEVC.2007.894200

Rarick, R., Simon, D., Villaseca, F. E., & Vyakaranam, B. (2009). Biogeography-Based Optimization and the Solution of the Power Flow Problem. In *Proceedings of the IEEE International Conference on Systems, Man, and Cybernetics* (pp. 1003–1008). doi: 10.1109/ICSMC.2009.5346046

Ratnaweera, A., Halgamuge, S. K., & Watson, H. C. (2004). Self Organizing Hierarchical Particle Swarm Optimization with time varying acceleration coefficients. *IEEE transactions on Evolutionary Transactions, 8*(3), 240-255.

Simon, D. (2008). Biogeography-Based Optimization. *IEEE Transactions on Evolutionary Computation, 12*(6), 712–713. doi:10.1109/TEVC.2008.919004

Simon, D., Ergezer, M., & Du, D. (2009). *Markov analysis of biogeography-based optimization.* Retrieved from http://academic.csuohio.edu/simond/bbo/markov/

Storn, R., & Price, K. (1997). Differential evolution – A simple and efficient heuristic for global optimization over continuous spaces. *Journal of Global Optimization, 11*(4), 341–359. doi:10.1023/A:1008202821328

Suganthan, P. N., Hansen, N., Liang, J. J., Deb, K., Chen, Y. P., & Auger, A. (2005). *Problem definitions and evaluation criteria for the CEC2005 special session on real-parameter optimization.* Singapore: Nanyang Technological University.

Sun, J., Zhang, Q., & Tsang, E. (2004). DE/EDA: A new evolutionary algorithm for global optimization. *Information Sciences, 169*(3-4), 249–262. doi:10.1016/j.ins.2004.06.009

Tseng, L., & Liang, S. (2006). A hybrid metaheuristic for the quadratic assignment problem. *Computational Optimization and Applications, 34*(1), 85–113. doi:10.1007/s10589-005-3069-9

Wang, L., Cui, Z., & Zeng, J. (2009). Particle Swarm Optimization with Group Decision Making. In *Proceedings of the 2009 Ninth International Conference on Hybrid Intelligent Systems* (Vol. 1, pp. 388-393).

Yao, X., & Liu, Y. (1997). Fast evolution strategies. *Control and Cybernetics, 26*(3), 467–496.

Yao, X., Liu, Y., & Lin, G. (1999). Evolutionary programming made faster. *IEEE Transactions on Evolutionary Computation, 3*(2), 82–102. doi:10.1109/4235.771163

Yilmaz, A. E., & Kuzuoglu, M. (2007). Calculation of Optimized Parameters of Rectangular Microstrip Patch Antenna using Particle Swarm Optimization. *Microwave and Optical Technology Letters, 49*(12), 2905–2907. doi:10.1002/mop.22918

This work was previously published in International Journal of Applied Evolutionary Computation, Volume 1, Issue 3, edited by Wei-Chiang Samuelson Hong, pp. 1-26, copyright 2010 by IGI Publishing (an imprint of IGI Global).

Chapter 10
Posterior Sampling using Particle Swarm Optimizers and Model Reduction Techniques

J. L. Fernández Martínez
Stanford University, University of California-Berkeley, USA & University of Oviedo, Spain

E. García Gonzalo
University of Oviedo, Spain

Z. Fernández Muñiz
University of Oviedo, Spain

G. Mariethoz
Stanford University, USA

T. Mukerji
Stanford University, USA

ABSTRACT

Inverse problems are ill-posed and posterior sampling is a way of providing an estimate of the uncertainty based on a finite set of the family of models that fit the observed data within the same tolerance. Monte Carlo methods are used for this purpose but are highly inefficient. Global optimization methods address the inverse problem as a sampling problem, particularly Particle Swarm, which is a very interesting algorithm that is typically used in an exploitative form. Although PSO has not been designed originally to perform importance sampling, the authors show practical applications in the domain of environmental geophysics, where it provides a proxy for the posterior distribution when it is used in its explorative form. Finally, this paper presents a hydrogeological example how to perform a similar task for inverse problems in high dimensional spaces through the combined use with model reduction techniques.

DOI: 10.4018/978-1-4666-1749-0.ch010

PARTICLE SWARM OPTIMIZATION (PSO) APPLIED TO INVERSE PROBLEMS

Particle swarm optimization is a stochastic evolutionary computation technique inspired by the social behavior of individuals (called particles) in nature, such as bird flocking and fish schooling (Kennedy & Eberhart, 1995).

Let us consider an inverse problem of the form $\mathbf{F}(\mathbf{m}) = \mathbf{d}$, where $\mathbf{m} \in \mathbf{M} \subset R^n$ are the model parameters, $\mathbf{d} \in R^s$ the discrete observed data, and

$$\mathbf{F}(\mathbf{m}) = (f_1(\mathbf{m}), f_2(\mathbf{m}), \ldots, f_s(\mathbf{m}))$$

is the vector field representing the forward operator and $f_j(\mathbf{m})$ is the scalar field that accounts for the *j*-th data. Inverse problems are very important in science and technology and sometimes referred to as, parameter identification, reverse modeling, etc. The "classical" goal of inversion given a particular data set (often affected by noise), is to find a unique set of parameters $\mathbf{m}$, such the data prediction error $\|\mathbf{F}(\mathbf{m}) - \mathbf{d}\|_p$ in a certain norm *p*, is minimized.

The PSO algorithm to approach this inverse problem is at first glance very easy to understand and implement:

1. A prismatic space of admissible models, $\mathbf{M}$, is defined:

$$l_j \leq m_{ij} \leq u_j, \quad 1 \leq j \leq n, \quad 1 \leq i \leq N_{size}$$

where l_j, u_j are the lower and upper limits for the *j*-th coordinate of each particle in the swarm, *n* is the number of parameters in the optimization problem and N_{size} is the swarm size.

2. The misfit for each particle of the swarm is calculated, $\|\mathbf{F}(\mathbf{m}) - \mathbf{d}\|_p$ and for each particle its local best position found so far (called $l_i(k)$) is determined as well as the minimum of all of them, called the global best ($\mathbf{g}(k)$).

3. The algorithm updates at each iteration the positions $\mathbf{x}_i(k)$ and velocities $\mathbf{v}_i(k)$ of each model in the swarm. The velocity of each particle *i* at each iteration *k* is a function of three major components:

   a. The inertia term, which consists of the old velocity of the particle, $\mathbf{v}_i(k)$ weighted by a real constant, ω, called inertia.

   b. The social learning term, which is the difference between the global best position found so far (called $\mathbf{g}(k)$) and the particle's current position ($\mathbf{x}_i(k)$).

   c. The cognitive learning term, which is the difference between the particle's best position (called $l_i(k)$) and the particle's current position ($\mathbf{x}_i(k)$):

$$\mathbf{v}_i(k+1) = \omega \mathbf{v}_i(k) + \phi_1(\mathbf{g}(k) - \mathbf{x}_i(k)) + \phi_1(\mathbf{l}_i(k) - \mathbf{x}_i(k))$$
$$\mathbf{x}_i(k+1) = \mathbf{x}_i(k) + \mathbf{v}_i(k+1)$$

ω, a_g, a_l are the PSO parameters: inertia and local and global acceleration constants; $\phi_1 = r_1 a_g$, $\phi_2 = r_2 a_l$ are the stochastic global and local accelerations, and r_1, r_2 are vectors of random numbers uniformly distributed in $(0, \ 1)$ to weight the global and local acceleration constants. In the classical PSO algorithm these parameters are the same for all the particles in the swarm.

In an inverse problem, the positions are the coordinates of the model $\mathbf{m}$ in the search space, and the velocities represent the perturbations needed to find the low misfit models.

The PSO algorithm can be physically interpreted as a particular discretization of a stochastic damped mass-spring system (Martínez et al., 2008; Martínez & Gonzalo, 2008):

$$\mathbf{x}_i''(t) + (1 - \omega)\mathbf{x}_i'(t) + (\phi_1 + \phi_2)\mathbf{x}_i(t) = \phi_1\mathbf{g}(t - t_0) + \phi_2\mathbf{l}_i(t - t_0). \tag{1}$$

This model has been addressed as the PSO continuous model since it describes (together with the initial conditions) the continuous movement of any particle coordinate in the swarm $\mathbf{x}_i(t)$, where i stands for the particle index, and $g(t)$ and $\mathbf{l}_i(t)$ are its local and global attractors. In model (1) the trajectories are allowed to be delayed a time t_0 with respect to the trajectories. Using this physical analogy we were able to analyze the PSO particle's trajectories (Martínez et al., 2008) and to explain the success in achieving convergence of some popular parameters sets found in the literature (Carlisle & Dozier, 2001; Clerc & Kennedy, 2002; Trelea, 2003). Also we derived a whole family of PSO algorithms (Martínez & Gonzalo, 2009; Gonzalo & Martínez, 2009) considering different differences schemes for $\mathbf{x}_i''(t)$ and $\mathbf{x}_i'(t)$:

1. GPSO or centered-regressive PSO ($t_0 = 0$).

$$v(t + \Delta t) = (1 - (1 - w)\Delta t)v(t)$$
$$+\phi1\Delta t(g(t) - x(t)) + \phi2\Delta t(l(t)) - x(t)),$$
$$x(t + \Delta t) = x(t) + v(t + \Delta t)\Delta t.$$

The GPSO algorithm is the generalization of the PSO algorithm for any time step Δt, (PSO is the particular case for $\Delta t = 1$). These expressions for the velocity and position are obtained by employing a regressive scheme in velocity and a centered scheme in acceleration.

2. CC-PSO or centered - centered PSO ($t_0 = 0$).

$$x(t + \Delta t) = x(t) +$$
$$\left[\frac{2 + (w - 1)\Delta t}{2}v(t) + \phi_1\frac{\Delta t}{2}(g(t) - x(t)) + \phi_2\frac{\Delta t}{2}(l(t) - x(t))\right]\Delta t,$$
$$v(t + \Delta t) = \frac{2 + (w - 1)\Delta t}{2 + (1 - w)\Delta t}v(t) +$$
$$\frac{\Delta t}{2 + (1 - w)\Delta t}\sum_{k=0}^{1}\begin{bmatrix}\phi_1(l(t + k\Delta t) - x(t + k\Delta t)) \\ \phi_2(g(t + k\Delta t) - x(t + k\Delta t))\end{bmatrix}$$

3. CP-PSO or centered-progressive PSO ($t_0 = \Delta t$).

$$v(t + \Delta t) =$$
$$\frac{(1 - \phi\Delta t^2)v(t) + \phi_1\Delta t(g(t) - x(t)) + \phi_2\Delta t(l(t) - x(t))}{1 + (1 - w)\Delta t},$$
$$x(t + \Delta t) = x(t) + v(t)\Delta t.$$

4. PP-PSO or progressive-progressive PSO ($t_0 = 0$).

$$v(t + \Delta t) = (1 - (1 - w)\Delta t)v(t)$$
$$+\phi1\Delta t(g(t) - x(t)) + \phi2\Delta t(l(t)) - x(t)),$$
$$x(t + \Delta t) = x(t) + v(t + \Delta t)\Delta t.$$

5. RR-PSO or regressive-regressive PSO ($t_0 = \Delta t$)-

$$v(t + \Delta t) =$$
$$\frac{v(t) + \phi_1\Delta t(g(t) - x(t)) + \phi_2\Delta t(l(t) - x(t))}{1 + (1 - w)\Delta t + \phi\Delta t^2},$$
$$x(t + \Delta t) = x(t) + v(t + \Delta t)\Delta t.$$

Comparing these versions it is also possible to observe that GPSO and RR-PSO act as integrators since first they update the velocity of the particle and thereafter its position. CC-PSO is a differentiator and uses two consecutive centers of attraction. Finally CP-PSO and PP-PSO update at the same time the position and velocity. Also in the case of CP-PSO and RR-PSO the centre of attraction and the trajectories are delayed. Thus, it is logical to conclude that these versions have the greater exploratory capabilities.

Also, we performed the full stochastic analysis of the PSO continuous and discrete models (GPSO) (Martínez & Gonzalo, 2009b; Martínez et al., 2010). This analysis served to investigate the GPSO second order trajectories, to show the convergence of the discrete versions (GPSO) to the continuous PSO model as the discretization time step goes to zero, and to explain the role of the cost function on the first and second order continuous and discrete dynamical systems.

The consistency of the different PSO family members has been related to the stability of their first and second order trajectories (Martínez et al., 2008; Martínez & Gonzalo, 2009). Figure 1 shows the first order stability regions for all family members and the corresponding spectral radii that control the attenuation of the mean trajectories. The type of mean trajectories depends on the character of the eigenvalues of the first order difference equation. Basically there are four kinds of trajectories: damped oscillatory in the complex eigenvalue region, symmetrically and asymmetrically zigzagging in the regions of negative real eigenvalues and almost monotonous decreasing character in the region of positive real eigenvalues. Maximum exploration in reached in the complex region.

The second order trajectories (Martínez & Gonzalo, 2009) show a similar kind of behavior. Similar to Figure 1, Figure 2 shows the second order stability regions for all family members and the corresponding spectral radii. The second order spectral radius controls the rate of attenuation of the second order moments of the particle trajectories (variance and temporal covariance between

$x(t)$ and $x(t + \Delta t)$). The second order moment (variance) becomes unbounded for points located outside the boundaries of the second order stability zone. This feature provides a more exploratory capability but can also affect negatively the convergence rate. Easy functions to optimize such as de Jong-f4 have the convergence zone inside the second order stability region, but difficult functions as Rosenbrock and/or Griewank benefit need points with higher exploration capabilities to succeed in locating the low misfit region. Other factor that has been proved important is the frequency of oscillation of the second order trajectories. In the RR-PSO algorithm the points with the best convergence have a high frequency oscillatory character for the second order trajectories..

These results have been confirmed by numerical experiments with different benchmark functions in several dimensions. Figure 3 shows for each family member the contour plots of the misfit error (in logarithmic scale) after a certain number of iterations (300) for the Rosenbrock function. Figure 4 shows similar results for the Griewank function.

Other benchmark functions can be used but basically these two functions show the numerical complexities that we are interested in for real inverse problems: minima located in very flat valleys and/or surrounded by many other local minima. This numerical analysis is done for a lattice of $(\omega, \bar{\phi})$ points located in the corresponding first order stability regions over 50 different simulations. For GPSO, CC-PSO and CP-PSO, better parameter sets ω, a_g, a_l are located on the first order complex region, close to the upper border of the second order stability region (where the variance of the trajectories becomes unbounded) and around the intersection to the median lines of the first stability regions (where the temporal covariance between trajectories is close to zero) (Martínez & Gonzalo, 2009). The PP-PSO

Figure 1. First order stability regions for different family members and corresponding spectral radii

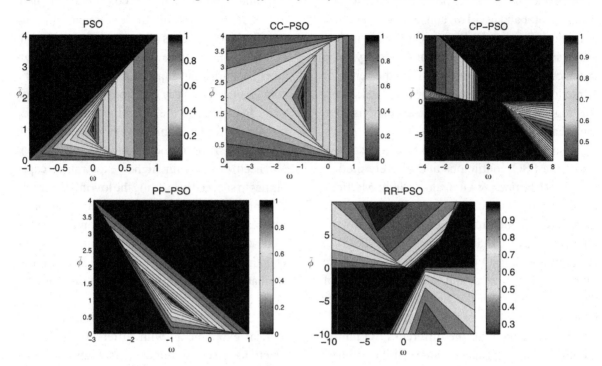

Figure 2. Second order stability regions for different family members and corresponding spectral radii

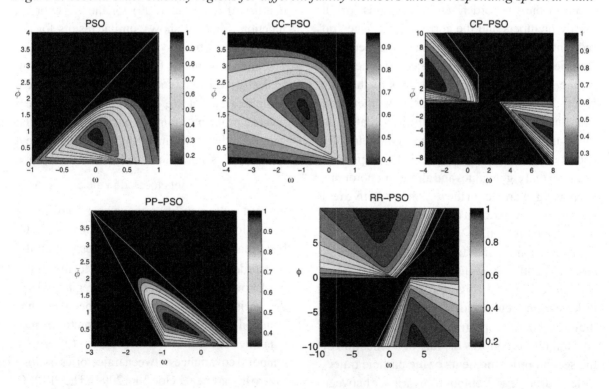

Figure 3. Logarithmic median misfit errors for the Rosenbrock function in 50 simulations (after 300 iterations) for different family members

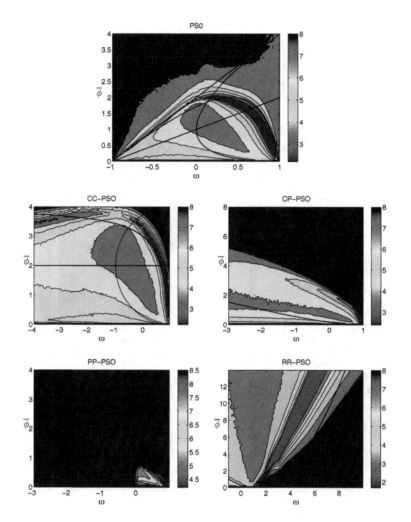

does not converge for $\omega < 0$, and the good parameter sets are in the complex region close to the limit of second order stability and to $\bar{\phi} = 0$. This result can be partially altered when the velocities are clamped or the time step is decreased. The good parameters sets for the RR-PSO are concentrated around the line $\bar{\phi} = 3(\omega - 3/2)$, mainly for inertia values greater than two. This line is located in a zone of medium attenuation and high frequency of trajectories.

WHY EXPLORATION IS NEEDED TO EVALUATE UNCERTAINTY

Most inverse problems can be written in discrete form as:

$$\mathbf{d} = \mathbf{F}(\mathbf{m}), \mathbf{d} \in R^s, \mathbf{m} \in R^n, \quad (2)$$

where $\mathbf{d}$ is the observed data, $\mathbf{m}$ is the vector containing the model parameters, and $\mathbf{F}$ is the physical model.

Given a particular observed data set, $\mathbf{d}_0$ the goal of inversion is to find a set of reasonable parameters, $\mathbf{m}_0$ such that $\mathbf{F}(\mathbf{m}_0) = \mathbf{d}_0$. Usually this problem either has no solution or many, and thus,

Figure 4. Logarithmic median misfit errors for the Griewank function in 50 simulations (after 300 iterations) for different family members

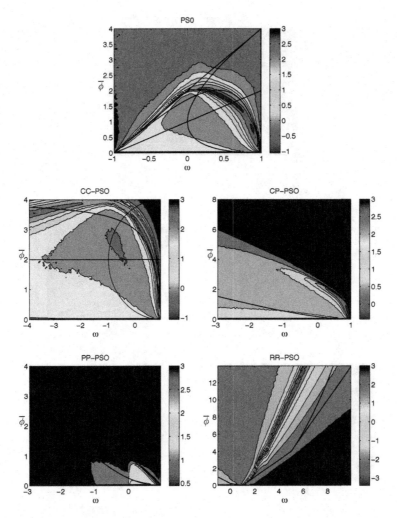

the solution of the inverse problem has to be constructed (Tarantola, 2004; Parker, 1994; Aster et al., 2005). The inverse problem is then solved as an optimization problem: finding $\mathbf{m}_0$ that minimizes the data prediction error, expressed in a certain norm, $\|\mathbf{d} - \mathbf{F}(\mathbf{m})\|_p$.

The above optimization problem turns out to be ill-posed and the main reasons are:

1. The forward model **F** is a simplification of reality, hypothesis and numerical approximations included.

2. Data are noisy and only partially sample the domain of interest.

3. Most applications of inverse modeling do not include enough (in quantity and quality) *a priori* knowledge to constrain the space of possible solutions.

These three points reveal inverse problems to be very different from other kind of optimization problems since physics and data are involved on the cost function, $\|\mathbf{d} - \mathbf{F}(\mathbf{m})\|_p$. Although a wide variety of optimization algorithms exist in the scientific literature, how to select the appropriate algorithm to solve an inverse problem is still an active subject of research. These methods involve different well known local and global optimization methods such as Bayesian approaches, neural networks, Kalman filters, kernel methods and support vector machines, etc. In addition, finding the global minima of the error function is often complicated by the presence of many local minima and/or the error space topography surrounding the global minima being very flat and oblong. Primarily, the nature of the error space topography is dependent upon the forward model, or physics, but the overall picture is a flat valley shape. To understand this fact, let us consider a model $\mathbf{m}_0$ located in the low misfit region, that is $\left\| \mathbf{F}(\mathbf{m}_0) - \mathbf{d} \right\|_2 < tol$. If we take a Taylor expansion of $\mathbf{F}(\mathbf{m})$ centered in $\mathbf{m}_0$, then:

$$\mathbf{F}(\mathbf{m}) - \mathbf{F}(\mathbf{m}_0) \approx \mathbf{JF}_{\mathbf{m}_0}(\mathbf{m} - \mathbf{m}_0),$$

$$\left\| \mathbf{F}(\mathbf{m}) - \mathbf{d} \right\|_2^2 = \left\| \Delta \mathbf{d} \right\|_2^2 + (\mathbf{m} - \mathbf{m}_0)^T$$
$$\mathbf{JF}_{\mathbf{m}_0}^T \mathbf{JF}_{\mathbf{m}_0}(\mathbf{m} - \mathbf{m}_0) + 2\Delta \mathbf{d}^T \mathbf{JF}_{\mathbf{m}_0}(\mathbf{m} - \mathbf{m}_0),$$

where $\Delta \mathbf{d} = \mathbf{F}(\mathbf{m}_0) - \mathbf{d}$. Therefore $\left\| \mathbf{F}(\mathbf{m}) - \mathbf{d} \right\|_2^2 = tol^2$ is the hyper quadric of equation:

$$(\mathbf{m} - \mathbf{m}_0)^T \mathbf{JF}_{\mathbf{m}_0}^T \mathbf{JF}_{\mathbf{m}_0}(\mathbf{m} - \mathbf{m}_0) +$$
$$2\Delta \mathbf{d}^T \mathbf{JF}_{\mathbf{m}_0}(\mathbf{m} - \mathbf{m}_0) + \left\| \Delta \mathbf{d} \right\|_2^2 = tol^2.$$

Introducing the singular value decomposition of the Jacobian matrix $\mathbf{JF}_{\mathbf{m}_0} = \mathbf{U}\pounds\mathbf{V}^T$, this equation transforms into:

$$''\mathbf{m}_{B_V}^T \pounds^{\mathbf{T}}\pounds\, ''\mathbf{m}_{B_V} +$$
$$2\Delta \mathbf{d}_{B_U}^T \pounds\, ''\mathbf{m}_{B_V} + \left\| \Delta \mathbf{d} \right\|_2^2 = tol^2,$$

where $''\mathbf{m}_{B_V}$ stands for the vector $\mathbf{m} - \mathbf{m}_0$ referred to the $\mathbf{V}$ base and $\Delta \mathbf{d}_{B_U}$ is the error data prediction $\mathbf{F}(\mathbf{m}_0) - \mathbf{d}$ referred to the base $\mathbf{U}$. The equivalent models locally in $\mathbf{m}_0$ will have the direction of the vectors of the $\mathbf{V}$ base and the axes are proportional to the inverse of the singular values $(1/\lambda_k)$ in each $\mathbf{v}_k$ direction. In the directions of the components that belong to the null-space of $\mathbf{JF}_{\mathbf{m}_0}$, the valley has infinite length. This means that along these directions the data are not sensible to model variations if the inverse problem was linear. Thus the equivalent region has locally a valley shape around model $\mathbf{m}_0$.

Additionally, data noise can lead to an increase in the size of the valley topography and/or in certain cases to an increased presence of local minima (see for instance, Alvarez et al., 2008; Martínez & González, 2008). Local optimization methods are not able to discriminate among the multiple choices consistent with the end criteria and may land quite unpredictably at any point on the valley region. These pathologies are treated through regularization techniques and the use of "good" prior information and/or initial guesses.

Once the solution of an inverse problem is found, an important issue is the model appraisal to quantify the uncertainty of the estimation. When using local optimization algorithms the appraisal is usually done through linearization of the inverse problem functional, $\mathbf{F}$. Bayesian approaches and Monte Carlo methods (Scales & Tenorio, 2001; Omre & Tjelmland, 1996; Mosegaard & Tarantola, 1995) can be used to solve the inverse problem in a different way accomplishing implicitly the model appraisal task. In this case, the inverse problem is formulated such that the posterior probability distribution is sampled many times in a random walk, with a bias towards increased sampling of areas of higher probability to accurately approximate the whole posterior probability (the so-called importance sampling). The drawback of such approaches is that they are computationally expensive, and they might not even be feasible at all in case of slow forward problems.

Posterior sampling techniques are closely related to global optimization algorithms, which can be used to provide a proxy for the true posterior distribution. In many practical situations, prior information is not available, and global optimization methods are a good alternative for avoiding the strong dependence of the solution upon noisy data. Most of these techniques are stochastic and heuristic and try to sample the low misfit region of model parameters, i.e., the region **E** of the model space **M** containing the models that fit the observed data within a given tolerance. As mentioned above, this sampling procedure acquires full sense in a Bayesian framework. Nevertheless, independent of the name that practitioners use to classify the inversion procedure, the main mechanism involved is sampling.

One of the peculiarities of global algorithms is that they do not try to solve the inverse problem as an optimization problem, but as a sampling problem, and thus, they do not need a prior model to stabilize the inversion. In fact the only prior information that these algorithms need is to specify the search space, which can be very large if no prior information is available. In some cases, the space of solutions is so large that some form of regularization is necessary to constrain the solution sampling to a range of acceptable limits.

Global optimization algorithms include, among others, well known techniques such as Genetic algorithms (Holland, 1992), Simulated Annealing (Kirkpatrick et al., 1983), Particle Swarm Optimization (Kennedy & Eberhart, 1995), Differential evolution (Storn & Price, 1997), the Neighborhood algorithm (Sambridge, 1999a). Previous work has shown that, under certain conditions, global algorithms can provide accurate measures for model uncertainty. Mosegaard and Tarantola (1995) used Simulated Tempering to perform importance sampling of the model parameters through the Metropolis-Hastings algorithm. More recently, Álvarez et al. (2008) have shown numerically

the ability of the binary Genetic Algorithms to perform an acceptable sampling of the posterior distribution when they are used in an exploration capacity. The Neighborhood Algorithm can also be used to accomplish this task (Sambridge, 1999b).

From this analysis we have shown that exploration is a very important property when we want to achieve a theoretically correct posterior sampling. In the case of genetic algorithms the exploration depends basically on the mutation probability. For simulated annealing the exploration is achieved by fixing the cooling parameter (temperature) to one.

Although PSO has not been designed to perform importance sampling, it provides a proxy for the posterior distribution for the model parameters if it is used in its explorative form (see for instance Martínez et al., 2010a). In the next section we show how to achieve exploration.

HOW TO ACHIEVE EXPLORATION USING PSO

PSO can be viewed as a set of algorithms that can be used for exploitation (looking for a unique global minimum) and/or exploration (sampling the low misfit region in the model space) purposes. The character of the PSO version (explorative or exploitative) depends on the PSO numerical parameters $\left(\omega, a_g, a_l, \Delta t\right)$.

The $\left(\omega, a_g, a_l\right)$ point that has been selected influences the algorithm explorative behavior. As we have already commented, the greatest explorative behavior is achieved when the $\left(\omega, a_g, a_l\right)$ point is close or even below the second order stability upper limit. The reason is that the variance increases its value with the mean acceleration $\bar{\phi}$. Above the second order stability limit, the variance does not attenuate with time (Martínez & Gonzalo, 2008, 2009). Also, the median of the first order stability region is the line where no temporal correlation exists at stagnation between trajectories, $x(t)$ and $x(t + \Delta t)$ (Martínez &

Gonzalo, 2008). In the transient state, this temporal correlation goes to zero within a very small number of iterations (Martínez & Gonzalo, 2009b).

This median line has also the following special properties:

1. If for a given ω value, the acceleration parameters a_g, a_l are chosen such that the mean value $\bar{\phi} = \dfrac{a_g + a_l}{2}$ falls on the median line. Then, every drawn value of $\phi = \phi_1 + \phi_2 = r_1 a_g + r_2 a_l$, will lie inside the first order stability region (Martínez et al., 2008).

2. The different set of parameters proposed in the literature for the PSO case (Carlisle & Dozier, 2001; Clerc & Kennedy, 2002; Trelea, 2003) lie close to the intersection of the median line and the upper limit hyperbola of second order stability (Martínez & Gonzalo, 2008). This fact has been also confirmed for all the PSO versions by means of numerical experiments (Martínez et al., 2009a).

Also, the total acceleration $\phi = \phi_1 + \phi_2 = r_1 a_g + r_2 a_l$, is a random variable with a trapezoidal density function centered on the mean value, $\bar{\phi} = \dfrac{a_g + a_l}{2}$, and with variance $\sigma^2 = \dfrac{a_g^2 + a_l^2}{12}$. Furthermore, if $a_g = a_l$, the density function becomes triangular. For the same total mean acceleration, $\bar{\phi} = \dfrac{a_g + a_l}{2}$, the use of dissimilar values of local and global accelerations terms, a_g, a_l, has the following consequences:

1. An increase in the dispersion of the total acceleration values at each PSO stage, since ϕ exhibits a trapezoidal distribution function with a greater variance than the corresponding of the triangular distribution function (case of $a_g = a_l$).

2. An increase of exploration when $a_l > a_g$, since particles are allowed to cover more freely the search space, making entrapment in local minima less likely.

3. Conversely, an increase of the exploitative task when $a_g > a_l$, since particles are strongly following the global leader direction. Entrapment around local minima becomes then more likely.

4. In the case $a_l = a_g$, the local and global terms have the same importance and the random draws for the total acceleration, $\phi = r_1 a_g + r_2 a_l$, are concentrated around its mean value $\bar{\phi} = a_g = a_l$.

The time step (Δt) parameter is a numerical constriction factor used to achieve stability. It is possible to show analytically that the first and second order stability regions increase their size and tend to $\left[\omega < 1, \bar{\phi} > 0\right]$ when Δt goes to zero. In this case, the exploration is increased around the global best solution. Conversely, when Δt is greater than one the first and second order stability regions shrink in size and the exploration is increased in the whole search space. This feature might help to avoid entrapment in local minima. This feature has inspired us to create the lime and sand algorithm that alternates values of Δt greater and lower than one depending on the iterations (Martínez & Gonzalo, 2008).

When the inertia value approaches to one, the damping coefficient $(1 - \omega)$ approaches zero, making the swarm explore a broader area of the search space. Stability is lost when $\omega = 1$. The role of the inertia constant ω is also to avoid elitism, since the **g** particle, which is the global best in iteration k $\left(\mathbf{x}_g(k) = \mathbf{g}(k)\right)$, will be on iteration *k+1*:

$$\mathbf{x}_g(k+1) = \mathbf{g}(k) + w\mathbf{v}_g(k),$$

i.e., its position will be changed by its velocity in iteration k, $\mathbf{v}_g(k)$, weighted by the inertia constant, w. Relationship (3) also shows that if the velocity $\mathbf{v}_g(k)$ is close to zero the swarm will collapse towards the global best, that is, the amount of exploration performed by PSO at the later stages of inversion is very limited and constrained to the global best neighborhood. This has the effect of oversampling the low misfit region.

Exploration can also be increased by:

1. Introducing repulsive forces into the dynamic of the swarm by switching to negative the sign of the acceleration constants. This repulsive effect is introduced when the mean distance between the particles of the swarm and the global best is less than a certain percentage (for instance 10%) of the initial mean dispersion. This percentage might depend on the inverse problem and the number of parameters used to describe the forward model. Also, in the posterior analysis we can take into account this effect by considering all the particles to be the same in each of these iterations.

2. Optimizing using the cloud versions (Gonzalo & Martínez, 2009; Martínez & Gonzalo, 2010) where each particle in the swarm has different inertia (damping) and acceleration (rigidity) constants. The results obtained for very hard benchmark functions in several dimensions using the PSO-cloud algorithm are comparable to the reference misfits published in the literature. This design avoids two main drawbacks of the PSO algorithm: the tuning of the PSO parameters and the clamping of the velocities. The criteria for choosing the cloud points it is not very rigid since points close to the second order convergence border achieve good results.

These strategies have been used to solve inverse problems in environmental geophysics (Martínez et al., 2009a, 2010a, b). Typically in these cases the number of parameters is low (tens to hundreds). These techniques can be also applied to inverse problems having a higher number of dimensions (thousands) by a combined use with model reduction techniques (Martínez at al., 2009c; Mukerji et al., 2009). In the next sections we show several examples in environmental geophysics and reservoir engineering.

APPLICATION TO ENVIRONMENTAL GEOPHYSICS

The VES method is a low-cost DC geophysical method to characterize the depth-variation of the subsurface resistivity distribution. This technique exhibits a wide range of environmental applications.

The VES data acquisition method deployed with the Schlumberger configuration is as follows:

1. On the surface at each station, two current and two potential electrodes are symmetrically laid on both sides of a fixed central point. In successive stations, the two external current electrodes are moved apart from each other increasing their mutual distance -s- while holding the two inner potential electrodes fixed in place at a much shorter distance, b.

2. At each position, the voltage difference $\Delta V(s)$ is measured and the apparent resistivity is calculated:

$$\rho_a^o(s;b) = K(s,b).\frac{\Delta V(s)}{I},$$

where $K(s,b)$ is a real constant with a known dependency on parameters $s,b,$ and I is the injected current.

In the VES model, the terrain is assumed to be horizontally stratified, characterized by the resistivities - ρ_k - and the thicknesses - t_k - of the electrical layers. The representation of the subsurface is accomplished by a vector $\mathbf{m} = (\rho_1, t_1, \rho_2, t_2, \ldots, \rho_{n-1}, t_{n-1}, \rho_n)$ belonging to a *2n-1* dimensional vector space $\mathbf{M}$, where *n* is the number of layers. The analysis of the VES mathematical model can be found for instance in Koefoed (1979) and involves the solution of the Laplace equation under cylindrical symmetry.

The inverse problem consists of estimating the model parameters of $\mathbf{m}$ given the measured data, $\acute{A}_a^o(\mathbf{s}) = (\rho_a^o(s_1), \rho_a^o(s_2), \ldots, \rho_a^o(s_{n_d}))$, for an array $\mathbf{s} = (s_1, s_2, \ldots, s_{n_d})$ of distances between the current electrodes (the so-called apparent resistivity curve), taking into account the physics of the problem. The VES inverse problem is nonlinear and over-determined since the number of available apparent resistivities, n_d, is often much higher than the number of geo-electrical parameters, *2n-1*. The number of geo-electrical layers, *n*, remains an additional unknown of the VES inverse problem. In the absence of prior information, the strategy adopted is to consider the lower number of geo-electrical layers that correctly fit the observed apparent resistivity curve such that the underdetermined part of the inverse problem is not increased. Although it has a low number of parameters, the VES inverse problem is a very challenging one due to its ill-posed character. Apart from the effect of noise, the main reason for ill-posedness of the VES inverse problem is that the spatial support of the resistivity field is unknown.

In this section we show the application of this geophysical method to monitor salt-water intrusion in a coastal aquifer in southern Spain, in a region where the use of groundwater for agriculture is very intensive.

The aim is to establish the depth of the intrusion probabilistically. For comparison purposes we have used Simulated Annealing with a temperature fixed to the value of one (no cooling) to correctly estimate the posterior distribution of the intrusion depth (Mosegaard & Tarantola, 1995). In all the cases, the swarm size was 200 models and the number of iterations 100. Initial seed was distributed uniformly on the model search space in $\mathbb{R}^{11}$. For the SA case, the algorithm was programmed in matrix form to run in parallel a swarm of 200 models, nevertheless each model execution was autonomous. We have also used binary GA with a high mutation probability (0.3) and the algorithm was not elitist (Álvarez et al., 2008). For the PSO family members (PSO, CC-PSO and CP-PSO) the (w, a_l, a_g) values adopted are located on the intersection of the median line of the first order stability region and the second order stability region with $a_l = 2a_g$. Figure 5 A shows the histogram of the depth of the intrusion for a resistivity cut-off of 10 Ohms-meter for different global algorithms. The histograms provided by the PSO family members have approximately the same mode, but PSO and CC-PSO overestimate the mode probability, considering SA to be the correct importance sampler. This means that PSO and CC-PSO oversample the low misfit error region. CP-PSO provides the more accurate histogram. The results obtained for PSO and CC-PSO can be improved working in points with a higher exploration rate (for example those located on the median line of temporal uncorrelation above the second order stability region) and/or introducing repulsive forces to disperse the swarm in the last iterations. Results are shown in Figure 5 B. The use of the cloud versions also improved the quality of the posterior histogram. In the absence of more concluding theoretical proofs, the experimental results shown in this section explain that exploration is the key to perform a correct posterior sampling.

HOW TO EXPLORE HIGH DIMENSIONAL SPACES? APPLICATION TO RESERVOIR ENGINEERING

The use of global optimization algorithms in inverse modeling is hampered mainly by two facts:

1. The computation time needed to solve each individual forward run.
2. The number of parameters needed to describe the inverse solution. In some cases the number of parameters used to solve the forward problem is very high (several thousands) due to the fine discretization used in the model space to achieve accurate data predictions. This also causes the inverse problem to be highly ill-posed.

Monte Carlo techniques and global optimization methods become unfeasible for high dimensional problems, although there are some attempts to deal with a high number of variables and fast forward evaluations (Cui et al., 2006, 2008). The main reason is that the base used to solve the inverse problem is the same than the one that is used to perform the forward predictions. We pro-pose to use global optimization algorithms (PSO in this case) in a reduced model space, that is, to adopt a "more-informed" base in which we solve the inverse problem. Model reduction techniques can be used for this purpose. Its use is based on the fact that the inverse model parameters are not independent. Conversely, there exist correlations between model parameters introduced by the physics of the forward problem in order to fit the observed data. We propose to take advantage of this fact to reduce the number of parameters that are used to solve the identification problem. To illustrate this idea let us consider an underdetermined linear inverse problem of the form:

$$\mathbf{Gm} = \mathbf{d}, \quad \mathbf{G} \in M(s,n), \quad n >> s,$$

where $\mathbf{G}$ is the forward linear operator and s, n stand respectively for the dimensions of the data and model spaces. The solution to this linear inverse problem is expanded as a linear combination of a set of independent models $\{\mathbf{v}_1, \mathbf{v}_2, ..., \mathbf{v}_q\}$:

$$\mathbf{m} \in \langle \mathbf{v}_1, \mathbf{v}_2, ..., \mathbf{v}_q \rangle = \sum_{k=1}^{q} \alpha_k \mathbf{v}_k, \quad q << n .$$

Figure 5. Posterior analysis on the region of 20% relative error. Comparison between the different depths of intrusion histograms. A) Results using standard versions. B) Results obtained using clouds and introducing repulsive forces.

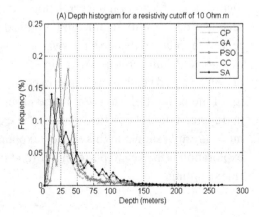
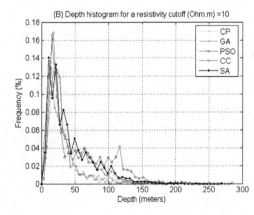

Now the inverse problem consists in finding a model $\mathbf{m}$ in a subspace of $\mathbb{R}^n$ of dimension q, fulfilling:

$$\mathbf{G V} \pm = \mathbf{d} \rightarrow \mathbf{G v}_i = \mathbf{b}_i \rightarrow \mathbf{B} \pm = \mathbf{d}, \quad \mathbf{B} \in M(s, q).$$

This amounts to finding the weights $\pm$ of the linear combination. Although this linear system might still be ill-posed, the effect of this methodology is to reduce the space of equivalent solutions. Additionally, depending on the values of s and q, the new linear system might be over-determined. This methodology can be easily generalized to nonlinear inverse problems, because once the base $\{\mathbf{v}_1, \mathbf{v}_2, ..., \mathbf{v}_q\}$ is determined, the search is performed on the $\pm$-space.

The use of a reduced set of basis vectors that are consistent with our prior knowledge allows to regularize the inverse problem and to reduce the space of possible solutions. Several techniques can be used to construct these bases such as the Principal Component Analysis (PCA) of the model covariance, the Singular Value Decomposition, the Discrete Cosine Transform (DCT) and the Discrete Wavelet Transform (Martínez et al., 2010c).

Between all these techniques, the Principal component analysis (Pearson, 1901) is very useful in geosciences because it allows inputting into the base different geological scenarios. This method has been extensively used in several fields, such as weather prediction and operational oceanography, fluid dynamics, turbulence, statistics, reservoir engineering, etc. Sometimes is also known under other terminologies such as Proper Orthogonal Decomposition or Orthogonal Empirical bases. The PCA transforms a number of correlated variables into a smaller number of uncorrelated variables called principal components. The resulting transformation is such that the first principal component accounts for as much of the variability and each succeeding component accounts for as much of the remaining variability as possible (Jolliffe, 2002).

Usually PCA is performed in the data space, but in this case it is used to reduce the dimensionality of the model space based on a priori models obtained from conditional geostatistical realizations that have been constrained to static data. Applied to our context, PCA consists in finding an orthogonal base of the experimental covariance matrix estimated with these prior geological models, and then selecting a subset of the most important eigenvalues and associated eigenvectors that are used as a reduced model space base.

The method works as follows:

1. First let us imagine that we are able to generate an ensemble $\mathbf{X} = [\mathbf{m}_1, \mathbf{m}_2, ..., \mathbf{m}_q]$ of plausible scenarios that are constrained using the available prior information. None of these scenarios obviously fit the observed data with the prescribed tolerance *tol*. Also these models might not constitute an independent set of vectors, that is, they might content redundant information. Random field simulations techniques can be used for this purpose. For instance, let us suppose that all the scenarios will be modeled as stochastic processes of the type $\mathbf{m}_i = \mathbf{t} + \mathbf{r}_i$, where $\mathbf{t}$ is a fixed deterministic trend and the residual $\mathbf{r}_i$ having a known prior covariance $\mathbf{C}$. It is then possible to generate different unconditional simulations by $\mathbf{m}_i = \mathbf{t} + \mathbf{L u}_i$, where $\mathbf{u}_i$ is a standard Gaussian process and $\mathbf{L}$ is the Cholesky decomposition of the covariance matrix $\mathbf{C} = \mathbf{L L}^T$. The different scenarios $\mathbf{m}_j$ can also correspond to different trends ($\mathbf{t}$) or spatial (time) covariance $\mathbf{C}$. These techniques can be implemented with two and three dimensional fields (Deutsch & Journel, 1992; Le Ravalec-Dupin et al., 2000; Remy et al., 2009).

2. The problem consists in finding a set of patterns $\{\mathbf{v}_1, \mathbf{v}_2, ..., \mathbf{v}_q\}$ that provide an accurate low dimensional representation of the

original set with q being much lower than the dimension of the model space. PCA does it by diagonalizing the prior experimental covariance matrix

$$C_{\text{prior}} = \frac{1}{N} \sum_{k=1}^{N} (m_k - \mu)(m_k - \mu)^T$$

where $\mu = \frac{1}{N} \sum_{k=1}^{N} m_k$ is the experimental ensemble mean. This ensemble covariance matrix is symmetric and semi-definite positive, hence, diagonalizable with orthogonal eigenvectors v_k, and real semi-definite positive eigenvalues. Eigenvectors v_k are called principal components. Eigenvalues can be ranged in decreasing order, and we can select a certain number of them to match most of the variability of the models. That is, the d first eigenvectors represent most of the variability in the model ensemble. The centered character of the experimental covariance is crucial to maintain consistency after reconstruction.

Then, any model in the reduced space is represented as a unique linear combination of the eigenmodels:

$$\mathbf{m} = \mu + \sum_{k=1}^{q} a_k \mathbf{v}_k.$$

where μ is the model experimental mean. The orthonormal character of the vectors provides to this base a telescopic (nested) character; that is, if we add the next eigenvector to the base, the vector will be expressed in these two bases as follows:

$$\mathbf{m} - \mu = \left(a_1, a_2, \ldots, a_q\right)_{\{v_1, v_2, \ldots, v_q\}}$$
$$= \left(a_1, a_2, \ldots, a_q, 0\right)_{\{v_1, v_2, \ldots, v_q, v_{q+1}\}}$$

This property allows an easy implementation of a multi-scale inversion approach adding more

eigenvalues to match higher frequencies to the model **m** as needed. Determining which level of detail we have to consider is an important question since all finer scales might not be informed by the observed data, that is, they might belong to the null space of our local linear forward operator. By truncating the number of PCA terms that we use in the expansion we are setting these finer scales of heterogeneity (high frequencies of the model) to zero, avoiding also the risk of over fitting the data. In other words, the use of a truncated PCA base provides a kind of natural smoothing of the solution.

The model covariance used in the PCA analysis, instead of being the prior covariance from a set of stochastic simulations, can also be a posterior covariance estimated by linearizing the forward operator about the last iteration, called $\mathbf{m}_f$. Based on linear inverse theory this posterior covariance can be computed using:

$$\mathbf{C}_{pos} \propto \left(\mathbf{JF}_{m_f}^T \mathbf{JF}_{m_f}\right)^{-1}$$

$\mathbf{JF}_{m_f}$ is the model Jacobian matrix computed at $\mathbf{m}_f$. This linear covariance matrix constitutes the prior information for our uncertainty estimation method and must be computed as the first step. The Jacobian matrix is rank deficient. The dimension of the null space of the Jacobian serves to account locally for the linear uncertainty analysis around the base model. To invert the matrix $\mathbf{JF}_{m_f}^T \mathbf{JF}_{m_f}$, truncation (Moore-Penrose pseudo-inverse) and/or damping techniques can be used. In this last case this inverse also gathers the influence of the left singular vectors that lie on the null space of $\mathbf{JF}_{m_f}$ and that are typically related to the high frequencies in the model. Finally another different estimate for the posterior covariance can be computed as an experimental covariance from the ensemble of sampled posterior models in a certain region of error tolerance (for instance 10%). In this case the change to the reduced base is performed when this sampled posterior covariance is calculated.

Application to Hydrogeological Inverse Problems

To illustrate this approach we use a synthetic problem where the transmissivity of an underground water reservoir has to be imaged using only the head measurements in nine wells. The problem was designed such that it has a large number of equivalent solutions, since the dimension of the model space is 10.000 and the number of data is only nine. To address this problem we include the prior information on a geologically consistent base. Figure 6 shows a set of scenarios that have been generated using multiple point geostatistics (Mariethoz et al., submitted; Mariethoz & Renard, 2010), with known prior information about this reservoir that consists in a training image displaying channels structures (Strebelle, 2002). Figure 7 shows the first 20 terms of the PCA base calculated using 2000 such scenarios. It can be observed that the terms of the PCA base reflect different features that are present on the original scenarios. The features' frequency becomes higher as their index increases. In this case we are using a PCA base reflecting the prior covariance. We solve this hydrogeological inverse problem using different numbers of PCA terms. Figure 8 shows the convergence rate curves deduced from this analysis. It can be observed that with 30, 50 and 100 PCA, PSO reaches the region of low misfits within 30 iterations. Also, when the number of PCA terms is increased to 200, the search becomes harder since the reservoir model has increased its high frequency content. Figure 9 shows the comparison between the posterior mean and standard deviation deduced from the samples having a relative misfit lower than 0.010 using an explorative version (CP-PSO), and those provided by a rejection algorithm that used 100.000 forward problem evaluations (Mariethoz et al.,

submitted). It can be observed that PSO gives a good approximation of the posterior distribution with only 1500 evaluations, sampling very different kinds of reservoir models.

Application to Reservoir Engineering: The History Matching Problem

The second application we would like to show is a petroleum engineering history matching problem. Numerical models and inverse problems are very much used in reservoir characterization to improve oil production. Solving the history matching problem provides to the reservoir engineers an update of the spatial distribution of physical reservoir properties that can be used in later stages for reservoir management. This problem has a very ill-posed character that increases with the noise level in the production data and with the reservoir complexity. In this case $\mathbf{F}(\mathbf{m})$ it is composed of multiple components: a reservoir flow simulator to predict the production data; a wave propagation model and inversion (diffraction tomography) to reconstruct the seismic velocities from the seismic traces measured at the boreholes; a geostatistical model to constrain the spatial structure of the reservoir, and finally a rock physics model that takes into account the facies-specific relations between porosity, permeability, saturations and elastic velocities. The reservoir model is composed of 4000 cells organized in ten layers of 20x20 pixels extracted from the Stanford VI sand and shale synthetic reservoir (Castro et al., 2005). The ensemble of plausible reservoirs (one thousand) was generated by geostatistical techniques (Strebelle, 2002). These realizations of the reservoir span what we think could be the variability of our model space. All these models are conditioned to the borehole data (facies measured at the wells). To perform the inversion we used the cloud versions (Gonzalo & Martínez, 2009; Martínez et al., 2010) of the different PSO

Figure 6. Different scenarios for a shale and sand reservoir generated by multiple-point geostatistics

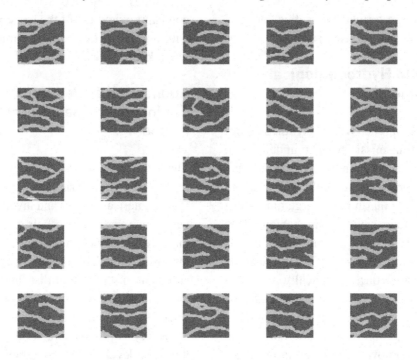

optimizers (Martínez & Gonzalo, 2009). As we have previously discussed, the cost function in real inverse problems involves observed data that are always noisy. This makes the optimization problem to be highly non-convex. Then, it is critical to explore the space of possible solutions and be able to sample the posterior distribution in the model space, rather than to achieve a very low misfit with the danger of over fitting the data. A good balance between exploitation and exploration is the key in this case. This feature is achieved for the particle swarm optimizers through the cloud design.

Figure 10 shows the optimum facies model found by the CP-PSO algorithm (the most explorative version) in the presence of 5% of Gaussian noise compared to the true model. We also show the uncertainty analysis deduced form the samples that can be associated to this "optimum" facies model and belong to the low misfit region. Although the true model is binary (sand and shale) the optimum facies model and the interquartile

range show a continuous color gradation due to the truncation adopted on the PCA base.

It can be observed that the inverted model approaches the true synthetic model, and although they are different, the uncertainty measures in each pixel serve to account for the difference between these models. In practice the uncertainty analysis is performed by taking into account the particles that have been collected on a certain region of the low misfit area, with a chosen misfit cut-off. We also keep track of the evolution of the median distance between the global best and the particles of the swarm. When this distance is smaller than a certain percentage of the initial value (5% for instance) this means that the swarm has collapsed towards the global best. Once this happens we can either stop the algorithm, or continue iterating, but in the posterior analysis we count all the particles in this collapsed swarm as one. Taking them into account individually has the effect of overestimating the probability in the low misfit area due to oversampling. The algorithm also has the possibility to increase the exploration

Figure 7. First twenty-five terms of the PCA base

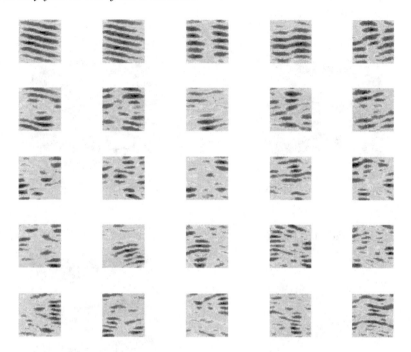

Figure 8. Convergence curves for PSO as a function of the number of PCA terms

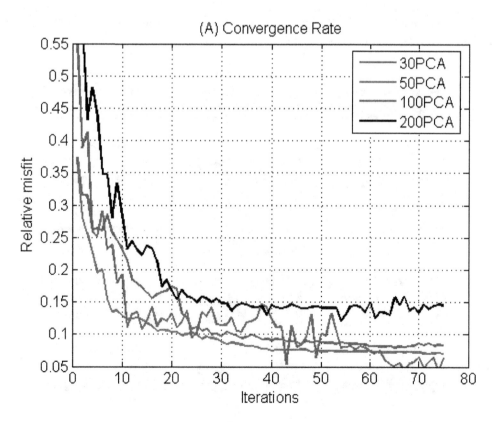

Figure 9. Comparison between the posterior mean and standard deviation deduced using CP-PSO with 30 PCA members, and the rejection algorithm

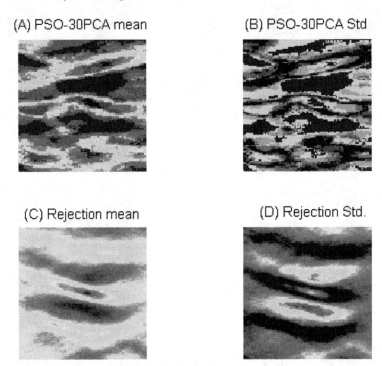

Figure 10. Five first horizontal slices from the synthetic reservoir showing the inverted solution, true model, and uncertainty on the model parameters (inter-quartile range)

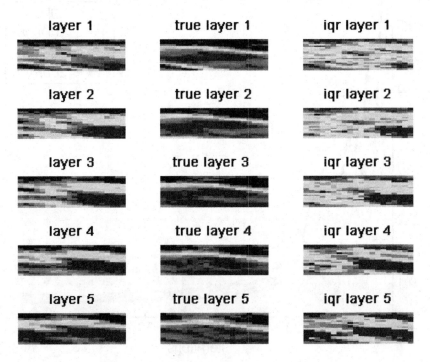

by adopting a new center of attraction based on previous statistics or by dispersing the swarm introducing repulsive forces by switching to negative the sign of the acceleration constants. Finally, based on the selected samples, it is possible to produce averages (E-types) over the samples and interquartile range maps to establish facies probabilities. The posterior marginal distributions indicate how any individual PCA term is resolved, and the posterior covariance helps us understanding the existing linear tradeoffs between model parameters. These last measures are related to the topography of the misfit surface.

In absence of more concluding theoretical proofs, the experimental results show that exploration is the key to perform a correct posterior sampling. By using these algorithms in explorative form, we can use the samples that are gathered in low misfit regions to deduce a proxy of uncertainty for the model parameters.

CONCLUSION

Inverse problems are ill posed. Uncertainty analysis around the best solution is always needed to perform risk analysis. Although the particle swarm optimizers have not been designed to perform posterior sampling, we show numerically that these algorithms can provide a proxy for the posterior distribution if they are used in their explorative form. Based on stochastic stability analysis, we show different ways to achieve exploration in particle swarm. Finally we show that the combined use of Particle Swarm Optimizers and model reduction techniques allows addressing real-world applications with thousands of parameters. The use of model reduction techniques is based on the fact that the inverse model parameters are not independent. Conversely, there exist correlations between model parameters introduced by the physics of the forward problem in order to fit the observed data.

ACKNOWLEDGMENT

This work benefited from one-year sabbatical grant (2008-2009) at the University of California Berkeley (Department of Civil and Environmental Engineering) given by the University of Oviedo (Spain), and by the "Secretaría de Estado de Universidades y de Investigación" of the Spanish Ministry of Science and Innovation. We also acknowledge the financial support for the present academic year coming from the University of California Berkeley, the Lawrence Berkeley National Laboratory (Earth Science Division), and the Energy Resources Engineering Department of Stanford University (Stanford Center for Reservoir Forecasting and Smart Fields Consortia). We also acknowledge David Echeverría and Eduardo Santos (Stanford University) for lending us the forward programs to model the oil reservoir example presented in this paper.

REFERENCES

Aster, R. C., Thurber, C. H., & Borchers, B. (2005). *Parameter estimation and Inverse problems*. New York: Elsevier Academic Press.

Carlisle, A., & Dozier, G. (2001). An off-the-shelf PSO. In *Proceedings of the Workshop on Particle Swarm Optimization 2001*, Indianapolis, IN.

Castro, S., Caers, J., & Mukerji, T. (2005). *The Stanford VI Reservoir*. Palo Alto, CA: Stanford Center for Reservoir Forecasting (SCRF).

Clerc, M., & Kennedy, J. (2002). The particle swarm-explosion, stability, and convergence in a multidimensional complex space. *IEEE Transactions on Evolutionary Computation, 6*(1), 58–73. doi:10.1109/4235.985692

Cui, Z., Cai, X., Zeng, J., & Sun, G. (2008). Particle swarm optimization with FUSS and RWS for high dimensional functions. *Applied Mathematics and Computation, 205*, 98–108. doi:10.1016/j.amc.2008.05.147

Cui, Z., Zeng, J., & Sun, G. (2006). A Fast Particle Swarm Optimization International. *Journal of Innovative Computing, 2,* 1365–1380.

Deutsch, C., & Journel, A. (1992). *GSLIB: Geostatistical Software Library* (p. 340). New York: Oxford University Press.

Echeverría, D., & Mukerji, T. (2009 July). A robust scheme for spatio-temporal inverse modelling of oil reservoirs. In R. S. Anderssen, R. D. Braddock, & L. T. H. Newham (Eds.), *18th World IMACS Congress and MODSIM09 International Congress on Modelling and Simulation. Modelling and Simulation Society of Australia and New Zealand and International Association for Mathematics and Computers in Simulation,* Cairns, Australia (pp. 4206-421).

Gonzalo, G. E., & Martínez, F. J. L. (2009a). Design of a simple and powerful Particle Swarm optimizer. In *Proceedings of the International Conference on Computational and Mathematical Methods in Science and Engineering (CMMSE2009),* Gijón, Spain.

Gonzalo, G. E., & Martínez, F. J. L. (2009b). *The PP-GPSO and RR-GPSO (Tech. Rep.).* Oviedo, Spain: University of Oviedo, Department of Mathematics.

Holland, J. (1992). Genetic algorithms. *Scientific American,* 66–72. doi:10.1038/scientificamerican0792-66

Jolliffe, I. T. (2002). *Principal Component Analysis* (p. 487). New York: Springer-Verlag.

Kennedy, J., & Eberhart, R. (1995). Particle swarm optimization. In *Proceedings of IEEE International Conference on Neural Networks (ICNN '95),* Perth, WA, Australia (pp. 1942-1948).

Kirkpatrick, S., Gelatt, C. D., & Vecchi, M. P. (1983). Optimization by simulated annealing. *Science, 220,* 671–680. doi:10.1126/science.220.4598.671

Koefoed, O. (1979). *Geosounding principles.* Amsterdam: Elsevier.

Le Ravalec-Dupin, L., Noetinger, B., & Hu, L. (2000). The FFT moving average (FFT-MA) generator: An efficient numerical method for generating and conditioning Gaussian simulations. *Mathematical Geology, 32*(6), 701–723. doi:10.1023/A:1007542406333

Mariethoz, G., & Renard, P. (2010). Reconstruction of incomplete data sets or images using Direct Sampling. *Mathematical Geosciences, 42*(3), 245–268. doi:10.1007/s11004-010-9270-0

Mariethoz, G., Renard, P., & Caers, J. (n.d.). Bayesian inverse problem and optimization with Iterative Spatial Resampling. *Water Resources Research.*

Mariethoz, G., Renard, P., & Straubhaar, J. (n.d.). The direct sampling method to perform multiple-points simulations. *Water Resources Research.*

Martínez, F. J. L., Álvarez, F. J. P., Gonzalo, G. E., Pérez, M. C. O., & Kuzma, H. A. (2008). Particle Swarm Optimization (PSO): A simple and powerful algorithm family for geophysical inversion. In *Proceedings of the SEG Annual Meeting, SEG Expanded Abstracts* (Vol. 27, p. 3568).

Martínez, F. J. L., & González, P. L. M. (2008). Anisotropic Mean traveltime curves: a method to estimate anisotropic parameters from 2D transmission tomographic data. *Mathematical Geosciences, 41*(2), 163–192. doi:10.1007/s11004-008-9202-4

Martínez, F. J. L., & Gonzalo, G. E. (2008). The generalized PSO: A new door for PSO evolution. *Journal of Artificial Evolution and Applications, 15.*

Martínez, F. J. L., & Gonzalo, G. E. (2009a). The PSO family: deduction, stochastic analysis and comparison. *Swarm Intelligence, 3,* 245–273. doi:10.1007/s11721-009-0034-8

Martínez, F. J. L., & Gonzalo, G. E. (2009b). *Stochastic stability analysis of the linear continuous and discrete PSO models (Tech. Rep.).* Oviedo, Spain: University of Oviedo, Department of Mathematics.

Martínez, F. J. L., & Gonzalo, G. E. (2010). *What makes Particle Swarm Optimization a very interesting and powerful algorithm? Handbook of Swarm Intelligence -- Concepts, Principles and Applications Series on Adaptation, Learning, and Optimization.* New York: Springer.

Martínez, F. J. L., & Gonzalo, G. E. (2010b). Advances in Particle Swarm Optimization. In *Proceedings of the Seventh Conference on Swarm Intelligence (Ants 2010).*

Martínez, F. J. L., Gonzalo, G. E., & Alvarez, F. J. P. (2008). Theoretical analysis of particle swarm trajectories through a mechanical analogy. *International Journal of Computational Intelligence Research, 4,* 93–104. Retrieved from http://www.ijcir.com/.

Martínez, F. J. L., Gonzalo, G. E., Álvarez, F. J. P., Kuzma, H. A., & Pérez, M. C. O. (2010a). *PSO: A Powerful Algorithm to Solve Geophysical Inverse Problems. Application to a 1D-DC Resistivity Case.* Jounal of Applied Geophysics.

Martínez, F. J. L., Gonzalo, G. E., Muñiz, F. Z., & Mukerji, T. (2010d). *How to design a powerful family of Particle Swarm Optimizers for inverse modeling. New Trends on Bio-inspired Computation.* Transactions of the Institute of Measurement and Control.

Martínez, F. J. L., Gonzalo, G. E., & Naudet, V. (2010b). *Particle Swarm Optimization applied to the solving and appraisal of the Streaming Potential inverse problem.* Geophysics. Hydrogeophysics Special Issue.

Martínez, F. J. L., Kuzma, H. A., García-Gonzalo, M. E., Díaz, F. J. M., Álvarez, F. J. P., & Pérez, M. C. O. (2009). Application of Global Optimization Algorithms to a Salt Water Intrusion Problem. In *Proceedings of the Symposium on the Application of Geophysics to Engineering and Environmental Problems, 22,* 252–260.

Martínez, F. J. L., Mukerji, T., Muñiz, F. Z., Gonzalo, G. E., Tompkins, M. J., & Alumbaugh, D. L. (2009b). *Complexity reduction in inverse problems: wavelet transforms, DCT, PCA and geological bases.* Eos. Trans.

Martínez, F. J. L., Tompkins, M. J., Muñiz, F. Z., & Mukerji, T. (2010c, September). How to construct geological bases for inversion and uncertainty appraisal? In *Proceedings of the International Groundwater Simposium,* Valencia, Spain.

Mosegaard, K., & Tarantola, A. (1995). Monte Carlo sampling of solutions to inverse problems. *Journal of Geophysical Research, 100*(B7), 12431–12447. doi:10.1029/94JB03097

Mukerji, T., Martínez, F. J. L., Ciaurri, E. D., & Gonzalo, G. E. (2009). Application of particle swarm optimization for enhanced reservoir characterization and inversion. *Eos, Transactions, American Geophysical Union, 90*(52).

Omre, H., & Tjelmland, H. (1996). *Petroleum geostatistics (Tech. Rep.).* Trondheim, Norway: Norwegian University of Science and Technology, Department of Mathematical Sciences.

Parker, R. L. (1994). *Geophysical Inverse Theory.* Princeton, NJ: Princeton University Press.

Pearson, K. (1901). Principal components analysis. *The London, Edinburgh and Dublin Philosophical Magazine and Journal, 6,* 566.

Remy, N., Boucher, A., & Wu, J. (2009). *Applied Geostatistics with SGeMS: A User's Guide* (p. 284). Cambridge, UK: Cambridge University Press.

Sambridge, M. (1999). Geophysical inversion with a neighborhood algorithm. I. Searching a parameter space. *Geophysical Journal International, 138*, 479–494. doi:10.1046/j.1365-246X.1999.00876.x

Scales, J. A., & Tenorio, L. (2001). Prior information and uncertainty in inverse problems. *Geophysics, 66*, 389–397. doi:10.1190/1.1444930

Storn, R., & Price, K. (1997). Differential evolution - a simple and efficient heuristic for global optimization over continuous spaces. *Journal of Global Optimization, 11*, 341–359. doi:10.1023/A:1008202821328

Strebelle, S. (2002). Conditional simulation of complex geological structures using multipoint statistics. *Mathematical Geology, 34*, 1–21. doi:10.1023/A:1014009426274

Tarantola, A. (2004). *Inverse Problem Theory and Model Parameter Estimation*. Philadelphia: SIAM.

Trelea, I. C. (2003). The particle swarm optimization algorithm: convergence analysis and parameter selection. *Information Processing Letters, 85*(6), 317–325. doi:10.1016/S0020-0190(02)00447-7

This work was previously published in International Journal of Applied Evolutionary Computation, Volume 1, Issue 3, edited by Wei-Chiang Samuelson Hong, pp. 27-48, copyright 2010 by IGI Publishing (an imprint of IGI Global).

Chapter 11
Reserve Constrained Multi–Area Economic Dispatch Employing Evolutionary Approach

Manisha Sharma
M.I.T.S., India

Manjaree Pandit
M.I.T.S., India

ABSTRACT

The objective of Multi-area economic dispatch (MAED) is to determine the generation levels and the interchange power between areas that minimize fuel costs, while satisfying power balance and generating limit and transmission constraints. If an area with excess power is not adjacent to a power deficient area, or the tie-line between the two areas is at transmission limit, it is necessary to find an alternative path between these two areas to transmit additional power. When a MAED problem is solved with spinning reserve constraints, the problem becomes further complicated. The power allocation to each unit is done in such a manner that after supplying the total load, some specified reserve is left behind. In this paper, the authors compare classic PSO and DE strategies and their variants for reserve constrained MAED. The superior constraint handling capability of these techniques enables them to produce high quality solutions. The performance is tested on a 2-area system having 4 generating units and a 4-area, 16-unit system.

INTRODUCTION

In the power sector, economic dispatch (ED) is used is to allocate power demand among available generators in the most economical manner, while satisfying all the physical and operational constraints. The cost of power generation, particularly in fossil fuel plants, is very high and

economic dispatch helps in saving a significant amount of revenue (Wood & Wollenberg, 1984). Many utilities and power pools have limits on power flow between different area/regions over tie lines. Each area/ region has its own pattern of load variation and generation characteristics. They also have separate spinning reserve constraints. The ED technique should select the units in each area in such a way that reserve requirements and transmission constraints are satisfied. The objec-

DOI: 10.4018/978-1-4666-1749-0.ch011

tive of MAED is to determine the generation levels and the interchange power between areas which minimize fuel costs in all areas while satisfying power balance, generating limit and transmission constraints. Power utilities try to achieve high operating efficiency to produce cheap electricity. Competition exists in the electricity supply industry in generation and in the marketing of electricity. The operating cost of a power pool can be reduced if the areas with more economic units generate larger power than their load and export the surplus power to other areas with more expensive units. The benefits thus gained will depend on several factors like the characteristics of a pool, the policies adopted by utilities, types of interconnections, tie-line limits and load distribution in different areas. Therefore, transmission capacity constraints and area reserve constraints are important issues in the operation and planning of electric power systems.

A complete formulation of multi-area generation scheduling with import/export constraints was presented in Shoults, Chang, Helmick, and Grady (1980). Desell et al. (1984) proposed an application of linear programming to transmission constrained production cost analysis. Farmer et al. (1990) presented a probabilistic method which was applied to the production costing of transmission constrained multi-area power systems. Hopfield neural network based approach was proposed to solve the MAED problem (Yalcinoz & Short, 1998). Doty and McIntyre (1982) solved multi-area economic dispatch problem by using spatial dynamic programming. Linear programming application is proposed in Desell, McClelland, Tammar, and Van Horne (1984) while area control error is solved in multi-area economic dispatch (Hemick & Shoults, 1985). Wang and Shahidehpour (1992) proposed a decomposition approach using expert systems. The Newton-Rapshon's method is applied to solve multi-area economic dispatch problem (Wernerus & Soder, 1995) by calculating short range margin cot based prices. An incremental network flow programming

algorithm was proposed for the MAED solution with tie-line constraints (Streifferet, 1995). The multi-area economic dispatch is solved by direct search method with considering transmission constraint (Chen & Chen, 2001). Evolutionary programming is proposed in Jayabarathi, Sadasivam, & Ramachandran, 2000) for multi-area economic dispatch problem. Recently covariance matrix adapted evolutionary strategy has been proposed for MAED problems where a Karush Kuhun Tucker (KKT) optimality based stopping criterion is applied to guarantee optimal convergence (Manoharan, Kannan, Baskar, & Willjuice, 2009).

When ED problem is solved with spinning reserve constraints the problem becomes further complicated. The power allocation to each unit is done in such a manner that after supplying the total load, some specified reserve is left behind (Nasr Azadani, Hosseinian, & Moradzadeh, 2010; Aruldoss, Victoire, & Jeyakumar, 2005; Wang & Singh, 2009; Lee & Breipohl, 1993). In MAED problems inter area reserve sharing can help in reducing the operational cost. Evolutionary methods are increasingly being proposed for ED problems with complex constraints due to their ease of implementation and random parallel search capability. The methods found in literature include tabu search, simulating annealing, neural networks (Yalcinoz & Short, 1998; Park, Kim, Eom, & Lee, 1993), genetic algorithm (Walter & Sheble, 1993), particle swarm optimization (Wang & Singh, 2009; Chaturvedi, Pandit, & Srivastava, 2009; Chaturvedi, Pandit, & Srivastava, 2008; Alrashidi & El-Hawary, 2007), harmony search (Vasebi, Fesanghary, & Bathaee, 2007), ant colony optimization (Song, Chou, & Stoham, 1999), bacterial foraging (Panigrahi & Pandi, 2009), artificial immune system (Vanaja, Hemamalini, & Simon, 2008) and differential evolution (DE) (Noman & Iba, 2008). Among these techniques, PSO, DE and their variants have been extensively popular due to their superior convergence characteristics, consistency and ease of implementation.

Although these methods do not always guarantee global best solutions, they often achieve a fast and near global optimal solution. Researchers have constantly observed that all these methods very quickly find a good local solution but get stuck there for a number of iterations without further improvement sometimes causing premature convergence. Time varying acceleration coefficients (TVAC) (Chaturvedi, Pandit, & Srivastava, 2009) are employed for countering the effect of premature convergence in PSO for solving nonconvex ED problems. The TVAC strategy strikes a proper balance between the cognitive and social component during the initial and latter part of the search and hence is found to avoid premature convergence of the swarm. The present paper aims to test the potential of all the basic DE variants in producing feasible solutions for the reserve constrained MAED problem formulated with many different constraints. The paper also compares the solution quality of DE variants with the PSO_TVAC strategy and classical PSO. The results of all three evolutionary strategies are found to be feasible and superior to reported results (Yalcinoz & Short, 1998; Chen & Chen, 2001; Manoharan, Kannan, Baskar, & Willjuice, 2009; Wang & Singh, 2009).

RESERVE CONSTRAINED MULTI-AREA ECONOMIC DISPATCH

The objective of MAED is to determine the generation levels and the interchange power between areas which would minimize total fuel costs in all areas while satisfying power balance, generating limit and transmission capacity constraints. Tie-line power flow between areas plays a very important role in deciding the operating cost in multi-area power systems. Taking into consideration the cost of transmission though each tie-line, the fuel input-power output cost function of ith unit is given as

$$F_i\left(P_i\right) = a_iP_i^2 + b_iP_i + c_i + \left|e_i \times \sin\left(f_i \times \left(P_i^{\min} - P_i\right)\right)\right|$$
$$(1)$$

where a_i, b_i and c_i are the fuel-cost coefficients of the ith unit, and e_i and f_i are the fuel cost-coefficients of the ith unit with valve-point effects. The ED problem is to determine the generated powers Pi of units for a total load of P_D so that the total fuel cost for the N number of generating units is minimized subject to the power balance constraint and unit upper and lower operating limits. Taking into consideration the cost of transmission though each tie-line, the objective function of MAED is given in Equation (2) as

$$Min F_T = \sum_{i=1}^{N} F_i(P_i) + \sum_{j}^{M-1} f_jT_{j(M-1)}$$
$$(2)$$

f_i is the cost function associated with tie line power flow from area j to area (M-1).

1. **Area Power Balance Constraints:** The power balance constraints for area m neglecting losses can be given as

$$\sum_{i=1}^{N} P_{im} = \left(P_{Dm} + \sum_{j}^{M-1} T_{j(M-1)}\right) = 0$$
$$(3)$$

for m=1,2........M (areas). P_{Dm} is the load demand in m^{th} area and T_j represents the tie line flows to the jth area from other areas.

2. **Generating Limit Constraints:** The power output of a unit must be allocated within the range bounded by its lower and upper limits of real power generation as given by

$$P_i^{\min} \leq P_i \leq P_i^{\max} \qquad i = 1, 2, ..., N \qquad (4)$$

3. **Tie-line Limit Constraints:** The tie line power flows to area j should be between the maximum and minimum

$$T_{j(M-1)}^{\min} \leq T_{j(M-1)} \leq T_{j(M-1)}^{\max} \qquad j = 1, 2, ..., M \tag{5}$$

where T_j is the power flow through the tie line.

Area wise spinning reserve constraints: In an area j, the spinning reserve requirement should be satisfied through multi-area reserve sharing:

$$\sum_{i=1}^{M_j} S_{ij} \geq S_{j,req} + \sum_{k, k \neq j} \mathrm{Re}\, s_{kj} \tag{6}$$

where j=1,2.............M; S_{ij} is the reserve existing on the ith unit of area j, and can be calculated as ($P_i^{\max} - P_i$), $S_{j,req}$ is the required spinning reserve in area j and Res_{kj} is the reserve contributed from area k to area j. When inter area aid is not available then Res_{kj} is zero and each area generation has to meet its own reserve.

EVOLUTIONARY OPTIMIZATION STRATEGIES

Researchers worldwide are increasingly proposing evolutionary soft computing methods as alternate approaches for solving power system optimization and other problems, as these methods are based on natural phenomena and hence are more robust and suitable for real world problems. Out of the different evolutionary techniques proposed PSO and DE have emerged as most popular, looking at the number of papers published during past few years. The present paper aims to present a brief review and comparison of both the techniques and their different variants using performance measures such as convergence behavior, consistency and solution quality for solving the reserve constrained MAED problem.

Classical PSO

A PSO is a population based modern heuristic search method that traces its evolution to the emergent motion of a flock of birds searching for food. It scatters random particles i.e., solutions into the problem space. These particles, called swarms, collect information from each other through their respective positions. The particles update their positions using their own experience and the experience of their neighbors. The update mode is termed as the velocity of particles. The position and velocity vectors of the ith particle of a d-dimensional search space can be represented as $X_i = (x_{i1}, x_{i2}, \ldots \ldots x_{id})$ and $V_i = (v_{i1}, v_{i2}, \ldots \ldots v_{id})$ respectively. On the basis of the value of the evaluation function, the best previous position of a particle is recorded and represented as $pbest_i = (p_{i1}, p_{i2}, \ldots \ldots p_{id})$. If the gth particle is the best among all particles in the group so far, it is represented as $pbest_g = gbest = (p_{g1}, p_{g2}, \ldots \ldots p_{gd})$. The particle tries to modify its position using the current velocity and the distance from. The modified velocity and position of each particle for fitness evaluation in the next iteration are calculated using the following equations:

$$v_{id}^{k+1} = C[w \times v_{id}^k + c_1 \times rand_1 \times (pbest_{id} - x_{id}) \tag{7}$$

$$x_{id}^{k+1} = x_{id} + v_{id}^{k+1} \tag{8}$$

Here w is the inertia weight parameter, C is constriction factor, c_1, c_2 are cognitive and social coefficients, and $rand_1, rand_2$ are random numbers between 0 and 1. A large inertia weight helps in good global search while a smaller value facilitates local exploration. Therefore, the practice is to use larger inertia weight factor during initial exploration and gradual reduction of its value as the search proceeds in further iterations. The time varying inertial weight is given by

$$w = (w_{\max} - w_{\min}) \times \frac{(iter_{\max} - iter)}{iter_{\max}} + w_{\min} \tag{9}$$

where *iter* is the current iteration number while is the maximum number of iterations. Usually the value of *w* is varied between 0.9 and 0.4.

PSO WITH TIME-VARYING ACCELERATION COEFFICIENTS (PSO_TVAC)

Though the PSO technique with time varying inertia weight can locate good solution at a significantly fast rate, its ability to fine tune the optimum solution is weak, mainly due to the lack of diversity at the end of the search. It has been observed by most researchers that in PSO, problem-based tuning of parameters is a key factor to find the optimum solution accurately and efficiently. Kennedy and Eberhart (1995) stated that a relatively higher value of the cognitive component, compared with the social component, results in roaming of individuals through a wide search space. On the other hand, a relatively high value of the social component leads particles to a local optimum prematurely. In population-based optimization methods, the policy is to encourage individuals to roam through the entire search space during the initial part of the search, without clustering around local optima. During the latter stages, convergence towards the global optima is encouraged, to find the optimal solution efficiently. The idea behind TVAC is to enhance the global search in the early part of the optimization and to encourage the particles to converge towards the global optima at the end of the search. This is achieved by changing the acceleration coefficients c_1 and c_2 with time in such a manner that the cognitive component is reduced while the social component is increased as the search proceeds. With a large cognitive component and small social component at the beginning, particles are allowed to move around the search space instead of moving toward the population best during early stages. On the other hand, a small cognitive component and a large social component allow the particles

to converge to the global optima in the latter part of the optimization process. The acceleration coefficients are expressed as (Ratnaweera, Halgamuge, & Watson, 2004):

$$c_1 = \left(c_{1f} - c_{1i}\right)\frac{iter}{iter_{max}} + c_{1i} \tag{10}$$

$$c_2 = \left(c_{2f} - c_{2i}\right)\frac{iter}{iter_{max}} + c_{2i} \tag{11}$$

where c1i, c1f, c2i and c2f are initial and final values of cognitive and social acceleration factors respectively.

Differential Evolution

DE is a population-based stochastic function minimizer (or maximizer) based on evolutionary computation, whose simple yet powerful and straightforward features make it very attractive for numerical optimization. DE differs from conventional genetic algorithms in its use of perturbing vectors, which are the difference between two randomly chosen parameter vectors; a concept borrowed from the operators of Nelder and Mead's simplex optimization technique. The DE algorithm was first introduced by Storn and Price (1995) and was successfully applied in the optimization of some well-known nonlinear, non-differentiable, and non-convex functions. DE works on three basic operations, namely mutation, crossover and selection.

Mutation is an operation that adds a vector differential to a population vector of individuals according to the chosen variant. The different variants of DE are classified using the notation DE, /α/β/δ where α indicates the method for selecting the parent chromosome that will form the base of the mutated vector, β indicates the number of difference vectors used to perturb the base chromosome, and δ indicates the recombination mechanism used to create the offspring population. Most papers have explored the variant DE / rand / 1 / bin (Coelho & Mariani, 2006). The best performing variant is found to be problem specific and needs detailed investigation. The donor or mutant vector for each population member is generated for different variants in classic DE as given below

1. DE/rand/1

$$Z_i(t+1) = x_{i,r1}(t) + f_m[x_{i,r2}(t) - x_{i,r3}(t)]$$

2. DE/best/1

$$Z_i(t+1) = x_{i,best}(t) + f_m[x_{i,r2}(t) - x_{i,r3}(t)]$$

3. DE/rand-to-best/1

$$Z_i(t+1) = x_i(t) + f_m[x_{i,best}(t) - x_i(t)] + fm[x_i r_1(t) - x_i r_2(t)]$$

4. DE/best/2

$$Z_i(t+1) = x_{ibest}(t) + f_m[x_{i,r1}(t) - x_i r_2(t)] + fm[x_i r_3(t) - x_i r_4(t)]$$

5. DE/rand/2

$$Z_i(t+1) = x_{ir5}(t) + f_m[x_{i,r1}(t) - x_i r_2(t)] + fm[x_i r_3(t) - x_i r_4(t)] \qquad (12)$$

where i = 1, 2 ..., R is the individual's index of population and j = 1, 2,...,N is the position in n-dimensional individual; t is the time (generation); r_1, r_2, r_3, r_4 and r_5 and are mutually different integers and also different from the running index, *i*, randomly selected with uniform distribution from the population set and fm > 0 is a real parameter called mutation factor, which controls the amplification of the difference between two individuals so as to avoid search stagnation and is usually taken from

the range [0, 2].Following the mutation operation, recombination is applied to the population. Recombination is employed to generate a trial vector by replacing certain parameters of the target vector with the corresponding parameters of the randomly generated donor vector.

$$U_{ij}(t+1) = \begin{cases} Z_{ij}(t+1),.....if(rand(j) \leq CR)or(j = rand\,\mathrm{int}(i)) \\ x_{ij}(t),.........if(rand(j) > CR)or(j \neq rand\,\mathrm{int}(i)) \end{cases}$$
$$(13)$$

In the above rand(j) is the jth evaluation of a uniform random number generation within range [0, 1], and CR is a crossover or recombination rate in the range [0, 1]. The performance of a DE algorithm usually depends on three variables; the population size N, the mutation factor f_m and the recombination rate CR. Selection is the procedure of producing better offspring. To decide whether or not the vector should be a member of the population comprising the next generation, it is compared with the corresponding vector. Thus, it denotes the objective function under minimization, and

$$x_i(t+1) = \begin{cases} U_i(t+1)......if(u(t+1) < f(x_i(t)) \\ x_i(t),.........otherwise \end{cases}$$
$$(14)$$

In this case, the cost of each trial vector $U_i(t+1)$ is compared with that of its parent target vector $x_i(t)$.

In this paper, a detailed study of all the basic DE variants is carried out to find the best strategy for a given MAED problem with reserve constraints. The performance is then compared with classical PSO and PSO_TVAC.

SOLUTION OF RESERVE CONSTRAINED MAED PROBLEM

The paper presents solution of MAED problem with reserve constraints employing PSO and DE strategies and critically compares their features for practical power system operation.

- **Parameter setup:** The PSO and DE parameters such as population size, the boundary constraints of optimization variables, cognitive and social acceleration coefficients, the mutation factor (fm), the crossover rate (CR), and the stopping criterion of maximum number of iterations (generations), Gmax are selected.

- **Initialization of an individual population:** For a population size R, the particles are randomly generated and normalized between the maximum and the minimum operating limits of the generators. If there are N generating units and M tie-lines, the ith particle is represented as

$$P_i = \begin{pmatrix} P_{i1}^n, P_{i2}^n, P_{i3}^n \ldots\ldots P_{iN}^n \ (T_{12}, T_{13,}\ldots\ldots\ldots T_{1M}), \\ (T_{23,} T_{24,}\ldots\ldots\ldots T_{2M}) \ldots\ldots T_{(M-1)M} \end{pmatrix} \tag{15}$$

The jth Dimension of The ith Particle is normalized as given below to satisfy the generation limit constraint given by (5). Here, $r \in [0,1]$.

$$P_{ij}^{\ n} = P_{ij\min} + r(P_{ij\max} - P_{ij\min}) \tag{16}$$

For initializing tie-line power flow variables their respective minimum and maximum limits are used in Equation (16).

- **Area wise reserve constraints:** The generated population is made to satisfy the area-wise reserve constraints specified by Equation (6). If the reserve of ith area is less than specified for a population, then the difference in reserve is distributed (in ratio of the ratings of generators in that area) among the units of that area, to satisfy the reserve constraints.

- **Evaluation of the individual population:** The strength of each individual particle in the swarm is evaluated to judge its merit using a fitness function called evaluation function. The evaluation function should be such that cost is minimized while constraints are satisfied. One of the methods for this is the popular penalty function method. In this method, the penalty functions composed of squared or absolute violations are incorporated in the fitness function, and are set to reduce the fitness of the particle according to the magnitude of the violation. The penalty parameters are chosen such that an infeasible solution is awarded lesser fitness than the weakest feasible particle string. Since two infeasible particles are not treated equally, the string further away from the feasibility boundary is more heavily penalized. The penalty function approach, thus, converts a constrained optimization problem into an unconstrained optimization problem. The fitness function values need to be calculated for each particle in order to find its merit. The evaluation function used here is given by

$$\min \sum_{i=1}^{N} F_i(P_i) + \alpha \left[\sum_{m=1}^{M} \sum_{i=1}^{N} P_{im} - \left(P_{Dm} + \sum_{j}^{(M-1)} T_{j(M-1)} \right) \right]^2 \tag{17}$$

Here, α is the penalty parameter. The second term imposes a penalty on the particle in terms of increased cost, if power balance constraints of all the areas are not satisfied. The first term is calculated using $F_i(P_i)$ from Equation (1). Transmission losses are neglected here for the sake of simplicity.

- **Iterative Parameter Updation:** In every iteration the parameters are updated to improve the fitness. In PSO the parameters are updated using Equation (7)- Equation

(11) while in DE mutation adds a vector differential to a population vector of individuals; the donor or mutant vector is generated by using Equation (12) corresponding to the chosen DE variant.

- **Recombination operation:** Recombination is applied in DE using Equation (13) to generate a trial vector by replacing certain parameters of the target vector with the corresponding parameters of the randomly generated donor in the step 4.

- **Selection operation:** Finally the selection operation produces better offspring. The values of the evaluation function are calculated for the updated positions of the particles. In PSO if the new value is better than the previous p*best,* the new value is set to p*best.* Similarly, value of g*best* is also updated as the best p*best.* In DE the trial vector $U_i(t+1)$ replaces its parent target vector $x_i(t)$ if its cost is found to be better otherwise the target vector is allowed to advance to the next generation.

- **Stopping criterion:** A stochastic optimization algorithm is stopped either based on the tolerance limit or maximum number of iterations. For comparison with other strategies, the number of iterations is adopted as the stopping criterion in this paper.

RESULTS AND DISCUSSIONS

The tie-line constraints, area wise spinning reserve constraints and area power balance constraints make the reserve constrained MAED problem much more complex and difficult to solve as compared to the classical ED problem. The PSO and DE based evolutionary strategies are tested for the proposed practical MAED problem on two systems having different sizes and complexities. The performance of both DE and PSO techniques is compared with previously published results

(Yalcinoz & Short, 1998; Chen & Chen, 2001; Manoharan, Kannan, Baskar, & Willjuice, 2009; Wang & Singh, 2009) and is found to be better.

Description of the Test Systems

1. The first test system consists of a two-area system with four generating units (Yalcinoz & Short, 1998; Chen & Chen, 2001) as shown in Figure 1. This system is considered here for the purpose of comparison with previous results. The percentage of the total load demand in area 1 is 70% and 30% in area 2. The cost coefficients and limits are taken from (Chen & Chen, 2001). The load demand (P_D) and tie-line flow limit are set at 1120 MW and 200MW respectively for solving MAED. The global best for this system has been reported at 10,605$ (Yalcinoz & Short, 1998; Chen & Chen, 2001). Manoharan, Kannan, Baskar, and Willjuice (2009) have reported $10,574 but the reported results are infeasible as they do not satisfy the area power balance constraints (solution satisfies only the power balance and generating limit constraints). Table 1 gives the comparison of reported results with already published results. The superiority of the reported results is evident from its ability to satisfy all constraints and produce feasible results. For solving reserve constrained dispatch the required area spinning reserves for the above system are taken as 40% (313.6MW)and 30% (100.8MW) of area load demand respectively, for area one and area two and the tie-line limit is assumed to be 300 MW.

2. The second system (Wang & Singh, 2009) has four areas and 4 generating units in each area as shown in Figure 2. The fuel characteristic data, unit operating limits and tie-line limits are taken from Wang and Singh (2009) and listed in Appendix. The area loads are 30MW, 50MW, 40MW and 60MW respectively. The area spinning

Figure 1. Two-area, four unit system

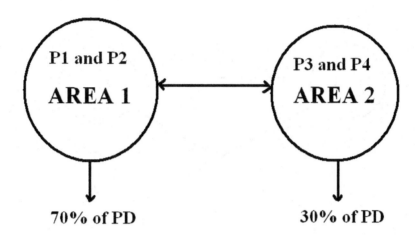

reserve requirement is 30% of area load demand in each area, i.e., 9 MW, 15 MW, 12 MW and 18 MW respectively for the four areas. The minimum cost reported for this system using PSO with local search (Wang & Singh, 2009) is $2166.82/h with inter area aid and $2191.14/h without inter area aid. DE and PSO_TVAC algorithms used in this paper have achieved better and feasible results for this system. Emission constraints are also applied in Wang and Singh (2009) but for the sake of comparison, only the best cost solution has been taken here.

The transmission costs are not considered for both the systems as they are normally small as compared to total fuel costs. In classical PSO both the acceleration coefficients are taken equal to 1.5 for all systems. Simulations were carried out using MATLAB 7.0.1 on a Pentium IV processor, 2.8 GHz. with 512 MB RAM.

Testing Strategies

The reserve constrained MAED problem was solved using the classical PSO, PSO_TVAC and DE and their performance was compared with some already reported results (Yalcinoz & Short, 1998; Chen & Chen, 2001; Manoharan, Kannan, Baskar, & Willjuice, 2009; Wang & Singh, 2009). The idea is to present an extensive comparison of DE and its hybrid variants with PSO and its variant for reserve constrained MAED problem with complex constraints. The paper i) Compares different DE variants for reserve constrained MAED problem ii) Compares the best DE variant with its close competitor PSO and its effective variant PSO_TVAC iii) Investigates the influence of

Table 1. Comparison of best results of evolutionary strategies for 4-area, 4-unit system

Strategy	P1	P2	P3	P4	P12	Cost($/H)	V1*	V2*
CMAES[17]	560.9383	168.9300	99.9890	290.1427	-194.39	10574	140.00	-140.00
DE	445.1223	138.8777	212.0427	323.9573	-200.0000	10604.6740	0.0000	0.0000
PSO-TVAC	444.8047	139.1953	211.0609	324.9391	-200.0000	10604.6781	0.0000	0.0000
PSO	449.4771	134.5786	202.0271	333.9173	-199.9443	10605.2022	0.0000	0.0000

* V1 and V2 are area power balance violations for the two areas

Figure 2. Four area sixteen generating unit system

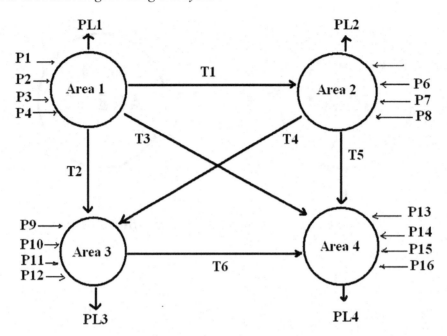

reserve constraints and inter area aid on the total fuel cost. In this paper DE/rand to best/1 variant of DE is applied for comparison with PSO and PSO_TVAC as it was found to be the best among various DE variants defined by Equation (12).

Effect of Tuning Parameters

Evolutionary strategies are known to depend heavily on the tuning parameters used for iterative convergence of the population. Many PSO and DE variants are being proposed for complex power system optimization problems these days. Here an attempt is made to compare the PSO and DE strategies in depth, to focus on their individual similarities and differences; merits and shortcomings; solution quality and consistency and dependence on tuning parameters. An insight into these strategies would result in saving a lot of time and effort which is otherwise spent in tuning the different parameters of these algorithms. The mean and standard deviation (S.D.) out of 50 trials for DE algorithm are tabulated in Table 2 for 2-area, 4-unit system and in Table 3 for 4-area,

16-unit system. From both tables it is evident that better results are available for f_m nearly equal to CR i.e., pairs roughly lying in a diagonal. When f_m is low it gives best results with lower value of CR and Higher f_m supports higher CR. Here, for reserve constrained MAED problem the best results are obtained for f_m=CR=0.9 for both the systems. However, for the 4-unit system zero S.D. was achieved for this combination, indicating global best results with full convergence where as for the more complex 16-unit system the S.D. was 1.84. It shows that with increase in problem dimension and complexity it becomes more difficult to achieve global best results. Sometimes, for some combinations of f_m and CR convergence is not achieved as can be seen from Table 1.

Ratnaweera, Halgamuge, and Watson (2004) have reported the best range of variation as 2.5-0.5 for c_1 and 0.5-2.5 for c_2. In Chaturvedi, Pandit, and Srivastava (2008) it is observed that initial value of the cognitive coefficient c_{1i} and final value of social coefficient c_{2f} control the range of the search space. Therefore in PSO_TVAC the values of c_{1i} and c_{2f} are varied between 2.5-1.8

Table 2. Effect of tuning parameters in DE for reserve constrained MAED (2-area, 4-unit system; 50 Trials)

f_m	CR=0.2	CR=0.4	CR=0.6	CR=0.8	CR=0.9
0.1	NON CONVERGENCE				
0.3	NON CONVERGENCE				
0.5	10588.5525 (13.6495)	**10587.8104 (13.1264)**	10592.5346 (16.1160)	29342049.6861 (3.8421e+007)	2061827.7318 (2.8644e+007)
0.7	10582.9070 (8.7853)	10568.1047 (0.6492)	10567.0219 (0.0831)	**10566.9973 (0.0828)**	10568.5141 (1.4469)
0.9	10567.7035 (8.6354)	10567.1912 (0.2093)	10566.9943 (0.0)	10566.9942 (0.0)	**10566.9942 (0.0)**

keeping c_{1f} and c_{2i} fixed at 0.2 (Chaturvedi, Pandit, & Srivastava, 2008). It is seen that a high initial value of the cognitive coefficient c_1 and a low social coefficient c_2 helps in avoiding premature convergence by maintaining right balance between exploration and exploitation. The search starts with high value of the cognitive coefficient c_1 to allow the swarm to explore, it is gradually decreased to reduce search space and c_2 is increased to accelerate the solution towards global convergence. This strategy is found to achieve better quality solutions as compared to classical PSO for all the tested functions.

Table 4 and Table 5 present the effect of acceleration coefficients on the MAED solution of 4-unit and 16-unit system by PSO_TVAC strategy. Best results for 4-unit system are found for $c_{1i} = c_{2f}$

=2.2 and for 16-unit system best results are found for c_{1i} = 2.2 and c_{2f} =2.5. It can be concluded from Table 4 and Table 5 that PSO_TVAC strategy achieves best results around $c_{1i} = c_{2f}$ =2.0. For the optimal combination of f_m and CR, the DE algorithm converges to the global best solution but it does not converge/or produces very high S.D for other combinations of tuning parameters. On the other hand PSO_TVAC produces near global results with low S.D. for almost all combinations of c_{1i} and c_{2f} as can be seen from Table 4 and Table 5. With these observations it can be concluded that DE is more sensitive to its tuning parameters that PSO_TVAC but the best value achieved by PSO_TVAC is slightly inferior to the best results of DE. For both strategies, the optimal parameter

Table 3. Effect of mutation factor and cross over rate on mean and S.D.in DE (4-area, 16-unit system; 50 Trials)

fm	CR=0.1	CR=0.2	CR=0.3	CR=0.5	CR=0.7	CR=0.9
0.1	**2181.10696 (9.0086)**	2189.55728 (20.6332)	2193.19845 (27.1880)	2195.20208 (27.8246)	2199.78698 (10424)	2199.79829 (137371)
0.3	2426.67283 (125.6497)	**2171.35686 (4.6344)**	2177.5432 (7.6774)	2180.33634 (5.0315)	2186.36895 (5.1065)	2183.13924 (5.0151)
0.5	3097.94904 (445.0659)	8534.2321` (234.3280)	**2160.9432 (4.780)**	2163.5291 (8.9943)	2196.6793 (15.1065)	2183.13924 (5.0151)
0.7	4324.28795 (1.0617e+003)	9734.10006 (9.5319e+003)	4561.03246 (5.2554e+003)	**2153.68508 (4.3857)**	2165.58999 (8.5268)	2170.45595 (11.5383)
0.9	2855.34363 (2190.32)	6993.55156 (2314)	2539.36171 (10395)	2314.57393 (129.3309)	2163.542 (8.7243)	**2134.1831 (1.8408)**

*the bracketed value indicates the standard deviation

combination is problem dependent and is found by trial and error approach.

Effect of Population Size

The population size is another important factor for achieving good results in evolutionary optimization methods. It has been reported that increasing population improved the performance of PSO algorithm (Chaturvedi, Pandit, & Srivastava, 2008; Alrashidi & El-Hawary, 2007). The optimal population size is found to depend on problem complexity and dimension. Storn and Price suggested a population size of 5-10 times that of problem dimension (Alrashidi & El-Hawary, 2007). In case of PSO, Chaturvedi, Pandit, and Srivastava (2008) clearly links population to performance while similar observations are reported for DE in Norman and Iba (2008) for various ED problems. Both references show that larger the dimension, larger is the population size required to achieve good results.

Different population sizes were tested and results can be seen in Table 6 and Table 7 for reserve constrained MAED problem for 4-unit and 16-unit systems for the DE algorithm. In Table 8 and Table 9 the results of the two test systems for PSO_TVAC algorithm are presented. Global best solution ($10566.9942/h) for the 4-unit reserve constrained system was achieved for a population size of 10 with a S.D. of 4.4263, but when population was increased to 20 the S.D. became zero. For the 4-area, 16-unit, test system also the results (minimum cost and S.D.) improved with population. The 4-area MAED problem is more complex, so S.D. did not drop to zero. For population higher than 250 there was only very slight improvement in S.D. and no change in minimum cost. It can be clearly seen that the PSO_TVAC strategy needs a higher population as compared to DE for similar performance. But it is interesting to note that DE does not converge when population size is 5 whereas PSO_TVAC converges to sub-optimal results though with a high S.D.

Table 4. Effect of acceleration coefficients on performance of PSO_TVAC (4 unit system; 50 trials)

S.No.	c_{1i}	c_{1f}	c_{2i}	c_{2f}	Minimum Cost($/h)	Mean cost($/h)	Max cost($/h)	S.D.
1	2.5	0.2	0.2	2.5	10571.1627	10603.7245	10651.3574	22.9119
2		0.2	0.2	2.2	10567.1017	10588.5628	10620.6481	15.7942
3		0.2	0.2	1.9	10572.4399	10597.2046	10646.1684	17.3088
4		0.2	0.2	1.6	10567.4208	10589.4200	10635.4442	20.9403
5	2.2	0.2	0.2	2.5	10568.5000	10585.4462	10608.1165	12.0717
6		**0.2**	**0.2**	**2.2**	**10567.0059**	**10585.3000**	**10613.7863**	**11.0512**
7		0.2	0.2	1.9	10573.7078	10598.0641	10629.8444	15.8550
8		0.2	0.2	1.6	10567.1314	10582.7097	10636.4196	15.9553
9	2	0.2	0.2	2.5	10570.7724	10605.4660	10652.2366	26.7054
10		0.2	0.2	2.2	10574.6925	10599.9216	10640.8692	17.7733
11		0.2	0.2	1.9	10569.8943	10608.8104	10660.8758	28.3077
12		0.2	0.2	1.6	10570.8181	10590.3793	10613.7086	13.3644
13	1.8	0.2	0.2	2.5	10574.4143	10589.6093	10642.3594	18.9789
14		0.2	0.2	2.2	10575.1141	10608.7149	10653.1403	26.4385
15		0.2	0.2	1.8	10580.0828	10585.4027	10635.5678	16.7408
16		0.2	0.2	1.7	10573.6622	10580.7429	10600.6508	7.6477

Table 5. Effect of acceleration coefficients on performance of PSO_TVAC (4-area, 16 unit system; 50 trials)

S.No.	c_{1i}	c_{1f}	c_{2i}	c_{2f}	Minimum Cost($/h)	Mean cost($/h)	Max cost($/h)	S.D.
1	2.5	0.2	0.2	2.5	2159.59506	2181.08503	2210.68277	9.3992
2		0.2	0.2	2.2	2161.12831	2193.92951	2213.26055	9.9184
3		0.2	0.2	1.9	2154.74795	2199.39777	2223.28707	11.0824
4		0.2	0.2	1.6	2159.97143	2193.50703	2217.16105	9.3707
5	2.2	0.2	0.2	2.5	2167.71805	2194.82667	2218.26802	10.7732
6		0.2	0.2	2.2	2160.65024	2198.99194	2222.22971	10.2540
7		0.2	0.2	1.9	2156.55619	2197.82993	2234.19736	15.3163
8		0.2	0.2	1.6	2158.32198	2198.86328	2233.25760	10.3980
9	2	0.2	0.2	2.5	**2146.44790**	**2194.11962**	**2225.70475**	**10.8107**
10		0.2	0.2	2.2	2157.07651	2191.00880	2226.59071	12.0115
11		0.2	0.2	1.9	2164.64675	2191.18872	2218.11009	10.6624
12		0.2	0.2	1.6	2161.81291	2192.57504	2222.42538	11.0344
13	1.8	0.2	0.2	2.5	2159.70801	2193.38596	2223.13262	12.8212
14		0.2	0.2	2.2	2156.72829	2192.45028	2223.72922	11.5096
15		0.2	0.2	1.8	2163.89457	2195.81629	2224.17805	9.0786
16		0.2	0.2	1.6	2160.58538	2190.14691	2212.44193	8.1415

Effect of Reserve Constraints

The results of MAED solution for the 2-area system using DE, PSO and PSO_TVAC with area reserve constraints are tabulated with tie-line capacity of 300MW in Table 10. Out of the three evolutionary strategies being compared here, the best performance (least cost and zero S.D) is achieved by DE, closely followed by PSO_TVAC. The classical PSO has found near global solution but the S.D. is very large indicating poor consistency. For the 4-area, 16-unit system the effect of area wise reserve constraints, on cost of operation was studied i) with inter area aid ii)

without inter area aid iii)Inter area reserve sharing. The results obtained by DE are compared with already published results (Wang & Singh, 2009) for the first two cases in Table 11.When area wise reserve constraints were imposed the best cost achieved by DE was $2131.74232/h against the already published $2166.82/h (Wang & Singh, 2009). In Wang and Singh (2009) the area reserve constraint of area 1 was violated and area balance constraints were also not fully satisfied. The cost increased to $2143.94836/h when no inter area aid was available. The results achieved by DE were superior to PSO (Wang & Singh, 2009) $2191.14/h in this case too, as the cost achieved

Table 6. Effect of population size on DE (reserve constrained 4 unit system; 50 trials) (F=CR=0.9)

Population	Minimum Cost	Mean Cost	Maximum Cost	S.D.
5	10592.7946	577569.1311	1343882956.0319	3.2646e+008
10	10566.9942	10567.1776	10591.6683	4.4263
15	10566.9942	10566.9942	10566.9942	0.3410
20	10566.9942	10566.9942	10566.9942	0.0

Table 7. Effect of population size on performance of DE (4-area, 16- unit system; 50 trials) (F=CR=0.9)

Population	Minimum Cost	Mean Cost	Maximum Cost	S.D.
5	Non convergence			
10	2183.89703	17747.65775	2357218.88740	1334970.0653
25	2167.57569	2183.44598	2198.96663	8.6539
50	2140.35424	2156.14664	2164.96996	7.1597
75	2134.81203	2148.77091	2156.64546	6.2455
100	2133.7132	2145.1432	2150.5642	5.5982
250	**2131.74232**	2134.1831	2140.5474	1.8408

Table 8. Effect of population size on performance of PSO_TVAC (2-area, 4-unit system; 50 trials)

Population	Minimum Cost	Mean Cost	Maximum Cost	S.D.
5	10567.5278	10646.5031	584510.0870	1.8399e+005
10	10574.6580	10598.5682	10634.8673	26.2295
25	10569.4409	10610.8046	10679.0515	17.5990
50	10568.6866	10567.6994	10636.9696	20.3451
100	10567.4672	10593.8420	10634.5229	19.6610
200	10567.0059	10585.3000	10613.7863	11.0512

Table 9. Effect of population size on performance of PSO_TVAC (4-area, 16- unit system; 50 trials)

Population	Minimum Cost	Mean Cost	Maximum Cost	S.D.
5	2164.76218	1.5117e+006	1.3401e+007	2.0890e+006
10	2149.78839	16537.9804	719711.51936	28127.0454
25	2163.98739	2193.93221	2211.92356	9.6196
50	2155.76388	2190.69271	2209.80704	9.3994
100	2171.22375	2194.20346	2213.28224	8.7987
200	2161.39630	2188.42678	2212.23175	9.6682
400	2157.62870	2187.54490	2209.98780	10.1966
600	**2146.44790**	2194.11962	2225.70475	10.8107

Table 10. Cost comparison with area reserve constraints and inter-area aid (2-area system; 50 trials)

Method	P1(MW)	P2(MW)	P3(MW)	P4(MW)	T12(MW)	Best Cost($/H)	Maximum Cost($/H)	S.D.
DE	369.5736	114.4263	296.0000	340.0000	-300.0000	10566.9942	10566.9942	0.0
PSO-TVAC	370.9293	113.0706	296.0000	340.0000	-300.0000	10567.0059	10613.7863	11.0512
PSO	383.7126	100.2874	296.0000	340.0000	-300.0000	10568.2696	10629.9326	3.120e+004

Table 11. Minimum fuel cost with, without inter-area aid and with total reserve constraint (4-area system; 50 trials)

Power output(MW)	w/inter-area aid [chanan singh]	w/inter-area reserve (DE)	w/o inter area aid [chanan singh]	w/o inter area aid(DE)	Total area reserve sharing (DE)
P1	13.20	13.99162	10.74	14.00000	13.99882
P2	6.49	9.98713	9.43	10.00000	9.99987
P3	12.01	4.52850	5.03	0.05000	5.69721
P4	11.28	11.40254	5.33	5.95000	11.98285
P5	20.47	24.98520	25.07	25.00000	24.99881
P6	6.57	10.49369	6.71	12.00000	11.99570
P7	13.16	0.07722	9.80	6.52533	10.94960
P8	15.03	16.93120	8.46	6.47466	8.36306
P9	5.72	0.17820	10.83	0.05001	0.07649
P10	9.71	0.09605	16.46	0.05000	0.05389
P11	6.63	20.02937	6.62	9.89999	18.17293
P12	22.78	28.05566	6.22	30.00000	29.99971
P13	7.59	9.78625	7.54	11.00000	10.99540
P14	11.23	0.07978	15.87	0.05000	0.05133
P15	5.20	29.26262	10.71	30.00000	22.60373
P16	14.02	0.11469	26.04	18.94999	0.06055
T1	-3.16	-5.99164	0.00000	0.00000	-4.31812
T2	-0.88	-3.97817	0.00000	0.00000	-3.99921
T3	16.99	19.87957	0.00000	0.00000	19.99604
T4	-3.20	-3.49963	0.00000	-0.00000	-3.49951
T5	5.16	-0.00441	0.00000	0.00000	5.48859
T6	0.48	0.88164	0.00000	0.00000	0.80430
Reserve Area1	6.02	9.09021	18.47	19.00000	7.32125
Reserve Area2	19.77	22.51268	24.96	25.00001	18.69282
Reserve Area3	75.16	71.64071	79.87	80.00000	71.69698
Reserve Area4	52.96	51.75667	30.84	31.00001	57.28899
Total reserve	153.91	155.00027	154.1400	155.00003	155.00004
Violation AR1	0.03	0.00	0.53	0.0000	0.0000
Violation AR2	0.11	-0.0047	0.04	-0.0001	0.0000
Violation AR3	0.28	-0.0002	0.13	-0.0001	0.0000
Violation AR4	0.67	0.0046	0.16	-0.0001	0.0001
COST($/h)	2166.82	2131.74232	2191.14	2143.94836	2127.81194

was less and constraints (area balance as well as area reserve) were fully satisfied. The cost was further reduced to $2127.81194/h when area wise reserve constraints were relaxed to total reserve constraint. The solution indicates that area 1 no longer has the required reserve of 9 MW as other areas are sharing its reserve requirement. The data for 4-area 16-unit system is given in Appendix from where it can be seen that all tie-lines are

Figure 3. Convergence characteristics of the three strategies for reserve constrained system (2-area, 4-unit system)

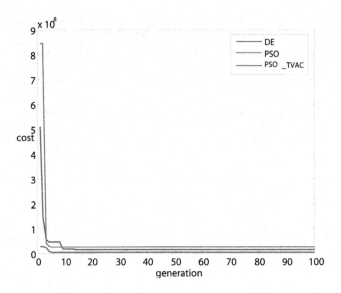

loaded to their capacity and no constraints defined by Equation (4)-(6) are violated.

Convergence Characteristics

The convergence behavior of DE, PSO and PSO_TVAC were tested using the same evalua-tion function and same initial population for same number of iterations. The results for all three strat-egies for one trial of 100 iterations are shown in Figure 3 for the 4-unit system. It can be seen that the TVAC strategy provides the PSO algorithm with optimal search capability due to the proper tuning of social and cognitive coefficients during

Figure 4. Best results of DE, PSO and PSO_TVAC for reserve constrained MAED (4-unit system); 50 trials

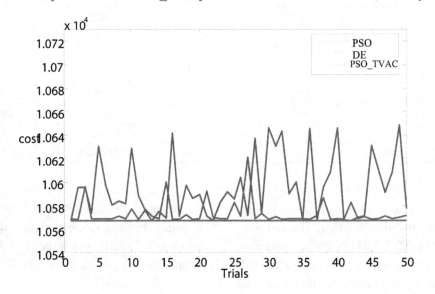

Figure 5. Best results of DE, PSO and PSO_TVAC variants (16-unit system); 50 trials

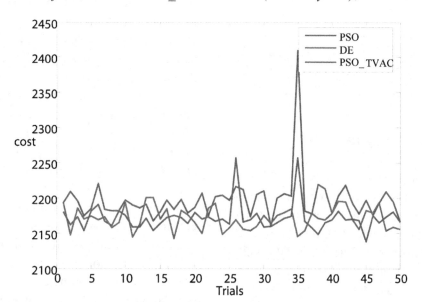

the search. When search advances and reaches a certain iteration count, the classical PSO character-istics saturates but the PSO_TVAC still continues to improve and thus shows the best convergence characteristics. It is seen that DE takes longer to converge than PSO_TVAC. Similar results were observed for the 4-area system also.

Consistency

The performance of evolutionary optimization algorithms is not judged by the results of a single run due to the randomness involved in their func-tioning. These techniques tend to converge to different optimal solutions in the neighborhood of the global optimum solution in different runs. Therefore, many trials with different initial popu-lations were carried out to test the consistency of the different evolutionary algorithms. The lowest cost for each of the 50 different trials has been plotted in Figure 4 and Figure 5 from which it can be seen that DE produces lowest cost with zero/near zero standard deviation indicating its highest consistency. The PSO_TVAC performs better than classical PSO and achieves near best results in many trials.

Table 12. Comparison of DE variants with PSO and PSO_TVAC (4-area, 16-unit system; 50 trials)

Strategy	Minimum Cost	Mean Cost	Maximum Cost	S.D.
DE/best/1	2164.13849	2234.70543	2291.19796	28.2408
DE/rand/1	2138.00903	2141.26909	2158.26342	5.9469
DE/rand to best /1	**2131.74232**	2134.1831	2140.5474	**1.8408**
DE/best/2	2209.42232	5544.91589	28786.22364	1.0373e+004
DE/rand/2	Non convergence			
PSO_TVAC	2146.44790	2194.11962	2225.70475	10.8107
PSO	2153.75742	2770.9073	30984.44153	1128.5403

Table 13. Time (cpu seconds) comparison of DE, PSO and PSO_TVAC

	DE	PSO	PSO_TVAC
2-area 4-unit	32.8174	10.3283	10.3404
4-area, 16 unit	98.6758	12.9106	13.0106

Comparative Analysis

Table 12 gives a detailed study of different classic DE variants out of 50 trials for reserve constrained 4-area system. It can be seen that out of the DE variants, the "DE/rand to best /1" strategy performs the best followed by DE/rand/1 and DE/best/1 strategies. This is clear from the minimum cost and standard deviation. The DE/rand/2 and DE/best/2 strategies do not converge in most trials. PSO_TVAC strategy gives better performance than the classical PSO and DE/best/1; it also reaches convergence for all values of acceleration coefficients, while DE does not. Another significant difference is that DE requires less population but takes larger number of iterations to converge while PSO works with larger populations and lesser iterations as reported in Table 13. The superiority of the reported results is evident from their ability to satisfy all constraints and produce feasible results. The solutions reported in Manoharan, Kannan, Baskar, and Willjuice (2009), and Wang and Singh (2009) do not satisfy the individual area balance constraints.

CONCLUSION

The paper presents an extensive comparison of classic PSO and DE strategies and their variants, which are increasingly being proposed for solving non-convex, discontinuous, multi-modal ED problems with complex constraints. In reserve constrained multi-area ED problem many additional constraints like the tie-line, area balance and area wise reserve constraints are introduced which

present difficulty in obtaining feasible solutions. The paper explores the ability of DE and PSO strategies to produce global best solutions for the complex reserve constrained MAED problems. A comparative study of classic DE variants with PSO and its variants is made to find their abilities and limitations. Simulations carried out on 2-area and 4-area systems clearly show that the *DE/rand to best/1* strategy performs the best for all tested systems closely followed by *DE/rand/1* and *DE/best/1* strategies. The other DE variants do not converge for tested problems with reserve constraints. A comparison of PSO_TVAC and classic DE reveals that the former converges to near global solutions in all trial runs, for all tested values of tuning parameters, and for all tested population sizes; DE on the other hand is highly sensitive to its tuning parameters f_m and CR. For some values of f_m and CR the DE algorithm does not converge at all or produces very high S.D. It can be concluded that DE converges to the global best solution with zero S.D. in a very narrow range of tuning parameters. But the best performance of DE is better than PSO in terms of cost as well as consistency (S.D). Also, the PSO_TVAC strategy needs a higher population as compared to DE for similar performance. Both DE and PSO_TVAC achieved better solutions than previously reported results, with full constraint satisfaction, for reserve constrained MAED problem for both with/without inter area aid cases. It has been shown that inter- area reserve sharing can help in reducing the operational cost. Both DE and PSO strategies are capable of solving ED problems with complex constraints very effectively.

ACKNOWLEDGMENT

The authors sincerely acknowledge the financial support provided by UGC under major research project entitled Power System Optimization and Security Assessment Using Soft Computing Techniques, vide F No.34-399/2008 (SR) dated,

24th December 2008 and AICTE New Delhi for financial assistance under RPS project F No 8023/RID/BOR/RPS-45/2005-06 dated 10/03/2006. The authors also thank the Director, M.I.T.S. Gwalior for providing facilities for carrying out this work.

REFERENCES

Alrashidi, M. R., & El-Hawary, M. E. (2007). Hybrid particle swarm optimization approach for solving the discrete OPF problem considering the valve loading effects. *IEEE Transactions on Power Systems, 22*(4), 2030–2038. doi:10.1109/TPWRS.2007.907375

Aruldoss, T., Victoire, A., & Jeyakumar, A. E. (2005). Reserve constrained dynamic dispatch of units with valve point effects. *IEEE Transactions on Power Systems, 20*(3), 1273–1282. doi:10.1109/TPWRS.2005.851958

Chaturvedi, K. T., Pandit, M., & Srivastava, L. (2008, August). Self-Organizing Hierarchical Particle Swarm Optimization for Nonconvex Economic Dispatch. *IEEE Transactions on Power Systems, 23*(3), 1079–1087. doi:10.1109/TPWRS.2008.926455

Chaturvedi, K. T., Pandit, M., & Srivastava, L. (2009). Particle Swarm Optimization with Time Varying Acceleration Coefficients for Nonconvex Economic Power Dispatch. *Electrical Power and Energy systems, 31*(6), 249-257.

Chen, C. L., & Chen, N. (2001). Direct search method for solving economic dispatch problem considering transmission capacity constraints. *IEEE Transactions on Power Systems, 16*(4), 764–769. doi:10.1109/59.962424

Coelho, L. S., & Mariani, V. C. (2006). Combining of chaotic differential evolution and quadratic programming for economic dispatch optimization with valve-point effect. *IEEE Transactions on Power Systems, 21*(2), 989–996. doi:10.1109/TPWRS.2006.873410

Desell, A. L., McClelland, E. C., Tammar, K., & Van Horne, R. R. (1984). Transmission constrained production cost analysis in power system planning. *IEEE Transactions on Power Apparatus and Systems, 103*(8), 2192–2198. doi:10.1109/TPAS.1984.318532

Desell, A. L., Tammar, K., McClelland, E. C., & Van Home, P. R. (1984). Transmission constrained production cost analysis in power system planning. *IEEE Transactions on Power Apparatus and Systems, 103*(8), 2192–2198. doi:10.1109/TPAS.1984.318532

Doty, K. W., & McEntire, P. L. (1982). An analysis of electrical power brokerage systems. *IEEE Transactions on Power Apparatus and Systems, 101*(2), 389–396. doi:10.1109/TPAS.1982.317119

Farmer, E. D., Grubb, M. J., & Vlahos, K. (1990). Probabilistic production costing of transmission-constrained power systems. In *Proceedings of the 10th PSCC Power System Computation Conference* (pp. 663-669).

Hemick, S. D., & Shoults, R. R. (1985). A practical approach to an interim multi-area economic dispatch using limited computer resources. *IEEE Transactions on Power Apparatus and Systems, 104*(6), 1400–1404. doi:10.1109/TPAS.1985.319244

Jayabarathi, T., Sadasivam, G., & Ramachandran, V. (2000). Evolutionary programming based multi-area economic dispatch with tie-line constraints. *Electrical Machines and Power Systems, 28*, 1165–1176. doi:10.1080/073135600449044

Kennedy, J., & Eberhart, R. (1995). Particle swarm optimization. In *Proceedings of the IEEE Conf. on Neural Networks (ICNN'95)*, Perth, Australia (Vol. 4, pp. 1942-48).

Lee, F. N., & Breipohl, J. D. A. M. (1993). Reserve constrained economic load dispatch with prohibited operating zones. *IEEE Transactions on Power Systems, 8*, 246–253. doi:10.1109/59.221233

Lin, C. E., & Viviani, G. L. (1984). Hierarchical economic load dispatch for piecewise quadratic cost functions. *IEEE Transactions on Power Apparatus and Systems, 103*, 1170–1175. doi:10.1109/TPAS.1984.318445

Manoharan, P. S., Kannan, S., Baskar, M., & Willjuice, I. (2009). Evolutionary algorithm solution and KKT based optimality verification to multi-area economic dispatch. *Electrical Power and Energy Systems, 31*, 365–373. doi:10.1016/j.ijepes.2009.03.010

Nasr Azadani, E., Hosseinian, S. H., & Moradzadeh, B. (2010). Generation and reserve dispatch in a competitive market using constrained particle swarm optimization. *Electrical power and energy systems, 32*, 79-86.

Noman, N., & Iba, H. (2008). Differential evolution for economic load dispatch problems. *Electric Power Systems Research, 78*, 1322–1331. doi:10.1016/j.epsr.2007.11.007

Panigrahi, B. K., & Pandi, V. R. (2009). Bacterial foraging optimisation: Nelder–Mead hybrid algorithm for economic load dispatch. *IET Generation. Transmission and Distribution, 2*(4), 556–565.

Park, J. H., & Kim, Y. S., Eom, & Lee, K. Y. (1993). Economic load dispatch for piecewise quadratic cost function using Hopfield neural network. *IEEE Transactions on Power Systems, 8*, 1030–1038. doi:10.1109/59.260897

Ratnaweera, A., Halgamuge, S. K., & Watson, H. C. (2004). Self-organizing hierarchical Particle swarm optimizer with time varying acceleration coefficients. *IEEE Transactions on Evolutionary Computation, 8*(3), 240–255. doi:10.1109/TEVC.2004.826071

Shoults, R. R., Chang, S. K., Helmick, S., & Grady, W. M. (1980). A practical approach to unit commitment, economic dispatch and savings allocation for multiple area pool operation with import/export constraints. *IEEE Transactions on Power Apparatus and Systems, 99*(2), 625–635. doi:10.1109/TPAS.1980.319654

Sinha, N., Chakraborty, R., & Chattopadhyay, P. K. (2003). Evolutionary programming techniques for economic load dispatch. *IEEE Transactions on Evolutionary Computation, 7*(1), 83–93. doi:10.1109/TEVC.2002.806788

Song, Y. S., Chou, C. S., & Stoham, T. J. (1999). Combined heat and power economic dispatch by improved ant colony search algorithm. *Electric Power Systems Research, 52*(2), 115–121. doi:10.1016/S0378-7796(99)00011-5

Storn, R. (1997). Differential evolution—a simple and efficient heuristic for global optimization over ontinuous spaces. *Journal of Global Optimization, 11*(4), 341–359. doi:10.1023/A:1008202821328

Storn, R., & Price, K. (1995). *Differential evolution: A simple and efficient adaptive scheme for global optimization over continuous spaces* (Tech. Rep. No. TR-95-012). Berkeley, CA: International Computer Science Institute.

Streifferet, D. (1995). Multi-Area economic dispatch with tie-line constraints. *IEEE Transactions on Power Systems, 10*(4), 1946–1951. doi:10.1109/59.476062

Vanaja, B., Hemamalini, S., & Simon, S. P. (2008, November 19-21). Artificial Immune based Economic Load Dispatch with valve-point effect. In *Proceedings of the IEEE Region 10 Conference (TENCON 2008)* (pp. 1-5).

Vasebi, A., Fesanghary, M., & Bathaee, S. M. T. (2007). Combined heat and power economic dispatch by harmony search algorithm. *Electrical Power and Energy systems, 29,* 713-719.

Walter, D. C., & Sheble, G. B. (1993). Genetic algorithm solution of economic load dispatch with valve point loading. *IEEE Transactions on Power Systems, 8*(3), 1325–1332. doi:10.1109/59.260861

Wang, C., & Shahidehpour, S. M. (1992). A decomposition approach to non -linear multi-area generation scheduling with tie-line constraints using expert sy*stem. IEEE Transactions on Power Apparatus and Systems, 7*(4), 1409–1418.

Wang, L., & Singh, C. (2009). Reserve constrained multi-area environmental/economic dispatch based on particle swarm optimization with local search. *Engineering Applications of Artificial Intelligence, 22,* 298–307. doi:10.1016/j.engappai.2008.07.007

Wernerus, J., & Soder, L. (1995). Area price based multi-area economic dispatch with tie-line losses and constraints. In *Proceedings of the IEEE/KTH Stockholm Power Tech Conference,* Sweden (pp. 710-15).

Wood, A. J., & Wollenberg, B. F. (1984). *Power generation, operation and control.* New York: John Wiley & Sons.

Yalcinoz, T., & Short, M. J. (1998). Neural Networks Approach for Solving Economic Dispatch Problem with Transmission Capacity Constraints. *IEEE Transactions on Power Systems, 13*(2), 307–313. doi:10.1109/59.667341

APPENDIX

Table A1. Cost coefficients, generation limits and tie-line limits of 4-area, 16-unit system [17]

Area	Power output(MW)	a	b	c	P_{max}	P_{min}
Area1	P1	0.000050	1.89	150	14	0.05
	P2	0.000055	2.00	115	10	0.05
	P3	0.000060	3.50	40	13	0.05
	P4	0.000050	3.15	122	12	0.05
Area 2	P5	0.000050	3.05	125	25	0.05
	P6	0.000070	2.75	70	12	0.05
	P7	0.000070	3.45	70	20	0.05
	P8	0.000070	3.45	70	18	0.05
Area 3	P9	0.000050	2.45	130	30	0.05
	P10	0.000050	2.45	130	30	0.05
	P11	0.000055	2.35	135	30	0.05
	P12	0.000045	1.30	200	30	0.05
Area 4	P13	0.000070	3.45	70	11	0.05
	P14	0.000060	3.89	45	20	0.05
	P15	0.000060	3.55	75	30	0.05
	P16	0.000080	3.70	100	30	0.05
Tie Lines	T1	-	-	-	6	0.1
	T2	-	-	-	4	0.1
	T3	-	-	-	20	0.1
	T4	-	-	-	3.5	0.1
	T5	-	-	-	5.5	0.1
	T6	-	-	-	0.9	0.1

This work was previously published in International Journal of Applied Evolutionary Computation, Volume 1, Issue 3, edited by Wei-Chiang Samuelson Hong, pp. 27-48, copyright 2010 by IGI Publishing (an imprint of IGI Global).

Chapter 12
Application of Machine Learning Techniques to Predict Software Reliability

Ramakanta Mohanty
Berhampur University, India

V. Ravi
Institute for Development and Research in Banking Technology, India

M. R. Patra
Berhampur University, India

ABSTRACT

In this paper, the authors employed machine learning techniques, specifically, Back propagation trained neural network (BPNN), Group method of data handling (GMDH), Counter propagation neural network (CPNN), Dynamic evolving neuro–fuzzy inference system (DENFIS), Genetic Programming (GP), TreeNet, statistical multiple linear regression (MLR), and multivariate adaptive regression splines (MARS), to accurately forecast software reliability. Their effectiveness is demonstrated on three datasets taken from literature, where performance is compared in terms of normalized root mean square error (NRMSE) obtained in the test set. From rigorous experiments conducted, it was observed that GP outperformed all techniques in all datasets, with GMDH coming a close second.

INTRODUCTION

Software reliability engineering has become a vital skill for both the software manager and software engineer. The software engineering knowledge is also important to managers and engineers of software oriented products and to users of the

products. The primary objective of software reliability engineering is to help the engineer, manager, or users to make more precise decisions. The secondary objective is to make everyone more concretely aware of software reliability by focusing attention on it. Better decisions can save money on a project or during the life cycle of a piece of software in many ways. In general, the

DOI: 10.4018/978-1-4666-1749-0.ch012

total savings can be more than 10 times greater than the cost of applying these ideas (Musa, 1998).

Reliability is probably the most important of the characteristics inherent in the concept "software quality". Software reliability is defined as the probability that the software will work without failure for a specified period of time (Musa, 1998). Software reliability is an important factor which is related to defects and faults. It differs from hardware reliability in that it reflects the design perfection, rather than manufacturing perfection. The principal factors that affect software reliability are (i) fault introduction (ii) fault removal and (iii) the environment. Fault introduction depends primarily on the characteristics of the product and the development process. The characteristics of development process include software engineering technologies and tools used the level of experience of the personnel, volatility of requirements, and other factors. Failure discovery, in turn, depends on the extent to which the software has been executed and the operational profile. Because some of the foregoing factors are probabilistic in nature and operate over time, software reliability models have generally been formulated in terms of random processes in execution time.

In the past few years much research work has been carried out in software reliability and forecasting but no single model could capture software characteristics.

In this paper, we investigate the performance of some of the well known machine learning techniques in predicting software reliability. The rest of the paper is organized as follows. In Literature review section, a brief review of the works carried out in area of software reliability prediction is presented. In the next section, the various stand-alone machine learning techniques applied in this paper are briefly described. In the next section, the experimental design followed in this paper is presented. It is followed by a section that discusses the results obtained. Finally, the last section concludes the paper.

LITERATURE SURVEY

Given the importance of software reliability in software engineering, its prediction becomes a very crucial issue. Machine learning and soft computing techniques have been dominating the statistical techniques in last two decades as far as their applications to software engineering are concerned. The most recent state-of-the-art review, by Mohanty et al. (2010), justifies this assertion. Cai et al. (1991) presented a review on software reliability modeling. The review discussed different types of probabilistic software reliability models and their shortcomings. Then, Karunanithi et al. (1991) employed the BPNN to predict the software reliability and found that the NN models were consistent in prediction and their performance is comparable to that of other parametric models. Later, Karunanithi et al. (1992b) predicted software reliability using a new connectionist approach which offers easy construction of complex models and estimation of parameters as well as good adaptability for different dataset. They used dataset collected from different software systems to compare the models. Based on the experiments, they found that the scaled representation of input–output variables provided better accuracy than the binary coded (or grey coded) representation. The experimental result obtained by them showed that the connectionist networks had less end point prediction errors than parametric models. Thereafter, Karunanithi et al. (1992a) presented a solution to the scaling problems in which they used a clipped linear unit in the output layer. The NN could predict positive values in any unbounded range with a clipped linear unit. They used different types of analytical models such as logarithmic model, inverse-polynomial, power model, delay S-shaped and exponential model. Among the models, the Jordan network model exhibits a better accuracy than the feed forward model. Khoshgoftaar et al. (1992) explored the use of NN for predicting the number of faults in a program. They used static reliability modeling and compared its performances with that of regression models. They used dataset obtained from Ada development environment for the command control of a military data line communication system. They found that the absolute relative error of NN is less compared to regression model.

Then, Khoshgoftaar and Szabo (1994) used the principal component analysis (PCA) on NN for improving predictive quality. They used regression modeling and NN modeling to predict the reliability and the number of faults. The datasets used for the prediction were collected from large commercial software system. They found that regression model did not correspond well in linking complexity and fault. Meanwhile, Sherer (1995) applied NN to predict software faults in several NASA projects. Further, Khoshgoftaar and Szabo (1996) used NN to investigate the application of PCA to predict the number of faults. The datasets used for prediction of faults collected from commercial software systems. They extracted PCA from these measures. They trained two NNs, one with observed data (raw) and other with principal components. They compared the predictive quality of two models and found that PCA based NN yielded better results. Furthermore, Khoshgoftaar et al. (1997) reported a case study of NN modeling techniques developed for early risk assessment of latent defect (EMERALD) for improving the reliability of telecommunication software products. They applied NN techniques to find out fault prone modules and also to detect the risk of operational problems. They used a variety of classification techniques to identify fault prone software including discriminant analysis and classification tress. They compared the NN model with non-discriminant model and found that NN model provided better accuracy. On the other hand, Dohi et al. (1999) used BPNN and recurrent NN to estimate the software release time for cost minimization problem. They interpreted cost minimization problem as a graphical one and showed that cost minimization problem could be reduced to a time series forecasting problem. They

used datasets of Lyu (1996) and found that the predictive performance of the optimal software release time by BPNN was better than the existing parametric SRGMs. Besides, Sitte (1999) reported that neural networks are not only much simpler to use than the recalibration method, but they are equal or better trend predictors for software reliability prediction. Later, Khoshgoftaar et al. (2000) employed CART to evaluate software quality models over several releases. They found that modules had accuracy that would be useful to predict the different new models releases about the accuracy. Cai et al. (2001) employed BPNN to predict the time between successive software failures observed in successive time intervals on a dynamic software reliability data. Tian and Noore (2005a, 20005b) proposed an evolutionary NN for software cumulative failure time prediction on multiple-delayed-input single-output architecture. However, a problem in this approach is that one has to predetermine the network architecture in terms of the number of hidden neurons and the numbers of hidden layers. Pai and Hong (2006) applied Support Vector Machines (SVMs) for forecasting software reliability where Simulated Annealing (SA) algorithm was used to select the parameters of the SVM model. Su and Huang (2006) applied NN to predict software reliability. Further, they made use of the NN approach to build a dynamic weighted combinational model (DWCM). Rajkiran and Ravi (2007a) developed an ensemble model to forecast software reliability. They used MLR, MARS, dynamic evolving neuro-fuzzy inference system (DENFIS) and TreeNet to develop the ensemble. They designed and tested three linear and one non-linear ensembles. They concluded that the non-linear ensemble outperformed all other ensembles and also the constituent's statistical and intelligent techniques. Later, Rajkiran and Ravi (2007b) proposed the use of Wavelets Neural Networks (WNN) with Morlet wavelet and Gaussian wavelet transfer functions to predict software reliability. They reported that the WNN outperformed Multiple Linear Regression

(MLR), Multivariate adaptive regression splines (MARS), BPNN, Threshold accepting trained neural network (TANN), Pi-Sigma Network (PSN), GRNN, dynamic evolving neuro-fuzzy inference system (DENFIS) and TreeNet in terms of normalized root mean square error (NRMSE) obtained on test data. Recently, Ravi et al. (2009) proposed the use of threshold accepting trained wavelet neural network (TAWNN) to predict operational risk in banks and firms by predicting software reliability. They observed that WNN based models outperformed TAWNN and other techniques over all the lags. Then, Aljahdali and Telbany (2009) employed Genetic Algorithm (GA) to solve the multi-objective optimization problems involving the objectives of NRMSE and correlation coefficient obtained by ensembling different auto regressive models to predict software reliability.

Most recently, Mohanty et al. (2009a, 2009b) employed group method of data handling (GMDH) and genetic programming (GP) respectively to predict software reliability on the Musa (1979a) dataset. They compared the performance of GMDH and GP with that of MLR, MARS, MLP, DENFIS, TreeNet and other techniques in terms of NRMSE obtained on test data. They found that GP outperformed all other techniques. In this paper, in addition to the above mentioned techniques, we employ CPNN, which is used for the first time in software reliability forecasting. Further, we conducted rigorous experiments with two other datasets (Musa, 1979b; Iyer & Lee, 1996) taken from literature.

OVERVIEW OF THE TECHNIQUES APPLIED

Here we present a brief overview of the machine learning, soft computing and statistical techniques that are employed in this paper. Since, BPNN, MLR are too popular to be overviewed here, rest of the techniques are presented here.

Group Method of Data Handling (GMDH)

The GMDH network is not like regular feed forward networks and was not originally represented as a network. The GMDH network is implemented with polynomial terms in the links and a genetic component to decide how many layers are to be built. The result of training at the output layer can be represented as a polynomial function of all or some of inputs. Ivakhnenko (1968) proposed it. The main idea behind GMDH is that it tries to build a function (called a polynomial model) that would behave in such a way that the predicted value of the output would be as close as possible to the actual value of output (http://www.inf.kiew.ua/gmdhhome).

GMDH (Farlow, 1984) is a heuristic self organizing method that models the input-output relationship of a complex system using a multilayered Rosenblatt's perception-type network structure. Each neuron in the network implements a non-linear equation of two inputs and its coefficients are determined by a regression analysis. Self selection thresholds are given at each layer in the network to delete those useless neurons which can not estimate the correct output. Only those neurons whose performance indices exceed the threshold are allowed to pass to succeeding layers, where more complex combination is formed. These steps are repeated until the convergence criterion is satisfied or a predetermined number of layers are reached. GMDH approach can be useful because (i) A small training set of data is required (ii) The computational burden is reduced (iii) The procedure automatically filters out redundant input variables (iv) A multilayer structure is a computationally feasible way to implement multinomials of high degree.

The concept of GMDH algorithm (Farlow, 1984) used in this paper is described as follows:

GMDH algorithm can be represented as a set of neurons in which different pairs of them in each layer are connected through a quadratic polynomial and thus produce new neuron in the next layer. Such representation can be used to map inputs to output. The formal definition of the identification is to find a function f in order to predict output Y for a given input vector $x = (x_1, x_2, x_3, \dots\dots\dots, x_n)$ as close as possible. Therefore, assume the output variable Y is a function of the input variable $(x_1, x_2, x_3, \dots\dots\dots x_n)$ as follows

$$Y = f(x_1, x_2, \dots\dots, x_n) \qquad (1)$$

At each layer, GMDH will build a polynomial like the following:

$$
\begin{aligned}
&\hat{Y} = f(x_j, x_k) = a_{0i} + a_{1i}x_j + a_{2i}x_k + \\
&a_{3i}x_j^2 + a_{4i}x_k^2 + a_{5i}x_j x_k \\
&i = 1, \dots q; j = 1, \dots n; k = 1 \dots\dots n - 1; q = \\
&\frac{n(n-1)}{2}
\end{aligned}
\qquad (2)
$$

Where a_0 is a constant; $a_1, a_2, a_3 \dots\dots$ are coefficients and $x_i, x_j, x_k \dots$ are input variables.

In the first layer, the input neurons are the input variables and the second layer neurons consist of polynomials like in Equation 3. When third layer is built, the input to the third layer polynomials can either be the original problem inputs, the polynomial from the second layer, or both. If inputs are polynomial, then a much more complicated polynomial will be built. In general, The Kolmogorov-Gabor polynomial (Farlow, 1984) can simulate

$$
\hat{Y} =
$$

$$
a_0 + \sum_{i=1}^{n} a_i x_i + \sum_{i=1}^{n}\sum_{j=1}^{n} a_{ij} x_i x_j + \qquad (3)
$$

$$
\sum_{i=1}^{n}\sum_{j=1}^{n}\sum_{k=1}^{n} a_{ijk} x_i x_j x_k
$$

It describes an input-output relationship perfectly and has been widely used as a complete description of the system model. By combining the so called partial polynomial of two variables in the multilayer, the GMDH can easily solve these problems.

Counter Propagation Neural network (CPNN)

In the counter propagation neural network (Hecht-Nielsen, 1987; Zupan et al., 1997; Zupan & Gasteiger, 1999), there are two layers. One layer is the competitive – Kohenen layer and other is the output layer. The input layer in CPNN performs the mapping of the multidimensional input data into lower dimensional array using competitive learning. The main steps of the training procedure of CPNN are presented on the flow chart.

The vectors with N input variables($x_s = x_{s,1}, \dots x_{s,i}, \dots x_{s,N}$) are compared only with the weights ($w_j = w_{j,1}, \dots w_{j,i}, \dots w_{j,N}$) of the neurons in the Kohonen layer. Once the winning (or central) neuron c is found among the neurons in the Kohonen layer, the weights of both layers (Kohonen and output layer) are adjusted according to the pairs of input and target vectors (x, y) using selected learning rate $\eta(t)$ and neighborhood function $a(d_j - d_c)$:

$$w_{j,i}^{new} = w_{j,i}^{old} + \eta(t) \cdot a(d_j - d_c) \cdot (xi - w_{j,i}^{old}) \qquad (4)$$

$$u_{j,i}^{new} = u_{j,i}^{old} + \eta(t) \cdot a(d_j - d_c) \cdot (y_i - u_{j,i}^{old}) \qquad (5)$$

The difference between $d_j - d_c$ in Equations (4) and (5) represents the topological distance between the winning neuron c and the neuron j in which weights are adjusted. $w_{j,i}^{old}$ and $w_{j,i}^{new}$ weights of the Kohonen layer before and after its adjustments were performed respectively, while $u_{j,i}^{old}$ and $u_{j,i}^{new}$ are the weights of the output layer before and after the performed adjustments respectively.

The learning rate $\eta(t)$ is a non increasing function which defines the intensity of the changes of the weights during the training process. Besides the changes of the weights of the central neuron, the weights of the neighboring neurons are also corrected. The intensity of the correction is determined by the shape of the neighborhood function. The width of the neighborhood defined by the topological distance between the central neuron and the furthest neuron is affected by the correction which is decreases during the training.

Multivariate Adaptive Regression Splines (MARS)

Friedman (1991) introduced Multivariate Adaptive Regression Splines (MARS). MARS automates the development and deployment of accurate and easy to understand regression models. MARS is used to solve problems such as predicting credit card holder balances, insurance claim losses, customer catalog orders, and cell phone usage. It excels at finding optimal variable transformations and interactions, the complex data structure that often hides in high dimensional data. In doing so, this new approach to regression modeling effectively uncovers important data patterns and relationships that are difficult, for other methods to reveal.

TreeNet

Friedman (1999) introduced the TreeNet. It makes use of a new concept of "ultra slow learning" in which layers of information are gradually peeled off to reveal structure in data. TreeNet models are typically composed of hundreds of small trees, each of which contributes just a tiny adjustment to the overall model. TreeNet is insensitive to data errors and needs no time-consuming data preprocessing or imputation of missing values. TreeNet is resistant to over training and is faster than a neural net. TreeNet available in (http://salford-systems.com/) was used in the paper.

Dynamic Evolving Neuro-Fuzzy Inference System (DENFIS)

DENFIS was introduced by Kasabov and Song (2002). DENFIS evolves through incremental, hybrid (supervised and unsupervised) learning and accommodates new input data, including new features, new classes, etc., through local element tuning. New fuzzy rules are created and updated during the operation of the system. At each time moment, the output of DENFIS is calculated through a fuzzy inference system based on -most activated fuzzy rules, which are dynamically chosen from a fuzzy rule set. A set of fuzzy rules can be inserted into DENFIS before or during its learning process. Fuzzy rules can also be extracted during or after the learning process.

Genetic Programming

GP is an extension of GA, which removes the restriction that the chromosome representing the individual has to be a fixed length binary string. In general, in GP, the chromosome is some type of program, which is then executed to obtain required results. One of the simplest forms of program, which is sufficient for this application, is a binary tree containing operators and operands. This means that each solution is an algebraic expression, which can be evaluated.

Koza (1992) "offers a large amount of empirical evidence to support the counter-intuitive and surprising conclusion that GP can be used to solve large number of seemingly different problems from many different fields". GP offers solutions in representations of computer programs. This offer the flexibility to (i) Perform operations in a hierarchical way (ii) Perform alternative computations conditioned on the outcome of intermediate calculations (iii) Perform iterations and recursions (iv) Perform computations on variables of different types (v) Define intermediate values and subprograms so that they can be subsequently reused.

The initial preparation for a GP system has several steps. First, it is necessary to choose a suitable alphabet of operands and operators. The operands are normally the independent input variables of the system and normally include a random number from within a range, e.g. 0 – 10. The operators should be rich enough to cover the type of functionality expected in solution but having too many operators can affect convergence. Secondly, it is necessary to construct an initial population. We use a set of randomly constructed trees from the specified alphabet, although this is dependent on the type of problem being solved and the representation chosen for the program. For initial population of trees, a good and common approach is called Ramped Half and Half. This means that half the trees are constructed as full trees, i.e. operands only occur at the maximum depth of tree, and half are trees with random shape. Within each half, an equal number of trees are constructed for each depth, between some minimum and maximum depths. This is found to give a good selection of trees in original population. The main genetic operations used are reproduction, mutation and crossover.

Reproduction is the copying of one individual from the previous generation into the next generation unchanged. This is elitism, where the top n% of the fitter solutions is copied straight into the next generation, where n varies between 1 and 10. The crossover operator chooses a node at random in the first chromosome, called crossover point 1 and the branch to that node is cut. Then it chooses a node at random in the second chromosome, called crossover point 2, and the branch to that node is cut. The sub-trees produced below the cuts are then swapped. The method of performing crossover is illustrated in Figure 1 (a) and (b). Although this example includes a variety of operations, for simplicity in this application only the set {+, -,*} were made available. More complex operators can be developed by combining these simple operations. Simple operators eliminate the bounding problems associated with more complex operations such as XOR, which is not defined for negative or non- integer values.

Figure 1. (a) Illustration of crossover operator before operation. The double lines indicate where the trees are cut, (b) Illustration of crossover operator after operation. The double line indicates where the sub-trees are swapped.

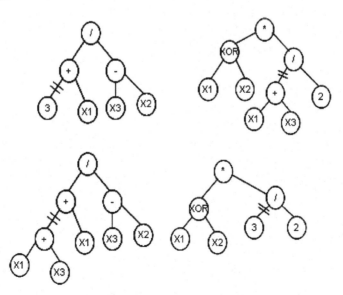

On average, 10% operands used were random constants in the range 0 – 10.

Illustration of the crossover operator

Parents before crossover:

$$(a)\frac{3+X_1}{X_3-X_2} \quad (b)\frac{(X_1XORX_2)*(X_1+3)}{2}$$

New children produced by cross over operation:-

$$(a)\frac{(X_1+3)+X_1}{X_3-X_2} \quad (b)\frac{(X_1XORX_2)*3}{2}$$

Thus two new individual are created, whose fitness is evaluated.

The important concept of GP is the fitness function, which determines how well a program is able to solve the problem. It varies greatly from one type of program to the next. Mutation is another important feature of genetic programming. The most commonly used form of mutation in GP (which we will call sub-tree mutation) randomly selects a mutation point in a tree and substitutes the sub-tree rooted there with a randomly generated sub-tree. This is illustrated in Figure 2.

Sub-tree mutation is sometimes implemented as crossover between a program and a newly generated random program. This operation is also known as "headless chicken" crossover (Angeline & Pollock, 1992). Another common form of mutation is point mutation, which is GP's equivalent of the bit-flip mutation used in GA (Goldberg, 1989). In point mutation, a random node is selected and the primitive stored there is replaced with a different random primitive of the same arity taken from the primitive set. If no other primitives with that arity exist, nothing happens to that node (but other nodes may still be mutated). The choice of which of the operators described above should be used to create an offspring is probabilistic. Operators in GP are normally mutually exclusive (unlike other evolutionary algorithms where offspring are sometimes obtained via a composition of operators). Their probabilities of application are called operator rates. Typically, crossover is applied with the highest probability, the crossover rate being 90% or higher. On the contrary, the mutation rate is much smaller, typically around 1%. When the rates of crossover and mutation add up to a value p which is less than 100%, an operator called reproduction is also used, with a rate of 1 – p. Reproduction involves the selection of an individual based on fitness and the insertion of a copy of it in the next generation is replaced with a different random primitive of the same type.

The major considerations in applying GP to pattern classification are (Poli, 2008): (i) GP-based techniques are data distribution-free, so no *a priori* knowledge is needed about statistical distribution of the data (ii) GP can directly operate on the data in its original form (iii) GP can detect the underlying, unknown relationship that exists among data (iv) GP can discover the most important discriminating features during the training phase (v) The generated expression can be easily used in the application environment.

Figure 2. Example of mutation

Parents   Offspring

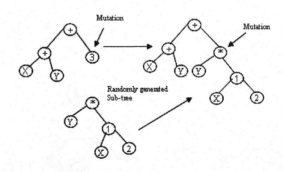

Parents Offspring

EXPERIMENTAL DESIGN

In our experiment, we followed general time series forecasting model because software reliability forecasting problem has only one dependent variable and no explanatory variables in their strict sense. The general time series can be presented as

$$X_t = f(X') \ldots\ldots \quad (6)$$

where X' is vector of lagged variables $\{x_{t-1}, x_{t-2} \ldots x_{t-p}\}$. Hence the key to finding the solution to the forecasting problems is to approximate the function 'f'. This can be done by iteratively adjusting the weights in the modeling process in the case of neural network solutions. Figure 3 depicts how training patterns can be rearranged so that they can be used to train a neural network (Xu et al., 2003). The data is rearranged in order to investigate if any autocorrelation exists in the data and the same rearrangement can be used to train other machine learning methods used in this paper.

In Figure 3, p denotes the number of lagged variables and *(t-p)* denotes the total number of training samples. In this representation, X is a set of *(t-p)* vectors of dimension p and Y is a vector of dimension *(t-p)*. X and Y represent the vector of explanatory variables and dependent variable in the transformed datasets respectively.

In this paper, the software failure data obtained from Musa (1979b) and Iyer and Lee (1996). It is used to demonstrate the forecasting performance of different types of machine learning and statistical techniques. Musa (1997a) contains 101 observations, Musa (1979b) dataset contains 163 observations and Iyer and Lee (1996) dataset contains 191 observations of the pair *(t, Y)* pertaining to software failure (see Table 1, Table 2, and Table 3). Here Y_t represents the time to failure of the software after the tth modification has been made. We created five datasets viz. lag # 1,2,3,4 and 5 in view of the foregoing discussion on generating lagged data sets out of a time series. The experiments are performed by dividing the data

Figure 3. Design of creating new dataset by rearranging the given dataset

	X			Y
x_1	x_2	....	x_p	x_{p+1}
x_2	x_3	....	x_{p+1}	x_{p+2}
x_3	x_4	....	x_{p+2}	x_{p+3}
.	.	....	.	.
.	.	...	.	.
.	.	...	.	.
x_{t-p}	x_{t-p+1}	....	x_{t-1}	x_t

into training and test set in the ratio of 80:20. The value of Normalized Root Mean Square Error (NRMSE) is used as the measurement criteria.

$$NRMSE = \sqrt{\frac{\sum_{i=1}^{n}(d_i - \hat{d}_i)^2}{\sum_{i=1}^{n} d_i^2}} \quad (7)$$

where n is the number of forecasting observations; d_i is the actual value at period i; and d_i is the forecast value of software reliability at period i.

RESULTS AND DISCUSSIONS

We conducted experiments with the above mentioned machine learning techniques on the software reliability datasets taken from Musa (1979a, 1979b) and Iyer and Lee (1996), which are presented in Tables 1-3. For each technique, the appropriate parameters specified by the algorithm are tweaked to get the least NRMSE values computed using Equation (7). Table 4, Table 5, and Table 6 respectively present the NRMSE values in the case of Musa (1979a, 1979b) and Iyer and

Table 1. Musa (1979a) dataset

t	Y_t	t	Y_t	t	Y_t	t	Y_t
0	5.7683	26	8.5941	52	10.0998	78	14.7824
1	9.5743	27	11.0399	53	12.6078	79	14.8969
2	9.105	28	10.1196	54	7.1546	80	12.1399
3	7.9655	29	10.1786	55	10.0033	81	9.7981
4	8.6482	30	5.8944	56	9.8601	82	12.0907
5	9.9887	31	9.546	57	7.8675	83	13.0977
6	10.1962	32	9.6197	58	10.5757	84	13.368
7	11.6399	33	10.3852	59	10.9294	85	12.7206
8	11.6275	34	10.6301	60	10.6604	86	14.192
9	6.4922	35	8.3333	61	12.4972	87	11.3704
10	7.901	36	11.315	62	11.3745	88	12.2021
11	10.2679	37	9.4871	63	11.9158	89	12.2793
12	7.6839	38	8.1391	64	9.575	90	11.3667
13	8.8905	39	8.6713	65	10.4504	91	11.3923
14	9.2933	40	6.4615	66	10.5866	92	14.4113
15	8.3499	41	6.4615	67	12.7201	93	8.3333
16	9.0431	42	7.6955	68	12.5982	94	8.0709
17	9.6027	43	4.7005	69	12.0859	95	12.2021
18	9.3736	44	10.0024	70	12.2766	96	12.7831
19	8.5869	45	11.0129	71	11.9602	97	13.1585
20	8.7877	46	10.8621	72	12.0246	98	12.753
21	8.7794	47	9.4372	73	9.2873	99	10.3533
22	8.0469	48	6.6644	74	12.495	100	12.4897
23	**10.8459**	**49**	**9.2294**	**75**	**14.5569**		
24	8.7416	50	8.9671	76	13.3279		
25	7.5443	51	10.3534	77	8.9464		

Lee (1996) for different lags of data obtained over different techniques.

In the case of Musa (1979a, 1979b) and Iyer and Lee (1996) datasets, GP provides the best NRMSE values, followed by GMDH. Further, we found that in the case of Musa (1979a) dataset the NRMSE values decrease with the increasing value of lag. However, in the case of Musa (1979b) and Iyer and Lee (1996) datasets, this trend is not observed. The best, average and worst results of GP over 30 runs for each lag on all datasets are presented in Table 7.

As regards the user-defined parameters, in GP, we took population size of (500, 1000, and 1500) and we run the experiment with different parameters viz. Mutation rate in the range of 0 to 0.95 in steps of 0.1; Crossover rate in the range of 0 to 0.95 in steps of 0.1; total number of runs: 0 to 100, and maximum depth of 100. The optimal parameter sets chosen for GP, which yielded the best results in the three datasets are presented in Table 8, Table 9, and Table 10.

From the experiments conducted on GP, we observed that to get best results, we needed to run the experiment for a period of at least one hour.

Table 2. Musa (1979b) dataset

t	Yt	t	Yt	t	Yt	t	yt
1	5.768321	42	6.461468	83	12.09066	124	12.34757
2	7.271704	43	6.461468	84	11.87757	125	12.46536
3	9.10498	44	7.965546	85	13.36797	126	12.12051
4	7.965546	45	4.70048	86	11.36674	127	8.188689
5	8.648221	46	10.00243	87	12.57072	128	11.87757
6	9.989665	47	11.01294	88	5.768321	129	9.574983
7	10.19616	48	10.86213	89	10.96128	130	11.36674
8	11.63991	49	9.437157	90	10.26813	131	11.60914
9	11.62748	50	6.664409	91	9.798127	132	10.26813
10	6.49224	51	11.52478	92	11.39234	133	10.6736
11	7.901007	52	8.967122	93	10.6736	134	10.96128
12	10.26789	53	10.35345	94	8.33327	135	10.75364
13	7.683864	54	10.09877	95	8.070906	136	13.76464
14	8.890548	55	12.60783	96	10.66429	137	12.90022
15	9.293302	56	7.154615	97	10.68281	138	13.69199
16	8.349957	57	10.00329	98	9.264829	139	12.51942
17	9.043577	58	9.860058	99	11.65443	140	12.97618
18	9.60272	59	7.867489	100	11.36674	141	13.66933
19	9.379577	60	10.57567	101	10.963	142	12.21899
20	8.586906	61	10.92942	102	10.26813	143	12.22293
21	8.787678	62	10.66036	103	12.97618	144	12.53422
22	8.779404	63	12.49725	104	12.75304	145	11.56172
23	8.04687	64	11.37451	105	11.65443	146	13.27092
24	10.84589	65	11.91576	106	10.70311	147	15.32711
25	9.741968	66	9.574983	107	9.259702	148	12.97618
26	7.544332	67	10.45045	108	12.08526	149	14.15995
27	8.594154	68	10.58658	109	12.39457	150	12.05989
28	11.03993	69	12.72008	110	11.8708	151	11.36674
29	10.11965	70	12.59817	111	12.51929	152	13.93169
30	10.17865	71	12.08613	112	12.15157	153	14.25711
31	5.894403	72	12.27663	113	12.05989	154	13.56397
32	9.546027	73	11.96017	114	9.980449	155	14.07479
33	9.619665	74	9.729134	115	11.07906	156	14.44252
34	10.3852	75	9.287301	116	12.61951	157	12.72368
35	10.63662	76	12.495	117	13.53074	158	13.73387
36	10.63662	77	10.44909	118	11.36674	159	13.85165
37	8.33327	78	8.946375	119	11.52089	160	14.36248
38	11.31496	79	10.53654	120	12.17767	161	13.56397
39	9.487138	80	9.3147	121	11.65443	162	10.96128
40	8.139149	81	12.13993	122	11.07906	163	9.757305
41	8.671287	82	9.798127	123	8.188689		

Table 3. Iyer and Lee (1996) dataset

t	Y_t	t	Y_t	t	Y_t	t	Y_t
1	9.989849	49	9.379239	97	13.69282	145	11.16321
2	8.757469	50	11.02339	98	13.70316	146	7.569928
3	10.21442	51	11.05414	99	13.76481	147	8.110427
4	11.7569	52	11.13708	100	13.76631	148	8.782476
5	12.15317	53	11.15538	101	13.77057	149	9.243872
6	8.165648	54	11.15622	102	13.78502	150	9.589051
7	9.410011	55	12.11349	103	13.79367	151	9.899128
8	9.582042	56	12.12096	104	14.51319	152	12.80252
9	8.789051	57	12.03785	105	14.51374	153	12.8067
10	11.48465	58	12.0414	106	14.5151	154	12.8082
11	10.01127	59	12.06069	107	14.51597	155	12.81368
12	6.982863	60	12.31419	108	14.5193	156	12.81829
13	7.063904	61	12.31715	109	14.84114	157	13.34396
14	6.486161	62	12.32046	110	14.92268	158	14.15527
15	6.632002	63	12.34527	111	14.92619	159	14.25293
16	6.192362	64	13.11372	112	14.92674	160	14.26656
17	5.971262	65	13.65588	113	14.92489	161	12.67102
18	4.828314	66	13.82387	114	6.257668	162	13.7524
19	9.899429	67	13.82502	115	12.17534	163	14.20219
20	12.87454	68	13.83676	116	12.98568	164	14.53763
21	6.652863	69	13.83803	117	12.99106	165	14.58584
22	7.929126	70	13.84461	118	13.74415	166	12.07316
23	8.195885	71	13.8747	119	13.74562	167	13.26607
24	8.764053	72	13.90696	120	13.94853	168	13.28284
25	9.268798	73	13.90982	121	13.94842	169	14.41135
26	9.544954	74	13.91387	122	5.135798	170	14.41653
27	9.897319	75	13.91617	123	5.278115	171	14.44412
28	9.970071	76	13.94068	124	8.705662	172	14.50544
29	10.09547	77	13.94258	125	12.42508	173	14.53652
30	10.13903	78	13.97001	126	13.14186	174	9.867809
31	12.47476	79	13.99294	127	13.65246	175	12.49195
32	12.78531	80	13.99611	128	13.65709	176	12.77024
33	12.82833	81	6.393591	129	13.92362	177	11.4086
34	13.81181	82	6.393591	130	14.49129	178	13.24415
35	8.54714	83	3.610918	131	7.46451	179	13.28787
36	8.672144	84	13.66246	132	11.07032	180	13.94611
37	8.672486	85	14.01192	133	12.97339	181	10.69716
38	8.677269	86	14.19584	134	13.02908	182	10.81555
39	8.640472	87	14.2961	135	14.10564	183	11.2806

continued on following page

Table 3. Continued

40	6.799056	88	14.2961	136	14.4552	184	11.84735
41	9.897067	89	14.29833	137	14.57073	185	12.65049
42	11.60008	90	14.29697	138	14.62154	186	12.68502
43	12.26156	91	5.680173	139	14.62173	187	13.18139
44	14.00518	92	7.678326	140	14.62746	188	13.18139
45	14.00704	93	8.014997	141	10.98658	189	13.18139
46	14.01054	94	8.044626	142	7.880804	190	13.18139
47	8.593228	95	8.395703	143	10.87654	191	13.1724
48	8.809415	96	8.691819	144	11.15618		

Table 4. NRMSE values on Test data for dataset (Musa, 1979a)

Techniques	Lag1	Lag2	Lag3	Lag4	Lag5
BPNN	0.171375	0.166086	0.1511429	0.144949	0.145541
MARS	0.170584	0.17091	0.161343	0.154821	0.15267
MLR	0.171448	0.167776	0.156537	0.151152	0.147881
TreeNet	0.168286	0.167865	0.168105	0.156998	0.161121
DENFIS	0.170907	0.167306	0.15425	0.148379	0.147641
CPNN	0.193323	0.185823	0.18323	0.164397	0.173707
GMDH	0.150875	0.152475	0.107226	0.103601	0.098616
GP	**0.105969**	**0.104682**	**0.099114**	**0.0.095674**	**0.089522**

Table 5. NRMSE values on Test data for dataset (Musa, 1979b)

Techniques	Lag1	Lag2	Lag3	Lag4	Lag5
BPNN	0.1041	0.106132	0.114087	0.109608	0.103557
MARS	0.226707	0.2271	0.224539	0.223312	0.222438
MLR	0.157898	0.140057	0.131448	0.127817	0.131533
TreeNet	0.141775	0.160957	0.163529	0.127548	0.164956
DENFIS	0.167327	0.136369	0.179573	0.160109	0.0.295278
CPNN	0.154288	0.108859	0.17994	0.118588	0.139657
GMDH	0.105225	0.113225	0.109538	0.10893	0.093866
GP	**0.082702**	**0.078978**	**0.086065**	**0.08653**	**0.089301**

But in GMDH, we need only three minutes to get the output. Thus, if time is the constraint to predict the software reliability, then we recommend GMDH rather than GP because GP is more time consuming than the GMDH. In this study, we employed CPNN, for the first time, to predict software reliability. Even though, it did not yield spectacular performance, it is not very bad either, by becoming the 5th or 6th best technique.

Future directions include building ensemble models using GP, GMDH and BPNN/TreeNet as the constituent members and GP as the arbitrator. Further, recurrent architectures are proposed to be built around the best techniques found out here.

Table 6. NRMSE values on Test data for dataset (Iyer & Lee, 1996)

Techniques	Lag1	Lag2	Lag3	Lag4	Lag5
BPNN	0.082288	0.083576	0.096399	0.092113	0.085457
MARS	0.157846	0.6772	0.093694	0.156401	0.157147
MLR	0.095836	0.094127	0.094791	0.095471	0.095106
TreeNet	0.083032	0.084868	0.085066	0.082558	0.081425
DENFIS	0.096238	0.093047	0.089964	0.107325	0.226197
CPNN	0.101627	0.107769	0.097465	0.107337	0.124073
GMDH	0.067046	0.078177	0.077253	0.07292	0.072352
GP	**0.019428**	**0.062886**	**0.023313**	**0.069001**	**0.069458**

Table 7. Best, Average and Worst results for GP

Lags	Musa(1979a)			Musa(1979a)			Iyer and Lee (1996)		
	Best	Average	Worst	Best	Average	Worst	Best	Average	Worst
Lag1	0.105969	0.126784	0.138567	0.082702	0.096398	0.105388	0.019428	0.076351	0.08512
Lag2	0.104682	0.127178	0.145616	0.078978	0.094543	0.099645	0.062886	0.083778	0.097474
Lag3	0.099114	0.1189307	0.132178	0.086065	0.095197	0.101366	0.023313	0.078123	0.099535
Lag4	0.095674	0.115252	0.13253	0.08653	0.095885	0.103023	0.069001	0.08088	0.087629
Lag5	0.089522	0.109657	0.137299	0.089301	0.094276	0.10057	0.069458	0.074761	0.091983

Table 8. Details of best NRMSE values, GP parameters for dataset (Musa, 1979a)

Parameters	Lag1	Lag2	Lag3	Lag4	Lag5
Population	500	1000	1000	1000	500
Mutation rate	0.10	0.60	0.95	0.95	0.95
Cross over rate	0.50	0.50	0.95	0.90	0.80
Total runs	68	61	93	75	87
Current step	6	6	8	6	7
NRMSE	0.105969	0.104682	0.099114	0.095674	0.089522

Table 9. Details of best NRMSE values, GP parameters for dataset (Musa, 1979b)

Parameters	Lag1	Lag2	Lag3	Lag4	Lag5
Population	500	1000	1000	1000	1000
Mutation rate	0.40	0.60	0.95	0.95	0.95
Cross over rate	0.95	0.95	0.90	0.50	0.50
Total runs	18	11	21	21	20
Current step	3	2	3	3	3
NRMSE	0.082702	0.078978	0.086065	0.08653	0.089301

Table 10. Details of best NRMSE values, GP parameters (Iyer & Lee, 1996)

Parameters	Lag1	Lag2	Lag3	Lag4	Lag5
Population	1000	500	500	500	500
Mutation rate	.95	.60	0.90	0.95	0.40
Cross over rate	0.7	0.95	0.95	0.70	0.95
Total runs	10	49	23	16	19
Current step	2	5	3	2	3
NRMSE	0.019428	0.062886	0.023313	0.069001	0.069458

CONCLUSION

In this paper, we employed various types of machine learning and statistical techniques viz., BPNN, GMDH, CPNN, DENFIS, TreeNet, MLR, MARS and GP to predict software reliability on three software failure dataset taken from literature. We observed that the performance of GP, in terms of NRMSE value, was superior to that of other techniques. Thus, we conclude after extensive experimentation, that GP holds a very good promise in the field of software reliability prediction.

ACKNOWLEDGMENT

We are very thankful to Mr. Frank Francone to give us permission us to use Discipulus Tool (Demo version) for conducting various experiments reported in this paper and also to B. Igor Kuzmanovski, Asst. Professor, Sts. Cyril and Methodius, University, Skopje, Republic of Macedonia for providing us with the MATLAB code for implementing CPNN.

REFERENCES

Aljahdali, S. H., & El-Telbany, M. E. (2009). Software reliability prediction using objective Genetic Algorithm. In *Proceedings of the ACS/ IEEE International Conference on Computer Systems and Applications* (pp. 293-300).

Angeline, P. J., & Pollack, J. B. (1992). The evolutionary induction of subroutines. In *Proceedings of the Fourteenth Annual Conference of the Cognitive Science Society* (pp. 236-241). Bloomington, IN: Lawrence Erlbaum. Retrieved from http://www.demo.cs.brandeis.edu/papers/glib92.pdf

Cai, K., Yuan, C., & Zhang, M. L. (1991). A critical review on software reliability modeling. *Reliability Engineering & System Safety, 32*, 357–371. doi:10.1016/0951-8320(91)90009-V

Cai, K. Y., Cai, L., Wang, W. D., Yu, Z. Y., & Zhang, D. (2001). On the neural network approach in software reliability modeling. *Journal of Systems and Software, 58*, 47–62. doi:10.1016/S0164-1212(01)00027-9

Discipulus tool. (n.d.). Retrieved from http://www.rmltech.com/

Dohi, T., Nishio, Y., & Osaki, S. (1999). Optional software release scheduling based on artificial neural networks. *Annals of Software Engineering, 8*, 167–185. doi:10.1023/A:1018962910992

Farlow, S. J. (1984). *Self-Organizing Methods in Modeling: GMDH type Algorithm.* New York: Bazel, Marcel Dekker Inc.

Friedman, J. H. (1991). Multivariate adaptive regression splines (with discussion). *Annals of Statistics, 19*, 1–141. doi:10.1214/aos/1176347963

Friedman, J. H. (1999). Stochastic gradient boosting. *Computational Statistics & Data Analysis, 38*(4), 367–378. doi:10.1016/S0167-9473(01)00065-2

Goldberg, D. E. (1989). *Genetic Algorithm in search, optimization and machining learning.* Reading, MA: Addison Wesley.

Hecht-Nielsen, R. (1987). Counterpropagation networks. *Applied Optics, 26,* 4979–4983. doi:10.1364/AO.26.004979

Ivakhnenko, A. G. (1968). The GMDH. A rival of stochastic approximation. *Sov. Autom. Control, 3,* 43.

Iyer, R. K., & Lee, I. (1996). Measurement-based analysis of software Reliability. In Lyu, M. R. (Ed.), *Handbook of Software Reliability Engineering* (pp. 303–358). New York: McGraw-Hill.

Karunanithi, N., Malaiya, Y. K., & Whitley, D. (1992a). The scaling problem in neural networks for software reliability prediction. In *Proceedings of the Third International IEEE Symposium of Software Reliability Engineering* (pp. 76-82). Washington, DC: IEEE.

Karunanithi, N., Whitley, D., & Malaiya, Y. K. (1991). Prediction of software reliability using neural networks. In *Proceedings of the International Symposium on Software Reliability* (pp. 124-130).

Karunanithi, N., Whitley, D., & Malaiya, Y. K. (1992b). Prediction of software reliability using connectionist models. *IEEE Transactions on Software Engineering, 18,* 563–574. doi:10.1109/32.148475

Kasabov, N. K., & Song, Q. (2002). DENFIS: dynamic evolving neural-fuzzy inference system and its application for time-series prediction. *IEEE Transactions on Fuzzy Systems, 10*(2). doi:10.1109/91.995117

Khoshgoftaar, T. M., Allen, E. B., Hudepohl, J. P., & Aud, S. J. (1997). Application of neural networks to software quality modeling of a very large telecommunications system. *IEEE Transactions on Neural Networks, 8*(4), 902–909. doi:10.1109/72.595888

Khoshgoftaar, T. M., Allen, E. B., Jones, W. D., & Hudepohl, J. P. (2000). Classification –Tree models of software quality over multiple releases. *IEEE Transactions on Reliability, 49*(1), 4–11. doi:10.1109/24.855532

Khoshgoftaar, T. M., Pandya, A. S., & More, H. B. (1992). A neural network approach for predicting software development faults. In *Proceedings of the third IEEE International Symposium on Software Reliability Engineering* (pp. 83-89). Washington, DC: IEEE.

Khoshgoftaar, T. M., & Szabo, R. M. (1994). Predicting software quality, during testing using neural network models: A comparative study. *International Journal of Reliability Quality and Safety Engineering, 1,* 303–319. doi:10.1142/S0218539394000222

Khoshgoftaar, T. M., & Szabo, R. M. (1996). Using neural networks to predict software faults during testing. *IEEE Transactions on Reliability, 45*(3), 456–462. doi:10.1109/24.537016

Koza, J. R. (1992). *Genetic Programming: On the Programming of Computers by Means of Natural Selection.* Cambridge, MA: The MIT Press.

Lyu, M. R. (1996). *Handbook of Software Reliability Engineering.* New York: McGraw-Hill.

Mohanty, R. K., Ravi, V., & Patra, M. R. (2009). Software Reliability Prediction Using Genetic Programming. In *Proceedings of the International Conferences on BICA, 2009,* 105–110.

Mohanty, R. K., Ravi, V., & Patra, M. R. (2010). *The Application of intelligent and soft-computing techniques to software engineering problems: A Review*. Int. J. Information and Decision Sciences.

Musa, J. D. (1979a). *Software reliability data*. IEEE Computer Society- Repository.

Musa, J. D. (1979b). *Software Reliability Data*. London: Bell Telephone Laboratories.

Musa, J. D. (1998). *Software Reliability Engineering*. New York: McGraw-Hill.

Pai, P. F., & Hong, W. C. (2006). Software reliability forecasting by support vector machine with simulated annealing algorithms. *Journal of Systems and Software, 79*(6), 747–755. doi:10.1016/j.jss.2005.02.025

Poli, R., Langdon, W. B., & Koza, J. R. (2008). *A field guide to Genetic Programming*. London: Lulu. ISBN: 978-1-4092-0073-4

Rajkiran, N., & Ravi, V. (2007a). Software Reliability prediction by soft computing technique. *Journal of Systems and Software, 81*(4), 576–583. doi:10.1016/j.jss.2007.05.005

Rajkiran, N., & Ravi, V. (2007b). Software Reliability prediction using wavelet Neural Networks. In *Proceedings of the International Conference on Computational Intelligence and Multimedia Application (ICCIMA, 2007)* (Vol. 1, pp. 195-197).

Ravi, V., Chauhan, N. J., & Rajkiran, N. (2009). Software reliability prediction using intelligent techniques: Application to operational risk prediction in Firms. *International Journal of Computational Intelligence and Applications, 8*(2), 181–194. doi:10.1142/S1469026809002588

Sherer, S. A. (1995). Software fault prediction. *Journal of Systems and Software, 29*(2), 97–105. doi:10.1016/0164-1212(94)00051-N

Sitte, R. (1999). Comparison of Software-Reliability-Growth Predictions: Neural Networks vs. Parametric-Recalibration. *IEEE Transactions on Reliability, 48*(3), 285–291. doi:10.1109/24.799900

Specht, D. F. (1991). A general regression neural network. *IEEE Transactions on Neural Networks, 2*(6), 568–576. doi:10.1109/72.97934

Su, Y. S., & Huang, C. Y. (2006). Neural-network-based approaches for software reliability estimation using dynamic weighted combinational models. *Journal of Systems and Software*. doi:. doi:10.1016/j.jss.2006.06.017

Tian, L., & Noore, A. (2005a). On-line prediction of software reliability using an evolutionary connectionist model. *Journal of Systems and Software, 77*, 173–180. doi:10.1016/j.jss.2004.08.023

Tian, L., & Noore, A. (2005b). Evolutionary neural network modeling for software cumulative failure time prediction. *Reliability Engineering & System Safety, 87*, 45–51. doi:10.1016/j.ress.2004.03.028

Xu, K., Xie, M., Tang, L. C., & Ho, S. L. (2003). Application of neural networks in forecasting engine systems reliability. *Applied Soft Computing, 2*, 255–268. doi:10.1016/S1568-4946(02)00059-5

Zupan, J., & Gasteiger, J. (1999). *Neural Networks in chemistry and Drug Design*. New York: Wiley Weinheim.

Zupan, J., Novie, M., Ruisanchez, M., & Chemomet, I. (1997)... *Intel Lab. Syst., 38*, 1. doi:10.1016/S0169-7439(97)00030-0

This work was previously published in International Journal of Applied Evolutionary Computation, Volume 1, Issue 3, edited by Wei-Chiang Samuelson Hong, pp. 70-86, copyright 2010 by IGI Publishing (an imprint of IGI Global).

Chapter 13
Buffer Management in Cellular IP Networks using Evolutionary Algorithms

Mohammad Anbar
Jawaharlal Nehru University, India

Deo Prakash Vidyarthi
Jawaharlal Nehru University, India

ABSTRACT

Real-time traffic in Cellular IP network is considered to be important and therefore given priority over non-real-time. Buffer is an important but scarce resource and to optimize Quality of Service by managing buffers of the network is an important and complex problem. Evolutionary Algorithms are quite useful in solving such complex optimization problems, and in this regard, a two-tier model for buffer, Gateway and Base Station, management in Cellular IP network has been proposed. The first tier applies a prioritization algorithm for prioritizing real-time packets in the buffer of the gateway with a specified threshold. Packets which couldn't be served, after the threshold, is given to the nearest cells of the network to be dealt with in the second tier, while Evolutionary Algorithm (EA) based procedures are applied in order to optimally store these packets in the buffer of the base stations. Experiments have been conducted to observe the performance of the proposed models and a comparative study of the models, GA based and PSO based, has been carried out to depict the advantage and disadvantage of the proposed models.

INTRODUCTION

Cellular IP protocol is a solution for mobility management at micro level. Being designed for micro level of mobility, Cellular IP supports frequently moving mobile hosts. It can also efficiently serve rarely moving or even stationary mobile hosts.

A Cellular IP network consists of interconnected nodes. These nodes accomplice the tasks to route IP packets inside the Cellular IP network and also communicate with the mobile hosts via wireless interface. Components of Cellular IP network are Cellular IP Base Station which controls and is responsible for the nodes in a cell, Cellular IP Gateway that connects Cellular IP network to Internet and stores the packets intended to be

DOI: 10.4018/978-1-4666-1749-0.ch013

sent through Internet in its buffer, and the Cellular IP Mobile Node which implements the Cellular IP protocol (Valkó, Gomez, Kim, & Campabell, 1999). Many operations such as routing, paging, and handoff etc. take place in Cellular IP network. Quality of Service (QoS) in Cellular IP network depends on number of factors and is insured according to the availability of the resources in the network. Buffer, an important resource should be managed and utilized in an effective manner to achieve better performance in the Cellular IP network.

In wireless communications packets are prone to be dropped, lost, or delayed which results in connection disturbance. Buffer space is a resource which is often in short supply and if handled properly may improve the performance of the network drastically. For the real-time and non real-time traffic there should be good schemes for buffer management that guarantee least packets drop/loss. Also the schemes for buffer management, especially in Cellular IP networks, must be as robust as possible that produce good results in terms of QoS.

In Cellular IP networks, when a packet is sent from a base station to the Gateway connecting the network with Internet, it will be queued for onward transmission to the corresponding node (network). If there is no available buffer space to put the packet in, the packet has to be discarded. To offer good quality of service, buffers can be reserved for real-time flow of packets so that this flow doesn't have to compete for buffers with other flows. In Cellular IP networks, due to data packet buffering at the air interface of the Gateway, the end-to-end bottleneck is a potential problem. Therefore buffer management is essential to support end-to-end QoS provision. Buffer reservation or buffer management must be done by giving the priority to real-time traffic over non real-time traffic and improve the QoS in the network. QoS can be achieved by increasing the Connection Completion Probability (CCP).

Evolutionary Algorithms (EAs) are often used to solve optimization problems that have no straightforward solutions. EAs maintain a population of structures (usually randomly generated initially) that evolves according to the rules of selection, cross-over, mutation etc. All individuals are evaluated against a fitness function. The fittest individuals are likely to be selected to generate new population in the next generation (Jain, Palade, & Srinivasan, 2007). Buffer management is an important issue to improve QoS in wireless networks especially in Cellular IP networks. With the increase in the number of flows this problem has become a complex one and involves a big search space. EAs can be applied successfully to solve this problem.

A two tier model is being proposed, in this work, for the buffer management. In the first tier, the real-time packets are prioritized and arranged in the front portion of the Gateway buffer. The packets are served from the front of the buffer till a specified threshold. Rest of the packets will be transferred back to the Cellular IP network rather than being dropped. In the second tier of the model, the returned packets are stored in the buffer of the network and for that an EA based procedure is applied in order to find a good solution. The model applies both GA and PSO based procedure in the second tier to observe the performance benefit of the buffer management with both the procedures. Eventually, the packets will be transferred to the Gateway buffer with higher priority. Most of the returned packets to the swarm (considered here as a group of cells) are normally (most probably) the non real-time packets. It is so because the real-time packets are given more priority for their service by putting them in the front of the buffer. Often the non real-time packets, considered less important, are further treated rather than discarding them straightforward. This is an important difference from few other similar models in which packets related to a non real-time application may be discarded that eventually may result in the application termination and disturbance in the service. Treatment of these packets will save the application though it may be delayed, thus make the system more reliable

The rest of the paper is organized presenting models that have been described, and both the EAs used in the model PSO and GA are explained. Next, insight of buffers in Cellular IP networks are given while elaborating on the proposed model. The results along with the comparative study will be mentioned, followed by observations and a conclusion.

PARTICLE SWARM OPTIMIZATION AND GENETIC ALGORITHM

As this work compares the performance of PSO and GA based method for the buffer management, both the methods (algorithms) have been briefed here.

Particle Swarm Optimization

Swarm intelligence is an intelligent paradigm to solve the hard problems. It is based on the behavior of the social insects such as bird flocks, fish school, ant colony etc. in which individual species change its position and velocity depending on its neighbor. This is done by mimicking the behavior of the creatures within their swarms or colonies. Particle Swarm Optimization (PSO) is an algorithm based on the swarm intelligence. The problem in hand (e.g., buffer management problem) is transformed to the function optimization problem. The swarm of individuals, called particles, is initialized with the random solutions. These particles move through many iterations to search a new and better solution for the problem. Each particle is represented by the two factors; one the position, where each particle has a specific position initialized by the initial position (x) and the other is the velocity (v), where each particle moves in the space according to a specific velocity. During the iteration time (t), the particles update

their position (x), and their velocity (v) (Nedjah & Mourelle, 2006; Seo, Im, Heo, Kim, Jung, & Lee, 2006).

In PSO algorithm there are two types of best values; one is Pbest which is the best position for each particle in the swarm and must be updated depending on the fitness value for each particle. The second best value is Gbest, which is the global best value for the swarm in general. This value must be checked in each iteration and be changed by Pbest if the Pbest for this iteration is better than Pbest for the last iteration.

The pseudo-code of the PSO algorithm is shown in Table 1.

In the pseudo code above,

- V_j^k is the velocity of particle j in iteration k
- *Pbest* is the best achieved solution for each individual so far
- *Gbest* is the global best value for the swarm
- X_j^k is the current position of particle j in iteration k
- w is inertia weight and is varied from 0.4 till 0.9
- r1, r2 are random numbers between 0 and 1
- c1, c2 are acceleration factors that determine the relative pull for each particle towards *Pbest* and *Gbest* and usually c1=c2=2
- Δt is the time step and usually 1

Genetic Algorithm

Genetic Algorithm is an automated search and optimization algorithm based on the mechanics of natural genetics and natural selection. Population in GA consists of number of individuals and each individual is considered as a solution to the given problem. The individual solution is also called chromosome that consists of many genes.

Some of the functions used in the GA are as follows.

Table 1. Pseudo-code of the PSO algorithm

```
PSO ()
{
    Initialize the swarm by giving initial and random values to each particle.
    For each particle do
    {Calculate the fitness function
    If the value of the fitness function for each particle at the current position is better than the fitness value at pbest then, set the current
value as the new Pbest.
    Choose the particle with the best fitness value of all the particles as the Gbest.
    Update the velocity of each particle as
```

$$V_j^{k+1} = w.V_j^k + c1.r1.(Pbest_j^k - X_j^k) + c2.r2.(Gbest^k - X_j^k)$$

Update the position of each particle as

$$X_j^{k+1} = X_j^k + V_j^k.\Delta t$$

```
}
    Until the solution converges
}
```

- *Selection:* Through selection operation, good produced offspring (solutions) are selected depending on their score obtained using fitness function for further operation.
- *Cross-over:* In this operation the parts of the two chromosomes are swapped to produce new offspring. Crossover can be either one site crossover or multiple sites crossover. Crossover operation is done according to a cross-over probability.
- *Mutation:* In mutation the parent chromosome is changed by mutating one or more gene for yielding a new offspring (Khanbary & Vidyarthi, 2008). Mutation operation is done according to the mutation probability which is often very low.

Table 2. Pseudo-code of the GA

```
GA ()
{
Create a random population of any size;
Evaluate the fitness function for each individual in the population;
For number of generations
{
Select parents for reproduction;
Perform crossover ();
Perform mutation ();
Evaluate population;
}
}
```

A pseudo-code of the GA is presented in Table 2.

PSO shares many common points with the GA. Both algorithms start with a group of randomly generated populations and both have fitness function to evaluate the population. Also, both update the population and search for the optimal solution with random techniques but in return both the algorithms don't guarantee to produce optimal values rather pacify with sub-optimal solution (Nedjah & Mourelle, 2006).

PSO doesn't have genetic operators like crossover and mutation. Particles update their position and velocity in every iteration. GA in this case might produce better chromosomes resulting after mutation. Particles in PSO might move towards the optimal solution faster than in GA. In GA the chromosomes share information with each other. In PSO only Gbest and Pbest give out the information to others. It is a one-way information sharing mechanism. The evolution only looks for the best solution. Compared to the GA all the particles tend to converge to the best solution quickly.

RELATED WORK

Quite a few works has been done for buffer management in Cellular IP network which have been listed in this section. (James, Hou, & Ho, 2007) proposed an application-driven MAC-layer buffer management framework. It is based on active dropping (AD) mechanism for real-time video streaming in IEEE 802.16 point-to- multipoint (PMP) networks. In this scheme the basic idea is that MAC-layer protocol data units (MPDUs) of video streams could be actively dropped at the Base Station (BS) if the corresponding frame is not with a sufficient confidence to be successfully delivered to the recipient within its application layer delay bound. (Lim & Qiu, 2001) proposed a predictive scheme for buffer management based on Fuzzy Logic in ATM networks referred as Fuzzy Logic Selective Cell Drop (FSCD). The basic idea of this scheme is its ability to accept or drop new incoming packets, dynamically, based on the predicted future buffer condition in the switch. Fuzzy Logic prediction has been used for the production of a drop factor based on which the packet dropping decision is taken.

A scheme for buffer management based on RED algorithm for Intelligent Gateway in wireless LAN has been presented by (Noh & Bae, 2007). This scheme is applicable in MAC layer of Gateway Gadget and depends on Random Early Discard (RED) algorithm. Simulation studies show the variation in the dropping rate with different number of thresholds.

Buffer management for real-time traffic over wireless networks based on Random Early Expiration Detection is studied by (Chen & Lemin, 2005). The basic idea behind this scheme is to predict whether new arrived packet can reach to the receiver under the limit of maximal delay bound. It randomly discards the packets based on an estimate result so as to prevent invalid transmission and at the meantime to minimize queue delay and to reduce expiration probability of the packets to be followed.

(Ryu & Koh, 1996) discussed dynamic buffer management technique for minimizing the necessary buffer space in continuous media server. It depends on window principle, where the service duration of clients is divided into several small time intervals called windows, and reallocates the buffer space in every window period. The effect of varying the window size on average necessary buffer size and average buffer utilization is studied and analyzed.

(Yousefi'zadeh & Jonckheere, 2005) introduced two dynamic buffer management techniques for queuing systems. These techniques depend on the adaptive learning power of perceptron of neural networks when applied to arriving traffic patterns. (Hou, Dapeng, Yao, & Takafumi, 2000) proposed a buffer management mechanism based on simple FIFO scheduling to support integrated transport of the PS service under the DiffServ model. Main property of this buffer management is to perform selective packet discarding from an embedded queue at a shared buffer. Buffer management to provide lossless service for guaranteed performance flows in network processors is proposed by Pan and Yang (2006). The authors in this work investigate the buffer size requirement and buffer allocation strategy.

Jardosh, Zunnun, Ranjan, and Srivastava (2008) propose an efficient buffer management scheme in wireless sensor networks based on random linear network coding. In this scheme, buffer requirement is distributed among the nodes on the path from the source to destination. In case of packet loss, the proposed scheme recovers packet from available information distributed on the path from source to destination. Markaki and Venieris (2000) presented a novel buffer management scheme called CBQ priority buffer management (CPBM) for IP routers using the class based queuing (CBQ) scheduler. This scheme deals with the various QoS requirements of the IP layer service classes to utilize the buffer space as efficiently as possible and to successfully coordinate with the

CBQ scheduling mechanism in order to improve packet loss performance.

Krifa, Baraka, and Spyropoulos (2008) have proposed an optimal buffer management policy based on global knowledge about the delay tolerant network. This policy can be turned either to minimize the average delivery delay or to maximize the average delivery rate. A new buffer management algorithm called BADT (Buffer Allocation with Dynamic Threshold) algorithm which uses dynamic threshold technique for the fairness index improvement is proposed by Krachodnok and Bemjapolakul (2001). How buffer management could be incorporated into HSDPA QoS framework for multimedia traffic QoS control is discussed by Yerima and Al-Begain (2007). Authors proposed a time space-priority (TSP) scheme which can be used for QoS control of heterogeneous multimedia service in the Node data buffer.

BUFFER IN CELLULAR IP NETWORKS

As mentioned before, there are three main components in Cellular IP networks. Based on these components, there are three kinds of buffers; Mobile Node buffer, Base Station buffer and Gateway buffer. Mobile Node buffer is the one in which the packets are arranged to be sent to the Base Station of the cell in which the Mobile Node is currently lying. Each Base Station of the network has its own buffer which is considered as a part of the total buffer of the swarm (group of cells) to which this Base Station belongs. Third kind of the buffer is the Gateway buffer connecting Cellular IP network to Internet and through which the packets are forwarded from Cellular IP network to the correspondent nodes in another network. Gateway buffer is important in Cellular IP network as all the packets will be stored here before further transmission through Internet. Buffer management is possible at two places; the Base Station's buffer and Gateway's buffer.

Base Station's buffer is managed by grouping the cells and applying evolutionary algorithm in order that the group of cells will be able to avail buffer space for storing the incoming packets. Gateway buffer can be managed by applying prioritization algorithm on the stored packets of this buffer. The priority algorithm assigns higher priority to the real-time packets.

Buffer, as mentioned before, is an important element in Cellular IP networks. Buffer in Cellular IP networks can be used to handle the handoff operation which is an important operation as Cellular IP protocol is a protocol for handling micro mobility and the mobile hosts are more likely to handoff from cell to another. Header Compression Context Transfer is an important operation; it is done depending on the buffer in Cellular IP networks. When a mobile host moves from one cell to another, no need to transfer the whole header but the header can be reconstructed again at the receiver. The buffer plays an important role in this issue where the established context during the header compression operation is stored in the old base station and later it is transferred to the buffer of the new base station before the mobile host handoffs to this base station (Anbar & Vidyarthi, 2008). Buffer, in Cellular IP, can play an important role in handling routing after handoff (Abduljalil & Bodhe, 2007). When Mobile host crosses cell boundary and receives an agent advertisement message; it sends a registration request to the new base station. The new base station then sends the path setup message to the old base station. The old base station forwards the buffer content to the new base station in multiple or single stream according to the scheme used.

As in Cellular IP networks both types of traffic (real-time and non real-time) exist, providing good QoS in these networks is determined by serving real-time users without any delay or packet drop. Though, non real-time users should also not be neglected. Base station buffer and Gateway buffer management should be the main concern in Cellular IP network. Real-time and non real-time packets can be served together in Cellular IP networks but with higher priority to the real-time packets. Therefore, the problem in buffer management is to prioritize the real-time packets without dropping non real-time packets. Out of the mentioned buffer, the model deals with the Gateway buffer and the base station buffer.

The model using Particle Swarm Optimization (PSO) Algorithm selects the seven cells as the swarm. Size of the Swarm usually depends on the problem being addressed. In Anbar and Vidyarthi (2009) a bandwidth management model using PSO with the swarm size seven is addressed. Selection of the swarm size is decided depending on the nature of the bandwidth problem. In many other researches such as Pant, Thangaraj, and Abraham (2007), swarm size was decided differently. The size of the swarm may be bigger or less and may affect the performance. We have selected seven cells as the shapes of the cells in network facilitate so and the way these cells communicate with each other. Every cell in the network is surrounded by six cells; therefore the group is taken as seven cells (Figure 1).

THE PROPOSED MODEL

The proposed model considers a Cellular IP network connecting to Internet through Gateway. Seven cells in Cellular IP networks are grouped together as shown in Figure. 1.

Packets are dispatched from Mobile Nodes in the network to the Base Stations and later on forwarded to the Gateway to be sent through Internet to the correspondent nodes. For two types of traffic, the model considers two types of packets; real-time packets and non real-time packets. The cell of the network is represented by the buffer of its Base Station. All the connecting links, i.e., Base Station to Base Station link, Base Station to Gateway link and Internet to Gateway link is wireless with capacity of 625 packets/sec. This

is in conformity with the similar models (Valkó, Gomez, Kim, & Campabell, 1999).

Buffer management is an optimization problem. It is an NP class of problems that implies big search space. Solving such type of problems can be done using evolutionary algorithms such as PSO and GA. One of the reasons of the success of EAs is their population based strategy which prevents them from getting trapped in a local optimal solution and consequently increases their probability of finding a global optimal solution. That was the motivation to use PSO and GA as soft computing tools to solve the problem of buffer management.

The model has been developed in two tiers described in Table 2.

Tier One (Prioritization of real-time packets in Gateway buffer)

This part considers the packets reaching to the Gateway buffer where these are stored and eventually served. The model depicts the real-time packets as (1) and the non real-time packets as (0). The Gateway buffer is shown in Figure. 2.

As packets (real-time and non real-time) arrive randomly to the buffer they are kept randomly as shown in Figure 3.

A prioritization algorithm is applied to search the real-time packets in the buffer. These real-time packets are arranged in the front positions of the

Figure 1. The system model

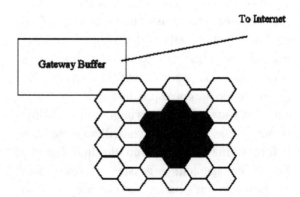

buffer followed by the non real time packets as shown in Figure 4.

After this, packet departure from the buffer takes place until a specific threshold is met. The packets after this threshold will not depart as shown in Figure. 5.

The mentioned packets in the model are TCP packets having an important field referred as TOS field. Through this field, the model can check what type of packet it is.

Buffer threshold setting is done in two ways (Markaki & Venieris, 2000). One is the static threshold (ST), in which buffer threshold is preset by the Network Management System (NMS). Number of departed packets from the front positions of the buffer depends on the threshold value. The other one is dynamic threshold (DT), in which buffer threshold is dynamically adjusted depending on the varying traffic load. For the proposed model, the buffer threshold selection is static where the threshold is chosen at the beginning of each experiment and fixed until the end of the experiment. The ST method is easy to implement.

Also the threshold point is randomly generated for the experiments. The packets that haven't been served from the buffer won't be dropped as doing so will cause connection termination. These packets will be returned back to the Cellular IP network for further services.

Tier Two (Storage Management)

In tier two, packets that have been returned to the network will reach to the nearest group of cells that consists of seven cells in the Cellular IP network. A PSO/GA based procedure is applied here to store these packets in the buffer space of the base stations. Eventually these packets will be returned to the gateway.

Assumptions

Assumptions used in the model are as follows.

* The cells are of hexagonal shape as shown in Figure 6.

Figure 2. Gateway buffer as considered in the model

Figure 3. Mixed packet arrangement in the buffer

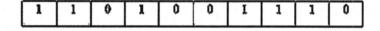

Figure 4. Arrangement of packets after prioritization

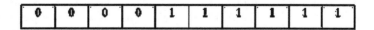

Figure 5. Serving packets till the specified threshold TH

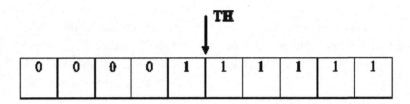

- Capacity of the buffer space for Base Station of the cell is measured in terms of packets.
- Packets returned from the buffer of the Gateway are of varying sizes.
- The buffer of each Base Station is depicted in two parts, one of them is the packets already stored in the buffer, and the other is the available buffer space.

Applying GA

For managing the buffer amongst the packets, Genetic Algorithm has been applied. Various functions used in the GA based model are as follows.

Encoding Used

The encoding of the chromosomes is as follows.

- A chromosome is an array of length 14 representing two types of information of 7 adjacent cells as it is evident from Figure 6 and Figure 7.
- Data representation in the chromosome is real and each gene represents the following.
  - Gene (0) is number of packets already stored in cell number 1.
  - Gene (1) is available buffer space in cell number 1 in terms of number of packets.
  - Gene (2) is number of packets already stored in cell number 2.
  - Gene (3) is available buffer space in cell number 2 in terms of number of packets.
  - Gene (4) is number of packets already stored in cell number 3.
  - Gene (5) is available buffer space in cell number 3 in terms of number of packets.
  - Gene (6) is number of packets already stored in cell number 4.
  - Gene (7) is available buffer space in cell number 4 in terms of number of packets.
  - Gene (8) is number of packets already stored in cell number 5.
  - Gene (9) is available buffer space in cell number 5 in terms of number of packets.
  - Gene (10) is number of packets already stored in cell number 6.
  - Gene (11) is available buffer space in cell number 6 in terms of number of packets.
  - Gene (12) is Number of packets already stored in cell number 7.
  - Gene (13) is available buffer space in cell number 7 in terms of number of packets.

Modules Used

Crossover: the crossover operation occurs between two chromosomes and generates two offspring from them. Crossover used in this algorithm is a single point crossover with probability one.

Figure 6. Group of seven cells where returned packets will be stored

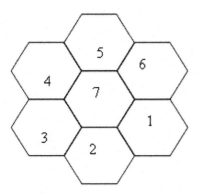

Mutation: this operation is used to generate new offspring by mutating one or more genes of the parents' chromosomes. It is done to overcome the local optimum. Mutation operation is used once in every 4 generations.

Fitness function: this function is used to measure the fitness values of the population. The chromosome with the good fitness value is selected for further crossover and mutation. Fitness function used in this model is the number of dropped packets and it is calculated as follows:

$$
\begin{aligned}
&\textit{Number of dropped packets} = \\
&\textit{Total number of packets} - \\
&\textit{Number of packets stored in} \\
&\textit{all seven cells}
\end{aligned} \tag{1}
$$

Selecting the fitness function is an important issue and depends on the problem. The fitness function chosen here was the number of dropped packets on which the performance of the model is

tested. Other fitness function may also be chosen but we have emphasized on this one only.

Algorithm

The Pseudo-Code for the GA based model is presented in Table 3.

Packets (real-time and non real-time) are randomly generated in the given range and sent through the Base Stations to the Gateway to be sent through Internet to the correspondent nodes. Buffer threshold is set using the ST method. Prioritization algorithm is applied and the packets in the front positions of the buffer are served. Remaining packets are sent back from the Gateway to the nearest group in the network consisting of seven cells. A solution for storing the returned packets and reducing the number of dropped packets as much as possible is designed based on the GA. The maximum available buffer space is also generated randomly in the specified range. After generating the first population, the chromosomes are evaluated against the fitness function, i.e., the number of dropped packets. Good chromosomes are selected based on the fitness value for further crossover and mutation. Crossover is performed with probability 1. To avoid the local minima, mutation is performed on the new generated chromosomes and the total new offspring is evaluated against the same fitness function to check the ability of the new offspring for survival. Selection operation is performed on the generated offspring and the procedure is repeated for 100 generations. Average value of the dropped packets is calculated and the minimum values in each generation are also stored. Experiment is repeated with different maximum available buffer

Figure 7. Chromosome structure used in the proposed model

0	1	2	3	4	5	6	7	8	9	10	11	12	13

Table 3. Algorithm 1: pseudo-code for the GA based model

```
Input (N); // number of returned packets
Input (pop_size); // population size
Input (max_avil); // maximum available buffer space

// Initialization of the population
For (int i=0; i<=pop_size; i++)
For (int j=0; j<=chrom_size-1; j++)
Oldpop[i].chrom[j] = rand () %max_avial+1; // gene has value between 0 and max_avil

Fitness_cump (Oldpop[i]); // evaluation of the generated population

Output (Oldpop[i].fitness);

Input (gene_no) // number of generations

For (i=0; i<=gene_no-1; i++) // repeating the procedure for number of generations
{
For (i=0; i<=pop_size-1; i++)
Sort (Oldpop[i]); //sorting the individuals according to the fitness values
For (i=0; i<=pop_size-1; i=i+2)
Crossover (Oldpop[i], i, i+1); // perform crossover module;

Mutation (Oldpop[i], site); // perform mutation with percentage 0.4%

//Storing the new generation
Temp=Newpop;
Newpop=Oldpop;
Oldpop=Temp;

Fitness_cump (Newpop[i]); // evaluation of the new generated population

Output (Newpop[i]. fitness); // output the fitness values for the new generation

}
```

space. After that the threshold will be set at the Gateway buffer in order to consider new number of returned packets.

Applying PSO

PSO has been applied for the same purpose. Various modules used in the PSO based model are as follows.

Encoding Used

- The buffer of each individual (cell) has two parts as shown in Figure 8.
- Part 1 represents the available buffer space in each cell in terms of number of packets.

This has been used as the position of the individual in the swarm.
- Part 2 represents the number of packets already stored in this buffer and has been used as the velocity of the individual in the swarm.

Modules Used

- *Initialize_swarm:* This module is used for initializing the positions and velocities of the individual in the swarm consisting of seven individuals.
- *Update_velocity:* Updating the velocities (number of packets already stored) of the individuals in the swarm is done in this module (Anbar & Vidyarthi, 2009)

Figure 8. Buffer structure used in PSO

Available Space	Used Space

- *Update_position:* A module used for updating positions (available buffer space) of the individuals in the swarm (Anbar & Vidyarthi, 2009)
- *Fitness functions:* used for evaluating the solutions and is the same as in the GA based model.

Algorithm

The Pseudo-Code for the model using the PSO is presented in Table 4.

The proposed model considers that the complete procedure starting from sending the packets from the Mobile Host to the Gateway and returning back the packets to the swarm (in PSO) or to the group of cells (in GA) is done at a specific point of time (t). The proposed model explains the problem of real-time dropping and avoiding this problem at a specific time. Naturally as a part of communication system, finding a solution for real-time packet drop involves an overhead in the form of the time taken to solve this problem. We did not mention it exclusively as PSO and GA are standard algorithms and the emphasis is to avoid the packet drop only.

EXPERIMENTS

In this section, the performance of the proposed model is evaluated. The experiment has been performed up to 100 generations for the GA based model and up to 100 iterations for the PSO-based model with the given input parameters.

Most of the data for experimental purposes has been taken from many references as specified below.

- **Gateway buffer capacity**: it can be: 8, 16, 28, 64, 128, 256, 512 (Shimonishi, Sanadidi, & Gerla, 2005).
- **Threshold value**: Noh and Bae (2007) specified the values of the threshold as follows: 30, 50, 70, 100, 128 packets. According to the threshold and to the Gateway buffer capacity, the number of returned packets can be estimated.
- **Gateway-Base Station link capacity (data rate)**: according to Abduljalil and Bodhe (2007) data rate can be considered as: 250 Kbps, 550 kbps, or 1Mbps. Taking data rates into account allows us to estimate the number of packets for transmission (returned) from the Gateway to the Base Station during a given period of time. The link and data rate are not considered in our work, instead of that the number of returned packets from the Gateway to the network is considered.
- **Packet Size**: Taking into account the TCP protocol, packet size considered is 1000 bytes. Packet size is important with data rate to decide the number of returned packets from the Gateway.

Experiment of GA Based Model

Experiment has been conducted with varying number of returned packets from the gateway buffer. The inputs for all the experiment is as follows. Maximum available buffer spaces: 5,

Table 4. Algorithm 2: pseudo-code for the model using the PSO

```
Input (N); // number of returned packets
Input (max_avil); // maximum available buffer space

// Initialization of the swarm, swarm size is 7
For (int i=0; i<=6; i++)
Initialize_swarm (Individual[i]);


For (i=0; i<=6;i++)
Fitness_cump (Individual[i]); // evaluation of the initialized individuals

// set the best position (number of stored packets) to the current position of each individual and the best global position to the current
position


For (i=0; i<=6; i++) {
Individual[i].Pbest = Individual[i].P;
Gbest=Individual[i].P;
}

For ( i=0; i<=iter_no-1; i++)
{
For (i=0; i<=6; i++)
Update_velocity (individual[i]); // velocity represents the available buffer space
```

$$// \ V_j^{k+1} = w.V_j^k + c1.r1.(Pbest_j^k - X_j^k) + c2.r2.(Gbest^k - X_j^k);$$

```
For (i=0; i<=6; i++)
Update_position (individual[i]); // position represents used buffer space
```

$$// \ X_i^{k+1} = X_j^k + V_j^k.\Delta t$$

```
For (i=0; i<=6; i++) // evaluation of the initialized individuals
Fitness_cump (Individual[i]);

// Update Pbest for each individual
For (i=0; i<=6; i++)
```
If (Individual[i].fitness ($Xbest^{k+1}$)) < Individual[i].fitness (X^k))

Individual[i] $Xbest^{k+1}$ =Individual[i] X^k ;

```
// Update Gbest for the swarm
For (i=0; i<=6; i++)
```
If ($Gbest^{k+1}$ < Individual[i].fitness ($Xbest^k$))

$Gbest^{k+1}$ = Individual[i]. $Xbest^k$;

```
// Compute number of dropped packets
NDP=N-Gbest;

// output the results
Output (NDP)
}
```

10, 15, 20 packets, number of generations for the experiment is 100.

Figure 9, Figure 10, Figure 11 and Figure 12 depict the graph when the number of returned packets is 100, 400, 600 and 900 respectively. Also an experiment in Figure13 depicts the best values for maximum available buffer spaces that make number of dropped packets zero. In this experiment number of returned packets varies from 50 to 1000.

Experiment Based on PSO

Again, experiment has been conducted with varying number of returned packets from the gateway buffer. The input for all the experiment is same as in GA based model.

Figures 14, Figure 15, Figure 16, and Figure 17 show the graph when the number of returned packets is 100, 400, 600 and 900 respectively. Also the experiment in Figure 18 depicts the best values for maximum available buffer spaces that make number of dropped packets zero. In this experiment number of returned packets varies from 50 to 1000.

Comparative Study

A comparative study has been conducted between the GA based model and PSO based model with 100 returned packets. Maximum available buffer space is again 5, 10, 15, 20 packets. Figure 19, Figure 20, Figure 21, and Figure 22 depict the graph for the comparative study. Comparison is also done between both the models for best maximum available buffer space that makes number of dropped packets close to zero in Figure 23.

Available Buffer Space Is 5 Packets

Figure 19 shows the number of dropped packets in PSO based model and GA based model when storing 100 returned packets from the Gateway to the network. Maximum available buffer space is 5

packets. X-axis represents the generation number for both the models. Y-axis represents the number of drooped packets out of 100 returned packets.

Available Buffer Space Is 10 Packets

In this experiment maximum available buffer space is 10 packets; number of returned packets from the Gateway buffer is 100. Figure 20 represent the performance.

Available Buffer Space Is 15 Packets

As the available buffer space is unknown, therefore the model must examine the performance of GA based model and PSO based model for different available buffer spaces. Available buffer space considered here is 15 packets. Number of returned packets is 100.

Available Buffer Space Is 20 Packets

Same number of returned packets is the input again for 20 packets available buffer space in each buffer of the base station. GA based model and PSO based model both try to store as many packets as possible from these returned packets. Performance of GA based model and PSO based model is shown in Figure 22.

Best Available Buffer Space to Store All the Returned Packets

It is clear from all the previously conducted experiments that there is packet loss. Therefore one might think why to waste the time of the network and return these packets back to store them in the network as some of them (sometimes a quite big number) are dropped? We evaluated this by conducting the experiments in which GA based model and PSO based model both decide the best maximum buffer spaces to be available and in turn they make the number of dropped packets to zero. This is clear from figure 23.

Figure 9. Storing 100 returned packets using GA

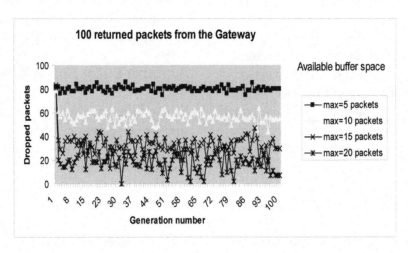

Figure 10. Storing 400 returned packets using GA

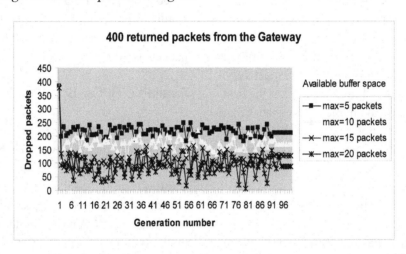

Figure 11. Storing 600 returned packets using GA

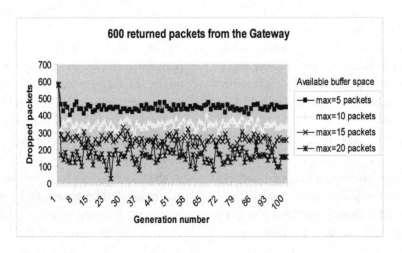

Figure 12. Storing 900 returned packets using GA

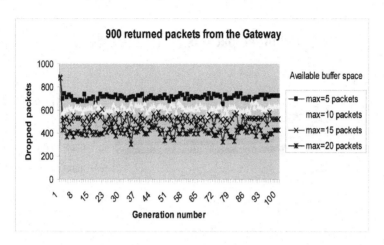

Figure 13. Best maximum buffer space required to store all returned packets using GA

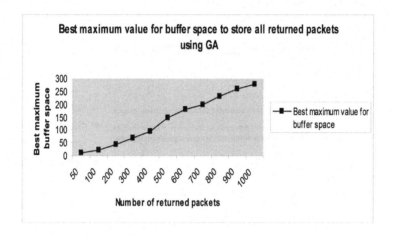

Figure 14. Storing 100 returned packets using PSO

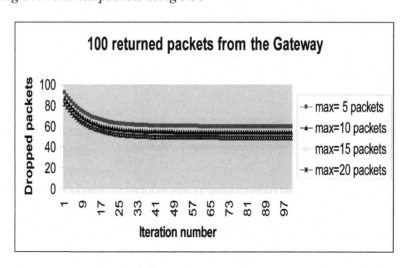

Figure 15. Storing 400 returned packets using PSO

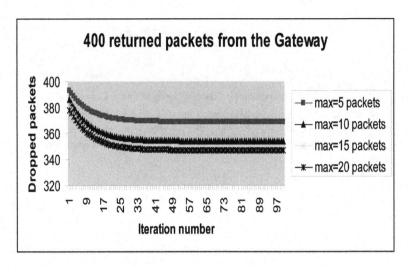

Figure 16. Storing 600 returned packets using PSO

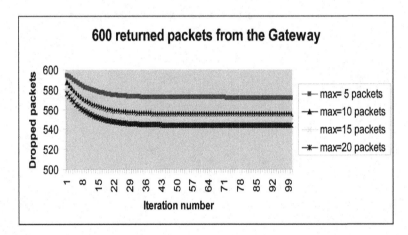

Figure 17. Storing 900 returned packets using PSO

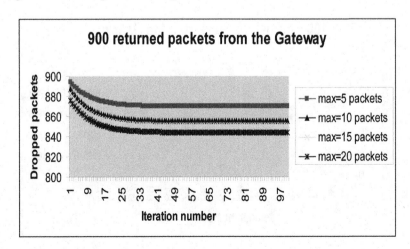

Figure 18. Best maximum buffer space required to store all returned packets using PSO

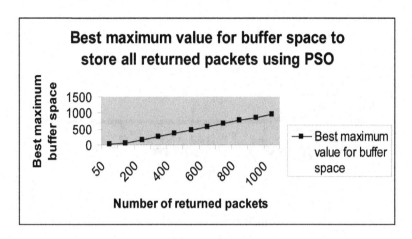

Figure 19. GA, PSO performances for maximum available buffer space 5 packets

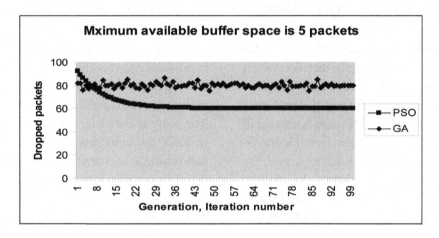

Figure 20. GA, PSO performances for maximum available buffer space 10 packets

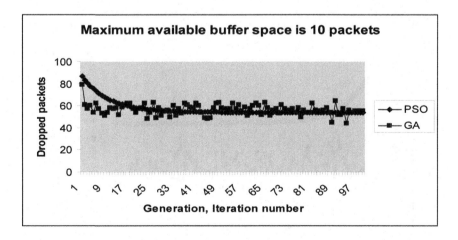

Figure 21. GA, PSO performances for maximum available buffer space 15 packets

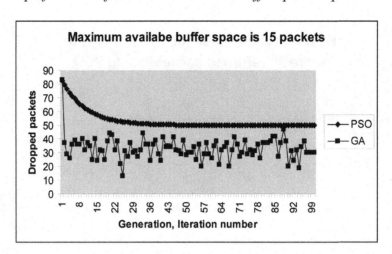

OBSERVATIONS AND CONCLUSION

Starting with 100 returned packets from the gateway to the swarm of seven cells, the observation is that PSO based model is performing better than GA based when the number of returned packets is small and the available buffer space is also small (maximum 5 packets) as evident from Figure 19.

When available buffer space is increased, the GA based model performs better. As obvious from Figure 20, both PSO and GA based models perform well (in terms of number of dropped packets) when maximum available buffer space is increased to 10.

As mutation and crossover operation in GA help in producing better offspring, it has been observed that the number of dropped packets decreases as the maximum available buffer space is increased. The same is not observed in PSO based model. In PSO, the individuals change their velocities and positions in search of optimal solution but this does not give better solutions in comparison to GA based model. It is evident from Figure 21 and Figure 22.

Figure 22. GA, PSO performances for maximum available buffer space 20 packets

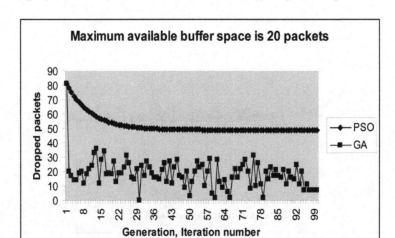

Figure 23. Maximum buffer space required to store all returned packets using GA and PSO

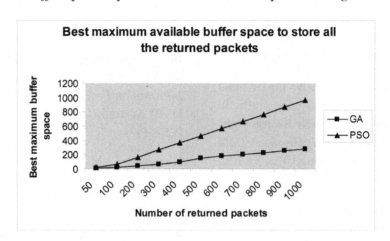

PSO is recommended for small number of returned packets but it is not recommended for higher number of returned packets. It is observed from the experiment that increasing the number of returned packets shows that GA improves the performance while PSO is satisfied by the values found until the end of the iterations.

As the number of returned packets is not same every time, the objective is to observe how well both PSO and GA behave in terms of number of dropped packets with different numbers of returned packets.

The experiment has also been carried out to check how much available buffer space is needed in both the models to reduce the number of dropped packets to zero (almost). This is depicted in Figure 23. The figure also indicates that the maximum buffer space needed by the GA based model is less than that needed by the PSO based model. GA in this experiment changes its behavior towards reaching the stable sub-optimal solution while PSO moves directly to the sub-optimal solution that it can find.

Due to the information exchange possibility among the individuals using crossover in GA; it is observed that all the solutions given by the GA based model are stable only after specific number of generations. Meaning thereby is that GA moves towards the sub-optimal solution in a non-stable

manner; while PSO moves towards its sub-optimal solution in a quite way without much deviation. Therefore PSO based model might take lesser time than GA based model in finding the solution but GA based model offers better end solution.

The authors would like to accord their sincere thanks to the anonymous reviewers for their useful suggestions that has resulted in the quality improvement of this paper.

REFERENCES

Abdelhalim, M. B., Salama, A. E., & Habib, S. E. D. (2006). Hardware Software Partitioning using Particle Swarm Optimization Technique. In *Proceedings of the 6th International Workshop on System on Chip for Real Time Applications*, Cairo, Egypt (pp. 189-194). Washington, DC: IEEE Press.

Abduljalil, F. M. A., & Bodhe, S. K. (2007). Forward-Based Handoff Mechanism In Cellular IP Access Networks. In *Proceedings of the Australian Conference on Wireless Broadband and Ultra Wideband Communications, AUSWireless*. Retrieved from http://epress.lib.uts.edu.au/dspace/bitstream/handle/2100/93/13_Abduljalil.pdf?sequence=1

Anbar, M., & Vidyarthi, D. P. (2009). Buffer Management in Cellular IP Network using PSO. *International Journal of Mobile Computing and Multimedia Communications, 1*(3), 78–93.

Anbar, M., & Vidyarthi, D. P. (2009). On Demand Bandwidth Reservation for Real-Time Traffic in Cellular IP Network using Particle Swarm Optimization. *International Journal of Business Data Communications and Networking, 5*(3), 53–65.

Chen, Y., & Lemin, L. (2005). A random early expiration detection based buffer management algorithm for real-time traffic over wireless networks. In *Proceedings of the IEEE International Conference on Computer and Information Technology (CIT 2005)*, Shanghai, China (pp. 507-511). Washington, DC: IEEE Press.

Hou, Y. T., Dapeng, W., Yao, J., & Takafumi, C. (2000). A core-stateless buffer management mechanism for differentiated services Internet. In *Proceedings of the 25th Annual IEEE Conference on Local Computer Networks (LCN 2000)*, Tampa, FL (pp.168-176). Washington, DC: IEEE Press.

Jain, L. C., Palade, V., & Srinivasan, D. (2007). *Advances in Evolutionary Computing for System Design*. Berlin: Springer Verlag.

James, S., Hou, F., & Ho, P. H. (2007). An Application-Driven MAC-layer Buffer Management with Active Dropping for Real-time Video Streaming in 802.16 Networks. In *Proceedings of the IEEE International Conference on Advanced Information Networking and Applications (AINA '07)*, Niagara Falls, ON (pp. 451-458). Washington, DC: IEEE Press.

Jardosh, S., Zunnun, N., Ranjan, P., & Srivastava, S. (2008). Effect of network coding on buffer management in wireless sensor network. In *Proceedings of the International Conference on Intelligent Sensors, Sensor Networks and Information Processing (ISSNIP 2008)*, Sydney, NSW, Australia (pp. 157-162). Washington, DC: IEEE Press.

Khanbary, L. M. O., & Vidyarthi, D. P. (2008). A GA-based effective fault-tolerant model for channel allocation in mobile computing. *IEEE Transactions on Vehicular Technology, 57*(3), 1823–1833. doi:10.1109/TVT.2007.907311

Krachodnok, P., & Bemjapolakul, W. (2001). Buffer management for TCP over GFR service in an ATM network. In *Proceedings of the Ninth IEEE International Conference on Networks* (pp. 302 - 307). Washington, DC: IEEE Press.

Krifa, A., Baraka, C., & Spyropoulos, T. (2008). Optimal Buffer Management Policies for Delay Tolerant Networks. In *Proceedings of the 5th Annual IEEE Communications Society Conference on Sensor, Mesh and Ad Hoc Communications and Networks (SECON '08)*, San Francisco (pp. 260-268). Washington, DC: IEEE Press.

Lim, H. H., & Qiu, B. (2001). Predictive fuzzy logic buffer management for TCP/IP over ATM-UBR and ATM-ABR. In *Proceedings of the IEEE International Conference on Global Telecommunications (GLOBECOM '01)*, San Antonio, TX (Vol. 4, pp. 2326-2330). Washington, DC: IEEE Press.

Markaki, M., & Venieris, I. S. (2000). A Novel Buffer Management Scheme for CBQ-based IP Routers in a Combined IntServ and DiffServ Architecture. In *Proceedings of the 5th IEEE Symposium on Computers and Communications*, Antibes-Juan les Pins, France (pp. 347-352). Washington, DC: IEEE Press.

Nedjah, N., & Mourelle, L. D. M. (2006). *Swarm Intelligent Systems*. Berlin: Springer Verlag. doi:10.1007/978-3-540-33869-7

Noh, K. J., & Bae, C. S. (2007). A QoS RED Buffer Management Scheme of Intelligent Gateway Gadget based on a Wireless LAN. In *Proceedings of the IEEE International Conference on Advanced Communication Technology (ICACT '07)*, Gangwon-Do, South Korea (Vol. 1, pp. 286-291). Washington, DC: IEEE Press.

Pan, D., & Yang, Y. (2006). Buffer Management for Lossless Service in Network Processors. In *Proceedings of the 14th IEEE Symposium on High-Performance interconnects*, Stanford, CA (pp. 81-86). Washington, DC: IEEE Press.

Pant, M., Thangaraj, R., & Abraham, A. (2007). A New PSO Algorithm with Crossover Operator for Global Optimization Problems. *Innovations in Hybrid Intelligent Systems Advances in Soft Computing*, *44*, 215–222. doi:10.1007/978-3-540-74972-1_29

Ryu, Y. S., & Koh, K. (1996). A dynamic buffer management technique for minimizing the necessary buffer space in a continuous media server. In *Proceedings of the third IEEE International Conference on Multimedia Computing and Systems (MMCS 1996)*, Hiroshima, Japan (pp. 181-185). Washington, DC: IEEE Press.

Seo, J. H., Im, C. H., Heo, C. G., Kim, J. K., Jung, H. K., & Lee, C. G. (2006). Multimodal function optimization based on particle swarm optimization. *IEEE Transactions on Magnetics*, *42*(4), 1095–1098. doi:10.1109/TMAG.2006.871568

Shimonishi, H. Sanadidi, & Gerla, M. (2005). Improving Efficiency-Friendliness Tradeoffs of TCP: Robustness to Router Buffer Capacity Variations. In *Proceedings of IEEE Global Telecommunications Conference*, St. Louis, MO (pp. 5-10).

Soudan, B., & Saad, M. (2008). An Evolutionary Dynamic Population Size PSO Implementation. In *Proceedings of the 3rd International Conference on Information & Communication Technologies: from Theory to Applications (ICTTA '08)*, Damascus, Syria (pp. 1-5). Washington, DC: IEEE Press.

Valkó, A. G., Gomez, J., Kim, S., & Compabell, A. T. (1999). On the Analysis of Cellular IP Access Networks. In *Proceedings of the IFIP Sixth International Workshop on Protocols for High Speed Networks VI*, Salem, MA (pp. 205-224).

Yerima, S. Y., & Al-Begain, K. (2007). Buffer Management for Multimedia QoS Control over HSDPA Downlink. In *Proceedings of the 21st International Conference on Advanced Information Networking and Applications Workshops (AINAW '07)*, Niagara Falls, ON (Vol. 1, pp. 912-917). Washington, DC: IEEE Press.

Ying, T., Ya-Ping, Y., & Jian-Chao, Z. (2006). An Enhanced Hybrid Quadratic Particle Swarm Optimization. In *Proceedings of the Sixth International Conference on Intelligent Systems Design and Applications (ISDA '06)*, Jinan, China (Vol. 2, pp. 980-985). Washington, DC: IEEE Press.

Yousefi'zadeh, H., & Jonckheere, E. A. (2005). Dynamic neural-based buffer management for queuing systems with self-similar characteristics. *IEEE Transactions on Neural Networks*, *16*(5), 1163–1173. doi:10.1109/TNN.2005.853417

This work was previously published in International Journal of Applied Evolutionary Computation, Volume 1, Issue 4, edited by Wei-Chiang Samuelson Hong, pp. 1-22, copyright 2010 by IGI Publishing (an imprint of IGI Global).

Chapter 14

Using Evolution Strategies to Perform Stellar Population Synthesis for Galaxy Spectra from SDSS

Juan Carlos Gomez
KULeuven, Belgium

Olac Fuentes
UTEP, USA

ABSTRACT

In this work, the authors employ Evolution Strategies (ES) to automatically extract a set of physical parameters, corresponding to stellar population synthesis, from a sample of galaxy spectra taken from the Sloan Digital Sky Survey (SDSS). This parameter extraction is presented as an optimization problem and being solved using ES. The idea is to reconstruct each galaxy spectrum by means of a linear combination of three different theoretical models for stellar population synthesis. This combination produces a model spectrum that is compared with the original spectrum using a simple difference function. The goal is to find a model that minimizes this difference, using ES as the algorithm to explore the parameter space. This paper presents experimental results using a set of 100 spectra from SDSS Data Release 2 that show that ES are very well suited to extract stellar population parameters from galaxy spectra. Additionally, in order to better understand the performance of ES in this problem, a comparison with two well known stochastic search algorithms, Genetic Algorithms (GA) and Simulated Annealing (SA), is presented.

INTRODUCTION

Evolution Strategy (ES) (Back, Hammel, & Schwefel, 1997; Rechenberg, 1973) is a very flexible and effective optimization algorithm (Ashlock, 2005), suitable to be employed in many areas and subjects such as mechanical design (Giraud-Moreau & Lafon, 2002), optics (Vazquez-Montiel, Sanchez-Escobar, & Fuentes, 2002) and control engineering (Fernandez, Muñoz, Sanchez, & Mayol, 1997). In this paper we introduce a novel application of this method to a very interesting problem in astronomy: the fitting

DOI: 10.4018/978-1-4666-1749-0.ch014

of galaxy spectra with models of stellar population synthesis; a problem that has been attacked following traditional approaches like χ^2 minimization (Wolf, Drory, Gebhardt, & Hill, 2007) or stochastic methods such as Simulated Annealing (SA) (Fernandes, Mateus, Sodré, Stasin'ska, & Gomes, 2005). However, these methods have some problems because they tend to be computationally expensive in terms of time, like χ^2, and sometimes converge to non-global optima, like SA.

Astronomy faces today an important set of difficult tasks that need to be tackled by sophisticated algorithms. Basically there are two types of problems in modern computational astronomy: problems with great computational complexity (e.g., n-body and cosmological simulations) (Gomez, Athanassoula, Fuentes, & Bosma, 2004) and problems where huge amounts of information must be analyzed (e.g., sky surveys, Abazajian et al., 2004). The problem presented here belongs to the second category.

Tasks where a huge amount of data have to be analyzed need to be performed automatically using reliable and efficient algorithms, as manual analysis is practically impossible because of the great amount of time required. In particular, the Sloan Digital Sky Survey (SDSS) (Abazajian et al., 2004) contains terabytes of information from galaxy images and spectra that need to be processed in order to extract important scientific knowledge. This massive amount of high quality data has the potential to enable enormous progress in our understanding of galaxies and the universe in general.

Galaxy spectra encode information about age and metallicity distributions of the constituent stars, which in turn reflect the star formation and chemical histories of the galaxies (Karttunen, Kroger, Oja, Poutanen, & Donner, 2000). Extracting such information from observational data in a reliable way is crucial for a deeper understanding of galaxy formation, composition, and evolution. In order to extract knowledge from SDSS spectra, a methodology must be set up to go from observed

spectra to the physical properties of galaxies, including reddening, age, metallicity, and contribution of each stellar population.

The main goal in this paper is to present a method based on ES for extracting parameter information about the stellar components of a given observed galaxy spectrum from SDSS, presented as an image. The idea is to do it by fitting, efficiently and automatically, the observed spectrum with a linear combination of simple theoretical stellar populations computed with evolutionary synthesis models at the same spectral resolution as that of the SDSS. ES works as an optimization algorithm by exploring the space of feasible parameters, trying to find the ones that produce the model that best matches the original galaxy spectrum image.

In this paper we have obtained results for a set of 100 spectra from SDSS Data Release 2 as a first approach to the use of ES in this problem, proving ES are very well suited to extract stellar population parameters from galaxy spectra automatically and efficiently. The rest of the document is structured by presenting a brief description of galaxy spectra and the information we can extract from them and describes the data from SDSS. Next, we detail the implementation of ES to solve the problem and then results are presented followed by a conclusion.

GALAXY SPECTRA

The light of a star can be dispersed into a spectrum by means of a prism or a diffraction grating. In this way we obtain the *stellar spectrum*, which is the distribution of the energy flux density over frequency. A stellar spectrum is made up by a continuum and by absorption and emission lines, which are produced by the different chemical elements present in the star (Karttunen, Kroger, Oja, Poutanen, & Donner, 2000). Each line is a fingerprint of some chemical element that is excited or ionized.

Almost all of the relevant information about physical properties of stars can be obtained more or less directly from studies of their spectra. The line shapes contain detailed information about chemical elements and atmospheric processes.

The spectrum of a galaxy, in fact, is the combination of spectra from the millions of stars in the galaxy. Thus the colors in a galaxy depend both on the ages of the stars (young stars are bluer) and on the abundance of heavy elements Z, or metallicity (stars with larger Z are redder). The interpretation of the observational results thus has to be based on detailed modeling of the stellar composition of galaxies, or stellar population synthesis, where several models of stellar populations are combined to reproduce galaxy spectra.

Studying the features of a galaxy spectrum tells us about the types of stars the galaxy contains, and the relative abundances of each type of stars. Stars of different spectral classes contribute with different characteristic absorption features to the galaxy spectrum. By observing the strength of various spectral features we can find out about

masses, ages, and chemical compositions of the stars that form the galaxy.

In galaxies we can distinguish three types of stellar populations: Type I that consists of young stars (hundreds of millions of years of age) with high metallicity, Type II that consists of old stars almost without metallicity and Type III, an intermediate population with ages between Types I and II. There exist libraries of models of entire stellar systems for each type of population, with different ages and metallicities. Combinations of models of these three types of populations are used in stellar population synthesis to reproduce galaxy spectra.

In this work we employ a library of 50 models from Bressan et al. (1994). These models cover the following ages: young = $[10^6, 10^{6.3}, 10^{6.6}, 10^7, 10^{7.3}]$ years, intermediate = $[10^{7.6}, 10^8, 10^{8.3}]$ years, and old = $[10^9, 10^{10.2}]$ years, and the following metallicities: $[0.0004, 0.004, 0.008, 0.02, 0.05]$ $Z_\odot$ (solar metallicity).

An example model of a galaxy spectrum is shown in Figure 1, where three models of stellar

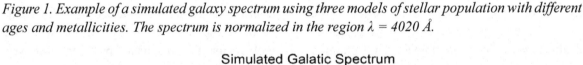

Figure 1. Example of a simulated galaxy spectrum using three models of stellar population with different ages and metallicities. The spectrum is normalized in the region $\lambda = 4020\ \mathring{A}$.

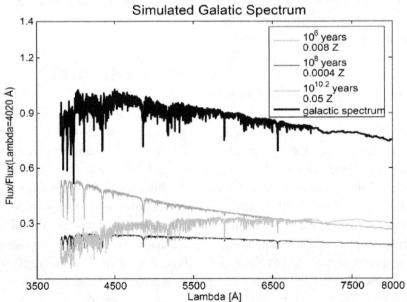

populations with different ages and metallicities are combined to create a simulated galaxy spectrum (thick line). In order to infer physical properties of galaxies (i.e., properties given by the models) from the observed spectra, it is necessary to find the best combination of models that fits the observed spectra. Performing this task is not easy, due to the number of parameters and the noise inherent to observational data, thus an effective and efficient algorithm must be employed to examine the space of potential solutions.

SDSS Data

SDSS is one of the most ambitious projects performed to survey the sky, trying to cover one quarter of the sky with high detail. To do this, the SDSS team has used a 2.5 meter telescope located in the observatory in Apache Point, New Mexico. This survey includes photometric and spectroscopic data.

Spectrography in SDSS is done using 2 spectrographs, covering a range from 3800Å to 9000Å, with a resolution of $R = \lambda/\Delta\lambda = 1800$. The Data Release (DR) 2 from SDSS contains the spectra from 574 plates with 640 fibers each, covering an area of 2,627 square degrees, with a total of 367,360 spectra of galaxies, quasars and stars. In Figure 2 we observe an example of a galaxy spectrum from SDSS DR2.

In this work we employ a sample of 100 spectra taken from SDSS DR2 (Figure 2) that were used and analyzed in (Bello, Terlevich, & Chávez, 2007). All the spectra from the sample were first passed through a preprocessing stage where they were brought to the rest frame, using the redshift given in the SDSS database, corrected for extinction, using the maps given by Schlegel, Finkbeiner, and Davis (1998) and the extinction law of Cardelli (1989), sampled from 3800Å to 8000Å in steps of 1Å and normalized by the median flux in the 4010Å - 4060Å. All this process is done to simplify the fitting task and it is necessary to standardize the data (the observed data and the models).

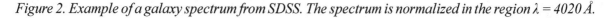

Figure 2. Example of a galaxy spectrum from SDSS. The spectrum is normalized in the region $\lambda = 4020 \, \text{Å}$.

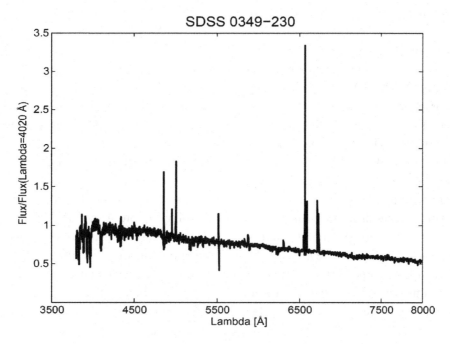

FITTING

In order to fit an observed spectrum, it is necessary to define a mathematical model that, using the library of stellar population spectra, can produce a simulated galaxy spectrum that matches the observation. From the spectra library we can define ages and metallicities for each stellar population; nevertheless, to produce more realistic galaxy spectra we also need to know the reddening term and the relative contribution for each stellar population. Thus, a model for a galaxy spectrum is constructed using the equation:

$$\mathbf{g} = \sum_{i=1}^{3} c_i s_i \left(a_i, m_i\right)\left(10^{-4r_i k}\right) \qquad (1)$$

where $s_i(a_i, m_i)$ represents a model of a stellar population from a library for specific age (a_i) and specific metallicity (m_i), $10^{-4r_i k}$ is the reddening term, and c_i is the relative contribution of each population.

Then, the final goal in this fitting task is to find, efficiently and automatically, the best combination for the following stellar population parameters: reddening (r_1, r_2, r_3), metallicities (m_1, m_2, m_3), ages (a_1, a_2, a_3) and relative contributions (c_1, c_2, c_3) for stellar populations, that produce a model that matches the observed spectrum.

The stellar population parameters are shown in Table 1 together with the domains where they can fall. The parameters for age and metallicity are discrete, since they are indexes in the simulated stellar population spectra library, while reddening and contribution are continuous.

The models of stellar populations from the library are defined only for the stellar component of galaxies, which means absorption lines. Even with this restriction, the models from the library are adequate to describe the main features of the spectra. Emission lines come from gas and dust in galaxies, so, since this component is not considered by the models, we need to discard the parts where emission lines are present in observed spectrum. There are some well known emission lines that are commonly present in galaxy spectra; such lines correspond to some chemical elements, and some of them can be observed in Figure 1. We have created a mask with the points where such emission lines are present to determine the parts of the spectra to be ignored by the optimization algorithm (the 0 values for w_λ described in the next subsection). The points masked are: $[\mathrm{Ne_{III}}]$ $\lambda = [3865,. . ., 3873]$ Å, H_e, H_δ, H_γ, H_β, $[\mathrm{O_{III}}]\lambda = [3865,. . ., 3873]$ Å, $[\mathrm{He_I}]\lambda = [5871,. . ., 5881]$ Å, $\mathrm{NaD}\lambda = [5885,. . ., 5895]$ Å, $[\mathrm{O_I}]\lambda = [6295,. . ., 6305]$ Å, $[\mathrm{N_{II}}],\mathrm{H}_\alpha\lambda = [6543,. . ., 6588]$ Å and $[\mathrm{S_{II}}]$ $\lambda = [6712,. . ., 6736]$ Å.

Stellar Population Synthesis as an Optimization Process

We have observed that the present fitting task can be posed as an optimization problem in the following way: let **o** be the observed galaxy spectrum as a vector containing fluxes, let **g** be the simulated spectrum with the same dimensionality as **o**. In order to measure how well a model **g** describes the spectrum **o** we use the following function:

$$f\left(\mathbf{g}\right) = \sum_{\lambda=3800}^{\lambda=8000} \left|o_\lambda - g_\lambda\right| w_\lambda \qquad (2)$$

where each w_λ takes a value of 0 for emission lines and 1 otherwise. This is the fitness function our evolutionary algorithm uses as fitness function. Thus, the goal of the optimization process is to obtain a model **g*** that minimizes the previous function, with $f(\mathbf{g}^*) = 0$.

The rationale to choose ES as the method to solve the problem of stellar population synthesis is that ES was designed since its origins as an optimization algorithm for problems with complex, real-valued parameters in static fitness functions (Back, Hammel, & Schwefel, 1997), like the problem shown here. On the other hand,

Table 1. Restricted domains for stellar population parameters

Parameter	Name	Domain
a_1	Young age	{1,2,3,4,5}
a_2	Intermediate age	{6,7,8}
a_3	Old age	{9,10}
m_1	Metallicity population I	{1,2,3,4,5}
m_2	Metallicity population II	{1,2,3,4,5}
m_3	Metallicity population III	{1,2,3,4,5}
r_1	Reddening population I	[-1,1]
r_2	Reddening population II	[-1,1]
r_3	Reddening population III	[-1,1]
c_1	Contribution population I	[0,1]
c_2	Contribution population II	[0,1]
c_3	Contribution population IIII	[0,1]

Simulated Annealing (SA) is better known to solve problems of discrete and combinatorial optimization (Kirkpatrick, Gelatt, & Vecchi, 1983), and Genetic Algorithm (GA) was originally developed to be a robust adaptive system that attempts to minimize expected looses over a series of samples from a state space of coding structures (Fogel, 1993), but discrete and combinatorial optimization is one of the main application area for these algorithms. This work contributes by showing another instance where ES is well suited to solve practical optimization problems with discrete and real parameters, by working directly with the numerical (phenotypic) representation of these parameters, as have been shown in other works (Fogel & Atmar, 1990). Additionally, a comparison between ES, GA and SA was carried out in order to better understand the behavior of these algorithms in the current problem.

Our implementation of ES for the present problem of fitting galaxy spectra with stellar population models is as follows: the initial population μ of ES, where $\mu = \{x_i\}$; $i = 1,\ldots, \mu$, with $x_i = [a_{1,i}, a_{2,i}, a_{3,i}, m_{1,i}, m_{2,i}, m_{3,i}, r_{1,i}, r_{2,i}, r_{3,i}, c_{1,i}, c_{2,i}, c_{3,i}]$ and their corresponding strategy parameters vectors σ_i $i =$ 1,…, μ is formed by randomly generated values for each parameter inside the domains defined in Table 1. Then, each set of parameters of the population (i.e., each x_i) is passed to a module that combines the stellar population models from the library following Equation 1 to create the simulated galaxy spectrum g_i. Afterwards, each g_i is evaluated using the fitness function (2).

The next step consists of an iterative process where if some model has a good match with the real spectrum we stop the process, otherwise we create a child population κ, containing κ new individuals x'_j $j = 1,\ldots, \kappa$ using recombination, mutation and average operators (described in detail below). Then we create their corresponding models g'_j and evaluate them using the fitness function (2). In the next step we combine the parent μ and child κ populations and afterward we select only the best μ individuals from this combined ($\mu + \kappa$) population. Finally, we return to the beginning to determine if some model has reached a good match with the observed.

Here we have employed a modified version of ES that includes some changes to the canonical version (Back, Hammel, & Schwefel, 1997). We create $\mu = 11$ parent individuals and $\kappa = 22$ children individuals; we use a ($\mu + \kappa$) scheme for selection, discrete recombination, and traditional mutation, but we also include a new way to create offspring with the average operator and dynamical mutation (Beyer, 1996) for strategy parameter vectors based on a simple, but effective and easy to understand, multiplication by constant factors. The pseudo-code of the ES algorithm for this problem is the following:

1. Create μ parent vectors x_i; $i = 1,\ldots, \mu$ where each vector contains 12 parameters $x_i = [a_{1,i}, a_{2,i}, a_{3,i}, m_{1,i}, m_{2,i}, m_{3,i}, r_{1,i}, r_{2,i}, r_{3,i}, c_{1,i}, c_{2,i}, c_{3,i}]$, and their corresponding strategy parameter vectors σ_i; $i = 1,\ldots, \mu$ where $\sigma_i = [\sigma_{1,i}, \sigma_{2,i}, \ldots, \sigma_{12,i}]$. Each parameter is chosen through a random process and satisfying the constraints of the problem

2. For each vector $\mathbf{x}_i$ produce a simulated galaxy spectrum $\mathbf{g}_i$

3. For each $\mathbf{g}_i$ compute the fitness function

$$f\left(\mathbf{g}_i\right) = \sum_{\lambda=3800}^{\lambda=8000} \left|o_\lambda - g_{i,\lambda}\right| w_\lambda$$

4. If some model $\mathbf{g}_i$ fits well the observed spectrum terminate, otherwise continue to next step

5. Create κ new individuals in the following way:

   ◦ Create 10% of κ population using discrete recombination. From two parents $\mathbf{x}_a$ and $\mathbf{x}_b$, chosen randomly, we create a new child $\mathbf{x}'_k$:

   $x'_{k,j} = x_{a,j}$ or $x_{b,j}$ with probability 0.5 for each one; $j = 1, 2,\ldots, 12$

   $\sigma'_{k,j} = \sigma_{a,j}$ or $\sigma_{b,j}$ with probability 0.5 for each one; $j = 1, 2,\ldots, 12$

   ◦ Create 10% of κ population using average operator. From two parents $\mathbf{x}_a$ and $\mathbf{x}_b$, chosen randomly, we create a new child $\mathbf{x}'_k$:

   $\mathbf{x}'_k = q\mathbf{x}_a + (1 - q)\mathbf{x}_b$
   $\mathbf{\sigma}'_k = q\mathbf{\sigma}_a + (1 - q)\mathbf{\sigma}_b$

   where q is a random number taken from a uniform distribution in the $[0,1]$ range

   ◦ Create 80% of κ population using mutation:

   $\mathbf{x}'_k = \mathbf{x}_a + N(0, \mathbf{\sigma}_a)$

6. For each vector $\mathbf{x}'_k$; $k = 1,\ldots, \kappa$ produce a simulated galaxy spectrum $\mathbf{g}'_k$

7. For each $\mathbf{g}'_k$ compute the fitness function

$$f\left(\mathbf{g}_k\right) = \sum_{\lambda=3800}^{\lambda=8000} \left|o_\lambda - g'_{k,\lambda}\right| w_\lambda$$

8. Merge $\mathbf{\mu}$ and $\mathbf{\kappa}$ populations to obtain a $(\mathbf{\mu} + \mathbf{\kappa})$ population

9. Sort the merged population by fitness function

10. Select the best μ individuals from the sorted population

11. Mutate strategy parameter vectors: $\mathbf{\sigma}'_i = 0.3\mathbf{\sigma}_i$ if $\mathbf{x}_i$ is a child or $\mathbf{\sigma}'_i = 3.3\mathbf{\sigma}_i$ if $\mathbf{x}_i$ is a parent; where these values have been selected experimentally. In this manner when we have successful populations (parent individuals) then we can explore farther regions from the current point, trying to improve the current best fitness; while when we have unsuccessful populations (children individuals) we explore nearer regions to current point with the same purpose.

12. If some model $\mathbf{g}_i$ fits the observed spectrum well or the maximum number of generations is reached terminate, otherwise return to 5

RESULTS

In order to evaluate the efficiency of the evolutionary method ES in this problem we have produced results for a sample of 100 spectra taken from SDSS DR2 and used in (Bello, Terlevich, & Chávez, 2007).

The fitting of one galaxy spectrum takes on average 1 minute on a PC with a PIV 3 GHz processor and 512 MB of RAM, using Matlab®. Computational time can be improved if we employ a compiled language such as C, C++ or FORTRAN rather than an interpreted one.

The fitness function (2) is not normalized, so it describes the fitness of each individual by measuring the direct difference of its corresponding model with respect to the observed spectrum. We say a model $\mathbf{g}^*$ matches perfectly the observed spectrum when $f(\mathbf{g}^*) = 0$, but since we are matching models with observational data, we do not expect to reach the theoretical minimum. Rather, we are interested in obtaining good approximations to the observed spectra.

After a set of experiments we determined that a value of 60 for the fitness function is good enough and the model can be acceptable. A smaller value for this threshold would lead to a better fit, albeit at an increase in computation time.

We illustrate the fitting with 12 examples presented in Figure 3 that shows spectra from

SDSS DR2 fitted by models approximated by ES. We can observe that, as stated before, emission lines are not fitted but the general distribution of absorption lines and the curve form are approximated very closely. A better fit is observed around the 4020Å region because of the normalization, and the less fitted part is at the end of the spectra because the models from the library are known not to be as accurate in this range of wavelengths. Also, as mentioned in the previous paragraph, we are not expecting to match perfectly the observed spectra, but to find good descriptions of the absorption lines.

Figure 3. Fitting for a sample of spectra from SDSS DR2, showing observed spectra in thin lines and models in thick lines. The spectra are normalized in the region λ = 4020 Å

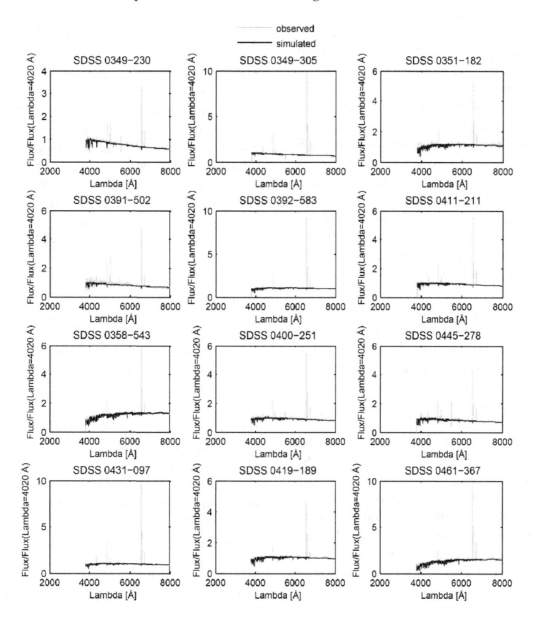

In Table 2 we present the summarized results for a sample of 100 galactic spectra. From this table we can observe that we have reached the goal threshold of 60 for fitness function in 85% of the analyses. In this work we established experimentally a limit of 5005 function evaluations (for a total of 455 generations) for ES, and a limit of 1 for the fitness function to terminate. We can see from the table that no fitting was able to reach the lower limit for the fitness function, and all of them spent the maximum number of allowable function evaluations. The average fitness function value for the successful fittings is 26.576, which means a good fitting for the great majority of the spectra, with a minimum value of 8.46 and a maximum value of 59.82, and a standard deviation of 12.65 for the sample, which means that we do not have a standard or uniform fitting, rather the fitting depends on the particular details of the observed spectrum. For comparison, we performed the spectral fitting using two other common stochastic algorithms: GA and SA. We used the implementations provided by the Matlab® Optimization Toolbox, using the same parameters for number of function evaluations and lower limit of the fitness function than in our algorithm. In Table 3 we see the results for these algorithms. In general ES outperforms GA and SA in terms of percentage of success and in average value of the fitness function; the later algorithms only present better standard deviations for the successful fittings, which means theirs results are more uniform, but these results depend on the number of successful fittings.

We have mentioned that a similar problem has been solved using other methods such as SA (Fernandes, Mateus, Sodré, Stasin'ska, & Gomes, 2005) and χ^2 minimization (Wolf, Drory, Gebhardt, & Hill, 2007), nevertheless we do not present comparisons with these works because they fit a different set of galaxy spectra and use a different library of spectra; then a direct comparison is not feasible.

Table 2. Results for a set of 100 galaxy spectra from SDSS DR2

Meth-od	Function Evalu-ations (average)	f(g) (aver-age)	Stan-dard Devia-tion for f(g)	Suc-cess (%)
ES	5005	**26.58**	12.65	**85**
GA	5016	27.18	11.22	79
SA	5005	27.87	**10.88**	80

CONCLUSION AND FUTURE WORK

In this paper we have presented a novel application of ES in astronomy, showing the versatility and good behavior of ES in difficult problems. Spectral fitting is a complex non-trivial problem with real-valued parameters and seemed a natural problem to be solved by ES. We presented a comparison of ES with other two stochastic search algorithms: GA and SA, showing the better performance of ES in terms of rate of success and average value of fitness function. In general ES was successful in spectral fitting; the algorithm was able to find good models in almost all the spectra from the sample, with a relatively low computational cost, taking on average 1 minute to fit one spectrum, which is a very good time if we take into account the fact that we are dealing with real data. In this manner ES has proved to be a very well suited method for this problem.

For future work we can employ a parallelized version of our ES algorithm to reduce computational time with larger samples of data, and also include a stop operator to break the ES process when the fitness function value cannot be reduced during a period of *n* generations. In addition, a better fit can be obtained if we use model libraries that take into account the gas component, and with better resolution for all the wavelength range. Also, we can obtain improvements if we include other effects such as velocity dispersion in the models.

ACKNOWLEDGMENT

This work was partially supported by CONACYT, Mexico, under grants C02-45258/A-1 and 144198.

REFERENCES

Abazajian, K. (2004). The second data release of the sloan digital sky survey. *The Astronomical Journal, 128*(1), 502–512. doi:10.1086/421365

Ashlock, D. (2005). *Evolutionary Computation for Modeling and Optimization*. New York: Springer.

Back, T., Hammel, U., & Schwefel, H. (1997). Evolutionary computation: Comments on the history and current state. *IEEE Transactions on Evolutionary Computation, 1*(1), 3–17. doi:10.1109/4235.585888

Bello, M., Terlevich, R., & Chavez, M. (2007). *Estudio de la evolución temporal del triplete de CaII*. Unpublished Master's thesis, INAOE.

Beyer, H. (1996). Toward a theory of evolution strategies: Self-adaptation. *Evolutionary Computation, 3*(3), 311–347. doi:10.1162/evco.1995.3.3.311

Bressan, A., Chiosi, C., & Fagotto, F. (1994). Spectrophotometric evolution of elliptical galaxies. 1: Ultraviolet excess and color-magnitude-redshift relations. *The Astrophysical Journal. Supplement Series, 94*(1), 63–115. doi:10.1086/192073

Cardelli, J., Clayton, G., & Mathis, J. (1989). The relationship between infrared, optical, and ultraviolet extinction. *The Astrophysical Journal, 345*(1), 245–256. doi:10.1086/167900

Fernandes, R. C., Mateus, A., Sodré, L., Stasin'ska, G., & Gomes, J. (2005). Semi-empirical analysis of sloan digital sky survey galaxies - I. spectral synthesis method. *Monthly Notices of the Royal Astronomical Society, 358*(2), 363–378. doi:10.1111/j.1365-2966.2005.08752.x

Fernandez, G., Muñoz, S., Sanchez, R., & Mayol, W. (1997). Simultaneous stabilization using evolutionary strategies. *International Journal of Control, 68*(6), 1417–1435. doi:10.1080/002071797223091

Fogel, D. B. (1993). On the philosophical differences between evolutionary algorithms and genetic algorithms. In *Proceedings of 2nd Annual Conference on Evolutionary Programming. Evolutionary Programming Society* (pp. 23-29).

Fogel, D. B., & Atmar, J. W. (1990). Comparing genetic operators with Gaussians mutations in simulated evolutionary processes using linear systems. *Biological Cybernetics, 63*(2), 111–114. doi:10.1007/BF00203032

Giraud-Moreau, L., & Lafon, P. (2002). A comparison of evolutionary algorithms for mechanical design components. *Engineering Optimization, 34*(1), 307–322. doi:10.1080/03052150211750

Gomez, J. C., Athanassoula, E., Fuentes, O., & Bosma, A. (2004). *Using evolution strategies to find a dynamical model for the m81 triplet* (LNAI 3215, pp. 404-410). New York: Springer.

Karttunen, H., Kroger, P., Oja, H., Poutanen, M., & Donner, K. (2000). *Fundamental Astronomy*. Berlin: Springer Verlag.

Kirkpatrick, S., Gelatt, C. D., & Vecchi, M. P. (1983). Optimization by simulated annealing. *Science, 220*(4598), 671–680. doi:10.1126/science.220.4598.671

Rechenberg, I. (1973). *Evolutionsstrategie: Optimierung Technischer Systeme nach Prinzipien der Biologischen Evolution*. Stuttgart, Germany: Frommann-Holzboog.

Schlegel, D., Finkbeiner, D., & Davis, M. (1998). Maps of dust infrared emission for use in estimation of reddening and cosmic microwave background radiation foregrounds. *The Astrophysical Journal, 500*(1), 525–553. doi:10.1086/305772

Vazquez-Montiel, S., Sanchez-Escobar, J., & Fuentes, O. (2002). Obtaining the phase of an interferogram by use of an evolution strategy: Part I. *Applied Optics*, *41*(17), 3448–3452. doi:10.1364/AO.41.003448

Wolf, M., Drory, N., Gebhardt, K., & Hill, G. (2007). Ages and metallicities of extra-galactic globular clusters from spectral and photometric fits of stellar population synthesis models. *The Astrophysical Journal*, *655*(1), 179–211. doi:10.1086/509768

This work was previously published in International Journal of Applied Evolutionary Computation, Volume 1, Issue 4, edited by Wei-Chiang Samuelson Hong, pp. 23-33, copyright 2010 by IGI Publishing (an imprint of IGI Global).

Chapter 15
A Novel Puzzle Based Compaction (PBC) Strategy for Enhancing the Utilization of Reconfigurable Resources

Ahmed I. Saleh
Mansoura University, Egypt

ABSTRACT

Partially reconfigurable field programmable gate arrays (FPGAs) can accommodate several independent tasks simultaneously. FPGA, as all reconfigurable chips, relies on the "host-then-compact-when-needed" strategy. Accordingly, it should have the ability to both place incoming tasks at run time and compact the chip whenever needed. Compaction is a proposed solution to alleviate external fragmentations problem, trying to move running tasks closer to each other in order to free a sufficient area for new tasks. However, compaction conditions the suspension of the running tasks, which introduces a high penalty. In order to increase the chip area utilization as well as not affecting the response times of tasks, efficient compaction techniques become increasingly important. Unfortunately, traditional compaction techniques suffer from a variety of faults. This paper introduces a novel Puzzle Based Compaction (PBC) technique that is a shape aware technique, which takes the tasks shapes into consideration. In this regard, it succeeded not only to eliminate the internal fragmentations but also to minimize the external fragmentations. This paper develops a novel formula, which is the first not to estimate, but to exactly calculate the amount of external fragmentations generated by accommodating a set of tasks inside the reconfigurable chip.

INTRODUCTION

In spite of its flexible architecture and good internal arrangement, FPGA usually suffers from external fragmentations (Roberto, Francesco, Massimo, Marco, & Donatella, 2009). As several tasks enter and leave the chip, the chip area becomes fragmented into small islands, which are unable to host newly incoming tasks (Marconi, Lu, Bertels, & Gaydadjiev, 2008). This decreases the chip ability to host new tasks, which in turn harmly affects both the chip area utilization as well as the response times of running and waiting

DOI: 10.4018/978-1-4666-1749-0.ch015

Figure 1. How external fragmentations affect the chip area

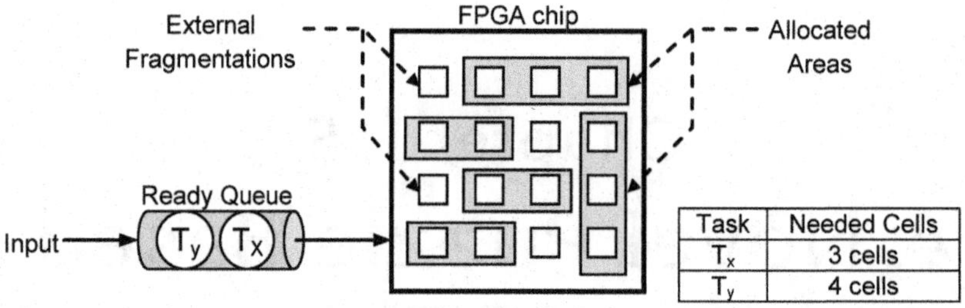

tasks (Giani, Redaelli, Santambrogio, & Sciuto, 2007) (Banerjee, Bozorgzadeh, & Dutt, 2005).

As illustrated in Figure 1, the chip is too fragmented to can host either task T_x or T_y. Hence, they are waiting in the ready queue despite there being available sufficient noncontiguous cells to host them. Accordingly, response times for those waiting tasks become longer and chip utilization is lower than it could be.

Generally, task arrangement in reconfigurable computing may be done in either offline or online scenarios (Banerjee, Bozorgzadeh, & Dutt, 2005). The offline scenario is similar to the traditional packing problem (Fekete, Kohler, & Teich, 2001) (Fekete & Schepers, 2004) where both tasks' size as well as its service time are known in advance. Accordingly, an optimal or near optimal task arrangements could be derived. However, such scenario becomes obsolete with the rapid development in the area of reconfigurable computing. New applications have been emerged in which each task has an arrival time and size that are unknown in advance. Hence, tasks of those applications need to be scheduled online, while the task placement is not the issue (Resano & Mozos, 2004). The challenge is then to find sufficient contiguous cells for those newly incoming online tasks.

Online task arrangement may be either static or dynamic (Banerjee, Bozorgzadeh, & Dutt, 2006). The static behavior conditions the no-preemption of running tasks, and so, it does not offer task rearrangement (Jean, Tomko, Yavagal, Shah,

& Cook, 1999; Fekete, Kohler, & Teich, 2001; Bazargan, Kastner, & Sarrafzadeh, 2000; Tabero, Septien, Mesha, Mozos, & Roman, 2003). On the other hand, the dynamic behavior for online task arrangement allows the scheduler to preempt the running tasks. Hence, preempted tasks can be rearranged to create a sufficient space for the incoming tasks when those new tasks have to wait. The process of task rearrangement, which aims to minimize the amount of external fragmentations (by making tasks closer to each others) is called the chip "compaction" (El Farag, Hatem, & Shaheen, 2007; Thomas, Yi, Koen, & Georgi, 2010).

Whenever a set of online arriving tasks are to be hosted into a reconfigurable chip, the chip will certainly suffer from internal and/or external fragmentations. To the best of our knowledge, almost all introduced online task placement techniques suffer from internal fragmentations. The reason is quite simple; "as they assume rectangular tasks". For non-rectangular tasks, the inclusive rectangle for the entire task is considered. Consequently, some area may get wasted, which is called internal fragmentations. In spite of its critical impact on the chip utilization, internal fragmentations problem has not been addressed yet. On the other hand, with the online task placement, as tasks are allocated and de-allocated over time, external fragmentations will unfortunately appear. External fragmentations may prevent a new task from being hosted into the chip although there exists a sufficient number of noncontiguous cells. Unlike internal fragmentations, external ones can be eliminated by compaction. Hence, compaction is to squeeze the neighboring tasks together so as to combine the interstitial free cells. Consequently, after compaction, the combined cells can be allocated to the incoming tasks.

In this paper a novel Puzzle based compaction (PBC), which is the first to consider both the internal and external fragmentations, has been introduced. PBC introduced the minimal amount of fragmentations, and accordingly the maximum amount of contiguous free cells after compaction. This happened because PBC eliminated internal fragmentations. The source of fragmentations in PBC is due to the external fragmentations only, which have been also minimized by considering the exact shape of the task. On the other hand, to the best of our knowledge, fragmentations in all other compaction techniques are due to both internal and external fragmentations.

As PBC takes both the internal and external fragmentations into account, it minimizes the chip wasted area. PBC relies on the principle that; "one additional free cell may allow a waiting task to run". This is simply because a task T_i of size n cells can not run inside an area of size n-1 cells. So, one more additional free cell may hardly affect the system performance as it may allow a waiting task to execute sooner. Moreover, PBC maximizes the degree of chip utilization (the number of running tasks) as it tries to utilize every chip fragments, which in turn maximizes the number of running tasks. The paper also develops a novel formula, which is the first not to estimate, but to exactly calculate the amount of external fragmentations generated by accommodating a set of tasks inside the reconfigurable chip. The proposed PBC has been compared against traditional compaction techniques. Experimental results have shown that PBC outperforms traditional compaction techniques as it introduces the minimal amount of fragmentations and accordingly maximizes the chip utilization.

BACKGROUND

In this section, a more detailed description about the reconfigurable computing as well as the compaction technology will be presented. Moreover, a novel view that simulates the compaction as a "Parkingman problem" will be addressed, which is the first to be introduced in this paper.

Reconfigurable Computing

FPGAs are designed to implement any logic circuit (Xilinx, 2008). They inherent reconfigurability from their programmable architecture. The main FPGA parts are; (i) the logic blocks (programmable cells), (ii) the input/output (I/O) blocks, and (iii) the routing infrastructure. All are programmable using static random-access memory (SRAM) to allow different connections and functionalities. The arrangement for an island-style FPGA is illustrated in Figure 2 in which logic blocks are distributed in an array with the routing fabric running between them (Xilinx, 2007). I/O blocks surround the logic blocks and routing tracks so that the direction of each I/O block (whether the block used for input or output) and connections to the routing tracks are configurable. Logic blocks can implement any arbitrary logic functions. Connections are made between them and

Figure 2. The arrangement of an island style FPGA

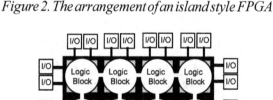

the programmable routing fabric so that the inputs and outputs of a logic block connect to some of the adjacent routing tracks.

FPGA Compaction

Area management for reconfigurable devices, such as FPGA, includes two main aspects, which are; (i) task placement, and, (ii) task compaction. The former decides where to map an incoming task into the reconfigurable area. If placement has failed, chip should be compacted by rearranging the running tasks close to each others. This impacts well the chip utilization by reducing the chip fragmentation, and then finds a place for the new task.

Compaction can be either full or partial, depending on whether all allocated tasks are moved, or just a subset of them. Simply, if all running tasks are involved in the compaction process, the compaction is full, otherwise it is partial (El Farag, Hatem, & Shaheen, 2007). Compaction requires the running tasks to be preempted, and then continue its execution at new locations (Thomas, Yi, Koen, & Georgi, 2010). Hence, it is needed to complete the compaction as quickly as possible so as to minimize the waiting and response times of both preempted and waiting tasks. Flowcharts illustrated in Figure 3 (A and B) describe the sequential steps needed for full and partial compactions.

As illustrated in Figure 3 (A), full compaction tries to move all tasks, if possible, to free as more

Figure 3. Compaction strategies (A) full compaction, (B) partial compaction

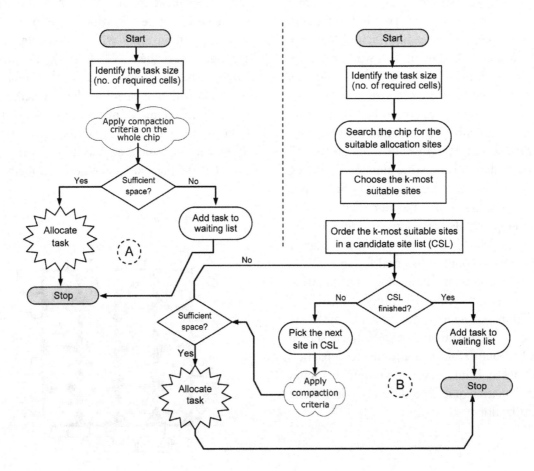

Figure 4. Illustrative example for applying partial and full compaction techniques

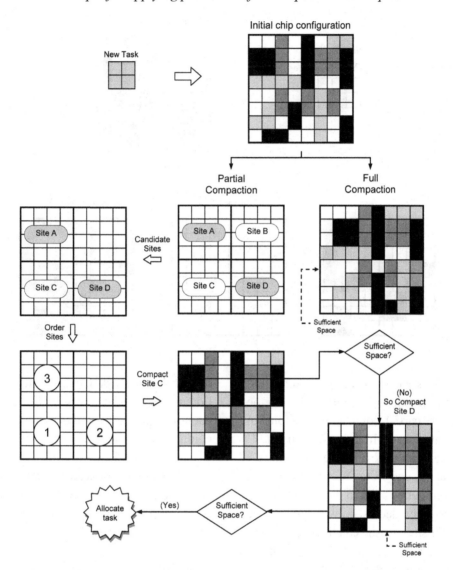

free contiguous area as possible. Hopefully, the freed area can accommodate the newly incoming task. On the other hand, partial compaction, as illustrated in Figure 3 (B), moves some tasks (at least one), to free an area that just fit the new task. Hence, only those tasks that help in the solution are preempted, other running tasks are not disturbed. However, partial compaction consumes more time to test all possible task movements so as to achieve the optimal solution. Moreover, choosing the compaction site (the portion of the

chip that will be compacted) is still a challenge. A more critical drawback of the partial compaction is that it introduces a short-term solution for the current incoming task (El Farag, Hatem, & Shaheen, 2007). It gives no interest to the future incoming tasks or the fragmentations of the reconfigurable area. An illustrative example for applying partial and full compaction techniques is presented in Figure 4.

As illustrated in Figure 4, the full compaction succeeded to find a sufficient free area for hosting

Figure 5. Hosting failure problem in the partial compaction

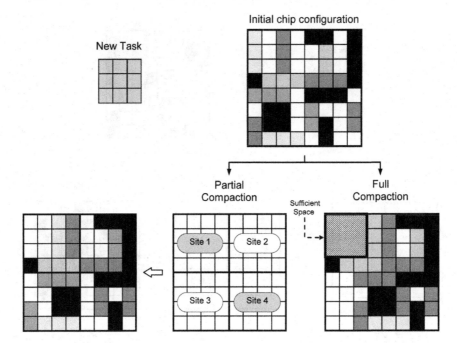

the new task. The strategy used by full compaction here is to shift all chip tasks to the right. On the other hand, the partial compaction is done in several sequential steps. Initially, the chip is divided into a number of sites, denotes as; "Site A", "Site B", "Site C", and "Site D". As the new task needs four contiguous cells to be hosted, hence Site A will be discarded as it owns only 3 free cells. The other sites are the candidate ones. The next step is to arrange the candidate sites in descending order using predefined criteria (the used criteria here is the number of free cells in the site). Partial compaction process is first start with "Site C" as it owns the maximum free cells. Initially "Site C" is virtually compacted (compaction that is done only by calculations). Hopefully, the freed area can accommodate the new task. Unfortunately, compaction fails to generate a sufficient area. Hence, the next candidate site, "Site D" in the example, is virtually compacted. Luckily, the virtual compaction of "Site D" succeeded to generate a sufficient number of contiguous cells

to host the new task. Consequently, the compaction unit decides to compact "Site D" (real compaction in this case), and then the freed area after compaction is allocated to the new task.

As illustrated in Figure 4, full compaction usually produces a wider area for hosting the new incoming task. However, for compacting the whole chip, all running tasks must be suspended. This has a great impact in maximizing not only the waiting time of the new task, but also the response time of the other chip tasks. On the other hand, partial compaction suspends only the tasks hosted inside the chosen site for compaction, while the remaining tasks can continue running.

For the first impression, partial compaction seems to be better than full compaction as it minimizes; (i) the waiting time for the new task, (ii) compaction impact on the response times of chip tasks, and (iii) the number of suspended chip tasks. However, partial compaction suffers from a major drawback, which is the "Hosting Failure" as it may fail to host the incoming task while the full compactions can succeed. Figure 5 illustrates as example for the hosting failure problem. Moreover, choosing the site to be partially compacted is still a challenge.

In spite of its reliability, full compaction usually suffers from high penalty as it not only maximizes the waiting time for the newly incoming task but also increases the response time for all the chip tasks (suspended tasks). The waiting time for the newly incoming task T_i when applying the full compaction (assuming the compaction succeeded to find a sufficient hole for T_i), denoted as $Delay(T_i)_F$, can be calculated using (1) as;

$$Delay(T_i)_F = V\_Comp\_Time(Chip) + Comp\_Time(Chip) + Load\_Time(T_i)$$
(1)

Where; $V\_Comp\_Time(Chip)$ is the time needed to virtually compact the chip (paper and pensile compaction) to determine whether the compaction will success to produce a sufficient area to host T_i or not (if not; the compaction process will discarded), $Comp\_Time(Chip)$ is the actual time needed to carry out the compaction process if the virtual compaction decides that the compaction will success, $load\_Time(T_i)$ is the time needed to load the configuration of T_i. Also, the response time of any suspended task T_s will be increased by R_F, which can be calculated using (2) as;

$$R_F = Comp\_Time(Chip) + Save\_State(T_s) + \mathrm{Re}load(T_s)$$
(2)

On the other hand, partial compaction tries to minimize the compaction penalty by reducing the compacted area. Assuming a reconfigurable chip of n sites is available. The partial compaction is to be applied to $Site_j$ with the aim to find a sufficient area to host task T_i where $j \leq n$. The waiting time for the newly incoming task T_i when applying the partial compaction (assuming $Site_j$ is the first site

that can accommodate T_i after compaction), denoted as $Delay(T_i)_P$, can be calculated using (3) as;

$$Delay(T_i)_P = \sum_{m=1}^{j} V\_Comp\_Time(Site_m) + Comp\_Time(Site_j) + Load\_Time(T_i)$$
(3)

Moreover, the response time of any suspended task T_s located in $Site_j$ will be increased by R_P which can be calculated using (4) as;

$$R_P = Comp\_Time(Site_j) + Save\_State(T_s) + \mathrm{Re}load(T_s)$$
(4)

Parking Man Problem

A good compaction process behaves like the parking man who wishes to utilize the area of the parking place so that to maximize the number of parked vehicles. To establish his aim, a parking man tries to find the best vehicles arrangement. When a vehicle leaves, other vehicles can be rearranged to create a sufficient area to host a new incoming one. Hence, as the parking man tries to maximize the parking place utilization, a good compaction algorithm is the one which maximize the chip area utilization so that it can host concurrently as more tasks as possible.

Figure 6. An example of the internal fragmentations

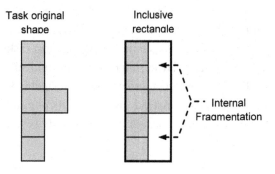

Figure 7. Driver versus parking man behavior compactions

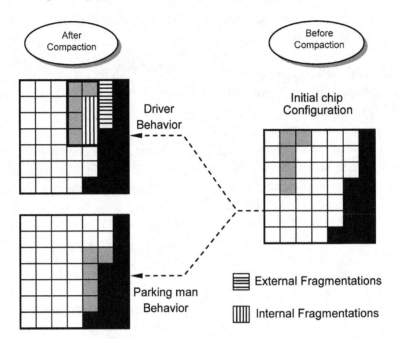

Puzzle based compaction (PBC), proposed in this paper, behaves just like the parking man, while the others behave like car drivers. A driver tries to park his vehicle beside its neighboring ones; however, he is not aware enough of the wasted area between his vehicle and its neighbors. On the other hand, the parking man aims, if he can, to arrange cars in a way that they touch each others.

A good compaction technique is the one that simulates the parking man behavior. Such technique is the one that compacts chip tasks at locations as much as possible touching their prior tasks. To the best of our knowledge, all compaction techniques assume rectangular tasks (Diessel, ElGindy, Middendorf, Schmeck, & Schmidt, 2000; El Farag, Hatem, & Shaheen, 2007; Thomas, Yi, Koen, & Georgi, 2010). However, such assumption is usually invalid as most tasks are non-rectangular in shape. To go around such hurdle, for non-rectangular tasks, the inclusive rectangle is used instead. In spite of its popularity and wide use, this assumption usually results

in internal fragmentations as some area of the inclusive rectangle may get wasted. Figure 6 gives an illustrative example.

Traditional compaction techniques simulate the driver behavior as they assume rectangular tasks. On the other hand, PBC simulates the parking man behavior as it considers the exact task shape instead of its inclusive rectangle. Consequently, PBC introduces the optimal task arrange-

Figure 8. The chip origin and Cell C23

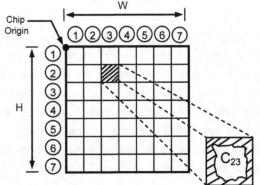

Figure 9. The chip surface face

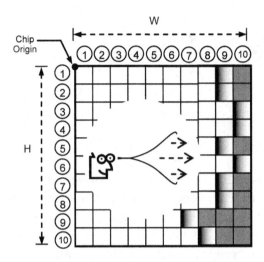

ment during the compaction process as it eliminates external fragmentations. Figure 7 gives an illustration.

RELATED WORK

A lot of work has been done in the placement of incoming tasks into reconfigurable devices such as FPGAs. In Steiger, Walder, and Platzner (2003), two algorithms, namely Horizon and Stuffing, have been introduced. The former arranges the incoming tasks then schedule them only when they do not overlap in both time and space with other scheduled tasks. The latter, on the other hand, schedules arriving tasks to arbitrary future expected free areas by imitating future tasks starts and terminations. Several recent modifications have been introduced on Stuffing algorithm (Chen, & Hsiung, 2003; Marconi, Lu, Bertels, & Gaydadjiev, 2008; Zhou, Wang, Huang, & Peng, 2006; Zhou, Wang, Huang, & Peng, 2007; Marconi, Lu, Bertels, & Gaydadjiev, 2009). However, in spite of using efficient task arrangement and placement techniques, the chip usually suffers from a huge amount of external fragmentations and need to be compacted.

In Diessel, ElGindy, Middendorf, Schmeck, and Schmidt (2000), a new ordered one dimensional compaction (ODC) technique is proposed. It moves some of tasks to one side of the chip with the aim to free the maximum number of contiguous cells. Then, it places the waiting tasks inside the freed area. Initially, ODC constructs a dependency graph, which records sufficient information about all chip running tasks as well as the relative distances between neighboring tasks and chip edges. A list of candidate locations for hosting the newly incoming tasks is constructed, and then the candidate list is searched to decide whether it is possible, with ODC compaction, to host a new task in any of the available locations.

In El Farag, Hatem, and Shaheen (2007), a two dimensional compaction algorithm called

Figure 10. The task shape illustration

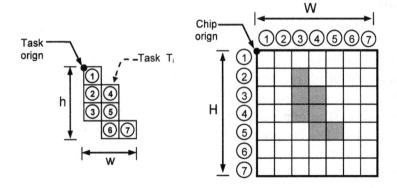

Figure 11. The left and right faces of an arbitrary task

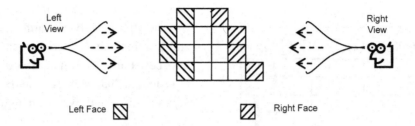

one corner compaction (OCC) has been proposed. OCC tries to shift some of the running tasks towards one of the chip corners to fee as wide area as possible. OCC is also extended by introducing a four corners compaction (FCC) technique (El Farag, Hatem, & Shaheen, 2007). FCC computes the task relative distance with respect to the chip corners, then each task is compacted towards the nearest chip corner.

In Thomas, Yi, Koen, and Georgi (2010), a novel blocking aware algorithm for task scheduling and placement on 2D partially reconfigurable devices has been proposed, which is called 3D compaction (3DC). It assumes a novel 3D total contiguous surface (3DTCS) heuristic, which adds the time as a new direction beside the other two directions of the reconfigurable device. In spite of its awareness of the blocking effect, the 3D compaction assumes the in advance availability of all task information (such as arrival, execution, finish times), which is usually difficult to be guaranteed in real time environments.

SYSTEM MODEL AND BASIC DEFINITIONS

Generally, two main categories of reconfigurable devices can be identified, which are; (i) homogenous and (iii) heterogeneous (Thomas, Yi, Koen, & Georgi, 2010). The former contains only one type of reconfigurable functional unit (cell or block). On the other hand, heterogeneous devices contain more than one type. Although

several heterogeneous devices have been recently emerged, homogenous devices are still the widely used ones. The Xilinx Vertex FPGA and Atmel APEX/ACEX FPGA families are examples of the homogenous devices (Xilinx, 2008). The work in this paper considers the homogenous reconfigurable devices. However, our work could be successfully applied to homogenous portions of heterogeneous reconfigurable devices (Hanad & Vemuri, 2004).

Device Characteristics

An $H \times W$ homogenous partially reconfigurable FPGA chip consists of H rows and W columns of configurable cells arranged as a grid is considered to implement the work in this paper. The upper left corner is the chip origin. The chip can be partially configured, that is any part of the chip can be configured without affecting the rest. We denote the ith row of cells as; Row_i and the jth column of cells as; Col_j. The intersection of Row_i and Col_j

Figure 12. Reading the normalized task face

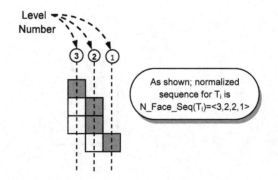

As shown; normalized sequence for T_i is N_Face_Seq(T_i)=<3,2,2,1>

is the cell C_{ij}. These notations are illustrated in Figure 8. Hence, for the chip shown in figure 8, $W=H=7$, and $Address(C_{23})=<2,3>$.

Definition 1: "*Cell Address*"

The address of the cell C_{ij} that lies in the intersection of Row_i and Col_j denoted as; $Address(C_{ij})$, can be represented by an ordered pair $<x,y>$, where $x=i$ and $y=j$.

Definition 2: "*Surface Face*"

The surface face for a reconfigurable chip at time t dented as; S_Face(Chip,t). It is defined as; " the ordered list of H items containing the addresses of all cells lies on the boundary between the compacted and un-compacted portions of the chip ordered from top to down at t". Hence, S_Face(Chip,t)=[Address(C)|∀ C∈ Boundary(Chip compacted portion, Chip un-compacted portion), cells picked from top to down].

Figure 9 shows an illustration to clarify the chip surface face. The surface face for the chip shown in Figure 9 at the current time t_0 can be expressed as; $S\_Face(Chip,t_0)=[<1,9>, <2, 9>, <3,8>, <4,8>, <5, 9>, <6,8>, <7,9>, <8,9>, <9,7>, <10,8>]$.

However, for simplicity, the chip surface face at time *t* can be expressed by an ordered concatenation of *H* numbers organized in an ordered set called Surface Face Sequence, and denoted as; *S_Face_Seq(Chip,t)*. Ordered numbers ∈ *S_Face_Seq(Chip,t)* are the column numbers of the ordered addresses ∈ Face_Seq(Chip,t). For illustration, *S_Face_Seq* of the chip shown in figure 9 at the current time t_0 can be expressed as; *S_Face_Seq(Chip, t_0)=<9, 9, 8, 8, 9, 8, 9, 9, 7, 8>*. Consider definition 3 for more clarification.

Definition 3: "*Surface Face Sequence*"

Surface Face Sequence for the chip at time t, denoted by S_Face_Seq(Chip,t) is an ordered

set of H numbers. Those numbers represent the column numbers (picked in order) of all cell addresses ∈ Face_Seq(Chip,t). Hence, S_Face_Seq(Chip,t)=<Col_j | Col_j is the column number of address(C); ∀ address(C) ∈ Face_Seq(Chip,t), where 1≤j≤H and column numbers are picked in order>.

Task Characteristics

It is assumed that tasks arrive online, queued and placed in the Ready Queue in the order as they have arrived. The task information including size, arrival time, and service time are not known in advance (Figure 10).

Several task parameters are considered, such as; *n* is the number of cells required by the task (task size), *h* is the number of task rows, *w* is the number of task columns. The following definitions present some other task parameters.

Definition 4: "*Task Shape*"

The shape of the task T_i is an ordered list of n items containing the addresses of all T_i cells ordered column by column from left to right. Hence, Shape(T_i)=[Address(C)|∀ C∈ T_i, cells picked column by column from left to right].

One of the attractive features of PBC is considering the exact shape of the task, which is illustrated in definition 4. To put such claim

Figure 13. The vertical movement range if Ti

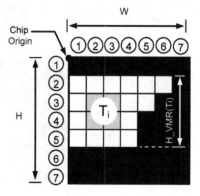

Figure 14. Steps for allocation and de-allocation of FPGA chip

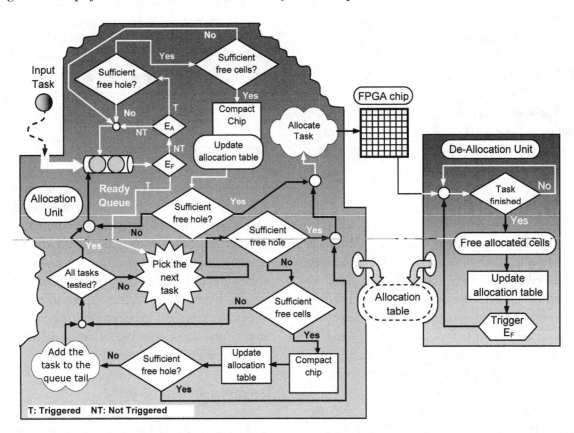

Figure 15. Illustrative example for the task allocation by the allocation unit

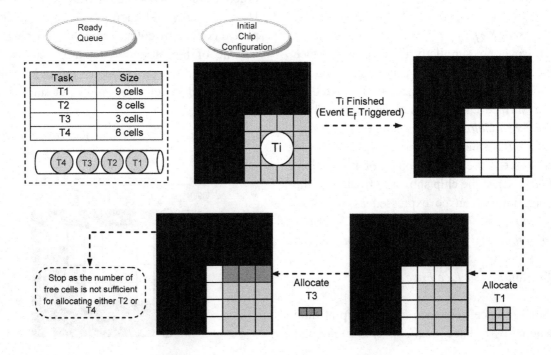

into perspective, consider the task T_i shown in Figure 10. To obtain the shape of T_i, denoted by Shape(T_i), all T_i cells are read in the order shown in Figure 10. Hence, Shape(T_i)=[<2,3>, <3,3>, <4,3>, <3,4>, <4,4>, <5,4>, <5,5>].

In order to minimize external fragmentations, chip tasks must be organized close to each others. To establish such aim, PBC should able to identify the task four faces. The left and right faces of an arbitrary task is shown in Figure 11. However, for simplicity, PBC tries to shift tasks to the right side of the chip, and accordingly, it considers only the right face of the task, which is denoted as; Face(T). Hence, Face(T_i) consists of all the addresses of the right most cells of the task ordered from top to down as depicted in definition 5. For illustration, consider the task T_i shown in Figure 10, Face(T_i)=[<2,3>, <3,4>, <4,4>, <5,5>].

Definition 5: *"Task Face"*

The face of the task T_i is an ordered list of h items containing the addresses of all T_i rightmost cells ordered from top to down. Hence, Face(T_i)=[Address(C)|$\forall$C$\in$ right_most_edge(T_i), cells picked from top to down].

Whenever PBC needs to move a task, it uses the face sequence of the task which is defined as the set of column numbers of those h cells that constitute the task face. For illustration, the face sequence of the task T_i shown in figure 10, denoted as; Face_Seq(T_i)=<3,4,4,5>.

Definition 6: *"Task Face Sequence"*

The face Sequence of the task T_i is an ordered list of h items containing the column numbers of those h cells that constitute the task face. Hence, Face_Seq(T_i)=<Column_number(C)|$\forall$C$\in$ right_most_edge(T_i), cells picked from top to down>.

However, PBC transfers the Face sequence for the task into another form called the normalized face sequence, denoted as N_Face_Seq. For illustration, consider the task T_i shown in

figure 10. While Face_Seq(T_i)=<3,4,4,5>, the corresponding normalized sequence for T_i is then N_Face_Seq(T_i)=<3,2,2,1>. The conversion is done by giving a label for each task column starting from 1 at the right most column, then read the normalized task face from top to down as illustrated in Figure 12.

Definition 7: *"Task Origin"*

The origin of task T_i is the address of its top left cell (denoted as; $C_{TL}(T_i)$), represented as; Origin(T_i)=address[$C_{TL}(T_i)$]=<x_i,y_i>, where x_i is the row number of $C_{TL}(T_i)$ and y_i is the column number of $C_{TL}(T_i)$.

Definition 8: *"Task Vertical Movement Range (VMR)"*

The vertical movement range of task T_i, denoted as; VMR(T_i) is the vertical range of cells in front of the task face in which the task can move through.

PBC tries to arrange the tasks close to each others in the R.H.S of the chip. Hence, it defines a vertical movement range for each movable task as illustrated in definition 8. The vertical movement range of task T_i, denoted as; *VMR(T_i)* defines the vertical range through which T_i can move. This is a critical definition as it may not be possible to move T_i along all the chip height. Some tasks may be blocked and can move within a smaller vertical range. The height of the tasks' VMR, denoted as VMR(Task) denotes the number of rows through which the task can move vertically. Consider task T_i shown in figure 13 in which *VMR(T_i)=[<2,7>, <3,6>, <4,5>, <5,5>], VMR_Seq(T_i)=<7,6,5,5>, and H_VMR(T_i)=4 (which indicates that T_i can move vertically through 4 rows)*.

Finally, prior to the compaction process, an arbitrary task T_i can be expressed as; *T_i=(n_i, h_i, w_i, x_i, y_i, Shape(T_i), Face(T_i), Face_Seq(T_i))*, where, n_i is the task size represented by the number of cells needed by the task, h_i is the task height represented by the number of task rows, w_i is the

Figure 16. The task allocation algorithm used by AU unit

Task Allocation Algorithm

- **Input:** a list L of ready tasks in RQ, L={T_1, T_2, T_3, ...}.
- **Output:** an allocated task list L'.
- **Conditions:** Lists L and L' are continuously updated at run time.
- **Steps:**

For each task $T_m \in L$ **do**
X= Get_Required_Cells(T_m)
L_FI= Get_Free_ Islands(Chip)   // where L_FI is a list of the free islands in the chip.
    For each island $d_k \in L\_FI$ **do**
    L_SFI [k]=Get_Size(L_FI [k]) // where L_SFI is a list storing all sizes of L_FI islands.
    Next
// Choosing the most suitable island for hosting T_m
For i=0 **to** L_FI.length-1
    If $X \le L\_SFI [i]$ **Then** Exit For
Next

If i=L_SFI.length **Then**
Compact_Chip()
// Check if there are suitable island for hosting T_m after compaction
L_FIC=Get_Free_Islands(Chip)
    For each island $d_n \in L\_FIC$ **do**
    L_SFIC [n]=Get_Size(L_FIC [n]) // L_SFIC stores sizes of L_FIC islands after compaction.
    Next
// Choosing the most suitable island for hosting T_m after compaction
For r=0 **to** L_FIC.length-1
    If $X \le L\_SFIC [r]$ **Then** Exit For
Next

If r=L_SFIC.length **Then**
    Inject(T_m, tail(RQ))
    Go to OUT
End if

// The first candidate allocation for T_m after compaction (first fit hole).
S=L_SFIC [r]   // S is the size of the allocated hole.
Location=r

// Search for the best fit hole after compaction for hosting T_m.
For j=r+1 **to** L_FIC.length-1
    If $X \le L\_SFIC [j]$ **AND** $S > L\_SFIC[j]$ **Then**
        S=L_SFIC [j]
        Location=j
        Allocate(T_m, L_FIC [location])
        Remove(T_m, RQ)
        Add(T_m, L')
        Update(allocation_Table)
        Go to out
    End if
Next
End if

// The first candidate allocation for T_m with no compaction (first fit hole).
S= L_SFI [i]
Location=i

// Search for the best fit hole with no compaction for hosting T_m.
For j=i+1 **to** L_FI.length-1
    If $X \le L\_SFI [j]$ **AND** $S > L\_SFI[j]$ **Then**
        S=L_SFI [j]
        Location=j
    End if
Next
Allocate(T_m, L_FI [location])
Remove(T_m, RQ)
Add(T_m, L')
Update(allocation_Table)
Out: **Next**

Figure 17. The puzzle based compaction algorithm used by AU unit

Puzzle Based Compaction Algorithm

- **Input:**
    - A reconfigurable chip with *n* active tasks.
    - A list X with *n* active tasks X={T$_i$| T_i =(n$_i$, h$_i$, w$_i$, x$_i$, y$_i$, Shape(T$_i$), Face(T$_i$), Face_Seq(T$_i$)), 1≤i≤n}

- **Output:**
    - A compacted list Y with *n* active tasks;
      Y={T$_q$| T_q =(n$_q$, h$_q$, w$_q$, x$'_q$, y$'_q$, Shape$'$(T$_q$), Face$'$(T$_q$), Face_Seq$'$(T$_q$)), 1≤q≤n}

- **Steps:**
    1. Identify the movable tasks set (MTS) at time *t as;*
       MTS(t)={ T_i| T_i can move in one or more directions *m* cells, m≥1, 0≤i≤n}
    2. If *MTS.length=0* then Exit Compaction
    3. For each task T_i ∈ *MTS* do
       3.1. Identify VMR(T$_i$)
       3.2. Find VMR_Seq(T$_i$).
       3.3. Divide VMR_Seq(T$_i$) into H_VMR(T$_i$)- h$_i$ +1 sequential sequences (Matching Patterns) and store sequences in set S, where;
          - S={S$_j$| 1≤j≤ (H_VMR(T$_i$)- h$_i$ +1)}
          - S$_j$=<s$_{1j}$, s$_{2j}$, s$_{3j}$, ..., s$_{hj}$>
          - Face_Seq(T$_i$)= <y$_{1i}$, y$_{2i}$, y$_{3i}$ ...., y$_{hi}$>
       3.4. Find the N_Face_Seq(T$_i$)
       3.5. Find N_S$_j$ ∀ S$_j$ ∈ S, where N_S$_j$ is the normalized sequence for S$_j$, then store normalized sequences in set N_S.
       3.6. Find Ext_Frag(N_Face_Seq(T$_i$), N_S$_j$) ∀ N_S$_j$ ∈ N_S
       3.7. $$S_{op} = \operatorname*{arg\,min}_{\forall N\_S_j \in N\_S} \left[Ext\_Frag\left(N\_Face\_Seq(T_m), N\_S_j \right) \right]$$
       3.8. Use S$_{op}$ to park T$_i$
       3.9. Add T$_i$ to set Y.
    4. Next

task width represented by the number of task columns, x_i is the row number of $C_{TL}(T_i)$, and y_i is the column number of $C_{TL}(T_i)$.

Chip tasks are re-locatable. Hence, an arriving task T_i can be placed at any sufficient free area within the reconfigurable device. Moreover, T_i can be suspended, moved to another free location, and then resumed again. Tasks arrive asynchronously in which the tasks service times are a priori unknown. For the task that arrives at time t_{ai}, starts at t_{si}, finishes at t_{fi} and has been suspended R times, the waiting time for T_i, denoted as; *wait*(T$_i$) can be calculated using (5) as;

$$wait(T_i) = t_{si} - t_{ai} + \sum_{j=1}^{R} Susp_j(T_i) \qquad (5)$$

Where $Susp_j(T_i)$ is the jth suspend interval of T_i. On the other hand, the response time of T_i can be calculated as; $\operatorname{Re} sp(T_i) = t_{fi} - t_{ai}$.

In spite of its effectiveness, task relocation may also involve some difficulties. Not only the wires between tasks and I/Os, but also the inter-task wires must be dynamically re-routed. However, PBC assumes that chip tasks are independent with no onboard communication. Moreover, re-routing wires among tasks and chip I/Os is outside the scope of this paper.

THE PROPOSED PUZZLE BASED COMPACTION (PBC) TECHNIQUE

The primary aim of the PBC is to maximize the degree of utilization of the reconfigurable chip, which is defined in Definition 9.

Definition 9: *"Degree of utilization of the reconfigurable chip"*

The degree of utilization of a reconfigurable chip at time t_i is defined as the number of running (active) tasks at t_i.

As illustrated in Figure 14, the system operations are involved into two main functional units, namely; (i) Allocation Unit (AU), and (ii) De-allocation Unit (DAU). The former tries to host the newly incoming tasks into the chip whenever possible, while the later immediately frees the set of allocated chip cells whose owner tasks have finished.

Incoming tasks are queued in a Ready Queue (RQ) as they arrive. On the other hand, AU attempts to find a sufficient space for the next task in RQ (i.e., find a set of contiguous cells sufficient

Figure 18. The reconfigurable chip used for the illustrative example

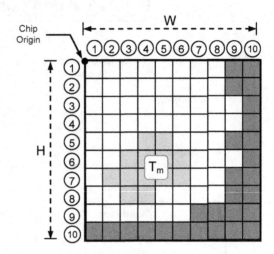

to host the new task). An allocation table is used to mirror both the location and allocated cells (and accordingly the shape) of each active task. It is continuously updated by both allocation and de-allocation units whenever a task enters or leaves the chip.

AU is triggered by two different events which are; (i) Task arrival (E_A) and (ii) Task Finish (E_F).

Table 1. The used Items and Abbreviations used by the task allocation algorithm

Item	Description
RQ	Ready Queue
L	List of ready tasks in RQ
L'	List containing all allocated tasks (tasks currently running inside the chip).
X	Size (no. of cells)of the current task.
Get_Required_Cells()	Returns the task size (no. of needed cells).
L_FI	A list of chip Free Islands.
Get_Free_Islands()	Searches the allocation table for free islands (hole) within the chip.
L_SFI	A list containing sizes of all islands $\in$ L_FI.
L_FIC	A list of chip Free Islands after compaction.
L_SFIC	A list containing sizes of all islands $\in$ L_FIC.
VMR(T_i)	The vertical movement range of task T_i.
VMR_Seq(T_i)	The ordered column numbers of each cell $\in$ VMR(T_i)
H_VMR(T_i)	The height of VMR(T_i), which represents the number of rows through which T_i can vertically move.

Figure 19. The amount of external fragmentations created by each normalized sequence

Matching pattern (Normalized sequence)	N_Face_Seq(T_m)	Amount of external fragmentations
<2,2,1,1>	<2,1,1,3>	Offset=1  Ext. Fragmentations=[0+(-1)+0+2]+4*1=5
<2,1,1,2>	<2,1,1,3>	Offset=0  Ext. Fragmentations=[0+0+0+1]+4*0=1
<1,1,2,1>	<2,1,1,3>	Offset=1 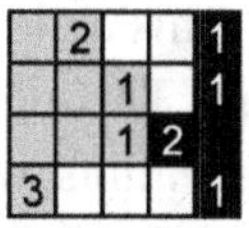 Ext. Fragmentations=[1+0+(-1)+2]+4*1=6
<1,2,1,2>	<2,1,1,3>	Offset=1  Ext. Fragmentations=[1+(-1)+0+1]+4*1=5
<2,1,2,2>	<2,1,1,3>	Offset=1  Ext. Fragmentations=[0+0+(-1)+1]+4*1=4
<1,2,2,4>	<2,1,1,3>	Offset=1  Ext. Fragmentations=[1+(-1)+(-1)+(-1)]+4*1=2

The former (i.e., E_A) is fired whenever a new task arrives. It triggers AU to scan the chip for a free hole sufficient enough to host a new task from RQ. This has a great impact in decreasing the waiting time of the incoming task if there exists a free hole sufficient to host it and accordingly eliminates the convoy effect. Hence, small tasks do not have to wait for the bigger ones to finish even if those bigger tasks come first. Clearly, this intelligent behavior of the allocation unit guarantees the maximum chip utilization as it utilizes any available free area. Moreover, AU behavior impacts well the system performance as it minimizes the average waiting time of an input group of tasks. Hence, AU uses the First Suitable First Serviced (FSFS) as a scheduling criteria. On the other hand, E_F is fired when a task terminates. It triggers AU to pick a suitable task from RQ to be packed into the chip. AU then checks the tasks in the order as they had arrived. However, after allocating the task at the head of the RQ (even if it failed to allocate it), AU tries to allocate more tasks. It tests then the remaining tasks in the RQ with the aim to allocate as much tasks as possible in the freed space. Consider the illustration in Figure 15.

Hence, before compacting the chip, the allocation table is checked to know whether there are sufficient numbers of non-contagious cells for hosting the new task. This action avoids the unnecessary compactions. The allocation unit employs two different algorithms, which are; (i) task allocation algorithm for the purpose of hosting a new task into the chip, and (ii) puzzle based compaction algorithm for compacting the chip whenever needed. Those algorithms are illustrated in Figure 16 and Figure 17 respectively. Table 1 lists the used terminologies as well as the abbreviations used by both algorithms.

To clarify how the puzzle based compaction algorithm works, consider the reconfigurable chip shown in Figure 18, which has $H=W=10$ and the current S_Face_Seq=<9,9,10,10,9,10,9,9,7,1>. Consider also the task $T_m=(n_m, h_m, w_m, x_m, y_m,$

Table 2. Different parameters of task T_m

Parameters	Description
n_m	13
h_m	4
w_m	5
x_m	6
y_m	2
Shape(T_m)	[<7,2>, <6,3>, <7,3>, <8,3>, <5,4>, <6,4>, <7,4>, <8,4>, <5,5>, <6,5>, <7,5>, <6,6>, <7,6>]
Face(T_m)	[<5,5>, <6,6>, <7,6>, <8,4>]
Face_Seq(T_m)	<5,6,6,4>

$Shape(T_m)$, $Face(T_m)$, $Face\_Seq(T_m)$) with parameters shown in Table 2.

Also $VMR(T_m)$ =[<1,9>, <2,9>, <3,10>, <4,10>, <5,9>, <6,10>, <7,9>, <8,9>, <9,7>], H_VMR(T_m)=9, and VMR_Seq(T_m)=<9,9,10,10,9,10,9,9,7>, which can be divided into H_VMR(T_m)-h_m+1=9-4+1=6 sequences that are called the "matching patterns", denoted as S_1, S_2, ..., S_6, and stored in the set S as depicted in table with the corresponding normalized sequences that are stored in the set N_S.

The normalized task face sequence N_Face_Seq(T_m)=<2,1,1,3> is now compared with each normalized sequence N_S$_j \in$ N_S in order to find the most similar sequence, which is called the "optimal sequence" S_{op}. The optimal sequence is the one which represents the minimal external fragmentations when it is used to park T_m, which is mathematically described in definition 10.

Definition 10: *"The Optimal Sequence S_{op}"*

For a task T_m with height h and Face_Seq(T_m)=$<y_{1m}, y_{2m}, ..., y_{hm}>$ and a set of matching patterns (Normalized Sequences) N_S= {N_S$_j$ | $1 \leq j \leq (H\_VMR(T_j)- h_i +1)$}, N_S_j=$<s_{1j}, s_{2j}, ..., s_{hm}>$. The optimal sequence for parking task T_m, denoted by $S_{op} \in N\_S$, which gives the minimal external fragmentations if it is used to park T_m, and can be calculated as;

$$S_{op} = \underset{\forall N\_S_j \in N\_S}{\arg\min}\left[Ext\_Frag\left(N\_Face\_Seq(T_m), N\_S_j\right)\right]$$

Where, Ext_Frag(N_Face_Seq(T_m), N_S$_j$) is the amount of external fragmentations that will be generated when using the sequence N_S$_j \in$ N_S to park task T_m, N_Face_Seq(T_m) is the normalized face sequence for task T_m, and N_S$_j \in$ N_S is the normalized sequence for the sequence S$_j \in$ S.

It is clear that S_{op} is the best place to park T_m as it introduces the minimal area lost in external fragmentations. For illustration, consider again

Figure 20. The considered shapes for task sizes of 2, 3, and 4 cells

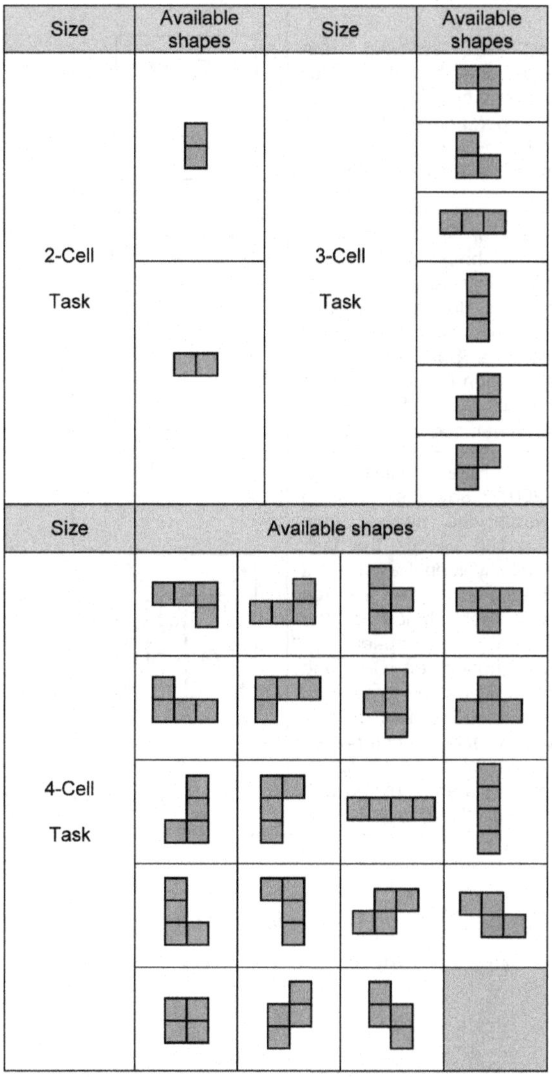

Table 3. Different sequences for VMR_Seq(T_m)

Sequence	Description	Normalized Sequence
S_1	<9,9,10,10>	<2,2,1,1>
S_2	<9,10,10,9>	<2,1,1,2>
S_3	<10,10,9,10>	<1,1,2,1>
S_4	<10,9,10,9>	<1,2,1,2>
S_5	<9,10,9,9>	<2,1,2,2>
S_6	<10,9,9,7>	<1,2,2,4>

the task T_m shown in Figure 18 with parameters illustrated in Table 2, and the set of matching patterns shown in Table 3. For finding the best place for parking T_m, the external fragmentations generated by parking T_m using each pattern "sequence" is first calculated, then the location that gives the minimal amount of external fragmentations is used to park T_m.

For calculating the amount of external fragmentations generated when using the sequence S_j $=<s_{1j}, s_{2j}, s_{3j}, ..., s_{hj}>$ to park task T with Face sequence $Face\_Seq(T)=<y_1, y_2, y_3, ..., y_h>$ with height h can be calculated by first normalizing both S_j and $Face\_Seq(T)$ to get $N\_S_j=<n\_s_1, n\_s_2, n\_s_3, ..., n\_s_h>$ and $N\_Face\_Seq(T) =<n\_y_1, n\_y_2, n\_y_3, ...,n\_y_h>$, then use (6).

$$Ext\_Frag(N\_Face\_Seq(T), N\_S_j) = \sum_{i=1}^{h}(n\_y_i - n\_s_{ij}) + h * Offset \quad (6)$$

Where;

$$Offset = \left| Min(n\_y_i - n\_s_{ij}) \right|$$
$$\forall n\_y_i \in N\_Face\_Seq(T) \ and \ n\_s_{ij} \in N\_S_j$$

Returning to task T_m shown in Table 2, finding the best location for parking T_m with N_Face_Seq(T_m)=<2,1,1,3> can be carried out by calculating the amount of external fragmentations generated when trying to park T_m using each normalized sequence shown in Table 3, then use the one which gives the minimal amount of external fragmentations. Calculating the amount of external fragmentations created by each normalized sequence is carried out with graphical notions in Figure 19.

EXCREMENTAL RESULTS

Through the experiments introduced in the next subsections, we assume a chip size of WxH where

Figure 21. Different competitors used in the next experiments

Compaction Technique	Category	Description	Implementation
One Dimensional Compaction (ODC)	One Dimensional	ODC tries to compact the reconfigurable chip by shifting all tasks towards one chip side. Through the next experiments, ODC is implemented by shifting tasks towards the right side of the chip.	
One Corner Compaction (OCC)	Two Dimensional	The philosophy of OCC is to move chip tasks in both vertical and horizontal directions towards one of the chip corners (top-right, top-left, bottom-right, or bottom-left) (El Farag, Hatem, & Shaheen, 2007). The implementation of this technique is carried out by shifting tasks towards the top-left corner)	
Four Corners Compaction (FCC)		In FCC (El Farag, Hatem, & Shaheen, 2007), any task can be shifted towards the nearest chip corners according. Hence the task location is initially identified, then it can be immediately shifted towards the nearest corner. Hence, as the chip has four corners; top-left C_{TL}, top-right C_{TR}, bottom-left C_{BL}, and bottom-right C_{BR}, all tasks are tested at first then divided into four groups. Finally, each group is compacted towards its nearest corner in which relative distances are calculated with respect to the selected corner.	

W=100 and H=100. Task sizes (number of cells) are randomly generated in the range [2→10], then a random shape is picked for the task from the available shapes based on the task size. Considered shapes for task sizes of 2, 3, and 4 cells are shown in Figure 20. Also, tasks execution times as well as tasks deadlines are randomly generated in the ranges [10→100] and [100→500] unit times respectively. Tasks arrival times are also randomly generated within the time test period.

Competitors

In this section, recent compaction techniques will be introduced for the purpose of comparing the proposed PBC against them. Generally, commonly used compaction techniques lie under two

Figure 22. Chip utilization for the different compaction techniques

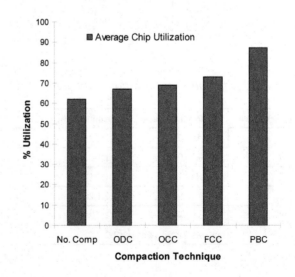

Figure 23. The percentage of AWT decrement compared with the "no compaction"

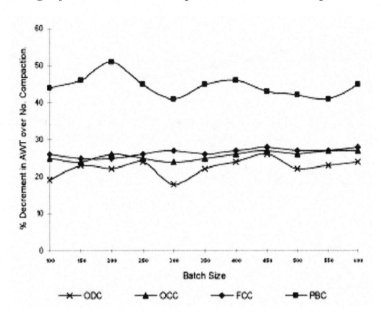

broad categories, which are; (i) one dimensional compaction, and (ii) two dimensional compaction. Figure 21, illustrates the different compaction techniques used in the next experiments. All those techniques as will as PBC try to find a sufficient area for the newly incoming task by employing the whole chip area in the compaction process (full compaction).

Experiment 1: Measuring System Performance

In this experiment, the average waiting time, average response time, overall execution time, and chip utilization are measured for a set of input batches. Each batch contains a group of tasks [100→600] with different sizes [2→10] cells, arrival and execution times [10→100] unit times. Initially the chip is filled with randomly generated tasks with different shapes, execution times, and locations. Then the input batches are allowed to enter the chip sequentially one after the other. For each batch, several parameters are measured using each compaction technique such as Average Waiting Time (AWT), Average

Response Time (ART), and chip utilization. The newly incoming batch task will take the shape of the freed hole if the compaction technique has succeeded to find a sufficient hole to host it. The reconfiguration delay per cell was fixed to 0.001 time units [20]. The average waiting time *AWT* for all techniques is measured assuming the first task arrives at time 0 using the batch *Batch$_j$* of *n* tasks using (7).

$$AWT(Batch_j) = \frac{\sum_{i=1}^{n} wait(T_i)}{n}$$

$$AWT(Batch_j) =$$
$$\frac{\sum_{i=1}^{n}\left(t_{si} - t_{ai} + \sum_{m=1}^{R} Susp_m(T_i)\right)}{n} \qquad (7)$$

Where t_{si} is the time in which task T_i starts execution, t_{ai} is the time in which task T_i arrives, R is the number of times in which T_i was suspended for reconfiguration, and $Susp_j(T)$ is the jth suspend interval of T_i. On the other hand, the

Figure 24. The percentage of ART decrement compared with the "no compaction"

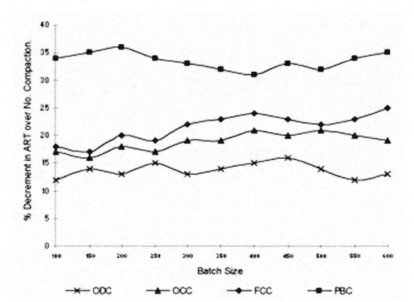

Figure 25. The number of utilized cells for each input batch

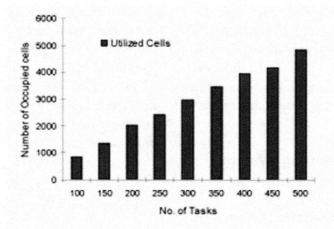

average response time *ART* of batch *Batch$_j$* can be calculated by (8).

$$ART(Batch_j) = \frac{\sum_{i=1}^{n}\left(t_{fi} - t_{ai}\right)}{n} \quad (8)$$

The overall execution time of *Batch$_j$* of *n* tasks, denoted as; *OET(Batch$_j$)=max(t$_{fi}$)∀ 1≤i≤n*. Finally the chip utilization for *Batch$_j$={T$_1$, T$_2$, ..., T$_n$}* of *n* tasks can be calculated by (9).

$$Chip\_Utilization(Batch_j) = \frac{\sum_{i=1}^{n}\left[Size(T_i) * \left(t_{fi} - t_{ai}\right)\right]}{OET(Batch_j) * H * W} * 100 \quad (9)$$

The average chip utilization for a set of B batches using different compaction techniques can be calculated by (10).

$$Avg\_Chip\_Utilization = \frac{\sum_{i=1}^{B} Chip\_Utilization(Batch_i)}{B} \quad (10)$$

During executing the batch tasks, as soon as a new task arrives, the chip is checked for a sufficient area for hosting the new task. If no sufficient area for the new task, the chip has to be compacted. When a task finishes its execution, the freed area is then checked if it is wide enough to host any waiting task, otherwise the chip is compacted to free more area. The operation continued until all batch tasks have been executed. For simplicity, real time tasks were not considered here, hence throughout this experiment, tasks are assumed to have no deadlines.

As PBC maximizes the number of running tasks, the chip is highly utilized as depicted in Figure 22. The chip utilization reaches 87% for PBC, while it reaches only 74% for FCC, which is the nearest competitor. In Figure 23, PBC can reach a decrement in the waiting time over the "no compaction" up to 52%. In Figure 24, PBC can reach a decrement in the response time over the "no compaction" up to 37%.

Hence, as depicted in Figure 22, Figure 23, and Figure 24, PBC outperforms all other compaction techniques as it minimizes both the average waiting and response times for an input batch of *n* tasks. Also, it maximizes the chip utilization.

Experiment 2: Measuring Fragmentations and Free Cells after Compaction

In this experiment a set of batches are formulated in which each batch consists of a number of tasks [100 →500] of different sizes and shapes. Each batch is separately allowed to enter the chip (assuming the chip able to host all batch tasks) in which different batch tasks are randomly hosted inside the chip. The number of utilized cells for

Figure 26. The amount of free cells after compaction for different techniques

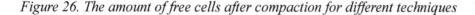
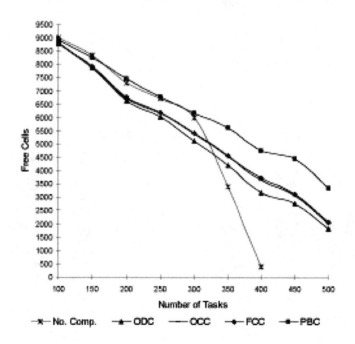

Figure 27. The amount of fragmentations after compaction for different techniques

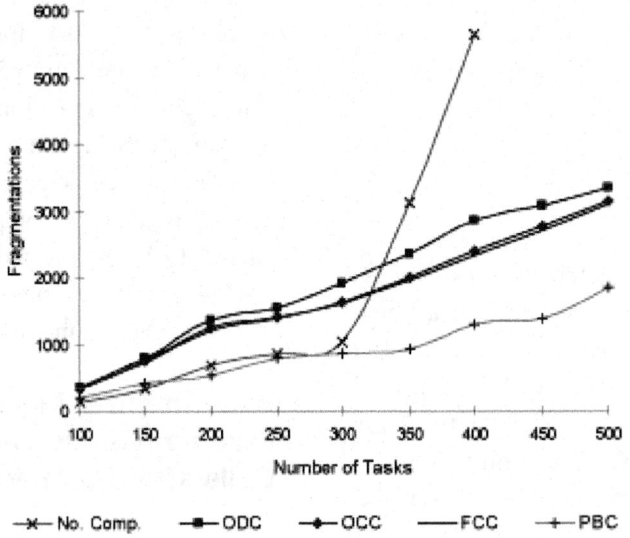

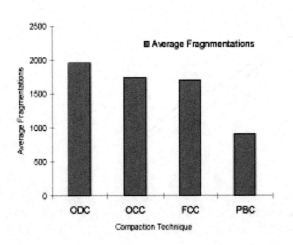

each input batch is illustrated in Figure 25. After hosting the batch tasks, different compaction techniques are applied, and then the number of fragmentations (internal and external) as well as the amount of contiguous free cells is calculated for each compaction technique. The best technique is the one that introduces the minimum fragmentations and accordingly the maximum amount of

contiguous free cells after compaction; results are illustrated in Table 4.

As depicted in Figure 26 and Figure 27, PBC introduced the minimal amount of fragmentations, and accordingly the maximum amount of contiguous free cells after compaction. This happened because PBC has no internal fragmentations. The source of fragmentations in PBC is due to the

Figure 28. The average amount of fragmentations for different techniques

Figure 29. The average free cells for different techniques

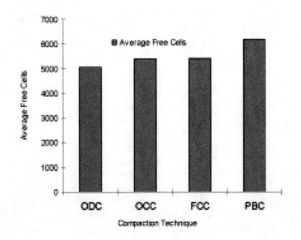

Table 4. Different amount of fragmentations and free cells generated by compaction techniques

Technique		Batch size (number of tasks in each batch)								
		100	150	200	250	300	350	400	450	500
No Compaction	Frag.s	123	321	691	862	1024	3121	5654	Can't be hosted	
	Free Cells	9006	8336	7290	6708	5995	3407	393		
ODC	Frag.s	341	789	1352	1543	1922	2341	2859	3072	3350
	Free Cells	8788	7868	6629	6027	5097	4187	3188	2764	1821
OCC	Frag.s	322	751	1261	1412	1623	1995	2394	2773	3142
	Free Cells	8807	7906	6720	6158	5396	4533	3653	3063	2029
FCC	Frag.s	334	734	1212	1390	1594	1961	2324	2709	3097
	Free Cells	8795	7923	6769	6180	5425	4567	3723	3127	2074
PBC	Frag.s	203	412	532	792	860	915	1302	1394	1842
	Free Cells	8926	8245	7449	6778	6159	5613	4745	4442	3329
Utilized Cells		871	1343	2019	2430	2981	3472	3953	4164	4829

external fragmentations only, which have been minimized by considering the exact shape of the task. On the other hand, fragmentations in other techniques are due to both internal and external fragmentations.

Again considering Table 4, without compaction, the chip starts with a small amount of fragmentations as tasks are added in random locations in the way that they are similar to isolated islands inside the chip. This results in a very small amount of external fragmentations and a huge amount of contiguous cells, fragmentations here are due to internal ones only. However, the chip able to host 437 tasks only. It fails to host more tasks because of the exponential increase in the amount of fragmentations with the addition of new tasks. On the other hand, although compaction introduces a huge amount of contiguous cells, it also results in a fast appearance of external fragmentations. Hence, other techniques (i.e., ODC, ODC, FDC, and PBC) suffer from a greater amount of fragmentations than "no compaction" at the beginning as illustrated in Figure 36. On the other hand, PBC introduces the minimal amount of fragmentations.

The average amount of free cells as well as the average amount of fragmentations for each compaction technique using n batches can be calculated using (11) and (12) respectively. Moreover, graphical representations are illustrated in Figure 28 and Figure 29 respectively. Detailed data are also shown in Table 5.

$$Average\_Free\_Cells = \frac{\sum_{i=1}^{n} Free\_Cells(Batch_i)}{n} \quad (11)$$

$$Average\_Fragmentations = \frac{\sum_{i=1}^{n} Fragmentations(Batch_i)}{n} \quad (12)$$

Table 5. Average amount of fragmentations and free cells for different compaction techniques

	ODC	OCC	FDC	PBC
Average Fragmentations	1952.121	1741.437	1706.189	916.8289
Average Free Cells	5041	5362.748	5398.241	6187.463

Figure 30. Loss factor for different compaction techniques

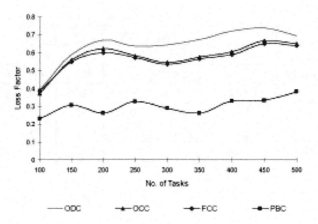

Another parameter that mirrors the chip utilization is the loss factor, which is the ratio between the amount of fragmentations and the utilized cells. The loss factor for each compaction technique can be calculated for each batch of the n input batches using (13). Results are illustrated in Table 6 and Figure 30.

$$Loss\_Factor(Batch_i) = \frac{Fragmentations(Batch_i)}{Occupied\_Cells(Batch_i)} \quad (13)$$

Then the average loss factor for each compaction technique considering the n batches can be calculated using (14). A graphical description is also illustrated in Figure 31.

$$Average\_Loss\_Factor = \frac{\sum_{i=1}^{n} Fragmentations(Batch_i)}{\sum_{i=1}^{n} Occupied\_Cells(Batch_i)} \Bigg/ n \quad (14)$$

Again, as PBC minimizes the amount of fragmentations, it introduced the minimal loss factor as illustrated in Figure 32 and Figure 33.

Figure 31. Average loss factor for different compaction techniques

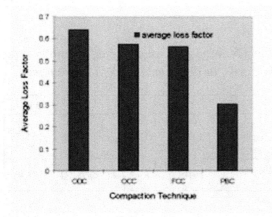

Figure 32. Measuring the system reliability when using different compaction techniques

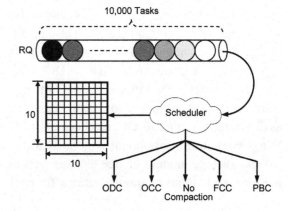

Figure 33. Number of succeeded tasks when using different compaction techniques

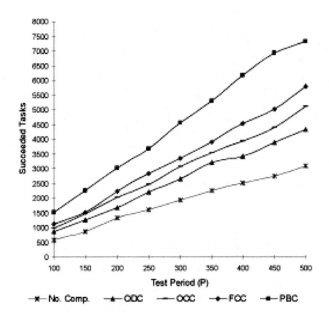

Table 6. The loss factor for each compaction technique

Technique	Batch size (number of tasks in each batch)								
	100	**150**	**200**	**250**	**300**	**350**	**400**	**450**	**500**
ODC	0.391504	0.587491	0.669638	0.634979	0.64475	0.674251	0.723248	0.737752	0.693725
OCC	0.36969	0.559196	0.624567	0.58107	0.544448	0.574597	0.605616	0.665946	0.650652
FCC	0.383467	0.546538	0.600297	0.572016	0.53472	0.564804	0.587908	0.650576	0.641334
PBC	0.233065	0.306776	0.263497	0.325926	0.288494	0.263537	0.32937	0.334774	0.381445

Table 7. TSTF and TFTF form different compaction techniques

Technique		Test Period P (measured in unit times)								
		100	**150**	**200**	**250**	**300**	**350**	**400**	**450**	**500**
No Compaction	TSTF	573	854	1321	1604	1931	2252	2513	2750	3092
	TFTF	9427	9146	8679	8396	8069	7748	7487	7250	6908
ODC	TSTF	849	1258	1674	2198	2643	3217	3411	3876	4321
	TFTF	9151	8742	8326	7802	7357	6783	6589	6124	5679
OCC	TSTF	983	1475	2014	2460	3061	3532	3931	4392	5125
	TFTF	9017	8525	7986	7540	6939	6468	6069	5608	4875
FCC	TSTF	1115	1519	2231	2831	3353	3912	4544	5025	5781
	TFTF	8885	8481	7769	7169	6647	6088	5456	4975	4219
PBC	TSTF	1503	2252	3021	3683	4559	5309	6167	6931	7314
	TFTF	8497	7748	6979	6317	5441	4691	3833	3069	2686

Table 8. The average number of active tasks for different compaction techniques

Technique	Test Period P (measured in unit time τ)																		
	100	150	200	250	300	350	400	450	500	550	600	650	700	750	800	850	900	950	1000
No Comp.	341	331	329	334	343	349	351	342	331	325	321	332	341	352	339	342	349	310	281
ODC	502	492	499	510	507	513	521	517	507	505	510	499	511	503	481	445	421	400	371
OCC	590	593	601	611	607	602	594	599	612	617	621	601	592	533	500	471	441	417	391
FCC	671	664	679	682	673	689	679	662	681	692	687	681	615	582	517	481	452	415	402
PBC	912	897	901	892	903	889	892	887	895	810	727	662	613	573	533	502	472	443	421

Figure 34. The number of failed tasks when using different compaction techniques

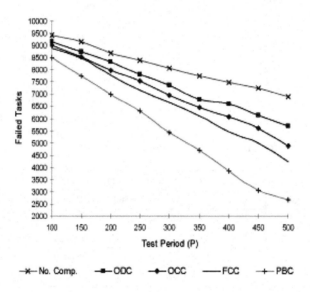

Experiment 3: Measuring System Reliability

Another important parameter that needs to be measured is the system reliability. The system reliability can be maximized by running as much tasks as possible this not only maximizes the chip utilization but also minimizes the number of tasks that may fail to finish its execution during the test period. In this experiment, as illustrated in Figure 32, a set of 10,000 tasks are prepared with random sizes [2→10] cells, shapes, and execution times [10→100] unit times. No deadlines are considered in this experiment. All tasks are assumed to be ready at time 0. Initially, the chip is randomly

Figure 35. The average succeeded tasks when using different compaction techniques

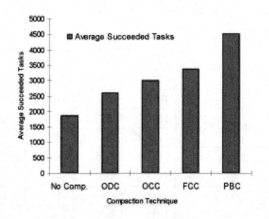

Figure 36. The average number of active tasks for different compaction techniques

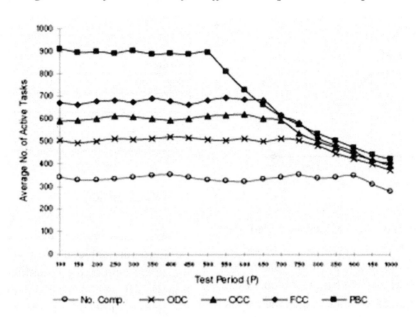

filled with a set of the available tasks (load as much tasks as possible until the chip is filled). PBC considers the exact shape of the task while other techniques use the inclusive rectangle for non-rectangular tasks. Then different compaction techniques compete to finish as much tasks as possible during an arbitrary test periods P[100 → 500] unit times. Again the reconfiguration delay per cell was fixed to 0.001 time units [20]. The number of tasks succeeded to finish (TSTF) as well as the number of tasks failed to finish (TFTF) are calculated for each compaction technique using different test periods. Results are illustrated in Table 7.

Figure 33 and Figure 34 illustrate respectively TSTF and TFTF when employing each compaction technique (as well as the "no compaction") using different test periods. The average TSTF for each compaction technique is also illustrated in Figure 35. Considering Figure 33, Figure 34 and Figure 35, it is clearly approved that PBC introduces the maximal TSTF and accordingly the minimal TFTF.

Experiment 4: Measuring the Average Number of Active Tasks

Using the same parameters as in experiment 3, a set of 10,000 tasks are prepared with random sizes [2→10] cells, shapes, and execution times [10→100] unit times. All tasks are assumed to be ready at time 0. The average number of active tasks is calculated for different compaction techniques. Using different test periods (measured in unit time τ, in τ=100 milliseconds) P∈[100 →1000], for each compaction technique, the number of active tasks is calculated every 10 τ, then the average number of active tasks is calculated for the entire period. Figure 36 and Table 8 illustrate the results, which prove that PBC can successfully manage the chip area for hosting more active tasks compared with other compaction techniques. This property improves the chip utilization and also reduces both the tasks response and waiting times.

As illustrated in Figure 36, for each compaction technique, the curve representing the number of the active tasks can be divided into two regions, which are; (i) steady region, and (ii) attenuation region, which are illustrated in Figure 37. The

Figure 37. The critical point notion

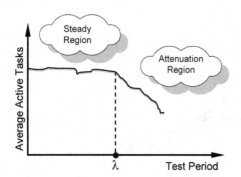

Table 9. Critical point for each compaction technique

Compaction Technique	λ
No Comp.	≈ 920
ODC	≈ 780
OCC	≈ 740
FCC	≈ 670
PBC	≈ 540

point separates the two regions is called the critical point, which is denoted as λ. It can be proved that the compaction technique that introduces the minimal λ is the best technique, as it can serve the input tasks quickly, then the chip is freed in less time. Table 9 shows the value of λ for different compaction techniques.

FUTURE WORK

The work in this paper is a "One Side Puzzle based Compaction" (OSPC) as it shifts all the active processes to the right to free as much as possible area in the left side of the chip. However, OSPC can be extended shift some of the active tasks to the right while the others are shifted to the left to free as much area as possible in the chip center. The new technique can be called then "Two Sides Puzzle based Compaction" (TSPC). Figure 38 gives an illustration.

CONCLUSION

Today's reconfigurable resources, especially the field-programmable gate arrays (FPGAs), increase in size and complexity. Accordingly, several operational hurdles should be handled carefully such as the placement of incoming tasks. However, even with the careful task placement, portions of chip area may be wasted due to internal and external fragmentations. Hence, to take full advantage of the partially reconfigurable fabric, the use of efficient compaction techniques becomes a must. This paper introduces a novel compaction technique called Puzzle Based Compaction (PBC). PBC introduced the minimal amount of fragmentations. This happened because PBC has no internal fragmentations. The source of fragmentations in PBC is due to the external fragmentations only, which have been minimized by considering the exact shape of the task. On the other hand, to the best of our knowledge, fragmentations in all other

Figure 38. Two sides versus one side puzzle based compaction

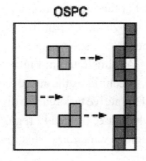

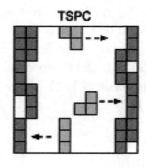

compaction techniques are due to both internal and external fragmentations.

The contributions of this paper can be summarized as; (i) developing a novel formula not to estimate, but to exactly calculate the amount of external fragmentations generated by accommodating a set of tasks inside the reconfigurable chip. (ii) Introducing a novel shape aware compaction technique (PBC) that is the first, to the best of our knowledge, to take the task shape into consideration. Hence, it succeeded not only to eliminate the internal fragmentations but also to minimize the external fragmentations. Experimental results have shown that PBC outperforms recent compaction techniques in which the chip utilization has reached to 87%.

REFERENCES

Banerjee, S., Bozorgzadeh, E., & Dutt, N. (2005a). Physically-aware HW–SW partitioning for reconfigurable architectures with partial dynamic reconfiguration. In *Proceedings of the DAC* (pp. 335-340).

Banerjee, S., Bozorgzadeh, E., & Dutt, N. (2005b). Considering run-time reconfiguration overhead in task graph transformation for dynamically reconfigurable architectures. In *Proceedings of the 13th Annual IEEE Symposium (FCCM)* (pp. 273-274).

Banerjee, S., Bozorgzadeh, E., & Dutt, N. (2006). Integrating physical constraints in HW–SW partitioning for architectures with partial dynamic reconfiguration. *IEEE Trans. Very Large Scale Integr. (VLSI). Syst.*, *14*(11), 1189–1202.

Bazargan, K., Kastner, R., & Sarrafzadeh, M. (2000). Fast template placement for reconfigurable computing systems. *IEEE Design & Test of Computers*, *17*, 68–83. doi:10.1109/54.825678

Chen, Y., & Hsiung, P. (2003). Hardware Task Scheduling and Placement in Operating Systems for Dynamically Reconfigurable SoC. In *Proceedings of the EUC* (pp. 489-498).

Diessel, O., ElGindy, H., Middendorf, M., Schmeck, H., & Schmidt, B. (2000). Dynamic Scheduling of Tasks on Partially Reconfigurable FPGAs. In *Proceedings on computers and digital techniques* (*Vol. 147*, pp. 181–188). Washington, DC: IEEE.

El Farag, A., Hatem, B., & Shaheen, S. (2007). Improving Utilization of Reconfigurable Resources Using Two-Dimensional Compaction. *International Journal of Super-Computing*, *42*, 235–250.

Fekete, S., Kohler, E., & Teich, J. (2001a). Higher-dimensional packing with order constrains. In *Proceedings of Algorithms and data structures (WADS 2001)* (LNCS 2125, pp. 192-204). Berlin: Springer.

Fekete, S., Kohler, E., & Teich, J. (2001b). Optimal FPGA module placement with temporal precedence constrains. In *Proceedings of design automation and test in Europe* (pp. 658–665). DATE.

Fekete, S., & Schepers, J. (2004). A combinational characterization of higher-dimensional orthogonal packing. *Mathematics of Operations Research*, *29*, 591–602. doi:10.1287/moor.1030.0079

Giani, M., Redaelli, M., Santambrogio, M., & Sciuto, D. (2007). Task partitioning for the scheduling on reconfigurable systems driven by specification self-similarity. In *Proceedings of the Int. Conf. (ERSA)* (pp. 78-84).

Hanad, M., & Vemuri, R. (2004). An efficient algorithm for finding empty space for online FPGA placement. In *Proceedigns of the Design automation conference*, San Diego, CA (pp. 960-965).

Jean, J., Tomko, K., Yavagal, V., Shah, J., & Cook, R. (1999). Dynamic reconfiguration to support concurrent applications. *IEEE Transactions on Computers, 48*(6), 591–602. doi:10.1109/12.773796

Marconi, T., Lu, Y., Bertels, K., & Gaydadjiev, G. (2008a). Intelligent Merging Online Task Placement Algorithm for Partial Reconfigurable Systems. In *Proceedings of DATE,* Munich, Germany (pp. 1346-1351).

Marconi, T., Lu, Y., Bertels, K., & Gaydadjiev, G. (2008b). Online Hardware Task Scheduling and Placement Algorithm on Partially Reconfigurable Devices. In R. Woods, K. Compton, C. Bouganis, & P. C. Diniz (Eds.), *Proceedings of the ARC 2008* (LNCS 4943, pp. 306-311).

Marconi, T., Lu, Y., Bertels, K., & Gaydadjiev, G. (2009). A Novel Fast Online Placement Algorithm on 2D Partially Reconfigurable Devices. In *Proceedings of the FPT* (pp. 296-299).

Resano, J., & Mozos, D. (2004). Specific scheduling support to minimize the reconfiguration overhead of dynamically reconfigurable hardware. In *Proceedings of the DAC* (pp. 119-124).

Roberto, C., Francesco, R., Massimo, A., Marco, D., & Donatella, S. (2009). Partitioning and Scheduling of Task Graphs on Partially Dynamically Reconfigurable FPGAs. *IEEE Transactions on Computer-Aided Design of Integrated Circuits and Systems, 28*(5).

Steiger, C., Walder, H., & Platzner, M. (2003). Heuristics for Online Scheduling Real-Time Tasks to Partially Reconfigurable Devices. In Y. K. Cheung & G. A. Constantinides (Eds.), *Proceedings of the FPL 2003* (LNCS 2778, pp. 575-584).

Tabero, J., Septien, J., Mesha, H., Mozos, D., & Roman, S. (2003). Efficient hardware multitasking through space multiplexing in 2D RTR FPGAs. In *Proceedings of the Euromicro digital system design conference.*

Thomas, M., Yi, L., Koen, B., & Georgi, G. (2010). 3D Compaction: A Novel Blocking-Aware Algorithm for Online Hardware Task Scheduling and Placement on 2D Partially Reconfigurable Devices. In *Proceedings of ARC 2010* (pp. 194-206). Berlin: Springer Verlag.

Xilinx. (2007). *Virtex-5 user guide* (Tech. Rep. No. UG190). San Jose, CA: Xilinx Inc.

Xilinx. (2008). *Virtex-4 FPGA Configuration User Guide* (Tech. Rep. No. UG071). San Jose, CA: Xilinx.

Zhou, X., Wang, Y., Huang, X., & Peng, C. (2006). *On-line Scheduling of Real-time Tasks for Reconfigurable Computing System* (pp. 57–64). FPT.

Zhou, X., Wang, Y., Huang, X., & Peng, C. (2007). *Fast On-line Task Placement and Scheduling on Reconfigurable Devices* (pp. 132–138). FPL.

This work was previously published in International Journal of Applied Evolutionary Computation, Volume 1, Issue 4, edited by Wei-Chiang Samuelson Hong, pp. 34-70, copyright 2010 by IGI Publishing (an imprint of IGI Global).

Chapter 16

A Comparative Study of Metaheuristic Methods for Transmission Network Expansion Planning

Ashu Verma
TERI University, India.

P. R. Bijwe
IIT, India

B. K. Panigrahi
IIT, India

ABSTRACT

Transmission network expansion planning is a very complex and computationally demanding problem due to the discrete nature of the optimization variables. This complexity has increased even more in a restructured deregulated environment. In this regard, there is a need for development of more rigorous optimization techniques. This paper presents a comparative analysis of three metaheuristic algorithms known as Bacteria foraging (BF), Genetic algorithm (GA), and Particle swarm optimization (PSO) for transmission network expansion planning with and without security constraints. The DC power flow based model is used for analysis and results for IEEE 24 bus system are obtained with the above three metaheuristic drawing a comparison of their performance characteristic.

INTRODUCTION

Transmission network expansion planning (TNEP) is an important part of the power system planning. It deals in finding the set of transmission lines to be constructed among the available candidate lines

for the transmission expansion, such that the cost of the expansion plan is minimum and there are no overloads during the planning horizon.

The complexity of the problem has increased even more due to restructuring of the power systems. The various factors affecting the TNEP are future load, generation scenarios, right of way

DOI: 10.4018/978-1-4666-1749-0.ch016

constraints, costs and capacities of lines etc. The transmission network expansion planning is of two types: static and dynamic. Static TNEP is done in a single planning horizon, whereas dynamic TNEP requires stage wise addition of lines over the planning horizon with varying stage wise loads. Basically, TNEP is dynamic in nature; however, most of the research work in the literature is for a simple static problem to keep the mathematical formulation simple.

This paper also considers the static TNEP model only. However, the algorithms can be extended for a multistage transmission network expansion planning. DC load flow model is used for simplicity.

Literature Survey

Several methods such as Linear programming, Garver (1970), Alguacil et al. (2003), and Villasana et al. (1985), Dynamic programming Dusonchet and Abiad (1973), Non-linear programming, Youssef and Hackam (1989), Mixed integer programming, Bahiense et al. (2001), Sharifnia and Aashtiani (1985), Benders decomposition, Binato et al. (2001), Oliveira et al. (1995), hierarchical decomposition Romero et al. (1994), Branch and bound algorithms, Haffner et al. (2000), Genetic Algorithms, Silva et al. (2000), Simulated Annealing (SA) Gallego et al.(1997), Tabu search, Gallego et al. (2000), Game theory, Contreras and Wu (2000), Expert systems, Teive et al. (1998), Greedy randomized adaptive search procedure (GRASP), Binato et al. (2001), have been used for the transmission expansion planning. A More detailed literature review has been presented in Latorre et al. (2003). These methods can be broadly classified into two categories: heuristic methods and mathematical optimization methods. However, there are methods that have characteristics of both types of models, known as meta-heuristic.

The TNEP problem is a complex mixed integer nonlinear programming problem due to the discrete nature of the optimization variables. Also, the number of options to be analyzed increases exponentially with the size of the network. Hence, it requires the use of heuristic and combinatorial optimization algorithms because they are able to find the better solutions as compared to those obtained with the classical optimization techniques.

The application of metaheuristic approaches for TNEP is increasing day by day due to their robust nature and ability to find global optimal solution. Few of these papers are discussed below.

Silva et al. (2006), developed two mathematical models and one methodology to solve STNEP (static transmission network expansion planning) considering uncertainty in demand. The first model considers the uncertainty in the system as a whole and the second one considers the uncertainty in demand at each individual bus. A specialized Genetic algorithm is used to solve the problem. Romero et al. (1996), proposed a simulated annealing (SA) approach for long-term TNEP. The SA approach is a generalization of the Monte Carlo method for examining the equations of states and frozen states of n-body system. The concept is based on the manner in which liquids freeze or metals recrystallize in an annealing process. Gallego et al. (1997) presented a parallel simulated annealing algorithm for long term TNEP. Gallego et al. (2000) discussed a Tabu search algorithm for TNEP. The proposed method is a third generation tabu search procedure which includes features of a variety of other approaches such as heuristic search, simulated annealing and genetic algorithms. Silva et al. (2001), presented a new variant of Tabu search for static TNEP. The intensification and diversification phases are designed using medium and long-term memory concepts. Gallego et al. (1998), presented an extended genetic algorithm for TNEP and a comparative analysis of SA, GA and tabu search in Gallego et al. (1998). A hybrid approach is then proposed which presents performances far better than the one presented by any of these algorithms individually. Da Silva et al. (2000), proposed an improved GA for TNEP. Some special features have been added to the basic GA to improve its performance. The genetic algorithm works on a set of candidate solutions know as population, and performs a number of operations. These operators recombine the information contained in the individuals to create new solutions (populations). A procedure based simulated annealing approach is implemented to improve the mutation mechanism in the presented approach. Escorbar et al. (2004) presented a GA based approach for multistage and coordinated planning of transmission expansions. An efficient form of generation of initial population is used in the proposed approach. Romero et al. (2007) presented a specialized GA for static and multistage TNEP. The proposed GA has some special characteristic such as 1) it uses fitness and unfitness functions to identify the value of objective function and unfeasibility of the tested solution 2) applies efficient strategy of local improvement for each individual tested. 3) it substitutes only one individual in the population for each iteration. Binato et al. (2001) presented a greedy randomized adaptive search procedure (GRASP) for solving TNEP. GRASP is an expert iterative sampling technique that has two phases for each iteration. The first phase is construction phase which finds out the feasible solution. The second phase is a local search procedure that seeks for improvements on the construction phase solution by local search. Jin et al. (2007) presented an application of new discrete method in particle swarm optimization for transmission network expansion planning. Maghouli et al. (2009) presented a multiobjective framework for TNEP in a deregulated environment. The problem is solved using non dominated sorting GA (NSGA II). Wang et al. (2008), proposed a multi objective approach for TNEP (MOTEP), considering transmission congestion. The proposed MOTEP approach optimizes three objectives simultaneously namely the congestion surplus, investment cost and power outage cost. An improved strength Pareto evolutionary algorithm

(SPEA) is adopted to solve the proposed model. A new algorithm known as Bacteria Foraging has recently been evolved for solving power system optimization problem in Biswas et al. (2007) and Dasgupta et al. (2009). However, the application of the above algorithm has not been investigated for TNEP so, far.

In view of above, the objective in this paper is to investigate the application of a bacteria foraging optimization (BF) algorithm for TNEP and its comparison with already existing metaheuristics known as Genetic Algorithm (GA) and Particle swarm optimization (PSO).A brief introduction of GA, PSO and details of BF are presented in the next section. An important aspect that must be considered in a power system is the system security. The *N-1* contingency analysis looks at the system state after a single line outage and is used to ensure the system security.

PROBLEM FORMULATION

In this Section, the mathematical models of transmission network expansion planning problem without/with security constrains, are presented.

Transmission Expansion Planning Without Security Constraints

The TNEP determines the set of new lines to be constructed such that the cost of expansion plan is minimum and no overloads are produced during the planning horizon. A DC power flow based model is used for TNEP. The DC power flow is a non iterative method to find power flows through an AC (alternating current) power system. The TNEP with security constraints, can be stated as follows,

$$\min \quad v = \sum_{l \in \Omega} c_l n_l \qquad (1)$$

s.t.

$$S f + g = d \qquad (2)$$

$$f_l - \gamma_l \left(n_l^0 + n_l \right) (\Delta \theta_l) = 0, \text{for } l \in 1,2.........., \qquad (3)$$

$$\left| f_l \right| \leq \left(n_l^0 + n_l \right) \overline{f_l} \text{ ,for } l \in 1,2.........., nl \qquad (4)$$

$$0 \leq n_l \leq \overline{\overline{n_l}}$$

f_l and θ_l are unbounded,

$n_l \geq 0$, and integer, for $l \in 1,2.........., nl,$

$l \in \Omega.$

$$(5)$$

c_l: cost of line added in l^{th} right-of-way,

S : branch-node incidence transposed matrix of the power system,

f : vector with elements f_l ,

γ_l : susceptance of the circuit that can be added to l^{th} right-of-way,

n_l : the number of circuits added in l^{th} right-of-way,

n_l^0 : number of circuits in the base case,

$\Delta \theta_l$: phase angle difference in l^{th} right-of way,

f_l : total real power flow by the circuit in l^{th} right-of-way,

$\overline{f_l}$: maximum allowed real power flow in the circuit in l^{th} right-of-way,

$\overline{n_l}$: maximum number of circuits that can be added in l^{th} right-of-way,

Ω : set of all right-of-ways,

nl: total number of lines in the circuit.

The objective is to minimize the total investment cost of the new transmission lines to be constructed, satisfying the constraint on real power flow in the lines of the network. Constraint (2) represents the power balance at each node. Constraint (3) is the real power flow equations in DC network. Constraint (4) represents the line real power flow constraint. Constraint (5) represents the restriction on the construction of lines per corridor (R.O.W). The transmission lines added in any right-of–way are the decision variables.

The fitness of each solution to the TNEP without security constraints can be obtained using the eq. (6) as shown below.

Minimize

$$f = \sum_{l \in \Omega} c_l n_l + W_1 \sum_{ol} (\text{abs } (f_l) - \overline{f_l}) + W_2 (n_l \text{-} \overline{n_l}) \qquad (6)$$

ol: represents the set of overloaded lines.

The objective of the TNEP is to find the set of transmission lines to be constructed such that the cost of expansion plan is minimum and no overloads are produced during the planning horizon. Hence, first term in the equation (6) indicates the total investment cost of a transmission expansion plan. The second term is added to the objective function for the real power flow constraint violations. The third term is added to the objective function if maximum number of circuits that can be added in l^{th} right-of-way exceeds the maximum limit. W_1, W_2 are constants. The second and third terms are added to the fitness function only in case of violations.

Transmission Expansion Planning with Security Constraints

System security is an important aspect that must be considered in the transmission network expansion planning. It ensures that the system will be secure even after any single line outage. The N-1 contingency analysis looks at the system state after a single line outage. For TNEP with security constraints, the mathematical model for the transmission network expansion planning problem without security constraints can be modified as follows.

A DC power flow based model is used for TNEP. The TNEP with security constraints, can be stated as follows,

$$\min \quad v = \sum_{l \in \Omega} c_l n_l \tag{7}$$

s.t.

$$S \, f^k + g = d \tag{8}$$

$$f_l^k - \gamma_l \left(n_l^0 + n_l \right)(\Delta \theta_l^k) = 0, \text{for } l \in 1,2\ldots\ldots, nl \, \& \, l \neq k \tag{9}$$

$$f_l^k - \gamma_l \left(n_l^0 + n_l - 1 \right)(\Delta \theta_l^k) = 0, \text{for } l=k \tag{10}$$

$$\left| f_l^k \right| \leq \left(n_l^0 + n_l \right) \overline{\overline{f_l}} \ , \text{for } l \in 1,2\ldots\ldots, nl \, \& \, l \neq k \tag{11}$$

$$\left| f_l^k \right| \leq \left(n_l^0 + n_l - 1 \right) \overline{\overline{f_l}} \ , \ \text{for } l=k \tag{12}$$

$0 \leq n_l \leq \overline{\overline{n_l}}$
f_l^k and θ_l^k are unbounded,
$n_l \geq 0$, and integer, for $l \in 1,2\ldots\ldots, nl \, \& \, l \neq k$,
$(n_l + n_l^0 - 1) \geq 0$, and integer, for $l = k$
$l \in \Omega$ and k=0,1,\ldots\ldots\ldots\ldots$NC$,
where, $k = 0$, represents the base case without any line outage.

$$\tag{13}$$

Where,

f^k: vector with elements f_l^k,

$\Delta\theta_l^k$: phase angle difference in l^{th} right-of way when k^{th} line is out,

f_l^k: total real power flow by the circuit in l^{th} right-of-way when k^{th} line is out,

NC: number of credible contingencies.

TNEP without security constraint is a special case of TNEP with security constraints with k=0 only.

The objective is to minimize the total investment cost of the new transmission lines to be constructed, satisfying the constraint on real power flow in the lines of the network, for base case and *N-1* contingency cases. Constraint (8) represents the power balance at each node for base case and *N-1* contingency cases. Constraints (9) and (10) are the real power flow equations in DC network for base case and *N-1* contingency cases. Constraints (11) and (12) represent the line real power flow constraint in base case and *N-1* contingency cases. Constraint (13) represents the restriction on the construction of lines per corridor (R.O.W).

The fitness of each solution to the TNEP with security constraints can be obtained using the eq. (14) as shown below.

Minimize

$$f = \sum_{l \in \Omega} c_l n_l + W_1 \sum_{k=0}^{NC} \sum_{ol(k)} (\text{abs } (f_l^k) - \overline{\overline{f_l}} \ ) + W_2 (n_l - \overline{n_l}) \tag{14}$$

ol(k): represents the set of overloaded lines for k^{th} topology.

The objective of the TNEP is to find the set of transmission lines to be constructed such that the cost of expansion plan is minimum and no overloads are produced during the planning horizon. Hence, first term in the equation (14) indicates the total investment cost of a transmission expansion plan. The second term is added to the objective function for the real power flow constraint violations in the base case, and *NC* contingency cases. The third term is added to the objective function if maximum number of circuits that can be added in l^{th} right-of-way exceeds the maximum limit. W_1, W_2 are constants. The second and third terms are added to the fitness function only in case of violations.

OVERVIEW OF GA, PSO AND BF

Genetic Algorithm (GA)

Genetic Algorithms (GAs) are used for many non-linear optimization problems. GA is a stochastic search algorithm based on the concept of natural selection, Goldberg (1989). They operate on a string structure called chromosomes. Chromosomes are typically a concatenated list of binary digits representing an encoding of the control parameters of a given problem. GAs consists of three basic operations, namely reproduction, crossover and mutation. The main purpose of reproduction is to make duplicates of good solutions and eliminate bad solutions, while keeping the population size constant. The higher the fitness, the more likely it is that the chromosome will be selected for the next generation. There are several strategies for selecting the individuals, e.g. roulette-wheel selection, ranking methods and tournament selection. In tournament selection, tournaments are played between two solutions and the better solution is chosen and placed in the mating pool. The crossover operator is mainly responsible for the global search property of the GA. The reproduction operator can not produce new solutions; it only makes more copies of good solutions. Crossover and mutation operators are responsible for creating the new solutions. Two child strings are generated from the parent strings in the process of crossover by complementing the child strings at selected bit positions in order to exchange the already existing information. Mutation is then applied on some of strings to introduce new information in the mating pool, with small probability. In order to maintain the best chromosome found so far, elitism is used. It always maintains the best chromosome called elites, in the mating pool at random, and some portion of the strings is exchanged to create a new string.

Pseudo Code for GA

1. Initialize population.
2. Evaluate the fitness of each individual in the population.
3. Repeat until termination.(maximum no. of fitness function evaluations or sufficient fitness achieved).
4. Perform reproduction (tournament selection is used here).
5. Breed new generation through crossover and mutation (genetic operations) and give birth to offspring.
6. Evaluate the individual fitness of the offspring.
7. Replace worst ranked part of population with offspring

Particle Swarm Optimization (PSO)

Particle swarm optimization was introduced by J. Kennedy and R. C. Eberhart (2001), for the optimization of nonlinear functions. The Particle Swarm Optimization method conducts search using a population of particles, corresponding to individuals. Each particle in the swarm represents a candidate solution to the problem. It starts with a random initialization of a population of individuals in the search space and works on the social behavior of the particles in the swarm like bird flocking, fish schooling and the swarm theory. Each solution in the population is assigned with a randomized velocity. Every particle is affected by three factors: its own velocity, the best solution it has achieved so far, pbest and the overall best position achieved by all particles called gbest.

Pseudo Code for PSO

1. For each particle
   Initialize particles.

2. Repeat until termination.(maximum no. of fitness function evaluations or sufficient fitness achieved).

3. For each particle
   Calculate fitness.
   if the fitness value is better than the best fitness value (pBest) in history. Set the current value as the new pBest.

4. Choose the particle with the best fitness value of all the particles as the gBest.

5. For each particle,
   a. Calculate the particle velocity using equation.
   b. Update the particle position according equation.

The equations used in PSO for updating velocity and positions of each particle are given as follows.

Updating velocity of each particle: the velocity of a particle is updated by the knowledge of its pbest and gbest locations. It also depends upon the current velocity as shown by Equation (15)

$$V_i^{k+1} = w V_i^k + c_1 r_1 (pbest_i - X_i^k) + c_2 r_2 (gbest - X_i^k)$$
(15)

Where, V_i^k :velocity of the particle i at generation k,

X_i^k : current position of particle i at generation k,

$pbest_i$: pbest of agent I,

$gbest$: gbest of the group,

w :inertia weight,

c_1, c_2 :Cognitive and social factors,

r_1, r_2 : uniformly distributed random number between 0 and 1.

The inertia weight at each generation can be calculated as

$$w = w_{\max} - \frac{w_{\max} - w_{\min}}{\text{Total no. of generation}} * \text{generation}$$
(16)

Updating location of each particle: each particle is moved to the position indicated by Equation (17)

$$X_i^{k+1} = X_i^k + V_i^{k+1}$$
(17)

Bacteria Foraging (BF)

The Bacterial Foraging algorithm was first proposed by K. M. Passino (2002) as a tool of optimization. This technique is motivated by the natural selection procedure which eliminates the animals with poor foraging strategy, and promotes the propagation of genes of those animals that have successful forging strategies. Some animals forage as individuals and others forage as groups. While performing a group foraging, an animal can gain advantage of the fact that it can exploit essentially the sensing capabilities of the group, the group can gang-up on large prey, individuals can obtain protection from predators while in a group, and in a certain sense the group can forage with a type of collective intelligence. This activity of foraging motivated the researchers to use it as an optimization process. The *E. coli* (bacteria present in our intestines), also undergo a foraging strategy which can be explained by four processes namely, chemotaxis, swarming, reproduction, and elimination and dispersal as presented below.

a. **Chemotaxis:** This process is achieved through swimming and tumbling via Flagella. Each left-handed helix configured flagellum either rotates counter clockwise to create the force against bacterium to push the cell or rotates in clockwise direction to pull at the cell. This mechanism of creating rotational forces is named as biological motor. An *E. coli* bacterium can move in two different ways, it can swim or it can tumble. The bacterium moves in a specified direction during swimming, while it does not have a set direction during tumbling and also the displacement is small. Generally, the bacterium alternates between these two modes of operation in its entire lifetime. This alternation between the two modes enables the bacteria to move in random directions and search for nutrients.

b. **Swarming:** When any one of the bacteria reaches a better location, it attracts other bacteria so that they converge in that location. For this, the *E. coli* cells provide an attraction signal to each other so that they swarm together. This is achieved by a cost function adjustment which depends on the relative distances of each bacterium from the fittest bacterium. When all the bacteria have emerged into the solution point this adjustment is stopped. The effect of swarming is to make the bacteria congregate into groups and move as concentric patterns with high bacterial density.

c. **Reproduction:** In this process the least healthy bacteria die and the other healthiest bacteria split into two at the same location thus ensuring that the population of the bacteria remains constant.

d. **Elimination and Dispersal:** This leads to the elimination of a set of bacteria and/or dispersion of them to a new environment, due to gradual or sudden changes in the location due to consumption of nutrients or some other influence. This reduces the chances of convergence at local optimal location.

The Bacterial Foraging Algorithm

Step1: Initialization

a. Number of bacteria (S).

b. Number of parameters (p) to be optimized.

c. Swimming length (N_s) is the maximum number of steps taken by each bacterium when it moves from low nutrient area to high nutrient area.

d. N_c is the number of chemotactic steps taken by each bacterium before reproduction
$(N_c > N_s)$.

e. N_{re} and N_{ed} are the number of reproduction and elimination dispersal events.

f. P_{ed} is the probability of elimination and dispersal.

g. Specifying the location of the initial position of bacteria by random numbers on [0,1].

h. The values of $d_{attract}$, $\omega_{attract}$, $h_{repellent}$, and $\omega_{repellent}$.

i. Random swim direction vector $\Delta(i)$ and run length vector C(i) = [C(1); C(2); … C(p)], where C(1), C(2),.., C(p) are the run length vector corresponding to the each parameter respectively.

Step2: Iterative Algorithm For Optimization

This explains the main part of the algorithm, i.e., evaluation of chemotaxis, swarming, reproduction, elimination and dispersal process. It starts with the calculation of *J error* for the initial bacterial population inside the innermost chemotaxis loop. Any i^{th} bacteria at the jth chemotactic, k^{th} reproduction and l^{th} elimination stage is represented by $\theta^i(j,k,l)$ and its corresponding error value is given by *J error* (i, j, k, l). (Initially, j=k=l=0).

The algorithm works as follows.

1. Starting of the Elimination-dispersal loop *(l=l+1)*

2. Starting of the Reproduction loop *(k=k+1)*

3. Starting of the chemotaxis loop *(j=j+1)*

    a. For all *i* = 1, 2, …, S, calculate *J error (i, j, k, l)*

    b. *J error (i, j, k, l)* is saved as *J errorold* so as to compare with other *J error* values.

    c. Tumble: Generate a random vector $\Delta(i)$ ε R^p with each element being a random number in the range [-1,1].

d. Move:

$$\theta^i(j+1,k,l) = \theta^i(j,k,l) + C(i)\frac{\Delta(i)}{\sqrt{\Delta(i)^T\Delta(i)}} \quad (18)$$

This results in a step size $C(i)$ in the direction of the tumble for i^{th} bacterium.

e. Calculate J error $(i, j+1, k, l)$

f. Swimming loop:
Let $m = 0$ (counter for swim length)
While $m < N_s$
$m = m+1$;
If J error $(i, j+1, k, l) < J$ errorold, then J errorold $= J$ error $(i, j+1, k, l)$ and

$$\theta^i(j+1,k,l) = \theta^i(j+1,k,l) + C(i)\frac{\Delta(i)}{\sqrt{\Delta(i)^T\Delta(i)}}$$
$$(19)$$

This $\theta^i(j+1,k,l)$ is then used to calculate new J error $(i, j+1, k, l)$.
Else $m = N_s$

g. Go to the next bacterium $(i+1)$ till all the bacteria undergo chemotaxis.

4. If $j < Nc$, go to step 3 and continue chemotaxis since the life of bacteria is not over, else continue.

5. Reproduction:
a. For the given k and l, and for each $i = 1,2,...S,$ let $J_{health}^i = \sum_{j=1}^{Nc+1} J_{error}(i,j,k,l)$ be the health of ith bacterium. The bacteria are sorted according to ascending order of J_{health}.
b. The bacteria with the highest J_{health} values die and those with minimum values split and the copies that are made already, now placed at the same location as their parent.

6. If $k < Nre,$ go to step 3, to start the next generation in the chemotactic loop, else go to step 7.

7. Elimination - dispersal: For $i = 1, 2 ...S,$ a random number is generated and if it is less than or equal to Ped, then that bacterium is dispersed to a new random location else it remains at its original location.

8. If $l < Ned$, go to step 2, else stop.

Step3: An Adaptive Strategy For Run Length Vector

The run length vector $C(i)$ plays an important role in the convergence of bacterial foraging. A small value of $C(i)$ causes slow convergence whereas a large value may fail to locate the minima by swimming through them without stopping. A careful selection of $C(i)$ has to be, therefore, done. Here an adaptive scheme to update $C(i)$ is used which ensures the convergence of bacterial foraging algorithm. Initially assuming the C(i) as 0.05 and during the evaluations it will be reduced as given in following steps.

Steps of Adaptive strategy:

a. Assume C(i) = 0.05.
b. Run the chemotaxis stage.
c. Now adjust the runlength C(i)=min{(C(i) − 0.0005),0.00001}.
d. Do steps (b) and (c) until all elimination and dispersal as well as reproduction stages are completed.

RESULTS AND DISCUSSIONS

In this section the results of transmission network expansion planning with and without security constraints for IEEE 24-bus system, Romero et al. (2005) are presented. This system consists of 24 buses, 41 candidate circuits, and a maximum of three lines per corridor can be added. The system is to be expanded to a future condition with the generation levels and the loads, three time their original values. Therefore, the system has enough generation capacity, but new lines are required to be installed to avoid overloads in the transmission system. The initial network and the electrical data can be found in Romero et al.

Table 1. Results for TNEP without security constraints for generation plan G_1 to G_4

	TNEP with GA	TNEP with PSO	TNEP with BFO
Generation Plan G_1	$n_{15-24}=1, n_{17-18}=1, n_{16-17}=1,$ $n_{15-21}=1, n_{14-16}=1, n_{3-24}=1, n_{1-5}=1,$ $n_{6-10}=1, n_{7-8}=2, n_{17-18}=1.$	$n_{15-24}=1, n_{17-18}=1, n_{16-17}=1, n_{15-21}=1,$ $n_{14-16}=1, n_{3-24}=1, n_{1-5}=1, n_{6-10}=1,$ $n_{7-8}=2, n_{17-18}=1.$	$n_{15-24}=1, n_{17-18}=1, n_{16-17}=1, n_{15-21}=1,$ $n_{14-16}=1, n_{3-24}=1, n_{1-5}=1, n_{6-10}=1,$ $n_{7-8}=2,$ $n_{17-18}=1.$
Total Number of Lines	11	11	11
Investment cost [10^6 US$]	**390**	**390**	**390**
Generation Plan G_2	$n_{10-11}=1, n_{6-10}=1, n_{1-5}=1,$ $n_{16-17}=1, n_{15-24}=1, n_{3-24}=1, n_{14-16}=1,$ $n_{7-8}=1, n_{17-18}=1.$	$n_{10-11}=1, n_{6-10}=1, n_{1-5}=1, n_{16-17}=1,$ $n_{15-24}=1, n_{3-24}=1, n_{14-16}=1, n_{7-8}=1,$ $n_{17-18}=1.$	$n_{10-11}=1, n_{6-10}=1, n_{1-5}=1, n_{16-17}=1,$ $n_{15-24}=1, n_{3-24}=1, n_{14-16}=1, n_{7-8}=1,$ $n_{17-18}=1.$
Total Number of Lines	9	9	9
Investment cost [10^6 US$]	**336**	**336**	**336**
Generation Plan G_3	$n_{16-19}=1, n_{14-16}=1, n_{6-10}=1, n_{7-8}=2,$ $n_{10-12}=1, n_{20-23}=1.$	$n_{16-19}=1, n_{14-16}=1, n_{6-10}=1, n_{7-8}=2,$ $n_{10-12}=1, n_{20-23}=1.$	$n_{16-19}=1, n_{14-16}=1, n_{6-10}=1, n_{7-8}=2,$ $n_{10-12}=1, n_{20-23}=1.$
Total Number of Lines	7	7	7
Investment cost [10^6 US$]	**214**	**214**	**214**
Generation Plan G_4	$n_{14-16}=1, n_{9-12}=1, n_{7-8}=2,$ $n_{12-13}=1, n_{6-10}=1, n_{15-16}=1, n_{10-11}=1.$	$n_{14-16}=1, n_{9-12}=1, n_{7-8}=2, n_{12-13}=1,$ $n_{6-10}=1, n_{15-16}=1, n_{10-11}=1.$	$n_{14-16}=1, n_{9-12}=1, n_{7-8}=2, n_{12-13}=1,$ $n_{6-10}=1, n_{15-16}=1, n_{10-11}=1.$
Total Number of Lines	8	8	8
Investment cost[10^6US$]	**292**	**292**	**292**

Table 2. Parametric study of BFO for generation plan G_1: S=50, iteration=1200

Parameters	Ns=1, C=0.05	Ns=1, C=0.03	Ns=1, C=0.01	Ns=1, C=adaptive	Ns=2, C=adaptive	Ns=3, C=adaptive
Number of trials in which the optimal solution is obtained out of 50 trials	11	7	8	2	2	**12**
Number of trials in which the solution without penalty is obtained out of 50 trials	47	50	50	50	48	**47**
Cost range Min	390	390	390	390	390	**390**
Max	532	577	557	588	576	**562**
Standard Deviation	45.132	51.97	47.14	49.42	47.1634	**42.15079**

Table 3. Parametric study of GA for generation plan G_1: Ngen=600, Npopu=200

Parameters	Number of trials in which the optimal solution is obtained out of 50 trials	Number of trials in which the solution without penalty is obtained out of 50 trials	Cost range		Standard Deviation
			Min	Max	
Pc=0.7, Pm=0.01	7	42	390	576	50.05103
Pc=0.8, Pm=0.01	**14**	**48**	**390**	**576**	**47.37868**
Pc=0.9, Pm=0.01	11	45	390	576	53.5214
Pc=1.0, Pm=0.01	14	45	390	576	48.711
Pc=0.8, Pm=0.02	10	44	390	562	48.813
Pc=0.8, Pm=0.03	4	43	390	595	57.67
Pc=0.8, Pm=0.04	1	30	390	622	52.744
Pc=0.8, Pm=0.05	0	21	438	580	38.314

Table 4. Parametric comparison of PSO for generation plan G_1: Ngen=600, Npopu=200

Parameters	Number of trials in which the optimal solution is obtained out of 50 trials	Number of trials in which the solution without penalty is obtained out of 50 trials	Cost range		Standard Deviation
			Min	Max	
$c_1=c_2=2.1, w_{max}=0.85, w_{min}=0.1$	0	48	396	1361	153.0326
$c_1=c_2=2.1, w_{max}=0.85, w_{min}=0.2$	**1**	**49**	**390**	**894**	**118.8022**
$c_1=c_2=2.1, w_{max}=0.85, w_{min}=0.3$	0	48	402	1120	127.5667
$c_1=c_2=2.1, w_{max}=0.85, w_{min}=0.4$	0	48	396	924	129.2105
$c_1=c_2=2.1, w_{max}=0.85, w_{min}=0.5$	0	44	439	1032	136.9843
$c_1=c_2=2.1, w_{max}=0.75, w_{min}=0.3$	1	48	390	1186	168.655
$c_1=c_2=2.1, w_{max}=0.65, w_{min}=0.3$	0	47	402	1310	179.8437
$c_1=c_2=2.1, w_{max}=0.55, w_{min}=0.3$	0	47	396	1196	191.2943
$c_1=c_2=2.1, w_{max}=0.95, w_{min}=0.3$	0	48	432	901	113.4699
$c_1=c_2=2.1, w_{max}=1.05, w_{min}=0.3$	0	49	396	868	80.60832
$c_1=c_2=2.2, w_{max}=0.85, w_{min}=0.3$	0	47	396	930	121.8973
$c_1=c_2=2.0, w_{max}=0.85, w_{min}=0.3$	0	45	396	1571	196.4241
$c_1=c_2=1.9, w_{max}=0.85, w_{min}=0.3$	0	47	438	986	122.6724

Table 5. Fitness function evaluations required by BFO, GA, PSO for generation plan G_1

Method	BFO	GA	PSO
No. of fitness function evaluations	10,650	11,200	13,800

Table 6. Comparison of performance of three methods for TNEP without security constraints, for generation plan G_1 to G_4

Generation Plan	G_1			G_2			G_3			G_4		
Method used	GA	PSO	BFO	GA	PSO	BFO	GA	PSO	BFO	GA	PSO	BFO
Number of trials in which the optimal solution is obtained out of 50 trials	6	1	20	15	6	5	3	3	3	1	2	40
Number of trials in which the solution without penalty is obtained out of 50 trials	43	49	50	49	46	49	49	49	50	34	48	50
Cost range Min	390	390	390	336	336	336	214	214	214	292	292	292
Max	579	1015	543	400	976	383	347	620	269	417	599	299
Standard Deviation	54	143	36	18	180	18	43	97	12	42	89	3
Mean Best Value	466	637	445	372	389	347	322	338	238	299	418	292

Table 7. Results for TNEP with security constraints for generation plan G1

Name of the Technique	TNEP	Total Number of Lines	Investment Cost [10^6 US\$]
GA	$n_{15-21}=2$, $n_{7-8}=3$, $n_{19-22}=1$, $n_{2-6}=2$, $n_{14-16}=2$, $n_{4-9}=1$, $n_{5-10}=1$, $n_{11-13}=1$, $n_{6-10}=1$, $n_{15-24}=2$, $n_{3-24}=2$, $n_{10-11}=1$, $n_{1-5}=1$, $n_{15-16}=1$.	21	1010
PSO	$n_{15-21}=2$, $n_{7-8}=3$, $n_{2-6}=1$, $n_{14-16}=2$, $n_{4-9}=1$, $n_{5-10}=1$, $n_{11-13}=1$, $n_{6-10}=2$, $n_{3-24}=1$, $n_{10-11}=1$, $n_{1-5}=1$, $n_{15-16}=2$, $n_{16-17}=2$, $n_{11-14}=1$, $n_{16-19}=1$, $n_{17-18}=1$, $n_{21-22}=1$, $n_{3-9}=1$, $n_{9-11}=1$, $n_{17-18}=1$, $n_{1-3}=1$.	27	1024
BFO	$n_{15-21}=1$, $n_{7-8}=3$, $n_{19-22}=1$, $n_{14-16}=2$, $n_{11-13}=1$, $n_{3-24}=2$, $n_{10-11}=1$, $n_{6-10}=1$, $n_{1-5}=1$, $n_{2-6}=2$, $n_{17-18}=2$, $n_{15-24}=2$, $n_{16-17}=2$.	21	980

Table 8. Performance comparison between three methods

Method used	GA	PSO	BF
Number of trials in which the optimal solution is obtained out of 50 trial	1	1	1
Number of trials in which the solution without penalty is obtained out of 50 trial	3	50	50
Cost range Min	1010	1024	980
Max	1326	2118	1278
Standard Deviation	140.1174	249.4742	83.18413
Mean Best Value	1052	1344	1015

Figure 1. (a) Performance comparison of GA, PSO and BF for generation plan G_1G_4. (b). Performance comparison of GA, PSO and BF for generation plan G_1G_4.

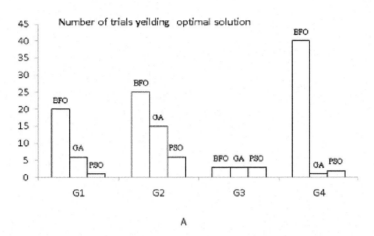

A

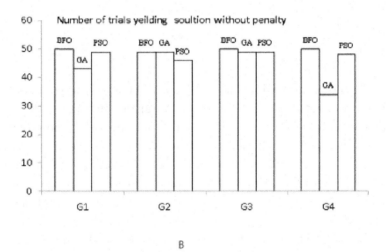

B

(2005). The system configuration and data used is also given in Appendix A for ready reference. The problem is solved with Bacteria Foraging (BF), Basic Binary GA and Particle swarm optimization (PSO) algorithms. A comparative study of the three methods for TNEP problem is presented.

Case 1. Transmission Network Expansion Planning without Security Constraints (TNEPWOSC)

In this case, results for transmission network expansion planning without security constraints

for four generation plans G_1 to G_4 [Appendix A], are obtained. The expansion plans obtained for the above mentioned cases are shown in Table 1, whereas performance comparison of the three methods is given in Table 6. It can be observed from Table 1, that for all generation plans G_1 to G_4, the optimal expansion plans obtained by the three methods are same. Comparing the cost of expansion plans obtained with the proposed algorithms and those reported in Romero et al. (2005), it can be observed that cost of expansion plan obtained for generation plan G_1 is 11% and for generation

Figure 2. Performance comparison of GA, PSO and BF for generation plan G₁

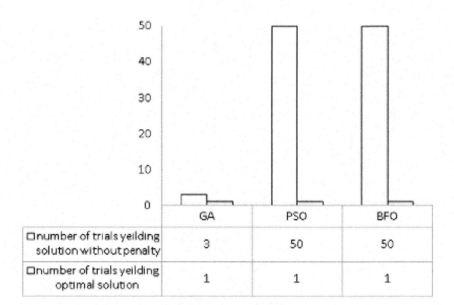

	GA	PSO	BFO
☐ number of trials yeilding solution without penalty	3	50	50
☐ number of trials yeilding optimal solution	1	1	1

plan G_4 1.8% lesser, with the proposed method than the one given in Romero et al. (2005).

To obtain a fair comparison between three algorithms parametric study of the three algorithms is done and the results are obtained with the best parameter setting for each algorithm. The parametric analysis of all BFO, GA and PSO is shown in Table 2, 3 and 4 respectively.

The number of fitness function evaluation required by three algorithms with their best parameter settings for plan G1 are shown in Table 5.

It can be observed from Table 5 that the BFO requires the least number of fitness function evaluation. GA requires fitness function lesser than PSO. These differences are more for TNEP with security constraints and for larger and more complex systems.

The detailed performance comparison of three methods is reported in Table 6 for the generation plans G_1-G_4. From Table 6 and Figure 1 a & b, it can be observed that the percentage of success,

i.e., yielding a solution without any penalty for the BFO algorithm is almost 100%. This demonstrates the robustness of the proposed algorithm, having least standard deviation and best convergence characteristics for all four cases G_1-G_4. The standard deviation is a measure of the variability in a data set. It indicates the closeness of the solutions obtained in different trial to the optimal solution. A low standard deviation means the solutions obtained in 50 trials tend to be very close to the same (mean) value, while a large standard deviation indicates that data are "spread out" over a large range of values.

Case 2. Transmission Network Expansion Planning with Security Constraints (TNEPWSC)

In this case, results for transmission network expansion planning with security constraints for generation plan G_1 [28], are obtained. The detailed results are given in Table 7, and the performance comparison, and performance characteristics of the three methods are shown in Table 8 and Figure 2 respectively.

It can be observed from the Table 8, that minimum cost expansion plan is obtained with the BFO. The performance comparison of three methods (Table 8) indicates the robustness and percentage of success of the BFO algorithm.

CONCLUSION

In this paper, a Bacteria Foraging optimization (BFO) scheme is used for transmission network expansion planning with and without security constraints. First the algorithm for base case transmission expansion planning has been presented. Then the algorithm has been extended to include security constraints. Results for IEEE 24 bus system are obtained **with** this method and also with other metaheuristic methods like GA and PSO for comparison. The BFO method is very robust and provides better results as compared to those with other two methods, in terms of least standard deviation and best convergence characteristics. Also, the cost of expansion plan is minimum with BFO, for TNEP with security constraints.

REFERENCES

Alguacil, N., Motto, A. L., & Conejo, A. J. (2003). Transmission expansion planning: a mixed-integer LP approach. *IEEE Transactions on Power Systems*, *18*(3), 1070–1077. doi:10.1109/TPWRS.2003.814891

Bahiense, L., Oliveira, G. C., Pereira, M., & Granville, S. (2001). A mixed integer disjunctive model for transmission network expansion. *IEEE Transactions on Power Systems*, *16*(3), 560–565. doi:10.1109/59.932295

Binato, S., de Oliveira, G. C., & de Araújo, J. L. (2001). A greedy randomized adaptive search procedure for transmission expansion planning. *IEEE Transactions on Power Systems*, *16*(2), 247–253. doi:10.1109/59.918294

Binato, S., Pereira, M. V. F., & Granville, S. (2001). A new Benders decomposition approach to solve power transmission network design problems. *IEEE Transactions on Power Systems*, *16*(2), 235–240. doi:10.1109/59.918292

Biswas, A., Dasgupta, S., Das, S., & Abraham, A. (2007). Synergy of PSO and Bacterial Foraging Optimization: A Comparative Study on Numerical Benchmarks. In E. Corchado et al. (Eds.), *Proceedings of the Second International Symposium on Hybrid Artificial Intelligent Systems (HAIS), Innovations in Hybrid Intelligent Systems (ASC 44)* (pp. 255-263).

Contreras, J., & Wu, F. F. (2000). A kernel-oriented algorithm for transmission expansion Planning. *IEEE Transactions on Power Systems*, *15*(4), 1434–1440. doi:10.1109/59.898124

da Silva, E. L., Gil, H. A., & Areiza, J. M. (2000). Transmission network expansion planning under an improved genetic algorithm. *IEEE Transactions on Power Systems*, *15*(3), 1168–1175. doi:10.1109/59.871750

da Silva, E. L., Ortiz, J. M. A., Oliveira, G. C., & Binato, S. (2001). Transmission network expansion planning under a tabu search approach. *IEEE Transactions on Power Systems*, *16*(1), 62–68. doi:10.1109/59.910782

Dasgupta, S., Das, S., Abraham, A., & Biswas, A. (2009). Adaptive Computational Chemotaxis in Bacterial Foraging Optimization: An Analysis. *IEEE Transactions on Evolutionary Computing*.

Dusonchet, Y. P., & El-Abiad, A. H. (1973). Transmission planning using discrete dynamic optimization. *IEEE Transactions on PAS*, *92*(4), 1358–1371.

Eberhart, R. C., & Shi, Y. (2001). Particle swarm optimization: developments, applications and resources. In *Proceedings of the Congress on Evolutionary Computation,* Piscataway, Soul (pp. 81-86).

Escobar, A. H., Gallego, R. A., & Romero, R. (2004). Multistage and Coordinated planning of the expansion of transmission systems. *IEEE Transactions on Power Systems, 19*(2), 735–744. doi:10.1109/TPWRS.2004.825920

Gallego, R. A., Alves, A. B., Monticelli, A., & Romero, R. (1997). Parallel simulated annealing approach applied to long term transmission network expansion planning. *IEEE Transactions on Power Systems, 12*(1), 181–188. doi:10.1109/59.574938

Gallego, R. A., Monticelli, A., & Romero, R. (1998). Transmission expansion planning by extended genetic algorithm. In *Proceedings of the Gener. Trans. Distr., 145*(3), 329-335.

Gallego, R. A., Monticelli, A., & Romero, R. (1998). Comparative studies of non-convex optimization methods for transmission network expansion planning. *IEEE Transactions on Power Systems, 13*(3), 822–828. doi:10.1109/59.708680

Gallego, R. A., Monticelli, A., & Romero, R. (2000). Tabu search algorithm for network synthesis. *IEEE Transactions on Power Systems, 15*(2), 490–495. doi:10.1109/59.867130

Garver, L. L. (1970). Transmission network estimation using linear programming.

Goldberg, D. E. (1989). *Genetic Algorithms in Search Optimization and Machine Learning.* Reading, MA: Addison Wesley.

Haffner, S., Monticelli, A., Garcia, A., Mantovani, J., & Romero, R. (2000). Branch and bound algorithm for transmission system expansion planning using a transportation model. *IEE Proceedings. Generation, Transmission and Distribution, 147*(3), 149–156. doi:10.1049/ip-gtd:20000337

Jin, Y. X., Cheng, H. Z., Yan, J. Y., & Zhang, L. (2007). New discrete particle swarm optimization and its application in transmission network expansion planning. *Electric Power Systems Research, 77*, 227–233. doi:10.1016/j.epsr.2006.02.016

Latorre, G., Cruz, R. D., Areiza, J. M., & Villegas, A. (2003). Classification of Publications and Models on Transmission Expansion Planning. *IEEE Transactions on Power Systems, 18*(2), 938–946. doi:10.1109/TPWRS.2003.811168

Maghouli, P., Hosseini, S. H., Buygi, M. O., & Shahidehpour, M. (2009). A multi-objective framework for transmission expansion planning in deregulated environments. *IEEE Transactions on Power Systems, 24*(2), 1051–1061. doi:10.1109/TPWRS.2009.2016499

Oliveira, G. C., Costa, A. P. C., & Binato, S. (1995). Large scale transmission network planning using optimization and heuristic techniques. *IEEE Transactions on Power Systems, 10*(4), 1828–1834. doi:10.1109/59.476047

Passino, K. M. (2002). Biomimicry of bacterial foraging for distributed optimization and control. *IEEE Control Systems Magazine,* 52–67. doi:10.1109/MCS.2002.1004010

Romero, R., Gallego, R. A., & Monticelli, A. (1996). Transmission network expansion planning by Simulated Annealing. *IEEE Transactions on Power Systems, 11*(1), 364–369. doi:10.1109/59.486119

Romero, R., & Monticelli, A. (1994). A hierarchical decomposition approach for transmission network expansion planning. *IEEE Transactions on Power Systems, 9*(1), 373–380. doi:10.1109/59.317588

Romero, R., Rider, M. J., & Silva, I. de J. (2007). A Metaheuristic to solve the Transmission Expansion Planning. *IEEE Transactions on Power Systems, 22*(4), 2289–2291. doi:10.1109/TPWRS.2007.907592

Romero, R., Rocha, C., Mantovani, J. R. S., & Slanchez, I. G. (2005). Constructive heuristic algorithm for the DC model in network transmission expansion planning. *IEE Proceedings. Generation, Transmission and Distribution, 152*(2), 277–282. doi:10.1049/ip-gtd:20041196

Sharifnia, A., & Aashtiani, H. Z. (1985). Transmission network planning: A method for synthesis of minimum-cost secure networks. *IEEE Transactions on Power Apparatus and Systems, 104*(8), 2026–2034. doi:10.1109/TPAS.1985.318777

Silva Irênio de, J., Rider Marcos, J., Romero, R., & Murari Carlos, A. F. (2006). Transmission network expansion planning considering uncertainty in demand.

Teive, R. C. G., Silva, E. L., & Fonseca, L. G. S. (1998). A cooperative expert system for transmission expansion planning of electrical power systems. *IEEE Transactions on Power Systems, 13*(2), 636–642. doi:10.1109/59.667393

Villasana, R., Garver, L. L., & Salon, S. J. (1985). Transmission network planning using linear programming. *IEEE Transactions on Power Apparatus and Systems, 104*(2), 349–356. doi:10.1109/TPAS.1985.319049

Wanga, Y., Chenga, H., Wang, C., Hu, Z., Yao, L., Mad, Z., & Zhud, Z. (2008). Pareto optimality-based multi-objective transmission planning considering transmission congestion. *Electric Power Systems Research, 78*, 1619–1626. doi:10.1016/j.epsr.2008.02.004

Youssef, H. K., & Hackam, R. (1989). New transmission planning model. *IEEE Transactions on Power Systems, 4*(2), 9–18. doi:10.1109/59.32451

APPENDIX A

Where, n_l^0: number of lines initially present in l^{th} right-of-way (before TNEP),

Cl: cost of new line added in l^{th} right-of-way,
f_{lmax}: maximum allowed flow in l^{th} right –of-way.

Figure 3. IEEE 24 Bus system

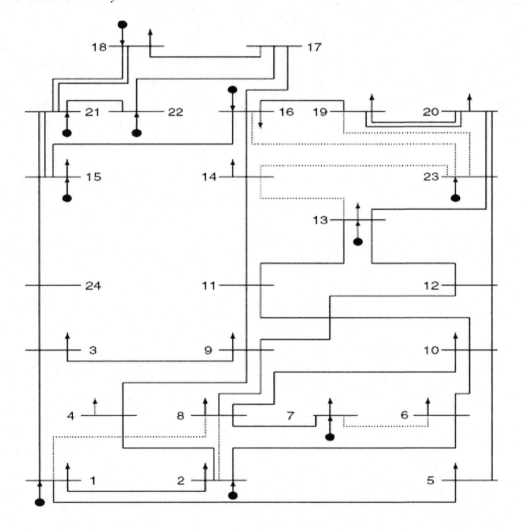

Table 9. Generation and load data in MW

Bus	G_1	G_2	G_3	G_4	D
1	576	465	576	520	324
2	576	576	576	520	291
3	0	0	0	0	540
4	0	0	0	0	222
5	0	0	0	0	213
6	0	0	0	0	408
7	900	722	900	812	375
8	0	0	0	0	513
9	0	0	0	0	525
10	0	0	0	0	585
11	0	0	0	0	0
12	0	0	0	0	0
13	1773	1424	1457	1599	795
14	0	0	0	0	582
15	645	645	325	581	951
16	465	465	282	419	300
17	0	0	0	0	0
18	1200	1200	603	718	999
19	0	0	0	0	543
20	0	0	0	0	384
21	1200	1200	951	1077	0
22	900	900	900	900	0
23	315	953	1980	1404	0
24	0	0	0	0	0

Table 10. Circuit data

From	To	n_i^0	reactance(p.u)	f_{lmax}(MW)	$C_i(10^4$US$)$
1	2	1	0.0139	175	3
1	3	1	0.2112	175	55
1	5	1	0.0845	175	22
2	4	1	0.1267	175	33
2	6	1	0.192	175	50
3	9	1	0.119	175	31
3	24	1	0.0839	400	50
4	9	1	0.1037	175	27
5	10	1	0.0883	175	23
6	10	1	0.0605	175	16
7	8	1	0.0614	175	16
8	9	1	0.1651	175	43
8	10	1	0.1651	175	43
9	11	1	0.0839	400	50
9	12	1	0.0839	400	50
10	11	1	0.0839	400	50
10	12	1	0.0839	400	50
11	13	1	0.0476	500	66
11	14	1	0.0418	500	58
12	13	1	0.0476	500	66
12	23	1	0.0966	500	134
13	23	1	0.0865	500	120
14	16	1	0.0389	500	54
15	16	1	0.0173	500	24
15	21	2	0.049	500	68
15	24	1	0.0519	500	72
16	17	1	0.0259	500	36
16	19	1	0.0231	500	32
17	18	1	0.0144	500	20
19	22	1	0.1053	500	146
18	21	2	0.0259	500	36
19	20	2	0.0396	500	55
20	23	2	0.0216	500	30
21	22	1	0.0678	500	94
1	8	0	0.1344	500	35

continued on following page

Table 10. Continued

From	To	n_l^0	reactance(p.u)	f_{lmax}(MW)	C_l(10^4US$)
2	8	0	0.1267	500	33
6	7	0	0.192	500	50
13	14	0	0.0447	500	62
14	23	0	0.062	500	86
16	23	0	0.0822	500	114
19	23	0	0.0606	500	84

This work was previously published in International Journal of Applied Evolutionary Computation, Volume 1, Issue 4, edited by Wei-Chiang Samuelson Hong, pp. 71-91, copyright 2010 by IGI Publishing (an imprint of IGI Global).

Compilation of References

Abarbanel, H. D. I. (1996). *Analysis of observed chaotic data*. New York: Springer-Verlag.

Abazajian, K. (2004). The second data release of the sloan digital sky survey. *The Astronomical Journal, 128*(1), 502–512. doi:10.1086/421365

Abdelhalim, M. B., Salama, A. E., & Habib, S. E. D. (2006). Hardware Software Partitioning using Particle Swarm Optimization Technique. In *Proceedings of the 6th International Workshop on System on Chip for Real Time Applications*, Cairo, Egypt (pp. 189-194). Washington, DC: IEEE Press.

Abduljalil, F. M. A., & Bodhe, S. K. (2007). Forward-Based Handoff Mechanism In Cellular IP Access Networks. In *Proceedings of the Australian Conference on Wireless Broadband and Ultra Wideband Communications, AUSWireless.* Retrieved from http://epress.lib.uts.edu.au/dspace/bitstream/handle/2100/93/13_Abduljalil.pdf?sequence=1

Aggarwal, M., Kent, R. D., & Ngom, A. (2005). Genetic Algorithm Based Scheduler for Computational Grids. In *Proceedings of the Nineteenth International Symposium on High Performance Computing Systems and Applications (HPCS'05)* (pp. 209-215). Washington, DC: IEEE.

Aggrawal, M., & Aggrawal, A. (2006). A Unified Scheduling Algorithm for Grid Applications. In *Proceedings of the International Symposium on High Performance Computing in an Advanced Colloborative Environment (HPCS'06)* (pp. 1-7).

Aghazadeh, R., Lesani, H., Sanaye-Pasand, M., & Ganji, B. (2005). New technique for frequency and amplitude Estimation of Power Signals. *IEE Proceedings. Generation, Transmission and Distribution, 152*(3), 435–440. doi:10.1049/ip-gtd:20041255

Ah King, R. T. F., Radha, B., & Rughooputh, H. C. S. (2003). A real-parameter genetic algorithm for optimal network reconfiguration. *IEEE International Conference on Industrial Technology, 1*, 54-59.

Ahlberg, J., & Forchheimer, R. (2003). Face tracking for model-based coding and face animation. *International Journal of Imaging Systems and Technology, 13*, 8–22. doi:10.1002/ima.10042

Aizawa, K., Harashima, H., & Saito, T. (1989). Model-based analysis-synthesis image coding (MBASIC) system for a person's face. *Signal Processing Image Communication, 1*, 139–152. doi:10.1016/0923-5965(89)90006-4

Alexandre, H. F., Dias, & Vasconcelos, J. A. (2002). Multiobjective Genetic Algorithms Applied to Solve Optimization Problems. *IEEE Transactions on Magnetics, 38*(2), 1133–1136. doi:10.1109/20.996290

Alguacil, N., Motto, A. L., & Conejo, A. J. (2003). Transmission expansion planning: a mixed-integer LP approach. *IEEE Transactions on Power Systems, 18*(3), 1070–1077. doi:10.1109/TPWRS.2003.814891

Ali, A. I., & Thiagarajan, H. (1989). A network relaxation based enumeration algorithm for set partitioning. *European Journal of Operational Research, 38*, 76–85. doi:10.1016/0377-2217(89)90471-2

Aljahdali, S. H., & El-Telbany, M. E. (2009). Software reliability prediction using objective Genetic Algorithm. In *Proceedings of the ACS/IEEE International Conference on Computer Systems and Applications* (pp. 293-300).

Alrashidi, M. R., & El-Hawary, M. E. (2007). Hybrid particle swarm optimization approach for solving the discrete OPF problem considering the valve loading effects. *IEEE Transactions on Power Systems, 22*(4), 2030–2038. doi:10.1109/TPWRS.2007.907375

Al-Sultan, K. S. (1995). A tabu search approach to the clustering problem. *Pattern Recognition, 28,* 1443–1451. doi:10.1016/0031-3203(95)00022-R

Amaki, H., Kita, H., & Kobayashi, S. (1996). Multi-Objective Optimization By Genetic Algorithms: A Review. In *Proceedings of IEEE International Conference on Evolutionary Computation* (pp. 517-522).

ANA. (n.d.). *Autonomic Network Architecture project.* Retrieved from http://www.ana-project.org/

Anbar, M., & Vidyarthi, D. P. (2009). Buffer Management in Cellular IP Network using PSO. *International Journal of Mobile Computing and Multimedia Communications, 1*(3), 78–93.

Anbar, M., & Vidyarthi, D. P. (2009). On Demand Bandwidth Reservation for Real-Time Traffic in Cellular IP Network using Particle Swarm Optimization. *International Journal of Business Data Communications and Networking, 5*(3), 53–65.

Angeline, P. J., & Pollack, J. B. (1992). The evolutionary induction of subroutines. In *Proceedings of the Fourteenth Annual Conference of the Cognitive Science Society* (pp. 236-241). Bloomington, IN: Lawrence Erlbaum. Retrieved from http://www.demo.cs.brandeis.edu/papers/glib92.pdf

Aoul, H., Mehaoua, A., & Skianis, C. (2007). A fuzzy logic-based AQM for real-time traffic over internet. *Computer Networks, 51,* 4617–4633. doi:10.1016/j.comnet.2007.06.007

Arrillaga, J., Watson, N. R., & Chen, S. (2000). *Power System Quality Assessment.* New York: John Wiley & Sons.

Aruldoss, T., Victoire, A., & Jeyakumar, A. E. (2005). Reserve constrained dynamic dispatch of units with valve point effects. *IEEE Transactions on Power Systems, 20*(3), 1273–1282. doi:10.1109/TPWRS.2005.851958

Arumugam, M. S., Rao, M. V. C., & Tan, A. W. C. (2009). A new novel and effective particle swarm optimization like algorithm with extrapolation technique. *International Journal of Applied Soft Computing, 9*(1), 308-320.

Arumugam, M. S., Rao, M. V. C., & Chandramohan, A. (2008). A new and improved version of particle swarm optimization algorithm with global-local best parameters. *Journal of Knowledge and Information System, 16*(3), 324–350.

Ashlock, D. (2005). *Evolutionary Computation for Modeling and Optimization.* New York: Springer.

Aster, R. C., Thurber, C. H., & Borchers, B. (2005). *Parameter estimation and Inverse problems.* New York: Elsevier Academic Press.

Azzag, H., Venturini, G., Oliver, A., & Guinot, C. (2007). A hierarchical and based clustering algorithm and its use in three real-world applications. *European Journal of Operational Research, 179,* 906–922. doi:10.1016/j.ejor.2005.03.062

Back, T. (1996). *Evolutionary algorithms in theory and practice.* Oxford, UK: Oxford University Press.

Back, T., Hammel, U., & Schwefel, H. (1997). Evolutionary computation: Comments on the history and current state. *IEEE Transactions on Evolutionary Computation, 1*(1), 3–17. doi:10.1109/4235.585888

Bahiense, L., Oliveira, G. C., Pereira, M., & Granville, S. (2001). A mixed integer disjunctive model for transmission network expansion. *IEEE Transactions on Power Systems, 16*(3), 560–565. doi:10.1109/59.932295

Bahl, I. J., & Bhartia, P. (1980). *Microstrip Antennas.* Dedham, MA: Artech House.

Banerjee, S., Bozorgzadeh, E., & Dutt, N. (2005). Considering run-time reconfiguration overhead in task graph transformation for dynamically reconfigurable architectures. In *Proceedings of the 13th Annual IEEE Symposium (FCCM)* (pp. 273-274).

Banerjee, S., Bozorgzadeh, E., & Dutt, N. (2005). Physically-aware HW–SW partitioning for reconfigurable architectures with partial dynamic reconfiguration. In *Proceedings of the DAC* (pp. 335-340).

Banerjee, S., Bozorgzadeh, E., & Dutt, N. (2006). Integrating physical constraints in HW–SW partitioning for architectures with partial dynamic reconfiguration. *IEEE Trans. Very Large Scale Integr. (VLSI). Syst., 14*(11), 1189–1202.

Baran, M. E., & Wu, F. F. (1989, April). Network reconfiguration in distribution systems for loss reduction and load balancing. *IEEE Transactions on Power Delivery, 4*(2), 1401–1409. doi:10.1109/61.25627

Barbuceanu, M., & Fox, M. (1994). *COOL - a language for describing coordination in multi-agent systems* (Tech. Rep.). Toronto, Ontario, Canada: Enterprise Integration Laboratory, University of Toronto.

Bartfai, G. (1996). An ART-based modular architecture for learning hierarchical clusterings. *Neurocomputing, 13,* 31–45. doi:10.1016/0925-2312(95)00077-1

Bazargan, K., Kastner, R., & Sarrafzadeh, M. (2000). Fast template placement for reconfigurable computing systems. *IEEE Design & Test of Computers, 17,* 68–83. doi:10.1109/54.825678

Bella, J. E., & McMullen, P. R. (2004). Ant colony optimization techniques for the vehicle routing problem. *Advanced Engineering Informatics, 18,* 41–48. doi:10.1016/j.aei.2004.07.001

Bello, M., Terlevich, R., & Chavez, M. (2007). *Estudio de la evolución temporal del triplete de CaII.* Unpublished Master's thesis, INAOE.

Bettayeb, M., & Qidwai, Q. (2003). A Hybrid Least Squares-GA based Algorithm for Harmonic Estimation. *IEEE Transactions on Power Delivery, 18*(2), 377–382. doi:10.1109/TPWRD.2002.807458

Beyer, H. (1996). Toward a theory of evolution strategies: Self-adaptation. *Evolutionary Computation, 3*(3), 311–347. doi:10.1162/evco.1995.3.3.311

Binato, S., de Oliveira, G. C., & de Araújo, J. L. (2001). A greedy randomized adaptive search procedure for transmission expansion planning. *IEEE Transactions on Power Systems, 16*(2), 247–253. doi:10.1109/59.918294

Binato, S., Oliveira, G. C., & Araújo, J. L. (2001). Greedy randomized adaptive search procedure for transmission expansion planning. *IEEE Transactions on Power Systems, 16*(2), 247–253. doi:10.1109/59.918294

Binato, S., Pereira, M. V. F., & Granville, S. (2001). A new Benders decomposition approach to solve power transmission network design problems. *IEEE Transactions on Power Systems, 16*(2), 235–240. doi:10.1109/59.918292

Biswas, A., Dasgupta, S., Das, S., & Abraham, A. (2007). Synergy of PSO and Bacterial Foraging Optimization: A Comparative Study on Numerical Benchmarks. In E. Corchado et al. (Eds.), *Proceedings of the Second International Symposium on Hybrid Artificial Intelligent Systems (HAIS), Innovations in Hybrid Intelligent Systems (ASC 44)* (pp. 255-263).

Biswas, A., Dasgupta, S., Das, S., & Abraham, A. (2007). Synergy of PSO and Bacterial Foraging Optimization- A Comparative Study on Numerical Benchmarks. In Corchado, E., Corchado, J. M., & Abraham, A. (Eds.), *Innovations in Hybrid Intelligent Systems, Advances in intelligent and soft computing* (*Vol. 44,* pp. 255–263). Berlin: Springer. doi:10.1007/978-3-540-74972-1_34

Black, D. et al. (1998). An architecture for differentiated service. *RFC 2475.*

Bollen, M. H. (2000). *Understanding Power Quality Problems: Voltage Sags and Interruptions.* New York: IEEE Press.

Bonnet, D., Labouisse, V., & Grumbach, A. (1997). δ-NARMA neural networks: A new approach to signal prediction. *IEEE Transactions on Signal Processing, 45,* 2878. doi:10.1109/78.650106

Braden, R. (1985). *Towards a transport service for transaction processing applications* (RFC 955). Los Angeles: UCLA OAC.

Bressan, A., Chiosi, C., & Fagotto, F. (1994). Spectrophotometric evolution of elliptical galaxies. 1: Ultraviolet excess and color-magnitude-redshift relations. *The Astrophysical Journal. Supplement Series, 94*(1), 63–115. doi:10.1086/192073

Brest, J., Greiner, S., Boskovic, B., Mernik, M., & Zumer, V. (2006). Self-adapting control parameters in differential evolution: A comparative study on numerical benchmark problems. *IEEE Transactions on Evolutionary Computation, 10*(6), 646–657. doi:10.1109/TEVC.2006.872133

Brucker, P. (1978). On the complexity of clustering problems. In M. Beckmenn, & H. P. Kunzi (Eds.), *Optimization and operations research* (LNEMS 157, pp. 45-54).

Buck, M. (1993). *Model based image sequence coding.* Berlin, Germany: Kluwer.

Cai, K. Y., Cai, L., Wang, W. D., Yu, Z. Y., & Zhang, D. (2001). On the neural network approach in software reliability modeling. *Journal of Systems and Software, 58,* 47–62. doi:10.1016/S0164-1212(01)00027-9

Cai, K., Yuan, C., & Zhang, M. L. (1991). A critical review on software reliability modeling. *Reliability Engineering & System Safety, 32,* 357–371. doi:10.1016/0951-8320(91)90009-V

Cai, Z., & Wang, Y. (2006). A multiobjective optimization-based evolutionary algorithm for constrained optimization. *IEEE Transactions on Evolutionary Computation, 10*(6), 658–675. doi:10.1109/TEVC.2006.872344

Cardelli, J., Clayton, G., & Mathis, J. (1989). The relationship between infrared, optical, and ultraviolet extinction. *The Astrophysical Journal, 345*(1), 245–256. doi:10.1086/167900

Carlisle, A., & Dozier, G. (2001). An off-the-shelf PSO. In *Proceedings of the Workshop on Particle Swarm Optimization 2001,* Indianapolis, IN.

Carlos, A., Coello, C., & Lechuga, M. S. (2002). MOPSO: A Proposal for Multiple Objective Particle Swarm Optimization. In *Proceedings of the Congress on Evolutionary Computation Vol.* (Vol. 2, pp. 1051-1056). doi: 10.1109/CEC.2002.1004388

Carlos, A., & Coello, C. (2000). An Updated Survey of GA-Based Multiobjective Optimization Techniques. *ACM Computing Surveys, 32*(2), 109–143. doi:10.1145/358923.358929

Carreras, I., Chlamtac, I., De Pellegrini, F., Kiraly, C., Miorandi, D., & Woesner, H. (2006). A biological approach to autonomic communication systems. In *Transactions on Computational Systems Biology IV* (LNCS 3939, pp. 76-82).

Carter, E. F. (1994). The generation and application of random numbers. *Forth Dimensions, 16,* 202–214.

CASCADAS. (n.d.). *CASCADAS project.* Retrieved from http://www.cascadas-project.org/index.html

Castro, S., Caers, J., & Mukerji, T. (2005). *The Stanford VI Reservoir.* Palo Alto, CA: Stanford Center for Reservoir Forecasting (SCRF).

Castro, L. N., & Timmis, J. (2002). *Artificial Immune System: A New Computational Intelligence Approach.* New York: Springer Verlag.

Castro, L. N., & Zuben, F. J. (2002). Learning and optimization using Clonal Selection principle. *IEEE Transactions on Evolutionary Computation, 6*(3), 239–251. doi:10.1109/TEVC.2002.1011539

Chang, H. C., & Kuo, C. C. (1994). Network reconfiguration in distribution system using simulated annealing. *Electric Power Systems Research, 29,* 227–238. doi:10.1016/0378-7796(94)90018-3

Chang, J. L., & Miaou, S. P. (1999). Real-time prediction of traffic flows using dynamic generalized linear models. *Transportation Research Record, 1678,* 168–178. doi:10.3141/1678-21

Chaturvedi, K. T., Pandit, M., & Srivastava, L. (2009). Particle Swarm Optimization with Time Varying Acceleration Coefficients for Nonconvex Economic Power Dispatch. *Electrical Power and Energy systems, 31*(6), 249-257.

Chaturvedi, K. T., Pandit, M., & Srivastava, L. (2008, August). Self-Organizing Hierarchical Particle Swarm Optimization for Nonconvex Economic Dispatch. *IEEE Transactions on Power Systems, 23*(3), 1079–1087. doi:10.1109/TPWRS.2008.926455

Chen, Q. (2003). *Objective Increment, Its Effect and Application in Multi-Objective Optimization Evolution.* Unpublished master's thesis, National University of Singapore, Singapore.

Chen, Y., & Hsiung, P. (2003). Hardware Task Scheduling and Placement in Operating Systems for Dynamically Reconfigurable SoC. In. *Proceedings of the EUC* (pp. 489-498).

Chen, Y., & Lemin, L. (2005). A random early expiration detection based buffer management algorithm for real-time traffic over wireless networks. In *Proceedings of the IEEE International Conference on Computer and Information Technology (CIT 2005),* Shanghai, China (pp. 507-511). Washington, DC: IEEE Press.

Chen, C. L., & Chen, N. (2001). Direct search method for solving economic dispatch problem considering transmission capacity constraints. *IEEE Transactions on Power Systems, 16*(4), 764–769. doi:10.1109/59.962424

Chen, M. (1997). Digital Algorithms for measurements of voltage flicker. *IEE Proceedings. Generation, Transmission and Distribution*, *144*(2), 175–180. doi:10.1049/ip-gtd:19970683

Chen, Q., & Guan, S. U. (2004, June). Incremental Multiple Objective Genetic Algorithms. *IEEE Transactions on System. Man and Cybernetics B*, *34*(3), 1325–1334. doi:10.1109/TSMCB.2003.822958

Cheriton, D. (1988). VMTP: Versatile Message Transaction Protocol. *RFC 1045*.

Chiou, Y. C., & Chou, S. C. (2005). *Ant-based clustering algorithms*. Paper presented at the International Conference of International Federation of Operational Research Societies, Hawaii.

Chiou, Y. C., & Lan, L. W. (2001). Genetic clustering algorithms. *European Journal of Operational Research*, *135*, 413–427. doi:10.1016/S0377-2217(00)00320-9

Choi, C. S., Aizawa, K., Harashima, H., & Takebe, T. (1994). Analysis and synthesis of facial image sequences in model-based image coding. *IEEE Transactions on Circuits and Systems for Video Technology*, *4*, 257–275. doi:10.1109/76.305871

Civanlar, S., Grainger, J. J., Yin, H., & Lee, S. S. H. (1998, July). Distribution feeder reconfiguration for loss reduction. *IEEE Transactions on Power Delivery*, *3*(3), 1217–1223. doi:10.1109/61.193906

Clark, S. D., Dougherty, M. S., & Kirby, H. R. (1993). *The use of neural networks and time series models for short term traffic forecasting: A comparative study*. Paper presented at Transportation Planning Method Conference, PTRC 21st Summer Annual Meeting, Manchester, UK.

Clerc, M., & Kennedy, J. (2002). The particle swarm-explosion, stability, and convergence in a multidimensional complex space. *IEEE Transactions on Evolutionary Computation*, *6*(1), 58–73. doi:10.1109/4235.985692

Coelho, L. S., & Mariani, V. C. (2006). Combining of chaotic differential evolution and quadratic programming for economic dispatch optimization with valve-point effect. *IEEE Transactions on Power Systems*, *21*(2), 989–996. doi:10.1109/TPWRS.2006.873410

Contreras, J., & Wu, F. F. (2000). A kernel-oriented algorithm for transmission expansion Planning. *IEEE Transactions on Power Systems*, *15*(4), 1434–1440. doi:10.1109/59.898124

Corne, D. W., Knowles, J. D., & Oates, M. J. (2000). The Pareto Envelope-Based Selection Algorithm For Multiobjective Optimization. In *Proceedings of the Sixth International Conference On Parallel Problem Solving from Nature*, France. Berlin: Springer Verlag. Retrieved from http://www.lania.mx/~ccoello/EMOO/knowles00d.ps.gz, 98-105

Cui, Z., Cai, X., Zeng, J., & Sun, G. (2008). Particle swarm optimization with FUSS and RWS for high dimensional functions. *Applied Mathematics and Computation*, *205*, 98–108. doi:10.1016/j.amc.2008.05.147

Cui, Z., Zeng, J., & Sun, G. (2006). A Fast Particle Swarm Optimization International. *Journal of Innovative Computing*, *2*, 1365–1380.

da Silva, E. L., Gil, H. A., & Areiza, J. M. (2000). Transmission network expansion planning under an improved genetic algorithm. *IEEE Transactions on Power Systems*, *15*(3), 1168–1175. doi:10.1109/59.871750

da Silva, E. L., Ortiz, J. M. A., Oliveira, G. C., & Binato, S. (2001). Transmission network expansion planning under a tabu search approach. *IEEE Transactions on Power Systems*, *16*(1), 62–68. doi:10.1109/59.910782

Das, D. (2006). A Fuzzy Multi objective Approach for Network Reconfiguration of Distribution Systems. *IEEE Transactions on Power Delivery*, *21*(1), 202–209. doi:10.1109/TPWRD.2005.852335

Dasgupta, S., Das, S., Abraham, A., & Biswas, A. (2009). Adaptive Computational Chemotaxis in Bacterial Foraging Optimization: An Analysis. *IEEE Transactions on Evolutionary Computing*.

Dash, P. K., Jena, R. K., Panda, G., & Routray, A. (2000). An extended complex Kalman filter for frequency measurement of distorted signals. *IEEE Transactions on Instrumentation and Measurement*, *49*, 746–753. doi:10.1109/19.863918

Dash, P. K., Pradhan, A. K., & Salama, M. A. (2002). Estimation of Voltage Flicker Magnitude and Frequency Using Fourier Linear Combiners to Improve Power Quality. *Electric Power Components and Systems, 29*, 1–13.

Dash, P. K., Swain, D. P., Liew, A. C., & Rahman, S. (1996). An Adaptive Linear Combiner for On-Line Tracking of Power System Harmonics. *IEEE Transactions on Power Systems, 11*(4), 1730–1735. doi:10.1109/59.544635

De Castro, L. N., & Von Zuben, F. J. (1999). *Artificial Immune Systems: Part I – Basic Theory and Applications* (Tech. Rep. No. RT DCA 01/99).

Deb, K., Agarwal, S., Pratap, A., & Meyarivan, T. (2000). A Fast Elitist Non-Dominated Sorting Genetic Algorithm For Multi-Objective Optimization: NSGA-II. In *Proceedings of the Parallel Problem Solving from Nature VI Conference*, France (849-858).

Deb, K. (1999). Multi-objective genetic algorithms: problems, difficulties, and construction of test problems. *Evolutionary Computation, 7*, 205–230. doi:10.1162/evco.1999.7.3.205

Deb, K., Agarwal, S., & Meyarivan, T. (2002). A Fast And Elitist Multi-Objective Genetic Algorithm: NSGA-II. *IEEE Transactions on Evolutionary Computation, 6*(2), 182–197. doi:10.1109/4235.996017

Deb, K., Pratap, A., Agarwal, S., & Meyarivan, T. (2002). A fast and elitist multiobjective genetic algorithm: NSGA-II. *IEEE Transactions on Evolutionary Computation, 6*, 182–197. doi:10.1109/4235.996017

Derneryd, A. G. (1978). A Theoretical Investigation of the Rectangular Microstrip Patch Antenna Element. *IEEE Transactions on Antennas and Propagation, 26*(4), 532–535. doi:10.1109/TAP.1978.1141890

Desell, A. L., McClelland, E. C., Tammar, K., & Van Horne, R. R. (1984). Transmission constrained production cost analysis in power system planning. *IEEE Transactions on Power Apparatus and Systems, 103*(8), 2192–2198. doi:10.1109/TPAS.1984.318532

Deutsch, C., & Journel, A. (1992). *GSLIB: Geostatistical Software Library* (p. 340). New York: Oxford University Press.

Diao, Y., Hellerstein, J. L., Parekh, S., Griffith, R., Kaiser, G. E., & Phung, D. (2005). A control theory foundation for self-managing computing systems. *IEEE Journal on Selected Areas in Communications, 23*, 2213–2222. doi:10.1109/JSAC.2005.857206

Diehl, N. (1991). Object motion estimation and segmentation on image sequences. *Signal Processing Image Communication, 3*, 23–56. doi:10.1016/0923-5965(91)90028-Z

Diessel, O., ElGindy, H., Middendorf, M., Schmeck, H., & Schmidt, B. (2000). Dynamic Scheduling of Tasks on Partially Reconfigurable FPGAs. In *Proceedings on computers and digital techniques* (*Vol. 147*, pp. 181–188). Washington, DC: IEEE.

Discipulus tool. (n.d.). Retreived from http://www.rmltech.com/

Dobson, S., Denazis, S., Fernández, A., Gaïti, D., Gelenbe, E., & Massacci, F. (2006). A survey of autonomic communications. *ACM Transactions on Autonomous and Adaptive Systems, 1*(2), 223–259. doi:10.1145/1186778.1186782

Dohi, T., Nishio, Y., & Osaki, S. (1999). Optional software release scheduling based on artificial neural networks. *Annals of Software Engineering, 8*, 167–185. doi:10.1023/A:1018962910992

Dorigo, M., & Gambardella, L. M. (1997). Ant colony system: A cooperative learning approach to the traveling salesman problem. *IEEE Transactions on Evolutionary Computation, 1*, 53–66. doi:10.1109/4235.585892

Dorigo, M., Maniezzo, V., & Colorni, A. (1996). Ant system: Optimization by a colony of cooperating agents. *IEEE Transactions on Systems, Man, and Cybernetics-Part B, 26*, 29–41. doi:10.1109/3477.484436

Dornaika, F., & Ahlberg, J. (2004). Fast and reliable active appearance model search for 3D face tracking. *IEEE Transactions on Systems, Man and Cybernetics. Part B, 34*, 1838–1853.

Dornaika, F., & Ahlberg, J. (2006). Fitting 3D face models for tracking and active appearance model training. *Image and Vision Computing, 24*, 1010–1024. doi:10.1016/j.imavis.2006.02.025

Doty, K. W., & McEntire, P. L. (1982). An analysis of electrical power brokerage systems. *IEEE Transactions on Power Apparatus and Systems*, *101*(2), 389–396. doi:10.1109/TPAS.1982.317119

Du, D., Simon, D., & Ergezer, M. (2009). Biogeography-Based Optimization Combined with Evolutionary Strategy and Immigration Refusal. In *Proceedings of the IEEE Conference on Systems, Man, and Cybernetics* (pp. 997-1002). doi: 10.1109/ICSMC.2009.5346055

Dugan, R. C., McGranaghan, M. F., & Beaty, H. W. (2000). *Electrical Power Systems Quality*. New York: McGraw-Hill Int.

Durbin, J. (2000). The Foreman lecture: The state space approach to time series analysis and its potential for official statistics. *Australian and New Zealand Journal of Statistics*, *42*(1), 1–23. doi:10.1111/1467-842X.00104

Dusonchet, Y. P., & El-Abiad, A. H. (1973). Transmission planning using discrete dynamic optimization. *IEEE Transactions on PAS*, *92*(4), 1358–1371.

Eberhart, R. C., & Shi, Y. (2000). Comparing inertia weights and constriction factors in particle swarm optimization. In *Proceedings of the 2000 Congress on Evolutionary Computation* (Vol. 1, pp. 84-88).

Eberhart, R., & Shi, Y. (2001). Particle swarm optimization: Developments, applications and resources. In *Proceedings of the IEEE congress on Evolutionary Computation* (Vol.1, pp. 81-86). doi: 10.1109/CEC.2001.934374

Eberhart, R., & Shi, Y. (2004). Special issue on particle swarm optimization. *IEEE Transactions on Evolutionary Computation*, *89*(3), 201–228. doi:10.1109/TEVC.2004.830335

Echeverría, D., & Mukerji, T. (2009 July). A robust scheme for spatio-temporal inverse modelling of oil reservoirs. In R. S. Anderssen, R. D. Braddock, & L. T. H. Newham (Eds.), *18th World IMACS Congress and MODSIM09 International Congress on Modelling and Simulation. Modelling and Simulation Society of Australia and New Zealand and International Association for Mathematics and Computers in Simulation*, Cairns, Australia (pp. 4206-421).

Edgar, T., Himmelblau, D., & Lasdon, L. (2001). *Optimization of chemical processes*. New York: McGraw-Hill.

EFIPSANS. (n.d.). *EFIPSANS project*. Retrieved from http://www.efipsans.org

Eisert, P. (2000). *Very low bit rate coding*. Unpublished doctoral dissertation, Fraunhofer Institute for Telecommunications, Germany.

Eisert, P. (2003). MPEG-4 facial animation in video analysis and synthesis. *International Journal of Imaging Systems and Technology*, *13*, 245–256. doi:10.1002/ima.10072

El Farag, A., Hatem, B., & Shaheen, S. (2007). Improving Utilization of Reconfigurable Resources Using Two-Dimensional Compaction. *International Journal of Super-Computing*, *42*, 235–250.

El-Darzi, E., & Mitra, G. (1995). Graph theoretic relaxations of set covering and set partitioning problems. *European Journal of Operational Research*, *87*, 109–121. doi:10.1016/0377-2217(94)00115-S

El-Naggar, K. M., & AL-Hasawi, W. M. (2006). A Genetic based algorithm for measurement of Power System Disturbances. *Electric Power Systems Research*, *76*, 808–814. doi:10.1016/j.epsr.2005.06.012

Elsayed, T., Hussein, M., Youssef, M., Nadeem, T., Youssef, A., & Iftode, L. (2003, December). ATP: Autnomous Transport Protocol. In *Proceedings of the 46th IEEE International Midwest Symposium on Circuits and Systems (MWSCAS'03)* (Vol. 1, pp. 436-439).

El-Zonkoly, A. (2005). Power system model validation for power quality assessment applications using genetic algorithm. *Expert Systems with Applications*, *29*, 941–944. doi:10.1016/j.eswa.2005.06.013

Ergezer, M., Simon, D., & Du, D. (2009). Oppositional Biogeography-Based Optimization. In *Proceedings of the IEEE Conference on Systems, Man, and Cybernetics* (pp. 1009–1014). doi: 10.1109/ICSMC.2009.5346043

Escobar, A. H., Gallego, R. A., & Romero, R. (2004). Multistage and Coordinated planning of the expansion of transmission systems. *IEEE Transactions on Power Systems*, *19*(2), 735–744. doi:10.1109/TPWRS.2004.825920

Farhang-Mehr, A., & Azarm, S. (2002). Diversity assessment of Pareto optimal solution sets: An entropy approach. In *Proceedings of the Congress Evolutionary Computation*, *1*, 723–728.

Farlow, S. J. (1984). *Self-Organizing Methods in Modeling: GMDH type Algorithm*. New York: Bazel, Marcel Dekker Inc.

Farmer, E. D., Grubb, M. J., & Vlahos, K. (1990). Probabilistic production costing of transmission-constrained power systems. In *Proceedings of the 10th PSCC Power System Computation Conference* (pp. 663-669).

Fekete, S., Kohler, E., & Teich, J. (2001). Higher-dimensional packing with order constrains. In *Proceedings of Algorithms and data structures (WADS 2001)* (LNCS 2125, pp. 192-204). Berlin: Springer.

Fekete, S., Kohler, E., & Teich, J. (2001). Optimal FPGA module placement with temporal precedence constrains. In *Proceedings of design automation and test in Europe* (pp. 658–665). DATE.

Fekete, S., & Schepers, J. (2004). A combinational characterization of higher-dimensional orthogonal packing. *Mathematics of Operations Research*, *29*, 591–602. doi:10.1287/moor.1030.0079

Feoktistov, V., & Janaqi, S. (2004). Generalization of the strategies in differential evolution. In *Proceedings of the 18th International Parallel and Distributed Processing Symposium* (pp. 165-170). doi: 10.1109/IPDPS.2004.1303160

Fernandes, R. C., Mateus, A., Sodré, L., Stasin'ska, G., & Gomes, J. (2005). Semi-empirical analysis of sloan digital sky survey galaxies - I. spectral synthesis method. *Monthly Notices of the Royal Astronomical Society*, *358*(2), 363–378. doi:10.1111/j.1365-2966.2005.08752.x

Fernandez, G., Muñoz, S., Sanchez, R., & Mayol, W. (1997). Simultaneous stabilization using evolutionary strategies. *International Journal of Control*, *68*(6), 1417–1435. doi:10.1080/002071797223091

Finin, T., McKay, D., Fritszson, R., & McEntire, R. (1994). KQML: An information and knowledge exchange protocol. In T. Yokoi (Ed.), *Knowledge building and knowledge sharing*. Amsterdam, The Netherlands: IOS Press.

Fogel, D. B. (1993). On the philosophical differences between evolutionary algorithms and genetic algorithms. In *Proceedings of 2nd Annual Conference on Evolutionary Programming. Evolutionary Programming Society* (pp. 23-29).

Fogel, D. B., & Atmar, J. W. (1990). Comparing genetic operators with Gaussians mutations in simulated evolutionary processes using linear systems. *Biological Cybernetics*, *63*(2), 111–114. doi:10.1007/BF00203032

Fonseca, C. M., & Fleming, P. J. (1993). Multiobjective genetic algorithms. *IEE colloquium on Genetic Algorithms for Control Systems Engineering* (Digest No. 1993/130). London, UK.

Fonseca, C. M., & Fleming, P. J. (1993, July 17-21). Genetic algorithms for multiobjective optimization: Formulation, discussion and generalization. In *Proceedings of the Fifth International Conference on Genetic Algorithm*, San Mateo, CA (pp. 416-423).

Fonseca, C. M., & Fleming, P. J. (1995). An Overview of Evolutionary Algorithms in Multiobjective Optimization. *Evolutionary Computation*, *3*(1), 1–16. doi:10.1162/evco.1995.3.1.1

Fonseca, C. M., & Fleming, P. J. (1998, January). Multiobjective optimization and multiple constraint handling with evolutionary algorithms. I. A unified formulation. *IEEE Transactions on System. Man and Cybernetics A*, *28*(1), 26–37. doi:10.1109/3468.650319

Forchheimer, R., & Kronander, T. (1989). Image coding–from waveforms to animation. *IEEE Transactions on Acoustics, Speech, and Signal Processing*, *37*, 2008–2023. doi:10.1109/29.45550

Friedman, J. H. (1991). Multivariate adaptive regression splines (with discussion). *Annals of Statistics*, *19*, 1–141. doi:10.1214/aos/1176347963

Friedman, J. H. (1999). Stochastic gradient boosting. *Computational Statistics & Data Analysis*, *38*(4), 367–378. doi:10.1016/S0167-9473(01)00065-2

Gallego, R. A., Monticelli, A., & Romero, R. (1998). Transmission expansion planning by extended genetic algorithm. In *Proceedings of the Gener. Trans. Distr.*, *145*(3), 329-335.

Gallego, R. A., Alves, A. B., Monticelli, A., & Romero, R. (1997). Parallel simulated annealing approach applied to long term transmission network expansion planning. *IEEE Transactions on Power Systems*, *12*(1), 181–188. doi:10.1109/59.574938

Gallego, R. A., Monticelli, A., & Romero, R. (1998). Comparative studies of non-convex optimization methods for transmission network expansion planning. *IEEE Transactions on Power Systems*, *13*(3), 822–828. doi:10.1109/59.708680

Gallego, R. A., Monticelli, A., & Romero, R. (2000). Tabu search algorithm for network synthesis. *IEEE Transactions on Power Systems*, *15*(2), 490–495. doi:10.1109/59.867130

Garai, G., & Chaudhuri, B. B. (2004). A novel genetic algorithm for automatic clustering. *Pattern Recognition Letters*, *25*, 173–187. doi:10.1016/j.patrec.2003.09.012

Garver, L. L. (1970). Transmission network estimation using linear programming.

Giani, M., Redaelli, M., Santambrogio, M., & Sciuto, D. (2007). Task partitioning for the scheduling on reconfigurable systems driven by specification self-similarity. In *Proceedings of the Int. Conf. (ERSA)* (pp. 78-84).

Giraud-Moreau, L., & Lafon, P. (2002). A comparison of evolutionary algorithms for mechanical design components. *Engineering Optimization*, *34*(1), 307–322. doi:10.1080/03052150211750

Girgis, A. A., & Ham, E. M. (1980). A Quantitive Study of Pit Falls in the FFT. *IEEE Trans. on AES*, *16*(4), 434–439.

Goldberg, D. E. (1989). *Genetic Algorithm in search, optimization and machining learning*. Reading, MA: Addison Wesley.

Gomez, J. C., Athanassoula, E., Fuentes, O., & Bosma, A. (2004). *Using evolution strategies to find a dynamical model for the m81 triplet* (LNAI 3215, pp. 404-410). New York: Springer.

Gong, W., Cai, Z., & Ling, C. X. (2009a). *A real-coded Biogeography-Based Optimization with neighborhood search operator*. Retrieved from http://academic.csuohio.edu/simond/bbo

Gong, W., Cai, Z., & Ling, C. X. (2009b). *DE/BBO: A hybrid differential evolution with biogeography-based optimization for global numerical optimization. Manuscript submitted for publication*. Retrieved from http://academic.csuohio.edu/simond/bbo

Gonzalo, G. E., & Martínez, F. J. L. (2009a). Design of a simple and powerful Particle Swarm optimizer. In *Proceedings of the International Conference on Computational and Mathematical Methods in Science and Engineering (CMMSE2009)*, Gijón, Spain.

Gonzalo, G. E., & Martínez, F. J. L. (2009b). *The PP-GPSO and RR-GPSO (Tech. Rep.)*. Oviedo, Spain: University of Oviedo, Department of Mathematics.

Goulden, C. H. (1956). *Methods of Statistical Analysis*. New York: Wiley.

Grosan, C., Abraham, A., & Helvik, B. (2007). *Multiobjective Evolutionary Algorithms for Scheduling Jobs on Computational Grids*. Retrieved from www.softcomputing.net/ac2007_2.pdf

Grosan, C., Abraham, A., & Ishibuchi, H. (Eds.). (2007). *Hybrid Evolutionary Algorithms*. Berlin: Springer.

Guan, S.-U., & Jiang, Z. (2000). *A new approach to implement self-modifying protocols*. Paper presented at the IEEE International Symposium on Intelligent Signal Processing and Communication Systems. HAGGLE. (n.d.). *HAGGLE project*. Retrieved from http://www.haggleproject.org/index.php/Main_Page

Guan, S. U., & Li, P. (2002). A Hierarchical Incremental Learning Approach to Task Decomposition. *Journal of Intelligent Systems*, *12*(3), 201–226.

Guan, S. U., & Li, P. (2004). Incremental Learning in Terms of Output Attributes. *Journal of Intelligent Systems*, *13*(2), 95–122.

Guan, S. U., & Li, S. C. (2001, December). Incremental Learning with Respect to New Incoming Input Attributes. *Neural Processing Letters*, *14*(3), 241–260. doi:10.1023/A:1012799113953

Guan, S. U., & Liu, J. (2002). Incremental Ordered Neural Network Training. *Journal of Intelligent Systems*, *12*(3), 137–172.

Guan, S. U., & Liu, J. (2004). Incremental Neural Network Training with an Increasing Input Dimension. *Journal of Intelligent Systems*, *13*(1), 45–70.

Guan, S. U., & Zhu, F. M. (2003, November). Incremental Learning of Collaborative Classifier Agents with New Class Acquisition – An Incremental Genetic Algorithm Approach. *International Journal of Intelligent Systems, 18*(11), 1173–1193. doi:10.1002/int.10145

Gu, X., Strassner, J., Xie, J., Wolf, L. C., & Suda, T. (2008, January). Autonomic multimedia communications: Where are we now? *Proceedings of the IEEE, 96*(1), 143–154. doi:10.1109/JPROC.2007.909880

Haffner, S., Monticelli, A., Garcia, A., Mantovani, J., & Romero, R. (2000). Branch and bound algorithm for transmission system expansion planning using a transportation model. *IEE Proceedings. Generation, Transmission and Distribution, 147*(3), 149–156. doi:10.1049/ip-gtd:20000337

Hanad, M., & Vemuri, R. (2004). An efficient algorithm for finding empty space for online FPGA placement. In *Proceedigns of the Design automation conference*, San Diego, CA (pp. 960-965).

Hansen, M. P., & Jaszkiewicz, A. (1998). *Evaluating the Quality of Approximations to the Nondominated Set* (Tech. Rep. No. IMM-REP-1998-7). Copenhagen, Denmark: Technical University of Denmark, Institute of Mathematical Modeling.

Hansen, P., & Jaumard, B. (1987). Minimum sum of diameters clustering. *Journal of Classification, 4*, 215–226. doi:10.1007/BF01896987

He, G., & Ma, S. (2002). A study on the short-term prediction of traffic volume based on wavelet analysis. In *Proceedings of the IEEE 5th International Conference on ITS* (pp. 731-735).

Head, K. L. (1995). Event-based short-term traffic flow prediction model. *Transportation Research Record, 1510*, 45–52.

Hecht-Nielsen, R. (1987). Counterpropagation networks. *Applied Optics, 26*, 4979–4983. doi:10.1364/AO.26.004979

Hemick, S. D., & Shoults, R. R. (1985). A practical approach to an interim multi-area economic dispatch using limited computer resources. *IEEE Transactions on Power Apparatus and Systems, 104*(6), 1400–1404. doi:10.1109/TPAS.1985.319244

Hendtlass, T. (2001). A combined swarm differential evolution algorithm for optimization problems. In L. Monostori, J. Vancza, & M. Ali (Eds.), *Proceedings of the 14th International Conference on Industrial and Engineering Applications of Artificial Intelligence and Expert System, Engineering of Intelligent Systems* (pp. 11-18). Berlin: Springer.

Hilborn, R. C. (2000). *Chaos and nonlinear dynamics.* New York: Oxford University Press.

Holland, J. (1992). Genetic algorithms. *Scientific American*, 66–72. doi:10.1038/scientificamerican0792-66

Hong, W. C. (2009). Hybrid evolutionary algorithms in a SVR-based electric load forecasting model. *International Journal of Electrical Power & Energy Systems, 31*(7-8), 409–417. doi:10.1016/j.ijepes.2009.03.020

Horn, J., Nafpliotis, N., & Goldberg, D. E. (1994, June 27-29). A Niched Pareto Genetic Algorithm For Multiobjective Optimization. In *Proceedings of the First IEEE Conference on Evolutionary Computation, IEEE world congress on computational intelligence*, Orlando, FL, USA (pp. 82-87).

Ho, S. L., Yang, S., Ni, G., & Wong, H. C. (2006). A Particle Swarm Optimization Method With Enhanced Global Search Ability for Design Optimizations of Electromagnetic Devices. *IEEE Transactions on Magnetics, 42*(4), 1107–1110. doi:10.1109/TMAG.2006.871426

Hou, Y. T., Dapeng, W., Yao, J., & Takafumi, C. (2000). A core-stateless buffer management mechanism for differentiated services Internet. In *Proceedings of the 25th Annual IEEE Conference on Local Computer Networks (LCN 2000)*, Tampa, FL (pp.168-176). Washington, DC: IEEE Press.

Hsiao, Y. T. (2004, February). Multiobjective evolution programming method for feeder reconfiguration. *IEEE Transactions on Power Systems, 19*(1), 594–599. doi:10.1109/TPWRS.2003.821430

Huang, T. S., & Tao, H. (2001). Visual face tracking and its application to 3D model-based video coding. In *Proceedings of Picture Coding Symposium*, Seoul, Korea (pp. 57-60).

Huang, Y. C. (2002, September). Enhanced genetic algorithm-based fuzzy multi-objective approach to distribution network reconfiguration. In *Proceedings of the IEE Gener. Transm. Distrib. Conf.* (Vol. 149, No. 5, pp. 615-620).

IEEE Trans. on Power Systems, 21(4), 1565-1573.

IEEE Transactions on PAS, 8 (7), 1688-1697.

IETF. *RFC1323*. Retrieved from http://www.ietf.org/rfc/rfc1323.txt?number=1323

Iokibe, T., Kanke, M., & Yasunari, F. (1995). Local fuzzy reconstruction model for short-term prediction on chaotic time series. *Fuzzy Set, 7*(1), 186–194.

Ishak, S., Kotha, P., & Alecsandru, C. (2003). Optimization of dynamic neural network performance for short-term traffic prediction. *Transportation Research Record, 1836,* 45–56. doi:10.3141/1836-07

ISTface. (2009). *wow25.fap* (Program from Instituto Superior Technico, standard FAP animation sequence).

Ivakhnenko, A. G. (1968). The GMDH. A rival of stochastic approximation. *Sov. Autom. Control, 3,* 43.

Iyer, R. K., & Lee, I. (1996). Measurement-based analysis of software Reliability. In Lyu, M. R. (Ed.), *Handbook of Software Reliability Engineering* (pp. 303–358). New York: McGraw-Hill.

Jain, L. C., Palade, V., & Srinivasan, D. (2007). *Advances in Evolutionary Computing for System Design.* Berlin: Springer Verlag.

James, S., Hou, F., & Ho, P. H. (2007). An Application-Driven MAC-layer Buffer Management with Active Dropping for Real-time Video Streaming in 802.16 Networks. In *Proceedings of the IEEE International Conference on Advanced Information Networking and Applications (AINA '07)*, Niagara Falls, ON (pp. 451-458). Washington, DC: IEEE Press.

Jardosh, S., Zunnun, N., Ranjan, P., & Srivastava, S. (2008). Effect of network coding on buffer management in wireless sensor network. In *Proceedings of the International Conference on Intelligent Sensors, Sensor Networks and Information Processing (ISSNIP 2008)*, Sydney, NSW, Australia (pp. 157-162). Washington, DC: IEEE Press.

Jayabarathi, T., Sadasivam, G., & Ramachandran, V. (2000). Evolutionary programming based multi-area economic dispatch with tie-line constraints. *Electrical Machines and Power Systems, 28,* 1165–1176. doi:10.1080/073135600449044

Jayaraman, V. K., Kulkarni, B. D., Karale, S., & Shelokar, P. (2000). Ant colony framework for optimal design and scheduling of batch plants. *Computers & Chemical Engineering, 24,* 1901–1912. doi:10.1016/S0098-1354(00)00592-5

Jean, J., Tomko, K., Yavagal, V., Shah, J., & Cook, R. (1999). Dynamic reconfiguration to support concurrent applications. *IEEE Transactions on Computers, 48*(6), 591–602. doi:10.1109/12.773796

Jennings, B., Meer, S. V. D., Balasubramaniam, S., Botvich, D., Foghlu, M. O., & Donnelly, W. (2007). Towards autonomic management of communications networks. *IEEE Communications Magazine, 45*(10), 112–121. doi:10.1109/MCOM.2007.4342833

Jensen, M. T. (2003). Reducing the Run-Time Complexity of Multiobjective EAs: The SGA-II and Other Algorithms. *IEEE Transactions on Evolutionary Computation, 7*(5), 503–515. doi:10.1109/TEVC.2003.817234

Jiang, J. H., Wang, J. H., Chu, X., & Yu, R. Q. (1997). Clustering data using a modified integer genetic algorithm (IGA). *Analytica Chimica Acta, 354,* 263–274. doi:10.1016/S0003-2670(97)00462-5

Jiang, J., Alwan, A., Keating, P. A., & Edward, T. A. (2002). On the relationship between face movements, tongue movements, and speech acoustics. *EURASIP Journal on Applied Signal Processing, 11,* 1174–1188. doi:10.1155/S1110865702206046

Jin, Y. X., Cheng, H. Z., Yan, J. Y., & Zhang, L. (2007). New discrete particle swarm optimization and its application in transmission network expansion planning. *Electric Power Systems Research, 77,* 227–233. doi:10.1016/j.epsr.2006.02.016

Jolliffe, I. T. (2002). *Principal Component Analysis* (p. 487). New York: Springer-Verlag.

Kaelo, P., & Ali, M. M. (2006). A numerical study of some modified differential evolution algorithms. *European Journal of Operational Research, 169*(3), 1176–1184. doi:10.1016/j.ejor.2004.08.047

Kandil, N., Sood, V. K., Khorasani, K., & Patel, R. V. (1992). Fault identification in an ac-dc transmission system using Neural Networks. *IEEE Transactions on Power Systems, 7*(2), 812–819. doi:10.1109/59.141790

Kantz, H., & Schreiber, T. (1997). *Nonlinear time series analysis*. Cambridge, UK: Cambridge University Press.

Kara, M. (1996a). Formulas for the Computation of the Physical Properties of Rectangular Microstrip Antenna Elements with Various Substrate Thicknesses. *Microwave and Optical Technology Letters, 12*(4), 234–239. doi:10.1002/(SICI)1098-2760(199607)12:4<234::AID-MOP15>3.0.CO;2-A

Kara, M. (1996b). The Resonant Frequency of Rectangular Microstrip Antenna Elements with Various Substrate Thicknesses. *Microwave and Optical Technology Letters, 11*(2), 55–59. doi:10.1002/(SICI)1098-2760(19960205)11:2<55::AID-MOP1>3.0.CO;2-N

Kara, M. (1997). Empirical Formulas for the Computation of the Physical Properties of Rectangular Microstrip Antenna Elements with Thick Substrates. *Microwave and Optical Technology Letters, 14*(2), 115–121. doi:10.1002/(SICI)1098-2760(19970205)14:2<115::AID-MOP12>3.0.CO;2-A

Karttunen, H., Kroger, P., Oja, H., Poutanen, M., & Donner, K. (2000). *Fundamental Astronomy*. Berlin: Springer Verlag.

Karunanithi, N., Malaiya, Y. K., & Whitley, D. (1992a). The scaling problem in neural networks for software reliability prediction. In *Proceedings of the Third International IEEE Symposium of Software Reliability Engineering* (pp. 76-82). Washington, DC: IEEE.

Karunanithi, N., Whitley, D., & Malaiya, Y. K. (1991). Prediction of software reliability using neural networks. In *Proceedings of the International Symposium on Software Reliability* (pp. 124-130).

Karunanithi, N., Whitley, D., & Malaiya, Y. K. (1992b). Prediction of software reliability using connectionist models. *IEEE Transactions on Software Engineering, 18*, 563–574. doi:10.1109/32.148475

Kasabov, N. K., & Song, Q. (2002). DENFIS: dynamic evolving neural-fuzzy inference system and its application for time-series prediction. *IEEE Transactions on Fuzzy Systems, 10*(2). doi:10.1109/91.995117

Kennedy, J., & Eberhart, R. (1995). Particle swarm optimization. In *Proceedings of IEEE International Conference on Neural Networks (ICNN '95)*, Perth, WA, Australia (pp. 1942-1948).

Kennedy, J., & Eberhart, R. (1995). Particle swarm optimization. In *Proceedings of the IEEE International Conference on Neural Networks, 4*, 1942–1948.

Kennel, M. B., Brown, R., & Abarbanel, H. D. I. (1992). Determining embedding dimension for phase-space reconstruction using a geometrical construction. *Physical Review, 45A*, 3403–3411.

Kephart, J. O., & Chess, D. M. (2003). The vision of autonomic computing. *Computer, 36*(1), 41–50. doi:10.1109/MC.2003.1160055

Khanbary, L. M. O., & Vidyarthi, D. P. (2008). A GA-based effective fault-tolerant model for channel allocation in mobile computing. *IEEE Transactions on Vehicular Technology, 57*(3), 1823–1833. doi:10.1109/TVT.2007.907311

Khanbary, L., Omer, M., & Vidyarthi, D. K. (2008). A GA-Based Effective Fault-Tolerant Model for Channel Allocation in Mobile Computing. *IEEE Transactions on Vehicular Technology, 57*(3), 1823–1833. doi:10.1109/TVT.2007.907311

Khanbary, L., Omer, M., & Vidyarthi, D. P. (2009). Channel Allocation in Cellular Network Using Modified Genetic Algorithm. *International Journal of Artificial Intelligence, 3*(A09), 126–148.

Khoshgoftaar, T. M., Pandya, A. S., & More, H. B. (1992). A neural network approach for predicting software development faults. In *Proceedings of the third IEEE International Symposium on Software Reliability Engineering* (pp. 83-89). Washington, DC: IEEE.

Khoshgoftaar, T. M., Allen, E. B., Hudepohl, J. P., & Aud, S. J. (1997). Application of neural networks to software quality modeling of a very large telecommunications system. *IEEE Transactions on Neural Networks, 8*(4), 902–909. doi:10.1109/72.595888

Khoshgoftaar, T. M., Allen, E. B., Jones, W. D., & Hudepohl, J. P. (2000). Classification–Tree models of software quality over multiple releases. *IEEE Transactions on Reliability, 49*(1), 4–11. doi:10.1109/24.855532

Khoshgoftaar, T. M., & Szabo, R. M. (1994). Predicting software quality, during testing using neural network models: A comparative study. *International Journal of Reliability Quality and Safety Engineering, 1*, 303–319. doi:10.1142/S0218539394000222

Khoshgoftaar, T. M., & Szabo, R. M. (1996). Using neural networks to predict software faults during testing. *IEEE Transactions on Reliability, 45*(3), 456–462. doi:10.1109/24.537016

Kim, D. H., Abraham, A., & Cho, J. H. (2007). A hybrid genetic algorithm and bacterial foraging approach for global optimization. *Information Sciences, 177*(18), 3918–3937. doi:10.1016/j.ins.2007.04.002

Kim, H., Ko, Y. K., & Jung, H. (1993, July). Artificial neural networks based feeder reconfiguration for loss reduction in distribution systems. *IEEE Transactions on Power Delivery, 8*, 1356–1366. doi:10.1109/61.252662

Kirby, H., Dougherty, M., & Watson, S. (1997). Should we use neural networks or statistical models for short term motorway traffic forecasting? *International Journal of Forecasting, 13*, 43–50. doi:10.1016/S0169-2070(96)00699-1

Kirkpatrick, S., Gelatt, C. D., & Vecchi, M. P. (1983). Optimization by simulated annealing. *Science, 220*, 671–680. doi:10.1126/science.220.4598.671

Klein, R. W., & Dubes, R. C. (1989). Experiments in projection and clustering by simulated annealing. *Pattern Recognition, 22*, 213–220. doi:10.1016/0031-3203(89)90067-8

Knowles, J. D., & Corne, D. W. (2002). On metrics for comparing nondominated sets in congress on evolutionary computation. In *Proceedings of the Congress on Evolut. Comput. (CEC'02)*, Piscataway, NJ (Vol. 1, pp. 711-716).

Knowles, J. D., Corne, D. W., Oates, M. J., et al. (2000). On the assessment of multiobjective approaches to the adaptive distributed database management problem. In M. Schoenauer, et al. (Eds.), Parallel Problem Solving From Nature—PPSN VI (pp. 869–878). Berlin: Springer-Verlag. doi:10.1007/3-540-45356-3_85doi:10.1007/3-540-45356-3_85

Knowles, J., & Corne, D. (1999, July 6-9). The Pareto Archived Evolution Strategy: A New Baseline Algorithm For Pareto Multiobjective Optimisation. In Proceedings Of The Congress On Evolutionary Computation (CEC99) (pp. 98–105). Washington, DC: IEEE.

Knowles, J. D., & Corne, D. W. (2000). Approximating the nondominated front using the pareto archived evolution strategy. *Evolutionary Computation, 8*(2), 149–172. doi:10.1162/106365600568167

Koefoed, O. (1979). *Geosounding principles*. Amsterdam: Elsevier.

Konak, A., Coit, D., & Smith, A. (2006). Multi-Objective Optimization Using Genetic Algorithms: A Tutorial. In *Reliability Engineering and System Safety* (pp. 992-1007). Atlanta, GA: Elsevier Ltd.

Koumousis, V. K., & Katsaras, C. P. (2006). A sawtooth genetic algorithm combining the effects of variable population size and reinitialization to enhance performance. *IEEE Transactions on Evolutionary Computation, 10*(1), 19–28. doi:10.1109/TEVC.2005.860765

Koza, J. R. (1992). *Genetic Programming: On the Programming of Computers by Means of Natural Selection*. Cambridge, MA: The MIT Press.

Krachodnok, P., & Bemjapolakul, W. (2001). Buffer management for TCP over GFR service in an ATM network. In *Proceedings of the Ninth IEEE International Conference on Networks* (pp. 302 - 307). Washington, DC: IEEE Press.

Krifa, A., Baraka, C., & Spyropoulos, T. (2008). Optimal Buffer Management Policies for Delay Tolerant Networks. In *Proceedings of the 5th Annual IEEE Communications Society Conference on Sensor, Mesh and Ad Hoc Communications and Networks (SECON '08)*, San Francisco (pp. 260-268). Washington, DC: IEEE Press.

Kuo, R. J., Wang, H. S., Hu, T. L., & Chou, S. H. (2005). Application of ant K-means on clustering analysis. *Computers and Mathematics with Application, 50*, 1709–1724. doi:10.1016/j.camwa.2005.05.009

Kursawe, F. (1991). A variant of evolution strategies for vector optimization. *Parallel Problem Solving from Nature*, 193-197.

Lam, W. H. K., Chan, K. S., Tam, M. L., & Shi, J. W. (2005). Short-term travel time forecasts for transport information system in Hong Kong. *Journal of Advanced Transportation, 39*(3), 289–306.

Lam, W. H. K., Tang, Y. F., & Tam, M. L. (2006). Comparison of two non-parametric models for daily traffic forecasting in Hong Kong. *Journal of Forecasting, 25*(3), 173–192. doi:10.1002/for.984

Lan, L. W., Lin, F. Y., & Huang, Y. S. (2004). Confined space fuzzy proportion model for short-term traffic flow prediction. In *Proceedings of the 9th Conference of Hong Kong Society for Transportation Studies* (pp. 370-379).

Lan, L. W., & Huang, Y. C. (2006). A rolling-trained fuzzy neural network approach for freeway incident detections. *Transportmetrica, 2*(1), 11–29. doi:10.1080/18128600608685653

Lan, L. W., Lin, F. Y., & Kuo, A. Y. (2003). Testing and prediction of traffic flow dynamics with chaos. *Journal of the Eastern Asia Society for Transportation Studies, 5*, 1975–1990.

Lan, L. W., Sheu, J. B., & Huang, Y. S. (2007). Prediction of short-interval traffic dynamics in multidimensional spaces. *Journal of the Eastern Asia Society for Transportation Studies, 7*, 2353–2367.

Lan, L. W., Sheu, J. B., & Huang, Y. S. (2008a). Features of traffic time-series on multidimensional spaces. *Journal of the Chinese Institute of Transportation, 20*(1), 91–118.

Lan, L. W., Sheu, J. B., & Huang, Y. S. (2008b). Investigation of temporal freeway traffic patterns in reconstructed state spaces. *Transportation Research, 16C*, 116–136.

Latorre, G., Cruz, R. D., Areiza, J. M., & Villegas, A. (2003). Classification of Publications and Models on Transmission Expansion Planning. *IEEE Transactions on Power Systems, 18*(2), 938–946. doi:10.1109/TPWRS.2003.811168

Laumanns, M., Rudolph, G., & Schwefel, H. P. (1998). A spatial predator-prey approach to multi-objective optimization. *Parallel Problem Solving from Nature, 5*, 241–249. doi:10.1007/BFb0056867

Le Ravalec-Dupin, L., Noetinger, B., & Hu, L. (2000). The FFT moving average (FFT-MA) generator: An efficient numerical method for generating and conditioning Gaussian simulations. *Mathematical Geology, 32*(6), 701–723. doi:10.1023/A:1007542406333

Lee, F. N., & Breipohl, J. D. A. M. (1993). Reserve constrained economic load dispatch with prohibited operating zones. *IEEE Transactions on Power Systems, 8*, 246–253. doi:10.1109/59.221233

Lee, S., & Fambro, D. B. (1999). Application of subset autoregressive integrated moving average model for short-term freeway traffic volume forecasting. *Transportation Research Record, 1678*, 179–188. doi:10.3141/1678-22

Lei, W., Qi, K., Hui, X., & Qidi, W. (2005). A modified adaptive particle swarm optimization algorithm. In *Proceedings of the IEEE International Conference on Industrial Technology (ICIT 2005)* (pp. 209-214).

Li, D., Gao, L., Zhang, J., & Li, Y. (2006). Power System Reactive Power Optimization Based on Adaptive Particle Swarm Optimization Algorithm. In *Proceedings of the 6th World Congress on Intelligent Control and Automation*, Dalian, China (pp. 7572-7576).

Li, S. (2002). Nonlinear combination of travel-time prediction model based on wavelet network. In *Proceedings of the IEEE 5th International Conference on ITS* (pp. 741-746).

Lim, H. H., & Qiu, B. (2001). Predictive fuzzy logic buffer management for TCP/IP over ATM-UBR and ATM-ABR. In *Proceedings of the IEEE International Conference on Global Telecommunications (GLOBECOM '01)*, San Antonio, TX (Vol. 4, pp. 2326-2330). Washington, DC: IEEE Press.

Limaye, K., Leangsuksun, B., Liu, Y., Greenwood, Z., Scott, S. L., Libby, R., & Chanchio, K. (2005). Reliability-Aware Resource Management For Computational Grid/Cluster Environments. In *Proceedings of the sixth IEEE/ACM International Workshop on Grid Computing* (pp. 211-218).

Lin, G., & Yao, X. (1997). Analysing crossover operators by search step size. In *Proceedings of the IEEE International Conference on Evolutionary Computation* (pp. 107-110).

Lin, J., & Wu, H. (2005). *A Task Duplication Based Scheduling Algorithm on GA in Grid Computing Systems* (LNCS 3612, pp. 225-234). Berlin: Springer-Verlag.

Lin, W. M., Cheng, F. S., & Tsay, M. T. (1999). Feeder loss reduction by switching operations with a hybrid programming technique. In *Proceedings of the IEEE Transm. Dist. Conf.* (Vol. 2, pp. 603-608).

Lin, C. E., & Viviani, G. L. (1984). Hierarchical economic load dispatch for piecewise quadratic cost functions. *IEEE Transactions on Power Apparatus and Systems, 103*, 1170–1175. doi:10.1109/TPAS.1984.318445

Lin, C.-L., & Guan, S.-U. (1996). The design and architecture of a video library system. *IEEE Communications, 34*(1), 86–91. doi:10.1109/35.482251

Lingras, P., Sharma, S. C., & Osborne, P. (2000). Traffic volume time-series analysis according to the type of road use. *Computer-Aided Civil and Infrastructure Engineering, 15*(5), 365–373. doi:10.1111/0885-9507.00200

Liu, C.-a., & Yuping, W. (2007). Dynamic Multi-objective Optimization Evolutionary Algorithm. In *Proceedings of the Third International Conference on Natural Computation* (pp. 456-459).

Liu, Y., Zhang, J., Jiang, M., Raymer, D., & Strassner, J. (2008, March). A case study: A model-based approach to retrofit a network fault management system with self-healing functionality. In *Proceedings of the 15th Annual IEEE International Conference and Workshop on the Engineering of Computer Based Systems (ECBS 2008)* (pp. 9-18).

Liu, C. C., Lee, S. J., & Venkata, S. S. (1988, May). An expert system operational aid for restoration and loss reduction of distribution system. *IEEE Transactions on Power Systems, 3*, 619–629. doi:10.1109/59.192914

Liu, C. C., Lee, S. J., & Vu, K. (1989, April). Loss minimization of distribution feeders: optimality and algorithms. *IEEE Transactions on Power Delivery, 4*(2), 1281–1289. doi:10.1109/61.25615

Lobos, T., Kozina, T., & Koglin, H. J. (2001). Power System Harmonics Estimation using Linear least squares method and SVD. *IEE Proceedings. Generation, Transmission and Distribution, 148*(6), 567–572. doi:10.1049/ip-gtd:20010563

Lohokare, M. R., Pattnaik, S. S., Devi, S., Panigrahi, B. K., Bakwad, K. M., & Joshi, J. G. (2009b). Modified BBO and Calculation of Resonant Frequency of Circular Microstrip Antenna. In *Proceedings of the World Congress on Nature and Biologically Inspired Computing* (pp. 487-492). doi: 10.1109/NABIC.2009.5393365

Lohokare, M. R., Pattnaik, S. S., Devi, S., Panigrahi, B. K., Das, S., & Bakwad, K. M. (2009a). Intelligent Biogeography-Based Optimization for Discrete Variables. In *Proceedings of the International Symposium on Biologically Inspired Computing and Applications* (pp. 1088-1091). doi: 10.1109/NABIC.2009.5393808

Lopez, E., Opazo, H., Garcia, L., & Poloujadoff, M. (2002, July). Minimal loss reconfiguration based on dynamic programming approach: Application to real systems. *Power Compon. Syst., 30*(7), 693–704. doi:10.1080/15325000290085145

Lu, C., Abdelzaher, T. F., Stankovic, J. A., & Son, S. H. (2001 June). Feedback control approach for guaranteeing relative delays in web servers. In *Proceedings of the IEEE Real-Time Technology and Applications Symposium*, Taipei, Taiwan (pp. 51-62).

Lu, H., & Yen, G. G. (2003). Rank-density-based multi-objective genetic algorithm and benchmark test function study. *IEEE Transactions on Evolutionary Computation, 7*, 325–343. doi:10.1109/TEVC.2003.812220

Lunchian, S., Lunchian, H., & Petriuc, M. (1994). Evolutionary automated classification. In *Proceedings of the First IEEE Conference on Evolutionary Computation* (pp. 585-589).

Lyu, M. R. (1996). *Handbook of Software Reliability Engineering*. New York: McGraw-Hill.

MacArthur, R., & Wilson, E. (1967). *The Theory of Biogeography*. Princeton, NJ: Princeton University Press.

MacQueen, J. (1967). Some methods for classification and analysis of multivariate observations. In *Proceedings of the Fifth Berkeley Symposium on Mathematical Statistics and Probability* (Vol. 1, pp. 281-297).

Maghouli, P., Hosseini, S. H., Buygi, M. O., & Shahidehpour, M. (2009). A multi-objective framework for transmission expansion planning in deregulated environments. *IEEE Transactions on Power Systems, 24*(2), 1051–1061. doi:10.1109/TPWRS.2009.2016499

Maniezzo, V., & Colorni, A. (1999). The ant system applied to the quadratic assignment problem. *IEEE Transactions on Knowledge and Data Engineering, 11*, 769–778. doi:10.1109/69.806935

Manoharan, P. S., Kannan, S., Baskar, M., & Willjuice, I. (2009). Evolutionary algorithm solution and KKT based optimality verification to multi-area economic dispatch. *Electrical Power and Energy Systems, 31*, 365–373. doi:10.1016/j.ijepes.2009.03.010

Marconi, T., Lu, Y., Bertels, K., & Gaydadjiev, G. (2008). Intelligent Merging Online Task Placement Algorithm for Partial Reconfigurable Systems. In *Proceedings of DATE,* Munich, Germany (pp. 1346-1351).

Marconi, T., Lu, Y., Bertels, K., & Gaydadjiev, G. (2008). Online Hardware Task Scheduling and Placement Algorithm on Partially Reconfigurable Devices. In R. Woods, K. Compton, C. Bouganis, & P. C. Diniz (Eds.), *Proceedings of the ARC 2008* (LNCS 4943, pp. 306-311).

Marconi, T., Lu, Y., Bertels, K., & Gaydadjiev, G. (2009). A Novel Fast Online Placement Algorithm on 2D Partially Reconfigurable Devices. In *Proceedings of the FPT* (pp. 296-299).

Mariethoz, G., & Renard, P. (2010). Reconstruction of incomplete data sets or images using Direct Sampling. *Mathematical Geosciences, 42*(3), 245–268. doi:10.1007/s11004-010-9270-0

Mariethoz, G., Renard, P., & Caers, J. (n.d.). Bayesian inverse problem and optimization with Iterative Spatial Resampling. *Water Resources Research*.

Mariethoz, G., Renard, P., & Straubhaar, J. (n.d.). The direct sampling method to perform multiple-points simulations. *Water Resources Research*.

Markaki, M., & Venieris, I. S. (2000). A Novel Buffer Management Scheme for CBQ-based IP Routers in a Combined IntServ and DiffServ Architecture. In *Proceedings of the 5th IEEE Symposium on Computers and Communications*, Antibes-Juan les Pins, France (pp. 347-352). Washington, DC: IEEE Press.

Martínez, F. J. L., & Gonzalo, G. E. (2008). The generalized PSO: A new door for PSO evolution. *Journal of Artificial Evolution and Applications, 15*.

Martínez, F. J. L., & Gonzalo, G. E. (2010b). Advances in Particle Swarm Optimization. In *Proceedings of the Seventh Conference on Swarm Intelligence (Ants 2010)*.

Martínez, F. J. L., Álvarez, F. J. P., Gonzalo, G. E., Pérez, M. C. O., & Kuzma, H. A. (2008). Particle Swarm Optimization (PSO): A simple and powerful algorithm family for geophysical inversion. In *Proceedings of the SEG Annual Meeting, SEG Expanded Abstracts* (Vol. 27, p. 3568).

Martínez, F. J. L., Tompkins, M. J., Muñiz, F. Z., & Mukerji, T. (2010c, September). How to construct geological bases for inversion and uncertainty appraisal? In *Proceedings of the International Groundwater Simposium*, Valencia, Spain.

Martínez, F. J. L., & González, P. L. M. (2008). Anisotropic Mean traveltime curves: a method to estimate anisotropic parameters from 2D transmission tomographic data. *Mathematical Geosciences, 41*(2), 163–192. doi:10.1007/s11004-008-9202-4

Martínez, F. J. L., & Gonzalo, G. E. (2009). The PSO family: deduction, stochastic analysis and comparison. *Swarm Intelligence, 3*, 245–273. doi:10.1007/s11721-009-0034-8

Martínez, F. J. L., & Gonzalo, G. E. (2009b). *Stochastic stability analysis of the linear continuous and discrete PSO models (Tech. Rep.)*. Oviedo, Spain: University of Oviedo, Department of Mathematics.

Martínez, F. J. L., & Gonzalo, G. E. (2010). *What makes Particle Swarm Optimization a very interesting and powerful algorithm? Handbook of Swarm Intelligence -- Concepts, Principles and Applications Series on Adaptation, Learning, and Optimization*. New York: Springer.

Martínez, F. J. L., Gonzalo, G. E., & Alvarez, F. J. P. (2008). Theoretical analysis of particle swarm trajectories through a mechanical analogy. *International Journal of Computational Intelligence Research, 4*, 93–104. Retrieved from http://www.ijcir.com/.

Martínez, F. J. L., Gonzalo, G. E., Álvarez, F. J. P., Kuzma, H. A., & Pérez, M. C. O. (2010a). *PSO: A Powerful Algorithm to Solve Geophysical Inverse Problems. Application to a 1D-DC Resistivity Case.* Jounal of Applied Geophysics.

Martínez, F. J. L., Gonzalo, G. E., Muñiz, F. Z., & Mukerji, T. (2010d). *How to design a powerful family of Particle Swarm Optimizers for inverse modeling. New Trends on Bio-inspired Computation.* Transactions of the Institute of Measurement and Control.

Martínez, F. J. L., Gonzalo, G. E., & Naudet, V. (2010b). *Particle Swarm Optimization applied to the solving and appraisal of the Streaming Potential inverse problem.* Geophysics. Hydrogeophysics Special Issue.

Martínez, F. J. L., Kuzma, H. A., García-Gonzalo, M. E., Díaz, F. J. M., Álvarez, F. J. P., & Pérez, M. C. O. (2009). Application of Global Optimization Algorithms to a Salt Water Intrusion Problem. In *Proceedings of the Symposium on the Application of Geophysics to Engineering and Environmental Problems, 22*, 252–260.

Martínez, F. J. L., Mukerji, T., Muñiz, F. Z., Gonzalo, G. E., Tompkins, M. J., & Alumbaugh, D. L. (2009b). *Complexity reduction in inverse problems: wavelet transforms, DCT, PCA and geological bases.* Eos. Trans.

Martins, R., Oliveira, A. D., & Goncalves, W. A. (2000). Expert Systems for the Analysis of Power Quality. In *Proceedings of the IEEE International Conference on Electric Utility Deregulation and Restructuring and Power Technologies,* City University, London (pp. 90-95).

MATLAB. (n.d.). *Math Works INC* (version 7.3). Retrieved from http://www.mathworks.com

Michalewicz, Z. (1992). *Genetic Algorithms + Data Structures= Evolution Programs.* New York: Springer.

Miettinen, K., & Neittaanmaki, P. (1999). *Evolutionary algorithms in engineering and computer science.* New York: John Wiley & Sons.

Milcher, B. (2004). Towards an autonomic framework: Self-configuring network services and developing autonomic applications. *Intel Technology Journal, 8(4).* Retrieved from http://developer.intel.com/technology/itj/index.htm

Mishra, S. (2005). A Hybrid Least Squares-Fuzzy Bacterial Foraging Strategy for Harmonic Estimation. *IEEE Transactions on Evolutionary Computation, 9*(1), 61–73. doi:10.1109/TEVC.2004.840144

Mo, W., & Guan, S. U. (2006). Particle Swarm Assisted Incremental Evolution Strategy for Function Optimization. In *Proceedings of the IEEE Conference on Cybernetics and Intelligent Systems* (pp. 1-6). doi: 10.1109/ICCIS.2006.252276

Moattar, E. Z., Rahmani, A. M., & Derakhshi, M. R. F. (2007). Scheduling in Multi Processor Architecture Using Genetic Algorithm. In *Proceedings of the fourth International Conference on Innovations in Information Technology* (pp. 248-251).

Mohanty, R. K., Ravi, V., & Patra, M. R. (2009). Software Reliability Prediction Using Group Method of Data Handling. In *Proceedings of the International conferences on RSFDGrC 2009* (LNAI 5908, pp. 344-351).

Mohanty, R. K., Ravi, V., & Patra, M. R. (2009). Software Reliability Prediction Using Genetic Programming. In *Proceedings of the International Conferences on BICA, 2009*, 105–110.

Mohanty, R. K., Ravi, V., & Patra, M. R. (2010). *The Application of intelligent and soft-computing techniques to software engineering problems: A Review.* Int. J. Information and Decision Sciences.

Mori, H. (1992). An Artificial Neural Network Based Method for Power System Voltage Harmonics. *IEEE Transactions on Power Delivery, 7*(1), 402–409. doi:10.1109/61.108934

Mortier, R., & Kiciman, E. (2006, September). *Autonomic network management: Some pragmatic considerations.* Paper presented at SIGCOMM'06 Workshops, Pisa, Italy. Motlabs.com. (n.d.). *Evolution of reconfiguration management and control system architecture* (IST FP6 project, E²RII, Deliverable 2.1). Retrieved from https://e2r2.motlabs.com/Deliverables/E2RII_WP2_D2.1_060807.pdf

Mosegaard, K., & Tarantola, A. (1995). Monte Carlo sampling of solutions to inverse problems. *Journal of Geophysical Research, 100*(B7), 12431–12447. doi:10.1029/94JB03097

Moshe, E. C., & Tovey, C. A. (1996). Ammons J-C. Circuit partitioning via set partitioning and column generation. *Operations Research, 44*, 65–76. doi:10.1287/opre.44.1.65

Mukerji, T., Martínez, F. J. L., Ciaurri, E. D., & Gonzalo, G. E. (2009). Application of particle swarm optimization for enhanced reservoir characterization and inversion. *Eos, Transactions, American Geophysical Union, 90*(52).

Mulvey, J. M., & Crowder, H. P. (1979). Cluster analysis: An application of Lagrangian relaxation. *Management Science, 25*, 329–340. doi:10.1287/mnsc.25.4.329

Musa, J. D. (1979a). *Software reliability data.* IEEE Computer Society- Repository.

Musa, J. D. (1979b). *Software Reliability Data.* London: Bell Telephone Laboratories.

Musa, J. D. (1998). *Software Reliability Engineering.* New York: McGraw-Hill.

Nara, K., Shiose, A., Kitagawa, M., & Ishihara, T. (1992, August). Implementation of genetic algorithm for distribution systems loss minimum reconfiguration. *IEEE Transactions on Power Systems, 7*(3), 1044–1051. doi:10.1109/59.207317

Nasr Azadani, E., Hosseinian, S. H., & Moradzadeh, B. (2010). Generation and reserve dispatch in a competitive market using constrained particle swarm optimization. *Electrical power and energy systems, 32*, 79-86.

Nedjah, N., & Mourelle, L. D. M. (2006). *Swarm Intelligent Systems.* Berlin: Springer Verlag. doi:10.1007/978-3-540-33869-7

Noh, K. J., & Bae, C. S. (2007). A QoS RED Buffer Management Scheme of Intelligent Gateway Gadget based on a Wireless LAN. In *Proceedings of the IEEE International Conference on Advanced Communication Technology (ICACT '07),* Gangwon-Do, South Korea (Vol. 1, pp. 286-291). Washington, DC: IEEE Press.

Noman, N., & Iba, H. (2008). Differential evolution for economic load dispatch problems. *Electric Power Systems Research, 78*, 1322–1331. doi:10.1016/j.epsr.2007.11.007

Okutani, I., & Stephanedes, Y. J. (1984). Dynamic prediction of traffic volume through Kalman filtering theory. *Transportation Research, 18B*, 1–11.

Oliveira, G. C., Costa, A. P. C., & Binato, S. (1995). Large scale transmission network planning using optimization and heuristic techniques. *IEEE Transactions on Power Systems, 10*(4), 1828–1834. doi:10.1109/59.476047

Omre, H., & Tjelmland, H. (1996). *Petroleum geostatistics (Tech. Rep.).* Trondheim, Norway: Norwegian University of Science and Technology, Department of Mathematical Sciences.

Osowski, S. (1992). Neural Network for estimation of harmonic components in a power system. *IEE Proceeding. Part C, 139*(2), 129–135.

Pai, P. F., & Hong, W. C. (2006). Software reliability forecasting by support vector machine with simulated annealing algorithms. *Journal of Systems and Software, 79*(6), 747–755. doi:10.1016/j.jss.2005.02.025

Pan, D., & Yang, Y. (2006). Buffer Management for Lossless Service in Network Processors. In *Proceedings of the 14th IEEE Symposium on High-Performance interconnects,* Stanford, CA (pp. 81-86). Washington, DC: IEEE Press.

Pandizic, I. S., & Forchheimer, R. (2002). *MPEG-4 facial animation: The standard, implementation, and applications.* New York: John Wiley.

Pandizic, I. S., Ahlberg, J., Wzorek, M., Rudol, P., & Mosmondor, M. (2003). Faces everywhere: Towards ubiquitous production and delivery of face animation. In *Proceedings of the 2nd International Conference on Mobile and Ubiquitous Media,* Norköping, Sweden (pp. 49-56).

Panigrahi, B. K., & Pandi, V. R. (2009). Bacterial foraging optimisation: Nelder–Mead hybrid algorithm for economic load dispatch. *IET Generation, Transmission and Distribution, 2*(4), 556–565.

Pant, M., Thangaraj, R., & Abraham, A. (2007). A New PSO Algorithm with Crossover Operator for Global Optimization Problems. *Innovations in Hybrid Intelligent Systems Advances in Soft Computing, 44*, 215–222. doi:10.1007/978-3-540-74972-1_29

Parke, F. I. (1982). Parameterized models for facial animation. *IEEE Computer Graphics and Applications, 2*, 61–68. doi:10.1109/MCG.1982.1674492

Parker, R. L. (1994). *Geophysical Inverse Theory*. Princeton, NJ: Princeton University Press.

Park, J. H., & Kim, Y. S., Eom, & Lee, K. Y. (1993). Economic load dispatch for piecewise quadratic cost function using Hopfield neural network. *IEEE Transactions on Power Systems, 8*, 1030–1038. doi:10.1109/59.260897

Passino, K. M. (2002). Biomimicry of bacterial foraging for distributed optimization and control. *IEEE Control Systems Magazine*, 52–67. doi:10.1109/MCS.2002.1004010

Pasupuleti, S., & Bhattiti, R. (2006). The Gregarious Particle Swarm Optimizer (G-PSO). In *Proceedings of the 8th Annual Conference on Genetic and Evolutionary Computation* (pp. 67-74). New York: ACM.

Pattnaik, S. S., Khuntia, B., Panda, D. C., Neog, D. K., & Devi, S. (2003). Calculation of optimized parameters of rectangular microstrip patch antenna using genetic algorithm. *Microwave and Optical Technology Letters, 37*(6), 431–433. doi:10.1002/mop.10940

Pearson, A. (1995). Developments in model-based image coding. *Proceedings of the IEEE, 83*, 892–906. doi:10.1109/5.387091

Pearson, K. (1901). Principal components analysis. *The London, Edinburgh and Dublin Philosophical Magazine and Journal, 6*, 566.

Pindyck, R. S., & Rubinfeld, D. L. (1998). *Econometric models and economic forecasts* (4th ed.). Singapore: Irwin/McGraw Hill.

Pique, R., & Torres, L. (2003). Efficient facial coding in video sequences combining adaptive principal component analysis and a hybrid codec approach. In *Proceedings of IEEE International Conference on Acoustic, Speech, and Signal Processing*, Hong Kong, China (pp. 629-632).

Poli, R., Langdon, W. B., & Koza, J. R. (2008). *A field guide to Genetic Programming*. London: Lulu. ISBN: 978-1-4092-0073-4

Pozar, D. M., & Schaubert, D. H. (Eds.). (1995). *Microwave Antennas: The Analysis and Design of Microstrip Antennas and Arrays*. New York: IEEE Press.

Prabhu, C. S. R. (2008). *Grid and Cluster Computing*. PHI Learning Private Limited.

Prasad, K., Ranjan, R., Sahoo, N. C., & Chaturvedi, A. (2005, April). Optimal reconfiguration of radial distribution systems using a fuzzy mutated genetic algorithm. *IEEE Transactions on Power Delivery, 20*(2), 1211–1213. doi:10.1109/TPWRD.2005.844245

Probabilistic aspects Task Force of the Harmonics Working Group Subcommittee. (1998). Time Varying Harmonics: Part – I – Characterizing Measured Data. *IEEE Transaction on Power Delivery, 13*(3), 938-944.

Purshouse, R. C., & Fleming, P. J. (2003, April). Conflict, Harmony, and Independence: Relationships in Evolutionary Multi-Criterion Optimization. In *Proceedings of the Evolutionary Multi-criterion Optimization* (pp. 8-11).

Qin, H., Zhou, J., Li, Y., Liu, L., & Lu, Y. (2008). Enhanced Strength Pareto Differential Evolution (ESPDE): An Extension of Differential Evolution for Multi-objective Optimization. In *Proceedings of the Fourth International Conference on Natural Computation (ICNC '08)* (pp. 191-196).

Rahnamayan, S., Tizhoosh, H. R., & Salama, M. M. A. (2008). Opposition-based differential evolution. *IEEE Transactions on Evolutionary Computation, 12*(1), 64–79. doi:10.1109/TEVC.2007.894200

Rajkiran, N., & Ravi, V. (2007b). Software Reliability prediction using wavelet Neural Networks. In *Proceedings of the International Conference on Computational Intelligence and Multimedia Application (ICCIMA, 2007)* (Vol. 1, pp. 195-197).

Rajkiran, N., & Ravi, V. (2007a). Software Reliability prediction by soft computing technique. *Journal of Systems and Software, 81*(4), 576–583. doi:10.1016/j.jss.2007.05.005

Rarick, R., Simon, D., Villaseca, F. E., & Vyakaranam, B. (2009). Biogeography-Based Optimization and the Solution of the Power Flow Problem. In *Proceedings of the IEEE International Conference on Systems, Man, and Cybernetics* (pp. 1003–1008). doi: 10.1109/ICSMC.2009.5346046

Ratnaweera, A., Halgamuge, S. K., & Watson, H. C. (2004). Self-organizing hierarchical Particle swarm optimizer with time varying acceleration coefficients. *IEEE Transactions on Evolutionary Computation, 8*(3), 240–255. doi:10.1109/TEVC.2004.826071

Ravi, V., Chauhan, N. J., & Rajkiran, N. (2009). Software reliability prediction using intelligent techniques: Application to operational risk prediction in Firms. *International Journal of Computational Intelligence and Applications, 8*(2), 181–194. doi:10.1142/S1469026809002588

Raymer, D., van der Meer, S., & Strassner, J. (2008 March). From autonomic computing to autonomic networking: An architectural perspective. In *Proceedings of the Fifth IEEE Workshop on Engineering of Autonomic and Autonomous Systems (EASE 2008)* (pp. 174-183).

Ray, T., & Smith, W. (2006). A Surrogate Assisted Parallel Multi-objective Evolutionary Algorithm for Robust Engineering Design. *Engineering Optimization, 38*(9), 997–1011. doi:10.1080/03052150600882538

Raza, Z., & Vidyarthi, D. P. (2008). A Fault Tolerant Grid Scheduling Model to Minimize Turnaround Time. In *Proceedings of the International conference on High Performance Computing, Networking and Communication Systems (HPCNCS'08)*, Orlando, Florida (pp. 167-175).

Raza, Z., & Vidyarthi, D. P. (2009a). GA Based Scheduling Model for Computational Grid to Minimize Turnaround Time. *International Journal of Grid and High Performance Computing, 1*(4), 70–90.

Raza, Z., & Vidyarthi, D. P. (2009b). Maximizing Reliability with Task Scheduling in a Computational Grid Using GA. *International Journal of Advancements in Computing Technology, 1*(2).

Raza, Z., & Vidyarthi, D. P. (2009c). A Computational Grid Scheduling Model To Minimize Turnaround Using Modified GA. *International Journal of Artificial Intelligence, 3*(A09), 86–106.

Rechenberg, I. (1973). *Evolutionsstrategie: Optimierung Technischer Systeme nach Prinzipien der Biologischen Evolution*. Stuttgart, Germany: Frommann-Holzboog.

Reklaitis, G., Ravindran, A., & Ragsdell, K. (2006). *Engineering optimization, methods and applications* (2nd ed.). New York: John Wiley.

Remy, N., Boucher, A., & Wu, J. (2009). *Applied Geostatistics with SGeMS: A User's Guide* (p. 284). Cambridge, UK: Cambridge University Press.

Resano, J., & Mozos, D. (2004). Specific scheduling support to minimize the reconfiguration overhead of dynamically reconfigurable hardware. In *Proceedings of the DAC* (pp. 119-124).

Roberto, C., Francesco, R., Massimo, A., Marco, D., & Donatella, S. (2009). Partitioning and Scheduling of Task Graphs on Partially Dynamically Reconfigurable FPGAs. *IEEE Transactions on Computer-Aided Design of Integrated Circuits and Systems, 28*(5).

Romero, R., Gallego, R. A., & Monticelli, A. (1996). Transmission network expansion planning by Simulated Annealing. *IEEE Transactions on Power Systems, 11*(1), 364–369. doi:10.1109/59.486119

Romero, R., & Monticelli, A. (1994). A hierarchical decomposition approach for transmission network expansion planning. *IEEE Transactions on Power Systems, 9*(1), 373–380. doi:10.1109/59.317588

Romero, R., Rider, M. J., & Silva, I. de J. (2007). A Metaheuristic to solve the Transmission Expansion Planning. *IEEE Transactions on Power Systems, 22*(4), 2289–2291. doi:10.1109/TPWRS.2007.907592

Romero, R., Rocha, C., Mantovani, J. R. S., & Slanchez, I. G. (2005). Constructive heuristic algorithm for the DC model in network transmission expansion planning. *IEE Proceedings. Generation, Transmission and Distribution, 152*(2), 277–282. doi:10.1049/ip-gtd:20041196

Routray, A., Pradhan, A. K., & Rao, K. P. (2002). A novel Kalman filter for frequency estimation of distorted signals in power system. *IEEE Transactions on Instrumentation and Measurement, 51*(3), 469–479. doi:10.1109/TIM.2002.1017717

Ryu, Y. S., & Koh, K. (1996). A dynamic buffer management technique for minimizing the necessary buffer space in a continuous media server. In *Proceedings of the third IEEE International Conference on Multimedia Computing and Systems (MMCS 1996)*, Hiroshima, Japan (pp. 181-185). Washington, DC: IEEE Press.

Rzadca, K., Tryatram, D., & Wierzbicki. (2007). Fair Game-Theoritic Resource Management in Dedicated Grids. In *Proceedings of the IEEE International Conference on Cluster Computing and the Grid (CCGrid'07)* (pp. 343-350).

Sachdev, M. S., & Giray, M. M. (1985). A Least Square Technique for Determining Power System Frequency. *IEEE Transactions on Power Apparatus and Systems*, *104*(2), 437–444. doi:10.1109/TPAS.1985.319059

Sakawa, M., Kosuke, K., & Ooura, K. (1998). A deterministic nonlinear prediction model through fuzzy reasoning using neighborhoods' difference and its application to actual time series data. *Fuzzy Set*, *10*(2), 381–386.

Sambridge, M. (1999). Geophysical inversion with a neighborhood algorithm. I. Searching a parameter space. *Geophysical Journal International*, *138*, 479–494. doi:10.1046/j.1365-246X.1999.00876.x

Sarker, R., & Abbass, H. (2004). Differential Evolution for Solving Multi-Objective Optimization Problems. *Asia-Pacific Journal of Operational Research*, *21*(2), 225–240. doi:10.1142/S0217595904000217

Sarker, R., Liang, K., & Newton, C. (2002). A New Evolutionary Algorithm for Multiobjective Optimization. *European Journal of Operational Research*, *140*(1), 12–23. doi:10.1016/S0377-2217(01)00190-4

Savelsbergh, M. (1997). A branch-and-price algorithm for the generalized assignment problem. *Operations Research*, *45*, 831–841. doi:10.1287/opre.45.6.831

Scales, J. A., & Tenorio, L. (2001). Prior information and uncertainty in inverse problems. *Geophysics*, *66*, 389–397. doi:10.1190/1.1444930

Schaffer, J. D. (1985). Multiple objective optimization with vector evaluated genetic algorithms. In *Proceedings of the 1st International Conference on Genetic Algorithms*, Pittsburgh, PA (pp. 93-100).

Schlegel, D., Finkbeiner, D., & Davis, M. (1998). Maps of dust infrared emission for use in estimation of reddening and cosmic microwave background radiation foregrounds. *The Astrophysical Journal*, *500*(1), 525–553. doi:10.1086/305772

Schroder, P. (1998). *Multivariable Control of active magnetic bearings*. Unpublished doctoral dissertation, University of Sheffield, Sheffield, South Yorkshire, England.

Schulzrinne, H., Fokus, G. M. D., Casner, S., Frederick, R., & Jacobson, V. (1996). *RTP: A transport protocol for real-time applications* (RFC 1889). Palo Alto, CA: Xerox Palo Alto Research Center, Lawrence Berkeley National Laboratory. SOCRATES. (n.d.). *SOCRATES project*. Retrieved from http://www.fp7-socrates.org

Selim, S. Z., & Al-Sultan, K. S. (1991). A simulated annealing algorithm for the clustering problem. *Pattern Recognition*, *24*, 1003–1008. doi:10.1016/0031-3203(91)90097-O

Senthil Arumugam, M., Chandramohan, A., & Rao, M. V. (2005). Competitive Approaches to PSO algorithm via New Acceleration Co-efficient Variant with Mutation operators. In *Proceedings of the sixth Intern. Conf. on Computational Intelligence and Multimedia Applications* (pp. 225-230).

Seo, J. H., Im, C. H., Heo, C. G., Kim, J. K., Jung, H. K., & Lee, C. G. (2006). Multimodal function optimization based on particle swarm optimization. *IEEE Transactions on Magnetics*, *42*(4), 1095–1098. doi:10.1109/TMAG.2006.871568

Sharifnia, A., & Aashtiani, H. Z. (1985). Transmission network planning: A method for synthesis of minimum-cost secure networks. *IEEE Transactions on Power Apparatus and Systems*, *104*(8), 2026–2034. doi:10.1109/TPAS.1985.318777

Shelokar, P. S., Jayaraman, V. K., & Kullkarni, B. D. (2004). An ant colony approach for clustering. *Analytica Chimica Acta*, *509*, 187–195. doi:10.1016/j.aca.2003.12.032

Sherer, S. A. (1995). Software fault prediction. *Journal of Systems and Software*, *29*(2), 97–105. doi:10.1016/0164-1212(94)00051-N

Sheu, J. B., Lan, L. W., & Huang, Y. S. (2009). Short-term prediction of traffic dynamics with real-time recurrent learning algorithms. *Transportmetrica*, *5*(1), 59–83. doi:10.1080/18128600802591681

Shimonishi, H. Sanadidi, & Gerla, M. (2005). Improving Efficiency-Friendliness Tradeoffs of TCP: Robustness to Router Buffer Capacity Variations. In *Proceedings of IEEE Global Telecommunications Conference*, St. Louis, MO (pp. 5-10).

Shirmohammadi, D., & Hong, W. H. (1989, April). Reconfiguration of electric distribution networks for resistive line losses reduction. *IEEE Transactions on Power Delivery*, *4*(2), 1492–1498. doi:10.1109/61.25637

Shi, Y., & Eberhart, R. C. (2001). Fuzzy Adaptive Particle Swarm Optimization. In *Proceedings of the Evolutionary Computation*, *1*, 101–106.

Shoults, R. R., Chang, S. K., Helmick, S., & Grady, W. M. (1980). A practical approach to unit commitment, economic dispatch and savings allocation for multiple area pool operation with import/export constraints. *IEEE Transactions on Power Apparatus and Systems*, *99*(2), 625–635. doi:10.1109/TPAS.1980.319654

Silva Irênio de, J., Rider Marcos, J., Romero, R., & Murari Carlos, A. F. (2006). Transmission network expansion planning considering uncertainty in demand.

Simon, D., Ergezer, M., & Du, D. (2009). *Markov analysis of biogeography-based optimization.* Retrieved from http://academic.csuohio.edu/simond/bbo/markov/

Simon, D. (2008). Biogeography-Based Optimization. *IEEE Transactions on Evolutionary Computation*, *12*(6), 712–713. doi:10.1109/TEVC.2008.919004

Sinha, N., Chakraborty, R., & Chattopadhyay, P. K. (2003). Evolutionary programming techniques for economic load dispatch. *IEEE Transactions on Evolutionary Computation*, *7*(1), 83–93. doi:10.1109/TEVC.2002.806788

Sitte, R. (1999). Comparison of Software-Reliability-Growth Predictions: Neural Networks vs. Parametric-Recalibration. *IEEE Transactions on Reliability*, *48*(3), 285–291. doi:10.1109/24.799900

Smith, B. L., & Demetsky, M. J. (1997). Traffic flow forecasting: Comparison of modeling approaches. *Journal of Transportation Engineering*, *123*(4), 261–266. doi:10.1061/(ASCE)0733-947X(1997)123:4(261)

Smith, B. L., Williams, B. M., & Oswald, R. K. (2002). Comparison of parametric and nonparametric models for traffic flow forecasting. *Transportation Research*, *10C*, 303–321.

Soliman, S. A., Christensen, G. S., Kelly, D. H., & El-Naggar, K. (1992). Least Absolute Value Based On Linear Programming Algorithm for Measurement of Power System Frequency from a Distorted Bus Voltage Signal. *Elect. Mach. and Power Systems*, *20*, 549–568. doi:10.1080/07313569208909620

Soliman, S. A., & El-Hawary, M. E. (1999). Measurement of Voltage Flicker Magnitude and Frequency in a power systems for power quality analysis. *Elect. Mach. and Power Systems*, *27*, 1289–1297. doi:10.1080/073135699268588

Soliman, S. A., Mantaway, A. H., & El-Hawary, M. E. (2004). Simulated Annealing Optimization Algorithm for Power System Quality Analysis. *Electric Power and Energy Systems*, *26*, 31–36. doi:10.1016/S0142-0615(03)00068-1

Soltani, S. (2002). On the use of the wavelet decomposition for time series prediction. *Neurocomputing*, *48*, 267–277. doi:10.1016/S0925-2312(01)00648-8

Song, Y. S., Chou, C. S., & Stoham, T. J. (1999). Combined heat and power economic dispatch by improved ant colony search algorithm. *Electric Power Systems Research*, *52*(2), 115–121. doi:10.1016/S0378-7796(99)00011-5

Soudan, B., & Saad, M. (2008). An Evolutionary Dynamic Population Size PSO Implementation. In *Proceedings of the 3rd International Conference on Information & Communication Technologies: from Theory to Applications (ICTTA'08)*, Damascus, Syria (pp. 1-5). Washington, DC: IEEE Press.

Specht, D. F. (1991). A general regression neural network. *IEEE Transactions on Neural Networks*, *2*(6), 568–576. doi:10.1109/72.97934

Sprott, J. C. (2003). *Chaos and time-series analysis.* New York: Oxford University Press.

Srinivas, N., & Deb, K. (1994). Multiobjective optimization using non-dominated sorting in genetic algorithms. *Evolutionary Computation*, *2*(3), 221–248. doi:10.1162/evco.1994.2.3.221

Standard, I. E. E. E. (1993). *IEEE Recommended Practices and Requirements for Harmonic Control in Electrical Power System* (pp. 519–1992). Washington, DC: IEEE Press.

Stathopoulos, A., & Karlaftis, M. G. (2003). A multivariate state space approach for urban traffic flow modeling and prediction. *Transportation Research*, *11C*, 121–135.

Steiger, C., Walder, H., & Platzner, M. (2003). Heuristics for Online Scheduling Real-Time Tasks to Partially Reconfigurable Devices. In Y. K. Cheung & G. A. Constantinides (Eds.), *Proceedings of the FPL 2003* (LNCS 2778, pp. 575-584).

Stephanedes, Y. J., Michalopoulos, P. G., & Plun, R. A. (1981). Improved estimation of traffic flow for real-time control. *Transportation Research Record*, *795*, 28–39.

Storn, R., & Price, K. (1995). *Differential evolution: A simple and efficient adaptive scheme for global optimization over continuous spaces* (Tech. Rep. No. TR-95-012). Berkeley, CA: International Computer Science Institute.

Storn, R. (1997). Differential evolution—a simple and efficient heuristic for global optimization over ontinuous spaces. *Journal of Global Optimization*, *11*(4), 341–359. doi:10.1023/A:1008202821328

Storn, R., & Price, K. (1997). Differential evolution – A simple and efficient heuristic for global optimization over continuous spaces. *Journal of Global Optimization*, *11*(4), 341–359. doi:10.1023/A:1008202821328

Strassner, J., Fleck, J., Lewis, D., Parashar, M., & Donnelly, W. (2008, March). The role of standardization in future autonomic communication systems. In *Proceedings of the Fifth IEEE Workshop on Engineering of Autonomic and Autonomous Systems (EASE 2008)* (pp. 65-173).

Strebelle, S. (2002). Conditional simulation of complex geological structures using multipoint statistics. *Mathematical Geology*, *34*, 1–21. doi:10.1023/A:1014009426274

Streifferet, D. (1995). Multi-Area economic dispatch with tie-line constraints. *IEEE Transactions on Power Systems*, *10*(4), 1946–1951. doi:10.1109/59.476062

Suganthan, P. N., Hansen, N., Liang, J. J., Deb, K., Chen, Y. P., & Auger, A. (2005). *Problem definitions and evaluation criteria for the CEC2005 special session on real-parameter optimization*. Singapore: Nanyang Technological University.

Sun, X., Munoz, L., & Horowitz, R. (2003). Highway traffic state estimation using improved mixture Kalman filters for effective ramp metering control. In *Proceedings of 42nd IEEE Conference on Decision and Control* (pp. 6333-6338).

Sung, C. S., & Jin, H. W. (2000). A tabu-search-based heuristic for clustering. *Pattern Recognition*, *33*, 849–858. doi:10.1016/S0031-3203(99)00090-4

Sun, J., Zhang, Q., & Tsang, E. (2004). DE/EDA: A new evolutionary algorithm for global optimization. *Information Sciences*, *169*(3-4), 249–262. doi:10.1016/j.ins.2004.06.009

Su, Y. S., & Huang, C. Y. (2006). Neural-network-based approaches for software reliability estimation using dynamic weighted combinational models. *Journal of Systems and Software*. doi:.doi:10.1016/j.jss.2006.06.017

Tabero, J., Septien, J., Mesha, H., Mozos, D., & Roman, S. (2003). Efficient hardware multitasking through space multiplexing in 2D RTR FPGAs. In *Proceedings of the Euromicro digital system design conference*.

Taha, H. A. (2003). *Operations Research: An Introduction*. Singapore: Prentice-Hall.

Takens, F. (1981). Detecting strange attractors in turbulence. In *Dynamical Systems and Turbulence, Warwick 1980* (LNM 898, pp. 366-381).

Tamaki, H., Kita, H., & Kobayashi, S. (1996, May 20-22). Multi-objective optimization by genetic algorithms: A review. In *Proceedings of the IEEE Conference on Evolutionary Computation (ICEC'96)*, Piscataway, NJ (pp. 517-522).

Tan, K. C., Goh, C. K., Yang, Y. J., & Lee, T. H. (2006). Evolving better population distribution and exploration in evolutionary multi-objective optimization. *European Journal of Operational Research*, *171*(2), 463–495. doi:10.1016/j.ejor.2004.08.038

Tarantola, A. (2004). *Inverse Problem Theory and Model Parameter Estimation*. Philadelphia: SIAM.

Tarricone, L., & Esposito, A. (2005). *Grid Computing for Electromagnetics*. Boston: Artech House Inc.

Taylor, I. J., & Harrison, A. (2009). *From P2P and Grids to Services on the Web- Evolving Distributed Communities* (2nd ed.). New York: Springer Verlag.

Teive, R. C. G., Silva, E. L., & Fonseca, L. G. S. (1998). A cooperative expert system for transmission expansion planning of electrical power systems. *IEEE Transactions on Power Systems, 13*(2), 636–642. doi:10.1109/59.667393

Tessema, B., & Yen, G. G. (2009). An adaptive penalty formulation for constrained evolutionary optimization. *IEEE Transactions on Systems, Man, and Cybernetics. Part A, Systems and Humans, 39*, 565–578. doi:10.1109/TSMCA.2009.2013333

Thomas, M., Yi, L., Koen, B., & Georgi, G. (2010). 3D Compaction: A Novel Blocking-Aware Algorithm for Online Hardware Task Scheduling and Placement on 2D Partially Reconfigurable Devices. In *Proceedings of ARC 2010* (pp. 194-206). Berlin: Springer Verlag.

Tian, L., & Noore, A. (2005a). On-line prediction of software reliability using an evolutionary connectionist model. *Journal of Systems and Software, 77*, 173–180. doi:10.1016/j.jss.2004.08.023

Tian, L., & Noore, A. (2005b). Evolutionary neural network modeling for software cumulative failure time prediction. *Reliability Engineering & System Safety, 87*, 45–51. doi:10.1016/j.ress.2004.03.028

TOP. (n.d.). *TOP, The Output Processor* (version 6.2). Retrieved from http://www.pqsoft.com

Trelea, I. C. (2003). The particle swarm optimization algorithm: convergence analysis and parameter selection. *Information Processing Letters, 85*(6), 317–325. doi:10.1016/S0020-0190(02)00447-7

Trick, M. A. (1992). A linear relaxation heuristic for the generalized assignment problem. *Naval Research Logistics, 39*, 137–152. doi:10.1002/1520-6750(199203)39:2<137::AID-NAV3220390202>3.0.CO;2-D

Tsai, C. F., Tsai, C. W., Wu, H. C., & Yang, T. (2004). ACODF: A novel data clustering approach for data mining in large databases. *Journal of Systems and Software, 73*, 133–145. doi:10.1016/S0164-1212(03)00216-4

Tseng, L., & Liang, S. (2006). A hybrid metaheuristic for the quadratic assignment problem. *Computational Optimization and Applications, 34*(1), 85–113. doi:10.1007/s10589-005-3069-9

Valkó, A. G., Gomez, J., Kim, S., & Compabell, A. T. (1999). On the Analysis of Cellular IP Access Networks. In *Proceedings of the IFIP Sixth International Workshop on Protocols for High Speed Networks VI,* Salem, MA (pp. 205-224).

Van Arem, B., Kirby, H. R., Van Der Vlist, M. J. M., & Whittaker, J. C. (1997). Recent advances in the field of short-term traffic forecasting. *International Journal of Forecasting, 13*, 1–12. doi:10.1016/S0169-2070(96)00695-4

Vanaja, B., Hemamalini, S., & Simon, S. P. (2008, November 19-21). Artificial Immune based Economic Load Dispatch with valve-point effect. In *Proceedings of the IEEE Region 10 Conference (TENCON 2008)* (pp. 1-5).

Vasebi, A., Fesanghary, M., & Bathaee, S. M. T. (2007). Combined heat and power economic dispatch by harmony search algorithm. *Electrical Power and Energy systems, 29*, 713-719.

Vazquez-Montiel, S., Sanchez-Escobar, J., & Fuentes, O. (2002). Obtaining the phase of an interferogram by use of an evolution strategy: Part I. *Applied Optics, 41*(17), 3448–3452. doi:10.1364/AO.41.003448

Venkatraman, S., & Yen, G. G. (2005). A generic framework for constrained optimization using genetic algorithms. *IEEE Transactions on Evolutionary Computation, 9*, 424–435. doi:10.1109/TEVC.2005.846817

Vesanto, J., & Alhonierni, E. (2000). Clustering of the self-organizing map. *IEEE Transactions on Neural Networks, 11*, 586–600. doi:10.1109/72.846731

Vidyarthi, D. P., Sarker, B. K., Tripathi, A. K., & Yang, L. T. (2009). *Scheduling in Distributed Computing Systems*. New York: Springer Verlag.

Vidyarthi, D. P., & Tripathi, A. K. (2001). Maximizing Reliability of Distributed Computing System with Task Allocation using Simple Genetic Algorithm. *Journal of Systems Architecture, 47*(6), 549–554. doi:10.1016/S1383-7621(01)00013-3

Vidyarthi, D. P., Tripathi, A. K., Sarker, B. K., & Yang, L. T. (2005). Performance Study of Reliability Maximization and Turnaround Minimization with GA based Task Allocation in DCS. In Yang, L. T., & Guo, M. (Eds.), *PART III - Scheduling and Resource Management, High Performance Computing: Paradigm and Infrastructure* (pp. 349–360). New York: John Wiley and Sons.

Villasana, R., Garver, L. L., & Salon, S. J. (1985). Transmission network planning using linear programming. *IEEE Transactions on Power Apparatus and Systems, 104*(2), 349–356. doi:10.1109/TPAS.1985.319049

Vlahogianni, E. I., Golia, J. C., & Karlaftis, M. G. (2004). Short-term traffic forecasting: Overview of objective and methods. *Transport Reviews, 24*, 533–557. doi:10.1080/0144164042000195072

Vlahogianni, E. I., Karlaftis, M. G., & Golias, J. C. (2005). Optimized and meta-optimized neural networks for short-term traffic flow prediction: A genetic approach. *Transportation Research, 13C*, 211–234.

Walter, D. C., & Sheble, G. B. (1993). Genetic algorithm solution of economic load dispatch with valve point loading. *IEEE Transactions on Power Systems, 8*(3), 1325–1332. doi:10.1109/59.260861

Wang, L., Cui, Z., & Zeng, J. (2009). Particle Swarm Optimization with Group Decision Making. In *Proceedings of the 2009 Ninth International Conference on Hybrid Intelligent Systems* (Vol. 1, pp. 388-393).

Wang, L., Xiong, S.-W., Yang, J., & Fan, J.-S. (2006). An Improved Elitist Strategy Multi-Objective Evolutionary Algorithm. In *Proceedings of the Fifth International Conference on Machine Learning and Cybernetics*, Dalian, China (pp. 2315-2319).

Wanga, Y., Chenga, H., Wang, C., Hu, Z., Yao, L., Mad, Z., & Zhud, Z. (2008). Pareto optimality-based multi-objective transmission planning considering transmission congestion. *Electric Power Systems Research, 78*, 1619–1626. doi:10.1016/j.epsr.2008.02.004

Wang, C., & Shahidehpour, S. M. (1992). A decomposition approach to non -linear multi-area generation scheduling with tie-line constraints using expert system. *IEEE Transactions on Power Apparatus and Systems, 7*(4), 1409–1418.

Wang, J. C., Chiang, H. D., & Darling, G. R. (1996, February). An efficient algorithm for real time network reconfiguration in large scale unbalanced distribution systems. *IEEE Transactions on Power Systems, 11*, 511–517. doi:10.1109/59.486141

Wang, L., & Singh, C. (2009). Reserve constrained multi-area environmental/economic dispatch based on particle swarm optimization with local search. *Engineering Applications of Artificial Intelligence, 22*, 298–307. doi:10.1016/j.engappai.2008.07.007

Wang, Y., & Papageorgiou, M. (2005). Real-time freeway traffic state estimation based on extended Kalman filter: A general approach. *Transportation Research, 39B*, 141–167.

Wang, Z., Bovik, A., Sheikh, H., & Simoncelli, E. (2004). Image quality assessment: From error visibility to structural similarity. *IEEE Transactions on Image Processing, 13*, 600–612. doi:10.1109/TIP.2003.819861

Ward, J. H. (1963). Hierarchical grouping to optimize an objective function. *Journal of the American Statistical Association, 58*, 236–244. doi:10.2307/2282967

Welch, J. W. (1983). Algorithmic complexity: three NP-hard problems in computational statistics. *Journal of Statistical Computation and Simulation, 15*, 17–25. doi:10.1080/00949658208810560

Wernerus, J., & Soder, L. (1995). Area price based multi-area economic dispatch with tie-line losses and constraints. In *Proceedings of the IEEE/KTH Stockholm Power Tech Conference*, Sweden (pp. 710-15).

Wolf, M., Drory, N., Gebhardt, K., & Hill, G. (2007). Ages and metallicities of extra-galactic globular clusters from spectral and photometric fits of stellar population synthesis models. *The Astrophysical Journal, 655*(1), 179–211. doi:10.1086/509768

Wood, A. J., & Wollenberg, B. F. (1984). *Power generation, operation and control*. New York: John Wiley & Sons.

Wu, S., & Chow, T. W. S. (2004). Clustering of the self-organizing map using a clustering validity index based on inter-cluster and intra-cluster density. *Pattern Recognition, 37*, 175–188. doi:10.1016/S0031-3203(03)00237-1

Xhafa, F., Alba, E., & Dorronsoro, B. (2007). Efficient Batch Job Scheduling in Grids using Cellular Memetic Algorithms. In *Proceedings of the IEEE International Symposium on Parallel and Distributed Processing (IPDPS 2007)*.

Xilinx. (2007). *Virtex-5 user guide* (Tech. Rep. No. UG190). San Jose, CA: Xilinx Inc.

Xilinx. (2008). *Virtex-4 FPGA Configuration User Guide* (Tech. Rep. No. UG071). San Jose, CA: Xilinx.

Xu, K., Xie, M., Tang, L. C., & Ho, S. L. (2003). Application of neural networks in forecasting engine systems reliability. *Applied Soft Computing, 2*, 255–268. doi:10.1016/S1568-4946(02)00059-5

Yalcinoz, T., & Short, M. J. (1998). Neural Networks Approach for Solving Economic Dispatch Problem with Transmission Capacity Constraints. *IEEE Transactions on Power Systems, 13*(2), 307–313. doi:10.1109/59.667341

Yang, Y., & Kamel, M. S. (2006). An aggregated clustering approach using multi-ant colonies algorithms. *Pattern Recognition, 39*, 1278–1289. doi:10.1016/j.patcog.2006.02.012

Yaojun, H., Changjun, J., & Xuemei, L. (2005). Resource Scheduling Model For Grid Computing Based On Sharing Synthesis Of Petri Net. In *Proceedings of the Ninth International Conference on Computer Supported Cooperative Work in Design*.

Yao, X., & Liu, Y. (1997). Fast evolution strategies. *Control and Cybernetics, 26*(3), 467–496.

Yao, X., Liu, Y., & Lin, G. (1999). Evolutionary programming made faster. *IEEE Transactions on Evolutionary Computation, 3*(2), 82–102. doi:10.1109/4235.771163

Yen, G. G., & Lu, H. (2003). Dynamic multiobjective evolutionary algorithm: Adaptive cell-based rank and density estimation. *IEEE Transactions on Evolutionary Computation, 7*, 253–274. doi:10.1109/TEVC.2003.810068

Yerima, S. Y., & Al-Begain, K. (2007). Buffer Management for Multimedia QoS Control over HSDPA Downlink. In *Proceedings of the 21st International Conference on Advanced Information Networking and Applications Workshops (AINAW '07)*, Niagara Falls, ON (Vol. 1, pp. 912-917). Washington, DC: IEEE Press.

Yilmaz, A. E., & Kuzuoglu, M. (2007). Calculation of Optimized Parameters of Rectangular Microstrip Patch Antenna using Particle Swarm Optimization. *Microwave and Optical Technology Letters, 49*(12), 2905–2907. doi:10.1002/mop.22918

Ying, T., Ya-Ping, Y., & Jian-Chao, Z. (2006). An Enhanced Hybrid Quadratic Particle Swarm Optimization. In *Proceedings of the Sixth International Conference on Intelligent Systems Design and Applications (ISDA'06)*, Jinan, China (Vol. 2, pp. 980-985). Washington, DC: IEEE Press.

Yousefi'zadeh, H., & Jonckheere, E. A. (2005). Dynamic neural-based buffer management for queuing systems with self-similar characteristics. *IEEE Transactions on Neural Networks, 16*(5), 1163–1173. doi:10.1109/TNN.2005.853417

Youssef, H. K., & Hackam, R. (1989). New transmission planning model. *IEEE Transactions on Power Systems, 4*(2), 9–18. doi:10.1109/59.32451

Zhang, L., Deering, S., Estrin, D., & Zappala, D. (1993). RSVP: A new resource reservation protocol. *IEEE Network Magazine*.

Zheng, J., & Li, M. (2008). An Efficient Method for Maintaining Diversity in Evolutionary Multi-objective Optimization. In *Proceedings of the Fourth International Conference on Natural Computation* (pp. 617-624).

Zhou, Q., Shirmohammadi, D., & Liu, W. H. E. (1997, May). Distribution feeder reconfiguration for service restoration and load balancing. *IEEE Transactions on Power Systems, 12*, 724–729. doi:10.1109/59.589664

Zhou, X., Wang, Y., Huang, X., & Peng, C. (2006). *Online Scheduling of Real-time Tasks for Reconfigurable Computing System* (pp. 57–64). FPT.

Zhou, X., Wang, Y., Huang, X., & Peng, C. (2007). *Fast On-line Task Placement and Scheduling on Reconfigurable Devices* (pp. 132–138). FPL.

Zhu, J. Z. (2002). Optimal reconfiguration of electrical distribution network using the refined genetic algorithm. *Electric Power Systems Research, 62*, 37–42. doi:10.1016/S0378-7796(02)00041-X

Zitzler, E. (1999, December). Evolutionary Algorithms for Multiobjective Optimization. *Methods and Applications*. Zurich, Switzerland: Swiss Federal Institute of Technology (ETH).

Zitzler, E., & Thiele, L. (1998). An evolutionary algorithm for multi-objective optimization: the strength rateto approach. *Swiss Federal Institute of Technology, TIK- Report*, (43).

Zitzler, E., Deb, K., & Thiele, L. (2000, April). Comparison of multiobjective evolutionary algorithms: Empirical results. *Evolutionary Computation*, 8(2), 173–195. doi:10.1162/106365600568202

Zitzler, E., Laumanns, M., & Thiele, L. (2001). *SPEA2: Improving the Strength Pareto Evolutionary Algorithm*. Zurich, Switzerland: Swiss Federal Institute Techonology.

Zitzler, E., & Thiele, L. (1999). Multiobjective Evolutionary Algorithms: A Comparative Case Study And the Strength Pareto Approach. *IEEE Transactions on Evolutionary Computation*, 3(4), 257–271. doi:10.1109/4235.797969

Zomaya, A. Y., & Wright, M. (2002). Observation on Using Genetic Algorithms for Channel Allocation in Mobile Computing. *IEEE Transactions on Parallel and Distributed Systems*, 13(9), 948–962. doi:10.1109/TPDS.2002.1036068

Zupan, J., & Gasteiger, J. (1999). *Neural Networks in chemistry and Drug Design*. New York: Wiley Weinheim.

Zupan, J., Novie, M., Ruisanchez, M., & Chemomet, I. (1997). *Intel Lab. Syst.*, 38, 1. doi:10.1016/S0169-7439(97)00030-0

About the Contributors

Wei-Chiang Samuelson Hong is an Associate Professor in the Department of Information Management at the Oriental Institute of Technology, Taiwan. His research interests mainly include computational intelligence (neural networks and evolutionary computation), and application of forecasting technology (ARIMA, support vector regression, and chaos theory), and tourism competitiveness evaluation and management. Dr. Hong's articles have been published in *Applied Mathematics and Computation, Applied Mathematical Modelling, Applied Soft Computing, Control and Cybernetics, Current Issues in Tourism, Decision Support Systems, Electric Power Systems Research, Energy, Energies, Energy Conversion and Management, Energy Policy, Hydrological Processes, IEEE Transactions on Fuzzy Systems, International Journal of Advanced Manufacturing Technology, International Journal of Electrical Power & Energy Systems, Journal of Systems and Software, Neural Computing and Applications, Neurocomputing,* and *Water Resources Management,* among others. Dr. Hong is currently on the editorial board of several journals, including *International Journal of Applied Evolutionary Computation, Neurocomputing, Neural Computing & Applications, Mathematical Problems in Engineering,* and *Energy Sources Part B: Economics, Planning, and Policy.* Dr. Hong presently teaches courses in the areas of forecasting methodologies and applications, hybridizing evolutionary algorithms, and conducts research in the areas of prediction modeling, simulation and optimization; artificial neural network, and novel forecasting development. Dr. Hong serves as the program committee of various international conferences including premium ones such as IEEE CEC, IEEE CIS, IEEE ICNSC, IEEE SMC, IEEE CASE, and IEEE SMCia, et cetera. He is a senior member of IIE and IEEE. He is indexed in the list of Who's Who in the World (25th-29th editions), Who's Who in Asia (2nd edition), and Who's Who in Science and Engineering (10th and 11th editions).

* * *

Mohammad Anbar received his B.Tech in Electronics Engineering from Tishreen University, Lattakia, Syria, in the year 2003, and M.Tech in Computer Science from Jawaharlal Nehru University, New Delhi, India in the year 2007. Currently, Mohammad Anbar is Ph.D student at the school of Computer and Systems Sciences, Jawaharlal Nehru University, New Delhi, India. His research interest includes Wireless Communication, Mobile Computing, Particle Swarm Optimization, and Genetic Algorithms.

P.R. Bijwe is a professor of electrical engineering at Indian Institute of technology, Delhi, India. His research interests include power system analysis and optimization, voltage stability, transmission expansion planning, and deregulation.

Yu-Chiun Chiou holds MSc and PhD degrees from National Chiao Tung University, Institute of Traffic and Transportation, where he teaches transportation economics, multivariate analysis, traffic flow theory and mathematical programming as an associate professor. His main areas of research are presently intelligent transportation system, sustainable transportation, transportation economics and intelligent research methods. He has published journal papers on fuzzy sets and systems, *European Journal of Operational Research*, Accident Analysis and Prevention, Transportmetrica, Transportation Research Part E, *Journal of Advanced Transportation* and other over ninety refereed journal papers and conference papers.

Shih-Ta Chou holds MSc degree from Feng Chia University, Department of Transportation Technology and Management. He is currently a logistic engineer for inventory control of China Technical Consultants, Inc. His main areas of research are transportation economics and intelligent research methods.

Olac Fuentes, was born in Chihuaha, Mexico, in 1966. He received the B.S. degree in Industrial Engineering from the Instituto Tecnologico de Chichuaha in 1989, the M.S. degree in computer science from the University of Texas at El Paso (UTEP) in 1991, and the Ph.D. degree in computer science from the University of Rochester in 1997. He currently leads the Vision and Learning Laboratory (VL2) at UTEP and I am also affiliated with the Interactive Systems Group (ISG). Also, he directs the UTEP REU Summer Site in Applied Intelligent Systems, an NSF-sponsored program to perform interdisciplinary research at UTEP. He is interested in Machine Learning and its applications to Computer Vision, Bioinformatics, Scientific Data Analysis, Robotics, and Natural Language Processing.

Juan Carlos Gomez, received the B.S. degree in Computer Systems Engineering from the Instituto Tecnologico de Queretaro, Mexico, in 1999, the M.S. degree in computational astrophysics from INAOE, Mexico, in 2002, and the Ph.D. degree in computer science from the same institute in 2007. He worked at KULeuven during two years as Research Assistant in the Language Intelligence and Information Retrieval (LIIR) group, developing algorithms for statistical feature extraction. He is currently a postdoctoral fellow in the Evolutionary Computing Cathedra in the ITESM, Mexico. He has published several papers in the field of machine learning, evolutionary computing, data mining and information retrieval.

Sheng-Uei Guan received his MSc & PhD from the University of North Carolina at Chapel Hill. He is currently a professor and head of the computer science and software engineering department at Xian Jiaotong-Liverpool University. Before joining XJTLU, he was a professor and chair in intelligent systems at Brunel University, UK. Prof. Guan has worked in a prestigious R&D organization for several years, serving as a design engineer, project leader, and manager. After leaving the industry, he joined Yuan-Ze University in Taiwan for three and half years. He served as deputy director for the Computing Center and the chairman for the Department of Information & Communication Technology. Later he joined the Electrical & Computer Engineering Department at National University of Singapore as an associate professor.

Mahmoud-Reza Haghifam received the BSc, MSc and PhD degrees in 1988, 1990 and 1995, respectively, all in electric power engineering. Currently, he is the full professor of electrical engineering at Tarbiat Modares University, Tehran, Iran. His main research interests are electric distribution systems, power system reliability and power system restructuring. He is a senior member of IEEE and research fellow of Alexander Van Humboldt, Germany.

Ilias Kiourktsidis received his BSc from the Technological Institute of Peiraias in Greece and his MSc from Brunel University. He was awarded a scholarship from the National Institute of Scholarships in Greece. Currently he is a PhD student in Brunel University.

April Y. Kuo is senior operations research specialist of service design and performance, BNSF Railway, USA. Dr. Kuo received her PhD from Department of Civil and Environmental Engineering, University of Maryland at College Park, USA in 2008. Her research interests include fuzzy neural networks, integral capacitated multicommodity network flow problems, systems optimization and heuristic algorithms.

Lawrence W. Lan is professor of Department of Global Marketing and Logistics, and the Dean of College of Management, MingDao University, Taiwan. He is also a lifetime Emeritus Professor of National Chiao Tung University, Taiwan. Dr. Lan received his PhD in transportation from University of California at Berkeley, USA in 1986. His research interests include traffic flow studies, transportation economics, and econometric modeling and forecasting.

Eric Larson received a BS degree in electrical engineering from Oklahoma State University in 2008. He is currently pursuing a MS degree from the University of Washington in Seattle, Washington. His research interests include evolutionary computation and its applications in image and video processing.

Feng-Yu Lin is adjunct assistant professor of Department of Criminal Investigation, Central Police University, Taiwan. Dr. Lin received his PhD from Institute of Traffic and Transportation, National Chiao Tung University, Taiwan in 2004. His research interests include time-series analysis, pattern recognition, and chaos theory.

Armin Ebrahimi Milani received the BSc degree in electric power engineering from Azad University, South Branch, Tehran, Iran, in 2006 and MSc degree in electric power engineering from Azad University, Science and Research Branch, Tehran, Iran, in 2009. Currently, he is with department of electrical engineering, Azad University, Iran. His main research interests are power system optimization and control, electric distribution systems and power system restructuring. He is a senior member of Young Researchers Club, Iran.

Wenting Mo received her BEng (Communication Engineering) from Huazhong University of Science and Technology (China) in 2003 and received her PhD degree from the National University of Singapore in 2008. She is currently working in IBM as an optimization consultant. Her research interests are in evolutionary computation, linear optimization algorithms and multi-objective optimization algorithms.

V. Ravikumar Pandi received his B.E. degree from Madurai Kamaraj University, Tamilnadu in 2003 and M.E. degree from Annamalai University, Tamilnadu in 2005. He worked as a Lecturer in Sri Venkateswara College of Engineering, Chennai, Tamilnadu. He is now working towards his Ph.D. degree at IIT Delhi, India. His research interest includes Numerical Optimization, Soft Computing, Power system analysis, power quality assessment and protection.

B. K. Panigrahi is working as an Assistant Professor in the Department of Electrical Engineering, IIT, New Delhi, India. Prior to joining IIT Delhi, he was working as Lecturer at University College of Engineering, Burla, Sambalpur, Orissa for about 13 years. The research interests of Dr. Panigrahi are in the areas of intelligent control of FACTS devices, Application of advanced DSP techniques for Power Quality assessment, Development of Soft Computing and Bio-inspired computing techniques for power system planning, operation and control applications.

Sadasivan Puthusserypady received the BTech degree in Electrical Engineering and the M.Tech degree in Instrumentation and Control Systems Engineering from University of Calicut, India, in 1986 and 1989, respectively. He obtained the PhD degree in Electrical Communication Engineering from the Indian Institute of Science, Bangalore, India, in 1995. During 1993-1996, he was a Research Associate at the Department of Psychopharmacology, National Institute of mental health and Neuroscience, Bangalore, India. He was a Postdoctoral Research Fellow at the Communications Research Laboratory, McMaster University, Hamilton, ON, Canada, from 1996 to 1998. From 1998 to 2000, he was a Senior Systems Engineer at Raytheon Systems Canada Ltd., Waterloo, ON, Canada. In 2000, he moved to the National University of Singapore and worked as an Assistant Professor in the Department of Electrical and Computer Engineering until 2009. Currently, he is an Associate Professor at the Department of Electrical Engineering, Technical University of Denmark, Denmark. His research interests are in signal processing, neural networks, evolutionary algorithms etc.

Zahid Raza is currently an Assistant Professor in the School of Computer and Systems Sciences, Jawaharlal Nehru University, India. He has a Master degree in Electronics as well as Computer Science and is pursuing Ph.D. from Jawaharlal Nehru University. Prior to joining Jawaharlal Nehru University he served as a Lecturer in Banasthali Vidyapith University, Rajasthan, India. His research interest is in the area of Grid Computing and has proposed a few models for job scheduling in a Computational Grid. He is a member of IEEE.

Ahmed Ibrahim Saleh received his B.Sc. in the department of Computer Engineering and Systems Department in the faculty of Engineering in Mansoura university, with general grade Excellent (1998). He got the master degree in the area of Mobile agents (2000). His PHD was in the area of web mining and search engines (2006). He has a good knowledge in networks Hardware and Software. Currently he is working as a Teacher at the faculty of Engineering, Mansoura University, Egypt. His interests are (Programming Languages, Networks and System Administration, and Database).

Ashu Verma received B'tech degree from National Institute of Technology, Hamirpur, India and M. Tech degree from Indian Institute of Technology, Delhi, India, in 2001 and 2002 respectively. Also, she completed her PhD in transmission network expansion planning in 2010, from Indian Institute of Technology, Delhi, India. She is currently working as Assistant Professor, in the Department of Energy and Environment, TERI University, India. Her areas of interest are power system analysis and optimization, transmission network expansion planning, integration of renewable energy sources to electric grid.

Deo Prakash Vidyarthi, received Master Degree in Computer Application from MMM Engineering College Gorakhpur and Ph.D. in Computer Science from Jabalpur University (worked in Banaras Hindu University, Varanasi). He was faculty in the Department of Computer Science of Banaras Hindu University, Varanasi for more than 12 years and currently working as Associate Professor in the School of Computer & System Sciences, Jawaharlal Nehru University, New Delhi. Research interest includes Parallel and Distributed System, Grid Computing, Mobile Computing. He has more than 50 publications in various journals of international repute. He can be approached at School of Computer & Systems Sciences, Jawaharlal Nehru University, New Delhi-67.He is member IEEE, ISRST and IACSIT.

Wenbing Yao received her PhD degree in communication and information systems from Huazhong University of Science and Technology, China, in 2001. She is currently a senior manager responsible for R&D collaborations in Huawei Technologies, Vodafone Business Unit. From 2003 to 2008, she was a lecturer in wireless communications in the School of Engineering and Design at Brunel University, West London. Prior to that, she was a postdoctoral research fellow in the Department of Electronic and Computer Engineering from Feb 2002. Between Aug 2001 and Feb 2002, she was a research scientist in the Wireless Technology Research Division of Hanwang High Technologies Inc., Wuhan, China. Her research works are mainly in wireless networking, mobility management, mobile ad hoc networks, and location technologies in wireless communication networks, etc. She is a member of IEEE and IET.

Gary G. Yen received the PhD degree in electrical and computer engineering from the University of Notre Dame in 1992. He is currently a professor in the School of Electrical and Computer Engineering, Oklahoma State University. Before joined OSU in 1997, he was with the Structure Control Division, U.S. Air Force Research Laboratory. His research is supported by the DoD, DoE, EPA, NASA, NSF, and Process Industry. His research interest includes intelligent control, computational intelligence, conditional health monitoring, signal processing and their industrial/defense applications. He is an IEEE Fellow.

Index

3D compaction (3DC) 296

A

ACO-based clustering algorithm with different favor
    (ACODF) 3
Adaptive Bacterial Foraging (ABF) 99, 110
Adaptive Particle Swarm Optimization (APSO) 99,
    101, 126
adaptive resonance theory 2
agglomerative hierarchical clustering method 2
ANTCLASS 3
ant clustering algorithms (ACAs) 1, 3
Ant Colony Optimization 1-2, 4, 14, 216
AntTree 3
area power balance constraints 217, 222
area wise spinning reserve constraints 218, 222
ARIMA models 17
ARMA models 17
autonomic communications (AutoComm) 36
Autonomic Management (AM) 37

B

Back propagation trained neural network (BPNN)
    237
bacteria foraging (bf) 319, 325, 331
Bacteria Foraging optimization (BFO) 333
Base Stations 254, 260-261, 263
Biogeography-Based Optimization (BBO) 165-166
branch-and-price 2, 15
buffer management 254-256, 258-260, 274-275

C

CBQ priority buffer management (CPBM) 258
chemotaxis 102-105, 325-327, 333
chip utilization 287-290, 303, 306-309, 312, 314-
    315, 317
class based queuing (CBQ) 258

Clonal Algorithm (CLONALOG) 99
clustering 1, 3
column generation 2, 15
Conflict level based objective ordering approach
    (CLOOA) 82
Connection Completion Probability (CCP) 255
Constriction based PSO 99, 106
counter propagation neural network (CPNN) 237,
    241
cyclic optimization 57, 62-63, 66, 71

D

Differential evolution 145, 162-163, 170, 189-191,
    200, 214-216, 219, 233-234
Difficulty based objective ordering approach
    (DOOA) 82
divisive hierarchical clustering method 2
dropped packets 254, 263, 267, 272-273
Dynamic Evolving Neuro-Fuzzy Inference System
    (DENFIS) 237, 239-240, 242
dynamic programming 2, 142, 216, 320
dynamic weighted combinational model (DWCM)
    239

E

economic dispatch (ED) 215
Estimation of Distribution Algorithm (EDA) 170
evolutionary multi-objective optimization (EMO) 75
Explicit Congestion Notification (ECN) 39
Extrapolated Biogeography-Based Optimization
    (eBBO) 165

F

facial animation parameters (FAPs) 60
facial definition parameters (FDPs) 60
facial feature tracking 57-58

fast self-organizing map combining with K-means (FSOM+K-means) 3

field programmable gate arrays (FPGAs) 287

fitness function 107-108, 135-136, 145-146, 150, 152, 161, 166, 172, 174, 221, 244, 255, 257, 263, 280-282, 284, 322, 324-325, 329, 332

fitness scaling 136

fitness uniform selection strategy (FUSS) 169

flowshop scheduling 3

fuzzy reasoning 16-17, 19-26, 30, 32, 34

G

galaxy spectra 276-278, 280-281, 284

generating limit constraints 217, 222

genetic clustering algorithm (GCA) 1, 4, 10

genetic K-means approach (GKA) 3

Genetic Programming (GP) 237, 240

gradient-based optimization 58

graph theoretic relaxations 2, 14

greedy randomized adaptive search procedure (GRASP) 320-321

group method of data handling (GMDH) 237, 240

H

habitat suitability index (HIS) 167

high dimensional spaces 192, 204

hyper-volume metrics 77-78, 94

I

Incremental Multiple Objective Genetic Algorithm (IMOGA) 72

INSGA-II 73, 75

intelligent BBO (IBBO) 170

K

Kalman filtering 17, 34, 100

Kalman filters 34, 199

K-means algorithm (KMA) 1, 10

knowledge utilization 276

L

Lagrangian relaxation 2, 15

linear relaxation 2, 15

M

machine learning 101, 164, 237-238, 240, 245, 251, 276, 334

Many Multiple Objective Genetic Algorithms (MO-GAs) 72

mathematical programming 1-2

metaheuristics 2-3, 319, 321

model–based coding 57

model-based facial coding (MBFC) 58

model reduction techniques 192, 202, 204, 211

Multi-area economic dispatch (MAED) 215

multi-objective optimization 57, 59, 61, 73, 75, 77-78, 81, 96-98, 132, 139, 143-146, 161-164, 240

multiobjective optimization problem (MOP) 59

multivariate adaptive regression splines (MARS) 237, 240, 242

multivariate state space approach 17, 34

N

NARMA model 17

Neighborhood Algorithm 200, 214

network programming 2

network relaxation 2, 14

Network Simulator (NS2) 36, 47

neural network 2, 17, 33, 97, 101, 128, 131, 216, 234, 237, 240-241, 245, 251-253

normalized root mean square error (NRMSE) 237, 240, 245

NSGA-II 59, 61-63, 66, 68-69, 71-73, 75, 84, 97, 143, 145-147, 151-152, 154-162

P

Pareto Archived Evolution Strategy (PAES) 72, 145

posterior sampling 192, 200, 203, 211

power quality (PQ) 100

Puzzle Based Compaction (PBC) 287, 289, 294, 302, 316

Q

quadratic assignment problem 3, 15, 170, 191

Quality of Service (QoS) 255

queen ant agent 3

R

random walk strategies (RWS) 169

Real Coded BBO (RCBBO) 167, 174

Reserve Constrained Multi-Area Economic Dispatch 215, 217

S

Self Evolvable Transaction Protocol (SETP) 36, 38

self-modifying protocols (SMP) 36, 38
self-organizing map (SOM) 2
simulated annealing 2-3, 14-15, 62, 69, 101, 129, 131, 141, 200, 203, 212, 239, 253, 276-277, 281, 285, 320-321, 334
Sloan Digital Sky Survey (SDSS) 276-277
software reliability engineering 237, 252-253
spatial confined (SC) method 24
spatial differences 22, 24, 26
spatial similarity 22, 24-26, 32
spatiotemporal confined (STC) method 22
spatiotemporal similarity 22-24
Spectrography 279
state-space prediction 18
static random-access memory (SRAM) 289
static transmission network expansion planning (STNEP) 320
statistical multiple linear regression (MLR) 237
statistics clustering 2
stellar content 276
stellar spectrum 277
Strength Pareto Evolutionary Algorithm (SPEA) 72, 145, 321
suitability index variables (SIV) 167
swarming 103, 326

T

temporal confined (TC) method 20
temporal differences 20, 22, 24
temporal similarity 20-22, 24, 32
tie-line limit constraints 217
time space-priority (TSP) 259
time varying acceleration coefficients (TVAC) 217
time varying inertia weight (TVIW) 169
traffic evolution 17
traffic time series data 16-17, 19-20, 22, 24, 32
Transmission Capacity Constraints 216-217, 233, 235
transmission network expansion planning (TNEP) 319
traveling salesman problem 3, 14
TreeNet 237, 239-240, 242, 249, 251

V

Vector Evaluated GA(VEGA) 145
vehicle routing problem 3, 14
voltage flicker 99-100, 107, 109-113, 127, 129

W

wavelet analysis 17, 33